P9-DND-092

Dreams
and
Inward
Journeys

Dreams
and
Inward
Journeys

A Rhetoric and Reader for Writers

Fifth Edition

Marjorie Ford
Stanford University

Jon Ford
De Anza College

PEARSON
Longman

New York Boston San Francisco
London Toronto Sydney Tokyo Singapore Madrid
Mexico City Munich Paris Cape Town Hong Kong Montreal

Senior Vice President/Publisher: Joseph Opiela
Acquisitions Editor: Lynn M. Huddon
Marketing Manager: Ann Stypuloski
Supplements Editor: Donna Campion
Production Manager: Denise Phillip
Project Coordination, Text Design, and Electronic Page Makeup: WestWords, Inc.
Cover Design Manager: Wendy Ann Fredericks
Cover Designer: Kay Petronio
Cover Art: Henri Rousseau (1844–1910), *The Sleeping Gypsy*. 1887. Oil on Canvas,
    51" x 6' 7". Gift of Mrs. Simon Guggenheim. (646.1939). Art Resource, New York, NY.
Photo Researcher: WestWords, Inc.
Manufacturing Buyer: Roy Pickering
Printer and Binder: R.R. Donnelley–Crawfordsville
Cover Printer: Lehigh Press, Inc.

For permission to use copyrighted material, grateful acknowledgment is made to the
copyright holders on pp. 564–567, which are hereby made part of this copyright page.

Library of Congress Cataloging-in-Publication Data
    Ford, Marjorie (Majorie A.)
        Dreams and inward journeys: a rhetoric and reader for writers / Majorie Ford, Jon
    Ford.—5th ed.
            p. cm
        Includes index.
        ISBN 0-321-12394-8
        1. College readers. 2. Report writing—Problems, exercises, etc. 3. English
    language—Rhetoric—Problems, exercises, etc. I. Ford, Jon. II. Title.

PE1417.D74 2004
808'.0427—dc21

                                                                2002043854

Copyright © 2004 by Pearson Education, Inc.

All rights reserved. No part of this publication may be reproduced, stored in a retrieval
system, or transmitted, in any form or by any means, electronic, mechanical,
photocopying, recording, or otherwise, without the prior written permission of the
publisher. Printed in the United States.

Please visit our website at http://www.ablongman.com

ISBN 0-321-12394-8

1 2 3 4 5 6 7 8 9 10—DOC—06 05 04 03

Contents

1 Discovering Ourselves in Writing and Reading   1

A Process View of Writing and Reading   2

The writing/reading processes are introduced, including prewriting, prereading and journal-keeping techniques.

The Writing Process and Self-discovery ■ Stages of the Writing Process ■ Strategies for Prewriting ■ Your Computer: Developing an Important Writing Partnership ■ The Reading Process ■ Personal and Interpretive Response ■ Critical and Evaluative Response ■ "Reading" Electronic Media

Thematic Introduction   13

Writing and reading are presented as processes of self-discovery rooted in personal experiences and the unconscious mind, including dreams, childhood memories, and everyday events. Each of the selections presents a unique perspective on the way people read, write, and interpret texts; selections also reflect on the ways that reading and writing play a part in the development of the inner life and imagination.

Readings

Wallace Stevens, "Of Modern Poetry" (poem)   15

"[A]n invisible audience listens,/to itself, expressed/in an emotion as of two people,/as of two emotions becoming one. . . ."

Stephen King, "The Symbolic Language of Dreams" (essay)   17

"I think that dreams are a way that people's minds illustrate the nature of their problems. Or maybe even illustrate the answers to their problems in symbolic language."

Student Writing

2 Visions of Nature   67

Student Writing

Bruno Bettelheim, "Fairy Tales and the Existential Predicament" (essay)   214

"[T]he form and structure of fairy tales suggest images to children by which they can structure their daydreams and with them give better direction to their life."

Four Versions of Cinderella   220

The many common elements found in versions from different periods and cultures of this story of an exploited young girl's rise in the world demonstrate the universality of fundamental story-lines in imaginative tales which teach and uplift young readers.

Student Writing

Joshua Groban, "Two Myths" (essay)   237

"The comparison of different creation myths . . . represents a reasoned approach to looking at God and creation and thus what true religious conviction really is."

Liz Scheps, "Cinderella: Politically Incorrect?" (essay)   240

"Garner creates a tale designed to entice and entertain people of all outlooks, while at the same time providing a strong and stinging critique of political correctness, and especially of feminism."

5   Obsessions and Transformation   246

6 Journeys in Sexuality and Gender   313

7   The Double/The Other   375

Argument and Dialogue   376

The argument essay is presented both as a type of dialogue between aspects of the writer's self and as a dialogue between writer and audience.

Traditional Argument ■ Dialogic Argument ■ Dialogue and Prewriting ■
Prewriting and the Audience ■ Defining Key Terms ■ Evaluating
Facts ■ Feelings in Argument

Thematic Introduction   515

The inward journey concludes with visions from the spiritual world which can help us to learn how to utilize our creative abilities to solve problems and to visualize and shape alternatives to the world as it is now.

Readings

Student Writing

Contents by Strategies and Modes

Process Analysis

Example and Illustration

Comparison and Contrast

Classification

Definition

Cause and Effect Analysis

Argument

Interpretation and Evaluation

Research Writing

Myths & Tales

Literary Fiction

Poetry

To the Student

> *Nothing said to us, nothing we can learn from others, reaches us so deep as that which we find in ourselves.*
> *Theodore Reik*

Each person has a unique understanding of the role and importance of dreams: We may value and analyze the dreams we have while asleep, our day time fantasies, our hopes and aspirations, our belief in the power of our own imagination and creativity. The lyrics of popular songs, the plots of movies and novels, advertisements and travel literature—all speak of the power of dreams and promise fulfillment of fantasies, romance, success, or peace of mind. As you think more about the presence and importance of dreams in your personal life and culture, you will begin to discover even more subtle meanings. Just as everyone dreams while sleeping, each person has a personal dream or vision that guides his or her waking life. Perhaps it is a dream that one is just starting to explore, a dream that one has been working to accomplish, or a dream that has just "come true."

We have designed this text using the concept of the dream as a common meeting ground, one that we hope will encourage you to better understand yourself, your family, friends, college, and professional acquaintances—and the world in which you live. Dreams and the insights they bring from the inner self, with the universality of their patterns, imagery, and meaning, also present a central metaphor that can be likened to the writing process that is often an inward journey that involves the imagination, creativity, and vision.

Dreams and Inward Journeys: A Reader for Writers, Fifth Edition, is composed of nine chapters. Each chapter presents an aspect of the book's theme as well as a writing strategy that we think will help you to understand yourself and your world while improving your writing fluency and skills. The earlier chapters ask you to reflect on your personal experiences as a reader and as a writer. As you progress through the book, you will be asked to relate your personal and imaginative experiences to the social and cultural realities that also help to shape your identity and values.

In Chapter 1, "Discovering Ourselves in Reading and Writing," you will explore the ways in which reading is an active process that encourages the reader to understand and clarify her or his inner resources and values in relation to the values and experiences that have been recorded in a text. The reading strategies introduced discuss techniques for activating and enriching your reading and language experience. We also emphasize how reading is closely related to writing, which is presented as a process that is often chaotic in its initial stages, but powerful and rewarding. Writing and revising help a writer to understand himself or herself better and to clarify thoughts and feelings. The writing techniques explained will help you to overcome writing-related anxieties and fears and to get you started on your writing. The dream journal project introduced in this chapter will provide you with the opportunity to discover the similarities between the writing process and dreaming—to discover the concerns of your unconscious mind.

In Chapter 2, "Observing Nature," the essays invite you to reflect on the way nature can inspire and help you reflect on the essential connections between human beings and the natural world. The selections in this chapter present a variety of experiences in nature that brought the writer to a revelation about the beauty of the natural world: the challenges of viewing magnificent natural formations, the wisdom that natural creatures show us when we watch listen to and recognize how they organize and value their own worlds. The strategies that we focus on—observing and capturing details, using words and images (both literally as well as metaphorically), and the essential power of revision through thinking about communicating with your audience—will help you to create striking accounts of what you see and have been affected by in the natural world.

The readings in Chapter 3, "Memories," explore how early experiences and memories, especially those inner experiences that are rooted in dreams, fantasies, or even obsessions, influence one's sense of self. The readings included in this section also suggest that the stories one created and remembered from childhood help to shape personal myths. In this chapter we discuss creative strategies for writing effective narratives. These strategies will help you when you write about your dreams and memories.

Chapter 4, "Dreams, Myths, and Fairy Tales," will help you develop perspective on your inward journey so that you can place it in a broader social and cultural context. Seeing how your self-concept and values have been influenced by ancient and popular myths and fairy tales may encourage you to seek out new meanings in your life experiences. Some of the readings in this chapter discuss the similarities and relationships between dreams and myths. Because you will be asked to compare different versions of fairy tales, to contrast an early memory of a favorite childhood book with a more recent reading of that book, or to create and evaluate a personal myth, in this chapter we discuss strategies used in comparison writing as well as approaches to making clear evaluative statements.

The readings included in Chapter 5, "Obsessions and Transformations," reveal situations in which the writer or the main character of a selection is overwhelmed by a submerged part of his or her self. Although the writers present the feeling of being overwhelmed as frightening, in each selection the obsession is ultimately transformed positively into greater self-understanding. The thinking and writing strategies discussed in this chapter will help you to define and draw distinctions among complex concepts such as dreams, myths, obsessions and fantasies. We also explore some common misuses of words and barriers to clear communication as well as the difference between the private and public meanings and associations of words.

Chapter 6, "Journeys in Sexuality and Gender," explores issues of gender and sexuality in both fiction and nonfiction works as they influence an individual's self-concept and role in society. The readings also examine ways that sexuality is reflected in dreams and emotional life, as well as the way that sexual feelings are channeled through myths and rituals. The writing and thinking strategy presented in this chapter, causal analysis, will help you to analyze and interpret the readings and will provide you with a structure for composing the essays you will be asked to write in response to the readings.

Chapter 7, "The Double/The Other," begins with a discussion of the double-sided nature of the human personality and presents readings, including a variety of classic stories, many of which are based on dreams or fantasies. These essays and stories reflect different forms of the dualistic struggle within the human mind: the good self as opposed to the evil self, the rational self as opposed to the irrational self. The writing strategies in this chapter focus on how to create a balanced argument through exploring opposing viewpoints, empathizing with your audience, making decisions, and taking a final position of your own.

To what extent have your self-concept and self-image been influenced by the dreams of our mass culture or the prevailing political ideology? What happens to those people who don't choose to fit into, or who feel excluded from, the predominant dream of their society? These are some of the questions that are considered in the readings included in Chapter 8, "Society's Dreams." The research writing strategies covered will help you to analyze social issues and to think critically about outside sources of opinion while maintaining your own personal perspective and sense of voice in research writing.

The book concludes with a chapter on "Visions of Spirituality." Dreams and visions that can present warnings or remind you of past experiences and help you to imagine a life beyond the familiar one. It is natural to wonder about what happens after a person dies. If you believe in a soul, some of the readings in this chapter will help you to think about the qualities of spiritual life in the here and now and also in the after life. Synthesis and problem solving, the writing strategies presented in this chapter, will help to reinforce your understanding of the chapter's readings and guide you in developing complex, creative essays.

Our experiences as writing teachers continue to confirm the importance of providing students with many opportunities to share their writing with their peers. We have included student essays for you to discuss in class. We hope, too, that you will share your own writing. We believe that you can gain confidence and motivation when you work on your writing with your peers and your instructor.

Although writing is a demanding and challenging activity, it can be a valuable and meaningful experience when you feel you are writing about something vital, something that engages your mind and your emotions. We have worked to provide opportunities for this type of engagement through the materials and activities included in this text. We hope that *Dreams and Inward Journeys* will guide and help you to uncover and understand more fully your personal and public dreams.

Marjorie Ford
Jon Ford

To the Instructor

Why have many of our greatest writers found inspiration or solved problems through their dreams? What can individuals learn from their
dreams that will make their waking lives and their writing more rewarding?
How does the unconscious mind inform the conscious mind using writing or
dreams as a medium? In what ways is the writing process like a dream? These
are questions that we have been exploring in our writing classes for more than
ten years now. Still they continue to remain as signposts; our search for these
answers to these questions has only grown more compelling through the years
of teaching *Dreams and Inward Journeys*.

Gathering the new materials and writing the Fifth Edition of *Dreams and
Inward Journeys*, we have felt very fortunate indeed to have the opportunity to
continue following our dreams. In this new edition we have built on the peda-
gogical foundation put in place by the earlier editions. We continue to support
a creative approach to teaching writing and reading that acknowledges the role
and importance of the unconscious mind, of dreams, of the imagination, of
the heart connected to the reasoning mind. Also fundamental to our approach
to teaching writing is the value of integrating rather than isolating the teaching
of literature and expository writing. We have seen our students' writing develop as they have experimented with different writing projects and genres,
from dream journals, poems and short stories to arguments; from practice with
essays based on the traditional modes such as comparison, causal analysis, and
definition to reflective essays that are primarily based on personal experiences.

As in previous editions of *Dreams*, we have enjoyed applying these assumptions in shaping the text around the theme of dreams, a topic that is intriguing,
revealing, and challenging. *Dreams and Inward Journeys* presents a rich mixture
of essays, stories, poems, and student writings thematically focused on dream-
related topics such as writing, reading, nature, memory, myths, obsessions, the
double, sexuality, gender roles, technology, popular culture, and spirituality.
Each chapter features rhetorical advice and strategies for writing and critical
thinking. All of the included selections have personal and social meanings that
encourage students to think about and develop new ways of seeing and understanding themselves in relation to fundamental social issues as well as universal
human concerns.

Special features of the Fifth Edition include:

- Thirty-eight new readings that continue to develop and update the text's
  thematic concept with more particular attention to social and political
  issues.

- A rhetorical advice section that opens each chapter and provides students with one particular writing and thinking strategy.
- Two new chapters: Chapter 2: "Observing Nature" and Chapter 9: "Spirituality."
- Classical artwork that supports the theme of each chapter, with related prompts that generate prewriting activities, informal, and formal writing projects.
- Two student essays in each chapter that present students' perspectives on the topics raised in the chapter and provide models of the rhetorical strategy outlined at the beginning of each chapter. Four of the student essays in the book are documented argumentative research papers.
- Information on keeping a dream journal as well as journal writing prompts before each reading to encourage informal, expressive, and spontaneous thinking and writing.
- One poem per chapter that explores the chapter's theme in a concrete, expressive, and literary form.
- New "Connection" questions as well as "Questions for Discussion" and "Ideas for Writing."
- "Topics for Research and Writing" questions at the end of each chapter. These questions give students suggestions for research and longer writing assignments, as well as film and URL suggestions for further viewing/reading/research.
- Two web sites related to each selection to encourage students to do further research on the topics raised in the reading.

In addition, an Instructor's Manual is available to teachers who adopt the Fifth Edition of *Dreams and Inward Journeys*. The Instructor's Manual presents instructors with three possible course constructions as well as teaching suggestions and possible responses to the study questions for each reading.

Acknowledgments

First, we thank our reviewers around the country whose advice guided us in this revision: Kitty Chen Dean, Nassau Community College; Stacey Donohue, Central Oregon Community College; Janet Carey Eldred, University of Kentucky; Suzanne Gates, El Camino College; Andrew Lamers, Bakersfield College; Rebecca Jones, University of North Carolina–Greensboro; Randall Pease, University of Southern Indiana; and Marianne Taylor, Kirkwood Community College.

We also give thanks to our editor, Lynn Huddon, who has helped us to interpret and apply the advice of the critics and to continue to help us develop the creative vision of the book. We thank Jami Darby of WestWords for her consistently supportive supervision of the manuscript's proofreading. We whould also like to thank Michael Ford for finding the web-sites that are included after each selection in this edition and Judy Moffett for her assistance with the study-question responses in the Instructor's Manual. Cindy Taylor managed the editing and formatting of the Manual; we would also like to thank her for her patience and helpful advice.

We thank our students at Stanford University and DeAnza College who have provided many valuable insights into ways that we could develop the manuscript's themes and keep the text lively. We are especially grateful to the students at Stanford: Melissa Burns, Tiffany Castillo, Elizabeth Matchett, Josh Spires, and Molly Thomas, all of whom wrote new essays for this edition, spending much time outside of their required writing assignments to produce works that we think will inspire your student writers.

We thank our friends and relatives who have provided encouragement and love: Olivia Hurd, Barbara Klein, Elizabeth Schave, and Cathy Young. Marjorie Ford would like to acknowledge and thank her doctors: Dr. Gayle Hylton and Dr. Jay Schlumpberger, whose wisdom and care helped her to recover from serious abdominal surgery while this edition of the *Dreams* book was being produced.

Finally we thank our loving children, Michael and Maya, whose lives bring us joy on a daily basis and make our own lives complete.

Marjorie Ford
Jon Ford

Discovering Ourselves in Reading and Writing

Johannes Vermeer (1632–1675)
A Lady Writing a Letter (1662–1664)

In his portraits of middle-class domestic life, seventeenth-century Dutch painter Vermeer was a master of clarity in light, composition, and space. The fashionably dressed, intelligent-looking young woman in *A Lady Writing a Letter* is caught in the moment as she looks up from her writing, both hands still resting on the page.

JOURNAL

Write about your thoughts as you engage in the act of writing: Do you become distracted, or do you find yourself in a deep state of concentration in which you are able to screen out external sounds and ideas unrelated to your writing?

Writing itself is one of the great, free human activities. . . . For the person who follows what occurs to him with trust and forgiveness, the world remains always ready and deep, an inexhaustible environment, with the combined vividness of an actuality and flexibility of a dream.

WILLIAM STAFFORD
The Way of Writing

A dream which is not understood is like a letter which is not opened.
The Talmud

Looking back, it's clear to me that I was reading as a creator, bringing myself . . . to a collaboration with the writer in the invention of an alternate world. These books were not collections of abstract symbols called words, printed on paper; they were real events that had happened to me.

PETE HAMILL
D'Artagnan on Ninth Street:
A Brooklyn Boy at the Library

A PROCESS VIEW OF WRITING AND READING

When people write and read, they are concerned with self-discovery just as they are when they explore their dreams. Both writing and reading are complex processes that a reader controls consciously and also experiences unconsciously. These processes, for most of us, begin almost at the same time, although we may have had experience having our parents or pre-school teachers read to us before we actually begin to study our ABCs and learn to write and to read. In the act of writing, a sort of internal conversation takes place between what we read and our own inner experiences and ideas that help us to come up with the words we put down on the page. Similarly, in the act of reading, as in a conversation, a dialogue takes place between the voice of the inner self and the voice of the text being read. A good conversation with a text can lead to the development and clarification of the writer's and the reader's values and ideas. Both reading and writing require some formal understanding of literary conventions and language codes. To write well, we must have done some reading: the more the better. Likewise writing down our responses to what we read helps to clarify our interpretations and evaluations of complex texts.

Because the processes are so interrelated, we could begin our discussion with either writing or reading. Since the course you are probably taking now is a "writing class," we will start with writing and move outward to the more public, responsive dimension of reading and writing about what we read.

The Writing Process and Self-discovery

William Stafford has said that "writing itself is one of the great, free human activities. There is scope for individuality, and elation, and discovery, in writing." At the same time, a good writer is also a patient craftsperson. Writing makes demands on both the creative and the rational sides of the mind. From the creative and intuitive mind it summons forth details, images, memories, dreams, and feelings; from the rational and logical mind it demands planning, development, evidence, rereading, rethinking, and revision.

Perhaps it is this basic duality associated with the act of writing that can sometimes make it feel like a complex and overwhelming task. Practicing and studying particular writing strategies such as those presented in each chapter of *Dreams and Inward Journeys*, along with drafting, revising, and sharing your writing with your peers and instructor, will help you to develop your self-confidence. As a writer you need to be aware of the feelings and fears of your unconscious self as well as the expectations of your rational mind. Balancing these two sides of your mind—knowing when, for example, to give your creative mind license to explore while controlling and quieting your critical mind—is an important part of the challenge of developing self-confidence and learning to write well.

Stages of the Writing Process

Most professional and student writers benefit from conceptualizing writing as a process with a number of stages. Although these stages do not need to be rigidly separated, an awareness of the different quality of thoughts and feelings that usually occur in each of the stages of writing is useful. Having a perspective on your writing process will encourage you to be patient and help you create a finished piece of writing that speaks clearly about your own concerns, values, and opinions. The stages of the writing process include the prewriting, drafting, and revision phases. As you become a more experienced and skillful writer, you may find that you want to adapt this process to the goals of your writing assignment. Perhaps you will find that you need to spend more time in preliminary reading to collect background information for a research essay, or that you don't have as much time to spend on prewriting if you are working on an essay that must be completed in a shorter time frame or during an in-class exam.

As preparation for writing the initial draft of an essay, prewriting allows you to pursue a variety of playful, creative activities that will help you to generate ideas and understand what you want to say about your subject. Drafting is your rapid first "take" on your topic and should be done after you have concentrated on your paper's subject and thought about the thesis or core concept around which you want to center the ideas and examples of your essay. You may find, however, that as you write your first draft, your thesis and focus shift or even change dramatically. Don't be concerned if this happens. Many professional writers have learned that although they begin the drafting phase feeling that they have a focus and thesis, the actual process of writing the draft changes their initial plan. Rewriting is a natural part of the writing process. As you return to your draft and continue to work to shape your thoughts into clear sentences, they will better capture your inner feelings and ideas.

While you will need to rewrite to clarify your thinking and ideas, the process of revision can also be approached in stages. They include revising for your paper's overall shape and meaning, which may involve outlining the rough draft; rearranging whole paragraphs or ideas and examples; developing and cutting redundancy within paragraphs; refining and clarifying sentences and individual words; and, finally, proofreading for grammar, spelling, and punctuation. The revision and editing stages of writing have become more exciting and less tedious since the invention of the computer and word processing software. Now your computer can help you because it includes commands for cutting and pasting text, outliners, spelling and grammar checkers, word and paragraph counters, and global search and replace functions that make it easier to correct any aspect of the entire essay. But revision is still a time-consuming and important element of the writing process, for it is through revision and editing that your essay moves from an approximate statement of a thought or insight into a well-crafted and moving verbal expression of your thoughts and purpose.

Strategies for Prewriting

Because writing begins with prewriting, we have chosen to focus on this stage here, at the beginning of your journey as a writer. The prewriting stage is enjoyable for those who enjoy creative expression, and helpful for people who don't have much confidence in themselves as writers, who feel it is hard to get warmed up to the task. If you are apprehensive about writing and don't see yourself as a creative thinker, prewriting activities may help you to discover new or forgotten images, memories, and ideas, as well as to make connections you may never have anticipated. You may find yourself liberating a creative spirit hidden in the recesses of your mind. You are the only person who needs to read and evaluate your prewriting; at this stage you determine what seems interesting and relevant.

Prewriting also makes the writing of later drafts easier because it helps you to clarify and organize your thoughts before they are put into a formal format. Drawing, freewriting, invisible writing, brainstorming, clustering, and journal keeping are all effective prewriting techniques that will help you to discover what you really want and need to say. Like the later stages of writing, all of these techniques can be practiced either with a pencil, a pen, or with sophisticated computer software. Although many students feel more comfortable and natural prewriting with a pencil, students who are familiar with the computer and have good keyboarding skills often find it helpful to do their prewritings on the computer so that they can save and possibly transform their initial ideas into details, images, and sentences for their drafts.

Drawing   Drawing a picture in response to a topic can help you understand what you think and feel. In the drawings in response to a topic included in this text, students used a computer program to capture their writing

A raindrop begins as a suspension of water. The instant it explodes upon a surface, it spreads and touches everything around it. Just as its potential for expansion increases the farther it falls, my writing process takes shape the deeper it progresses. At first, I begin with nothing, like the blank regions in this background. Then, an idea buds, and I find that the crescendo of my thoughts is like the descent of this raindrop, until it finally bursts and my idea flowers into a new creation. Just as the water is transformed into a broad palette of colors, my writing welcomes potential and growth in various forms.

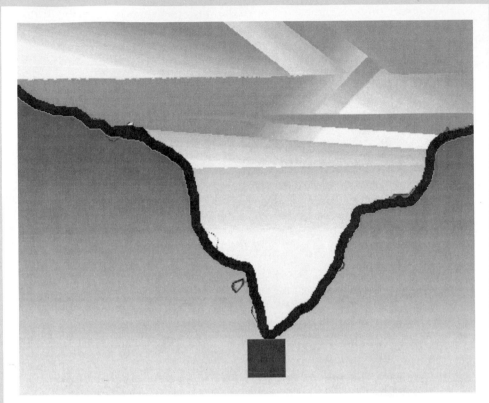

You should "read" my picture from top to bottom. My writing process, as with anybody's, begins with human creativity, an entity as vast and varied as the endless blue skies. When I am called upon to write, I channel my creativity amidst a sea of red, seething frustration. I constantly try to convey my thoughts exactly to my reader, a tedious process. As the channel narrows, the frustration decreases in intensity and I get closer to my final product. At last, when the channel reaches its apex, my pains are rewarded. The result is green, new and fresh, and square, rigid to my expectations.

processes and responses to readings, but you may feel more comfortable using colored pencils, watercolors, charcoal, or ink. A number of professional writers have spoken of the value of drawing as a way to develop ideas or understand a new text. In *The Nature and Aim of Fiction* Flannery O'Connor maintains, "Any discipline can help your writing . . . particularly drawing. Anything that helps you to see, anything that makes you look." While drawing an image from a complex text you are reading, you will be able to focus your thoughts on the details that may have already unconsciously captured your imagination. This process of drawing about a piece of writing will increase your engagement with it and help you clarify your response as you make that response more tangible.

Freewriting   A freewrite can start anywhere and usually lasts from 5 to 15 minutes. During these brief writing sessions, it is important to continue to write and not to censor any idea or feeling that comes to your mind. If you seem to run out of thoughts, just write, "I have no more to say," or anything you wish until a new thought emerges. After ten minutes of freewriting, read what you have written and try to sum up the central idea or feeling of the piece. You can then proceed to another freewrite, using the summary statement as a new starting point. Writers often do several freewrites before they decide how to focus their thoughts.

Invisible Writing   With invisible writing, the writer creates "invisible" words, or words that can't be seen while the writer is working. Some writers never even look at the words generated in an invisible writing exercise but instead use the exercise as a rehearsal, a building of mental pathways that will make the actual writing of their paper less halting and painful. Many writers find new insights in their thoughts that were produced invisibly. Invisible writing can be done by writing on the back of a piece of carbon paper onto a piece of notebook paper or by keyboarding with a dimmed computer screen. While you are freewriting and doing invisible writing, do not consciously pay attention to central ideas, relationships between ideas, organizational patterns, or grammatical or spelling errors. Concentrate instead on getting your ideas and feelings out in words.

Brainstorming   Brainstorming, which can be done effectively in groups or individually, involves writing a list of words, phrases, ideas, descriptions, thoughts, and questions that come to your mind in response to a topic or issue. As in freewriting, it is essential not to stop to censor, judge, or correct ideas or feelings. The process of listing will, itself, bring up new ideas and associations. Ideas will build on one another, leading to thoughts that are original and fresh, while creating a list will help you to see relationships between ideas that may have previously seemed disconnected. When your list is complete, normally in 15 to 20 minutes, go back to find patterns of thought or main ideas that you have uncovered. Bracketing or circling related ideas and details may help you form an organizational plan. Through brainstorming, you can formulate a rough outline for your essay that will guide you in the drafting phase of writing.

Clustering   Clustering, or mapping, closely reflects the way the mind functions in making nonlinear connections between ideas. Combined with brainstorming or freewriting, clustering can also help you to perceive relationships between ideas. Start your cluster by placing the topic to be explored in the center of the page. Draw a circle around it, and then draw lines out from your central circle in different directions to connect it with other circles containing additional ideas, phrases, or clues to experiences. The words in these circles will naturally develop their own offshoots as new associations emerge. The pattern being created by the clustering process continually changes in complex ways because any new idea will relate to all of the ideas already recorded. As in freewriting, clustering should be done without stopping. Once the cluster feels completed to you, write for a few minutes about what you have discovered. Completing a cluster and a related freewrite can help you understand how you want to focus your topic and organize the major relationships between ideas, examples, and details.

Journal Keeping   Daily writing in a notebook or journal will help you develop a record of your thoughts and feelings. Keeping a journal is similar to the type of prewriting assignments we have just discussed in that it allows you freedom to explore parts of your inner world, knowing that your writing will not be evaluated. Keeping a journal of your responses to the journal topics and study questions in a text, using either a small notebook or computer, is one of the most effective ways to develop your confidence and skills as a writer. Both of the student essays included in this chapter were developed from journal entries that focused on strong inner experiences and images that initially seemed very private but were clarified and made public through drafting, revising, peer sharing, and more revision.

The Dream Journal   Because this text has been developed around the theme of dreams, and because the process of understanding your dreams may lead you to new insights and images that you may find useful in more formal writing, we recommend that you extend your journal keeping into the night world by writing down your dreams—a process used by many professional writers. Through keeping a dream journal you can improve your ability to recall dreams, and you can capture unconscious images that intrigue or possibly disturb you. Perhaps, too, you will notice more similarities between your dream images and some of the dream-like stories in this text. Your appreciation of metaphors and symbols will increase.

By keeping your dream journal, you will also realize how understanding your writing process is similar to understanding your dreams. The first written draft of your dream is like a prewrite of an essay: a set of strong, if chaotic, images that you can work with thoughtfully and creatively. As you bring form and meaning to a dream through analysis and interpretation, you bring form and meaning to an essay through drafting and revising those first generative ideas that begin the process of writing an essay, story, or poem.

Keep your dream journal at your bedside along with a pen or dark pencil. The best time to write in your dream journal is in the early morning or immediately on awaking from a vivid dream. Some students have even used a tape recorder to capture their "dream voice," its sounds and rhythms. Try to write in your dream journal three or four times a week, even if you have only a dim or fleeting image or impression to record. Write down all the details you can remember, indicating a shift, jump in time, or unclear portion of the dream with a question mark or ellipsis. Try not to censor or "clean up" the dream imagery, even if the thinking seems illogical, chaotic, or even embarrassing to you. Avoid interpreting your dream as you are recording it, although you might list in the margins any associations that immediately come to mind in relation to the images as you record them. Later, as you reread your dream journal entries over a period of several days, you may see patterns and more complex associations emerging and you may want to write about them.

Your Computer: Developing an Important Writing Partnership

More and more students come to their college writing classes with basic computer skills. You may already use e-mail and the Internet on a daily basis. You will also find that your computer will help to facilitate and streamline your writing process. Computers are not just "keyboarding tools," or for printing out text. As mentioned previously, in the later stages of revising and editing, computers are invaluable, making it possible to reorganize your paper easily by moving around large sections of your essay, adding in concise examples and details, fine tuning grammar, syntax, and word choice. The spelling checker on your computer will help you prepare your draft for final presentation, while an on-line dictionary and thesaurus make it possible to find just the right word for precise and powerful expression. Some students find that the flexibility that computers provide to generate new ideas, experiment, and change sentences, paragraphs, details, examples, and refine major ideas helps them to overcome writing blocks.

In fact, all of the strategies for prewriting mentioned here, particularly the technique of invisible writing can be completed on a computer and saved. Other exploratory techniques work only on a computer, such as engaging in an on-line conversation on a subject for writing using a chat program or e-mail, and then saving the conversation for later use. You might decide to copy sections from any of your prewritings into the first or a later draft of your essay; this is much easier to do if you write them on a computer rather than on a piece of paper.

Prewriting strategies are more frequently used in the generative stage of the writing process, but we encourage you to use these techniques whenever you feel yourself getting blocked in your work. During the drafting stage of writing, or even after an instructor has returned your paper to you with corrections on it and you are working on a major revision, the exercises discussed here can continue to help you keep in touch with what you really want to say—with your own inner voice.

Discovering Ourselves in Reading: The Reading Process

Once absorbed in the complex mental process of reading, readers desire to identify with the characters, the ideas, the emotions, and the cultural and social assumptions of the text. Readers then are able to experience new and different realities vicariously; these encounters can contribute to the reader's personal growth as they present new intellectual and emotional experiences that help readers to build their inner resources. As a person becomes a better reader and develops a richer life through reading, his or her writing may also become more fluent and varied as the reader becomes more conscious of public values, opinions, and cultures that are different from his or her personal experiences.

Writing is one of the most valuable ways to respond to what you read. Writing about what you're reading will help you articulate and clarify your responses and will improve your writing as you develop your writer's voice through connecting to the words and thoughts of others. As with any form of writing, responses to reading can move through a series of phases or stages, each one building upon the next, moving gradually from prereading strategies to interpretation and evaluation.

Prereading/Early Reading

In the prereading phase you examine what you plan to read, browsing through titles, subheadings, noting epigraphs, topic sentences, headnotes and footnotes, just as you probably did when you first picked up this textbook. Prereading can be a very helpful process if you combine it with writing down basic questions that you have during this initial browsing stage. Does this work seem like fact or fiction? Was it written recently or in the distant past? Is its style experimental or traditional? Is the writer American or is he or she from a different culture and country? Is the writer male or female? Is the subject a familiar one? Do you need more background knowledge to understand the subject? Asking and answering such questions can help you become involved with the text and can help put you into a receptive frame of mind. After previewing the work, proceed to the second part of the first stage in reading, the "early reading" phase. In this phase as in writing a first draft, you simply plunge in, reading the work quickly to get an overall sense of its meaning, perhaps noting a few key passages or putting a question mark by an idea or detail that seems unfamiliar or confusing. At this stage of reading, avoid negative preconceptions about the content of the reading; don't tell yourself, "This is about a subject in which I have absolutely no interest." Try instead to be open to the reading. Avoid evaluating the text before you give yourself a chance to become engaged with it.

Personal and Interpretive Response

In this second stage, the interpretive response phase, put the reading aside for a moment and write down a few immediate, personal reactions: Is this piece what I expected it to be? Did it make me angry? Sad? Elated? How did the piece challenge me? What didn't I understand after the first reading? Reread your notes and questions before attempting another reading. The second time, read more slowly and reflectively. Try to answer some of your initial questions as well as to move toward an overview and interpretation of the piece as a whole—its meaning, or your view of its meaning at this stage in your reading.

   Look for those patterns that support an interpretation or view of the work: metaphors, plot and subplot, character relationships and conflicts, point of view, evolving persona, narrative voice. Mark your book, placing circles around and drawing lines to connect ideas and images that you believe form a pattern of meaning. Ask yourself how much of the work is meant to be responded to literally, and how much is meant to be considered as ironic or symbolic. Record responses to this stage of the reading process in writing, including some particular quotations and references to the text. Also compare your reactions at this stage of reading with your written responses to the first reading of the text. You will probably find that your ideas have deepened considerably and that you have a more complete and interpretive view of the work than you did initially.

Critical and Evaluative Response

For the third stage in your reading/writing process, the "critical" phase, reread the story again more rapidly, after reviewing your second written response and your textual references. Now write a final response, clarifying how this reading confirms, expands on, or causes you to question or revise your earlier readings. Using particular elements in the text that you noticed in your earlier readings as evidence, try to draw some larger evaluative conclusions about the work and your response to it: Is your overall response to the values, ideas, and emotions in the work positive or negative? How do you feel about the unity of the piece, its quality as writing? How do the values of this selection reflect or illuminate issues of concern to you and to your community? Was there something new and special about the experience of reading this work? Did it remind you of or seem to build upon other, similar works with which you are familiar? After finishing the text, did you want to read more by this writer or learn more about the theme of the work by reading related works by other writers? Would you recommend the work to other readers?

"Reading" Nonprint, Multimedia, and Online Texts

Although some theorists believe that the traditional act of reading is passé in this electronic age, the perceptual and critical thinking process for decoding, analyzing, interpreting, and evaluating materials that involve images along with printed words or even with no words at all is not as different from book reading as it might seem. Whether you are reading a book, watching a film, viewing a television show, or scrolling through Web pages, you need to pay close attention to all clues for meaning available. You will need to look for patterns of imagery, symbols, significant character interaction, plotlines, and crucial meaning statements, whether in the form of speeches by characters, key bits of dialogue, or voice-overs (in the case of a film).

   Whether reading a book, viewing a film, or examining a Web page, you also need to know something about the author (director/screenwriter, in the case of a film, or, in the case of many Web pages, the organization that has produced the page and its objectives). You need to know how this work builds on other works by the same writer or organization, as well as what cultural assumptions and traditions (of writing, filmmaking, or multimedia) the work issues from.

Finally, whether you are reading a book, watching a film/TV show, or even cruising the Internet, you need the opportunity for a second reading/viewing, to get closer to the work through repeated exposure to grasp its full significance and to make interpretations and connections with other similar works. While this is easier and cheaper to do with a book, you can always watch a film a second time, take notes, videotape a TV show, or, in the case of Web pages, bookmark the page or save the text on disk for instant replay later on. Note that in nonprint media or multi-media you have to learn to read visual images for intellectual suggestions and emotional impact, just as you examine the words in a written text closely for their connotations or shadings of meaning. In multimedia, you need to be alert to a complex interplay between words, images, and even sounds.

What makes a person a good reader, interpreter, and judge of electronic media are precisely the kind of good study habits that an experienced reader brings to a book. You need to resist the passive mood many people sink into in front of TV sets or the "surf" mentality that involves clicking rapidly and restlessly from one link to another on the Internet. When studying media, writing can be an especially helpful way to develop critical responses. Try keeping a journal of media you watch and listen to, responding actively by using the kind of entries suggested above in the section on the reader's journal: preliminary responses and entries, interpretive entries, and evaluative entries for a repeated viewing of material that looks interesting. In this way, you can become a strong reader, sensitive to the world of books as well as an able critic of the electronic media that surround us daily, which at times overwhelm our abilities to respond or to take a position.

In reading and writing about the essays, stories, and poems selected for this textbook as well as the different media that you encounter, try to practice the slow, three-stage reading and written response process outlined above, taking time to write down questions and responses in your notebook and in the margins of the text. Give yourself enough time to absorb and think about what you have read and viewed. Your patience will yield you both heightened understanding as well as deeper pleasure in all your learning experiences.

THEMATIC INTRODUCTION: DISCOVERING OURSELVES IN WRITING AND READING

Writing and reading can be described as inward journeys. Discovering what resides within your mind and your spirit begins anew each time you start a writing or reading project. Many people find it difficult to begin, wondering how they will be able to untangle all of their thoughts and feelings, and how they will finally decide on the most accurate words and sentence patterns to make their statement clear and compelling. You may feel overwhelmed by the possibilities of all that is waiting to be discovered within you, and, at the same time, you may feel a sense of wonder and excitement, anticipating pleasures and rewards of uncovering and expressing new parts of your mind, imagination, and spirit.

The complex feelings often experienced at the beginning of the writing/reading process have been eloquently described by many authors whose language, images, and ideas can serve as your guides. They experience writing and reading as processes of self-discovery and self-understanding that are rooted in their unconscious and conscious mind, in their dreams and memories of childhood, and in their everyday lives and goals. At the same time, reading and writing are about communication with the public world as well as the inner world.

This chapter's readings begin with Wallace Steven's powerful poem "Of Modern Poetry." Stevens defines reading and writing poetry in ways that can apply generally to the writing/reading process. He sees modern poetry as engaged in finding "what will suffice"—a living form of expression involving the "speech of the place"—not just academic language—as well as the concerns close to contemporary men and women, such as war. Stevens also sees poetry (as is the case with other forms of writing), as being essentially a dialogue between writer and reader, "an emotion as of two people, as of two emotions becoming one." In the selection that follows, "The Symbolic Language of Dreams," popular novelist Stephen King discusses the ways in which his dreams have helped him to solve problems that he has had in writing. He compares his writing process to a dream state. In "Teaching Two Kinds of Thinking by Teaching Writing," English professor Peter Elbow, like King, presents an approach to writing in which he encourages the creative, intuitive unconscious mind to work separately but supportively with logical, critical modes of thinking and reasoning that are concerned with communicating clearly and effectively with the reader.

Virginia Woolf, in her classic essay, "Professions for Women," explores how social, economic, and gender status has an impact on a person's writing. She takes the position that writers need a particular place free of distraction to pursue their craft, noting that gender-bias in the patriarchal society of her time caused women writers to have difficulty accessing the dream and fantasy worlds that seems so available to authors like Stephen King. In her essay "Mother Tongue," best-selling novelist Amy Tan reveals how she developed her talents by incorporating all that she and her mother, a nonnative speaker, knew about language and about life — "what language ability tests can never reveal: her [mother's] intent, her passion, her imagery, the rhythms of her speech and the nature of her thoughts."

Reading can be a very active, intriguing, and creative process. Several of the authors in this chapter reflect on the ways that reading plays a part in the development of the reader's inner life and imagination. A reader with a calm mind can come to feel like a part of a book that he or she is reading. Frederick Douglass in "Learning to Read," shares his passion for reading; he speaks of his awakening to freedom through the knowledge he uncovers in the books of the great writers of his time. As a Southern African-American during the time of slavery, Douglass had to be very resourceful to gain the privilege of learning to read.

In contrast, in "Don't Look Back," software executive Steven Holtzman argues that we can't turn our backs on the new ways that reading is presented to us through technology. Holtzman believes that technology is already such an inextricable part of our lives that it has changed our experience of reading and the nature of the book itself. Journalist Linton Weeks in his essay, "The No-Book Report: Skim It and Weep," presents a different perspective on the impact of the electronic age on reading, providing evidence which suggests that many "aliterate" Americans are choosing to read as little as possible despite modern technology's ability to provide quick access to an abundance of information.

The two student essays that conclude this chapter give further insights into how writing and reading shape an individual's inner growth and identity. Joyce Chang, in her essay "Drive Becarefully," a reading response to Amy Tan's "Mother Tongue," discusses her inner struggle to accept her mother's language as fundamental to both of their identities. Student writer Molly Thomas responds to Steven Holtzman's "Don't Look Back," pointing out some of the contradictions seen in his and other contemporary positions taken on the electronic media and its impact on our culture.

As you embark on your journey through the readings in this chapter, we hope that you will reflect on the universal yet changing nature of writing and reading. We know that these interrelated processes have the power to engage your mind in lively, imaginative and provocative adventures.

Wallace Stevens

Of Modern Poetry

*One of America's foremost poets of ideas, Wallace Stevens (1879–1955) was edu-
cated at Harvard University as a lawyer and spent most of his life working as an executive of the Hartford Accident and Indemnity Company. Stevens published his
poetry in reviews, and his first book of poems,* Harmonium, *came out in 1923. He
received national acclaim when he was awarded the Pulitzer Prize for his* Collected
Poems *in 1954. Many of Stevens's poems explore the structured visions of the world
provided by the arts. As you read the following poem, which appeared in Stevens's
book* Parts of a World *(1942), notice how Stevens explores through metaphors of the
theater the relationship between the literary work and its reader.*

JOURNAL

Describe the sense of relatedness you experience when you write: Do you feel you
are most often writing only for yourself, or for some imagined or actual reader?

The poem of the mind in the act of finding
What will suffice. It has not always had
To find: the scene was set; it repeated what
Was in the script.
5   Then the theatre was changed
To something else. Its past was a souvenir.

It has to be living, to learn the speech of the place.
It has to face the men of the time and to meet
The women of the time. It has to think about war
10 And it has to find what will suffice. It has
To construct a new stage. It has to be on that stage
And, like an insatiable actor, slowly and
With meditation, speak words that in the ear,
In the delicatest ear of the mind, repeat,
15 Exactly, that which it wants to hear, at the sound
Of which, an invisible audience listens,
Not to the play, but to itself, expressed
In an emotion as of two people, as of two
Emotions becoming one. The actor is
20 A metaphysician in the dark, twanging
An instrument, twanging a wiry string that gives
Sounds passing through sudden rightnesses, wholly

Containing the mind, below which it cannot descend,
Beyond which it has no will to rise.
25   It must
Be the finding of a satisfaction, and may
Be of a man skating, a woman dancing, a woman
Combing. The poem of the act of the mind.

QUESTIONS FOR DISCUSSION

1. How is modern poetry defined in the first few lines of the poem? How and why has it changed? What is suggested by "the act of finding/What will suffice"?

2. Why and how does Stevens use theatrical terms such as *scene, script, actor,* and *stage* in his effort to explain the nature of modern poetry?

3. In the second stanza, Stevens lists some of the qualities of modern poetry, what "it has to be." What four qualities does he list, and why do you think these qualities are so important to poetry in the modern age?

4. In the middle of the second stanza, how is the communication process of the poem described? Why is it so important that the poem "slowly and/With meditation, speak"? What is the emotional relationship between a poem and its "invisible audience"?

5. At the end of the second stanza we can say that the role of the actor-poem shifts to that of a "metaphysician . . . twanging an instrument" whose sounds contain only "the mind," rather than the body or spirit. Explain this shift from the earlier part of the poem, in which the poem seemed to be dealing with more emotional, everyday matters.

6. In what way does the third stanza attempt to reconcile the split between the view of poetry in the early part of the poem and that expressed at the end of the second stanza? What is the significance of the expression "the finding of a satisfaction" and the three examples of poetic subjects? Comment on the difference between the first line of the poem and the last line, "Combing. The poem of the act of the mind."

CONNECTION

Compare and contrast Stevens' view of writing and reading with Steven Holtzman's in "Don't Look Back" (see page 48). What would Stevens think of the new media for reading that Holtzman describes?

IDEAS FOR WRITING

1. Have you ever written or read a poem (or any other text) in the way that Stevens describes in his poem? Write a paper in which you describe your experience of writing or reading a poem or story that is especially meaningful to you. Be specific about why and how the book had an impact on your life. Refer to passages in the book when relevant.

2. "Of Modern Poetry" suggests that writing and reading can be slow, deeply focused inner experiences like meditation. Based on your own experiences and research, write an essay that explains why and how writing and/or reading can be a meditative experience.

RELATED WEB SITES

WALLACE STEVENS
http://www.wesleyan.edu/wstevens/stevens.html
This web site includes information about the author and his work, discussion groups, relevant links, as well as audio recordings.

READING POETRY
http://www.bedfordstmartins.com/litlinks/poetry/readpoet.htm
This excellent web site displays a practical guide to reading poetry and includes a vast amount of information on authors of fiction, drama, critical theory, and essays, as well as links to understanding different literary periods.

THE POETRY ARCHIVE
http://www.emule.com/poetry/?page=author list
An educational resource dedicated to researching poetry that includes an on-line archive of poetry by numerous authors with categories of "what's new," top poems, top authors, a chat forum, and books.

Stephen King

The Symbolic Language of Dreams

Stephen King (b. 1947) is originally from Portland, Maine, where he continues to reside. After graduating from the University of Maine in 1970 with a B.A. in English, King taught high school and worked at odd jobs before finding time to write his first novel Carrie *(1974), a story of psychic powers and the cruelty of adolescence.* Carrie *was an immediate best-seller and was made into a classic horror film, and King has continued to be one of the most popular contemporary writers of horror novels. Some of his best known works include* The Shining *(1977; film version 1980),* Firestarter *(1980; film version 1984),* Misery *(1987; film version 1990),* The Dark Half *(1989),* Desperation *(1996),* Bag of Bones *(1998),* The Girl Who Loved Tom Gordon *(1999), and* Hearts in Atlantis *(1999). King's fiction takes on some serious themes related to writing and creation: the double life of the writer, the responsibility of the writer to his fans, and the role of dreams and early childhood memory in the creative process. In the following essay, King describes some of the ways dreams have helped him with his writing.*

Write about how one of your dreams or intuitions helped you to solve a writing problem or to understand an issue in your life.

One of the things that I've been able to use dreams for in my stories is to show things in a symbolic way that I wouldn't want to come right out and say directly. I've always used dreams the way you'd use mirrors to look at something you couldn't see head-on—the way that you use a mirror to look at your hair in the back. To me that's what dreams are supposed to do. I think that dreams are a way that people's minds illustrate the nature of their problems. Or maybe even illustrate the answers to their problems in symbolic language.

When we look back on our dreams, a lot of times they decompose as soon as the light hits them. So, you can have a dream, and you can remember very vividly what it's about, but ten or fifteen minutes later, unless it's an extraordinarily vivid dream or an extraordinarily good dream, it's gone. It's like the mind is this hard rubber and you really have to hit it hard to leave an impression that won't eventually just erase.

One of the things that we're familiar with in dreams is the sense that familiar or prosaic objects are being put in very bizarre circumstances or situations. And since that's what I write about, the use of dreams is an obvious way to create that feeling of weirdness in the real world. I guess probably the most striking example of using a dream in my fiction was connected to the writing of *Salem's Lot*.

Now, I can think of only maybe five or six really horrible nightmares in the course of my life—which isn't bad when you think that that life stretches over 44 years—but I can remember having an extremely bad dream when I was probably nine or ten years old.

5   It was a dream where I came up a hill and there was a gallows on top of this hill with birds all flying around it. There was a hangman there. He had died, not by having his neck broken, but by strangulation. I could tell because his face was all puffy and purple. And as I came close to him he opened his eyes, reached his hands out and grabbed me.

I woke up in my bed, sitting bolt upright, screaming. I was hot and cold at the same time and covered with goosebumps. And not only was I unable to go back to sleep for hours after that, but I was really afraid to turn out the lights for weeks. I can still see it as clearly now as when it happened.

Years later I began to work on *Salem's Lot*. Now, I knew that the story was going to be about a vampire that came from abroad to the United States and I wanted to put him in a spooky old house. I got about that far in my thinking and, by whatever way it is that your mind connects things, as I was looking around for a spooky house, a guy who works in the creative department of my brain said, Well what about that nightmare you had when you were eight or nine years old? Will that work? And I remembered the nightmare and I thought, Yes, it's perfect.

I turned the dead man into a guy named Hubie Marston who owned a bad house and pretty much repeated the story of the dream in terms of the way he died. In the story, Hubie Marston hangs himself. He's some sort of black artist of the Aleister Crowley kind—some sort of a dark magician—and I kind of combined him with a stock character in American tabloidism—the wealthy guy who lives and dies in squalor.

For me, once the actual act of creation starts, writing is like this high-speed version of the flip books you have when you're a kid, where you mix and match. The cover of the book will say, "You Can Make Thousands of Faces!" You can put maybe six or seven different eyes with different noses. Except that there aren't just thousands of faces, there are literally billions of different events, personalities, and things that you can flip together. And it happens at a very rapid rate. Dreams are just one of those flip strips that you can flip in there. But they also work in terms of advancing the story.

Sometimes when I write I can use dreams to have a sort of precognitive effect on the story. Precognitive dreams are a staple of our supernatural folklore. You know, the person who dreamed that flight 17 was going to crash and changed his reservation and sure enough, flight 17 crashed. But it's like those urban fairy tales: you always hear somebody say, "I have a friend that this happened to." I've never actually heard anyone say, "This happened to *me*."

The closest that I can come to a precognitive experience is that I can be in a situation where a really strong feeling of déjà vu washes over me. I'm sure that I've been there before. A lot of times I make the association that, at some point, I had a dream about this place and this series of actions, and forgot it with my conscious mind when I awoke.

Every now and then dreams can come in handy. When I was working on *It*—which was this really long book—a dream made a difference.

I had a lot of time and a lot of my sense of craft invested in the idea of being able to finish this huge, long book. Now, when I'm working on something, I see books, completed books. And in some fashion that thing is already there. I'm not really making it so much as I am digging it up, the way that you would an artifact, out of the sand. The trick is to get as much of that object as you possibly can, to get the whole thing out, so it's usable, without breaking it. You always break it somewhat—I mean you never get a complete thing—but if you're really careful and if you're really lucky, you can get most of it.

When I'm working I never know what the end is going to be or how things are going to come out. I've got an idea what direction I want the story to go in, or hope it will go in, but mostly I feel like the tail on a kite. I don't feel like the kite itself, of like the wind that blows on the kite—I'm just the tail of it. And if I know when I sit down what's happening or what's going to happen, that day and the next day and the day after, I'm happy. But with *It* I got to a point where I couldn't see ahead any more. And every day I got closer to the place where this young girl, who was one of my people—I don't think of them as good people or bad people, just my people—was going to be and they were going to find her.

15   I didn't know what was going to happen to her. And that made me extremely nervous. Because that's the way books don't get done. All at once you just get to a point where there is no more. It's like pulling a little string out of a hole and all at once it's broken and you don't get whatever prize there was on the end of it.

So I had seven, eight hundred pages and I just couldn't stand it. I remember going to bed one night saying, I've got to have an idea. I've got to have an idea! I fell asleep and dreamed that I was in a junk yard, which was where this part of the story was set.

Apparently, I was the girl. There was no girl in the dream. There was just me. And there were all these discarded refrigerators in this dump. I opened one of them and there were these things inside, hanging from the various rusty shelves. They looked like macaroni shells and they were all just sort of trembling in a breeze. Then one of them opened up these wings, flew out and landed on the back of my hand. There was a sensation of warmth, almost like when you get a subcutaneous shot of Novocain or something, and this thing started to turn from white to red. I realized it had anesthetized my hand and it was sucking my blood out. Then they all started to fly out of this refrigerator and to land on me. They were these leeches that looked like macaroni shells. And they were swelling up.

I woke up and I was very frightened. But I was also very happy. Because then I knew what was going to happen. I just took the dream as it was and put it in the book. Dropped it in. I didn't change anything.

In the story "The Body," there's an incident where several boys find themselves covered with leeches. That was something that actually happened to me. There's a lot of stuff in "The Body" that's just simply history that's been tarted up a little bit. These friends and I all went into this pond about a mile and half from the house where I grew up and when we came out we were just covered with those babies. It was awful. I don't remember that I had nightmares about the incident then but of course I had this leech dream years later.

20   I really think what happened with this dream was that I went to sleep and the subconscious went right on working and finally sent up this dream the way that you would send somebody an interoffice message in a pneumatic tube.

In the Freudian sense, I don't think there is any subconscious, any unconscious where things are going on. I think that consciousness is like an ocean. Whether you're an inch below the surface or whether you're down a mile and half deep, it's all water. All H_2O.

I think that our minds are the same nutrient bath all the way down to the bottom and different things live at different levels. Some of them are a little bit harder to see because we don't get down that deep. But whatever's going on in our daily lives, our daily thoughts, the things that the surface of our minds are concerned with eddy down—trickle down—and then they have some sort of an influence down there. And the messages that we get a lot of times are nothing more than symbolic reworkings of the things that we're concerned with. I don't think they're very prophetic or anything like that. I think a lot of times dreams are nothing more than a kind of mental or spiritual flatulence. They're a way of relieving pressure.

One way of looking at this water metaphor might be to talk about jumbo shrimp, everybody's favorite oxymoron. They're the big shrimp that nobody ate in restaurants until 1955 or 1960 because, until then, nobody thought of going shrimping after dark. They were there all the time, living their prosaic shrimp lives, but nobody caught them. So when they finally caught them it was, "Hello! Look at this. This is something entirely new." And if the shrimp could talk they'd say, "Shit, we're not new. We've been around for a couple of thousand years. You were just too dumb to look for us."

A slightly different way of looking at this is that there are certain fish that we get used to looking at. There are carp, goldfish, catfish, shad, cod— they're fish that are more or less surface fish. They go down to a depth of maybe fifty, sixty, or a hundred feet. People catch them, and we get used to seeing them. Not only do we see them in aquariums or as pictures in books, we see them on our plates. We cook them. We see them in the supermarket in the fish case. Whereas if you go down in a bathysphere, if you go down real deep, you see all these bright fluorescent, weird, strange things with membranous umbrellas and weird skirts that flare out from their bodies. Those are creatures that we don't see very often because they explode if we bring them up close to the surface. They are to surface fish what dreams are to our surface thoughts. Deep fish are like dreams of surface fish. They change shape, they change form.

25   There are dreams and there are deep dreams. There are dreams where you're able to tap sources that are a lot deeper. I'm sure that if you wanted to extend this metaphor you could say that within the human psyche, within human thought, there really are Mindanao trenches, places that are very very deep, where there are probably some extremely strange things floating around. And what the conscious mind brings up may be the equivalent of an exploded fish. It may just be a mess. It may be something that's gorgeous in its own habitat but when it gets up to the sun it just dries out. And then it's very gray and dull.

I remember about six months ago having this really vivid dream.

I was in some sort of an apartment building, a cheesy little apartment building. The front door was open and I could see all these black people going back and forth. They were talking and having a wonderful time. Somebody was playing music somewhere. And then the door shut.

In the dream I went back and got into bed. I think I must have shut the door myself. My brother was in bed with me, behind me, and he started to strangle me. My brother had gone crazy. It was awful!

I remember saying, with the last of my breath, "I think there's somebody out there." And he got up from the bed and went out. As soon as he was out I went up and closed the door and locked it. And then I went back to bed. That is, I started to lie down in this dream.

30   Then I began to worry that I hadn't really locked the door. This is the sort of thing that I'm always afraid of in real life. Did I turn off the burners on the stove? Did I leave a light on when I left the house? So, I got up to check the door and sure enough it was unlocked. I realized that he was still in there with me. Somewhere.

I screamed in the dream, "He's still in the house." I screamed so loud I woke myself up. Except I wasn't screaming when I woke up. I was just sort of muttering it over and over again: He's in the house, he's in the house. I was terrified.

Now, I keep a glass of ice water beside the bed where I sleep and the ice cubes hadn't melted yet, so it had happened almost immediately after I fell asleep. That's usually when I have the dreams that I remember most vividly.

Part of my function as a writer is to dream awake. And that usually happens. If I sit down to write in the morning, in the beginning of that writing session and the ending of that session, I'm aware that I'm writing. I'm aware of my surroundings. It's like shallow sleep on both ends, when you go to bed and when you wake up. But in the middle, the world is gone and I'm able to see better.

Creative imaging and dreaming are just so similar that they've got to be related.

35   In a story like "The Body" or *It,* which is set around the late fifties or the early sixties, I'm literally able to regress so that I can remember things that I'd forgotten. Time goes by and events pile up on the surface of your mind like snow, and it covers all these other previous layers. But if you're able to put yourself into that sort of semidreaming state—whether you're dreaming or whether you're writing creatively the brainwaves are apparently interchangeable—you're able to get a lot of that stuff back. That might be deep dreaming.

I'm aware, particularly in recent years, how precious that state is, I mean the ability to go in there when one is awake. I'm also aware, as an adult, of the vividness of my sleeping dreams when I have them. But I don't have any way of stacking up the number of dreams that I have as opposed to anybody else. My sense is I probably dream a little bit less at night because I'm taking off some of the pressure in the daytime. But I don't have an inherent proof of that.

I can remember finding that state for the first time and being delighted. It's a little bit like finding a secret door in a room but not knowing exactly how you got in. I can't remember exactly how I first found that state except that I would sit down to write every day, and I would pretty much do that whether the work went well or the work went badly. And after doing that for a while it was a little bit like having a posthypnotic suggestion.

I know that there are certain things that I do if I sit down to write: I have a glass of water or I have a cup of tea. There's a certain time I sit down around eight o'clock—or 8:15 or 8:30—somewhere within that half-hour every morning. I have my vitamin pill; I have my music; I have my same seat; and the papers are all arranged in the same places. It's a series of things. The cumulative purpose of doing those things the same way every day seems to be a way of saying to the mind: you're going to be dreaming soon.

It's not really any different than a bedtime routine. Do you go to bed a different way every night? Is there a certain side that you sleep on? I mean I brush my teeth. I wash my hands. Why would anybody wash their hands before they go to bed? I don't know. And the pillows: the pillows are supposed to be pointed a certain way. The open side of the pillowcase is supposed to be pointed *in* toward the other side of the bed. I don't know why.

40　　And the sleeping position is the same: turn to the right, turn to the left. I think it's a way of your mind saying to your body, or your body saying to your mind—maybe they're communicating with each other saying—we're gonna go to sleep now. And probably dreaming follows the same pattern if you don't interrupt it with things like drug use, alcohol, or whatever.

The dreams that I remember most clearly are almost always early dreams. And they're not always bad dreams. I don't want to give you that impression. I can remember one very clearly. It was a flying dream. I was over the turnpike and I was flying along wearing a pair of pajama bottoms. I didn't have any shirt on. I'm just buzzing along under overpasses—*kazipp*—and I'm reminding myself in the dream to stay high enough so that I don't get disemboweled by car antennas sticking up from the cars. That's a fairly mechanistic detail but when I woke up from this dream my feeling was not fear or loathing but just real exhilaration, pleasure and happiness.

It wasn't an out of control flying dream. I can remember as a kid, having a lot of falling dreams but this is the only flying dream that I can remember in detail.

I don't have a lot of repetitive dreams but I do have an anxiety dream: I'm working very hard in a little hot room—it seems to be the room where I lived as a teenager—and I'm aware that there's a madwoman in the attic. There's a little tiny door under the eave that goes to the attic, and I have to finish my work. I have to get that work done or she'll come out and get me. At some point in the dream that door always bursts open and this hideous woman—with all this white hair stuck up around her head like a gone-to-seed dandelion—jumps out with a scalpel.

45　　And I wake up.

I still have that dream when I'm backed up on my work and trying to fill all these ridiculous commitments I've made for myself.

QUESTIONS FOR DISCUSSION

1. King says, "I think that dreams are a way that people's minds illustrate the nature of their problems. Or maybe even illustrate the answers to their problems in symbolic language." How does he develop this insight about dreams through the personal examples provided in the essay?
2. Discuss several different ways in which King uses his dreams in his writing. Which approach seems to have been most productive for him?
3. King is known as a vivid and detailed writer, particularly in the construction of the fantasy scenes in his novels. Give examples of King's use of

specific detail and effective choice of language in describing the dreams he refers to in this essay.

4. What conclusions about the way in which the mind functions does King develop through his metaphors of the mind as an ocean, as a nutrient bath, as water? What different roles do the analogies he makes with jumbo shrimp and different kinds of fish play in his explanations?

5. What relationship does King find between his process of writing and his process of dreaming? Why does King believe that "creative imaging and dreaming are just so similar that they've got to be related"? Explain why you agree or disagree with him.

6. Although King is primarily a novelist, how do you think you will be able to use his insights about the role of dreams in your own writing?

CONNECTION

Compare and contrast King's and Woolf's use of their dreams and fantasies in their writing (see page 32).

IDEAS FOR WRITING

1. Write down a dream or nightmare that is vivid in your mind but that has never been recorded in words; then write an analysis of the dream. Discuss what you have learned about yourself from recording the dream.

2. King gives us a good sense of the types of dreams that he has, the impact that his dreams have had on him, and the detailed fabric of his dreams. Write an essay in which you compare and contrast your dreams to King's dreams. What does this comparison and contrast suggest to you about how dreams might have a significant impact on waking life?

RELATED WEB SITES

STEPHEN KING
http://www.stephenking.com
This official site for author Stephen King provides the latest news about the author as well as relevant links. The site also includes information on Steven King's past and his upcoming projects.

ONLINE SYMBOLISM DICTIONARY
http://www.umich.edu/~umfandsf/symbolismproject/symbolism.html/index.html
This online dictionary of symbols in dreams, literature, and the visual arts will serve as a helpful guide to readers, writers, or curious dreamers. Browse or search by key word.

Peter Elbow

Teaching Two Kinds of Thinking by Teaching Writing

Peter Elbow (b. 1935) was raised in New York and completed his Ph.D. at Brandeis University (1969). Elbow, who has taught at a number of universities including the Massachusetts Institute of Technology and the State University of New York at Stony Brook, is currently a professor emeritus of English at the University Of Massachusetts at Amherst. His books about writing include Writing Without Teachers *(1973, 1998),* Writing with Power *(1981, 1998),* Embracing Contraries: Explorations in Learning and Teaching *(1986),* A Community of Writers *(1988, 1994), and* What is English? *(1990). Elbow has contributed numerous articles on the teaching of writing to national English teacher's journals and speaks at many national conferences for writing teachers. His work emphasizes the importance of the development of the student's authentic voice in writing through processes such as freewriting. He also acknowledges revision and critical reflection as essential to the writing process.*

JOURNAL

Discuss activities that have helped you to discover new ideas in your writing. How do you make the transition between these new insights in to writing a final draft?

When I celebrate freewriting and fast exploratory writing on first drafts—the postponing of vigilance and control during the early stages of writing—it seems to many listeners as though I'm celebrating *holidays* from thinking. Some say "Yes, good, we all need holidays from thinking." Others say, "Horrors! Their vigilance muscles will get flabby and they'll lose their ability to think critically." But I insist that I'm teaching thinking.

Of course it's not the only way I teach thinking through writing. I also teach it by teaching careful, conscious, critical revising. Thus I teach two kinds of thinking. I'll call them first-order thinking and second-order thinking.

First-order thinking is intuitive and creative and doesn't strive for conscious direction or control. We use it when we get hunches or see gestalts. We use it when we sense analogies or ride on metaphors or arrange the pieces in a collage. We use it when we write fast without censoring and let the words lead us to associations and intuitions we hadn't foreseen. Second-order thinking is conscious, directed, controlled thinking. We steer; we scrutinize each link in the chain. Second-order thinking is committed to accuracy and strives for logic and control: we examine our premises and assess the validity of each inference. Second-order thinking is what most people have in mind when they talk about "critical thinking."

Each kind of thinking has its own characteristic strengths and weaknesses. I like to emphasize how second-order thinking often brings our people's worst thinking. If you want to get people to seem dumber than they are, try asking them a hard question and then saying, "Now think carefully." Thinking carefully means trying to examine your thinking while using it too—trying to think about thinking while also thinking about something else—which often leads people to foolishness. This is one of the main reasons why shrewd and sensible students often write essays asserting things they don't really believe and defending them with wooden reasoning they wouldn't dream of using if they were just talking thoughtfully with a friend.

5   First-order thinking, on the other hand, often heightens intelligence. If you want to get people to be remarkably insightful, try asking them the hard question and then saying, "Don't do any careful thinking yet, just write three or four stories or incidents that come to mind in connection with that question; and then do some fast exploratory freewriting." It turns out that such unplanned narrative and descriptive exploratory writing (or speaking) will almost invariably lead the person spontaneously to formulate *conceptual* insights that are remarkably shrewd. These are fresh insights which are rooted in experience and thus they usually get around the person's prejudices, stock responses, or desires for mere consistency; they are usually shrewder than the person's long-held convictions. (See "The Loop Writing Process" in my *Writing With Power*.) In addition (to bring up a writerly concern), these insights are usually expressed in lively, human, and experienced language. In short, to use Polanyi's terms, we know more tacitly than we do focally. Finally (to raise another writerly concern), when someone really gets going in a sustained piece of generative writing and manages, as it were, to stand out of the way and relinquish planning and control—when someone manages to let the words and images and ideas choose more words, images, and ideas—a more elegant shape or organization often emerges, one more integral to the material than careful outlining or conscious planning can produce. It's not that the rough draft writing will itself be well organized in its totality—though that occasionally happens. What's more common is that the exploratory zigzagging leads finally to a click where the writer suddenly sees, "Yes, that's the right handle for this whole issue, now I've got the right point of view, and now I see the right organization or progression of parts. I couldn't find it when I just tried to think, plan, and outline."

Yet despite my fascination with the conceptual power of creative intuitive thinking—of what might seem to some like "careless thinking"—I have learned not to forget to tell the other side of the story. That is, we are also likely to be *fooled* by first-order thinking. In first-order thinking we don't reflect on what we are doing and hence we are more likely to be steered by our unaware assumptions, our unconscious prejudices, our unexamined point of view. And often enough, no shape or organization emerges at all—just randomly ordered thoughts. We cannot *count on* first-order thinking to give us something valuable.

Thus the two kinds of thinking have the opposite virtues and vices. Second-order thinking is a way to check our thinking, to be more aware, to steer instead of being steered. In particular, we must not trust the fruits of intuitive and experiential first-order thinking unless we have carefully assessed them with second-order thinking. Yet we probably won't *have* enough interesting ideas or hypotheses to assess if we use only our assessing muscles: we need first-order thinking to generate a rich array of insights. And first-order thinking doesn't just give us more; it is faster too. Our early steps in second-order thinking (or our early steps at a higher level of second-order thinking than we are practiced at) are often slow backward steps into wrong-headedness (Bruner, 1966.) Yet this is no argument against the need for second-order thinking. Indeed I suspect that the way we enlarge the penumbra of our tacit knowledge is by searching harder and further with the beam of our focal knowledge.

We are in the habit—in the academic culture anyway—of assuming that thinking is not thinking unless it is wholly logical or critically aware of itself at every step. But I cannot resist calling first-order thinking a bona fide kind of thinking because it is a process of making sense and figuring out: thought not consciously steered or controlled, it is nevertheless purposive and skillful.

There is an obvious link between the writing process and these two kinds of thinking. I link first-order intuitive or creative thinking with freewriting and first-draft exploratory writing in which one defers planning, control, organizing, and censoring. I link second-order thinking with slow, thoughtful rewriting or revising where one constantly subjects everything to critical scrutiny.

But I'm not content merely to assert a link. The two writing processes enhance the two thinking processes.

It is obvious how careful revising enhances second-order thinking. If having any language at all (any "second signaling system") gives us more power over our thinking, it is obvious that a *written* language vastly increases that power. By writing down our thoughts we can put them aside and come back to them with renewed critical energy and a fresh point of view. We can criticize better because writing helps us achieve the perennially difficult task of standing outside our own thinking. Thus outlines are more helpful while revising than at the start of the writing process because finally there's something rich and interesting to outline. Revising is when I use the "X-ray" or "skeleton" exercise—asking both the writer and her readers to isolate the central core of inference in a paper: What is the assertion and what premises and reasons does it rest on? This is the best practice for critical thinking, because instead of being a canned exercise with artificial ingredients unconnected to the student, it is an exercise in assessing and strengthening the thinking which is embodied in one's own or someone else's live discourse. Since we are trying for the tricky goal of thinking about our subject but at the same time thinking about our thinking about it, putting our thoughts on paper gives us a fighting chance. But notice that what most heightens this critical awareness is not so much the writing down of words in the first place, though of course that helps, but the *coming back* to a text and re-seeing it from the outside (in space) instead of just hearing it from the inside (in time).

But does freewriting or uncensored, generative writing really enhance creative first-order thinking? You might say that speaking is a better way to enhance creative thinking—either through brainstorming or through the back and forth of discussion or debate. But that only works if we *have* other people available, people we trust, and people skilled at enhancing our creative thinking. Free exploratory writing, on the other hand, though we must learn to use it, is always available. And since the goal in creative thinking is to harness intuition—to get the imagination to take the reins in its own hands—solitary writing for no audience is often more productive than speaking. Speaking is almost invariably to an audience, and an audience puts pressure on us to make sense and avoid inferences we cannot explain.

You might also argue that intuitive thinking is better enhanced by silent musing; or going for a walk or sleeping on it or any of a host of other ways to push a question away from focal attention back to the preconscious. But such attempts at nonlinguistic processing often merely postpone thinking instead of actually enriching it. Freewriting and exploratory writing, on the other hand, are almost invariably productive because they exploit the autonomous generative powers of language and syntax themselves. Once you manage to get yourself writing in an exploratory but uncensored fashion, the ongoing string of language and syntax itself becomes a lively and surprising force for generation. Words call up words, ideas call up more ideas. A momentum of language and thinking develops and one learns to nurture it by keeping the pen moving. With a bit of practice, you can usually bring yourself to the place where you can stop and say, "Look at that! I've been led by this unrolling string of words to an insight or connection or structure that I had no premonition of. I could never have proposed it if I were just musing or making an outline. I wasn't steering, I was being taken for a ride." Heuristic prewriting techniques that involve only list-making or diagram-making tend to lack the generative force that comes from the use of actual syntax—speech on paper.

I'm not trying to disparage spoken discourse or nonverbal back-burner work. They can be wonderful. But they are not as reliable as writing for enhancing first-order thinking.

15   "Taken for a ride." The metaphor evokes what's good but also what's fearful about first-order thinking and uncensored writing. It is dangerous to be taken for a ride, literally by a horse or metaphorically by a shark. "Eternal vigilance." But the goal of first-order thinking or writing is to *relax* vigilance and be taken on as many rides as possible: *as long as* we remember that this is only half the process. We must assess the results with second-order thinking or revising. In short, by using the writing process in this two-sided way, I can foster contraries: our ability to let go and be taken on surprising rides; yet also our ability critically to assess the resulting views.

Practical Consequences   I am not concluding from all this that there is only one right way to think or write. We all know too many good thinkers or writers who contradict each other and even themselves in their methods. But his notion of opposite extremes gives a constructive and specific picture of what we're looking for in good thinking and writing. That is, even though there are many good ways to think and write, it seems clear that excellence must involve finding *some* way to be both abundantly inventive yet toughmindedly critical. Indeed this model of conflicting goals suggests why good writers and thinkers are so various in their technique: if they are managing to harness opposites—in particular, opposites that tend to interfere with each other— they are doing something mysterious. Success is liable to take many forms, some of them surprising.

As a teacher, it helps me to have these two clear goals in mind when I come across a student about whom I must say, "She clearly *is* a smart person, but why is she so often wrong?" Or "She clearly thinks hard and carefully, but why is she so characteristically uninteresting or unproductive in her work?" I can ask of any person or performance, "Is there enough rich material to build from?" and, "Is there a careful and critical enough assessment of the material?"

If I am careful to acknowledge to my students that things are complex and that there is no single best way to think or write—and that excellence in these realms is a mystery that can be mastered in surprising ways—then I may justifiably turn around and stress simplicity by harping on two practical rules of thumb.

First, since creative and critical thinking are opposite and involve mentalities that tend to conflict with each other, it helps most people to learn to work on them separately or one at a time by moving back and forth between them. If we are trying to think creatively to write generatively, it usually hinders us if we try at the same time to think critically or to revise it: it makes us reject what we are engaged in thinking before we've really worked it out at all— or to cross out what we've written before we've finished the sentence or paragraph and allowed something to develop. But if we hold off criticism or revising for a while, we can build a safe place for generative thinking or writing. Similarly, if we devote certain times to wholehearted critical thinking or revising, we can be more acute and powerful in our critical assessment.

20   For one of the main things that holds us back from being as creative as we could be is fear of looking silly or being wrong. But that worry dissipates when we know we will soon turn to wholehearted criticism and revising and weed out what is foolish. Similarly, one of the main things that holds us back from being as critical as we could be is fear that we'll have to reject everything and be left with nothing at all. But that worry also dissipates when we know we've already generated an extremely rich set of materials to work on (or if we haven't, we know we can do so quickly whenever we turn to wholehearted generating). In short, even though creative and critical thinking can magically coalesce in the hands of masters and at certain special moments when the rest of us are at our best, it usually helps us to work on them separately so they can flourish yet reinforce each other.

Second rule of thumb. It usually helps to *start with* creative thinking and exploratory writing and then engage in critical assessment and revision afterward— after we have gotten ourselves going and there is already lots to assess. It's not that we should necessarily try to force our writing into two self-contained steps (though I aim for this when all goes smoothly). Often I cannot finish all generating or all first-order thinking before I need to do some revising or criticizing—which will sometimes force a new burst of generating. We are never finished with generating—and having generated, we always need to criticize and revise. I used to think that I should try to finish getting my students good at creative generating before I went on to work on revising and being critical. But I've discovered that some students won't let go and allow themselves to be creative till after we do some hard work on critical thinking and revising. They don't feel safe relaxing their vigilance till I demonstrate that I'm also teaching heightened vigilance. Sometimes, early in the semester, I ask students to rethink and revise a paper in order to prove to them that they are not stuck with what they put down in early drafts, and that careful critical thinking can make a big difference.

But the fact remains that most people get more and better thinking—and less time-wasting—if they start off generating. My main agenda for the beginning of a semester is always to enforce generating and brainstorming and deferral of criticism in order to build students' confidence and show them that they can quickly learn to come up with a great quantity of words and ideas. Then gradually we progress to a back-and-forth movement between generating and criticizing. I find I help my own writing and thinking and that of my students by consciously training ourselves to start with first-order thinking and generating and to take it on longer and longer rides—to hold off longer and longer the transition to criticizing and logic. Back and forth, yes, but in longer spells so that each mentality has more time to flourish before we move on to its opposite.

Mutual Reinforcement   Because the history of our culture is often experienced as a battle between reason and feeling, between rationality and irrationality, between logic and impulse—and because intuitive first-order thinking is indissolubly mixed up with feeling, irrationality, and impulse—we end up with disciplined critical thinking and uncensored creative thinking dug into opposed trenches with their guns trained on each other. Logic and reason have won the battle to be our standard for thinking, but not the battle for hearts and minds, and therefore champions of logic and reason understandably criticize all relaxations of critical vigilance. Similarly, champions of creative first-order thinking sometimes feel they must criticize critical thinking if only to win some legitimacy for themselves. But this is an unfortunate historical and developmental accident. If we would see clearly how it really is with thinking and writing, we would see that the situation isn't either/or, it's both/and: the more first-order thinking, the more second-order thinking; the more generative uncensored writing, the more critical revising; and vice versa. It's a matter of learning to work on opposites one at a time in a generous spirit of mutual reinforcement rather than in a spirit of restrictive combat.

QUESTIONS FOR DISCUSSION

1. Why does Elbow teach two kinds of thinking? Why does he consider the intuitive and creative mode "first order" and the critical mode "second order"?
2. Elbow gives examples of each kind of thinking. Why does he believe that we need to engage in both kinds of thinking to produce good writing? Explain why you agree or disagree with him.
3. According to Elbow, why is freewriting preferable to brainstorming aloud or "silent musing" as a way to generate ideas? Do you agree? Explain your point of view and process.
4. Discuss the meaning of the metaphor "taken for a ride" in relationship to the two kinds of thinking. What is positive and what is "fearful" about this expression in relation to writing? Why and how does Elbow seek to "foster contraries"?
5. What does Elbow expect when he asks us to "work on opposites one at a time in a generous spirit of mutual reinforcement"? Provide an example from your own writing process that supports or refutes his expectation.
6. What is Elbow's most recent position on whether students should begin their writing process with creative generation or with critical thinking and planning? Why has he changed his original position somewhat? What does Elbow continue to believe works best?

CONNECTION

Compare and contrast Peter Elbow's and Virginia Woolf's ideas about the writing process. How does each emphasize a need for a separation between the writer's creative and critical mind (see page 32)?

IDEAS FOR WRITING

1. Write an essay that describes your writing process using comparisons and metaphors. You might want to begin with a picture (a visualization) of your writing process that could help clarify your explanation of how you approach the completion of a writing project.
2. Write an essay in response to Elbow's approach to thinking and writing. Discuss the reasons why you agree and/or disagree with his ideas. Develop examples and evidence from your own writing experiences to support your major points.

RELATED WEB SITES

PETER ELBOW
http://www.iupui.edu/~sharrin/5365/huang.htm
This URL shares a brief introduction to the work of Peter Elbow. A useful annotated bibliography is also provided.

LAWYER AS WRITER
http://www.wvu.edu/~lawfac/jelkins/writeshop/links.html
Several links to writings related to the ideas of Peter Elbow can be found at
this web site. The site focuses on free writing and exploratory writing.

WRITING AS CREATIVE DESIGN
http://www.cogs.susx.ac.uk/users/mike/wa/writingdesign.html
In this essay posted online, Mike Sharples of the University of Sussex, England presents his ideas on creativity, cognition, and the writing process.

Virginia Woolf

Professions for Women

*Virginia Woolf (1882–1941) grew up in London as the daughter of the eminent Vic-
torian literary critic and agnostic, Leslie Stephen. Since women were not sent to
school at that time, she educated herself in her father's extensive library. As a young
woman, Woolf was a member of the intellectual circle known as the Bloomsbury
group. Woolf is best known for her experimental, stream of consciousness novels*
Mrs. Dalloway *(1925),* To the Lighthouse *(1927), and* The Waves *(1931). Her
extended essay,* A Room of One's Own *(1929) is considered one of the most important feminist texts of the twentieth century. The essay that follows, "Professions for
Women," reflects Woolf's deep concern about the status of women writers in any society dominated by males. The essay was first delivered in 1925 to a professional
women's club and is included in* Death of a Moth and Other Essays *(1942).*

JOURNAL

Discuss what it would be like to have your own special writing room. What would
the room be like? Where would it be? How might you furnish it?

When your secretary invited me to come here, she told me that your Society
is concerned with the employment of women and she suggested that I
might tell you something about my own professional experiences. It is true I am
a woman: it is true I am employed; but what professional experiences have I
had? It is difficult to say. My profession is literature; and in that profession there
are fewer experiences for women than in any other, with the exception of the
stage—fewer, I mean, that are peculiar to women. For the road was cut many
years ago—by Fanny Burney, by Aphra Behn, by Harriet Martineau, by Jane
Austen, by George Eliot—many famous women, and many more unknown and
forgotten, have been before me, making the path smooth, and regulating my
steps. Thus, when I came to write, there were very few material obstacles in my

way. Writing was a reputable and harmless occupation. The family peace was not broken by the scratching of a pen. No demand was made upon the family purse. For ten and sixpence one can buy paper enough to write all the plays of Shakespeare—if one has a mind that way. Pianos and models, Paris, Vienna and Berlin, masters and mistresses, are not needed by a writer. The cheapness of writing is, of course, the reason why women have succeeded as writers before they have succeeded in the other professions.

But to tell you my story—it is a simple one. You have only got to figure to yourselves a girl in a bedroom with a pen in her hand. She had only to move that pen from left to right—from ten o'clock to one. Then it occurred to her to do what is simple and cheap enough for all—to slip a few of those pages into an envelope, fix a penny stamp in the corner, and drop the envelope into the red box at the corner. It was thus that I became a journalist; and my effort was rewarded on the first day of the following month—a very glorious day it was for me—by a letter from an editor containing a cheque for one pound ten shillings and sixpence. But to show you how little I deserve to be called a professional woman, how little I know of the struggles and difficulties of such lives, I have to admit that instead of spending that sum upon bread and butter, rent, shoes and stockings, or butcher's bills, I went out and bought a cat—a beautiful cat, a Persian cat, which very soon involved me in bitter disputes with my neighbours.

What could be easier than to write articles and to buy Persian cats with the profits? But wait a moment. Articles have to be about something. Mine, I seem to remember, was about a novel by a famous man. And while I was writing this review, I discovered that if I were going to review books I should need to do battle with a certain phantom. And the phantom was a woman, and when I came to know her better I called her after the heroine of a famous poem, The Angel in the House. It was she who used to come between me and my paper when I was writing reviews. It was she who bothered me and wasted my time and so tormented me that at last I killed her. You who come of a younger and happier generation may not have heard of her—you may not know what I mean by the Angel in the House. I will describe her as shortly as I can. She was intensely sympathetic. She was immensely charming. She was utterly unselfish. She excelled in the difficult arts of family life. She sacrificed herself daily. If there was a chicken, she took the leg; if there was a draught she sat in it—in short she was so constituted that she never had a mind or a wish of her own, but preferred to sympathize always with the minds and wishes of others. Above all—I need not say it—she was pure. Her purity was supposed to be her chief beauty—her blushes, her great grace. In those days—the last of Queen Victoria—every house had its Angel. And when I came to write I encountered her with the very first words. The shadow of her wings fell on my page; I heard the rustling of her skirts in the room. Directly, that is to say, I took my pen in hand to review that novel by a famous man, she slipped behind me and whispered: "My dear, you are a young woman. You are writing about a book that has been written by a man. Be sympathetic; be tender; flatter; deceive; use all the arts and wiles of our sex. Never let anybody guess that you have a mind of your own. Above all, be pure." And she made as if to guide my pen. I now record the one act for which I take some credit to myself, though the credit rightly belongs to some excellent ancestors of mine who left me a certain sum of money—shall we say five hundred pounds a year?—so that it was not necessary for me to depend solely on charm for my living. I turned upon her and caught her by the throat. I did my best to kill her. My excuse, if I were to be had up in a court of law, would be that I acted in self-defence. Had I not killed her she would have killed me. She would have plucked the heart out of my writing. For, as I found, directly I put pen to paper, you cannot review even a novel without having a mind of your own, without expressing what you think to be the truth about human relations, morality, sex. And all these questions, according to the Angel in the House, cannot be dealt with freely and openly by women; they must charm, they must conciliate, they must—to put it bluntly—tell lies if they are to succeed. Thus, whenever I felt the shadow of her wing or the radiance of her halo upon my page, I took up the inkpot and flung it at her. She died hard. Her fictitious nature was of great assistance to her. It is far harder to kill a phantom than a reality. She was always creeping back when I thought I had despatched her. Though I flatter myself that I killed her in the end, the struggle was severe; it took much time that had better have been spent upon learning Greek grammar; or in roaming the world in search of adventures. But it was a real experience; it was an experience that was bound to befall all women writers at that time. Killing the Angel in the House was part of the occupation of a woman writer.

But to continue my story. The Angel was dead; what then remained? You may say that what remained was a simple and common object—a young woman in a bedroom with an inkpot. In other words, now that she had rid herself of falsehood, that young woman had only to be herself. Ah, but what is "herself"? I mean, what is a woman? I assure you, I do not know. I do not believe that you know. I do not believe that anybody can know until she has expressed herself in all the arts and professions open to human skill. That indeed is one of the reasons why I have come here—out of respect for you, who are in process of showing us by your experiments what a woman is, who are in process of providing us, by your failures and successes, with that extremely important piece of information.

5   But to continue the story of my professional experiences. I made one pound ten and six by my first review; and I bought a Persian cat with the proceeds. Then I grew ambitious. A Persian cat is all very well, I said; but a Persian cat is not enough. I must have a motor car. And it was thus that I became a novelist—for it is a very strange thing that people will give you a motor car if you will tell them a story. It is a still stranger thing that there is nothing so delightful in the world as telling stories. It is far pleasanter than writing reviews of famous novels. And yet, if I am to obey your secretary and tell you my professional experiences as a novelist, I must tell you about a very strange experience that befell me as a novelist. And to understand it you must try first to imagine a novelist's state of mind. I hope I am not giving away professional secrets if I say that a novelist's chief desire is to be as unconscious as possible. He has to induce in himself a state of perpetual lethargy. He wants life to proceed with the utmost

quiet and regularity. He wants to see the same faces, to read the same books, to do the same things day after day, month after month, while he is writing, so that nothing may break the illusion in which he is living—so that nothing may disturb or disquiet the mysterious nosings about, feelings round, darts, dashes and sudden discoveries of that very shy and illusive spirit, the imagination. I suspect that this state is the same both for men and women. Be that as it may, I want you to imagine me writing a novel in a state of trance. I want you to figure to yourselves a girl sitting with a pen in her hand, which for minutes, and indeed for hours, she never dips into the inkpot. The image that comes to my mind when I think of this girl is the image of a fisherman lying sunk in dreams on the verge of a deep lake with a rod held out over the water. She was letting her imagination sweep unchecked round every rock and cranny of the world that lies submerged in the depths of our unconscious being. Now came the experience, the experience that I believe to be far commoner with women writers than with men. The line raced through the girl's fingers. Her imagination had rushed away. It had sought the pools, the depths, the dark places where the largest fish slumber. And then there was a smash. There was an explosion. There was foam and confusion. The imagination had dashed itself against something hard. The girl was roused from her dream. She was indeed in a state of the most acute and difficult distress. To speak without figure she had thought of something, something about the body, about the passions which it was unfitting for her as a woman to say. Men, her reason told her, would be shocked. The consciousness of what men will say of a woman who speaks the truth about her passions had roused her from her artist's state of unconsciousness. She could write no more. The trance was over. Her imagination could work no longer. This I believe to be a very common experience with women writers—they are impeded by the extreme conventionality of the other sex. For though men sensibly allow themselves great freedom in these respects, I doubt that they realize or can control the extreme severity with which they condemn such freedom in women.

These then were two very genuine experiences of my own. These were two of the adventures of my professional life. The first—killing the Angel in the House—I think I solved. She died. But the second, telling the truth about my own experiences as a body, I do not think I solved. I doubt that any woman has solved it yet. The obstacles against her are still immensely powerful—and yet they are very difficult to define. Outwardly, what is simpler than to write books? Outwardly, what obstacles are there for a woman rather than for a man? Inwardly, I think, the case is very different; she has still many ghosts to fight, many prejudices to overcome. Indeed it will be a long time still, I think, before a woman can sit down to write a book without finding a phantom to be slain, a rock to be dashed against. And if this is so in literature, the freest of all professions for women, how is it in the new professions which you are now for the first time entering?

Those are the questions that I should like, had I time, to ask you. And indeed, if I have laid stress upon these professional experiences of mine, it is because I believe that they are, though in different forms, yours also. Even when the path is nominally open—when there is nothing to prevent a woman from being a doctor, a lawyer, a civil servant—there are many phantoms and obstacles, as I believe, looming in her way. To discuss and define them is I think of great value and importance; for thus only can the labour be shared, the difficulties be solved. But besides this, it is necessary also to discuss the ends and the aims for which we are fighting, for which we are doing battle with these formidible obstacles. Those aims cannot be taken for granted; they must be perpetually questioned and examined. The whole position, as I see it—here in this hall surrounded by women practising for the first time in history I know not how many different professions—is one of extraordinary interest and importance. You have won rooms of your own in the house hitherto exclusively owned by men. You are able, though not without great labour and effort, to pay the rent. You are earning your five hundred pounds a year. But this freedom is only a beginning; the room is your own, but it is still bare. It has to be furnished; it has to be decorated; it has to be shared. How are you going to furnish it, how are you going to decorate it? With whom are you going to share it, and upon what terms? These, I think are questions of the utmost importance and interest. For the first time in history you are able to ask them; for the first time you are able to decide for yourselves what the answers should be. Willingly would I stay and discuss those questions and answers—but not tonight. My time is up; and I must cease.

QUESTIONS FOR DISCUSSION

1. Explain why Woolf's opening paragraph is ironic. Is her use of irony effective? Explain.
2. Describe the angel-like phantom that torments Woolf when she tries to write reviews of men's work. What does the angel represent for Woolf? Do you ever think that you, too, have an angel-like figure that sometimes controls your thoughts and actions?
3. Why is it so difficult for Woolf to kill the phantom angel? Why was killing the phantom angel an important concern of any woman writer of Woolf's age? Do you think that women writers today still struggle against a phantom angel?
4. How does Woolf get into her writer's frame of mind? Why does Woolf rely on her unconscious mind when she writes? What rouses the woman from her artist's state of unconsciousness? Do women today still face this type of obstacle?
5. Why does Woolf rely on metaphors and images (such as the phantom angel and the young girl who wants to write becoming "the image of a fisherman lying sunk in dreams on the verge of a deep lake with a rod held out over the water") to illustrate her ideas about writing? Are her metaphors and images persuasive and effective? Explain.
6. Why does Woolf think that the inward obstacles women writers face are the hardest to overcome? In your own life as a writer, what are the most difficult challenges that you must overcome?

CONNECTION

Compare Woolf's reliance on dreams and reverie to Steven King's comments on his use of dream material (see page 17).

IDEAS FOR WRITING

1. Write an essay that discusses the relevance of Woolf's ideas for men who are struggling to become writers.
2. Create your own phantom angel, the visual and mental image that tries to keep you from expressing yourself in your writing. Begin by drawing (with pens and paper or on a computer program) this inner critic. Then write a dialogue between your inner critic and your creative self. In conclusion write a paragraph that discuses what you learned from this activity.

RELATED WEB SITES

VIRGINIA WOOLF

http://hubcap.clemson.edu/aah/ws/vw6links.html

Learn all about Virginia Woolf at this web site of links to useful research materials about the author. It not only includes large collections of links, but also courses and course materials, chronologies, online texts, bibliographies, and books on Woolf.

FEMINIST THEORY—AN OVERVIEW

http://www.victorianweb.org/victorian/gender/temtheory.html

Visit "The Victorian Web" and read a brief overview of Feminist Theory. Link to information about Gender Studies as well as other various topics surrounding "The Victorians."

Amy Tan

Mother Tongue

Born in Oakland, California, in 1952 to immigrant parents, Amy Tan received an M.A. (1974) from San Jose State University, where she studied linguistics. Her first best-selling novel, The Joy Luck Club *(1989), was inspired by the stories told by Chinese-American women of her mother's generation. Tan has written three other novels,* The Kitchen God's Wife *(1991),* The One Hundred Secret Senses *(1995), and* The Bonesetter's Daughter *(2001), as well as a number of essays in which she explores cultural and linguistic issues. As you read the following essay, notice how Tan uses her experiences growing up bilingual in a Chinese-American family to challenge the traditional expectations of academic writing achievement tests.*

In her essay, Amy Tan states that she is "fascinated by language in daily life." Discuss several striking examples of creative uses of language that you have noticed recently in your everyday life or in conversations with friends.

I am not a scholar of English or literature. I cannot give you much more than personal opinions on the English language and its variations in this country or others.

I am a writer. And by that definition, I am someone who has always loved language. I am fascinated by language in daily life. I spend a great deal of my time thinking about the power of language—the way it can evoke an emotion, a visual image, a complex idea, or a simple truth. Language is the tool of any trade. And I use them all—all the Englishes I grew up with.

Recently, I was made keenly aware of the different Englishes I do use. I was giving a talk to a large group of people, the same talk I had already given to half a dozen other groups. The nature of the talk was about my writing, my life, and my book, *The Joy Luck Club*. The talk was going along well enough, until I remembered one major difference that made the whole talk sound wrong. My mother was in the room. And it was perhaps the first time she had heard me give a lengthy speech, using the kind of English I have never used with her. I was saying things like, "The intersection of memory upon imagination" and "There is an aspect of my fiction that relates to thus-and-thus"—a speech filled with carefully wrought grammatical phrases, burdened, it suddenly seemed to me, with nominalized forms, past perfect tenses, conditional phrases, all the forms of standard English that I had learned in school and through books, the forms of English I did not use at home with my mother.

Just last week, I was walking down the street with my mother, and I again found myself conscious of the English I was using, the English I use with her. We were talking about the price of new and used furniture, and I heard myself saying this: "Not waste money that way." My husband was with us as well, and he didn't notice any switch in my English. And then I realized why. It's because over the twenty years we've been together, I've often used that same kind of English with him, and sometimes he even uses it with me. It has become our language of intimacy, a different sort of English that relates to family talk, the language I grew up with.

5   So you'll have some idea of what this family talk I heard sounds like I'll quote what my mother said during a recent conversation which I videotaped and then transcribed. During this conversation, my mother was talking about a political gangster in Shanghai who had the same last name as her family's, Du, and how the gangster in his early years wanted to be adopted by her family, which was rich by comparison. Later, the gangster became more powerful, far richer than my mother's family, and one day showed up at my mother's wedding to pay his respects. Here's what she said in part:

"Du Yusong having business like fruit stand. Like off the street kind. He is Du like Du Zong—but not Tsung-ming Island people. The local people call pu-tong, the near east side, he belong to that side local people. That man want to ask Du Zong father take him in like become own family. Du Zong father wasn't look down on him, but didn't take seriously, until that man big like become a mafia. Now important person, very hard to inviting him. Chinese way, came only to show respect, don't stay for dinner. Respect for making big celebration, he shows up. Man gives lots of respect. Chinese custom. Chinese social life that way. If too important won't have to stay too long. He come to my wedding. I didn't see, I heard it. I gone to boy's side, they have YMCA dinner. Chinese age I was nineteen."

You should know that my mother's expressive command of English belies how much she actually understands. She reads the *Forbes* report, listens to *Wall Street Week*, converses daily with her stockbroker, reads all of Shirley MacLaine's books with ease—all kinds of things I can't begin to understand. Yet some of my friends tell me they understand 50 percent of what my mother says. Some say they understand 80 to 90 percent. Some say they understand none of it, as if she were speaking pure Chinese. But to me, my mother's English is perfectly clear, perfectly natural. It's my mother tongue. Her language, as I hear it, is vivid, direct, full of observation and imagery. That was the language that helped shape the way I saw things, expressed things, made sense of the world.

Lately, I've been giving more thought to the kind of English my mother speaks. Like others, I have described it to people as "broken" or "fractured" English. But I wince when I say that. It has always bothered me that I can think of no way to describe it other than "broken," as if it were damaged and needed to be fixed, as if it lacked a certain wholeness and soundness. I've heard other terms used, "limited English," for example. But they seem just as bad, as if everything is limited, including people's perceptions of the limited English speaker.

I know this for a fact, because when I was growing up, my mother's "limited" English limited *my* perception of her. I was ashamed of her English. I believed that her English reflected the quality of what she had to say. That is, because she expressed them imperfectly her thoughts were imperfect. And I had plenty of empirical evidence to support me: the fact that people in department stores, at banks, and at restaurants did not take her seriously, did not give her good service, pretended not to understand her, or even acted as if they did not hear her.

10   My mother had long realized the limitations of her English as well. When I was fifteen, she used to have me call people on the phone to pretend I was she. In this guise, I was forced to ask for information or even to complain and yell at people who had been rude to her. One time it was a call to her stockbroker in New York. She had cashed out her small portfolio and it just so happened we were going to go to New York the next week, our very first trip outside California. I had to get on the phone and say in an adolescent voice that was not very convincing, "This is Mrs. Tan."

And my mother was standing in the back whispering loudly, "Why he don't send me check, already two weeks late. So mad he lie to me, losing me money."

And then I said in perfect English, "Yes, I'm getting rather concerned. You had agreed to send the check two weeks ago, but it hasn't arrived."

Then she began to talk more loudly. "What he want, I come to New York tell him front of his boss, you cheating me?" And I was trying to calm her down, make her be quiet, while telling the stockbroker, "I can't tolerate any more excuses. If I don't receive the check immediately, I am going to have to speak to your manager when I'm in New York next week." And sure enough, the following week there we were in front of this astonished stockbroker, and I was sitting there red-faced and quiet, and my mother, the real Mrs. Tan, was shouting at his boss in her impeccable broken English.

We used a similar routine just five days ago, for a situation that was far less humorous. My mother had gone to the hospital for an appointment, to find out about a benign brain tumor a CAT scan had revealed a month ago. She said she had spoken very good English, her best English, no mistakes. Still, she said, the hospital did not apologize when they said they had lost the CAT scan and she had come for nothing. She said they did not seem to have any sympathy when she told them she was anxious to know the exact diagnosis, since her husband and son had both died of brain tumors. She said they would not give her any more information until the next time and she would have to make another appointment for that. So she said she would not leave until the doctor called daughter. She wouldn't budge. And when the doctor finally called her daughter, me, who spoke in perfect English—lo and behold—we had assurances the CAT scan would be found, promises that a conference call on Monday would be held, and apologies for any suffering my mother had gone through for a most regrettable mistake.

15   I think my mother's English almost had an effect on limiting my possibilities in life as well. Sociologists and linguists probably will tell you that a person's developing language skills are more influenced by peers. But I do think that the language spoken in the family, especially in immigrant families which are more insular, plays a large role in shaping the language of the child. And I believe that it affected my results on achievement tests, IQ Tests, and the SAT. While my English skills were never judged as poor, compared to math, English could not be considered my strong suit. In grade school I did moderately well, getting perhaps B's, sometimes B-pluses, in English and scoring perhaps in the sixtieth or seventieth percentile on achievement tests. But those scores were not good enough to override the opinion that my true abilities lay in math and science, because in those areas I achieved A's and scored in the ninetieth percentile or higher.

This was understandable. Math is precise; there is only one correct answer. Whereas, for me at least, the answers on English tests were always a judgement call, a matter of opinion and personal experience. Those tests were constructed around items like fill-in-the-blank sentence completion, such as "Even though Tom was _____, Mary thought he was _____." And the correct answer always seemed to be the most bland combinations of thoughts, for example, "Even though Tom was shy, Mary thought he was charming," with the grammatical structure "even though" limiting the correct answer to some sort of semantic opposites, so you wouldn't get answers like, "Even though Tom was foolish, Mary thought he was ridiculous." Well, according to my mother, there were very few limitations as to what Tom could have been and what Mary might have thought of him. So I never did well on tests like that.

The same was true with word analogies, pairs of words in which you were supposed to find some sort of logical, semantic relationship—for example, "*Sunset* is to *nightfall* as _____ is to _____." And here you would be presented with a list of four possible pairs, one of which showed the same kind of relationship: *red* is to *stoplight, bus* is to *arrival, chills* is to *fever, yawn* is to *boring*. Well, I could never think that way. I knew what the tests were asking, but I could not block out of my mind the images already created by the first pair "*sunset* is to *nightfall*"—and I would see a burst of colors against a darkening sky, the moon rising, the lowering of a curtain of stars. And all the other pairs of words—red, bus, stoplight, boring—just threw up a mass of confusing images, making it impossible for me to sort out something as logical as saying: "A sunset precedes nightfall" is the same as "a chill precedes a fever." The only way I would have gotten that answer right would have been to imagine an associative situation, for example, my being disobedient and staying out past sunset, catching a chill at night, which turns into feverish pneumonia as punishment, which indeed did happen to me.

I have been thinking about all this lately, about my mother's English, about achievement tests. Because lately I've been asked, as a writer, why there are not more Asian-Americans represented in American literature. Why are there few Asian-Americans enrolled in creative writing programs? Why do so many Chinese students go into engineering? Well, theses are broad sociological questions I can't begin to answer. But I have noticed in surveys—in fact, just last week—that Asian students, as a whole, always do significantly better on math achievement tests than in English. And this makes me think that there are other Asian-American students whose English spoken in the home might also be described as "broken" or "limited." And perhaps they also have teachers who are steering them away from writing and into math and science, which is what happened to me.

Fortunately, I happen to be rebellious in nature and enjoy the challenge of disproving assumptions made about me. I became an English major my first year in college, after being enrolled as pre-med. I started writing nonfiction as a freelancer the week after I was told by my former boss that writing was my worst skill and I should hone my talents toward account management.

20   But it wasn't until 1985 that I finally began to write fiction. And at first I wrote using what I thought to be wittily crafted sentences, sentences that would finally prove I had mastery over the English language. Here's an example from the first draft of a story that later made its way into *The Joy Luck Club,* but without this line: "That was my mental quandary in its nascent state." A terrible line, which I can barely pronounce.

Fortunately, for reasons I won't get into today, I later decided I should envision a reader for the stories I would write. And the reader I decided upon was my mother, because these were stories about mothers. So with this reader in mind—and in fact she did read my early drafts—I began to write stories using all the Englishes I grew up with: the English I spoke to my mother, which for lack of a better term might be described as "simple"; the English she used with me, which for lack of a better term might be described as "broken"; my translation of her Chinese, which could certainly be described as "watered down"; and what I imagined to be her translation of her Chinese if she could speak in perfect English, her internal language, and for that I sought to preserve the essence, but neither an English nor a Chinese structure. I wanted to capture what language ability tests can never reveal: her intent, her passion, her imagery, the rhythms of her speech and the nature of her thoughts.

Apart from what any critic had to say about my writing, I knew I had succeeded where it counted when my mother finished reading my book and gave me her verdict: "So easy to read."

QUESTIONS FOR DISCUSSION

1. Tan discusses her awareness of using language differently when speaking with different audiences and on different occasions. Keep a log for several days that records the situations when you change the way you use English for a specific group of friends, teachers, relatives, or a work situation. Share your observations and conclusions with your classmates.

2. Why is Tan critical of the descriptive term "limited English"? How did this term influence her perception of her own mother?

3. Why is the article entitled "Mother Tongue"? What do Tan's examples about how she would often speak for her mother suggest?

4. Why is Tan critical of the achievement tests she was given as an adolescent? Do you agree or disagree with her point of view and conclusions? Explain your point of view.

5. Why does Tan believe that high school teachers encourage Asian students to study math and science rather than writing? How does she explain her success as a writer in spite of the evaluations provided by her teachers and employer?

6. According to Tan, what is the real test of a writer? What advice does Tan offer to the person who aspires to be a successful writer?

CONNECTION

Compare Tan's views on the role of different "Englishes" in her writer's life and in her relationship with her mother with the views of Joyce Chang in her essay "Drive Becarefully" (see page 59).

IDEAS FOR WRITING

1. "I am a writer. And by definition, I am someone who has always loved language. I am fascinated by language in daily life." Develop Tan's ideas

on language into an essay, using personal experiences and examples from your reading that illustrate language's complexity and power.
2. Write an essay in which you discuss how your rebellion against a cultural or social myth helped you to develop a skill and talent that is both useful and rewarding.

RELATED WEB SITES

AMY TAN
http://www.luminarium.org/contemporary/amytan/
This excellent, extensive online resource on author Amy Tan includes interviews, book reviews, essays, links, and biographical information.

ASIAN-AMERICAN STUDIES RESOURCES
http//sun3.lib.uci.edu/~dtsang/aas2.htm
This site contains hundreds of links to topics in Asian-American Studies, such as bibliographies, magazines, journals, audio visual resources, research institutes, programs, and libraries.

Frederick Douglass

Learning to Read and Write

An important figure in the history of African-American thought and writing, Frederick Douglass (1818–1895) was born in Maryland into slavery. After escaping to the North, he wrote of his journey to freedom in The Narrative Life of Frederick Douglass *(1845). He also became the publisher of two radical newspapers:* North Star *and the* Frederick Douglass Paper, *which had a very significant impact on the antislavery movement. Douglass helped hundreds of slaves make their way to freedom on the Underground Railroad. During the Civil War Douglass served as an advisor to President Abraham Lincoln, and after 1872, he served as an international diplomat. In the short excerpt from his autobiography included below, Douglass describes how learning to read developed his intellect, pride, and resourcefulness.*

JOURNAL

How did you learn to read? What do you appreciate most about reading?

I lived in Master Hugh's family about seven years. During this time, I succeeded in learning to read and write. In accomplishing this, I was compelled to resort to various stratagems. I had no regular teacher. My mistress, who kindly commenced to instruct me, had, in compliance with the advice and direction of her husband, not only ceased to instruct, but had set her face against my being instructed by any one else. It is due, however, to my mistress to say of her, that she did not adopt this course of treatment immediately. She at first lacked the depravity indispensable to shutting me up in mental darkness. It was at least necessary for her to have some training in the exercise of irresponsible power, to make her equal to the task of treating me as though I were a brute.

My mistress was, as I have said, a kind and tender-hearted woman; and in the simplicity of her soul she commenced, when I first went to live with her, to treat me as she supposed one human being ought to treat another. In entering upon the duties of a slaveholder, she did not seem to perceive that I sustained to her the relation of a mere chattel, and that for her to treat me as a human being was not only wrong, but dangerously so. Slavery proved as injurious to her as it did to me. When I went there, she was a pious, warm, and tender-hearted woman. There was no sorrow or suffering for which she had not a tear. She had bread for the hungry, clothes for the naked, and comfort for every mourner that came within her reach. Slavery soon proved its ability to divest her of these heavenly qualities. Under its influence, the tender heart became stone, and the lamb-like disposition gave way to one of tiger-like fierceness. The first step in her downward course was in her ceasing to instruct me. She now commenced to practise her husband's precepts. She finally became even more violent in her opposition than her husband himself. She was not satisfied with simply doing as well as he had commanded; she seemed anxious to do better. Nothing seemed to make her more angry than to see me with a newspaper. She seemed to think that here lay the danger. I have had her rush at me with a face made all up of fury, and snatch from me a newspaper, in a manner that fully revealed her apprehension. She was an apt woman; and a little experience soon demonstrated, to her satisfaction, that education and slavery were incompatible with each other.

From this time I was most narrowly watched. If I was in a separate room any considerable length of time, I was sure to be suspected of having a book, and was at once called to give an account of myself. All this, however, was too late. The first step had been taken. Mistress, in teaching me the alphabet, had given me the *inch,* and no precaution could prevent me from taking the *ell.*

The plan which I adopted, and the one by which I was most successful, was that of making friends of all the little white boys whom I met in the street. As many of these as I could, I converted into teachers. With their kindly aid, obtained at different times and in different places, I finally succeeded in learning to read. When I was sent on errands, I always took my book with me, and by doing one part of my errand quickly, I found time to get a lesson before my return. I used also to carry bread with me, enough of which was always in the house, and to which I was always welcome; for I was much better off in this regard than many of the poor white children in our neighborhood. This bread I used to bestow upon the hungry little urchins, who, in return, would give me that more valuable bread of knowledge. I am strongly tempted to give the names of two or three of those little boys, as a testimonial of the gratitude and affection I bear them; but prudence forbids;—not that it would injure me, but it might embarrass them; for it is almost an unpardonable offence to teach slaves to read in this Christian country. It is enough to say of the dear little fellows, that they lived on Philpot Street, very near Durgin and Bailey's shipyard. I used to talk this matter of slavery over with them. I would sometimes say to them, I wished I could be as free as they would be when they got to be men. "You will be free as soon as you are twenty-one, *but I am a slave for life!* Have not I as good a right to be free as you have?" These words used to trouble them; they would express for me the liveliest sympathy, and console me with the hope that something would occur by which I might be free.

5   I was now about twelve years old, and the thought of being *a slave for life* began to bear heavily upon my heart. Just about this time, I got hold of a book entitled "The Columbian Orator." Every opportunity I got, I used to read this book. Among much of other interesting matter, I found in it a dialogue between a master and his slave. The slave was represented as having run away from his master three times. The dialogue represented the conversation which took place between them, when the slave was retaken the third time. In this dialogue, the whole argument in behalf of slavery was brought forward by the master, all of which was disposed of by the slave. The slave was made to say some very smart as well as impressive things in reply to his master—things which had the desired though unexpected effect; for the conversation resulted in the voluntary emancipation of the slave on the part of the master.

In the same book, I met with one of Sheridan's mighty speeches on and in behalf of Catholic emancipation. These were choice documents to me. I read them over and over again with unabated interest. They gave tongue to interesting thoughts of my own soul, which had frequently flashed through my mind, and died away for want of utterance. The moral which I gained from the dialogue was the power of truth over the conscience of even a slaveholder. What I got from Sheridan was a bold denunciation of slavery, and a powerful vindication of human rights. The reading of these documents enabled me to utter my thoughts, and to meet the arguments brought forward to sustain slavery; but while they relieved me of one difficulty, they brought on another even more painful than the one of which I was relieved. The more I read, the more I was led to abhor and detest my enslavers. I could regard them in no other light than a band of successful robbers, who had left their homes, and gone to Africa, and stolen us from our homes, and in a strange land reduced us to slavery. I loathed them as being the meanest as well as the most wicked of men. As I read and contemplated the subject, behold! that very discontentment which Master Hugh had predicted would follow my learning to read had already come, to torment and sting my soul to unutterable anguish. As I writhed under it, I would at times feel that learning to read had been a curse rather than a blessing. It had given me a view of my wretched condition, without the remedy. It opened my eyes to the horrible pit, but to no ladder upon which to get out. In moments of agony, I envied my fellow-slaves for their stupidity. I have often wished myself a beast. I preferred the condition of the meanest reptile to my own. Any thing, no matter what, to get rid of thinking! It was this everlasting thinking of my condition that tormented me. There was no getting rid of it. It was pressed upon me by every object within sight or hearing, animate or inanimate. The silver trump of freedom had roused my soul to eternal wakefulness. Freedom now appeared, to disappear no more forever. It was heard in every sound, and seen in every thing. It was ever present to torment me with a sense of my wretched condition. I saw nothing without seeing it, I heard nothing without hearing it, and felt nothing without feeling it. It looked from every star, it smiled in every calm, breathed in every wind, and moved in every storm.

I often found myself regretting my own existence, and wishing myself dead; and but for the hope of being free, I have no doubt but that I should have killed myself, or done something for which I should have been killed. While in this state of mind, I was eager to hear anyone speak of slavery. I was a ready listener. Every little while, I could hear something about the abolitionists. It was some time before I found what the word meant. It was always used in such connections as to make it an interesting word to me. If a slave ran away and succeeded in getting clear, or if a slave killed his master, set fire to a barn, or did any thing very wrong in the mind of a slaveholder, it was spoken of as the fruit of *abolition.* Hearing the word in this connection very often, I set about learning what it meant. The dictionary afforded me little or no help. I found it was "the act of abolishing;" but then I did not know what was to be abolished. Here I was perplexed. I did not dare to ask any one about its meaning, for I was satisfied that it was something they wanted me to know very little about. After a patient waiting, I got one of our city papers, containing an account of the number of petitions from the north, praying for the abolition of slavery in the District of Columbia, and of the slave trade between the States. From this time I understood the words *abolition* and *abolitionist,* and always drew near when that word was spoken, expecting to hear something of importance to myself and fellow-slaves. The light broke in upon me by degrees. I went one day down on the wharf of Mr. Waters; and seeing two Irishmen unloading a scow of stone, I went, unasked, and helped them. When we had finished, one of them came to me and asked me if I were a slave. I told him I was. He asked, "Are ye a slave for life?" I told him that I was. The good Irishman seemed to be deeply affected by the statement. He said to the other that it was a pity so fine a little fellow as myself should be a slave for life. He said it was a shame to hold me. They both advised me to run away to the north; that I should find friends there, and that I should be free. I pretended not to be interested in what they said, and treated them as if I did not understand them; for I feared they might be treacherous. White men have been known to encourage slaves to escape, and then, to get the reward, catch them and return them to their masters. I was afraid that these seemingly good men might use me so; but I nevertheless remembered their advice, and from that time I resolved to run away.

Questions for Discussion

1. Why does the relationship between Frederick Douglass and his mistress change? What is the nature of their power struggle?
2. How did Douglass learn to read?
3. Discuss two of the incidents from the selection that show that Douglass has resourcefulness and an understanding of human nature, as well as an ability to listen, think critically, and learn from his experience.
4. Why does Douglass grow more and more tormented by what he is reading and thinking? How does he combat his deep feelings of frustration and despair on his journey to becoming an educated and free man?
5. Why and how does Douglass finally join the Abolitionist's cause?
6. What connections between education and freedom does Douglass make in this excerpt from his autobiography? What relationships have you seen between education and freedom in your own life?

Ideas for Writing

1. Becoming educated through reading allowed Douglass to gain his freedom and help many other slaves to gain their freedom. Write an essay that explores different ways in which your education through reading has helped you to gain more freedom and independence.
2. Using the resources at your college library and on the Internet, find out more about how slaves learned to read and write, and how their education helped them to gain their freedom.

Connection

Compare Linton Weeks's and Douglass's views on the importance of reading. Why do you think reading was more important to Douglass than it is for many young people today (see page 53)?

Related Web Sites

Frederick Douglass
www.history.rochester.edu/class/douglass/home.html
This biography of Frederick Douglass by Sandra Thomas will give you more insight into the struggles and challenges that Douglass overcame in his fight to gain his own freedom and the freedom of his people.

Frederick Douglass National Historic Site
www.nps.gov/frdo/freddoug.html
The Frederick Douglass National Historic Site is dedicated to preserving the legacy of the most famous African-Americans of the nineteenth century. The museum is located at the final home that Douglass purchased in 1877, which he named Cedar Hill.

FREDERICK DOUGLASS PAPERS
`www.iupui.edu/~douglass/`
Housed at Indiana University-Purdue University at Indianapolis, The Frederick Douglass Papers project collects and publishes his speeches and writings.

Steven Holtzman

Don't Look Back

Steven Holtzman (b. 1947) is interested in computers, philosophy, and creativity. He holds both an undergraduate degree in Western and Eastern philosophy and a Ph.D. in computer science from the University of Edinburgh. He is also founder and Vice President of Optimal Networks in Palo Alto, California. Using computer techniques, he has composed a number of musical works that have been performed in Europe and the United States, some of which can be found on a CD he has produced, Digital Mantras (Shriek! Records, 1994). He also has written two books that examine the new types of creative expression possible in the age of computers and cyberspace: Digital Mantras: The Language of Abstract and Virtual Worlds *(1994), and* Digital Mosaics: The Aesthetics of Cyberspace *(1997). Holtzman's books are aesthetically appealing as well as intellectually provocative. In the following excerpt from* Digital Mosaics, *he argues that we can't turn our backs on today's digital technology as it is already an inextricable part of our lives.*

JOURNAL

Write about your experience with reading books and other texts online: Have you found this kind of reading rewarding?

For centuries, the book has been the primary vehicle for recording, storing, and transferring knowledge. But it's hard to imagine that paper will be the preferred format in a hundred years. Digital media will marginalize this earlier form of communication, relegating it to a niche just as music CDs have replaced LPs. The book will be forced to redefine itself, just as TV forced radio to redefine itself, and radio and TV together transformed the newspaper's role. The process is survival of the fittest—competition in the market to be a useful medium. Whatever the book's future is, clearly its role will never be the same. The book has lost its preeminence.

The print medium of newspaper is also fading. Almost every major newspaper in the United States is experiencing significant declines in circulation. (The exception is *USA Today*—characterized by itself as "TV on paper.") More than 70 percent of Americans under the age of thirty don't read newspapers. And this trend isn't about to change.

The powers of the media business today understand this. As part of the frenzied convergence of media, communications, and the digital world, we're witnessing a dizzying tangle of corporate alliances and mega-mergers. Companies are jockeying for position for this epochal change. The list includes many multibillion-dollar companies—AT&T, Bertelsmann, Disney, Microsoft, Time Warner, Viacom—and many, many more small startup technology companies. They all want to position themselves as preeminent new media companies.

Clinging to the Past

Members of the literary establishment can also see this imminent change. Yet, for the most part, they take a dim view of these new digital worlds. Beyond the loss of their cherished culture, what disturbs many critics is that they find new digital media like CD-ROMs and the World Wide Web completely unsatisfying.

5   The literary critic Sven Birkerts eloquently laments that the generation growing up in the digital age is incapable of enjoying literature. Teaching at college has brought Birkerts to despair because his students aren't able to appreciate the literary culture he so values. After only a proudly self-confessed "glimpse of the future" of CD-ROMs, he declares he is "clinging all the more tightly to my books."

The disillusionment with the digital experience is summed up by the *New York Times Book Review* critic Sarah Lyall. She complains that multimedia CD-ROMs

> still don't come close to matching the experience of reading a paper-and-print book while curled up in a chair, in bed, on the train, under a tree, in an airplane. . . . After all, the modern book is the result of centuries of trial and error during which people wrote on bark, on parchment, on vellum, on clay, on scrolls, on stone, chiseling characters into surfaces or copying them out by hand.

Okay, I thought as I read Birkerts and Lyall, these are members of a dying cultural heritage who—like seemingly every generation—are uncomfortable with new. Unable to shift their perspective, they'll be casualties of change. After all, Birkerts boasts that he doesn't own a computer and still uses only a typewriter.

Birkerts clings not to his books, but to the past. I was reminded of a comment by the cultural critic William Irwin Thompson, who is also wary of the consequences of digital technology:

> It is not the literary intelligentsia of *The New York Review of Books* [or *The New York Times,* as the case may be] that is bringing forth this new culture, for it is as repugnant to them as the Reformation was to the Catholic Church. . . . This new cyberpunk, technological culture is brought forth by Top and Pop, electronic science and pop music, and both the hackers and the rockers are anti-intellectual and unsympathetic to the previous Mental level expressed by the genius of European civilization.

This helped me dismiss the backlash from those looking in the rearview mirror. But then I came across a book by Clifford Stoll.

Muddier Mud

10   Stoll, who was introduced to computers twenty years ago, is a longtime member of the digerati. In his book *Silicone Snake Oil,* he claims to expose the true emptiness of the digital experience.

In opening, Stoll explains that "every time someone mentions MUDs [multi-user dungeons, a type of interactive adventure game] and virtual reality, I think of a genuine reality with muddier mud than anything a computer can deliver." Stoll then nostalgically recounts the story of the first time he went crawling through caves in his college days. "We start in, trailing a string through the muddy tunnel—everything's covered with gunk, as are the six of us crawling behind [the guide]. Not your ordinary slimy, brown, backyard mud, either. This is the goop of inner-earth that works its way into your hair, socks, and underwear."

Stoll's general theme: "You're viewing a world that doesn't exist. During that week you spend online, you could have planted a tomato garden. . . . While the Internet beckons brightly, seductively flashing an icon of knowledge-as-power, this nonplace lures us to surrender our time on earth."

I suppose this excludes any experience that might distract us from the real—a novel, a Beethoven symphony, a movie. (A tomato garden?)

And then we get the same theme that Birtkerts and Lyall hit on.

I've rarely met anyone who prefers to read digital books. I don't want my morning newspaper delivered over computer, or a CD-ROM stuffed with National Geographic photographs. Call me a troglodyte; I'd rather peruse those photos alongside my sweetheart, catch the newspaper on the way to work, and page through a real book. . . . Now, I'm hardly a judge of aesthetics, but of the scores of electronic multimedia productions I've seen, I don't remember any as being beautiful.

A CD-ROM Is Not a Book

15   These laments totally miss the point. No, a CD-ROM isn't a book. Nor is a virtual world—whether a MUD or a simulation of rolling in the mud—the same as the real experience. This is *exactly* the point! A CD-ROM isn't a book; it's something completely new and different. A MUD on the Internet isn't like mud in a cave. A virtual world isn't the real world; it offers possibilities unlike anything we've known before.

Birkerts, Lyall, and Stoll dismiss the digital experience to justify staying in the familiar and comfortable worlds of their past. Yet what's exciting to me about these digital worlds is precisely that they're new, they're unfamiliar, and they're our future.

It's not that I disagree with the literati's assertions. We will lose part of our literary culture and tradition. Kids today are so attuned to the rapid rhythms of MTV that they're unresponsive to the patient patterns of literary prose. They are indeed so seduced by the flickeringly powerful identifications of the screen as to be deaf to the inner voices of print. Literary culture—like classical music and opera—will become marginalized as mainstream culture pursues a digital path.

There never will be a substitute for a book. And today's multimedia CD-ROM—even surfing the World Wide Web—is still for the most part a static and unsatisfying experience. But it's rather early to conclude anything about their ultimate potential.

Patience Is a Virtue

It puzzles me that there are people who expect that, in almost no time at all, we'd find great works by those who have mastered the subtleties of such completely new digital worlds. We are seeing the first experiments with a new medium. It took a long time to master the medium of film. Or the book, for that matter. It will also take time to master new digital worlds.

20   It's challenging to create a multimedia digital world today. The enabling technologies that will make radically new digital worlds possible—Java, VRML, and a string of acronymic technologies—are still emerging. Artists, writers, and musicians must also be software programmers. Today, a rare combination of passion, artistry, and technical knowledge is required. Yet, over time, these skills will become common. Even more important than the technical mastery of new digital media, a new conceptual framework and aesthetic must also be established for digital worlds.

When this conceptual and technical mastery is achieved, we'll discover the true possibilities of digital expression. In a few decades—or possibly in just five years—we'll look on today's explorations as primitive. Until then, we will continue to explore these new digital worlds and seek to learn their true potential.

Embracing the Digital

There will be nothing to replace the reading of a book or newspaper in bed. Curling up by a fireside to read a poem with an electronic tablet won't have the same intimacy as doing so with a book. But curling up by a fireside with an electronic tablet is itself simply an example of substituting electronic technology for an existing medium—extrapolating from today's flat-paneled handheld computers to an "electronic book." We need to develop a new aesthetic—a digital aesthetic. And the emerging backlash from the literati makes clear to me how urgently we need it.

When we've mastered digital media, we won't be talking about anything that has much to do with the antiquated form of the book. I imagine myself curled up in bed with laser images projected on my retinas, allowing me to view and travel through an imaginary three-dimensional virtual world. A story about the distant past flashes a quaint image of a young woman sitting and reading a book, which seems just as remote as the idea of a cluster of Navajo Indians sitting around a campfire and listening to a master of the long-lost tradition of storytelling. In a hundred years, we'll think of the book as we do the storyteller today.

Will we lose a part of our cultural heritage as we assimilate new media? No doubt. Is this disturbing? Absolutely. Today's traditional media will be further marginalized. Is there much value in decrying an inevitable future? Probably not. The music of *today* is written on electric instruments. Hollywood creates our theater. And soon digital media will be *our* media. Digital technology and new digital media—for better or worse—are here to stay.

25   That's not to say that all things digital are good. Perhaps, like the Luddites in Britain during the first half of the nineteenth century, the literati raise a flag of warning, raise awareness, and create debate, debunking some of the myths of a utopian digital future. But in the end, for better or for worse, the efforts of the Luddites were futile when it came to stopping the industrial revolution.

Likewise, today you can't turn off the Internet. Digital technology isn't going away. There are already thousands of multimedia CD-ROMs and hundreds of thousands of sites on the World Wide Web; soon there will be thousands of channels of on-demand digital worlds.

Digital technology is part of our lives, a part of our lives that we know will only continue to grow. We can't afford to dismiss it. Rather we must embrace it—not indiscriminately, but thoughtfully. We must seize the opportunities generated by the birth of a new medium to do things we've never been able to do before. Don't look back.

QUESTIONS FOR DISCUSSION

1. Why does Holtzman believe that the power and popularity of books and newspapers are fading? Do you agree?
2. According to William Thompson, why do the members of the "literary intelligentsia" find the "new culture" of CD-ROMs and the Internet to be repugnant? What other reasons for the rejection might there be?
3. What is computer scientist Cliff Stoll's primary reason for rejecting the Internet as a learning experience for children? How does Holtzman attempt to refute Stoll? Is he successful? With whose point of view do you agree?
4. What features of the book do the traditional critics such as Birkerts consider to be irreplaceable? Do these critics have valid arguments? Explain.
5. What do you think Holtzman means by his concluding statement that we must embrace digital media "not indiscriminately, but thoughtfully"? Do you think his essay is a good example of the thoughtful approach he recommends? Explain your point of view.

CONNECTION

Compare Holtzman's view of reading and its significance with Linton Weeks's reading. How would Holtzman respond to Weeks's critique of modern reading habits (see page 53)?

IDEAS FOR WRITING

1. Write an essay in which you compare your own experience with the World Wide Web or a learning program on multimedia CD-ROM disk to reading a regular book or textbook on the same subject. Which experi-

ence did you find more useful and worthwhile? Use examples to support each of your main ideas?

2. Write an essay that explores and predicts the changing roles that books and printed media will play in contrast to the roles of the Internet and other digital media in the next five years. Consider specific environments such as the home, schools, the work place, and governmental agencies.

RELATED WEB SITES

STEVEN HOLTZMAN
http://www.beatrice.com/interviews/holtzman/
Learn more about the author, Steven Holtzman, and his ideas on the revolution of art and writing in the "new digital media age."

THE SCENE! DIGITAL EXPRESSION
http://www.inthescene.com/digitexp/
This web site shares new writing, art, and music "in the digital realm." Here one can view the latest in digital expressions from artists, musicians and writers.

Linton Weeks

The No-Book Report: Skim it and Weep

Linton Weeks was born and raised in Memphis, Tennessee. He received a B.A. in English from Rhodes College in Memphis in 1976. Weeks founded Southern Magazine *in Little Rock in 1986, moving on to the* Washington Post *in 1990, where he became managing editor. In 1994 he became the first director of the* Washington Post's *online service. The following article appeared in the* Washington Post *in May 2001.*

JOURNAL

Write about the differences you perceive between an aliterate and an illiterate. What reactions do you have to an aliterate? To an illiterate?

Jeremy Spreitzer probably wouldn't read this story if it weren't about him. He is an aliterate—someone who can read, but chooses not to.

A graduate student in public affairs at Park University in Kansas City, Mo., Spreitzer, 25, gleans most of his news from TV. He skims required texts, draws themes from dust jackets and, when he absolutely, positively has to read something, reaches for the audiobook.

"I am fairly lazy when it comes to certain tasks," says Spreitzer, a long-distance runner who hopes to compete in the 2004 Olympics. "Reading is one of them."

As he grows older, Spreitzer finds he has less time to read. And less inclination. In fact, he says, if he weren't in school, he probably wouldn't read at all.

He's not alone. According to the survey firm NDP Group—which tracked the everyday habits of thousands of people through the 1990s—this country is reading printed versions of books, magazines and newspapers less and less. In 1991, more than half of all Americans read a half-hour or more every day. By 1999, that had dropped to 45 percent.

A 1999 Gallup Poll found that only 7 percent of Americans were voracious readers, reading more than a book a week, while some 59 percent said they had read fewer than 10 books in the previous year. Though book clubs seem popular now, only 6 percent of those who read belong to one. The number of people who don't read at all, the poll concluded, has been rising for the past 20 years.

The reports on changes in reading cut to the quick of American culture. We pride ourselves on being a largely literate First World country while at the same time we rush to build a visually powerful environment in which reading is not required.

The results are inevitable. Aliteracy is all around. Just ask:

- Internet developers. At the Terra Lycos portal design lab in Waltham, Mass., researcher William Albert has noticed that the human guinea pigs in his focus groups are too impatient to read much. When people look up information on the Internet today, Albert explains, they are "basically scanning. There's very little actual comprehension that's going on." People, Albert adds, prefer to get info in short bursts, with bullets, rather than in large blocks of text.
- Transportation gurus. Chandra Clayton, who oversees the design of road signs and signals for the Virginia Department of Transportation, says, "Symbols can quickly give you a message that might take too long to read in text." The department is using logos and symbols more and more. When it comes to highway safety and getting lifesaving information quickly, she adds, "a picture *is* worth a thousand words."
- Packaging designers. "People don't take the time to read anything," explains Jim Peters, editor of BrandPackaging magazine. "Marketers and packagers are giving them colors and shapes as ways of communicating." For effective marketing, Peters says, "researchers tell us that the hierarchy is colors, shapes, icons and, dead last, words."

Some of this shift away from words—and toward images—can be attributed to our ever-growing multilingual population. But for many people, reading is passe or impractical or, like, so totally unnecessary in this day and age.

To Jim Trelease, author of "The Read-Aloud Handbook," this trend away from the written word is more than worrisome. It's wicked. It's tearing apart our culture. People who have stopped reading, he says, "base their future decisions on what they used to know."

"If you don't read much, you really don't know much," he says. "You're dangerous."

Losing a Heritage

"The man who does not read good books has no advantage over the man who cannot read them."

—Mark Twain

One thing you can say for illiteracy: It can be identified, nailed down. And combated. Scores of programs such as the Greater Washington Literacy Council and the International Reading Association are geared toward fighting read-inglessness in the home, the school and the workplace.

Aliteracy, on the other hand, is like an invisible liquid, seeping through our culture, nigh impossible to pinpoint or defend against. It's the kid who spends hours and hours with video games instead of books, who knows Sim Cities better than "A Tale of Two Cities."

It's the thousands of business people who subscribe to executive book summaries—for example, Soundview's easy-to-swallow eight-page pamphlets
15 that take simply written management books such as "Secrets of Question-Based Selling" by Thomas A. Freese and make them even simpler.

It's the parent who pops the crummy movie of "Stuart Little" into a machine for his kid instead of reading E. B. White's marvelous novel aloud. Or the teacher who assigns the made-for-TV movie "Gettysburg" instead of the book it was based on, "The Killer Angels" by Michael Shaara.

There may be untold collateral damage in a society that can read but doesn't. "So much of our culture is embedded in literature," says Philip A. Thompsen, professor of communications at West Chester University in West Chester, Pa. Thompsen has been watching the rise of aliteracy in the classroom for 20 years, and "students today are less capable of getting full value from textbooks than they were 10 years ago."

He adds that these aliterate students are "missing out on our cultural heritage."

That literature-based past included a reverence for reading, a celebration of the works and a worshipful awe of those who wrote.
20 To draw you a picture: Where we once deified the lifestyles of writers such as Ernest Hemingway and F. Scott Fitzgerald, we now fantasize about rock-and-roll gods, movie starlets or NBA super-studs (e.g. MTV's "Cribs"). The notion of writer-as-culture-hero is dead and gone. Comedic monologuists such as Jay Leno or David Letterman have more sex appeal than serious fiction writers. The grail quest for the Great American Novel has ended; it *was* a myth after all.

Where we once drew our mass-cult references from books ("He's a veritable Simon Legree"*), we now allude to visual works—a Seinfeld episode (not that

---

* Simon Legree: a cruel slave dealer in the novel *Uncle Tom's Cabin* by Harriet Beecher Stowe.

there's anything *wrong* with that . . .) or "The Silence of the Lambs" (the movie, not the book). A recent story in Salon* speaks of "learning to read a movie."

Where we once believed that a well-read populace leads to a healthy democracy, many people now rely on whole TV broadcast operations built around politics and elections. Quick, name a Wolf Blitzer book.

Non-readers abound. Ask "Politically Incorrect" talk show host Bill Maher, who once boasted in print that he hadn't read a book in years. Or Noel Gallagher of the rock band Oasis, who has been quoted as saying he'd *never* read a book. You can walk through whole neighborhoods of houses in the country that do not contain books or magazines—unless you count catalogues.

American historian Daniel Boorstin saw this coming. In 1984, while Boorstin was serving as librarian of Congress, the library issued a landmark report: "Books in Our Future." Citing recent statistics that only about half of all Americans read regularly every year, he referred to the "twin menaces" of illiteracy and aliteracy.

25   "In the United States today," Boorstin wrote, "aliteracy is widespread."

Several of the articles in the report alluded to the growing number of non-readers. In one essay, "The Computer and the Book," Edmund D. Pellegrino, a former president of Catholic University who is now a bioethicist at Georgetown University, observed: "The computer is simply the most effective, efficient and attractive form for transmittal of processed information. Added to the other nonbook devices like films, tapes, television and the popular media, the computer accelerates the atrophy of the intellectual skills acquired for personally reading the books from which the information is extracted."

Reading for Bliss

30   Kylene Beers has talked about the evils of aliteracy for so long and so loud, she's losing her voice. Today she's in the lecture hall of Oakton High School bending the ears of 100 or so middle school teachers.

If someone graduates from high school and is aliterate, Beers believes, that person will probably never become a habitual reader.

One of the few academics who have written about the phenomenon, Beers, a professor of reading at the University of Houston, says there are two types of reading: efferent and aesthetic.

Efferent, which comes from the Latin word *efferre* (meaning to carry away), is purposeful reading, the kind students are taught day after day in schools. Efferent readers connect cognitively with the words and plan to take something useful from it—such as answers for a test.

Aesthetic is reading for the sheer bliss of it, as when you dive deep into Dostoevski or get lost in Louisa May Alcott. Aesthetic readers connect emotionally to the story. Beers believes that more students must be shown the marvels of reading for pleasure.

On this late afternoon, she is mapping out strategies for teachers who hope to engage reluctant middle school readers. Teaching grammar and parts of

---

* Salon: an on-line news and entertainment magazine at <www.salon.com>.

speech, such as dangling participles, is the kiss of death, she says. "You don't want to talk about dangling anythings with middleschoolers," she says in her Texas drawl. And the room laughs.

Aliteracy, she continues, is no laughing matter. Using an overhead projector, she explains that alitcrate people just don't get it. Unlike accomplished readers, aliterates don't understand that sometimes you have to read efferently and sometimes you have to read aesthetically; that even the best readers occasionally read the same paragraph over and over to understand it and that to be a good reader you have to visualize the text.

To engage non-reading students—and adults—she proposes reading strategies, such as turning a chapter of a hard book into a dramatic production or relating tough words to easier words.

35   She writes the word "tepid" on the acetate sheet. Then she asks the audience to supply other words that describe water temperature. "Hot," someone calls out. "Freezing," somebody clse says. Others suggest: cold, warm and boiling. Beers arranges the words in a linear fashion, from the coldest word, "freezing," to the hottest, "boiling." "Tepid" falls in the middle of the list. This method, she says, will help reluctant readers to connect words they don't know to words they do know. "Aliterates," she tells the teachers, "don't see relationships."

Apparently, teachers don't always see the relationships either. Jim Trelease is concerned that teachers do not read. The aliteracy rate among teachers, he says, is about the same, 50 percent, as among the general public.

There is some good news on the reading front, according to Trelease and others. The Harry Potter series has turned on a lot of young readers and megabookstores, such as Barnes & Noble and Borders, are acrawl with people.

But there is plenty of bad news, too. Lots of aliterates, according to Trelease, say they just don't have time to read anymore. "The time argument is the biggest hoax of all," he says. According to time studics, we have more leisure time than ever. "If people didn't have time, the malls would be empty, cable companies would be broke, video stores would go out of business. It's not a time problem, it's a value problem. You have 50 percent in the country who don't value reading."

Like Beers, Trelease believes that youngsters should be encouraged to read aesthetically. Reading aloud to children, according to Trelease and other reading specialists, is the single best way to ensure that someone will become a lifelong reader.

40   "Even Daniel Boorstin wasn't born wanting to read," Trelease says. "Michael Jordan wasn't born wanting to play basketball. The desire has to be planted."

Surfing through Grad School

Trelease and Beers and others are scrambling for ways to engage aliterates. For all kinds of reasons. "What aliteracy does is breed illiteracy," Beers explains. "If you go through school having learned to read and then you leave school not wanting to read, chances are you won't put your own children into a reading environment."

"What you have to do is play hardball," says Trelease. He suggests running public awareness campaigns on TV. "That's where the aliterates are."

Trelease says we should try to eradicate aliteracy in the way we went after to-bacco. We should let people know, Trelease says, "what the consequences are to your family and children if you don't read."

"Aliteracy may be a significant problem today," says Philip Thompsen. "But on the other hand, a narrow view of literacy—one that defines literacy as the ability to read verbal texts—may be a significant problem as well."

45   Many of the messages that we have to interpret in day-to-day life, Thompsen says, "use multiple communication media. I think it is important to realize that as our society becomes more accustomed to using multimedia messages, we must also expand our thinking about what it means to be 'literate.'"

Olympic hopeful Jeremy Spreitzer plans to become a teacher and maybe go into politics someday. For now, he's just trying to get through graduate school.

He watches a lot of television. "I'm a major surfer," he says. He watches the History Channel, A&E, Turner Classic Movies and all of the news stations.

"I'm required to do a lot of reading," he says. "But I do a minimum of what I need to do."

But how do you get through grad school without reading? Spreitzer is asked.

50   He gives an example. One of his required texts is the recently published "Bowling Alone: The Collapse and Revival of American Community" by Robert Putnam. In the book, Putnam argues, among other things, that television has fragmented our society.

Spreitzer thumbed through the book, dipped into a few chapters and spent a while "skipping around" here and there.

He feels, however, that he understands Putnam and Putnam's theories as well as if he had read the book.

How is that? he is asked.

Putnam, he explains, has been on TV a lot. "He's on the news all the time," Spreitzer says. "On MSNBC and other places. Those interviews with him are more invaluable than anything else."

QUESTIONS FOR DISCUSSION

1. Why does Weeks open and conclude his article with the example of Jeremy Spreitzer's attitude and approach to reading? In what ways is Spreitzer representative of an American aliterate?

2. According to the article, how are the increasing numbers of people who are aliterate affecting American culture? What is your response to the figures reported by the 1999 Gallup Poll on the reading habits of Americans?

3. What is the difference between efferent reading and aesthetic reading? Why does Beers, a professor of reading at the University of Houston, be-lieve that more students must read for aesthetic pleasure? Explain why you agree or disagree with Beers's point of view.

4. Why does Jim Trelease argue that people do have the time to read? Why does he believe that most Americans don't read?

5. What solutions to the problem of aliteracy does the article offer? Do the solutions seem adequate? Do you have any other solutions?

6. Do you think that Weeks's article is convincing? In what ways? What else do you think should be done to improve the reading habits of Americans?

CONNECTION

Compare the presentation of a positive reading experience in "Of Modern Poetry" to the modern view of reading among "aliterates" (see page 16).

IDEAS FOR WRITING

1. Jim Trelease, author of *The Read-Aloud Handbook,* believes that the "trend away from the written word is tearing apart our culture . . . If you don't read much, you really don't know much . . . You're dangerous." Write an essay that presents a response to Trelease's claims. Refer to specific examples from your own experiences and what you have learned from the media and the Internet to support your thesis and main ideas.

2. Write an essay that discusses some of Weeks's conclusions about possible solutions for aliteracy; then present some specific ideas of your own for making people more interested and engaged in the act of reading.

RELATED WEB SITES

UNDERSTANDING AND ENCOURAGING A RELUCTANT READER
http://npin.org/pnews/2002/pncw302/int302b.html
This URL shares an article that provides useful ways to battle against the growing trend of "aliteracy" in America described by Linton Weeks. Book lists for interesting reading are also included.

ALL AMERICA READS
http://www.allamericareads.org/

READING MATTERS: INTEREST AND ENJOYMENT
http://www.vm.robcol.k12.tr/~jroyce/read6.htm
This website presents a series of articles and bibliographies by educator John Royce on creative approaches to presenting reading in the classroom in order to heighten children's pleasure in reading.

Joyce Chang

Drive Becarefully

Student writer Joyce Chang (b. 1975) was raised in northern California. Living in a predominantly white neighborhood and growing up in a traditional, close-knit Asian family, Chang struggled to integrate her Chinese heritage with mainstream American culture. In the essay that follows, written originally for an introductory writing class, she explores the problem of coming to terms with her mother's nonstandard English in light of reading Amy Tan's essay, "Mother Tongue."

"My mother's 'limited' English limited my perception of her. I was ashamed of her English." Amy Tan's self-evaluation in her essay, "Mother Tongue," clung to my conscience as I continued reading. I could have said those words myself. I have definitely thought those words a million times. Like Tan, I too used to be ashamed of my mother's English. I used to shudder whenever I heard an incorrect verb tense, misplaced adverb, or incorrect pronoun come from her lips. Like many people, I couldn't look beyond my mother's incorrect grammar to see the intent and beauty behind her words.

My mother immigrated to the United States in the 1970s, speaking only a few words of English. As time went on, she gradually learned more and more words, although her sentence structure remained very basic. As a young working woman and mother of two, my mother didn't have much of a chance to improve her grammar. Taking ESL courses was not one of her immediate concerns—trying to beat rush hour Chicago traffic to get home in time to make dinner was what she worried about. So my mother went on using phrases like "He go to the store."

Since I had the advantage of being born and raised in the United States, my English abilities quickly surpassed those of my mother by the time I was in grade school. I knew all about auxiliary verbs, the subjunctive, and plurals—my mother didn't. I could form sentences like "He treated her as if she were still a child." For my mother to convey that same idea, she could only say, "He treat her like child."

My mother's comprehension of the English language was comparable to her speaking abilities. When I was with her, I learned early on not to try any of the complicated, flowery, descriptive sentences that I had been praised for in school. Anything beyond a simple subject-verb-object construction was poorly received. When I was very young, I did not think much about having to use a different English with my mother. The two Englishes in my life were just different—one was not better than the other. However, that feeling quickly changed in third grade.

5   My young mind could not always switch between the two Englishes with ease. I usually knew which English belonged in which world, but sometimes my Englishes crossed over. I remember one day in third grade when I was supposed to bring something for a "cultural show-and-tell." It must have been sometime in winter—around Chinese New Year. My mother had given me a "red bag" for show-and-tell. A "red bag" is an envelope that contains money. Chinese people give and receive these envelopes of money as gifts for the new year. As my mother described it to me, "The bag for good fortune . . . you rich for New Year." When I tried to explain the meaning of the red envelope to my class, I used my mother's words, "The bag for good fortune. . . ." I do not think my classmates noticed my grammatical shortcomings, or maybe they did notice but chose not to comment. In any case, my teacher had an alarmed look on her face and sharply demanded, "What did you say?" She seemed to be in complete bewilderment at how one of her students who spoke "good English" could sud-

denly speak "bad English." Thinking that she just didn't hear me the first time, I innocently repeated the exact same phrase I had said before.

"Where did you learn *that* English?" she questioned. "It's wrong! Please speak correctly!" she commanded.

After her admonishment, it took me a while to continue speaking. When I finally opened my mouth to utter my first word, all I could think of was, "I hope this is correct." I was relieved when I finished with no further interruptions.

Hearing my teacher say that my mother's English was wrong had a lasting impression on me. When I went home that day, all I could think about when my mother spoke was the "wrongness" of her English, and the "wrongness" of her as a person. I took her awkward phrases, sentence fragments, and other incorrect phrases as a sign that she somehow was "incorrect." I became irritated with her when she made grammatical mistakes at home. I became ashamed of her when she made those same mistakes outside of the house.

By the time I entered high school I was tired of being ashamed of my mother's English. I thought I would do her a favor and take on a mission to improve her English. The mission turned out to be a lot more difficult than I thought it would be. No matter how many times I would tell her something that she said was wrong, she would still say the same phrase over and over again. For example, whenever I left the house, my mother would say, "Drive becarefully." After the first time she said that, I told her it was wrong. I would then add, "The correct way to say that is 'drive carefully' or 'be careful driving.'" She would then nod and say good-bye. However, the next day as I headed out the door, mother would come up to me and say "drive becarefully" again. I would get incredibly frustrated because she never seemed to learn. I was glad, however, that at least I was the only one to hear such an "incorrect" statement.

10   One day, however, a friend of mine was with me as we headed out the door. As usual my mother screamed out "drive becarefully" as we walked toward the car. I immediately rolled my eyes and muttered, "It's 'drive carefully.' Get it right."

Later, as I drove my friend back home, she asked me a question that I will never forget. "Is it your mom who wants to improve her English or is it you who wants to 'improve' her?" I was stunned at first by my friend's question. I had no response. After a lot of thinking, I realized my friend was right. My mom was satisfied with her English. She could convey her thoughts and didn't care that she did it in a way that was different from the standard. She had no problem with her use of language—I did.

After that conversation, I began to accept the idea that there are many different Englishes and that one is not necessarily better than the other. As long as a person is understood, it is not necessary to speak textbook perfect English. Presently, I am very concerned with how people treat others who speak "limited" English. I understand how easy it is to misperceive and mistreat people. In her essay "Mother Tongue," Tan also writes about how people are perceived differently just because of their "limited" English. She describes the problems her mother encounters day to day, "people in department stores, at banks, and at restaurants did not take her seriously, did not give her good service, pretended not to understand her, or even acted as if they did not hear her." Although I am very angry when I read about how a person with "limited" English is mistreated, I still understand how it is all too easy for a person not to take someone seriously when he/she does not speak the same English as that person. It is also easy to assume a person who speaks "broken" English wants someone to help him "fix" it.

Now, when I find myself talking with people who speak "another" English, I try to look for the meaning, the intent of what they say, and ignore the perhaps awkward structure of their statements. Also when I encounter someone who speaks an English different from my own, I try not to assume that he or she wants to "improve" it.

As Tan concludes her essay, the importance of what is spoken lies in a person's ". . . intent, . . . passion, . . . imagery, . . . and nature of . . . thoughts." These are the things I now look for when someone speaks to me. Incorrect verb tenses, misplaced adverbs, and incorrect pronouns are less significant issues. As I begin to realize this more, I feel more comfortable with not only my mom's different English but my own. My mom's English is the one I grew up with at 15 home. It is one of the Englishes I speak.

The other day I went home to help my mom run errands.

"Go to store," she said.

"Buy what?"

"Juice and eggs. Drive becarefully!" my mom warned.

I couldn't help but to smile. I like hearing that now.

Questions for Discussion

1. How has Chang applied insights and experiences of Amy Tan in "Mother Tongue" to her own relationship with her mother?
2. Could you identify with any aspects of Chang's feelings and attitudes about her mother's English or with her struggle to accept her mother for who she is rather than to "fix her"?
3. Do you agree or disagree with Chang's teacher's attitude and her definition of correct English? Explain your point of view.
4. Do you agree or disagree with Chang's conclusion, "As long as a person is understood, it is not necessary to speak textbook perfect English"?

Molly Thomas

Response to "Don't Look Back"

Student writer Molly Thomas wrote the following essay after reading "Don't Look Back," a reading selection included in this chapter. In the essay that follows, notice how she writes using a number of the response strategies suggested at the beginning of the chapter: giving some background on the piece and its central debate, then moving to analyze some of its strategies of refutation and audience, and finally taking her own evaluative position on the piece itself and the larger debate over technology and the book.

Today the debate over the long-lasting effects of digital technology on literacy and the culture of the book provoke many heated and widespread disputes that often pit different generations against one another. In "Don't Look Back," a chapter from his book Digital Mosaics, Steven Holtzman heralds the onset of the digital age and the opportunities it will provide, dismissing the extreme negative critics of digital learning and culture even as he expresses regret about its potential effects on the high culture of books and print literacy. Holtzman's arguments are subtly contradictory enough to undermine some of his initial claims supporting technology.

In both the pro and antitechnology sides of the argument, there is an impending feeling that the spread of digital technology is inevitable. For Holtzman, this fact rests on the nature of the technology itself. He writes, "For centuries, the book has been the primary vehicle for recording, storing, and transferring knowledge. But it's hard to imagine that paper will be the preferred format in 100 years." In Holtzman's model, technology takes the more active role, driven by sheer Darwinian evolution and a search for convenience. As is the case with most technological developments, digital technology itself develops at a rate far faster than the consideration of its moral and cultural implications. For Holtzman, the argument seems to be simply over the technology itself, the actual practical differences between writing information on a piece of paper versus a computer. Later on in his argument, Holtzman goes on to compare the opponents of digital technology to the machine-smashing Luddites who rebelled against the rise of industrialization in nineteenth century Britain. The connotation today of a "Luddite" is of someone who appears antiquated in his or her approach to the world and as a result out of tune with reality. According to this view, people may have a say in how technology is created, but once it is in circulation it becomes self-propagating and as a result any opposition to its spread is futile.

In disqualifying opposition to his pro-digital argument, Holtzman quotes critic William Irwin Thompson who observes, "This new cyberpunk, technological culture is brought forth by . . . electronic science and pop music, and both the hackers and the rockers are antiintellectual and unsympathetic to the previous Mental level expressed by the genius of European civilization." For Thompson, these digital advancements are less about the technology itself and instead are more defined by the community that fosters technological growth. This opinion is clearly very one-sided, and easy to refute as it only attributes digital creativity to those who have been traditionally classified as outlying, destructive and "anti-intellectual" deviants of modern culture such as hackers and rockers. From this perspective, the debate over digital technology versus books is less about the technology itself; it rather centers on how technology is fostered by a disinterest or aversion to learning and the intellectual.

Holtzman goes on to cite another dissenting opinion of technology from author Clifford Stoll who argues, "During that week you spend online, you could have planted a tomato garden. . . . While the Internet beckons brightly, seductively flashing an icon of knowledge-as-power, this nonplace lures us to surrender our time on earth." Holtzman is right to point out ironically that books and symphonies similarly deter us from direct, physical ways of acquiring knowledge through observation and action, although he could have developed his critique further. Stoll's imagery of the Internet seducing its youthful viewers is really a stereotype or cartoon image of evil technological tools that inevitably alienate youngsters from the world of experiential learning. Stoll is creating an either-or dilemma in response to technology: Why should manual labor provide more essential understanding than the Internet, rather than an equal and complementary insight into the world around us and the distant worlds of foreign cultures, geographies, and planetary systems?

5   Despite his deft refutation of Stoll, Holtzman's argument loses some of its power through the use of rhetorical strategies that suggest his audience is predominantly one that shares his point of view. For example, after excerpting Thompson's quote on "cyberpunks" Holtzman states his response very briefly: "This helped me dismiss the backlash from those looking in the rearview mirror." Throughout the first half of his piece, Holtzman creates a distance between himself and those who espouse an anti-digital perspective by creating a casual dialogue-like tone between himself and the reader as he walks through the process of reaffirming his own beliefs. Again we see from the use of dismissive words like "rear-view mirror" and "backlash" that those who are responding as antiquated "Luddites" are only protesting a technology that has and will inevitably spread.

However, Holtzman seems to draw back from fully supporting technology-based culture and learning by espousing some of the rhetoric associated with the opposing side of the debate. He writes, "There never will be a substitute for a book. And today's multimedia CD-ROM—even surfing the World Wide Web—is still for the most part a static and unsatisfying experience." It's true that no technology will be able to replicate a book exactly, but it's certainly an exaggeration to suggest that multimedia provides an "unsatisfying experience." Like the authors he criticizes, Holtzman seems to make a hierarchical distinction between reading and using the Internet. It might have helped for him to qualify this statement by specifying in what ways books *and* the Internet can be both rewarding and not. Holtzman goes on to inquire, "Will we lose part of our cultural heritage as we assimilate new media? No doubt. Is this disturbing? Absolutely." Here again, he fails to explain exactly what will be lost and what new culture might replace it. Although Holtzman begins his piece by suggesting that his argument is fundamentally one over the fated evolution of technology, he ends by conceding that books still give us insight into a world that will never be matched by technology.

Why is it, then, that books are unquestioningly associated with learning and intellectual growth while technology becomes defined as just the opposite? The answer lies in the fact that learning itself is frequently viewed as a tool of privilege; those who feel that the digital world is alien to them in turn cling to traditional means of learning that they do understand, means which are slowly becoming alien to today's youngest generations. As Holtzman concedes, "Kids today are so attuned to the rapid rhythms of MTV that they're unresponsive to the patient pattern of literary prose. . . . Literary culture—like classical music and opera—will become marginalized as mainstream culture pursues a digital path." Unlike the technological arguments that we saw earlier, the distinction he now makes seems more class-based. It would be sad indeed if books did meet the same fate that classical music and opera have met in modern culture, if they become part of a culturally elitist group that excludes its membership from mass culture. Holtzman cites one writer who prides himself in using only a typewriter and not even owning a computer. Many, like this writer, hide behind the façade of intellectualism to avoid integrating themselves into the digital world. In a sense, Holtzman seems to accept this position by similarly classifying books into a unique, unchanging and irreplaceable aspect of culture instead of seeing them as an evolving means of cultural communication. It's only when the cultures of readers and technology users become polarized that we really have to worry about one group having a superficial relationship with their surrounding world.

While opponents of the digital revolution claim that technology is "dumbing us down" and drawing us away from real learning, the reality is quite different. To the average person with access to an inexpensive home computer and a modem, the Internet alone has opened up doors to more sources of knowledge than anyone in history has ever had access to. For thousands of years, this type of access to vast knowledge contained previously only in world-class libraries has been limited by access to high-level literacy and quality education to a lucky few. Today the Internet has become the digital printing press of our generation. It's unfortunate, then, that there are those who still wish to deter the development of digital technology, and in turn maintain access to knowledge and learning as a privilege, not a right. Now that this privilege has become a widespread commodity, we shouldn't discourage its growth; rather we should help it to evolve into a universal tool for cultural expression.

QUESTIONS FOR DISCUSSION

1. In the first paragraph, how clearly does Thomas state both the subject of Holtzman's essay and his perspective on the debate between pro and anti technology forces? Is her position on the essay clear?

2. In the second paragraph, how does Thomas use references to "Luddites" and Darwinian evolution theories to contrast the conflicting positions on technology of Holtzman and his opponents? Is her explanation of these terms clear?

3. Thomas uses both paraphrase and direct quoting from Holtzman's essay, as well quoting and paraphrasing some of his critics. How effectively are these quotations and paraphrases used? Are there places where you would have liked to see quoting rather than paraphrase, or more introduction or explanation of a quotation?

4. In the two paragraphs before the conclusion, Thomas criticizes Holtzman for conceding too much to the antitechnology argument which comes from a "high culture," traditional perspective. Does her criticism seem justified and supported?

TOPICS FOR RESEARCH AND WRITING

1. Drawing on evidence from the selections in this chapter such as the essays by King and Elbow, outside reading and Internet research, and your own experiences, write an essay that examines the role of dreams and the unconscious mind in the reading and writing processes.

2. Although several authors in this chapter discuss ways in which they have been influenced to become readers and writers, in contrast, Linton Weeks discusses reasons why people in today's society feel no motivation to practice higher literacy skills and seldom read books at all. Taking into consideration the experiences of these authors as well as those of others you have read about or interviewed, write an essay in which you examine some of the influences that either encourage or discourage a person's interest in becoming a reader and/or a writer.

3. Tan, Woolf, Wright and King value reading and writing as a process of self-discovery and healing. Write an essay in which you explore this perspective on reading and writing, taking into account these writers' ideas, those of other writers you read about, as well as your own experiences.

4. Woolf and Stevens discuss the social, ethical, and spiritual values involved in the art of writing. Taking into account their ideas and those of other authors, discuss some of the ways that reading and writing have a positive influence on beliefs, values, and social behavior.

5. Several of the writers in the chapter present insights into the nature of creativity and the creative process. After doing some further research into this issue, write an essay in which you present and evaluate several current theories about creative thinking and the creative process in writing.

6. Holtzman suggests that the wide availability of computers, e-mail, and Internet chat groups are changing the way writers work and relate to their audience. After doing some research into new web-based literary ideas, writers' groups, and online publications, write an essay about new directions for writing and interactions of writers and audiences that are arising as a direct result of the cyberspace revolution.

7. See one of the following films that approach the life of the writer and/or the reader: *The Postman, Dreamchild, Naked Lunch, Misery, The Color Purple, Shakespeare in Love, Finding Forrester, Dangerous Minds, Wonder Boys, Dead Poet's Society, Stanley and Iris, Educating Rita, The Miracle Worker, Nora*. Making reference to such elements of the film as plot, dialogue, voice-over, characters, images, and visual symbolism, write an essay that discusses the ways in which the film explores the inner world of the writer and/or the reader.

Visions of Nature 2

Henri Rousseau (1844–1910)
The Repast of the Lion (1907)

Henri Rousseau, who worked at the Paris Customs Office for over 20 years, created colorful paintings of natural scenes inspired by his active fantasy life rather than firsthand observations of the wilderness. The intensity of his vision communicates on a level that continues to inspire viewers, just as it did for Picasso and the artists of the Surrealist movement who hailed his art as the work of an "untaught genius."

JOURNAL

Write a description of a scene from nature as you imagine it; then reflect on what readings or images you have had contact with that may have led you to depict it in this manner.

It is the marriage of the soul with Nature that makes the intellect fruitful, and give birth to the imagination.
                                    HENRY DAVID THOREAU

Nature is what we know—
Yet have no art to say—

                                    EMILY DICKINSON

Unless I call my attention to what passes before my eyes, I simply won't see it.
                                    ANNIE DILLARD

OBSERVING NATURE AND WRITING DESCRIPTIONS

When we describe, we try to create powerful impressions of our experiences so that others can share our visions, feeling what we have felt, seeing through our eyes, and sharing other senses as well—hearing, taste, smell, and touch. Descriptions need to be written with great care to detail, in specific language, and with much thought as to the choice of material in order to communicate your meaning to your audience.

Observing

The more awake and alert your senses are to the world around you, the more fully you experience your world, the more likely it is that you will be able to collect the relevant, unique and interesting details you will need to create an expressive description. To train your senses to be receptive to your surroundings and to help you write a vivid description, spend some time in quiet observation of a particular object or place you want to describe. Try observing your subject from various perspectives, walking around it, looking at it in different lights, and experiencing it through your different senses. Can you listen to it? Touch it? Smell it? While you observe, try asking yourself these questions: Why am I doing this observation? How do I feel about my subject? How do my feelings influence the way I perceive the subject? Spend ten minutes or so in quiet observation before you begin to write; then jot down as many details as you can about your subject. Read your list over to see if you can add more sensory details. Share your list of details with a classmate who may be able to help you to think about details you had forgotten.

Words and Images

Writer Annie Dillard has noted that "Seeing is . . . verbalization." When describing a person, place, thing, or even something so seemingly imprecise as an emotion, it is important to verbalize your response using specific, carefully chosen words. When you use words effectively, you can create a series of images, or sensory clusters of detail, which, taken together, convey to your readers an intimate or intense description of your experiences. Notice how in the following example from her travel memoir *Russian Journal,* Andrea Lee used a series of images that evoke specific colors (*gold, yellow*), a sense of touch (*stuck, cold*) and a concrete impression of textures and forms (*decayed grotesque, peeling front*) and a specific place or area (*a mansion in the Arbat*): "In Moscow I found more demanding pleasures of nature and architecture: rain on the gold domes inside the Kremlin walls, yellow leaves stuck to a wet pavement; a decayed stone grotesque on the peeling front of a mansion in the Arbat; a face in a subway crowd."

An image may be clarified by a comparison (a simile or a metaphor) that helps to explain more fully the quality of an experience by linking it imaginatively or literally to other, related experiences or things. This is a technique Farley Mowat uses in his essay "Learning to See" to capture his confusion as he notices something mysterious and white that looks like a feather boa at first, yet turns out to be the tails of two huge, playful wolves: "Without warning, both boas turned toward me; began rising higher and higher, and finally revealed themselves as the tails of two wolves beginning to top the esker." A reader of such a comparison is imaginatively drawn into the image and the author's attempt to create meaning for it. Use specific images and comparisons in your writing in order to invite your readers to become imaginatively engaged in your thoughts and descriptions.

Revising Initial Descriptions

Look back through your journal to find several descriptive passages of physical objects, places, people, or moods. Try to replace observations or descriptions, in particular any words that now seem too general, generic, or imprecise with specific, concrete, close up words or with imaginative images and comparisons that will involve your readers' minds and emotions. In the following two paragraphs written by a student, notice the differences between the initial version, in which the student describes a cattle feedlot in generalized terms, and the second paragraph which presents a more vivid and emotionally involving description of the same scene.

Original Version   Once I visited a feedlot. In and around the wood and metal barn at the center of the lot were stalls where a number of, dull-colored, dirty, smelly, cattle were penned, eating from long metal troughs.

Approximately fifty animals per pen were huddled in four structures surrounding the barn.

Revised Version   Last winter I had the depressing experience of visiting a feedlot. A ram-shackle, unpainted oak barn leaned against the yellowish metal of a prefabricated structure, the juxtaposed structures clashing like images from a nightmare. The cattle huddled in dejected, segregated groups of approximately fifty animals per pen in four battered wooden structures surrounding the barn. The dull-colored, dusty cattle blended into the unpainted desolation of the winter day, standing in munching fortitude before a long metal trough extending the entire length of their outdoor prison. Their jaws worked with ceaseless rhythm: a lifestyle of breathing, chewing; breathing, chewing.

Establishing Vantage Point and Tone

A descriptive writer, like a painter or a photographer, is interested in establishing a coherent, unified impression. To create this impression it is necessary to focus the description from a particular vantage point, to let the reader see the scene from one special window. The student writer above began her description of the feedlot from a distance, gradually moved closer to the cattle, and concluded with a close look at their endlessly chewing jaws.

Notice how Annie Dillard in her essay "A Field of Silence" (from Chapter 9 of this book) begins her account of a visionary experience that takes place on a farm she enjoys visiting. First, she establishes a clear geographical, spatially precise backdrop for her subsequent description: "I loved the place, and still do. It was an ordinary farm, a calf raising, hay making farm, and very beautiful. Its flat, messy pastures ran along one side of the central position of a quarter-mile road in the central part of an island, an island in Puget Sound, so that from the high end of the road you could look west toward the Pacific." While Annie Dillard establishes a clear vantage point in the passage above, she also draws us into her description of a free, open environment through the positive emotions that she associates with her subject: "I loved the place, and still do." As you write descriptions, remember to pay close attention to the emotional associations evoked by the physical qualities of the subject you are describing, as the student writing about a feedlot does through her use of emotional words such as "depressing," "huddled," and "desolate," or as Dillard does in her use of paradoxical words as "ordinary" and "beautiful" to describe the complex impression made upon her by the farm.

Thinking About Your Purpose and Audience

Although descriptions are often written for the pleasure of capturing an experience with accuracy, description serves other purposes in writing, depending in part upon the occasion for and intended audience of the piece. The selection from the student essay on a feedlot, for example, was intended to make a comment on the nature of apathy, and was directed to an audience of students and city dwellers who might never have seen a feedlot. By including details appropriate to the dull existence of the cattle on the lot, the student both shocks and prepares her audience for a commentary on human apathy and indifference. Annie Dillard has a very different purpose for her description in her essay "Field of Silence": to make the remote farm reflect "ordinary" beauty, which heightens the contrast that she will introduce later in the essay between familiar peace and contentment, and the other-worldly intensity of a vision she had one morning while exploring the farm. Dillard assumes that her readers share her interest in nature and visionary experience, whereas the student writer assumes that her classmates would naturally share her feelings of outrage and anger over the unfortunate condition of cattle in the feedlot. Try taking a look at some of the descriptive writing in this chapter and ask yourself what assumptions the authors are making about the tastes, needs, and interests of their readers, particularly as regards the level of involvement with nature that the readers have. How do the writers try to satisfy these needs by the details and images they have chosen to include in their essays?

Now that you have had some practice observing a familiar place or object, selecting a purpose and tone, audience, and vantage point, you are ready to write a precise, imaginative and expressive description of a place that holds strong meaning for you. Finding the words to describe what you see, selecting the pertinent details, images, and comparisons to clarify and support your ideas and opinions are skills that you will need to master as you continue to improve your ability to describe. As you become more adept at using these strategies, you will discover above all that powerful writing is also writing that reveals, that lights up the darkness around you.

THEMATIC INTRODUCTION: VISIONS OF NATURE

Nature has always had the power to nourish, heal, and inspire. Many naturalists believe that nature is our greatest teacher, embodying the truth through the dangers, challenges, and beauty it presents to us: a remarkable sunset, an isolated beach at dawn, ancient rock formations in the desert as well as a devastating earthquake, flood, or forest fire. Nature is extraordinary with the power to nourish and to destroy. Despite our efforts to control nature for our own benefit, it continues to act upon us, to have the last word, for we are inextricably a part of it. Yet how often do we think seriously about the natural world, or even pause to observe its beauty and its laws? Most of us live in communities that are largely defined by laws and technology. Intent on getting through our daily routines and on maintaining a comfortable life style, it is easy to forget about how much the natural world has to provide: adventure, beauty, perspective, and peace. Nature is in great part what we are, where we came from, and where we are going as we move through our lives.

The selections in this chapter present a variety of experiences in nature that will give the reader insights about the beauty and interdependence of the natural world. The writers we have included have experienced nature first hand; many of them are trained scientists, explorers, and naturalists. They rely on close observations, vivid descriptions, and intense inner awareness to create the moments of revelation that make up the texts that follow.

The chapter opens with Lorna Dee Cervantes's poem, "Emplumada," which offers a rich snapshot of nature's rhythm and power through description and powerful symbolism of the death and rebirth of flowers and the bravery and determination of mating birds.

The next two selections show us what we can learn from the animal world. In "Dreaming Elands," nature writer Peter Steinhart addresses a fundamental concern about the limited exposure to nature and animals, in particular, that people have in modern day life, arguing that as we are destroying the ecological balance of our communities and distancing ourselves from the animal world, we are diminishing our capacity to think and to imagine: "We are drawn to animals, not just because they are lively and pretty, but because we think through them. And a world without an abundance of kinds is bound to be a different world." In the next selection, "Learning to See," scientist Farley Mowat shares what he has learned while applying his scientific knowledge and equipment to study the wolf population in the Canadian Arctic. His scientific study becomes a process of self-education and, by extension, reader enlightenment.

Adventurers and travel writers Donovan Webster and Jon Krakauer describe their challenging adventures exploring two of nature's most breathtaking and dangerous terrains, leading us into the fiery depths and the icy heights of the earth. "In the Volcano" is Webster's account of his climb down into a high volcano in the South Pacific. Reading his description of his adventure will not only heighten your appreciation for the beauty and danger of a volcano, but it will make you wonder why some men and women are driven to explore such dangerous parts of the natural world. In the "Khumbu Icefall," Jon Krakauer describes the challenges and practical strategies of climbing the most demanding and terrifying glacial icefall on the route to Mount Everest. He concludes with a deeply aesthetic realization: "As dawn washed the darkness from the sky, the shattered glacier was revealed to be a three-dimensional landscape of phantasmal beauty."

The two essays that follow proceed slowly and reflectively, considering insights and natural changes that occur over long periods of time. In "Walking," Native American poet Linda Hogan encourages us to think about the way nature reveals itself to us over a long cycle of time and seasonal change. She creates a representative micro-community around a sunflower that she observes repeatedly over a year of walking in nature. Finally, naturalist Loren Eiseley believes that people must spend time alone with nature in different settings, opening oneself to chance happenings and unusual visions of natural creatures. In his essay "The Judgment of the Birds," Eiseley portrays a number of revelations he had through watching the natural world and "discerning in the flow of ordinary events the point at which the mundane world gives way to quite another dimension."

Student Essays

In "Strawberry Creek," student writer David Kerr describes a childhood excursion into a natural world long hidden from surface explorers: the world of a creek rerouted through concrete tunnels. Through their excursion to find the origins of Strawberry Creek, David and his friends discover something significant about the place of nature in modern urban environments. In our final student essay, "Dian Fossey and Me," student writer Lindsey Munro explores Fossey's legacy as a champion of an endangered species of gorillas. An idealistic researcher, Munro also hopes to develop a practical and realistic perspective on how to approach problems related to endangered species.

Powerful writing is nurtured through connections: between the inner world of dreams and the imagination, between the world of experience and knowledge, between one's own feeling for and mastery of the conventions of language and written expression. As you gain more experience expressing and crafting your ideas about yourself, the natural world around you, and your hopes for the future, we hope that writing will become a vital and versatile means for expressing your thoughts, feelings, hopes, and visions.

Lorna Dee Cervantes

Emplumada

Lorna Dee Cervantes was born in 1954 and was raised in northern California. She received her B. A. at San Jose State in northern California and has also studied at the University of California at Santa Cruz. Currently she is the Director of Creative Writing at the University of Colorado at Boulder. Her books of poems include Emplumada *(1981), which won an American Book Award, and* From the Cables of Genocide: Poems on Love and Hunger *(1991). Her work has appeared in a number of anthologies, and she also serves as coeditor of the poetry journal* Red Dirt. *Her poems often depict racial, gender, and class struggles, but she also has a strong interest in nature and the environment, as can be seen in the poem below, which appeared originally in* Emplumada.

JOURNAL

Describe a seasonal change in nature that touched your mind and your heart.

When summer ended
the leaves of snapdragons withered
taking their shrill-colored mouths with them.
They were still, so quiet. They were
5   violet where umber now is. She hated
and she hated to see
them go. Flowers

born when the weather was good—this
she thinks of, watching the branch of peaches
10 daring their ways above the fence, and further,
two hummingbirds, hovering, stuck to each other,
arcing their bodies in grim determination
to find what is good, what is
given them to find. These are warriors

15 distancing themselves from history.
They find peace
in the way they contain the wind
and are gone.

Questions for Discussion

1. What does *emplumada* mean? Why is it a suitable title for this poem?
2. What does the description of the snapdragons and their death represent about the natural world? Why does "she" hate to see them go? Who is the "she" in the poem?

3. What is the symbolism of the branch of peaches? How does the poem describe their gradual movement and growth? In what ways are the peaches "daring"?
4. Why does the poet use the term "grim determination" to describe how the hummingbirds arc their bodies?
5. What is the "good" that the hummingbirds are seeking?
6. Why are the two humming birds described as warriors? Why do the hummingbirds need to distance themselves from history to find peace? How do you imagine that they find peace?

CONNECTION

Compare Cervantes's meditation on hummingbirds with Steinhart's dream of elands in the essay that follows. What do both authors see as the importance of living creatures to our imagination and understanding of the world and of ourselves?

IDEAS FOR WRITING

1. Develop your journal entry into a descriptive and analytical essay.
2. The poem makes a contrast between the nature of human history and the natural sense of change. Write an essay that contrasts this reality using examples from human history as well as natural changes or the annual changes that you have experienced in nature.

RELATED WEB SITES

LORNA DEE CERVANTES
http://voices.cla.umn.edu/authors/LornaDeeCervantes.html
Biographical and bibliographical information can both be found at this URL on Lorna Dee Cervantes. Related links to the author, as well as reviews of her work, will also be found here.

POETRY AND NATURE PROTECTION
http://www.phii.unt.edu/show/001.htm
This web site explores the connection between poetry and nature, as well as the history of human perceptions of nature.

Peter Steinhart

Dreaming Elands

Born in 1943 in San Francisco, California, Peter Steinhart has had a lifetime interest in the wildlife of the Pacific Coast region and is particularly concerned about the damage to the ecosystem and the loss of many species of animal life due to excessive development and atmospheric pollution. Steinhart has taught Ecology and English at Stanford University and has written a number of books including Tracks in the Sky *(1988) about the Pacific Coast area, its creatures and its menaced wetlands,* The Company of Wolves *(1995) and* Two Eagles *(1994). Steinhart was a longtime contributor to* Audubon *magazine. He often explores scientific and ecological issues using literary style, personal voice and imagination, as can be seen in "Dreaming Elands," which first appeared in* Audubon *in 1982. As you read the essay, notice how Steinhart's dream narrative leads to a provocative meditation on the place of animal life in the human imagination and spirit.*

JOURNAL

Write about a dream you have had involving birds or animals. What did your dream suggest about how your imagination works and about your sense of kinship with or alienation from the animal kingdom?

Sometimes I dream about elands. They don't talk to me or leap over rooftops or turn into pretty damsels. They just lope silently along the horizon of a blue-skied plain. They are big, alert, and stately. They move like cows with their ancestral wildness and long-legged grace restored.

That is how I saw elands long ago in Africa, and the dreams give me a feeling of satisfaction. But I don't know why I dream of them or what elands mean.

I do know, however, that we all dream and think in terms of animals. Leonardo da Vinci was beset by the dream of a vulture perched over his childhood crib. Modern Brazilians may choose lottery numbers on the basis of the animal seen in a recent dream. Malays believe being snakebit in a dream promises luck in love. Sometimes we dream half-animals, as when Alexander dreamed of a satyr dancing on his shield and so foresaw victory in his siege of Tyre. Or we think men into animals, turn Dr. Jekyll into Mr. Hyde or football players into apes to suggest psychological changes. Animals are far more fundamental to our thinking than we suppose. They are not just a part of the fabric of thought: they are a part of the loom.

Animals are what men use to wrap ideas into visible form. We can see it in the development of our own language. We make abstractions manifest by embodying them in animals, and our language is a vast, shadowy bestiary. We call muscles "muscles" because the Romans thought they resembled mice (Latin: *mus*) running under the skin. Erosion is what happens when rodents nibble on wood, a little at a time, out of sight and mind. An auspicious occasion is one in which the birds (Latin: *avis*) are seen (as in "spectate") to fly in the right direction. A person is said to be chubby because he resembles a fish that swims in the Thames River. A cynic is, in Greek, a surly dog. Sarcasm is the tearing of flesh, as by dogs, and the word transposes the snarl of the dog to the expression on our faces when we say something nasty. We are bullish and bearish, hawkish and dovelike, shrewish and bovine, busy as beavers, timid as rabbits, mad as hornets, sly as foxes.

5   Animals let us represent feelings that are otherwise undefinable. We can be happy as larks or cross as a bear. Freud noted that when children have family problems that are too threatening to deal with, they typically fantasize about animals. And if something strikes us as out of place, we are apt to mark it with a monster, an amalgam of animal forms which suggests the essential qualities of the conflict. A werewolf is half-human sociability, half-lupine hunger. Dragons are the evil we attribute to snakes, but magnified by wings, claws, and fire.

Once we nail concepts to animals, we arrange them into roadmaps of custom. In traditional societies, animal symbols preserved the rules of conduct. Classless societies kept the rules of marriage, inheritance, and authority in ancestral totems, which were generally wild animals. A man who traced his descent from the ancestral turtle might have a specific kind of relationship to a man who descended from the eagle. By thinking about the ecological and mythological relationships between totems, the people carried about in their minds their Constitutions and Magna Cartas.

Folktales continue this tradition. They contain rules for the use of love, power, and cooperation that we cannot fit into legal or religious documents. A people who celebrate foxes carry in their fables ideas about how the individual may challenge the will of the group. Modern animal stories, such as *Watership Down*, hold similar rules. And C. S. Lewis described the character of Badger in Kenneth Grahame's *Wind in the Willows* as an "extraordinary amalgam of high rank, coarse manners, gruffness, shyness, and goodness . . . The child who has once met Mr. Badger has ever afterwards in his bones a knowledge of humanity and of English social history which he could not get in any other way."

The tradition of keeping rules and ideas in animal form is rich even in modern societies. Our unreasoning fear of snakes hearkens back to an ancient notion that evil spirits live in the earth. We still put bird wings on angels. Athletic teams and military units select bears and bluejays as mascots. The industrial arm of this tradition uses animals to sell us detergents, beer, and the services of bankers. When we sell automobiles, for example, we offer as symbols hawks, mustangs, cougars, skylarks, and impalas. We sell no turkeys or Holsteins because they are not symbols of freedom, and we buy cars, above all, as engines of personal independence.

If advertising animals seems contrived, what children do with animals is not. Children love to name animals and explore the differences between them. My two-year-old daughter shouts with glee when she sees a horse. She delights in pictures of elephants and monkeys and turtles and wants to talk about their eyes, ears, and tails. Animals are part of her capacity for joy.

10   That joy is not simply a matter of fictitious companions and imaginary adventures. It is the joy of recognizing and understanding life outside of one's own form. It was programmed into human childhood long ago. Traditional societies encourage children to collect names, for as adults they must know many more animals and plants than they use for food and fiber. The Penobscot Indians, for example, classify snakes into genus and species but have no practical or

ritual use for them. The Hanunóo of the Philippines know 1,800 plants, 500 more than botanists can find in their neighborhood. And when traditional children aren't looking at nature, they are fed animal images in myth and folklore.

Likewise, in modern life, we feed our children fables, give them teddy bears and rocking horses and embroider duckies and bunnies on their bibs. We encourage them to shout the names of animals as they wander through picture books and zoos. They play games like "Foxes and Geese," assuming alternately the roles of predator and prey, weak and strong.

All children thereby find special qualities in parrots, camels, or frogs, and the qualities become synonymous with the animal. We use such images as substitutes for people in our thoughts. People are too complex and too close to us to yield to such simplification. A wolf may always in our thoughts be a cunning killer. One's father may be a headhunter or a Congolese mercenary, but may nevertheless cry at weddings and be baffled by tax forms. Cunning is much clearer when we think of it as a wolf. And it is safer to talk of such things as greed or aggression in lions or bears than in a brother or a neighbor, for we can focus upon the quality without exposing our human relationships to conflict.

In all societies, animals give our children images of order and diversity. We are teaching them to think, not just about food on the table or fangs in the bushes, but about ourselves. We are teaching them to separate human qualities from human beings, but not from life. Animals thus enable us to add the reach of the eye to the reach of the heart. And that makes us braver and more patient with adversity in our own lives. It makes us better able to get along with one another.

Paul Shepard, professor of natural philosophy at Pitzer College, believes the human mind was shaped by the act of watching animals. In *Thinking Animals,* Shepard writes, "Animals are among the first inhabitants of the mind's eye. They are basic to the development of speech and thought . . . indispensable to our becoming human in the fullest sense."

15   Shepard believes animals are essential to the act of classification because they are lively and diverse. He notes that children also classify household tools, kinds of automobiles, and parts of things, but "with animals, the categories are all living. And a lively image is more potent." And animal forms tend to grade into one another, so that they test one's perceptions rigorously and require skill in making distinctions. Only animals fit the need, and, concludes Shepard, "From the standpoint of the developing brain, an assembly, say, of horselike animals—donkeys, tarpans, zebras, asses, and other groups of their odd-toed relatives—is as essential as blood."

The process of classifying animals, Shepard believes, is inborn and scheduled for the first twelve years of life. "That part of the young brain combining signals from vision, sound, and touch in the inferior parietal lobule physically matures, or becomes myelinated, with the end of childhood," he writes. "Names pass through a part of it, the Wernicke's area, like beasts entering Noah's Ark, and with the transitional period of puberty, the door closes on the real world, that is on the raw materials from which a cosmos is to be created." Adolescents typically lose their interest in animals.

For the process to work, the animals must exist in real life. Says Shepard, "It wouldn't work unless there were an order [in] which animals really participate, an ecosystem as organic and as whole and as lively as our bodies are. The games of animal imitation are hollow if we never have any external evidence that the things we imitate have a stable and good relationship in the world."

Shepard warns that the trend toward extinction of wild animals is a threat to human thought. If we eliminate animals, we eliminate much of the naming and classifying and reduce the number and quality of ideas we may embody. "Just as you blind a young animal for life by covering its eyes at the time when the final neural connections are being made," he writes, "if you deprive a child of natural diversity, you curb its mental development."

The most important result of "minding animals," Shepard believes, is that the animal images teach us that the separateness of other creatures is not threatening, and so teach us to live with diversity. If, despite the conflict of deer and wolf or plankton and whale, life survives, then we may also hope to survive our conflicts with the strangers who crowd the human world. If we can master our fear of disorder by naming lions and pythons, perhaps we can master our fears of men and live with the difficulties of race, class, and locality.

20 Shepard suggests that as we lose natural diversity we will suffer a form of insanity. He notes that we see an increasing number of adults who cannot deal with fear, control, dominance, or acceptance, and who seem unable to fit themselves into some kind of order with other people or with their setting. We see, too, many people who oversimplify human diversity in order to make life seem less fearsome, or who hide behind locked doors because life's categories are simply overwhelming.

"The loss of natural diversity probably shapes our whole notion about the world," says Shepard. "Instead of a world that grows, a world in which we deal with mysterious forces we have to feel some humility about, we see it as a machine." We view our brains as computers, our bodies as puzzles for doctors to assemble, and our societies merely as devices made for the distribution of goods.

The solution, Shepard thinks, may be to make environment and animals the setting, rather than the subject, of education. He suggests that we send our children out of the cities, where they can be spared the false sameness, the man-centeredness and the mechanical determinism of modern life. In the countryside, Shepard believes, children may pass through the age of naming with an opportunity to see the true breadth and variety of life.

Some of these thoughts leave me a bit breathless. I have no doubt that a natural world, being the world in which our minds evolved, encourages our minds to be what they have been. I am not sure what evolutionary effects cities may have upon our minds. They may stupefy and simplify, rob us of the common sense of diversity and give us over to fantasy and fear. Then again, they may not. Perhaps we *could* survive without animals. Our minds, like it or not, are still evolving, and we have no way of seeing over the evolutionary horizon.

But I believe with Paul Shepard that animals are a part of our minds, a part of the room upon which we spin out thoughts. We are drawn to animals, not just because they are lively and pretty, but because we think through them. And a world without an abundance of kinds is bound to be a different world. A humanity without abundant animals is bound to be a different humanity. Despite its flaws, I like the humanity we have. Perhaps that is why I dream about elands.

Questions for Discussion

1. Do you think the dream narration Steinhart uses to begin his essay is effective? How does it prepare readers for what will follow? Steinhart says that he doesn't know why he dreams of elands or what they signify. How would you interpret his dream, based on the concerns he reveals in the essay? Why does Steinhart conclude with a return to the dream about elands?
2. What does Steinhart mean when he says that animals are "not just a part of the fabric of thought: they are a part of the loom"? In what ways are animals important to our thinking processes?
3. What examples does Steinhart use to illustrate how our language was developed through animal comparisons and metaphors? Can you think of other examples to add to Steinhart's list?
4. According to Steinhart, how do we clarify both emotions and concepts through references and comparisons to animals? How do we make use of animals in literature and visual representations to emphasize values and beliefs?
5. Why does philosopher Paul Shepard believe that animals are "essential to the act of classification"? Why does he also believe that they "teach us to live with diversity" and that the loss of diversity can lead to insanity?
6. What is Steinhart's response to Shepard's views on the importance of animals to the inner life? What is Steinhart's vision of the future?

Connection

Compare and contrast the reasons why Steinhart and Eiseley value animals as sources that nurture our inner life, our imagination, and well being (see page 104).

Ideas for Writing

1. Imagine a world where there would be a healthy balance between animals and people. After describing this world, give several reasons to explain why the balance that you have established is healthy and will help people to live more rewarding, peaceful and spiritual lives.
2. Develop an essay in which you examine the use of animal names and comparisons to form the words that are central to your ways of thinking and feeling about yourself, other people, and the world we all live in. Draw

some conclusions about how animals influence people's perceptions and expressions of thoughts and feelings. Use specific examples to illustrate your claims.

RELATED WEB SITES

"THE CRY OF THE OCEAN" BY PETER STEINHART
www.motherjones.com/mother_jones/JA94/steinhart.html
Visit this URL for Peter Steinhart's article, "The Cry of the Ocean," which warns against the increasing harm done to our oceans through the actions of humankind.

A NEW ENVIRONMENTALISM
http://www.newenvironmentalism.org/
This project identifies and promotes innovative approaches to addressing serious environmental challenges. The program has been created by the "Reason Public Policy Institute" and promotes innovative and forward-looking environmentalist thought.

Farley Mowat

Learning to See

One of Canada's most highly respected and best-loved nature writers, Farley Mowat was born in Belleville, Ontario, in 1921. After serving in the Canadian Army during World War II, Mowat moved to the Canadian Arctic. His writing expresses deep sympathy for threatened species and cultures. Some of his more widely read works include The Snow Walker *(1975),* Sea of Slaughter *(1984),* Woman in the Mists: The Story of Dian Fossey and The Mountain Gorillas of Africa *(1987), and* Rescue the Earth *(1990). The selection that follows is from* Never Cry Wolf *(1963), an account of his adventures working for the Canadian government's wildlife services as a field biologist studying the Arctic wolves in northern Canada. Mowat's book was transformed into a film in 1983.*

JOURNAL

What do you know about wolves and how they survive in nature? Do you believe the wolf to be a savage killer?

I was very thoughtful for the balance of the day, and there were moments when I wondered if my hopes of gaining the confidence of the wolves might not be overly optimistic. As to demonstrating that I bore them no ill will—this I felt would be easy enough to do, but would be of little value unless the wolves felt like reciprocating.

The next morning I undertook to clean up the Stygian mess in the cabin, and in the process I uncovered my compass. I set it on the windowsill while I continued with my work, but the sun caught its brass surface and it glittered at me so accusingly that I resigned myself to making another effort to restore the lost contact between me and the wolves.

My progress on this second safari was even slower, since I was carrying my rifle, shotgun, pistol and pistol belt, a small hatchet and my hunting knife, together with a flask of wolf-juice in case I fell into one of the icy streams.

It was a hot day, and spring days in the subarctic can be nearly as hot as in the tropics. The first mosquitoes were already heralding the approach of the sky-filling swarms which would soon make travel on the Barrens a veritable trip through hell. I located the wolf tracks and resolutely set out upon the trail.

5   It led directly across the muskeg for several miles; but although the wolf had sunk in only three or four inches, my steps sank in until I reached solid ice a foot beneath the surface. It was with great relief that I finally breasted another gravel ridge and lost all trace of the wolf tracks.

My attempts to find them again were perfunctory. As I gazed around me at the morose world of rolling muskeg and frost-shattered stone that stretched uninterruptedly to a horizon so distant it might as well have been the horizon of the sea, I felt lonelier than I had ever felt in all my life. No friendly sound of aircraft engines broke the silence of that empty sky. No distant rumble of traffic set the ground beneath my feet to shaking. Only the disembodied whistling of an unseen plover gave any indication that life existed anywhere in all this lunar land where no tree grew.

I found a niche amongst some lichen-covered rocks and, having firmly jammed myself into it, ate and drank my lunch. Then I picked up the binoculars and began to scan the barren landscape for some signs of life.

Directly in front of me was the ice-covered bay of a great lake, and on the far side of this bay was something which at least relieved the somber monochrome of the muskeg colorings. It was a yellow sand esker, rising to a height of fifty or sixty feet and winding sinuously away into the distance like a gigantic snake.

These barren land eskers are the inverted beds of long-vanished rivers which once flowed through and over the glaciers that, ten thousand years ago, covered the Keewatin Barrens to a depth of several thousand feet. When the ice melted, sandy riverbeds were deposited on the land below, where they now provide almost the sole visual relief in the bleak monotony of the tundra plains.

10   I gazed at this one with affection, studying it closely; and as I swept it with my glasses I saw something move. The distance was great, but the impression I had was of someone, just the other side of the esker crest, waving his arm above his head. Much excited, I stumbled to my feet and trotted along the ridge to its termination on the shore of the bay. I was then not more than three hundred yards from the esker and when I got my breath back I took another look through the glasses.

The object I had previously glimpsed was still in view, but now it looked like a white feather boa being vehemently waved by persons or person unseen. It was a most inexplicable object, and nothing I had ever heard of in my study of natural history seemed to fit it. As I stared in perplexity, the first boa was joined by a second one, also waving furiously, and both boas began to move slowly along, parallel to the crest of the esker.

I began to feel somewhat uneasy, for here was a phenomenon which did not seem to be subject to scientific explanation. In fact I was on the point of abandoning my interest in the spectacle until some expert in psychic research happened along—when, without warning, both boas turned toward me, began rising higher and higher, and finally revealed themselves as the tails of two wolves proceeding to top the esker.

The esker overlooked my position on the bay's shore, and I felt as nakedly exposed as the lady in the famous brassiére advertisement. Hunkering down to make myself as small as possible, I wormed my way into the rocks and did my best to be unobtrusive. I need not have worried. The wolves paid no attention to me, if indeed they even saw me. They were far too engrossed in their own affairs, which, as I slowly and incredulously began to realize, were at that moment centered around the playing of a game of tag.

It was difficult to believe my eyes. They were romping like a pair of month-old pups! The smaller wolf (who soon gave concrete evidence that she was a female) took the initiative. Putting her head down on her forepaws and elevating her posterior in a most undignified manner, she suddenly pounced toward the much larger male whom I now recognized as my acquaintance of two days earlier. He, in his attempt to evade her, tripped and went sprawling. Instantly she was upon him, nipping him smartly in the backside, before leaping away to run around him in frenzied circles. The male scrambled to his feet and gave chase, but only by the most strenuous efforts was he able to close the gap until he, in his turn, was able to nip *her* backside. Thereupon the roles were again reversed, and the female began to pursue the male, who led her on a wild scrabble up, over, down, and back across the esker until finally both wolves lost their footing on the steep slope and went skidding down it inextricably locked together.

15 When they reached the bottom they separated, shook the sand out of their hair, and stood panting heavily, almost nose to nose. Then the female reared up and quite literally embraced the male with both forepaws while she proceeded to smother him in long-tongued kisses.

The male appeared to be enduring this overt display of affection, rather than enjoying it. He kept trying to avert his head, to no avail. Involuntarily I felt my sympathy warming toward him, for, in truth, it was a disgusting exhibition of wanton passion. Nevertheless he bore it with what stoicism he could muster until the female tired. Turning from him, she climbed halfway up the esker slope and . . . disappeared.

She seemed to have vanished off the face of the earth without leaving a trace behind her. Not until I swung the glasses back toward a dark shadow in a fold of the esker near where I had last seen her did I understand. The dark shadow was the mouth of a cave, or den, and the female wolf had almost certainly gone into it.

I was so elated by the realization that I had not only located a pair of wolves, but by an incredible stroke of fortune had found their den as well, that I forgot all caution and ran to a nearby knoll in order to gain a better view of the den mouth.

The male wolf, who had been loafing about the foot of the esker after the departure of his wife, instantly saw me. In three or four bounds he reached the ridge of the esker, where he stood facing me in an attitude of tense and threatening vigilance. As I looked up at him my sense of exhilaration waned rapidly. He no longer seemed like a playful pup, but had metamorphosed into a magnificent engine of destruction which impressed me so much that the neck of my flask positively rattled against my teeth.

20   I decided I had better not disturb the wolf family any more that day, for fear of upsetting them and perhaps forcing them to move away. So I withdrew. It was not an easy withdrawal, for one of the most difficult things I know of is to walk backward up a broken rocky slope for three quarters of a mile encumbered, as I was, by the complex hardware of a scientist's trade.

When I reached the ridge from which I had first seen the wolves I took a last quick look through the binoculars. The female was still invisible, and the male had so far relaxed his attitude of vigilance as to lie down on the crest of the esker. While I watched he turned around two or three times, as a dog will, and then settled himself, nose under tail, with the evident intention of having a nap.

I was much relieved to see he was no longer interested in me, for it would have been a tragedy if my accidental intrusion had unduly disturbed these wolves, thereby prejudicing what promised to be a unique opportunity to study the beasts I had come so far to find.

The lack of sustained interest which the big male wolf had displayed toward me was encouraging enough to tempt me to visit the den again the next morning; but this time, instead of the shotgun and the hatchet (I still retained the rifle, pistol and hunting knife) I carried a high-powered periscopic telescope and a tripod on which to mount it.

It was a fine sunny morning with enough breeze to keep the mosquito vanguard down. When I reached the bay where the esker was, I chose a prominent knoll of rock some four hundred yards from the den, behind which I could set up my telescope so that its objective lenses peered over the crest, but left me in hiding. Using consummate fieldcraft, I approached the chosen observation point in such a manner that the wolves could not possibly have seen me and, since the wind was from them to me, I was assured that they would have had no suspicion of my arrival.

25   When all was in order, I focused the telescope; but to my chagrin I could see no wolves. The magnification of the instrument was such that I could almost distinguish the individual grains of sand in the esker; yet, though I searched every inch of it for a distance of a mile on each side of the den, I could find no indication that wolves were about, or had ever been about. By noon, I had a

bad case of eye-strain and a worse one of cramps, and I had almost concluded that my hypothesis of the previous day was grievously at fault and that the den was just a fortuitous hole in the sand.

This was discouraging, for it had begun to dawn on me that all of the intricate study plans and schedules which I had drawn up were not going to be of much use without a great deal of co-operation on the part of the wolves. In country as open and as vast as this one was, the prospects of getting within visual range of a wolf except by the luckiest of accidents (and I had already had more than my ration of these) were negligible. I realized that if this was not a wolves' den which I had found, I had about as much chance of locating the actual den in this faceless wilderness as I had of finding a diamond mine.

Glumly I went back to my unproductive survey through the telescope. The esker remained deserted. The hot sand began sending up heat waves which increased my eyestrain. By 2:00 P.M. I had given up hope. There seemed no further point in concealment, so I got stiffly to my feet and prepared to relieve myself.

Now it is a remarkable fact that a man, even though he may be alone in a small boat in mid-ocean, or isolated in the midst of the trackless forest, finds that the very process of unbuttoning causes him to become peculiarly sensitive to the possibility that he may be under observation. At this critical juncture none but the most self-assured of men, no matter how certain he may be of his privacy, can refrain from casting a surreptitious glance around to reassure himself that he really is alone.

To say I was chagrined to discover I was *not* alone would be an understatement; for sitting directly behind me, and not twenty yards away, were the missing wolves.

30 They appeared to be quite relaxed and comfortable, as if they had been sitting there behind my back for hours. The big male seemed a trifle bored; but the female's gaze was fixed on me with what I took to be an expression of unabashed and even prurient curiosity.

The human psyche is truly an amazing thing. Under almost any other circumstances I would probably have been panic-stricken, and I think few would have blamed me for it. But these were not ordinary circumstances and my reaction was one of violent indignation. Outraged, I turned my back on the watching wolves and with fingers which were shaking with vexation, hurriedly did up my buttons. When decency, if not my dignity, had been restored, I rounded on those wolves with a virulence which surprised even me.

"Shoo!" I screamed at them. "What the hell do you think you're at, you . . . you . . . peeping Toms! Go away, for heaven's sake!"

The wolves were startled. They sprang to their feet, glanced at each other with a wild surmise, and then trotted off, passed down a draw, and disappeared in the direction of the esker. They did not once look back.

With their departure I experienced a reaction of another kind. The realization that they had been sitting almost within jumping distance of my unprotected back for God knows how long set up such a turmoil of the spirit that I had to give up all thought of carrying on where my discovery of the wolves had forced me to leave off. Suffering from both mental and physical strain, therefore, I hurriedly packed my gear and set out for the cabin.

35   My thoughts that evening were confused. True, my prayer had been answered, and the wolves had certainly co-operated by reappearing; but on the other hand I was becoming prey to a small but nagging doubt as to just *who* was watching *whom.* I felt that I, because of my specific superiority as a member of *Homo sapiens,* together with my intensive technical training, was entitled to pride of place. The sneaking suspicion that this pride had been denied and that, in point of fact, *I* was the one who was under observation, had an unsettling effect upon my ego.

In order to establish my ascendancy once and for all, I determined to visit the wolf esker itself the following morning and make a detailed examination of the presumed den. I decided to go by canoe, since the rivers were now clear and the rafting lake ice was being driven offshore by a stiff northerly breeze.

It was a fine, leisurely trip to Wolf House Bay, as I had now named it. The annual spring caribou migration north from the forested areas of Manitoba toward the distant tundra plains near Dubawnt Lake was under way, and from my canoe I could see countless skeins of caribou crisscrossing the muskegs and the rolling hills in all directions. No wolves were in evidence as I neared the esker, and I assumed they were away hunting a caribou for lunch.

I ran the canoe ashore and, fearfully laden with cameras, guns, binoculars and other gear, laboriously climbed the shifting sands of the esker to the shadowy place where the female wolf had disappeared. En route I found unmistakable proof that this esker was, if not the home, at least one of the favorite promenades of the wolves. It was liberally strewn with scats and covered with wolf tracks which in many places formed well-defined paths.

The den was located in a small wadi in the esker, and was so well concealed that I was on the point of walking past without seeing it, when a series of small squeaks attracted my attention. I stopped and turned to look, and there, not fifteen feet below me, were four small, gray beasties engaged in a free-for-all wrestling match.

40   At first I did not recognize them for what they were. The fat, fox faces with pinprick ears; the butterball bodies; as round as pumpkins; the short, bowed legs and the tiny upthrust sprigs of tails were so far from my conception of a wolf that my brain refused to make the logical connection.

Suddenly one of the pups caught my scent. He stopped in the midst of attempting to bite off a brother's tail and turned smoky blue eyes up toward me. What he saw evidently intrigued him. Lurching free of the scrimmage, he padded toward me with a rolling, wobbly gait: but a flea bit him unexpectedly before he had gone far, and he had to sit down to scratch it.

At this instant an adult wolf let loose a full-throated howl vibrant with alarm and warning, not more than fifty yards from me.

The idyllic scene exploded into frenzied action.

The pups became gray streaks which vanished into the gaping darkness of the den mouth. I spun around to face the adult wolf, lost my footing, and started to skid down the loose slope toward the den. In trying to regain my balance I thrust the muzzle of the rifle deep into the sand, where it stuck fast until the carrying-strap dragged it free as I slid rapidly away from it. I fumbled wildly at my revolver, but so cluttered was I with cameras and equipment straps that I did not succeed in getting the weapon clear as, accompanied by a growing avalanche of sand, I shot past the den mouth, over the lip of the main ridge and down the full length of the esker slope. Miraculously, I kept my feet; but only by dint of superhuman contortions during which I was alternately bent forward like a skier going over a jump, or leaning backward at such an acute angle I thought my backbone was going to snap.

45   It must have been quite a show. When I got myself straightened out and glanced back up the esker, it was to see *three* adult wolves ranged side by side like spectators in the Royal Box, all peering down at me with expressions of incredulous delight.

I lost my temper. This is something a scientist seldom does, but I lost mine. My dignity had been too heavily eroded during the past several days and my scientific detachment was no longer equal to the strain. With a snarl of exasperation I raised the rifle but, fortunately, the thing was so clogged with sand that when I pressed the trigger nothing happened.

The wolves did not appear alarmed until they saw me begin to dance up and down in helpless fury, waving the useless rifle and hurling imprecations at their cocked ears; whereupon they exchanged quizzical looks and silently withdrew out of my sight.

I too withdrew, for I was in no fit mental state to carry on with my exacting scientific duties. To tell the truth, I was in no fit mental state to do anything except hurry home to Mike's and seek solace for my tattered nerves and frayed vanity in the bottom of a jar of wolf-juice.

I had a long and salutary session with the stuff that night, and as my spiritual bruises became less painful under its healing influence I reviewed the incidents of the past few days. Inescapably, the realization was being borne in upon my preconditioned mind that the centuries-old and universally accepted human concept of wolf character was a palpable lie. On three separate occasions in less than a week I had been completely at the mercy of these "savage killers"; but far from attempting to tear me limb from limb, they had displayed a restraint verging on contempt, even when I invaded their home and appeared to be posing a direct threat to the young pups.

50   This much was obvious, yet I was still strangely reluctant to let the myth go down the drain. Part of this reluctance was no doubt due to the thought that, by discarding the accepted concepts of wolf nature, I would be committing scientific treason; part of it to the knowledge that recognition of the truth would deprive my mission of its fine aura of danger and high adventure; and not the least part of that reluctance was probably due to my unwillingness to accept the fact that I had been made to look like a blithering idiot—not by my fellow man, but by mere brute beasts.

Nevertheless I persevered.

When I emerged from my session with the wolf-juice the following morning I was somewhat the worse for wear in a physical sense; but I was cleansed and purified spiritually. I had wrestled with my devils and I had won. I had made my decision that, from this hour onward, I would go open-minded into the lupine world and learn to see and know the wolves, not for what they were supposed to be, but for what they actually were.

QUESTIONS FOR DISCUSSION

1. What leads to Mowat's encounter with the wolves? What range of feelings does he experience once he realizes that the wolves have been watching him?
2. What role does Mowat's scientific knowledge play in his understanding and study of the wolves? In what sense does his knowledge make it harder for him to perceive the wolves as they are?
3. How does Mowat characterize himself through his encounters with the wolves? Do you think that he is an able and objective scientist? Explain.
4. Examine each of Mowat's encounters with the wolves. Does he use effective and relevant descriptive detail to portray these encounters? Give examples. What does he learn from each encounter? Why does he finally decide, "I would go open-minded into the lupine world and learn to see and know the wolves, not for what they were supposed to be, but for what they actually were"?
5. As his observations continue, Mowat begins to perceive the wolves as similar to humans—playful and silly at times, concerned about their families, watchful and observant. We might say he makes them seem like humans in his mind, almost identifying with them. How does his perspective affect his ability to understand the wolves and their behavior?
6. How does Mowat explain his spiritual cleansing? How does this emphasis on cleansing add to the tone and power of the story?

CONNECTION

Compare and contrast the way that Linda Hogan and Farley Mowat learn to see. What do both of them learn from their education (see page 101)?

IDEAS FOR WRITING

1. Write an essay about an encounter that you have had with unfamiliar animals. What myths about the animals did you believe before your encounter? In what ways were your attitudes changed as a result of your experience?
2. Write an essay that explores why people become leaders in a field of study that involves understanding and protecting a particular animal group. Focus on one leader, such as Farley Mowat, Dian Fossey, or Jane Goodall.

What dream or vision of animals motivated this leader to strike out on such a new and risk taking path? What inspiration do we draw from such a person's life?

RELATED WEB SITES

FARLEY MOWAT

http://schwinger.harvard.edu/~terning/bios/Mowat.html
Facts and a bibliography on the author Farley Mowat will be found at this URL. The site also includes a link to more detailed biographic information about the writer and adventurer.

NEVER CRY WOLF — THE FILM

http://www.wafflemovies.com/nevercrywolf.html
Visit this URL for a review on the film *Never Cry Wolf,* based on Farley Mowat's book with the same title.

Donovan Webster

Inside the Volcano

After studying at Kenyon College and Middlebury College, Donovan Webster devoted himself to a career in writing and travel. He has been a senior editor for Outside *magazine, and has written on subjects ranging from the Underground Railroad to feathered dinosaurs for such national publications as* The National Geographic, The New Yorker, The New York Times Magazine, *and* The Smithsonian. *His book on landmines and other leftover toxics from wars,* Aftermath: Cleaning Up a Century of World War *(1996), won the Lionel Gelber Prize in 1997 and was made into a documentary film in 2001. He is currently working on a history of relations between China, Burma, and India during World War II, tentatively entitled* The Burma Road. *Webster was a founder of the Chicago-based Physicians against Land Mines/Center for International Rehabilitation.*

JOURNAL

Write a description of an unusual natural spot you have visited, trying to choose descriptive details that create a unified impression of the place as well as your response to it.

The volcano's summit is a dead zone, a cindered plain swirling with poisonous chlorine and sulfur gases, its air further thickened by nonstop siftings of new volcanic ash. No life can survive this environment for long. On the ash plain's edge, always threatening to make the island an aboveground hell, sit two active vents, Marum and Benbow, constantly shaking the earth and spewing globs of molten rock into the air. Yet across the black soil of the plain come all nine of us, a team of explorers, photographers, a film crew, a volcanologist, and me. We have hacked through dense jungles on this island called Ambrym, one of some eighty islands making up the South Pacific nation of Vanuatu, and entered this inhospitable landscape to camp and explore for two weeks. We've tightroped up miles of eroded, inches-wide ridgeline—with deep canyons plummeting hundreds of feet on either side—to totter at the lip of the volcanic pit of Benbow. The pit's malevolent red eye—obscured by gases and a balcony ledge of new volcanic rock—sits just a few hundred feet below.

"Okay, your turn," Chris Heinlein shouts above the volcano's roar.

A sinewy and friendly German engineer, Heinlein hands me the expedition's climbing rope, which leads down, inside the volcano. Clipping the rope into a rappelling device on my belt—which helps control my descent—I step into the air above the pit.

A dozen feet of rope slips between my gloved fingers. I lower myself into the volcano. Acidic gas bites my nose and eyes. The sulfur dioxide is mixing with the day's spitting drizzle, creating a sulfuric-acid rain so strong it will eat the metal frames of my eyeglasses within days, turning them to crumbly rust. The breathing of Benbow's pit is deafening, like up-close jet engines mixed with a cosmic belch. Each new breath from the volcano heaves the air so violently my ears pop in the changing pressure—then the temperature momentarily soars. Somewhere not too far below, red-hot, pumpkin-size globs of ejected lava are flying through the air.

5   I let more rope slip. With each slide deeper inside, I can only wonder: Why would anyone *do* this? And what drives the guy on the rope below me—the German photographer and longtime volcano obsessive Carsten Peter—to do it again and again?

We have come to see Ambrym's volcano close up and to witness the lava lakes in these paired pits, which fulminate constantly but rarely erupt. Yet suspended hundreds of feet above lava up to 2,200 degrees Fahrenheit that reaches toward the center of the Earth, I'm also discovering there's more. It is stupefyingly beautiful. The enormous noise. The deep, orangy red light from spattering lava. And those dark and brittle strands called Pele's hair: Filaments of lava that follow large blobs out of the pit, they cool quickly in the updraft and create six-inch-long, glassy threads that drift on the wind. It is like nowhere else on Earth.

Our first night on Ambrym we make camp in a beachside town called Port-Vato at the base of the 4,167-foot-high volcano. Shortly after sunrise the next morning, at the start of a demanding hike up the side of the volcano—walking a dry riverbed through thick jungle—I try to extract Peter's reasons for coming. As we crunch along the floor of black volcanic cinders, scrambling over shiny cliffs of cold lava that become waterfalls in the rainy season, Peter, forty-one, is grinning with excitement. Overhead dark silhouettes of large bats called flying foxes crease the morning sky like pterodactyls.

"I was fifteen years old and on vacation in Italy with my parents. They took me to see Mount Etna," he says. "As soon as I saw it, I was drawn to the crater's edge. I was *fascinated.* My parents went back to the tour bus. They honked the horn for me to come—but I couldn't leave. I edged closer, seeing the smoke inside, imagining the boiling magma below. At that moment I became infected."

Since then Peter has traveled the world examining volcanoes. His trips have taken him to Iceland, Ethiopia, Indonesia, Hawaii, and beyond. "And of course," he says, "I have been back to Etna, my home volcano, many times."

10 Using single-rope descending and climbing techniques developed by cave explorers and adapted for volcanoes, Peter has been dropping into volcanoes now for nearly a decade. "The size and power of a volcano is like nothing else on Earth," he says. "You think you understand the Earth and its geology, but once you look down into a volcanic crater and see what's there, well, you realize you will never completely understand. It is that powerful. That big." He grins. "You'll find out what I mean, I think."

After a five-hour walk uphill I get my first glimpse of that power as the expedition emerges from the steep, heavily vegetated sides of the volcano's cone and onto the caldera. In the course of a few hundred yards the trail flattens out, and the palm trees and eight foot-tall cane grasses that lushly lined the trail behind us become gnarled and dead, their life force snuffed by a world of swirling gas clouds and acid rain.

This is Ambrym's ash plain. Seven miles across, it's a severely eroded ash-and-lava cap hundreds of feet thick. Across the plain Benbow and Marum jut almost a thousand feet into the sky.

To protect ourselves from the harsh environment, our team quickly establishes a base camp near the caldera's edge. Shielded behind a low bluff separating the caldera from the jungle, the camp stretches through a grove of palms and tree-size ferns, the black soil dotted with purple orchids bobbing on long green stalks. For the remainder of this first afternoon we set up tents and create acid-rain-tight storage areas. The camp is a paradise perched on the edge of disaster. As night falls, we eat chicken soup fortified with cellophane noodles and plan tomorrow's exploration, the volcano rumbling regularly in the background as we talk.

After dinner we follow Carsten Peter to the edge of the ash plain and watch the vents light the gas clouds, wreathing each peak in ghostly red glows. "Look there," Peter says, pointing to a third red cauldron halfway up Marum's side. "That must be Niri Taten. Tomorrow we'll start there."

15 All night long the rumbling keeps awakening us. Just a few miles away lava boils and the Earth roars while each of us—lying quietly in a flimsy tent—anxiously dreams of those swirling red clouds. Tomorrow night at this time, I resolve as I drift off to sleep once again, one thing is certain: It will have been a day like none I've ever had.

In the morning, shortly after a sunrise breakfast, we strike out toward Niri Taten, several miles uphill. As we follow dry and eroded riverbeds toward the volcanic cones, a gentle rain falls.

"What does Niri Taten mean?" I ask our local guide, Jimmy.

"Niri Taten is a small pig," he replies. "A small mad pig. A crazy pig. A small pig that causes trouble to men."

Haraldur Sigurdsson, one of the world's premier volcanologists, walks alongside me in the dry riverbed, examining sheer cliff faces. He points out strata of tephra, a mixture of volcanic material. By examining these layers, volcanologists can tell a volcano's level of activity. Larger and coarser tephra far from a volcanic pit means a more powerful volcano, since heavier matter is thrown farther as more explosive energy is supplied.

20   It's true. The closer we hike to the craters, the more the character of the riverbed beneath our feet changes from silty black grit to charcoal-size stones—not unlike old-time furnace clinkers. "Each volcano has its own chemical fingerprint," Sigurdsson says. "Each volcano's mineral and elemental content is different because of the nature of the volcano itself: its rock and the shape of its vent. It helps volcanologists a lot in their study.

"Like the Tambora eruption of 1815 in Indonesia," Sigurdsson says. "We've found Tambora ash by its particular chemical signature almost everywhere on Earth. One of that magnitude happens about every thousand years." The Tambora explosion is said to have given off so much ash and sulfur dioxide—both of which blocked and reflected sunlight—that 1816 was a "year without a summer" across much of the world. There was crop-killing frost throughout the summer in New England. In northern Europe harvests were a disaster.

Suddenly, from two miles upwind behind us, Benbow gives a huge belch. We turn to look back. "Uh-oh" Sigurdsson says. "Ashfall on the way." Instead of the usual bluish white clouds of steam and gas, the plume issuing from the cone is heavy and black, trailing earthward in a dark curtain. Slowly it drifts our way on the wind. Five minutes later the ashfall finds us, covering our rucksacks, clothing, faces, boots, and ponchos with a sandy grit the color of wet cocoa mix.

Under the ashfall we climb Marum, pressing forward through the dead volcanic soil for another hour. Each step takes us closer to Niri Taten, a crater that tunnels straight down into the basaltic rock like a massive, steaming worm burrow 200 yards across. As we approach, a rising wind and thick clouds of chlorine gas force us to pause and pull on safety helmets and industrial-style gas masks that cover our noses and mouths. Without them, between the flying bits of stone and grit carried on the fifty-mile-an-hour winds and the thick clouds of gas roaring upward from the vent, time spent near the pit's lip would be painfully dangerous if not impossible.

Even with these protections the howling wind and gas often force us to shut our eyes and suspend breathing until the heaviest gas clouds pass. We lean against the high winds, brace at the crater's edge, and look inside.

25   Five hundred feet below, the vent's opening is obscured by rocky ledges. But if we can't see the lava itself, there is a consolation. Every inch of rocky surface

inside the vent's cone is painted with color. Sunshine yellow sulfur coats some of the crater's sheer rock faces. Iron washes other sections of rock with flaming orange. Pastel green deposits of manganese glaze rock nearest the vent, like a carpet of immortal moss. Other patches of stone have been bleached white by chlorine and fluorine gases pouring from the vent.

Besides the wind and dangerous concentration of gases, the edges of Niri Taten are too crumbly to allow safe descent. Anyone climbing down a rope inside the crater could be dislodging loose boulders, some the size of cars, that could crash on anyone below. Carsten Peter pulls out his camera and long lens—whose coating immediately becomes corroded in the noxious air. The howling gusts twice knock expedition members to the ground.

After an hour it's decided that we should examine the Marum crater itself. "We can get two volcanoes in one day!" Carsten Peter says with glee. Our helmeted heads tucked down, we continue breathing scuba-diver slow into our masks for maximum benefit, and we push on.

The walk to Marum's opening isn't far, but what it lacks in distance it makes up for in danger. No matter which route you choose, you have to traverse the mountain's steep slopes, many of which are gouged with deep, unclimbable erosion gullies. We decide to cross where the gullies are smallest: along Niri Taten's knife-edged lip, within a foot of a sheer drop into the crater.

We step gingerly where the slope looks most reliable, but our footing remains dangerously slick. The slope's top layer is crumbly tephra, sometimes as big as charcoal briquettes. Making things more difficult, we've moved downwind of Niri Taten. All around us clouds of sulfur dioxide, chlorine, and fluorine gases swirl so thick they sometimes obscure our vision and force us to stop and bury our gas-masked faces inside our arms for extra protection.

30   It's a slog. Minutes stretch into an hour. Every step could be our last. Finally we reach the summit of the crater's edge and begin down its other side. Protected by the lip behind us, the environment changes. Sunshine blankets the tilting black ash, and the cold gales calm into balmy breezes.

Two expedition members, Franck Tessier and Irène Margaritis, hustle downslope with me toward Marum. As we approach its lip, the thirty-nine-year-old Tessier—a genial and easygoing French biologist with impressive rope and rock-climbing skills honed by years of adventures like this one—rips off his gas mask and begins to hoot with pleasure.

I know why. Ahead of us Marum's volcanic pit stretches as open and clear as a visionary's painting. In the pit, three step-down ledges—each deeper and wider than the one uphill of it—are marbled with layers of black ash and pale, bleached basaltic andesite. The layers of lava inside the vent form as a crust over a cooling lava lake that gets blown out like a massive champagne cork when volcanic activity resumes. Small wall vents called fumaroles—created where heated groundwater and escaping volcanic gas reach the surface—let off steady plumes of steam. Inside Marum's crater it looks as if the world is being born.

And there, in the bottom of the third and largest pit—some 1,200 feet below—sits the lava lake. Its fury pushes lava through three skylight holes in a roof that partly covers the lake like a canopy. Bright orange and red spatters fly unpredictably from the circular opening of the largest skylight, a hole perhaps fifty yards across.

Lava is three times as dense as water. Despite its up to 2,200 degrees-Fahrenheit heat, lava moves, burbles, and flies through the air with the consistency of syrup. Every few minutes huge molten blobs seem to soar in slow motion. A second or two later a noise from beneath the earth—a rumbling *booooom*—fills the pit and rolls across the sculpted ash plain beyond. It's mesmerizing: lava sloshing back and forth, bubbles emerging and popping like a thick stew. As we survey Marum's lip and crater, I can't take my eyes off the lava. Suddenly I understand Peter's obsession. As evening cloaks the pit's deepest recesses in shade, the lava lake and explosive bubbles glow more seductively. The spatterings glisten like enormous, otherworldly fireworks as they sail through the shadowed air.

35   Dangling inside Benbow's crater the following afternoon, I have time to reflect. This morning we followed the narrow ridge to Benbow's pit—which was firm enough to climb down. We fixed our rope, ate lunch in a spitting acid rain, and began our descent into the volcano.

Now, on the rope below me, Carsten Peter works his way deeper inside the crater. I let more rope slide through my hands, easing myself deeper as well.

With each drop the air shakes more violently; the clouds of poison gas grow thicker. Waves of pressurized air rumble past me.

Grasping the rope tightly, I halt my descent at the edge of an overhung cliff and stare deeper inside. The lava lake waits below, ejecting orange bombs and smaller drops. Then, in a heartbeat, a wall of thick clouds blows between me and the pit, enveloping everything around me in a world of gray. In the shuddering air and disorienting noise, gravity, direction, and time seem to fade away. There is only the volcano, its existence a direct result of two tectonic plates colliding below me. Benbow roars again. The earth shakes.

In this moment I know I've gotten close enough to the fire at the center of the Earth. At that same second the clouds part and Benbow reappears. Fumaroles smoke, and steam swirls from the pit's walls. The Technicolor wash swarms around me like a kaleidoscope. Below, Carsten Peter hits the end of the rope just above Benbow's explosive vent. He pulls a camera from his bag and lifts it to his eye.

40   Torrential rains will frustrate another attempt to explore Benbow. Then dissension breaks out among some of the expedition's porters who helped carry gear up the volcano's steep cone, and it becomes clear that the team will have to leave Ambrym as soon as possible. In a last-ditch, eighteen-hour marathon, team members drop 1,200 feet into Marum and photograph its lava lake nonstop. They emerge from the crater and find a fractious camp. Jimmy cannot persuade the disgruntled porters to bend, and the tension escalates. With a satchel full of photographs, Carsten Peter finally agrees to abandon the volcano—even as he vows to return.

QUESTIONS FOR DISCUSSION

1. Explain how Webster's opening paragraph uses descriptive detail to provide the background, setting, and purpose of his essay.
2. The paragraphs that follow the introduction bring the reader into the volcano along with the other climbers. Point out how Webster uses details that appeal to all of the senses in order to evoke the atmosphere of the volcano and its physical impact.
3. Comment on the way Webster uses details and dialogue to characterize the other explorers on his expedition, particularly Carsten Peter, the "longtime volcano obsessive"? How do these characters engage readers' interest while helping them to better understand the nature of volcanoes?
4. How does Webster use contrast and color description to bring out the beauty of particular aspects of the volcano's interior? Give examples.
5. How does the description of the lava in Mayum volcanic pit prepare the reader for Webster's realization: "Suddenly I understand Peter's obsession"?
6. Examine the final paragraphs of the essay: How is Webster's response to the volcano similar to Peter's, yet ultimately different? Point out details and word-choice that underscore the two men's different levels of engagement.

CONNECTION

Compare Webster's description of a hazardous "extreme" natural place with that of the Khumbu Icefall. How do the authors use description differently to appeal to their respective audiences (see page 96)?

IDEAS FOR WRITING

1. Develop your journal writing into an essay in which you create a dramatic descriptive account of a visit to an unusual natural place. Reflect at the end on what seeing this place and engaging in it with all of your senses has meant to you.
2. Look at some back issues of *National Geographic*. Read some of the stories and study the accompanying photographs to get a feel for the interests of the typical reader of the publication as well as the typical style and "reader appeal" of such a story. Then analyze "Inside the Volcano," pointing out specific aspects of its descriptive style, characterization, and information that would appeal strongly to the publication's readers.

RELATED WEB SITES

MICHIGAN TECHNOLOGICAL UNIVERSITY VOLCANOES PAGE
http://www.geo.mtu.edu/volcanoes/
Visit the "MTU Volcanoes" web site to find out "anything you ever wanted to know about volcanoes" and about specific volcanoes all around the world.

NATURE LINKS
http://www.connix.com/~fmusante/nature/nature_links.htm
This is a web page of links devoted to nature writing and the philosophy of
nature. The links are divided into sections on "nature writing" with miscella-
neous related links.

Jon Krakauer

The Khumbu Icefall

*Jon Krakauer was born in 1954 and raised in Corvalis, Oregon. He traces his obses-
sion with mountain climbing to his first climbing experiences when he was only eight
years old. After graduating from college in 1975, Krakauer worked as an itinerant
carpenter to make money to support his expeditions. In 1981 he began his career as a
journalist, writing about what he loves most. A collection of his essays was published
in* Eiger Dreams *(1992). His second book,* Into the Wild *(1996), is the story of a
young adventurer who gets lost in the vast Alaska territory; his most recent work returns to a similar subject with* The Land of White Death: An Epic Story of Survival in the Siberian Arctic *(2000). In the following excerpt, from his best-selling
account of a failed climbing expedition to Mount Everest,* Into Thin Air *(1997),
Krakauer captures one of the most dramatic episodes in the days leading up to the
deadly summit attempt. He also shows how commercialization and high tech equipment have affected the challenges of mountain climbing.*

JOURNAL

Try to get inside the mind of a mountain climber and imagine his thoughts and
feelings before embarking on a challenging climb. Imagine what has led this person to risk his or her life just to "get to the top."

Our route to the summit would follow the Khumbu Glacier up the lower half
of the mountain. From the *bergschrund** at 23,000 feet that marked its upper end, this great river of ice flowed two and a half miles down a relatively gentle
valley called the Western Cwm. As the glacier inched over humps and dips in the
Cwm's underlying strata, it fractured into countless vertical fissures—crevasses.
Some of these crevasses were narrow enough to step across; others were eighty
feet wide, several hundred feet deep, and ran half a mile from end to end. The

---

*A *bergschrund* is a deep slit that delineates a glacier's upper terminus; it forms as the body of ice slides away
from the steeper wall immediately above, leaving a gap between glacier and rock.

big ones were apt to be vexing obstacles to our ascent, and when hidden beneath a crust of snow they would pose a serious hazard, but the challenges presented by the crevasses in the Cwm had proven over the years to be predictable and manageable.

The Icefall was a different story. No part of the South Col route was feared more by climbers. At around 20,000 feet, where the glacier emerged from the lower end of the Cwm, it pitched abruptly over a precipitous drop. This was the infamous Khumbu Icefall, the most technically demanding section on the entire route.

The movement of the glacier in the Icefall has been measured at between three and four feet a day. As it skids down the steep, irregular terrain in fits and starts, the mass of ice splinters into a jumble of huge, tottering blocks called *seracs,* some as large as office buildings. Because the climbing route wove under, around, and between hundreds of these unstable towers, each trip through the Icefall was a little like playing a round of Russian roulette: sooner or later any given serac was going to fall over without warning, and you could only hope you weren't beneath it when it toppled. Since 1963, when . . . Jake Breitenbach was crushed by an avalanching serac to become the Icefall's first victim, eighteen other climbers had died here.

The previous winter, as he had done in winters past, Hall had consulted with the leaders of all the expeditions planning to climb Everest in the spring, and together they'd agreed on one team among them who would be responsible for establishing and maintaining a route through the Icefall. For its trouble, the designated team was to be paid $2,200 from each of the other expeditions on the mountain. In recent years this cooperative approach had been met with wide, if not universal, acceptance, but it wasn't always so.

5   The first time one expedition thought to charge another to travel through the ice was in 1988, when a lavishly funded American team announced that any expedition that intended to follow the route they'd engineered up the Icefall would have to fork over $2,000. Some of the other teams on the mountain that year, failing to understand that Everest was no longer merely a mountain but a commodity as well, were incensed. And the greatest hue and cry came from Rob Hall, who was leading a small, impecunious New Zealand team.

Hall carped that the Americans were "violating the spirit of the hills" and practicing a shameful form of alpine extortion, but Jim Frush, the unsentimental attorney who was the leader of the American group, remained unmoved. Hall eventually agreed through clenched teeth to send Frush a check and was granted passage through the Icefall. (Frush later reported that Hall never made good on his IOU.)

Within two years, however, Hall did an about-face and came to see the logic of treating the Icefall as a toll road. Indeed, from 1993 through '95 he volunteered to put in the route and collect the toll himself. In the spring of 1996 he elected not to assume responsibility for the Icefall, but he was happy to pay the leader of a rival commercial* expedition—a Scottish Everest veteran named Mal Duff—to take over the job. Long before we'd even arrived at Base Camp, a team of Sherpas employed by Duff had blazed a zigzag path through the seracs, stringing out more than a mile of rope and installing some sixty aluminum ladders over the broken surface of the glacier. The ladders belonged to an enterprising Sherpa from the village of Gorak Shep who turned a nice profit by renting them out each season.

So it came to pass that at 4:45 A.M. on Saturday, April 13, I found myself at the foot of the fabled Icefall, strapping on my crampons in the frigid predawn gloom.

Crusty old alpinists who've survived a lifetime of close scrapes like to counsel young protégés that staying alive hinges on listening carefully to one's "inner voice." Tales abound of one or another climber who decided to remain in his or her sleeping bag after detecting some inauspicious vibe in the ether and thereby survived a catastrophe that wiped out others who failed to heed the portents.

10   I didn't doubt the potential value of paying attention to subconscious cues. As I waited for Rob to lead the way, the ice underfoot emitted a series of loud cracking noises, like small trees being snapped in two, and I felt myself wince with each pop and rumble from the glacier's shifting depths. Problem was, my inner voice resembled Chicken Little: it was screaming that I was about to die, but it did that almost every time I laced up my climbing boots. I therefore did my damnedest to ignore my histrionic imagination and grimly followed Rob into the eerie blue labyrinth.

Although I'd never been in an icefall as frightening as the Khumbu, I'd climbed many other icefalls. They typically have vertical or even overhanging passages that demand considerable expertise with ice ax and crampons. There was certainly no lack of steep ice in the Khumbu Icefall, but all of it had been rigged with ladders or ropes or both, rendering the conventional tools and techniques of ice climbing largely superfluous.

I soon learned that on Everest not even the rope—the quintessential climber's accoutrement—was to be utilized in the time-honored manner. Ordinarily, one climber is tied to one or two partners with a 150-foot length of rope, making each person directly responsible for the life of the others; roping up in this fashion is a serious and very intimate act. In the Icefall, though, expediency dictated that each of us climb independently, without being physically connected to one another in any way.

Mal Duff's Sherpas had anchored a static line of rope that extended from the bottom of the Icefall to its top. Attached to my waist was a three-foot-long safety tether with a carabiner, or snap-link, at the distal end. Security was achieved not

---

*Although I use "commercial" to denote any expedition organized as a money-making venture, not all commercial expeditions are guided. For instance, Mal Duff—who charged his clients considerably less than the $65,000 fee requested by Hall and Fischer—provided leadership and the essential infrastructure necessary to climb Everest (food, tents, bottled oxygen, fixed ropes, Sherpa support staff, and so on) but did not purport to act as a guide; the climbers on his team were assumed to be sufficiently skilled to get themselves safely up Everest and back down again.

by roping myself to a teammate but rather by clipping my safety tether to the fixed line and sliding it up the rope as I ascended. Climbing in this fashion, we would be able to move as quickly as possible through the most dangerous parts of the Icefall, and we wouldn't have to entrust our lives to teammates whose skill and experience were unknown. As it turned out, not once during the entire expedition would I ever have reason to rope myself to another climber.

If the Icefall required few orthodox climbing techniques, it demanded a whole new repertoire of skills in their stead—for instance, the ability to tiptoe in mountaineering boots and crampons across three wobbly ladders lashed end to end, bridging a sphincter-clenching chasm. There were many such crossings, and I never got used to them.

15   At one point I was balanced on an unsteady ladder in the predawn gloaming, stepping tenuously from one bent rung to the next, when the ice supporting the ladder on either end began to quiver as if an earthquake had struck. A moment later came an explosive roar as a large serac somewhere close above came crashing down. I froze, my heart in my throat, but the avalanching ice passed fifty yards to the left, out of sight, without doing any damage. After waiting a few minutes to regain my composure I resumed my herky-jerky passage to the far side of the ladder.

The glacier's continual and often violent state of flux added an element of uncertainty to every ladder crossing. As the glacier moved, crevasses would sometimes compress, buckling ladders like toothpicks; other times a crevasse might expand, leaving a ladder dangling in the air, only tenuously supported, with neither end mounted on solid ice. Anchors* securing the ladders and lines routinely melted out when the afternoon sun warmed the surrounding ice and snow. Despite daily maintenance, there was a very real danger that any given rope might pull loose under body weight.

But if the Icefall was strenuous and terrifying, it had a surprising allure as well. As dawn washed the darkness from the sky, the shattered glacier was revealed to be a three-dimensional landscape of phantasmal beauty. The temperature was six degrees Fahrenheit. My crampons crunched reassuringly into the glacier's rind. Following the fixed line, I meandered through a vertical maze of crystalline blue stalagmites. Sheer rock buttresses seamed with ice pressed in from both edges of the glacier, rising like the shoulders of a malevolent god. Absorbed by my surroundings and the gravity of the labor, I lost myself in the unfettered pleasures of ascent, and for an hour or two actually forgot to be afraid.

Three-quarters of the way to Camp One, Hall remarked at a rest stop that the Icefall was in better shape than he'd ever seen it: "The route's a bloody freeway this season." But only slightly higher, at 19,000 feet, the ropes brought us to the base of a gargantuan, perilously balanced serac. As massive as a twelve-story building, it

---

*Three-foot long aluminum stakes called pickets were used to anchor ropes and ladders to snow slopes; when the terrain was hard glacial ice, "ice screws" were employed: hollow, threaded tubes about ten inches long that were twisted into the frozen glacier.

loomed over our heads, leaning 30 degrees past vertical. The route followed a natural catwalk that angled sharply up the overhanging face: we would have to climb
up and over the entire off-kilter tower to escape its threatening tonnage.

Safety, I understood, hinged on speed. I huffed toward the relative security
of the serac's crest with all the haste I could muster, but since I wasn't acclima-
tized my fastest pace was no better than a crawl. Every four or five steps I'd have
to stop, lean against the rope, and suck desperately at the thin, bitter air, sear-
ing my lungs in the process.

20   I reached the top of the serac without it collapsing and flopped breathless
onto its flat summit, my heart pounding like a jackhammer. A little later,
around 8:30 A.M., I arrived at the top of the Icefall itself, just beyond the last of
the seracs. The safety of Camp One didn't supply much peace of mind, however: I couldn't stop thinking about the ominously tilted slab a short distance
below, and the fact that I would have to pass beneath its faltering bulk at least
seven more times if I was going to make it to the summit of Everest. Climbers
who snidely denigrate this as the Yak Route, I decided, had obviously never
been through the Khumbu Icefall.

QUESTIONS FOR DISCUSSION

1. According to Krakauer, what factors make climbing the Khumbu Icefall the
   most demanding challenge on the route to the summit of Mount Everest?
2. Why has the icefall been made into a toll road? Does this seem like an
   overcommercialization of a natural place? Is it necessary?
3. Why does Krakauer reflect on the alpine climbers who listen to their inner voices, or subconscious, before embarking on a dangerous journey?
   How does Krakauer handle his fear?
4. Give examples of Krakauer's use of descriptive detail in passages where
   he tries to give clear impressions of the terrain of the glacier and the place-
   ments of the ladders. Do you get a good sense of what it was like to climb
   the ladders? Could he have included other details?
5. Give examples of ways that Krakauer uses description to clarify the different techniques of ice climbing used on the Khumbu Icefall as well as
   the glacier's "continual and violent state of flux."
6. In this climb two highly respected climbers, Rob Hall and Scott Fisher,
   died when they were caught in a storm at the summit. Give examples of
   physical and emotional observations made by Krakauer here that could be
   said to foreshadow the disaster that lies ahead.

CONNECTION

Compare Krakauer's use of descriptive detail with Webster's (see page 89).

IDEAS FOR WRITING

1. Write a paper about a natural challenge that you have experienced or that
   you intend to experience. What will or did you do? How did you or are

you preparing yourself? Why did you or why are you going on this journey? If you have completed this journey, what did you learn? What insights did you gain?

2. Describe an ordinary process that you participate in that could be said to be dangerous at times, such as driving in heavy traffic in the rain or snow through a mountain pass. Describe the process involved in this activity in clear details, indicating some of the close calls you have had performing the activity. Provide insights into your feelings of fear and exhilaration.

RELATED WEB SITES

JON KRAKAUER
http://www.cwu.edu/~geograph/krakauer.htm
This URL includes biographical and bibliographical information on Krakauer, as well as a critical assessment of the writer and links to other relevant web sites.

MOUNT EVEREST
http://www.mnteverest.net/
Information about Mount Everest can be found at this extensive web devoted to the world's highest peak. The site includes several interesting links for climbers and trekkers.

Linda Hogan

Walking

Linda Hogan (b. 1947), a member of the Chickasaw tribe, was raised in Denver, Colorado. She completed her M.A. at the University of Colorado at Boulder in 1978. Hogan began her career teaching creative writing and Native American literature at the University of Colorado at Boulder and went on to teach poetry and literature in outreach programs in Colorado and Oklahoma. Since 1989 she has been an associate professor of English at the University of Colorado at Boulder. Her books include Eclipse *(1983),* Seeing Through the Sun *(1985), the novel* Mean Spirit *(1990),* Confronting The Truth *(2000), and* The Woman who Watches Over the World *(2001). Hogan has dedicated her writing to "gentle women" and their children, and her work looks to reconciliation's for the survival of the family, community, and the natural world with visions of Indian continuance and a strong sense of place. The following selection, "Walking," a chronicle of observation in nature over a period of time, is excerpted from her essay collection,* Dwellings *(1995).*

JOURNAL

Write about a solitary walk that you took repeatedly in a nature area. What changes did you notice in the environment over time?

It began in dark and underground weather, a slow hunger moving toward light. It grew in a dry gully beside the road where I live, a place where entire hillsides are sometimes yellow, windblown tides of sunflower plants. But this plant was different. It was alone and larger than the countless others that had established their lives farther up the hill. This one was a traveler, a settler, and like a dream beginning in conflict, it grew where the land had been disturbed.

I saw it first in early summer. It was a green and sleeping bud, raising itself toward the sun. Ants worked around the unopened bloom, gathering aphids and sap. A few days later, it was a tender young flower, soft and new, with a pale green center and a troop of silver-gray insects climbing up and down the stalk. Over the summer this sunflower grew into a plant of incredible beauty, turning its face daily toward the sun in the most subtle of ways, the black center of it dark and alive with a deep blue light, as if flint had sparked an elemental fire there, in community with rain, mineral, mountain air, and sand.

As summer changed from green to yellow there were new visitors daily, the lace-winged insects, the bees whose legs were fat with pollen, and grasshoppers with their clattering wings and desperate hunger. There were other lives I missed, those too small or hidden to see. It was as if the plant with its host of lives was a society, one in which moment by moment, depending on light and moisture, there was great and diverse change.

There were changes in the next larger world around the plant as well. One day I rounded a bend in the road to find the disturbing sight of a dead horse, black and still against a hillside, eyes rolled back. Another day I was nearly lifted by a wind and sandstorm so fierce and hot that I had to wait for it to pass before I could return home. On this day the faded dry petals of the sunflower were swept across the land. That was when the birds arrived to carry the new seeds to another future.

5   In this one plant, in one summer season, a drama of need and survival took place. Hungers were filled. Insects coupled. There was escape, exhaustion, and death. Lives touched down a moment and were gone.

I was an outsider. I only watched. I never learned the sunflower's golden language or the tongues of its citizens. I had a small understanding, nothing more than a shallow observation of the flower, insects, and birds. But they knew what to do, how to live. An old voice from somewhere, gene or cell, told the plant how to evade the pull of gravity and find its way upward, how to open. It was instinct, intuition, necessity. A certain knowing directed the seed-bearing birds on paths to ancestral homelands they had never seen. They believed it. They followed.

There are other summons and calls, some even more mysterious than those commandments to birds or those survival journeys of insects. In bamboo plants, for instance, with their thin green canopy of light and golden stalks that creak in the wind. Once a century, all of a certain kind of bamboo flower on the same day. Neither the plants' location, in Malaysia or in a greenhouse in Minnesota, nor their age or size make a difference. They flower. Some current of an inner language passes among them, through space and separation, in ways we cannot explain in our language. They are all, somehow, one plant, each with a share of communal knowledge.

John Hay, in *The Immortal Wilderness,* has written: "There are occasions when you can hear the mysterious language of the Earth, in water, or coming through the trees, emanating from the mosses, seeping through the undercurrents of the soil, but you have to be willing to wait and receive."

Sometimes I hear it talking. The light of the sunflower was one language, but there are others more audible. Once, in the redwood forest, I heard a beat, something like a drum or heart coming from the ground and trees and wind. That underground current stirred a kind of knowing inside me, a kinship and longing, a dream barely remembered that disappeared back to the body. Another time, there was the booming voice of an ocean storm thundering from far out to sea, telling about what lived in the distance, about the rough water that would arrive, wave after wave revealing the disturbance at center.

10 Tonight I walk. I am watching the sky. I think of the people who came before me and how they knew the placement of stars in the sky, watched the moving sun long and hard enough to witness how a certain angle of light touched a stone only once a year. Without written records, they knew the gods of every night, the small, fine details of the world around them and of immensity above them.

Walking, I can almost hear the redwoods beating. And the oceans are above me here, rolling clouds, heavy and dark, considering snow. On the dry, red road, I pass the place of sunflower, that dark and secret location where creation took place. I wonder if it will return this summer, if it will multiply and move up to the other stand of flowers in a territorial struggle.

It's winter and there is smoke from the fires. The square, lighted windows of houses are fogging over. It is a world of elemental attention, of all things working together, listening to what speaks in the blood. Whichever road I follow, I walk in the land of many gods, and they love and eat one another. Walking, I am listening to a deeper way. Suddenly all my ancestors are behind me. Be still, they say. Watch and listen. You are the result of the love of thousands.

QUESTIONS FOR DISCUSSION

1. Why does the essay begin by anticipating the birth of the sunflower? Explain the logic behind Hogan's organization of her ideas in this essay.

2. Why does Hogan personify the sunflower is a "traveler, a settler, like a dream beginning in conflict"?

3. Hogan describes herself as an outsider and an observer: "I never learned the sunflower's golden language or the tongues of its citizens." How and why does she believe that those within the sunflower's world communicated? What does their ability to communicate exemplify for Hogan?

4. What relationship between life and death, love and hate is Hogan developing in this essay?

5. What does Hogan believe that observers and walkers can learn from the natural world? Explain why you agree or disagree with her assumptions.

6. Why is the essay entitled "Walking"? Discuss several different ways that walking is a meaningful activity in this essay.

CONNECTION

Compare and contrast how Hogan and Steinhart see nonverbal language systems at work in the natural world (see page 75).

IDEAS FOR WRITING

1. Hogan concludes, "Walking, I am listening to a deeper way." Write an essay that is developed from observational walks in which you try to be aware of what Hogan describes about the changes in nature over time.

2. Hogan quotes from John Hay's *Immortal Wilderness:* "There are occasions when you can hear the mysterious language of the Earth, in water, or coming through the trees, . . . but you have to be willing to wait and receive." Write an essay about a time when you heard or sensed one form of the mysterious language of the earth.

RELATED WEB SITES

LINDA HOGAN
http://voices.cla.umn.edu/authors/LindaHogan.html
Learn about Linda Hogan's work and biography at this URL from "Voices from the Gaps." Related links and interviews with the author are also included.

WRITING AND WALKING
http://www.humanities.ualberta.ca/agora/Articles.cfm?
ArticleNo=116
Read this interesting and philosophical article about the relationship between walking and writing at this URL. The essay is entitled, "Recursivity: Navigating Composition and Space," by Jason Snart and Dean Swinford.

Loren Eiseley

The Judgment of the Birds

A native of Nebraska, Loren Eiseley (1901–1977) spent most of his life as a professor of anthropology and history of science at the University of Pennsylvania. He is known for his powerful prose writing on scientific topics for the general public. His works include Firmament of Time *(1960),* The Night Country *(1971), and* The Star Thrower *(1978). He also published several volumes of poetry. Using a blend of anthropology, archaeology, natural history, and the history of science. Eiseley's work is dramatic, complex and poetic. Eiseley often pondered the relationship between human awareness and nature: "No longer . . . can the world be accepted as given. It has to be perceived and consciously thought about, abstracted, and considered. The moment one does so, one is outside of the natural; objects are each one surrounded with an aura radiating meaning to man alone."*

JOURNAL

Write about a time when you had a revelation or a moment of heightened, awareness after a period of close observation of a natural creature or event.

It is a commonplace of all religious thought, even the most primitive, that the man seeking visions and insight must go apart from his fellows and live for a time in the wilderness. If he is of the proper sort, he will return with a message. It may not be a message from the god he set out to seek, but even if he has failed in that particular, he will have had a vision or seen a marvel, and these are always worth listening to and thinking about.

The world, I have come to believe, is a very queer place, but we have been part of this queerness for so long that we tend to take it for granted. We rush to and fro like Mad Hatters upon our peculiar errands, all the time imagining our surroundings to be dull and ourselves quite ordinary creatures. Actually, there is nothing in the world to encourage this idea, but such is the mind of man, and this is why he finds it necessary from time to time to send emissaries into the wilderness in the hope of learning of great events, or plans in store for him, that will resuscitate his waning taste for life. His great news services, his worldwide radio network, he knows with a last remnant of healthy distrust will be of no use to him in this matter. No miracle can withstand a radio broadcast, and it is certain that it would be no miracle if it could. One must seek, then, what only the solitary approach can give—a natural revelation.

Let it be understood that I am not the sort of man to whom is entrusted direct knowledge of great events or prophecies. A naturalist, however, spends much of his life alone, and my life is no exception. Even in New York City there are patches of wilderness, and a man by himself is bound to undergo certain experiences falling into the class of which I speak. I set mine down, therefore: a matter of pigeons, a flight of chemicals, and a judgment of birds, in the hope that they will come to the eye of those who have retained a true taste for the marvelous, and who are capable of discerning in the flow of ordinary events the point at which the mundane world gives way to quite another dimension.

New York is not, on the whole, the best place to enjoy the downright miraculous nature of the planet. There are, I do not doubt, many remarkable stories to be heard there and many strange sights to be seen, but to grasp a marvel fully it must be savored from all aspects. This cannot be done while one is being jostled and hustled along a crowded street. Nevertheless, in any city there are true wildernesses where a man can be alone. It can happen in a hotel room, or on the high roofs at dawn.

5   One night on the twentieth floor of a midtown hotel I awoke in the dark and grew restless. On an impulse I climbed upon the broad old-fashioned window sill, opened the curtains, and peered out. It was the hour just before dawn, the hour when men sigh in their sleep or, if awake, strive to focus their wavering eyesight upon a world emerging from the shadows. I leaned out sleepily through the open window. I had expected depths, but not the sight I saw.

I found I was looking down from that great height into a series of curious cupolas or lofts that I could just barely make out in the darkness. As I looked, the outlines of these lofts became more distinct because the light was being reflected from the wings of pigeons who, in utter silence, were beginning to float outward upon the city. In and out through the open slits in the cupolas passed the white-winged birds on their mysterious errands. At this hour the city was theirs, and quietly, without the brush of a single wing tip against stone in that high, eerie place, they were taking over the spires of Manhattan. They were pouring upward in a light that was not yet perceptible to human eyes, while far down in the black darkness of the alleys it was still midnight.

As I crouched half-asleep across the sill, I had a moment's illusion that the world had changed in the night, as in some immense snowfall, and that, if I were to leave, it would have to be as these other inhabitants were doing, by the window. I should have to launch out into that great bottomless void with the simple confidence of young birds reared high up there among the familiar chimney pots and interposed horrors of the abyss.

I leaned farther out. To and fro went the white wings, to and fro. There were no sounds from any of them. They knew man was asleep and this light for a little while was theirs. Or perhaps I had only dreamed about man in this city of wings—which he could surely never have built. Perhaps I, myself, was one of these birds dreaming unpleasantly a moment of old dangers far below as I teetered on a window ledge.

Around and around went the wings. It needed only a little courage, only a little shove from the window ledge, to enter that city of light. The muscles of my hands were already making little premonitory lunges. I wanted to enter that city and go away over the roofs in the first dawn. I wanted to enter it so badly that I drew back carefully into the room and opened the hall door. I found my coat on the chair, and it slowly became clear to me that there was a way down through the floors, that I was, after all, only a man.

10   I dressed then and went back to my own kind, and I have been rather more than usually careful ever since not to look into the city of light. I had seen, just once, man's greatest creation from a strange inverted angle, and it was not really his at all. I will never forget how those wings went round and round, and how, by the merest pressure of the fingers and a feeling for air, one might go

away over the roofs. It is a knowledge, however, that is better kept to oneself. I think of it sometimes in such a way that the wings, beginning far down in the black depths of the mind, begin to rise and whirl till all the mind is lit by their spinning, and there is a sense of things passing away, but lightly, as a wing might veer over an obstacle.

To see from an inverted angle, however, is not a gift allotted merely to the human imagination. I have come to suspect that within their degree it is sensed by animals, though perhaps as rarely as among men. The time has to be right; one has to be, by chance or intention, upon the border of two worlds. And sometimes these two borders may shift or interpenetrate and one sees the miraculous.

I once saw this happen to a crow.

This crow lives near my house, and though I have never injured him, he takes good care to stay up in the very highest trees and, in general, to avoid humanity. His world begins at about the limit of my eyesight.

On the particular morning when this episode occurred, the whole countryside was buried in one of the thickest fogs in years. The ceiling was absolutely zero. All planes were grounded, and even a pedestrian could hardly see his outstretched hand before him.

15   I was groping across a field in the general direction of the railroad station, following a dimly outlined path. Suddenly out of the fog, at about the level of my eyes, and so closely that I flinched, there flashed a pair of immense black wings and a huge beak. The whole bird rushed over my head with a frantic cawing outcry of such hideous terror as I have never heard in a crow's voice before and never expect to hear again.

He was lost and startled, I thought, as I recovered my poise. He ought not to have flown out in this fog. He'd knock his silly brains out.

All afternoon that great awkward cry rang in my head. Merely being lost in a fog seemed scarcely to account for it—especially in a tough, intelligent old bandit such as I knew that particular crow to be. I even looked once in the mirror to see what it might be about me that had so revolted him that he had cried out in protest to the very stones.

Finally, as I worked my way homeward along the path, the solution came to me. It should have been clear before. The borders of our worlds had shifted. It was the fog that had done it. That crow, and I knew him well, never under normal circumstances flew low near men. He had been lost all right, but it was more than that. He had thought he was high up, and when he encountered me looming gigantically through the fog, he had perceived a ghastly and, to the crow mind, unnatural sight. He had seen a man walking on air, desecrating the very heart of the crow kingdom, a harbinger of the most profound evil a crow mind could conceive of—air-walking men. The encounter, he must have thought, had taken place a hundred feet over the roofs.

He caws now when he sees me leaving for the station in the morning, and I fancy that in that note I catch the uncertainty of a mind that has come to know things are not always what they seem. He has seen a marvel in his heights of air and is no longer as other crows. He has experienced the human world from an unlikely perspective. He and I share a viewpoint in common: our worlds have interpenetrated, and we both have faith in the miraculous.

20   It is a faith that in my own case has been augmented by two remarkable sights. I once saw some very odd chemicals fly across a waste so dead it might have been upon the moon, and once, by an even more fantastic piece of luck, I was present when a group of birds passed a judgment upon life.

On the maps of the old voyageurs it is called *Mauvaises Terres,* the evil lands, and, slurred a little with the passage through many minds, it has come down to us anglicized as the badlands. The soft shuffle of moccasins has passed through its canyons on the grim business of war and flight, but the last of those slight disturbances of immemorial silences died out almost a century ago. The land, if one can call it a land, is a waste as lifeless as that valley in which lie the kings of Egypt. Like the Valley of the Kings, it is a mausoleum, a place of dry bones in what once was a place of life. Now it has silences as deep as those in the moon's airless chasms.

Nothing grows among its pinnacles; there is no shade except under great toadstools of sandstone whose bases have been eaten to the shape of wine glasses by the wind. Everything is flaking, cracking, disintegrating, wearing away in the long, imperceptible weather of time. The ash of ancient volcanic outbursts still sterilizes its soil, and its colors in that waste are the colors that flame in the lonely sunsets on dead planets. Men come there but rarely, and for one purpose only, the collection of bones.

It was a late hour on a cold, wind-bitten autumn day when I climbed a great hill spined like a dinosaur's back and tried to take my bearings. The tumbled waste fell away in waves in all directions. Blue air was darkening into purple along the bases of the hills. I shifted my knapsack, heavy with the petrified bones of long-vanished creatures, and studied my compass. I wanted to be out of there by nightfall, and already the sun was going sullenly down in the west.

It was then that I saw the flight coming on. It was moving like a little close-knit body of black specks that danced and darted and closed again. It was pouring from the north and heading toward me with the undeviating relentlessness of a compass needle. It streamed through the shadows rising out of monstrous gorges. It rushed over towering pinnacles in the red light of the sun or momentarily sank from sight within their shade. Across that desert of eroding clay and wind-worn stone they came with a faint wild twittering that filled all the air about me as those tiny living bullets hurtled past into the night.

25   It may not strike you as a marvel. It would not, perhaps, unless you stood in the middle of a dead world at sunset, but that was where I stood. Fifty million years lay under my feet, fifty million years of bellowing monsters moving in a green world now gone so utterly that its very light was traveling on the farther edge of space. The chemicals of all that vanished age lay about me in the ground. Around me still lay the shearing molars of dead titanotheres, the delicate sabers of soft-stepping cats, the hollow sockets that had held the eyes of many a strange, outmoded beast. Those eyes had looked out upon a world as

real as ours; dark, savage brains had roamed and roared their challenges into the steaming night.

Now they were still here, or, put it as you will, the chemicals that made them were here about me in the ground. The carbon that had driven them ran blackly in the eroding stone. The stain of iron was in the clays. The iron did not remember the blood it had once moved within, the phosphorus had forgot the savage brain. The little individual moment had ebbed from all those strange combinations of chemicals as it would ebb from our living bodies into the sinks and runnels of oncoming time.

I had lifted up a fistful of that ground. I held it while that wild flight of southbound warblers hurtled over me into the oncoming dark. There went phosphorus, there went iron, there went carbon, there beat the calcium in those hurrying wings. Alone on a dead planet I watched that incredible miracle speeding past. It ran by some true compass over field and waste land. It cried its individual ecstasies into the air until the gullies rang. It swerved like a single body, it knew itself, and, lonely, it bunched close in the racing darkness, its individual entities feeling about them the rising night. And so, crying to each other their identity, they passed away out of my view.

I dropped my fistful of earth. I heard it roll inanimate back into the gully at the base of the hill: iron, carbon, the chemicals of life. Like men from those wild tribes who had haunted these hills before me seeking visions, I made my sign to the great darkness. It was not a mocking sign, and I was not mocked. As I walked into my camp late that night, one man, rousing from his blankets beside the fire, asked sleepily, "What did you see?"

"I think, a miracle," I said softly, but I said it to myself. Behind me that vast waste began to glow under the rising moon.

30   I have said that I saw a judgment upon life, and that it was not passed by men. Those who stare at birds in cages or who test minds by their closeness to our own may not care for it. It comes from far away out of my past, in a place of pouring waters and green leaves. I shall never see an episode like it again if I live to be a hundred, nor do I think that one man in a million has ever seen it, because man is an intruder into such silences. The light must be right, and the observer must remain unseen. No man sets up such an experiment. What he sees, he sees by chance.

You may put it that I had come over a mountain, that I had slogged through fern and pine needles for half a long day, and that on the edge of a little glade with one long, crooked branch extending across it, I had sat down to rest with my back against a stump. Through accident I was concealed from the glade, although I could see into it perfectly.

The sun was warm there, and the murmurs of forest life blurred softly away into my sleep. When I awoke, dimly aware of some commotion and outcry in the clearing, the light was slanting down through the pines in such a way that the glade was lit like some vast cathedral. I could see the dust motes of wood pollen in the long shaft of light, and there on the extended branch sat an enormous raven with a red and squirming nestling in his beak.

The sound that awoke me was the outraged cries of the nestling's parents, who flew helplessly in circles about the clearing. The sleek black monster was indifferent to them. He gulped, whetted his beak on the dead branch a moment, and sat still. Up to that point the little tragedy had followed the usual pattern. But suddenly, out of all that area of woodland, a soft sound of complaint began to rise. Into the glade fluttered small birds of half a dozen varieties drawn by the anguished outcries of the tiny parents.

No one dared to attack the raven. But they cried there in some instinctive common misery, the bereaved and the unbereaved. The glade filled with their soft rustling and their cries. They fluttered as though to point their wings at the murderer. There was a dim intangible ethic he had violated, that they knew. He was a bird of death.

35   And he, the murderer, the black bird at the heart of life, sat on there, glistening in the common light, formidable, unmoving, unperturbed, untouchable.

The sighing died. It was then I saw the judgment. It was the judgment of life against death. I will never see it again so forcefully presented. I will never hear it again in notes so tragically prolonged. For in the midst of protest, they forgot the violence. There, in that clearing, the crystal note of a song sparrow lifted hesitantly in the hush. And finally, after painful fluttering, another took the song, and then another, the song passing from one bird to another, doubtfully at first, as though some evil thing were being slowly forgotten. Till suddenly they took heart and sang from many throats joyously together as birds are known to sing. They sang because life is sweet and sunlight beautiful. They sang under the brooding shadow of the raven. In simple truth they had forgotten the raven, for they were the singers of life, and not of death.

I was not of that airy company. My limbs were the heavy limbs of an earthbound creature who could climb mountains, even the mountains of the mind, only by a great effort of will. I knew I had seen a marvel and observed a judgment, but the mind which was my human endowment was sure to question it and to be at me day by day with its heresies until I grew to doubt the meaning of what I had seen. Eventually darkness and subtleties would ring me round once more.

And so it proved until, on the top of a stepladder, I made one more observation upon life. It was cold that autumn evening, and, standing under a suburban street light in a spate of leaves and beginning snow, I was suddenly conscious of some huge and hairy shadows dancing over the pavement. They seemed attached to an odd, globular shape that was magnified above me. There was no mistaking it. I was standing under the shadow of an orb-weaving spider. Gigantically projected against the street, she was about her spinning when everything was going underground. Even her cables were magnified upon the sidewalk and already I was half-entangled in their shadows.

"Good Lord," I thought, "she has found herself a kind of minor sun and is going to upset the course of nature."

40   I procured a ladder from my yard and climbed up to inspect the situation. There she was, the universe running down around her, warmly arranged

among her guy ropes attached to the lamp supports—a great black and yellow embodiment of the life force, not giving up to either frost or stepladders. She ignored me and went on tightening and improving her web.

I stood over her on the ladder, a faint snow touching my cheeks, and surveyed her universe. There were a couple of iridescent green beetle cases turning slowly on a loose strand of web, a fragment of luminescent eye from a moth's wing and a large indeterminable object, perhaps a cicada, that had struggled and been wrapped in silk. There were also little bits and slivers, little red and blue flashes from the scales of anonymous wings that had crashed there.

Some days, I thought, they will be dull and gray and the shine will be out of them; then the dew will polish them again and drops hang on the silk until everything is gleaming and turning in the light. It is like a mind, really, where everything changes but remains, and in the end you have these eaten-out bits of experience like beetle wings.

I stood over her a moment longer, comprehending somewhat reluctantly that her adventure against the great blind forces of winter, her seizure of this warming globe of light, would come to nothing and was hopeless. Nevertheless it brought the birds back into my mind, and that faraway song which had traveled with growing strength around a forest clearing years ago—a kind of heroism, a world where even a spider refuses to lie down and die if a rope can still be spun on to a star. Maybe man himself will fight like this in the end, I thought, slowly realizing that the web and its threatening yellow occupant had been added to some luminous store of experience, shining for a moment in the fogbound reaches of my brain.

The mind, it came to me as I slowly descended the ladder, is a very remarkable thing; it has gotten itself a kind of courage by looking at a spider in a street lamp. Here was something that ought to be passed on to those who will fight our final freezing battle with the void. I thought of setting it down carefully as a message to the future: *In the days of the frost seek a minor sun.*

45   But as I hesitated, it became plain that something was wrong. The marvel was escaping—a sense of bigness beyond man's power to grasp, the essence of life in its great dealings with the universe. It was better, I decided, for the emissaries returning from the wilderness, even if they were merely descending from a stepladder, to record their marvel, not to define its meaning. In that way it would go echoing on through the minds of men, each grasping at that beyond out of which the miracles emerge, and which, once defined, ceases to satisfy the human need for symbols.

In the end I merely made a mental note: One specimen of Epeira observed building a web in a street light. Late autumn and cold for spiders. Cold for men, too. I shivered and left the lamp glowing there in my mind. The last I saw of Epeira she was hauling steadily on a cable. I stepped carefully over her shadow as I walked away.

QUESTIONS FOR DISCUSSION

1. Why does Eiseley believe it is important to enter the wilderness, to remain apart from other humans, in order to experience profound insights and revelations? Do you agree with Eiseley? Explain your answer.

2. What was the "patch of wilderness" that Eiseley encountered in New York City? How does he describe it and what revelation about nature did he have there? What did Eiseley learn about nature from his encounter with the crow? In what ways was this encounter both different from and similar to his previous one with the pigeons?

3. What new, deeper insight into the natural world and its elements does Eiseley gain from his encounter with the flock of warblers in the desert?

4. The essay takes its title from a fourth natural revelation, in which the author feels that a flock of birds is judging an intruder, a bird of prey. Why does Eiseley believe the smaller birds are judging the raven? What evidence does he present for his inference about the birds? Does his inference seem accurate? Do you think Eiseley makes a projection onto the birds of his humanistic values?

5. Eiseley's final revelation is much less dramatic than the others in his essay. Why does Eiseley conclude with the anecdote of the spider? What new meaning does he perceive in the spider's activity?

6. At the end of his essay, Eiseley seems to retreat from some of the meaning he has seen in the spider's act and, presumably, those of the creatures he observed earlier. Why does he feel that it is inappropriate to create meanings to explain natural phenomena? Do you agree with his reasoning here?

CONNECTION

Compare Eiseley's revelations from his observations of birds with Cervantes's observations and insights in "Emplumada." Which author seems the most inclined to project human values onto natural creatures? Whose perspective on the meaning of the life cycle of natural creatures is closest to your own (see page 74)?

IDEAS FOR WRITING

1. Write an essay in response to Eiseley's conclusion. Do you feel that people should or should not refrain from projecting human meaning and values onto nature?

2. Develop a narrative about an observation of nature and a revelation you have had about a living creature. From this experience what did you learn about yourself, your values, and the way you observe, think, and feel?

RELATED WEB SITES

LOREN EISELEY
http://www.geocities.com/Athens/4189/
Find more information on the author, Loren Eiseley, at this URL. Biographical, bibliographical and other relevant topics are provided here at the site, which includes excerpts from some his most powerful work.

NATURE WRITING
http://www.connix.com/~fmusante/nature/nature.htm
This attractive web site offers an answer to the question, "What is nature writing?" It shares an essay "on the themes, history, and character of nature writing over the last 200-plus years," as well as many nature writing links to resources.

David Kerr

Strawberry Creek: A Search for Origins

David Kerr, a longtime resident of Berkeley, California, wrote the following paper for his critical thinking class and published it in a class anthology on nature. In his paper David Kerr uses his own boyhood explorations in an attempt to understand and to define the history and secret pattern of a buried urban creek.

On warm summer days as if there were some great parental conspiracy, my friends and I would be sent out of our respective homes to "get some sun" and "go for a hike and explore nature." The irony of these requests would be that we would very often explore nature without ever getting any sun at all.

Once we decided to trace Strawberry Creek from the flatlands where I lived to its hidden beginnings. This had to be done underground. Our starting point was alongside a road in lower Berkeley (we often called lower Berkeley the flatlands or flats). Here the creek exited a tunnel on its way to the Bay. At an early period in the city's history, those in charge of such things decided to bury all of the creeks in the flatlands in order to build homes there as well as all over downtown. Even though the creeks had been covered over, they still flowed through these now ancient tunnels, perfect kid-size tunnels with small tunnel mouths.

Armed with flashlights, candles, lighters and matches, we entered the tunnel for Strawberry Creek at a small, partially concealed outlet on the side of the road among the bushes. Our plan was to wind our way through the city underground. A big part of the adventure for us was finding out if this was truly the same Strawberry Creek that coursed through the university and Strawberry Canyon. There was no other way of knowing without tracing the creek backwards.

Entering the tunnel we tried to balance ourselves on any flat rocks we could find, some of which were covered with a fine green moss from the occasional flow of water that passed over them. We tried our best to stay dry, something that was to be a losing battle. Inside, we discovered that there was a small dry ledge upon which we could walk. Our strange mixture of lights created long and short dancing shadows on the walls and on the rushing water. The rocks in the creek seemed almost alive as our flashlight beams crossed over them. The whole scene was straight out of some old horror movie, making us all a little nervous.

5   In the tunnel, we discovered after a short while that there were a number of side tunnels. In the hope of finding out what these side tunnels were for, we entered one. There was no flowing water as in the main tunnel; this tunnel was dry. The ground was very smooth and silky with soft ripples like an ancient ocean bed hidden for years. As our steps left the impressions of our tennis shoes, it was like being the first man on the moon. Someone in the group, not being able to resist, argued, "I'm just sure that this has nothing to do with the creek. We're following an old sewer line. Let's turn back before someone decides to flush." I replied, "I don't think so; I'm sure it would smell if that were true."

As we continued on, we could see the roots of trees dangling down above our heads. Leonard observed, "Don't you feel like you're in a cartoon or something?" He grabbed a large root and started to swing around from it. I asked, "What the hell do you think you're doing, Leonard?" He came back with authority, "Trying to pull the tree into the tunnel of course." Well, there was no arguing with that, so we let him swing. This little side tunnel somehow ended up back at the main tunnel; at least we hoped this was the main tunnel. Here it was not so easy to walk as in the side tunnels, because there was flowing water and no dry, silted mud to walk on.

More often than not, as we traversed the tunnel, we had to walk in the creek water because the dry edges had become too small to walk on. As we walked with the creek water rushing over our feet and soaking our shoes, we started making jokes about coming across giant rats or some great albino alligator who would gobble us up. We had heard stories of children bringing back alligators from Florida that end up in the sewers of New York. These alligators supposedly attack sewer workers there; so why not here? Never mind that we are on the other side of the country. Then of course there were the giant mutant rats lurking around the next bend. It had to be true. My friend Leonard also pointed out that in this great exploration of nature, "Strawberry Creek does run through the university." He commented with his best all-knowing voice, "Some careless student has dumped something radioactive into the creek." This without question had given birth to giant mutant rats which were certainly going to eat us for a tasty little snack. We never did get eaten; we did, on the other hand, come to the end of the tunnel at the entrance of the university. At least one mystery was solved: It is the same creek.

Strawberry Creek enters the tunnel at the university around Center and Oxford streets where we had just exited. The creek at this point is surrounded by a small grove of redwoods through which the sun was still shining as we emerged. It was a bit of a shock to see the sun again after having spent the last few hours underground. We were tired and a bit wet; nonetheless, we were only half done in our search for the creek's origins.

As we followed the creek through the university, we wound around buildings and under bridges rather than underground. The creek led us through different groves of trees, some bay laurel, some redwood and some live oak. At a point near the Life Sciences building, there is a calm area that has created a pond. There is an abundance of water life here; it provided a momentary stop in our search. We cupped our hands and tried to scoop up water striders. They raced away the second our hands touched the water, yet always returned (as if to torture us) to where we had placed our hands in the water. Somehow we were never able to capture any at all. After giving up our efforts with the water striders, we followed the creek to the other side of the campus. Here, much to our dismay, we could no longer follow the creek; the tunnel under the stadium was too small for us. Crossing over to the other side of the stadium we tried to pick up Strawberry Creek where it starts before it enters the tunnel. I don't remember whether we ever found that end of the tunnel, but we eventually picked up our journey for the origins of the creek in Strawberry Canyon.

10   As we hiked up the canyon alongside the creek, the creek started to split into different tributaries. We followed one of them, which led us to a fenced area, the botanical gardens for the university. Unable to continue here, we followed a fire trail that this part of the creek had led us to. As we hiked up the trail, we could see another part of the creek continuing up the canyon. This again led us to another part of the botanical gardens fence through which we could pass.

At this point, we gave up our search for the mythical origins of Strawberry Creek, yet we continued on to a part of the canyon called Woodbridge Memorial Grove. When we arrived at this small grove of redwoods with its tilted bay tree from which we, as others have, once hung a rope to swing from, we found our rope had once again been cut away from the tree. The day was gone, so we headed home where dinner awaited.

QUESTIONS FOR DISCUSSION

1. How does David Kerr's essay add to our sense of definition and understanding of Strawberry Creek through the process of exploration? Give examples from the essay of what it taught you about the history, origins, and form of the creek.

2. Kerr writes his essay from the point of view of several children on a nature expedition. How does he capture the voice and typical sense of expression and concerns of children in nature?

3. Kerr uses dialogue in his essay not only to capture the way children speak, but also to communicate some observations about the creek. Give examples of effective uses of dialogue in the essay.
4. Give examples of closely observed, clear description from the essay that adds to your understanding of the creek and its surrounding environment.
5. It could be argued that Kerr's essay has no conclusion; the friends simply give up and go home for supper. Do you consider this an effective ending, or would you rather have seen a more formal conclusion that emphasized Kerr's understanding of the creek? What advice would you have for Kerr in revising his essay?

Lindsey Munro

Dian Fossey and Me

Lindsey Munro wrote the following essay after completing a longer research project on the life of Dian Fossey. An International relations major, Munro is especially interested in environmental and development policy. In her essay, Munro reflects on her response to Dian Fossey's radical perspective on the preservation of wildlife.

JOURNAL

Discuss a person who inspires you. Discuss why you admire the person's values and courage and how he or she has influenced you to build a life that has values that you believe in strongly.

So many of us young people seek a hero. Usually our heroes share our passions and epitomize the kind of people we want to be. As I am concerned about the welfare of wildlife, Dian Fossey is certainly a hero of mine. When Fossey began her field work only 242 gorillas survived in the Virunga mountains; they were dangerously approaching extinction. To save the "gentle giants" Fossey spent 17 years living in the somewhat makeshift Karisoke Research Center she established. Most of these were lonely years, as Fossey was separated from her family and friends back in the United States; she was isolated even from most of the local people who did not live in the high altitudes of the mountain gorillas' habitat. Not only did Fossey sacrifice comfort and companionship high up in the Virungas, she also sacrificed her own safety by fighting for the gorillas' sake against the poachers and corrupt Rwandan government officials. Looking at her life and tragic murder by a still unidentified enemy, I am inspired by the legacy of unlimited courage and devotion that she has left for the world.

Yet Fossey has left a legacy that I cannot wholly accept. Fossey belonged to the school of conservationists that are better called preservationists because of their romantic view of nature. Preservationists believe nature should not be in any way spoiled by the world of humans. Such was the attitude Fossey expressed with her insistence that those students and employees who worked with her gorillas "must remember that the rights of the animal supersede human interests" (Fossey 14). Fossey's inability to compromise her preservationist ideals conflicts with my conservationist view that we must consider different perspectives when trying to save threatened wildlife; most important, we must consider the perspectives of the people who live with the wildlife. Although her commitment truly is inspiring, I cannot agree with Fossey that the needs of all humans must be subordinate to those of wildlife. The issue of wildlife tourism illustrates why my opinion must differ from Fossey's.

Fossey cherished the wild, uncorrupted environment of the Virungas. With every new tourist center built to bring wealthy Westerners to the habitat of the mountain gorillas, she felt the mountains were corrupted by the artificial "civilized" world (22). Conceding that tourism could provide much-needed revenue to Rwanda (241), Fossey still insisted that promotion of tourism was only "theoretical" conservation. "Active conservation" was the only approach that Fossey believed could really save the gorillas from the brink of extinction (242). Fossey believed that active conservation means doing whatever necessary to stop all immediate threats to the gorillas, including "frequent patrols in wildlife areas to destroy poacher equipment and weapons" (242). Such methods need to be "supplemented by longer term projects" such as tourism, indicating that any such efforts to promote a tourist industry were of secondary importance.

Dividing conservation methods between "active" and "theoretical" implies that tourism is of minor importance in the fight to preserve the gorillas, as well as elephants and other wildlife all over Africa. Idealistically I agree that the wildlife ought to come first, and that efforts to save animals in their natural habitat should prevail over all other considerations. The preservationist within me finds the idea of using tours and safaris to profit off the animals distasteful; likewise, I hate to see the pristine mountain world of the gorillas or the savannas of the elephants invaded by gawking, noisy tourists eager to snap some pictures.

5   Yet I cannot help but be realistic. My concern for the marginalized people living with wildlife in places like Rwanda prevents me from staunchly following Fossey's idealistic position. Living in a nice house in a safe, economically advantaged area, it is easy for me to agree that the needs of the animals must be held above all else. However, for a poor African living in an impoverished, unhealthy, and crowded area Fossey's romantic ideals hold little meaning. For example, a campaign by Kenyans protesting the preservationist approach of Kenya's wildlife policy has the slogan, "Stop policies that put more value on elephants than on human beings" (Herman and Moldway 41). Tribal

leader William Ole Ntimama reflects the view of many Africans who argue that the needs of people living with wildlife are ignored, saying, "Our people have always lived alongside the wildlife. Now we hate it" (qtd. in Herman and Moldway 42).

This conflict between preservationist and conservationist approaches to wildlife is occurring throughout Africa today. Conservationists believe wildlife tourism is the best way to help wildlife to pay for themselves. Most Africans do not benefit from living wildlife, and this puts the animals in danger because the Africans will kill them to survive. Elephants trample their crops and gorillas deprive Rwandans of much-needed space for agriculture or cattle grazing, while poaching gives Africans the opportunity to profit from dead animals; consequently gorillas are hunted for their head and hands and African elephants are poached for their ivory.

By making wildlife tourism a viable industry, many conservationists hope to make living animals valuable to Africans. If tourists bring revenue to the underdeveloped areas, the people will benefit economically from conserving the animals rather than killing them. Thus, the wildlife can be protected while simultaneously helping the African people. The idea of making wildlife pay for itself runs contrary to Fossey's preservationist perspective. I, too, find the idea of assigning animals economic value somehow insulting to wildlife, but how can I not support the economic argument with the knowledge that nine out of ten Africans live in absolute poverty and that black Africa has the highest infant mortality rate in the world? How can I consider myself an ethical person if I only try to save wildlife while ignoring the tragic situation of millions of African people? I know that I cannot. Gorilla tours provided the third largest source of desperately needed foreign currency to Rwanda before war broke out in 1994 (Wallace 35). Since I cannot in good conscience adopt Fossey's uncompromising opinions and try to deny the Rwandan people this money that they need, I support tourism as one of the few ways to save both the wildlife and the people who live with it.

After careful consideration I am left with the conclusion that the wildness of wildlife must be made available to the tourism industry so that people will have incentives to keep the animals alive. While this conclusion is disheartening from the perspective of an idealistic preservationist, from the viewpoint of a conservationist who values people as well as wildlife, tourism provides hope that human and animal life can both be saved, each learning from one another, each making some sacrifices to live in harmony.

Knowing there are ways to succeed at the balancing act between the needs of people and the needs of the wildlife encourages me as I struggle to find my own way while also finding inspiration in Fossey's legacy. Compromising ideals is one of the most difficult things a human being must do; I understand why Fossey would not make compromises. I can admire her for never conceding. Most important, her life inspires me to strive to have the same strength as she had to fight for what one believes is right.

WORKS CITED

Fossey, Dian. <u>Gorillas in the Mist</u>. Boston: Houghton Mifflin, 1983.

Herman, Kai, and Milhaly Moldway. "Are Elephants Protected to Death?" <u>World Press Review</u>, April 1995: 41–42. First published in <u>Stein</u>, 19 January 1995.

Wallace, Bruce. "High Above it All: How War Brought Peace to Rwanda's Gorillas." <u>Maclean's</u>, 6 February 1995: 35.

QUESTIONS FOR DISCUSSION

1. Why is Munro inspired by Fossey and yet unable to completely accept the legacy of her work with the gorilla population in Rwanda? How effectively does she explain her position?
2. What is the difference between a preservationist and a conservationist? Do you think that this is a significant distinction?
3. What does Munro consider most important when evaluating a strategy for saving endangered wildlife?
4. How does the issue of wildlife tourism illustrate why Munro disagrees with Fossey's preservationist perspective? What other examples and evidence could she have used to make her argument stronger?

TOPICS FOR RESEARCH AND WRITING

1. Some of the essays in this chapter, such as those by Krakauer and Webster, raise disturbing issues about the presence of humans in pristine natural spots. Do some research and write about the impact on the environment of ecotourism and other forms of recreational uses of the wilderness. Write about your findings with some conclusions about what kind of regulation could make such uses of nature less damaging and intrusive.

2. Develop an ideal program for educating today's children to live in harmony with nature. What emphasis would you put on science and technology? How would you introduce dreams, myths, and imaginative literature? How would you present history, social science, and politics? What books would you assign, and why? Discuss particular projects and field trip experiences that you might have your students complete.

3. Several of the texts in the chapter comment on the importance of the relationship between humans and natural creatures. Do some research into this subject and write an essay that examines several consequences of the severing of the relations between humans and other living beings.

4. The poem by Cervantes and the essays by Eiseley and Mowat examine the way we project human values, fears, and stereotypical beliefs onto animals, at times preventing us from seeing and appreciating them as they are. Do some research into this tendency on the part of humans to "anthropomorphize" living creatures and write an essay in which you evaluate the problems it might cause.

5. The poem and essays in this chapter all reveal a skilled ability to observe nature and its creatures. Using examples from the works in this chapter as well as other nature writing that you have read, write an essay in which you offer the beginning writer advice about improving his or her ability to observe closely and to make an accurate and interesting record of her or his observations of nature.

6. One of the most intriguing aspects of nature is the ceaseless process of change, which features a myriad of births, seeming deaths, transformations and rebirths of living things over fairly short periods of time as well as larger historical changes to the environment. Taking the area where you live or another region with which you are familiar, do some research and then write an essay describing some of the changes in the "natural" and "artificial" landscapes as well as the population of various living creatures that have taken place over the past 50 to 100 years.

7. A number of films have been made that provide powerful images of nature as well as its relation to humanity and human values. Select and view a film that presents a vision of nature; then discuss the vision of the filmmaker. You might select a film from the following list: *Dreams* (Kurosawa*), Never Cry Wolf, Mindwalk, Dances with Wolves, Out of Africa, Gorillas in the Mist, The Horse Whisperer, The Medicine Man,* and *Himalaya.*

Memories 3

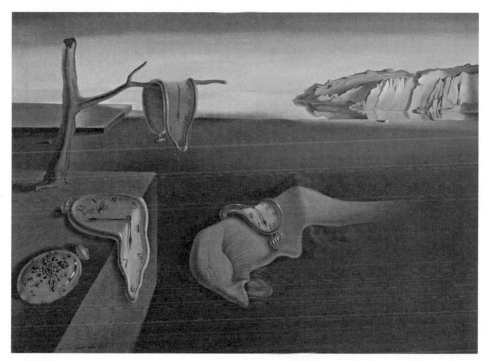

Salvador Dali (1904–1989)
The Persistence of Memory (1931)

Salvador Dali was born and died in Figueres, Spain. Dali was a leader of the international Surrealist movement in the arts; he termed his paintings "hand-painted dream photographs." Dali's *The Persistence of Memory*, with its melting watches giving different times and attacked by voracious ants, seems to suggest that time and memory are extremely subjective realities.

JOURNAL

Write about a memory that you find confusing, strange, and dreamlike.

In the New Age the Daughters of Memory shall become the Daughters of Inspiration.

WILLIAM BLAKE

Nothing can be brought to an end in the unconscious; nothing is past or forgotten.

SIGMUND FREUD

Often I felt as though I was in a trance at my typewriter, that the shape of a particular memory was decided not by my conscious mind but by all that is dark and deep within me, unconscious but present.

BELL HOOKS
Writing Autobiography

NARRATION, MEMORY, AND SELF-AWARENESS

You will read a number of narrative accounts of childhood experiences in this chapter. Narratives serve two important functions for a writer: they can bring about a process of self-discovery, and they are fundamental sources and building blocks of both fiction and nonfiction writing. The brief stories or extended examples that develop, illustrate, and support points made in expository and argumentative essays are among the best resources writers have for presenting ideas in a clear, vivid, and convincing manner.

When you create a narrative, you draw on many inner resources and skills: memories of life experiences, dreams, your imagination, the ability to imitate the voices of others, and the skill required to develop a suspenseful plot that will hold your readers' attention. While not everyone can entertain friends with a natural storytelling ability, most of us can learn how to write a clear and engaging story.

Making Associations

As in other forms of writing, the first phase of narrative writing involves generating ideas and images to write about, experiences that come in part from your past and in part from your imagination that can later be shaped into a story with an overall theme. You can begin as Patricia Hampl does in her first draft of her essay, "Memory and Imagination," with what you think you remember: "When I was seven, my father . . . led me by the hand down a long, unlit corridor in St. Luke's basement, a sort of tunnel that ended in a room full of pianos." Later Hampl rereads her draft and realizes that her efforts to make emotional sense of a rather unpleasant childhood experience have led her to make numerous distortions in the actual facts of the first visit to her future piano teacher. She is willing to keep many of these alterations because they feel emotionally right if not factually so. This marks an important distinction between personal narrative and the kind of close description of nature that we saw in some of the essays in the previous chapter.

How do you find ideas and events for your writing, however, if the only memories you have of your early years are vague or sketchy? Notice the following initial account of a student's childhood in Sacramento: "As a child, I lived for five years on B Street in Sacramento. It was always hot in the summer there." Writing strategies such as drawing, freewriting, invisible writing, brainstorming, and clustering can help you to generate details, images, and ideas associated with a particular time and place in your life. For example, you could start with a significant part of an address and do a cluster or ten minute freewrite around it, letting one detail lead to another: "B Street, hot, barren, dusty, fire hydrant out front turned on in the summer, the ice cream wagon's jingle. . . ." If you follow this process long enough, you will begin to imagine and re-create a number of details you thought you had forgotten, and you will have begun to gather the words, thoughts, and images that you can later shape into an essay.

Focusing and Concentration: The Inner Screen

In developing your narrative it is also important to try to focus on the most significant aspect of your memory. For example, you might visualize a particular room or the backyard of your house on a summer day when something significant happened to you: a fateful accident, a moment of serious conflict, an unexpected gift, a moment of friendship or intimacy. Close your eyes and try to visualize all the objects, colors, forms, people, and expressions associated with that place and a particular time there. Then try to visualize the movements within the scene, as movement in time and space are essential elements of narration. When did certain people arrive and leave? How did they walk? What gestures did they make? What activities did they perform? What did they say to one another? After visualizing and naming specific colors, try to recall other sensations: textures, warmth or coolness, smells, tastes, sounds. Take notes as you begin to remember and imagine sensations, forms, and movements.

Dialogue and Characters

While not all people have vivid auditory memories, including some conversation in your narrative will help bring it to life. Focus on the way each person in your scene speaks; jot down some of the typical brief exchanges that the group could have had, and then try to understand each character more fully through role-playing. Imagine that you have become each person in the scene, one at a time. As you role-play, speak out loud in the voice of each person, then write down a paragraph in which you try to capture their typical concerns and rhythms of speech. Finally, try to construct a conversation between the people in the scene.

Main Idea or Dominant Impression

Now you should be ready to write about the strong ideas or feelings that underlie or dominate your scene. Brainstorm or cluster around key details in your notes. Which emotions does the remembered moment call up for you? What ideas, what "lessons" does it suggest? Develop a statement that you can later clarify and qualify: "That evening was one of waiting and apprehension"; "The morning was a joyful one for my family, yet tinged by regret." Writing this type of dominant impression statement will guide you in adding more details and bits of dialogue and in selecting and ordering your material. A central idea for your narrative will help you to achieve a sense of focus and purpose that will help you to engage your readers' interest; most importantly, it will help you clarify what you have gained from the experience. The process of writing the narrative will contribute to your personal growth and self-awareness.

Drafting and Shaping the Narrative

Using your central idea or dominant impression as a guide in selecting and ordering details and events, write a rapid first draft, including what is relevant from the notes you generated in your preliminary brainstorming. Leave out any details or events that introduce a tone or feeling that conflicts, detracts, or clashes with the one you want to emphasize. Relevant but not particularly interesting events and periods of time do not need to be narrated in detail and can be summed up in a sentence or two: "For hours I played with my dog, waiting eagerly for my father to return from work."

Try to order the events of your narrative to emphasize your main idea as well. Although most writers use a chronological sequence in shaping a narrative, your dominant idea may demand withholding a key event for purposes of suspense or creating a powerful conclusion, as Maya Angelou does with the powerful fantasy in "The Angel of the Candy Counter," included in this chapter. You might also consider the use of flashbacks, beginning perhaps with a brief scene that occurs at the end of the action and then revealing the sequence of events leading up to the initially described event. Any order is acceptable as long as you clarify shifts of time for the reader with transitions and make sure that your order serves the overall purpose of your story. While writing different drafts of your narrative, don't hesitate to experiment with rearranging the parts of the story or essay until you find a clear, comfortable fit between the structure and meaning of your work. This rearrangement process is made much easier if you are revising on a computer, as the cut and paste functions of your word processor make it easy to see how different sequences work. You might try saving different versions of your narrative with different file names, each using a different sequence of events, printing each out and reading them over to see more clearly what may be the advantages of each version.

Revising the Narrative: Point of View, Transition and Style

Point of View and Transition   As you move from the early stages into the final drafting of your narrative, pay special attention to your point of view and style. Your narrative will probably use the first person "I" pronoun, unless you are writing about someone else's experience. As is the case with the essays in this chapter, narrative essays are most frequently told from the perspective of an adult looking back on the past and are known as memoir narratives. Be sure to maintain a consistent point of view. If you decide to move into your mind as a young person, indicate this shift with a clear transition ("Then I thought to myself . . ."), after which you could write in language that is typical of the younger "you."

Notice in Patricia Hampl's narrative of her piano lesson with Sister Olive how effectively she uses transition to indicate the shift of perspective and time that occurs with each next paragraph, beginning with a straightforward account of her trip through the corridor, moving in the second paragraph to a scene setting, extended description of the nun, then getting the father out of the picture in paragraph three "My father left me to discover the piano . . ." She then gets down to the business of the lesson with paragraph four: "But first Sister Olive must do her work," moving through a series of stages until in paragraphs 11 and 12 we find Mary Katherine Reilly's final appraisal of young Hampl (and Hampl's appraisal of her): "Sized me up and found a person ready to be dominated."

Word Choice and Transition   Like descriptions, narratives are seldom written in highly formal, abstract, or generalized language, so try to make your narrative voice down to earth, using common and concrete language as you try to capture the mood and feeling of the events being revealed and the characters involved, as Hampl does in the passages quoted above. In refining the style of your narrative, ask yourself some questions about your word and sentence choices, questions similar to those you use in realistic descriptive writing, but with more emphasis on emotional tonality. For instance, have you used specific, concrete nouns, adjectives, verbs, and adverbs, and clear transitions indicating time lapses and movements in order to capture the emotional feel of the experience you are describing? Always search for the word that best fits your meaning and mood. A thesaurus (paper or online) can be very helpful in finding specific replacements for tired, imprecise, general terms. When it seems as though no word exists to communicate your exact sensory impression or mood, try using literal or figurative comparisons as in descriptive writing, but with an imaginative twist. Always try for originality in your figurative comparisons, as clichés like "she looked like an angel" or "it was as dark as a dungeon" can tarnish the original impression that you are trying to create.

Sentence Patterns   Your writing style is also created through the way you put words together. Thus your sentence patterns are a vital part of your narrative, as they should be in everything you write. Vary your sentence length for emphasis, using short sentences to slow down the action and to emphasize climactic moments. Try, too, to capture the voice rhythms of your characters through your punctuation. Remember that you can use a number of different sentence patterns (simple, compound, complex) as well as different ordering possibilities for the parts of your sentences. Again, in writing on your computer, try saving different versions of key sentences with different strategies for combination and punctuation; print them out and decide which works best in context. Consult your grammar text repeatedly to review the range of sentence patterns and punctuation strategies; experiment to heighten the dramatic effects of your writing.

Writing an engaging narrative is a challenge. It can also be a fulfilling writing experience that will bring you in touch with your past experiences, feelings, values, and identity.

THEMATIC INTRODUCTION: MEMORIES

Self-concept, imagination, dreams, and memories—all are born in child-hood. A person's identity as a writer begins there, too. Through writing about your memories, you will begin to rediscover yourself through places, people, events, and stories that are still alive in your mind. These formative memories may have kindled your dreams while creating the foundation of your self-concept. Because writing is a process of self-discovery that has its roots in childhood, some of the poems, essays, and stories that we have included address issues of childhood identity in relationship to dreams and fantasies, expectations, and goals. In many of the selections that follow, essayists and fiction writers create vividly narrated moments, some positive and some painful, from their earliest remembered experiences. Some of the selections present perspectives on the nature and the effects of memory itself.

The chapter begins with a poem by Li-Young Lee, in "For a New Citizen of These United States." Lee's poem re-creates the double-edged quality of memories for an immigrant, memories that can remind us of painful past experiences and that sometimes interfere with bonding within the new society we have decided to call home. Yet these memories also give life a full-ness and depth that can easily be lost in making the difficult transition into a new culture. Another kind of immigrant, N. Scott Momaday, in his essay "The Way to Rainy Mountain," writes from a Native American perspective about leaving and returning to the place of his ancestors, Rainy Mountain, to visit his grandmother's grave: "Here and there on the dark stones were ancestral names. Looking back once, I saw the mountain and came away."

Our next selection, Patricia Hampl's "Memory and Imagination," also journeys back in to the past, but with a desire to re-create a childhood world in the form of a sustained memoir. Hampl acknowledges the immense role played by the imagination in our efforts to reenter and communicate remembered worlds from the distant past.

The next selections present traumatic, turning point memories of family life. In "The Angel of the Candy Counter," from Maya Angelou's autobiography, *I Know Why the Caged Bird Sings*, the reader comes to understand Angelou's great respect for her grandmother and how a childhood fantasy of revenge helped Angelou to overcome her anger and humiliation at a white dentist's cruel and prejudiced refusal to grant her grandmother's request to pull Maya's aching tooth. The next narrative, "Silent Dancing," by Judith Ortiz Cofer, who was born in Puerto Rico and raised in New Jersey, explores how Cofer's childhood memories of her native culture and relatives continue to have a powerful influence on her understanding and fears about her life in the United States. Memoirist bell hooks also writes about how she looks first to her memories as the cornerstone of her identity, presenting in "Writing Autobiography" ways that writing acts as a way helping us to accept the past through revealing forgotten secrets of pain that emerge through the writing process.

Do our memories represent the deepest truth, or do they sometimes cloud and distort our pasts? In our final professional selection, "Muller Bros. Moving & Storage," acclaimed scientist and writer Stephen Jay Gould reflects on his own relationship with his grandfather as he asks his readers to think about why people continue to cherish memories of the past, despite the fact that these memories often do not represent the truth.

The chapter closes with two student essays, each exploring an issue of memory. In "Enter Dragon," Tin Le, a Vietnamese-American student, presents disturbing memories of a childhood in which his fantasies of power and revenge gave him courage in the face of the prejudice and bullying of his classmates. In contrast, student writer and musician Melissa Burns explores poignant recollections of her grandfather, who died when she was very young, and examines how her memories of him helped to provide her with the motivation to succeed.

Although most people mature and learn to function in the rational world, the dreams and ghosts of their childhoods continue to shape, haunt, and inspire their waking lives. Writing about the past can be one of the best ways to face and come to terms with the ghosts of memory. This type of writing can help us to formulate and construct realistic and positive dreams for the future.

Li-Young Lee

For A New Citizen of These United States

Born in 1957 in Jakarta, Indonesia, Li-Young Lee is from a Christian Chinese family, forced to leave China during the Maoist regime. In 1959, after spending a year as political prisoners, Lee's family fled from Indonesia, traveling in Hong Kong, Macau, and Japan, before finally arriving in America in 1964. Currently residing in Chicago, Lee studied at several universities and taught at the University of Iowa and at Northwestern. He has been featured in Bill Moyers' public television program, Voices of Memory, and has published two collections of his work: Rose (1986) and The City in Which I Love You (1990), as well as a memoir The Winged Seed (1995), and Book of My Nights (2000). Lee's poetry is characterized by a focus on language, memory, and imagination, as can be seen in the poem that follows, "For a New Citizen of These United States," from The City in Which I Love You. Directed to immigrants who feel they must put aside their culture and their memories of homeland, this poem employs the kind of strong emotion and rich sensory imagery that make Lee's poetry so intriguing.

JOURNAL

Write about a time when you "migrated," either from country to country or from one state, city, or neighborhood to another. What did you have to forget? What do you continue to remember from your "past life"?

Forgive me for thinking I saw
the irregular postage stamp of death;
a black moth the size of my left
thumbnail is all I've trapped in the damask.
5 There is no need for alarm. And

there is no need for sadness, if
the rain at the window now reminds you
of nothing; not even of that
parlor, long like a nave, where cloud-shadow,
10 wing-shadow, where father-shadow
continually confused the light. In flight,
leaf throng and, later, soldiers and
flags deepened those windows to submarine.

But you don't remember, I know,
15 so I won't mention that house where Chung hid,
Lin wizened, you languished, and Ming—
Ming hush-hushed us with small song. And since you
don't recall the missionary
bells chiming the hour, or those words whose sounds
20 alone exhaust the heart—*garden,
heaven, amen*—I'll mention none of it.

After all, it was just our life,
merely years in a book of years. It was
1960, and we stood with
25 the other families on a crowded
railroad platform. The trains came, then
the rains, and then we got separated.

And in the interval between
familiar faces, events occurred, which
30 one of us faithfully pencilled
in a day-book bound by a rubber band.

But birds, as you say, fly forward.
So I won't show you letters and the shawl
I've so meaninglessly preserved.
35 And I won't hum along, if you don't, when
our mothers sing *Nights in Shanghai*.
I won't, each Spring, each time I smell lilac,
recall my mother, patiently
stitching money inside my coat lining,
40 if you don't remember your mother
preparing for your own escape.

After all, it was only our
life, our life and its forgetting.

QUESTIONS FOR DISCUSSION

1. From whom does Lee's narrator ask forgiveness and for what reason?
2. What is the significance of the "irregular postage stamp of death"? What has died, or is about to die?
3. Do you think that the speaker is being ironic when he says "there is no need for alarm . . . no need for sadness"? What is there to be sad about?
4. What specific images are provided as examples of forgetting? How are these images and examples representative of the heroic struggle of many immigrants?
5. Why does the poem focus on language, storytelling, and writing as ways of preserving memories? Is the preservation of these records seen by the narrator as a "meaningless" act?
6. Evaluate the ironic message of the poem's final lines: "After all, it was only our/ life, our life and its forgetting." What, if anything, does the poem suggest will be provided for the new citizen in exchange for "our life and its forgetting"?

CONNECTION

Contrast and compare Li-Young Lee's view of the importance of reconciling our feelings towards the past with that of Naomi Remen in her essay "Remembering" in Chapter 5 (see page 262).

IDEAS FOR WRITING

1. Develop your journal entry into a longer narrative essay about the experience of immigration and the impact it has had on your memories of your past.
2. Write an essay designed as a response to the advice given by the speaker in this poem. What advice would you have for a new citizen? For instance, is it possible for the citizen to maintain a former cultural identity and sense of vital memory of the past while still taking an active role in the cultural life of "these United States"?

RELATED WEB SITES

LI-YOUNG LEE

http://www.poets.org/poets/poets.cfm?prmID=309

Presenting a brief history and picture of Li-Young Lee, as well as many interesting links surrounding the author, this site is an excellent entrance into Lee's work and life.

THE POETRY ARCHIVE

http://www.emule.com/poetry/?page=author_list

An educational resource dedicated to poetry will be found at this web site. It includes an online archive of poetry by numerous authors with categories of "what's new," top poems, top authors, a chat forum, and books.

THE IMMIGRANT EXPERIENCE BOOKLIST

http://www.nypl.org/branch/cos/publications/immigrants.html

This New York Public Library web site offers an extensive list of book titles for all age levels written by immigrants who came to America from many different countries of origin.

N. Scott Momaday

The Way to Rainy Mountain

N. Scott Momaday's ancestors came from different Native American tribes; his father was Kiowa and his mother was part Cherokee. Born in 1934, Momaday grew up on his family's reservation in Oklahoma and later moved to New Mexico where his parents worked among the Jemez Indians in the state's high canyon and mountain country. He earned a B.A. from the University of New Mexico (1958) and a Ph.D. in English at Stanford University (1963). Momaday taught at a number of universities, including the University of California at Santa Barbara and at Berkeley, as well as at Stanford. Since 1982, he has been a professor of English at the University of Arizona. His first novel, House Made of Dawn *(1968) was awarded the Pulitzer Prize for fiction. His second work,* The Way to Rainy Mountain *(1969) interweaves stories from Kiowa elders, short historical and personal commentaries, poems and three lyrical essays in retelling Kiowa history. Momaday's more recent work includes* The Ancient Child *(1989) and A Native American Christmas Story (1995). In the section from* The Way to Rainy Mountain *that follows, Momaday develops a compelling symbol of his tribe's historical and spiritual community through the image of the mountain where his grandmother was buried.*

JOURNAL

Write about a natural place that has meaning to you and your family.

A single knoll rises out of the plain in Oklahoma, north and west of the Wichita Range. For my people, the Kiowas, it is an old landmark, and they gave it the name Rainy Mountain. The hardest weather in the world is there. Winter brings blizzards, hot tornadic winds arise in the spring, and in summer the prairie is an anvil's edge. The grass runs brittle and brown, and it cracks beneath your feet. There are green belts along the rivers and creeks, linear groves of hickory and pecan, willow and witch hazel. At a distance in July or August the steaming foliage seems almost to writhe in fire. Great green and yellow grasshoppers are everywhere in the tall grass, popping up like corn to sting the flesh, and tortoises crawl about on the red earth, going nowhere in the plenty of time. Loneliness is an aspect of the land. All things in the plain are isolated; there is no confusion of objects in the eye, but *one* hill or *one* tree or *one* man. To look upon that landscape in the early morning, with the sun at your back, is to lose the sense of proportion. Your imagination comes to life, and this, you think, is where Creation was begun.

I returned to Rainy Mountain in July. My grandmother had died in the spring, and I wanted to be at her grave. She had lived to be very old and at last infirm. Her only living daughter was with her when she died, and I was told that in death her face was that of a child.

I like to think of her as a child. When she was born, the Kiowas were living the last great moment of their history. For more than a hundred years they had controlled the open range from the Smoky Hill River to the Red, from the headwaters of the Canadian to the fork of the Arkansas and Cimarron. In alliance with the Comanches, they had ruled the whole of the southern Plains. War was their sacred business, and they were among the finest horsemen the world has ever known. But warfare for the Kiowas was preeminently a matter of disposition rather than of survival, and they never understood the grim, unrelenting advance of the U.S. Cavalry. When at last, divided and ill-provisioned, they were driven onto the Staked Plains in the cold rains of autumn, they fell into panic. In Palo Duro Canyon they abandoned their crucial stores to pillage and had nothing then but their lives. In order to save themselves, they surrendered to the soldiers at Fort Sill and were imprisoned in the old stone corral that now stands as a military museum. My grandmother was spared the humiliation of those high gray walls by eight or ten years, but she must have known from birth the affliction of defeat, the dark brooding of old warriors.

Her name was Aho, and she belonged to the last culture to evolve in North America. Her forebears came down from the high country in western Montana nearly three centuries ago. They were a mountain people, a mysterious tribe of hunters whose language has never been positively classified in any major group. In the late seventeenth century they began a long migration to the south and east. It was a journey toward the dawn, and it led to a golden age. Along the way the Kiowas were befriended by the Crows, who gave them the culture and religion of the Plains. They acquired horses, and their ancient nomadic spirit was suddenly free of the ground. They acquired Tai-me, the sacred Sun Dance doll, from that moment the object and symbol of their worship, and so shared in the divinity of the sun. Not least, they acquired the sense of destiny, therefore courage and pride. When they entered upon the southern Plains they had been transformed. No longer were they slaves to the simple necessity of survival; they were a lordly and dangerous society of fighters and thieves, hunters and priests of the sun. According to their origin myth, they entered the world through a hollow log. From one point of view, their migration was the fruit of an old prophecy, for indeed they emerged from a sunless world.

5   Although my grandmother lived out her long life in the shadow of Rainy Mountain, the immense landscape of the continental interior lay like memory in her blood. She could tell of the Crows, whom she had never seen, and of the Black Hills, where she had never been. I wanted to see in reality what she had seen more perfectly in the mind's eye, and traveled fifteen hundred miles to begin my pilgrimage.

Yellowstone, it seemed to me, was the top of the world, a region of deep lakes and dark timber, canyons and waterfalls. But, beautiful as it is, one might have the sense of confinement there. The skyline in all directions is close at hand, the high wall of the woods and deep cleavages of shade. There is a perfect freedom in the mountains, but it belongs to the eagle and the elk, the badger and the bear. The Kiowas reckoned their stature by the distance they could see, and they were bent and blind in the wilderness.

Descending eastward, the highland meadows are a stairway to the plain. In July the inland slope of the Rockies is luxuriant with flax and buckwheat, stonecrop and larkspur. The earth unfolds and the limit of the land recedes. Clusters of trees, and animals grazing far in the distance, cause the vision to reach away and wonder to build upon the mind. The sun follows a longer course in the day, and the sky is immense beyond all comparison. The great billowing clouds that sail upon it are the shadows that move upon the grain like water, dividing light. Farther down, in the land of the Crows and Blackfeet, the plain is yellow. Sweet clover takes hold of the hills and bends upon itself to cover and seal the soil. There the Kiowas paused on their way; they had come to the place where they must change their lives. The sun is at home on the plains. Precisely there does it have the certain character of a god. When the Kiowas came to the land of the Crows, they could see the dark lees of the hills at dawn across the Bighorn River, the profusion of light on the grain shelves, the oldest deity ranging after the solstices. Not yet would they veer southward to the caldron of the land that lay below; they must wean their blood from the northern winter and hold the mountains a while longer in their view. They bore Tai-me in procession to the east.

A dark mist lay over the Black Hills, and the land was like iron. At the top of a ridge I caught sight of Devil's Tower upthrust against the gray sky as if in the birth of time the core of the earth had broken through its crust and the motion of the world was begun. There are things in nature that engender an awful quiet in the heart of man; Devil's Tower is one of them. Two centuries ago, because they could not do otherwise, the Kiowas made a legend at the base of the rock. My grandmother said:

Eight children were at play, seven sisters and their brother. Suddenly the boy was struck dumb; he trembled and began to run upon his hands and feet. His fingers became claws, and his body was covered with fur. Directly there was a bear where the boy had been. The sisters were terrified; they ran, and the bear after them. They came to the stump of a great tree, and the tree spoke to them. It bade them climb upon it, and as they did so it began to rise into the air. The bear came to kill them, but they were just beyond its reach. It reared against the tree and scored the bark all around with its claws. The seven sisters were borne into the sky, and they became the stars of the Big Dipper.

From that moment, and so long as the legend lives, the Kiowas have kinsmen in the night sky. Whatever they were in the mountains, they could be no more. However, tenuous their well-being, however much they had suffered and would suffer again, they had found a way out of the wilderness.

10   My grandmother had a reverence for the sun, a holy regard that now is all but gone out of mankind. There was a wariness in her, and an ancient awe. She was a Christian in her later years, but she had come a long way about, and she never forgot her birthright. As a child she had been to the Sun Dances; she had taken part in those annual rites, and by them she had learned the restoration of her people in the presence of Tai-me. She was about seven when the last Kiowa Sun Dance was held in 1887 on the Washita River above Rainy Mountain Creek. The buffalo were gone. In order to consummate the ancient sacrifice—to impale the head of a buffalo bull upon the medicine tree—a delegation of old men journeyed into Texas, there to beg and barter for an animal from the Goodnight herd. She was ten when the Kiowas came together for the last time as a living Sun Dance culture. They could find no buffalo; they had to hang an old hide from the sacred tree. Before the dance could begin, a company of soldiers rode out from Fort Sill under orders to disperse the tribe. Forbidden without cause the essential act of their faith, having seen the wild herds slaughtered and left to rot upon the ground, the Kiowas backed away forever from the medicine tree. That was July 20, 1890, at the great bend of the Washita. My grandmother was there. Without bitterness, and for as long as she lived, she bore a vision of deicide.

Now that I can have her only in memory, I see my grandmother in the several postures that were peculiar to her: standing at the wood stove on a winter morning and turning meat in a great iron skillet; sitting at the south window, bent above her beadwork, and afterwards, when her vision failed, looking down for a long time into the fold of her hands; going out upon a cane, very slowly as she did when the weight of age came upon her; praying. I remember her most often at prayer. She made long, rambling prayers out of suffering and hope, having seen many things. I was never sure that I had the right to hear, so exclusive were they of all mere custom and company. The last time I saw her she prayed standing by the side of her bed at night, naked to the waist, the light of a kerosene lamp moving upon her dark skin. Her long, black hair, always drawn and braided in the day, lay upon her shoulders and against her breasts like a shawl. I do not speak Kiowa, and I never understood her prayers, but there was something inherently sad in the sound, some merest hesitation upon the syllables of sorrow. She began in a high and descending pitch, exhausting her breath to silence; then again and again—and always the same intensity of effort, of something that is, and is not, like urgency in the human voice. Transported so in the dancing light among the shadows of her room, she seemed beyond the reach of time. But that was illusion; I think I knew then that I should not see her again.

Houses are like sentinels in the plain, old keepers of the weather watch. There, in a very little while, wood takes on the appearance of great age. All colors wear soon away in the wind and rain, and then the wood is burned gray and the grain appears and the nails turn red with rust. The windowpanes are black and opaque; you imagine there is nothing within, and indeed there are many ghosts, bones given up to the land. They stand here and there against the sky, and you approach them for a longer time than you expect. They belong in the distance; it is their domain.

Once there was a lot of sound in my grandmother's house, a lot of coming and going, feasting and talk. The summers there were full of excitement and reunion. The Kiowas are a summer people; they abide the cold and keep to themselves, but when the season turns and the land becomes warm and vital they cannot hold still; an old love of going returns upon them. The aged visitors who came to my grandmother's house when I was a child were made of lean and leather, and they bore themselves upright. They wore great back hats and bright ample shirts that shook in the wind. They rubbed fat upon their hair and wound their braids with strips of colored cloth. Some of them painted their faces and carried the scars of old and cherished enmities. They were an old council of warlords, come to remind and be reminded of who they were. Their wives and daughters served them well. The women might indulge themselves; gossip was at once the mark and compensation of their servitude. They made loud and elaborate talk among themselves, full of jest and gesture, fright and false alarm. They went abroad in fringed and flowered shawls, bright beadwork and German silver. They were at home in the kitchen, and they prepared meals that were banquets.

There were frequent prayer meetings, and great nocturnal feasts. When I was a child I played with my cousins outside, where the lamplight fell upon the ground and the singing of the old people rose up around us and carried away into the darkness. There were a lot of good things to eat, a lot of laughter and surprise. And afterwards, when the quiet returned, I lay down with my grandmother and could hear the frogs away by the river and feel the motion of the air.

15 Now there is a funeral silence in the rooms, the endless wake of some final word. The walls have closed in upon my grandmother's house. When I returned to it in mourning, I saw for the first time in my life how small it was. It was late at night, and there was a white moon, nearly full. I sat for a long time on the stone steps by the kitchen door. From there I could see out across the

land; I could see the long row of trees by the creek, the low light upon the rolling plains, and the stars of the Big Dipper. Once I looked at the moon and caught sight of a strange thing. A cricket had perched upon the handrail, only a few inches away from me. My line of vision was such that the creature filled the moon like a fossil. It had gone there, I thought, to live and die, for there, of all places, was its small definition made whole and eternal. A warm wind rose up and purled like the longing within me.

The next morning I awoke at dawn and went out on the dirt road to Rainy Mountain. It was already hot, and the grasshoppers began to fill the air. Still, it was early in the morning, and the birds sang out of the shadows. The long yellow grass on the mountain shone in the bright light, and a scissortail hied above the land. There, where it ought to be, at the end of a long and legendary way, was my grandmother's grave. Here and there on the dark stones were ancestral names. Looking back once, I saw the mountain and came away.

QUESTIONS FOR DISCUSSION

1. Discuss several of the metaphors and similes in the first paragraph that you think are especially vivid. What is the effect of Momaday describing Rainy Mountain before letting his reader know that he is going there to visit his grandmother's grave?
2. "Whatever they were in the mountains, they could be no more." How do the Kiowas maintain their legacy of spiritual power, community, and destiny in the face of conflict and change?
3. How does Momaday re-create the legacy of the Kiowa tribe through his narrative of tribal legends and myths, intertwined with actual events from his grandmother's life? Give examples of the different types of narration or story telling used in the essay.
4. In our culture we sometimes associate "memory" with what we have ourselves experienced directly. Contrast the complex sources of memory involved in Momaday's narrative to more individual memories. Would it be accurate to call this essay an example of tribal memory?
5. Discuss the way Momaday employs contrastive description and narrative in his vivid remembered account of his mother's house. Notice how in the next to last paragraph present-day observations of the house as "funereal" and "small," present the home in a much larger perspective that includes surrounding trees, plains, and the stars. What is the effect of this contrast?
6. Compare the "close up" description of Rainy Mountain at the end of the essay with the distant, framing description at the beginning. What is the emotional affect of this change of perspective? How are the natural world, the Native American community, and immortality linked through the symbol and legend of Rainy Mountain?

CONNECTION

Compare and contrast Momaday's and Gould's use of description and narrative of remembered (yet changed) scenes from their early years. What different purposes do the narrative and description serve in each essay (see page 167)?

IDEAS FOR WRITING

1. Visit a familiar place you remember from your childhood that has changed considerably over the years. Write an essay in which you contrast your memories of the place with your current observations. Consider how much of the "change" has been purely physical, and how much lies within you and your memories.

2. Write about a journey to a place of community and personal significance. After narrating the journey, discuss what you learned on your trip about your heritage, about the importance of physical surroundings to your community, and about yourself.

RELATED WEB SITES

N. SCOTT MOMADAY

http://www.english.uiuc.edu/maps/poets/m_r/momaday/momaday.htm

This web site is devoted to understanding the life and works of authors of modern American poetry. Explore information on Momaday and his Native American culture.

NATIVE AMERICAN AUTHORS

http://www.ipl.org/ref/native/aboutus.html

The Native American Authors web site was created for the Internet Public Library by five graduate students at the University of Michigan to help people around the world learn about and celebrate the achievements, lives and works of these important writers.

Patricia Hampl

Memory and Imagination

Born in St. Paul, Minnesota in 1946, Patricia Hampl is a poet and memoirist who writes about the importance of history, place, and beauty as revealed through memories. She earned her B.A. in English from the University of Minnesota in 1968 and her MFA from the University of Iowa in 1970. Hampl has taught English and creative writing at the University of Minnesota since 1984. In 1992 she was awarded the prestigious MacArthur Award for creative achievement. Hampl is also the author of A Romantic Education *(1981),* Virgin Time *(1992), her account of her quest for religious understanding, and* I Could Tell You Stories: Sojourns in the Land of Memory *(1999). The article that follows, "Memory and Imagination," is included in* The Anatomy of Memory: An Anthology, *edited by James Hofstadter (1996).*

JOURNAL

Write about a memory that has remained important to you although you have never recorded it in words.

When I was seven, my father, who played the violin on Sundays with a nicely tortured flair which we considered artistic, led me by the hand down a long, unlit corridor in St. Luke's School basement, a sort of tunnel that ended in a room full of pianos. There many little girls and a single sad boy were playing truly tortured scales and arpeggios in a mash of troubled sound. My father gave me over to Sister Olive Marie, who did look remarkably like an olive.

Her oily face gleamed as if it had just been rolled out of a can and laid on the white plate of her broad, spotless wimple. She was a small, plump woman; her body and the small window of her face seemed to interpret the entire alphabet of olive: her face was a sallow green olive placed upon the jumbo ripe olive of her black habit. I trusted her instantly and smiled, glad to have my hand placed in the hand of a woman who made sense, who provided the satisfaction of being what she was: an Olive who looked like an Olive.

My father left me to discover the piano with Sister Olive Marie so that one day I would join him in mutually tortured piano-violin duets for the edification of my mother and brother who sat at the table meditatively spooning in the last of their pineapple sherbet until their part was called for: they put down their spoons and clapped while we bowed, while the sweet ice in their bowls melted, while the music melted, and we all melted a little into each other for a moment.

But first Sister Olive must do her work. I was shown middle C, which Sister seemed to think terribly important. I stared at middle C and then glanced away for a second. When my eye returned, middle C was gone, its slim finger lost in the complicated grasp of the keyboard. Sister Olive struck it again, finding it with laughable ease. She emphasized the importance of middle C, its central position, a sort of North Star of sound. I remember thinking, "Middle C is the belly button of the piano," an insight whose originality and accuracy stunned me with pride. For the first time in my life I was astonished by metaphor. I hesitated to tell the kindly Olive for some reason; apparently I understood a true metaphor is a risky business, revealing of the self. In fact, I have never, until this moment of writing it down, told my first metaphor to anyone.

5   Sunlight flooded the room; the pianos, all black, gleamed. Sister Olive, dressed in the colors of the keyboard, gleamed; middle C shimmered with meaning and I resolved never—never—to forget its location: it was the center of the world.

Then Sister Olive, who had had to show me middle C twice but who seemed to have drawn no bad conclusions about me anyway, got up and went to the windows on the opposite wall. She pulled the shades down, one after the other. The sun was too bright, she said. She sneezed as she stood at the windows with the sun shedding its glare over her. She sneezed and sneezed, crazy little convulsive sneezes, one after another, as helpless as if she had the hiccups.

"The sun makes me sneeze," she said when the fit was over and she was back at the piano. This was odd, too odd to grasp in the mind. I associated sneezing with colds, and colds with rain, fog, snow and bad weather. The sun, however, had caused Sister Olive to sneeze in this wild way, Sister Olive who gleamed benignly and who was so certain of the location of the center of the world. The universe wobbled a bit and became unreliable. Things were not, after all, necessarily what they seemed. Appearance deceived. Here was the sun acting totally out of character, hurling this woman into sneezes, a woman so mild that she was named, so it seemed, for a bland object on a relish tray.

I was given a red book, the first Thompson book, and told to play the first piece over and over at one of the black pianos where the other children were crashing away. This, I was told, was called practicing. It sounded alluringly adult, practicing. The piece itself consisted mainly of middle C, and I excelled, thrilled by my savvy at being able to locate that central note amidst the cunning camouflage of all the other white keys before me. Thrilled too by the shiny red book that gleamed, as the pianos did, as Sister Olive did, as my eager eyes probably did. I sat at the formidable machine of the piano and got to know middle C intimately, preparing to be as tortured as I could manage one day soon with my father's violin at my side.

But at the moment Mary Katherine Reilly was at my side, playing something at least two or three lessons more sophisticated than my piece. I believe she even struck a chord. I glanced at her from the peasantry of single notes, shy, ready to pay homage. She turned toward me, stopped playing, and sized me up.

10   Sized me up and found a person ready to be dominated. Without introduction she said, "My grandfather invented the collapsible opera hat."

I nodded, I acquiesced, I was hers. With that little stroke it was decided between us—that she should be the leader, and I the side-kick. My job was admiration. Even when she added, "But he didn't make a penny from it. He didn't have a patent"—even then, I knew and she knew that this was not an admission of powerlessness, but the easy candor of a master, of one who can afford a weakness or two.

With the clairvoyance of all fated relationships based on dominance and submission, it was decided in advance: that when the time came for us to play duets, I should always play second piano, that I should spend my allowance to buy her the Twinkies she craved but was not allowed to have, that finally, I should let her copy from my test paper, and when confronted by our teacher, confess with convincing hysteria that it was I, I who had cheated, who had reached above myself to steal what clearly belonged to the rightful heir of the inventor of the collapsible opera hat. . . .

There must be a reason I remember that little story about my first piano lesson. In fact, it isn't a story, just a moment, the beginning of what could perhaps become a story. For the memoirist, more than for the fiction writer, the story seems already *there*, already accomplished and fully achieved in history ("in reality," as we naively say). For the memoirist, the writing of the story is a matter of transcription.

That, anyway, is the myth. But no memoirist writes for long without experiencing an unsettling disbelief about the reliability of memory, a hunch that memory is not, after all, *just* memory. I don't know why I remembered this fragment about my first piano lesson. I don't, for instance, have a single recollection of my first arithmetic lesson, the first time I studied Latin, the first time my grandmother tried to teach me to knit. Yet these things occurred too, and must have their stories.

15   It is the piano lesson that has trudged forward, clearing the haze of forgetfulness, showing itself bright with detail more than thirty years after the event. I did not choose to remember the piano lesson. It was simply there, like a book that has always been on the shelf, whether I ever read it or not, the binding and title showing as I skim across the contents of my life. On the day I wrote this fragment I happened to take that memory, not some other, from the shelf and paged through it. I found more detail, more event, perhaps a little more entertainment than I had expected, but the memory itself was there from the start. Waiting for me.

Or was it? When I reread what I had written just after I finished it, I realized that I had told a number of lies. I *think* it was my father who took me the first time for my piano lesson—but maybe he only took me to meet my teacher and there was no actual lesson that day. And did I even know then that he played the violin—didn't he take up his violin again much later, as a result of my piano playing, and not the reverse? And is it even remotely accurate to describe as "tortured" the musicianship of a man who began every day by belting out "Oh What a Beautiful Morning" as he shaved?

More: Sister Olive Marie did sneeze in the sun, but was her name Olive? As for her skin tone—I would have sworn it was olive-like; I would have been willing to spend the better part of an afternoon trying to write the exact description of imported Italian or Greek olive her face suggested: I wanted to get it right. But now, were I to write that passage over, it is her intense black eyebrows I would see, for suddenly they seem the central fact of that face, some indicative mark of her serious and patient nature. But the truth is, I don't remember the woman at all. She's a sneeze in the sun and a finger touching middle C. That, at least, is steady and clear.

Worse: I didn't have the Thompson book as my piano text. I'm sure of that because I remember envying children who did have this wonderful book with its pictures of children and animals printed on the pages of music.

As for Mary Katherine Reilly. She didn't even go to grade school with me (and her name isn't Mary Katherine Reilly—but I made that change on purpose). I met her in Girl Scouts and only went to school with her later, in high school. Our relationship was not really one of leader and follower; I played first piano most of the time in duets. She certainly never copied anything from a test paper of mine: she was a better student, and cheating just wasn't a possibility with her. Though her grandfather (or someone in her family) did invent the collapsible opera hat and I remember that she was proud of that fact, she didn't tell me this news as a deft move in a childish power play.

20   So, what was I doing in this brief memoir? Is it simply an example of the curious relation a fiction writer has to the material of her own life? Maybe. That may have some value in itself. But to tell the truth (if anyone still believes me capable of telling the truth), I wasn't writing fiction. I was writing memoir—or was trying to. My desire was to be accurate. I wished to embody the myth of memoir: to write as an act of dutiful transcription.

Yet clearly the work of writing narrative caused me to do something very different from transcription. I am forced to admit that memoir is not a matter of transcription, that memory itself is not a warehouse of finished stories, not a static gallery of framed pictures. I must admit that I invented. Buy why?

Two whys: why did I invent, and then, if a memoirist must inevitably invent rather than transcribe, why do I—why should anybody—write memoir at all?

I must respond to these impertinent questions because they, like the bumper sticker I saw the other day commanding all who read it to QUESTION AUTHORITY, challenge my authority as a memoirist and as a witness.

It still comes as a shock to realize that I don't write about what I know: I write in order to find out what I know. Is it possible to convey to a reader the enormous degree of blankness, confusion, hunch and uncertainty lurking in the act of writing? When I am the reader, not the writer, I too fall into the lovely illusion that the words before me (in a story by Mavis Gallant, an essay by Carol Bly, a memoir by M. F. K. Fisher), which *read* so inevitably, must also have been *written* exactly as they appear, rhythm and cadence, language and syntax, the powerful waves of the sentences laying themselves on the smooth beach of the page one after another faultlessly.

25   But here I sit before a yellow legal pad, and the long page of the preceding two paragraphs is a jumble of crossed-out lines, false starts, confused order. A mess. The mess of my mind trying to find out what it wants to say. This is a writer's frantic, grabby mind, not the poised mind of a reader ready to be edified or entertained.

I sometimes think of the reader as a cat, endlessly fastidious, capable, by turns, of mordant indifference and riveted attention, luxurious, recumbent, and ever poised. Whereas the writer is absolutely a dog, panting and moping, too eager for an affectionate scratch behind the ears, lunging frantically after any old stick thrown in the distance.

The blankness, of a new page never fails to intrigue and terrify me. Sometimes, in fact, I think my habit of writing on long yellow sheets comes from an atavistic fear of the writer's stereotypic "blank white page." At least when I begin writing, my page isn't utterly blank; at least it has a wash of color on it, even if the absence of words must finally be faced on a yellow sheet as truly as on a blank white one. Well, we all have our ways of whistling in the dark.

If I approach writing from memory with the assumption that I know what I wish to say, I assume that intentionality is running the show. Things are not that simple. Or perhaps writing is even more profoundly simple, more telegraphic and immediate in its choices than the grating wheels and chugging engine of logic and rational intention. The heart, the guardian of intuition with its secret, often fearful intentions, is the boss. Its commands are what a writer obeys—often without knowing it. Or, I do.

That's why I'm a strong adherent of the first draft. And why it's worth pausing for a moment to consider what first draft really is. By my lights, the piano lesson memoir is a first draft. That doesn't mean it exists here exactly as I first wrote it. I like to think I've cleaned it up from the first time I put it down on paper. I've cut some adjectives here, toned down the hyperbole there, smoothed a transition, cut a repetition—that sort of housekeeperly tidying-up. But the piece remains a first draft because I haven't yet gotten to know it, haven't given it a chance to tell me anything. For me, writing a first draft is a little like meeting someone for the first time. I come away with a wary acquaintanceship, but the real friendship (if any) and genuine intimacy—that's all down the road. Intimacy with a piece of writing, as with a person, comes from paying attention to the revelations it is capable of giving, not by imposing my own preconceived notions, no matter how well-intentioned they might be.

30   I try to let pretty much anything happen in a first draft. A careful first draft is a failed first draft. That may be why there are so many inaccuracies in the piano lesson memoir: I didn't censor, I didn't judge. I kept moving. But I would not publish this piece as a memoir on its own in its present state. It isn't the "lies" in the piece that give me pause, though a reader has a right to expect a memoir to be as accurate as the writer's memory can make it. No, it isn't the lies themselves that makes the piano lesson memoir a first draft and therefore "unpublishable."

The real trouble: the piece hasn't yet found its subject; it isn't yet about what it wants to be about. Note: what *it* wants, not what I want. The difference has to do with the relation a memoirist—any writer, in fact—has to unconscious or half-known intentions and impulses in composition.

Now that I have the fragment down on paper, I can read this little piece as a mystery which drops clues to the riddle of my feelings, like a culprit who wishes to be apprehended. My narrative self (the culprit who has invented) wishes to be discovered by my reflective self, the self who wants to understand and make sense of a half-remembered story about a nun sneezing in the sun. . . .

We only store in memory images of value. The value may be lost over the passage of time (I was baffled about why I remembered that sneezing nun, for example), but that's the implacable judgment of feeling: *this,* we say somewhere deep within us, is something I'm hanging on to. And of course, often we cleave to things because they possess heavy negative charges. Pain likes to be vivid.

Over time, the value (the feeling) and the stored memory (the image) may become estranged. Memoir seeks a permanent home for feeling and image, a habitation where they can live together in harmony. Naturally, I've had a lot of experiences since I packed away that one from the basement of St. Luke's School; that piano lesson has been effaced by waves of feeling for other moments and episodes. I persist in believing the event has value—after all, I remember it—but in writing the memoir I did not simply relive the experience. Rather, I explored the mysterious relationship between all the images I could round up and the even more impacted feelings that caused me to store the images safely away in memory. Stalking the relationship, seeking the congruence between stored image and hidden emotion—that's the real job of memoir.

35   By writing about the first piano lesson, I've come to know things I could not know otherwise. But I only know these things as a result of reading this first draft. While I was writing, I was following the images, letting the details fill the room of the page and use the furniture as they wished. I was their dutiful servant—or thought I was. In fact, I was the faithful retainer of my hidden feelings which were giving the commands.

I really did feel, for instance, that Mary Katherine Reilly was far superior to me. She was smarter, funnier, more wonderful in every way—that's how I saw it. Our friendship (or she herself) did not require that I become her vassal, yet perhaps in my heart that was something I wanted; I wanted a way to express my feeling of admiration. I suppose I waited until this memoir to begin to find the way.

Just as, in the memoir, I finally possess that red Thompson book with the barking dogs and bleating lambs and winsome children. I couldn't (and still can't) remember what my own music book was, so I grabbed the name and image of the one book I could remember. It was only in reviewing the piece after writing it that I saw my inaccuracy. In pondering this "lie," I came to see what I was up to: I was getting what I wanted. At last.

The truth of many circumstances and episodes in the past emerges for the memoirist through details (the red music book, the fascination with a nun's name and gleaming face), but these details are not merely information, not flat facts. Such details are not allowed to lounge. They must work. Their work is the creation of symbol. But it's more accurate to call it the *recognition* of symbol. For meaning is not "attached" to the detail by the memoirist; meaning is revealed. That's why a first draft is important. Just as the first meeting (good or bad) with someone who later becomes the beloved is important and is often reviewed for signals, meanings, omens and indications.

Now I can look at that music book and see it not only as "a detail," but for what it is, how it *acts*. See it as the small red door leading straight into the dark room of my childhood longing and disappointment. That red book *becomes* the palpable evidence of that longing. In other words, it becomes symbol. There is no symbol, no life-of-the-spirit in the general or the abstract. Yet a writer wishes—indeed all of us wish—to speak about profound matters that are, like it or not, general and abstract. We wish to talk to each other about life and death, about love, despair, loss, and innocence. We sense that in order to live together we must learn to speak of peace, of history, of meaning and values. Those are a few.

40   We seek a means of exchange, a language which will renew these ancient concerns and make them wholly and pulsingly ours. Instinctively, we go to our store of private images and associations for our authority to speak of these weighty issues. We find, in our details and broken and obscured images, the language of symbol. Here memory impulsively reaches out its arms and embraces imagination. That is the resort to invention. It isn't a lie, but an act of necessity, as the innate urge to locate personal truth always is.

All right. Invention is inevitable. But why write memoir? Why not call it fiction and be done with all the hashing about, wondering where memory stops and imagination begins? And if memoir seeks to talk about "the big issues," about history and peace, death and love—why not leave these reflections to those with expert and scholarly knowledge? Why let the common or garden variety memoirist into the club? I'm thinking again of the bumper sticker: why Question Authority?

My answer, of course, is a memoirist's answer. Memoir must be written because each of us must have a created version of the past. Created: that is, real, tangible, made of the stuff of a life lived in place and in history. And the down side of any created thing as well: we must live with a version that attaches us to our limitations, to the inevitable subjectivity of our points of view. We must acquiesce to our experience and our gift to transform experience into meaning and value. You tell me your story, I'll tell you my story.

If we refuse to do the work of creating this personal version of the past, someone else will do it for us. That is a scary political fact. "The struggle of man against power," a character in Milan Kundera's novel *The Book of Laughter and Forgetting* says, "is the struggle of memory against forgetting." He refers to willful political forgetting, the habit of nations and those in power (Question Authority!) to deny the truth of memory in order to disarm moral and ethical power. It's an efficient way of controlling masses of people. It doesn't even require much bloodshed, as long as people are entirely willing to give over their personal memories. Whole histories can be rewritten. As Czeslaw Milosz said in his 1980 Nobel Prize lecture, the number of books published that seek to deny the existence of the Nazi death camps now exceeds one hundred.

What is remembered is what *becomes* reality. If we "forget" Auschwitz, if we "forget" My Lai, what then do we remember? And what is the purpose of our remembering? If we think of memory naively, as a simple story, logged like a documentary in the archive of the mind, we miss its beauty but also its function. The beauty of memory rests in its talent for rendering detail, for paying homage to the senses, its capacity to love the particles of life, the richness and idiosyncrasy of our existence. The function of memory, on the other hand, is intensely personal and surprisingly political.

45   Our capacity to move forward as developing beings rests on a healthy relation with the past. Psychotherapy, that widespread method of mental health,
relies heavily on memory and on the ability to retrieve and organize images
and events from the personal past. We carry our wounds and perhaps even
worse, our capacity to wound, forward with us. If we learn not only to tell our
stories but to listen to what our stories tell us—to write the first draft and then
return for the second draft—we are doing the work of memoir.

Memoir is the intersection of narration and reflection, of story-telling and
essay-writing. It can present its story *and* reflect and consider the meaning of
the story. It is a peculiarly open form, inviting broken and incomplete images,
half-recollected fragments, all the mass (and mess) of detail. It offers to shape
this confusion—and in shaping, of course it necessarily creates a work of art,
not a legal document. But then, even legal documents are only valiant attempts
to consign the truth, the whole truth and nothing but the truth to paper. Even
they remain versions.

Locating touchstones—the red music book, the olive Olive, my father's violin playing—is deeply satisfying. Who knows why? Perhaps we all sense that we
can't grasp the whole truth and nothing but the truth of our experience. Just
can't be done. What can be achieved, however, is a version of its swirling,
changing wholeness. A memoirist must acquiesce to selectivity, like any artist.
The version we dare to write is the only truth, the only relationship we can have
with the past. Refuse to write your life and you have no life. At least, that is the
stern view of the memoirist.

Personal history, logged in memory, is a sort of slide projector flashing images on the wall of the mind. And there's precious little order to the slides in
the rotating carousel. Beyond that confusion, who knows who is running the
projector? A memoirist steps into this darkened room of flashing, unorga-
nized images and stands blinking for a while. Maybe for a long while. But
eventually, as with any attempt to tell a story, it is necessary to put something
first, then something else. And so on, to the end. That's a first draft. Not necessarily the truth, not even *a* truth sometimes, but the first attempt to create a
shape.

The first thing I usually notice at this stage of composition is the appalling
inaccuracy of the piece. Witness my first piano lesson draft. Invention is
screamingly evident in what I intended to be transcription. But here's the further truth: I feel no shame. In fact, it's only now that my interest in the piece
truly quickens. For I can see what isn't there, what is shyly hugging the walls,
hoping not to be seen. I see the filmy shape of the next draft. I see a more
acute version of the episode or—this is more likely—an entirely new piece rising from the ashes of the first attempt.

50   The next draft of the piece would have to be a true re-vision, a new seeing of
the materials of the first draft. Nothing merely cosmetic will do—no rouge buff-
ing up the opening sentence, no glossy adjective to lift a sagging line, nothing
to attempt covering a patch of gray writing. None of that. I can't say for sure,
but my hunch is the revision would lead me to more writing about my father

(why was I so impressed by that ancestral inventor of the collapsible opera hat? Did I feel I had nothing as remarkable in my own background? Did this make me feel inadequate?). I begin to think perhaps Sister Olive is less central to this business than she is in this draft. She is meant to be a moment, not a character.

And so I might proceed, if I were to undertake a new draft of the memoir. I begin to feel a relationship developing between a former self and me.

And, even more compelling, a relationship between an old world and me. Some people think of autobiographical writing as the precious occupation of a particularly self-absorbed person. Maybe, but I don't buy that. True memoir is written in an attempt to find not only a self but a world.

The self-absorption that seems to be the impetus and embarrassment of autobiography turns into (or perhaps always was) a hunger for the world. Actually, it begins as hunger for *a* world, one gone or lost, effaced by time or a more sudden brutality. But in the act of remembering, the personal environment expands, resonates beyond itself, beyond its "subect," into the endless and tragic recollection that is history.

We look at old family photographs in which we stand next to black, boxy Fords and are wearing period costumes, and we do not gaze fascinated because there we are young again, or there we are standing, as we never will again in life, next to our mother. We stare and drift because there we are . . . historical. It is the dress, the black car that dazzle us now and draw us beyond our mother's bright arms which once caught us. We reach into the attractive impersonality of something more significant than ourselves. We write memoir, in other words. We accept the humble position of writing a version rather than "the whole truth."

55   I suppose I write memoir because of the radiance of the past—it draws me back and back to it. Not that the past is beautiful. In our commercial memoir, in history, the death camps *are* back there. In intimate life too, the record is usually pretty mixed. "I could tell you stories . . ." people say and drift off, meaning terrible things have happened to them.

But the past is radiant. It has the light of lived life. A memoirist wishes to touch it. No one owns the past, though typically the first act of new political regimes, whether of the left or the right, is to attempt to re-write history, to grab the past and make it over so the end comes out right. So their power looks inevitable.

No one owns the past, but it is a grave error (another age would have said a grave sin) not to inhabit memory. Sometimes I think it is all we really have. But that may be a trifle melodramatic. At any rate, memory possesses authority for the fearful self in a world where it is necessary to have authority in order to Question Authority.

There may be no more pressing intellectual need in our culture than for people to become sophisticated about the function of memory. The political implications of the loss of memory are obvious. The authority of memory is a personal confirmation of selfhood. To write one's life is to live it twice, and the second living is both spiritual and historical, for a memoir reaches deep within the personality as it seeks its narrative form and also grasps the life-of-the-times as no political treatise can.

Our most ancient metaphor says life is a journey. Memoir is travel writing, then, notes taken along the way, telling how things looked and what thoughts occurred. But I cannot think of the memoirist as a tourist. This is the traveller who goes on foot, living the journey, taking on mountains, enduring deserts, marveling at the lush green places. Moving through it all faithfully, not so much a survivor with a harrowing tale to tell as a pilgrim, seeking, wondering.

QUESTIONS FOR DISCUSSION

1. According to Hampl, what is the role and importance of a first draft? Why shouldn't a first draft be a "careful" draft?
2. Hampl states that the heart is the "boss" of her writing process? What do you think she means in this statement? Is your heart the boss of your writing process? In what ways is Hampl's insight significant to you?
3. Why does Hampl tell the story of Sister Olive and Mary Katherine Reilly only to later show that her memory could not possibly reflect the actual relationship that she had with them? Why is her memory more important to her than what actually happened?
4. How has reading this essay changed your understanding of the relationships among truth, fact, memory, and the imagination of a writer?
5. What does Hampl mean when she says, if you "refuse to write your life . . . you have no life"? What examples does she provide in her memoir to support her claim? Do you agree or disagree with Hampl?
6. Identify several of Hampl's comparisons or metaphors that you found especially effective and persuasive. Explain how these metaphors help to illustrate her meanings.

CONNECTION

Compare Hampl's use of examples of the unreliability of memory to those used by Stephen Jay Gould in his essay in this chapter. What different conclusions do the authors draw from their examples (see page 167)?

IDEAS FOR WRITING

1. Working through several drafts, develop your journal entry above into a memory narrative. Then discuss how writing about the memory has affected you. Has it changed your understanding of the memory's meaning and importance? What did you learn about yourself through writing your memory narrative?
2. Write an essay that explores the differences between memoir and fiction. You should refer to Hampl's essay, but also do some research into the topic and explore the views of other writers to support your claims and conclusions.

RELATED WEB SITES

PATRICIA HAMPL
http://english.cla.umn.edu/faculty/hampl/hampl.htm
Visit this URL for information on Patricia Hampl, including her achievements,
works, background, and central interests. A link to her teaching philosophy is
also included.

MEMOIR WRITING LINKS
http://www.kporterfield.com/memoir/Memoir Links.html
Several links to sites about memoir writing on the web will be found at this
URL as well as links to creativity, journaling, the arts, and healing.

Maya Angelou

The Angel of the Candy Counter

*Maya Angelou (b. 1928) grew up in Stamps, Arkansas, where she spent her child-
hood with her grandmother, a storekeeper and a leader in the African-American community of Stamps. Currently she is a professor of American Studies at Wake Forest
University. Angelou has worked as a dancer, actress, teacher, and screenwriter. She
has lectured all over the world, speaking as an advocate of civil rights. Angelou's most
recent works include* Wouldn't Take Nothing for My Journey Now *(1993),*
Complete Collected Poems *(1994),* The Challenge of Creative Leadership
(1996), Even the Stars Look Lonesome *(1997), and* A Song Flying Up To
Heaven *(2002). Her autobiographical writings reflect on the impact of poverty and
racism on the black community, as well as presenting moments of joy, insight, and
creative expression that sometimes can ease the pain of oppression. In the following
selection excerpted from the first book of her memoir,* I Know Why the Caged Bird
Sings *(1970), Angelou remembers the fierce courage and determination of her
grandmother.*

JOURNAL

Write about a time in your childhood when you retreated into fantasy to help protect yourself from feelings of rejection or loss. How did the fantasy help you to
cope with your situation ?

The Angel of the candy counter had found me out at last, and was exacting
excruciating penance for all the stolen Milky Ways, Mounds, Mr. Goodbars
and Hersheys with Almonds. I had two cavities that were rotten to the gums.
The pain was beyond the bailiwick of crushed aspirins or oil of cloves. Only one

thing could help me, so I prayed earnestly that I'd be allowed to sit under the house and have the building collapse on my left jaw. Since there was no Negro dentist in Stamps, nor doctor either, for that matter, Momma had dealt with previous toothaches by pulling them out (a string tied to the tooth with the other end looped over her fist), pain killers and prayer. In this particular instance the medicine had proved ineffective; there wasn't enough enamel left to hook a string on, and the prayers were being ignored because the Balancing Angel was blocking their passage.

I lived a few days and nights in blinding pain, not so much toying with as seriously considering the idea of jumping in the well, and Momma decided I had to be taken to a dentist. The nearest Negro dentist was in Texarkana, twenty-five miles away, and I was certain that I'd be dead long before we reached half the distance. Momma said we'd go to Dr. Lincoln, right in Stamps, and he'd take care of me. She said he owed her a favor.

I knew that there were a number of whitefolks in town that owed her favors. Bailey and I had seen the books which showed how she had lent money to Blacks and whites alike during the Depression, and most still owed her. But I couldn't aptly remember seeing Dr. Lincoln's name, nor had I ever heard of a Negro's going to him as a patient. However, Momma said we were going, and put water on the stove for our baths. I had never been to a doctor, so she told me that after the bath (which would make my mouth feel better) I had to put on freshly starched and ironed underclothes from inside out. The ache failed to respond to the bath, and I knew then that the pain was more serious than that which anyone had ever suffered.

Before we left the Store, she ordered me to brush my teeth and then wash my mouth with Listerine. The idea of even opening my clamped jaws increased the pain, but upon her explanation that when you go to a doctor you have to clean yourself all over, but most especially the part that's to be examined, I screwed up my courage and unlocked my teeth. The cool air in my mouth and the jarring of my molars dislodged what little remained of my reason. I had frozen to the pain, my family nearly had to tie me down to take the toothbrush away. It was no small effort to get me started on the road to the dentist. Momma spoke to all the passers by, but didn't stop to chat. She explained over her shoulder that we were going to the doctor and she'd "pass the time of day" on our way home.

5   Until we reached the pond the pain was my world, an aura that haloed me for three feet around. Crossing the bridge into whitefolks' country, pieces of sanity pushed themselves forward. I had to stop moaning and start walking straight. The white towel, which was drawn under my chin and tied over my head, had to be arranged. If one was dying, it had to be done in style if the dying took place in whitefolks' part of town.

On the other side of the bridge the ache seemed to lessen as if a whitebreeze blew off the whitefolks and cushioned everything in their neighborhood— including my jaw. The gravel road was smoother, the stones smaller and the tree branches hung down around the path and nearly covered us. If the pain didn't diminish then, the familiar yet strange sights hypnotized me into believing that it had.

But my head continued to throb with the measured insistence of a bass drum, and how could a toothache pass the calaboose, hear the songs of the prisoners, their blues and laughter, and not be changed? How could one or two or even a mouthful of angry tooth roots meet a wagonload of powhitetrash children, endure their idiotic snobbery and not feel less important?

Behind the building which housed the dentist's office ran a small path used by servants and those tradespeople who catered to the butcher and Stamps' one restaurant. Momma and I followed that lane to the backstairs of Dentist Lincoln's office. The sun was bright and gave the day a hard reality as we climbed up the steps to the second floor.

Momma knocked on the back door and a young white girl opened it to show surprise at seeing us there. Momma said she wanted to see Dentist Lincoln and to tell him Annie was there. The girl closed the door firmly. Now the humiliation of hearing Momma describe herself as if she had no last name to the young white girl was equal to the physical pain. It seemed terribly unfair to have a toothache and a headache and have to bear at the same time the heavy burden of Blackness.

10   It was always possible that the teeth would quiet down and maybe drop out of their own accord. Momma said we would wait. We leaned in the harsh sunlight on the shaky railings of the dentist's back porch for over an hour.

He opened the door and looked at Momma. "Well, Annie, what can I do for you?"

He didn't see the towel around my jaw or notice my swollen face.

Momma said, "Dentist Lincoln. It's my grandbaby here. She got two rotten teeth that's giving her a fit."

She waited for him to acknowledge the truth of her statement. He made no comment, orally or facially.

15   "She had this toothache purt' near four days now, and today I said, 'Young lady, you going to the Dentist.'"

"Annie?"

"Yes, sir, Dentist Lincoln."

He was choosing words the way people hunt for shells. "Annie, you know I don't treat nigra, colored people."

"I know, Dentist Lincoln. But this here is just my little grandbaby, and she ain't gone be no trouble to you . . ."

20   "Annie, everybody has a policy. In this world you have to have a policy. Now, my policy is I don't treat colored people."

The sun had baked the oil out of Momma's skin and melted the Vaseline in her hair. She shone greasily as she leaned out of the dentist's shadow.

"Seem like to me, Dentist Lincoln, you might look after her, she ain't nothing but a little mite. And seems like maybe you owe me a favor or two."

He reddened slightly. "Favor or no favor. The money has all been repaid to you and that's the end of it. Sorry, Annie." He had his hand on the doorknob. "Sorry." His voice was a bit kinder on the second "Sorry," as if he really was.

Momma said, "I wouldn't press on you like this for myself but I can't take
No. Not for my grandbaby. When you come to borrow my money you didn't
have to beg. You asked me, and I lent it. Now, it wasn't my policy. I ain't no
moneylender, but you stood to lose this building and I tried to help you out."

25 "It's been paid, and raising your voice won't make me change my mind. My
policy . . ." He let go of the door and stepped nearer Momma. The three of us
were crowded on the small landing. "Annie, my policy is I'd rather stick my
hand in a dog's mouth than in a nigger's."

He had never once looked at me. He turned his back and went through the
door into the cool beyond. Momma backed up inside herself for a few minutes.
I forget everything except her face which was almost a new one to me. She
leaned over and took the doorknob, and in her everyday soft voice she said,
"Sister, go on downstairs. Wait for me. I'll be there directly."

Under the most common of circumstances I knew it did no good to argue
with Momma. So I walked down the steep stairs, afraid to look back and afraid
not to do so. I turned as the door slammed, and she was gone.

Momma walked in that room as if she owned it. She shoved that silly nurse aside with
one hand and strode into the dentist's office. He was sitting in his chair, sharpening his
mean instruments and putting extra sting into his medicines. Her eyes were blazing like
live coals and her arms had doubled themselves in length. He looked up at her just before
she caught him by the collar of his white jacket.

"Stand up when you see a lady, you contemptuous scoundrel." Her tongue had
thinned and the words rolled off well enunciated. Enunciated and sharp like little claps
of thunder.

30 *The dentist had no choice but to stand at R.O.T.C. attention. His head dropped after*
a minute and his voice was humble. "Yes, ma'am, Mrs. Henderson."

"You knave, do you think you acted like a gentleman, speaking to me like that in front
of my granddaughter?" She didn't shake him, although she had the power. She simply
held him upright.

"No, ma'am, Mrs. Henderson."

"No, ma'am, Mrs. Henderson, what?" Then she did give him the tiniest of shakes,
but because of her strength the action set his head and arms to shaking loose on the ends
of his body. He stuttered much worse than Uncle Willie. "No, ma'am. Mrs. Henderson,
I'm sorry."

With just an edge of her disgust showing, Momma slung him back in his dentist's
chair. "Sorry is as sorry does, and you're about the sorriest dentist I ever laid my eyes
on." (She could afford to slip into the vernacular because she had such eloquent com-
mand of English.)

35 *"I didn't ask you to apologize in front of Marguerite, because I don't want her to know*
my power, but I order you, now and herewith. Leave Stamps by sundown."

"Mrs. Henderson, I can't get my equipment . . ." He was shaking terribly now.

"Now, that brings me to my second order. You will never again practice dentistry.
Never! When you get settled in your next place, you will be a veterinarian caring for dogs
with the mange, cats with the cholera and cows with the epizootic. Is that clear?"

The saliva ran down his chin and his eyes filled with tears. "Yes, ma'am. Thank you
for not killing me. Thank you, Mrs. Henderson."

Momma pulled herself back from being ten feet tall with eight-foot arms and said,
"You're welcome for nothing, you varlet, I wouldn't waste a killing on the likes of you."

40   *On her way out she waved her handkerchief at the nurse and turned her into a crocus*
sack of chicken feed.

Momma looked tired when she came down the stairs, but who wouldn't be
tired if they had gone through what she had. She came close to me and adjusted the towel under my jaw (I had forgotten the toothache; I only knew that
she made her hands gentle in order not to awaken the pain). She took my
hand. Her voice never changed. "Come on, Sister."

I reckoned we were going home where she would concoct a brew to eliminate the pain and maybe give me new teeth too. New teeth that would grow
overnight out of my gums. She led me toward the drugstore, which was in the
opposite direction from the Store. "I'm taking you to Dentist Baker in
Texarkana."

I was glad after all that I had bathed and put on Mum and Cashmere Bou-
quet talcum powder. It was a wonderful surprise. My toothache had quieted to
solemn pain, Momma had obliterated the evil white man, and we were going
on a trip to Texarkana, just the two of us.

On the Greyhound she took an inside seat in the back, and I sat beside her.
I was so proud of being her granddaughter and sure that some of her magic
must have come down to me. She asked if I was scared. I only shook my head
and leaned over on her cool brown upper arm. There was no chance that a
dentist, especially a Negro dentist, would dare hurt me then. Not with Momma
there. The trip was uneventful, except that she put her arm around me, which
was very unusual for Momma to do.

45   The dentist showed me the medicine and the needle before he deadened
my gums, but if he hadn't I wouldn't have worried. Momma stood right behind
him. Her arms were folded and she checked on everything he did. The teeth
were extracted and she bought me an ice cream cone from the side window of
a drug counter. The trip back to Stamps was quiet, except that I had to spit into
a very small empty snuff can which she had gotten for me and it was difficult
with the bus humping and jerking on our country roads.

At home, I was given a warm salt solution, and when I washed out my
mouth I showed Bailey the empty holes, where the clotted blood sat like filling in a pie crust. He said I was quite brave, and that was my cue to reveal
our confrontation with the peckerwood dentist and Momma's incredible
powers.

I had to admit that I didn't hear the conversation, but what else could she
have said than what I said she said? What else done? He agreed with my analysis
in a lukewarm way, and I happily (after all, I'd been sick) flounced into the
Store. Momma was preparing our evening meal and Uncle Willie leaned on
the door sill. She gave her version.

"Dentist Lincoln got right uppity. Said he'd rather put his hand in a dog's
mouth. And when I reminded him of the favor, he brushed it off like a piece of
lint. Well, I sent Sister downstairs and went inside. I hadn't never been in his

office before, but I found the door to where he takes out teeth, and him and the nurse was in there thick as thieves. I just stood there till he caught sight of me." Crash bang the pots on the stove. "He jumped just like he was sitting on a pin. He said, 'Annie, I done tole you, I ain't gonna mess around in no niggah's mouth.' I said, 'Somebody's got to do it then,' and he said, 'Take her to Texarkana to the colored dentist' and that's when I said, 'If you paid me my money I could afford to take her.' He said, 'It's all been paid.' I tole him every-thing but the interest had been paid. He said, 'Twasn't no interest.' I said, 'Tis now. I'll take ten dollars as payment in full.' You know, Willie, it wasn't no right thing to do, 'cause I lent that money without thinking about it.

"He tole that little snippity nurse of his'n to give me ten dollars and make me sign a 'paid in full' receipt. She gave it to me and I signed the papers. Even though by rights he was paid up before, I figger, he gonna be that kind of nasty, he gonna have to pay for it."

50   Momma and her son laughed and laughed over the white man's evilness and her retributive sin.

I preferred, much preferred, my version.

QUESTIONS FOR DISCUSSION

1. Why does Momma think the white dentist, Dr. Lincoln, will pull Maya's tooth? What type of woman is Maya's grandmother?
2. Angelou contrasts the physical pain of her toothache with the painful realiza-tion of the doctor's prejudice. Which pain do you think was more hurtful for Maya? Why?
3. Contrast the types of discrimination against Blacks in the South and elsewhere in this country today to the discrimination that Angelou describes in her story.
4. What does Maya learn about Momma on her trip to Dr. Lincoln's?
5. What does Maya's revenge fantasy reveal about her self-concept and self-esteem? Why does she prefer her version of what happened?
6. Point out instances of effective dialogue, dialect, setting, details, and im-agery that help make this an especially moving memoir.

CONNECTION

Compare Angelou's presentation of her painful childhood experience with bell hooks' exploration of her painful childhood memories. How does each writer use the memory in a unique way? How do the memories presented have a different long-term impact on the writers (see page 162)?

IDEAS FOR WRITING

1. Develop your journal entry into an essay that discusses what you have learned from living through situations when you were discriminated against, humiliated, or rejected.

2. Write about a childhood fantasy that helped you to overcome feelings of inadequacy and rejection and develop courage and inner strength. What conclusions can you make? What conclusions about the role that childhood fantasies of power and heroism play in helping children to make the transition into adulthood?

RELATED WEB SITES

MAYA ANGELOU
http://www.empirezine.com/spotlight/maya/maya1.htm
This web site displays pictures, relevant links, biographical, and bibliographical information on Maya Angelou. It also shares excerpts from books, poetry, and has a special discussion forum.

WOMEN WRITERS OF COLOR
http://voices.cla.umn.edu/wwwsites.html
Entitled "Voice from the Gaps," this web site shares information on and work by African-American writers, as well as Asian-American, Arab-American, Latin American, and Native American writers.

Judith Ortiz Cofer

Silent Dancing

Born in Puerto Rico in 1952, Judith Ortiz Cofer came to New Jersey with her family when she was a child. After receiving an M.A. from Florida Atlantic University, Cofer taught English and Spanish at the University of Miami and currently teaches at the University of Georgia. Cofer's works include, Silent Dancing: A Partial Remembrance of a Puerto Rican Childhood *(1990),* Latin Deli: Prose and Poetry *(1993),* Island Like You: Stories of the Barrio *(1995) and* Women In Front of the Sun *(2000). In the following selection from* Silent Dancing, *Cofer recalls memories of a childhood spent in two strikingly different cultures.*

JOURNAL

Write about a photograph or a home movie that evokes memories of your childhood.

We have a home movie of this party. Several times my mother and I have watched it together, and I have asked questions about the silent revellers coming in and out of focus. It is grainy and of short duration but a great visual aid to my first memory of life in Paterson at that time. And it is in color—the only complete scene in color I can recall from those years.

We lived in Puerto Rico until my brother was born in 1954. Soon after, because of economic pressures on our growing family, my father joined the United States Navy. He was assigned to duty on a ship in Brooklyn Yard, New York City—a place of cement and steel that was to be his home base in the States until his retirement more than twenty years later. He left the Island first, tracking down his uncle who lived with his family across the Hudson River, in Paterson, New Jersey. There he found a tiny apartment in a huge apartment building that had once housed Jewish families and was just being transformed into a tenement by Puerto Ricans overflowing from New York City. In 1955 he sent for us. My mother was only twenty years old, I was not quite three, and my brother was a toddler when we arrived at *El Building*, as the place had been christened by its new residents.

My memories of life in Paterson during those first few years are in shades of gray. Maybe I was too young to absorb vivid colors and details, or to discriminate between the slate blue of the winter sky and the darker hues of the snow-bearing clouds, but the single color washes over the whole period. The building we lived in was gray, the streets were gray with slush the first few months of my life there, the coat my father had bought for me was dark in color and too big. It sat heavily on my thin frame.

I do remember the way the heater pipes banged and rattled, startling all of us out of sleep until we got so used to the sound that we automatically either shut it out or raised our voices above the racket. The hiss from the valve punctuated my sleep, which has always been fitful, like a nonhuman presence in the room—the dragon sleeping at the entrance of my childhood. But the pipes were a connection to all the other lives being lived around us. Having come from a house made for a single family back in Puerto Rico—my mother's extended-family home—it was curious to know that strangers lived under our floor and above our heads, and that the heater pipe went through everyone's apartment. (My first spanking in Paterson came as a result of playing tunes on the pipes in my room to see if there would be an answer.) My mother was as new to this concept of beehive life as I was, but had been given strict orders by my father to keep the doors locked, the noise down, ourselves to ourselves.

5 It seems that Father had learned some painful lessons about prejudice while searching for an apartment in Paterson. Not until years later did I hear how much resistance he had encountered with landlords who were panicking at the influx of Latinos into a neighborhood that had been Jewish for a couple of generations. But it was the American phenomenon of ethnic turnover that was changing the urban core of Paterson, and the human flood could not be held back with an accusing finger.

"You Cuban?" the man had asked my father, pointing a finger at his name tag on the Navy uniform—even though my father had the fair skin and light brown hair of his northern Spanish family background and our name is as common in Puerto Rico as Johnson is in the U.S.

"No," my father had answered looking past the finger into his adversary's angry eyes, "I'm Puerto Rican."

"Same shit." And the door closed. My father could have passed as European, but we couldn't. My brother and I both have our mother's black hair and olive skin, and so we lived in El Building and visited our great-uncle and his fair children on the next block. It was their private joke that they were the German branch of the family. Not many years later that area too would be mainly Puerto Rican. It was as if the heart of the city map were being gradually colored in brown—*café-con-leche* brown. Our color.

The movie opens with a sweep of the living room. It is "typical" immigrant Puerto Rican decor for the time: the sofa and chairs are square and hard-looking, upholstered in bright colors (blue and yellow in this instance, and covered in the transparent plastic) that furniture salesmen then were adept at making women buy. The linoleum on the floor is light blue, and if it was subjected to the spike heels as it was in most places, there were dime-sized indentations all over it that cannot be seen in this movie. The room is full of people dressed in mainly two colors: dark suits for the men, red dresses for the women. I have asked my mother why most of the women are in red that night, and she shrugs, "I don't remember. Just a coincidence." She doesn't have my obsession for assigning symbolism to everything.

10   *The three women in red sitting on the couch are my mother, my eighteen-year-old cousin, and her brother's girlfriend. The "novia" is just up from the Island, which is apparent in her body language. She sits up formally, and her dress is carefully pulled over her knees. She is a pretty girl but her posture makes her look insecure, lost in her full skirted red dress which she has carefully tucked around her to make room for my gorgeous cousin, her future sister-in-law. My cousin has grown up in Paterson and is in her last year of high school. She doesn't have a trace of what Puerto Ricans call "la mancha" (literally, the stain: the mark of the new immigrant—something about the posture, the voice, or the humble demeanor making it obvious to everyone that that person has just arrived on the mainland; has not yet acquired the polished look of the city dweller). My cousin is wearing a tight red-sequined cocktail dress. Her brown hair has been lightened with peroxide around the bangs, and she is holding a cigarette very expertly between her fingers, bringing it up to her mouth in a sensuous arc of her arm to her as she talks animatedly with my mother, who has come up to sit between the two women, both only a few years younger than herself. My mother is somewhere halfway between the poles they represent in our culture.*

It became my father's obsession to get out of the barrio, and thus we were never permitted to form bonds with the place or with the people who lived there. Yet the building was a comfort to my mother, who never got over yearning for *la isla*. She felt surrounded by her language: the walls were thin, and voices speaking and arguing in Spanish could be heard all day. *Salsas* blasted out of radios turned on early in the morning and left on for company. Women seemed to cook rice and beans perpetually—the strong aroma of red kidney beans boiling permeated the hallways.

Though Father preferred that we do our grocery shopping at the supermarket when he came home on weekend leaves, my mother insisted that she could cook only with products whose labels she could read, and so, during the week, I accompanied her and my little brother to *La Bodega*—a hole-in-the-wall grocery store across the street from *El Building*. There we squeezed down three narrow aisles jammed with various products. Goya and Libby's—those were the trademarks trusted by her Mamá, and so my mother bought cans of Goya beans, soups and condiments. She bought little cans of Libby's fruit juices for us. And she bought Colgate toothpaste and Palmolive soap. (The final *e* is pronounced in both those products in Spanish, and for many years I believed that they were manufactured on the Island. I remember my surprise at first hearing a commercial on television for the toothpaste in which Colgate rhymed with "ate.") We would linger at La Bodega, for it was there that mother breathed best, taking in the familiar aromas of the foods she knew from Mamá's kitchen, and it was also there that she got to speak to the other women of El Building without violating outright Father's dictates against fraternizing with our neighbors.

But he did his best to make our "assimilation" painless. I can still see him carrying a Christmas tree up several flights of stairs to our apartment, leaving a trail of aromatic pine. He carried it formally, as if it were a flag in a parade. We were the only ones in El Building that I knew of who got presents on both Christmas Day and on *Día de Reyes,* the day when the Three Kings brought gifts to Christ and to Hispanic children.

Our greatest luxury in El Building was having our own television set. It must have been a result of Father's guilty feelings over the isolation he had imposed on us, but we were one of the first families in the barrio to have one. My brother quickly became an avid watcher of Captain Kangaroo and Jungle Jim. I loved all the family series, and by the time I started first grade in school, I could have drawn a map of Middle America as exemplified by the lives of characters in "Father Knows Best," "The Donna Reed Show," "Leave It to Beaver," "My Three Sons," and (my favorite) "Bachelor Father," where John Forsythe treated his adopted teenage daughter like a princess because he was rich and had a Chinese houseboy to do everything for him. Compared to our neighbors in El Building, we were rich. My father's Navy check provided us with financial security and a standard of life that the factory workers envied. The only thing his money could not buy us was a place to live away from the barrio—his greatest wish and Mother's greatest fear.

15   *In the home movie the men are shown next, sitting around a card table set up in one corner of the living room, playing dominoes. The clack of the ivory pieces is a sound familiar. I heard it in many houses on the Island and in many apartments in Paterson. In "Leave It to Beaver," the Cleavers played bridge in every other episode; in my childhood, the men started every social occasion with a hotly debated round of dominoes: the women would sit around and watch, but they never participated in the games.*

Here and there you can see a small child. Children were always brought to parties and, whenever they got sleepy, put to bed in the host's bedrooms. Babysitting was a concept unrecognized by the Puerto Rican women I knew: a responsible mother did not leave her children with any stranger. And in a culture where children are not considered intrusive, there is no need to leave children at home. We went where our mother went.

Of my preschool years I have only impressions: the sharp bite of the wind in December as we walked with our parents towards the brightly lit stores downtown, how I felt like a stuffed doll in my heavy coat, boots and mittens; how good it was to walk into the five-and-dime and sit at the counter drinking hot chocolate.

On Saturdays our whole family would walk downtown to shop at the big department stores on Broadway. Mother bought all our clothes at Penney's and Sears, and she liked to buy her dresses at the women's specialty shops like Lerner's and Diana's. At some point we would go into Woolworth's and sit at the soda fountain to eat.

We never ran into other Latinos at these stores or eating out, and it became clear to me only years later that the women from El Building shopped mainly at other places—stores owned either by other Puerto Ricans, or by Jewish merchants who had philosophically accepted our presence in the city and decided to make us their good customers, if not neighbors and friends. These establishments were located not downtown, but in the blocks around our street, and they were referred to generically as *La Tienda, El Bazar, La Bodega, La Botánica.* Everyone knew what was meant. These were the stores where your face did not turn a clerk to stone, where your money was as green as anyone else's.

20   On New Year's Eve we were dressed up like child models in the Sears catalogue—my brother in a miniature man's suit and bow tie, and I in black patent leather shoes and a frilly dress with several layers of crinolines underneath. My mother wore a bright red dress that night, I remember, and spike heels; her long black hair hung to her waist. Father, who usually wore his Navy uniform during his short visits home, had put on a dark civilian suit for the occasion: we had been invited to his uncle's house for a big celebration. Everyone was excited because my mother's brother, Hernán—a bachelor who could indulge himself in such luxuries—had bought a movie camera which he would be trying out that night.

Even the home movie cannot fill in the sensory details such a gathering left imprinted in a child's brain. The thick sweetness of women's perfume mixing with the ever-present smells of food cooking in the kitchen: meat and plantain *pasteles,* the ubiquitous rice dish made special with pigeon peas—*gandules*—and seasoned with the precious *sofrito* sent up from the island by somebody's mother or smuggled in by a recent traveler. *Sofrito* was one of the items that women hoarded, since it was hardly ever in stock at La Bodega. It was the flavor of Puerto Rico.

The men drank Palo Viejo rum and some of the younger ones got weepy. The first time I saw a grown man cry was at a New Year's Eve party. He had been reminded of his mother by the smells in the kitchen. But what I remember most were the boiled *pasteles*—boiled plantain or yucca rectangles stuffed with corned beef or other meats, olives, and many other savory ingredients, all wrapped in banana leaves. Everyone had to fish one out with a fork. There was always a "trick" pastel—one without stuffing—and whoever got that one was the "New Year's Fool."

There was also the music. Long-playing albums were treated like precious china in these homes. Mexican recordings were popular, but the songs that brought tears to my mother's eyes were sung by the melancholic Daniel Santos, whose life as a drug addict was the stuff of legend. Felipe Rodríguez was a particular favorite of couples. He sang about faithless women and broken-hearted men. There is a snatch of a lyric that has stuck in my mind like a needle on a worn groove: "De piedra ha de ser mi cama, de piedra la cabecera . . . la mujer que a mí me quiera . . . ha de quererme de veras. Ay, Ay, corazón, ¿por qué no amas . . . ?" I must have heard it a thousand times since the idea of a bed made of stone, and its connection to love, first troubled me with its disturbing images.

The five-minute home movie ends with people dancing in a circle. The creative filmmaker must have asked them to do that so that they could file past him. It is both comical and sad to watch silent dancing. Since there is no justification for the absurd movements that music provides for some of us, people appear frantic, their faces embarrassingly intense. It's as if you were watching sex. Yet for years, I've had dreams in the form of this home movie. In a recurring scene, familiar faces push themselves forward into my mind's eye, plastering their features into distorted close-ups. And I'm asking them: "Who is she? Who is the woman I don't recognize? Is she an aunt? Somebody's wife? Tell me who she is. Tell me who these people are."

25 "No, see the beauty mark on her cheek as big as a hill on the lunar landscape of her face—well, that runs in the family. The women on your father's side of the family wrinkle early; it's the price they pay for that fair skin. The young girl with the green stain on her wedding dress is *La Novia*—just up from the island. See, she lowers her eyes as she approaches the camera like she's supposed to. Decent girls never look you directly in the face. *Humilde*, humble, a girl should express humility in all her actions. She will make a good wife for your cousin. He should consider himself lucky to have met her only weeks after she arrived here. If he married her quickly, she will make him a good Puerto Rican-style wife; but if he waits too long, she will be corrupted by the city, just like your cousin there."

"She means me. I do what I want. This is not some primitive island I live on. Do they expect me to wear a black *mantilla* on my head and go to mass every day? Not me. I'm an American woman and I will do as I please. I can type faster than anyone in my senior class at Central High, and I'm going to be a secretary to a lawyer when I graduate. I can pass for an American girl anywhere—I've tried it—at least for Italian, anyway. I never speak Spanish in public. I hate these parties, but I wanted the dress. I look better than any of these *humildes* here. My life is going to be different. I have an American boyfriend. He is older and has a car. My parents don't know it, but I sneak out of the house late at night sometimes to be with him. If I marry him, even my name will be American. I hate rice and beans. It's what makes these women fat."

"Your *prima* is pregnant by that man she's been sneaking around with. Would I lie to you? I'm your great-uncle's common-law wife—the one he abandoned on the island to marry your cousin's mother. I was not invited to this party, but I came anyway. I came to tell you that story about your cousin that you've always wanted to hear. Remember that comment your mother made to a neighbor that has always haunted you? The only thing you heard was your cousin's name and then you saw your mother pick up your doll from the couch and say: 'It was as big as this doll when they flushed it down the toilet.' This image has bothered you for years, hasn't it? You had nightmares about babies being flushed down the toilet, and you wondered why anyone would do such a horrible thing. You didn't dare ask your mother about it. She would only tell you that you had not heard her right and yell at you for listening to adult conversations. But later, when you were old enough to know about abortions, you suspected. I am here to tell you that you were right. Your cousin was growing an *Americanito* in her belly when this movie was made. Soon after she put something long and pointy into her pretty self, thinking maybe she could get rid of the problem before breakfast and still make it to her first class at the high school. Well, Niña, her screams could be heard downtown. Your aunt, her Mamá, who had been a midwife on the Island, managed to pull the little thing out. Yes, they probably flushed it down the toilet, what else could they do with it—give it a Christian burial in a little white casket with blue bows and ribbons? Nobody wanted that baby— least of all the father, a teacher at her school with a house in West Paterson that he was filling with real children, and a wife who was a natural blond.

"Girl, the scandal sent your uncle back to the bottle. And guess where your cousin ended up? Irony of ironies. She was sent to a village in Puerto Rico to live with a relative on her mother's side: a place so far away from civilization that you have to ride a mule to reach it. A real change in scenery. She found a man there. Women like that cannot live without male company. But believe me, the men in Puerto Rico know how to put a saddle on a woman like her. *La Gringa,* they call her. ha, ha. ha. *La Gringa* is what she always wanted to be . . ."

The old woman's mouth becomes a cavernous black hole I fall into. And as I fall, I can feel the reverberations of her laughter. I hear the echoes of her last mocking words: *La Gringa, La Gringa!* And the conga line keeps moving silently past me. There is no music in my dream for the dancers.

30   When Odysseus visits Hades asking to see the spirit of his mother, he makes an offering of sacrificial blood, but since all of the souls crave an audience with the living, he has to listen to many of them before he can ask questions. I, too, have to hear the dead and the forgotten speak in my dream. Those who are still part of my life remain silent, going around and around in their dance. The others keep pressing their faces forward to say things about the past.

My father's uncle is last in line. He is dying of alcoholism, shrunken and shriveled like a monkey, his face is a mass of wrinkles and broken arteries. As he comes closer I realize that in his features I can see my whole family. If you were to stretch that rubbery flesh, you could find my father's face, and deep within *that* face—mine. I don't want to look into those eyes ringed in purple. In a few years he will retreat into silence, and take a long, long time to die. *Move back, Tío,* I tell him. *I don't want to hear what you have to say. Give the dancers room to move, soon it will be midnight. Who is the New Year's Fool this time?*

QUESTIONS FOR DISCUSSION

1. Which cultural and lifestyle differences affect Cofer most strikingly when she first arrived in Paterson? What prejudice does her family encounter there?
2. What do the television programs that she watches teach Cofer about American family life and how to adapt to it?
3. How do Cofer's father and mother relate differently to their neighborhood environment? With whose values does Cofer identify?
4. How does Cofer respond to the La Gringa story? Why does she respond in this way? What dream continues to haunt Cofer?
5. What dreamlike images and symbols does Cofer use in her narrative? How do these images contribute to the story and its power?
6. Interpret the meaning of the title, "Silent Dancing." Why is the dancing "silent"?

CONNECTION

Compare and contrast Cofer's and Li-Young Lee's ways of adjusting to a new life in America and dealing with memories of the culture each left behind (see page 128).

IDEAS FOR WRITING

1. Write an essay in which you discuss a conflict that you or a close friend experienced because you or your friend was not a member of the dominant cultural group in your community. What did you learn from this conflict and how did it help shape your perceptions and expectations of the world?
2. Develop your journal entry into an essay. You might discuss a series of photographs or two or three films or videos made over a period of years. What do these images reveal to you about you and your family's evolving values and concerns?

RELATED WEB SITES

JUDITH ORTIZ COFER
http://parallel.park.uga.edu/~jcofer/
Judith Ortiz Cofer's personal web site includes a short biography as well as several interesting links to other sites that feature her work, life, and interviews.

PUERTO RICANS
http://lab2.cc.wmich.edu/mgeasler/fcs568/rican/
This web site from Western Michigan University features extensive information on the Puerto Rican culture and immigrant experience in America. It includes information on racism and prejudice against Puerto Ricans, child rearing practices, religious practices, family structure, cultural values, and annotated related links.

bell hooks

Writing Autobiography

Gloria Watkins (b. 1952) uses the pen name bell hooks for her writing. She earned a Ph.D. at Stanford University and has taught English and African-American Literature at City University of New York, Yale University, and Oberlin College in Ohio. She has written many books and essay collections including Ain't I a Woman *(1981),* Talking Back, Thinking Feminist, Thinking Black *(1989),* Yearning: Race, Gender, and Cultural Politics *(1990),* Bone Black *(1996),* All About Love: New Visions *(2000), and* Communion *(2002). In writing about cultural and gender issues, hooks always reflects deeply on her own experiences. As you read the following selection from* Talking Back, *notice how hooks emphasizes the role that pain and memory play in the writing process, as well as how writing can be a healing experience.*

JOURNAL

Discuss why it is difficult for you to write about childhood memories, especially those that were very intense. Or write about an intense childhood memory that you have never explored in writing.

To me, telling the story of my growing up years was intimately connected with the longing to kill the self I was without really having to die. I wanted to kill that self in writing. Once that self was gone—out of my life forever—I could more easily become the me of me. It was clearly the Gloria Jean of my tormented and anguished childhood that I wanted to be rid of, the girl who was always wrong, always punished, always subjected to some humiliation or other, always crying, the girl who was to end up in a mental institution because she could not be anything but crazy, or so they told her. She was the girl who sat a hot iron on her arm pleading with them to leave her alone, the girl who wore her scar as a brand marking her madness. Even now I can hear the voices of my sisters saying "mama make Gloria stop crying." By writing the autobiography, it was not just this Gloria I would be rid of, but the past that had a hold on me, that kept me from the present. I wanted not to forget the past but to break its hold. This death in writing was to be liberatory.

Until I began to try and write an autobiography, I thought that it would be a simple task this telling of one's story. And yet I tried year after year, never writing more than a few pages. My inability to write out the story I interpreted as an indication that I was not ready to let go of the past, that I was not ready to be fully in the present. Psychologically, I considered the possibility that I had become attached to the wounds and sorrows of my childhood, that I held to them in a manner that blocked my efforts to be self-realized, whole, to be healed. A key message in Toni Cade Bambara's novel *The Salteaters,* which tells the story of Velma's suicide attempt, her breakdown, is expressed when the healer asks her "are you sure sweetheart, that you want to be well?"

There was very clearly something blocking my ability to tell my story. Perhaps it was remembered scoldings and punishments when mama heard me saying something to a friend or stranger that she did not think should be said. Secrecy and silence—these were central issues. Secrecy about family, about what went on in the domestic household was a bond between us—was part of what made us family. There was a dread one felt about breaking that bond. And yet I could not grow inside the atmosphere of secrecy that had pervaded our lives and the lives of other families about us. Strange that I had always challenged the secrecy, always let something slip that should not be known growing up, yet as a writer staring into the solitary space of paper, I was bound, trapped in the fear that a bond is lost or broken in the telling. I did not want to be the traitor, the teller of family secrets— and yet I wanted to be a writer. Surely, I told myself, I could write a purely imaginative work—a work that would not hint at personal private realities. And so I tried. But always there were the intruding traces, those elements of real life however disguised. Claiming the freedom to grow as an imaginative writer was connected for me with having the courage to open, to be able to tell the truth of one's life as I had experienced it in writing. To talk about one's life—that I could do. To write about it, to leave a trace—that was frightening.

The longer it took me to begin the process of writing autobiography, the further removed from those memories I was becoming. Each year, a memory seemed less and less clear. I wanted not to lose the vividness, the recall and felt an urgent need to begin the work and complete it. Yet I could not begin even though I had begun to confront some of the reasons I was blocked, as I am blocked just now in writing this piece because I am afraid to express in writing the experience that served as a catalyst for that block to move.

5   I had met a young black man. We were having an affair. It is important that he was black. He was in some mysterious way a link to this past that I had been struggling to grapple with, to name in writing. With him I remembered incidents, moments of the past that I had completely suppressed. It was as though there was something about the passion of contact that was hypnotic, that enabled me to drop barriers and thus enter fully, rather reenter those past experiences. A key aspect seemed to be the way he smelled, the combined odors of cigarettes, occasionally alcohol, and his body smells. I thought often of the phrase "scent of memory," for it was those smells that carried me back. And there were specific occasions when it was very evident that the experience of being in his company was the catalyst for this remembering.

Two specific incidents come to mind. One day in the middle of the afternoon we met at his place. We were drinking cognac and dancing to music from the radio. He was smoking cigarettes (not only do I not smoke, but I usually make an effort to avoid smoke). As we held each other dancing those mingled odors of alcohol, sweat, and cigarettes led me to say, quite without thinking about it, "Uncle Pete." It was not that I had forgotten Uncle Pete. It was more that I had forgotten the childhood experience of meeting him. He drank often, smoked cigarettes, and always on the few occasions that we met him, he held us children in tight embraces. It was the memory of those embraces—of the way I hated and longed to resist them—that I recalled.

Another day we went to a favorite park to feed ducks and parked the car in front of tall bushes. As we were sitting there, we suddenly heard the sound of an oncoming train—a sound which startled me so that it evoked another long-suppressed memory: that of crossing the train tracks in my father's car. I recalled an incident where the car stopped on the tracks and my father left us sitting there while he raised the hood of the car and worked to repair it. This is an incident that I am not certain actually happened. As a child, I had been terrified of just such an incident occurring, perhaps so terrified that it played itself out in my mind as though it had happened. These are just two ways this encounter acted as a catalyst breaking down barriers enabling me to finally write this long-desired autobiography of my childhood.

Each day I sat at the typewriter and different memories were written about in short vignettes. They came in a rush, as though they were a sudden thunderstorm. They came in a surreal, dreamlike style which made me cease to think of them as strictly autobiographical because it seemed that myth, dream, and reality had merged. There were many incidents that I would talk about with my siblings to see if they recalled them. Often we remembered together a general outline of an incident but the details were different for us. This fact was a constant reminder of the limitations of autobiography, of the extent to which autobiography is a very personal storytelling—a unique recounting of events not so much as they had happened but as we remember and invent them. One memory that I would have sworn was "the truth and nothing but the truth" concerned a wagon that my brother and I shared as a child. I remembered that we played with this toy only at my grandfather's house, that we shared it, that I would ride it and my brother would push me. Yet one facet of the memory was puzzling, I remembered always returning home with bruises or scratches from this toy. When I called my mother, she said there had never been any wagon, that we had shared a red wheelbarrow, that it had always been at my grandfather's house because there were sidewalks on that part of town. We lived in the hills where there were no sidewalks. Again I was compelled to face the fiction that is a part of all retelling, remembering. I began to think of the work I was doing as both fiction and autobiography. It seemed to fall in the category of writing that Audre Lorde, in her autobiographically-based work *Zami,* calls bio-mythography. As I wrote, I felt that I was not as concerned with accuracy of detail as I was with evoking in writing the state of mind, the spirit of a particular moment.

The longing to tell one's story and the process of telling is symbolically a gesture of longing to recover the past in such a way that one experiences both a sense of reunion and a sense of release. It was the longing for release that compelled the writing but concurrently it was the joy of reunion that enabled me to see that the act of writing one's autobiography is a way to find again that aspect of self and experience that may no longer be an actual part of one's life but is a living memory shaping and informing the present. Autobiographical writing was a way for me to evoke the particular experience of growing up southern and black in segregated communities. It was a way to recapture the richness of southern black culture. The need to remember and hold to the legacy of that experience and what it taught me has been all the more important since I have since lived in predominately white communities and taught at predominately white colleges. Black southern folk experience was the foundation of the life around me when I was a child; that experience no longer exists in many places where it was once all of life that we knew. Capitalism, upward mobility, assimilation of other values have all led to rapid disintegration of black folk experience or in some cases the gradual wearing away of that experience.

Within the world of my childhood, we held onto the legacy of a distinct black culture by listening to the elders tell their stories. Autobiography was experienced most actively in the art of telling one's story. I can recall sitting at Baba's (my grandmother on my mother's side) at 1200 Broad Street—listening to people come and recount their life experience. In those days, whenever I brought a playmate to my grandmother's house, Baba would want a brief outline of their autobiography before we would begin playing. She wanted not only to know who their people were but what their values were. It was sometimes an awesome and terrifying experience to stand answering these questions or witness another playmate being subjected to the process and yet this was the way we would come to know our own and one another's family history. It is the absence of such a tradition in my adult life that makes the written narrative of my girlhood all the more important. As the years pass and these glorious memories grow much more vague, there will remain the clarity contained within the written words.

Conceptually, the autobiography was framed in the manner of a hope chest. I remembered my mother's hope chest, with its wonderful odor of cedar and thought about her taking the most precious items and placing them there for safekeeping. Certain memories were for me a similar treasure. I wanted to place them somewhere for safekeeping. An autobiographical narrative seemed an appropriate place. Each particular incident, encounter, experience had its own story, sometimes told from the first person, sometimes told from the third person. Often I felt as though I was in a trance at my typewriter, that the shape of a particular memory was decided not by my conscious mind but by all that is dark and deep within me, unconscious but present. It was the act of making it present, bringing it into the open, so to speak, that was liberating.

From the perspective of trying to understand my psyche, it was also interesting to read the narrative in its entirety after I had completed the work. It had not occurred to me that bringing one's past, one's memories together in a complete narrative would allow one to view them from a different perspective, not as singular isolated events but as part of a continuum. Reading the completed manuscript, I felt as though I had an overview not so much of my childhood but of those experiences that were deeply imprinted in my consciousness. Significantly, that which was absent, left out, not included also was important. I was shocked to find at the end of my narrative that there were few incidents I recalled that involved my five sisters. Most of the incidents with siblings were with me and my brother. There was a sense of alienation from my sisters present in childhood, a sense of estrangement. This was reflected in the narrative. Another aspect of the completed manuscript that is interesting to me is the way in which the incidents describing adult men suggest that I feared them intensely, with the exception of my grandfather and a few old men. Writing the autobiographical narrative enabled me to look at my past from a different perspective and to use this knowledge as a means of self-growth and change in a practical way.

In the end I did not feel as though I had killed the Gloria of my childhood. Instead I had rescued her. She was no longer the enemy within, the little girl who had to be annihilated for the woman to come into being. In writing about her, I reclaimed that part of myself I had long ago rejected, left uncared for, just as she had often felt alone and uncared for as a child. Remembering was part of a cycle of reunion, a joining of fragments, "the bits and pieces of my heart" that the narrative made whole again.

QUESTIONS FOR DISCUSSION

1. "To me, telling the story of my growing up years was intimately connected with the longing to kill the self I was without really having to die." What was your initial response to hooks's opening sentence? After reading the entire essay, go back and reinterpret the meaning of the statement.
2. Why is it difficult for hooks to write her autobiography? What helps her to get beyond her writer's block? Do you think her technique might help you in your own writing? Why or why not?
3. How does hooks experience the recollection of her memories? What specific events, sensations, and images in the present helped her to recall past memories? Have you experienced the recollection of memories in similar ways? What helps you to get in touch with your memories?
4. Why does hooks believe that autobiography involves invention and imagination as well as the reporting of events? Do you agree with her? Why or why not?
5. "Often I felt as though I was in a trance at my typewriter, that the shape of a particular memory was decided not by my conscious mind but by all that is dark and deep within me, unconscious but present," hooks writes. Have you ever experienced writing in this way? Explain.
6. Hooks describes the influence that the legacy of African-American oral storytelling had on her ability to frame her past experiences in writing. Was there a similar type of legacy in your own family? If so, do you think that you could draw on it as a source for your writing?

CONNECTION

Compare bell hooks' discussion of the reasons for the distortion and gaps in her memories to Stephen Jay Gould's discussion of his insights into his own childhood memories (see below).

IDEAS FOR WRITING

1. Write about an incident from your past about which you still have mixed feelings, a part of the past you still don't quite understand or to which you don't yet feel reconciled. (If it is relevant, compare your experiences of self-understanding with those that hooks experienced in writing her autobiography.) How did your feelings toward the material you were writing about change in the course of doing the writing? What did you learn about the event and yourself in the writing process?

2. Hooks discusses her writer's block and how she works through it. Develop an essay that explores the topic of writer's block. Do some research on the Internet and then present some strategies for overcoming the problem of writer's block that have worked for you or other writers.

RELATED WEB SITES

bell hooks

http://www.education.miami.edu/ep/contemporaryed/Bell_Hooks/bell_hooks.html

This site provides historical and bibliographical information on bell hooks. It also shares links to other useful sites surrounding hooks and interviews with her.

WRITING TO HEAL, WRITING TO GROW

http://www.writingtoheal.com/aboutwth.htm

This web site shares information about writing as a way of healing based on research that shows the positive results of this powerful approach. Additionally, it offers writing courses to examine and understand life's events, and includes other relevant links.

Stephen Jay Gould

Muller Bros. Moving & Storage

A long-time professor of biology, geology, and the history of science at Harvard University, Stephen Jay Gould (b. 1941–2002) is well known for his views on evolution, creationism, and race. He is widely read by thinkers in many different disciplines as his works often point out relationships between scientific and humanistic thought, making technical subjects understandable to nonscientific readers. Gould was the recipient of a number of distinguished awards, including grants from the National Science Foundation and the MacArthur Foundation. He wrote many essays; his most recent collections are Questioning the Millennium *(1997),* Leonardo's Mountain of Clams and the Diet of Worms: Essays On Natural History *(1998), and* Rocks Of Ages: Science and Religion In the Fullness of Life *(1999),* The Structure of Evolutionary Theory *(2002), and* I Have Landed: The End of a Beginning in Natural History *(2002). As you read the following essay, which first appeared in* Natural History Magazine *(1990), notice how Gould shows his readers the limitations of factual recall in memories while illustrating the emotional power that recollections of the past can have in shaping an individual's values.*

JOURNAL

Write about a possession a relative gave you that you cherish for the memories it embodies.

I own many old and beautiful books, classics of natural history bound in leather and illustrated with hand-colored plates. But no item in my collection comes close in personal value to a modest volume, bound in gray cloth and published in 1892: "Studies of English Grammar," by J. M. Greenwood, superintendent of schools in Kansas City. The book belonged to my grandfather, a Hungarian immigrant. He wrote on the title page, in an elegant European hand: "Prop. of Joseph A. Rosenberg, New York." Just underneath, he added in pencil the most eloquent of all possible lines: "I have landed. Sept. 11, 1901."

Papa Joe died when I was 13, before I could properly distill his deepest experiences, but long enough into my own ontogeny for the precious gifts of extensive memory and lasting influence. He was a man of great artistic sensibility and limited opportunity for expression. I am told that he sang beautifully as a young man, although increasing deafness and a pledge to the memory of his mother (never to sing again after her death) stilled his voice long before my birth.

He never used his remarkable talent for drawing in any effort of fine arts, although he marshaled these skills to rise from cloth-cutting in the sweatshops to middle-class life as a brassiere and corset designer. (The content of his chosen expression titillated me as a child, but I now appreciate the primary theme of economic emancipation through the practical application of artistic talent.)

Yet, above all, he expressed his artistic sensibilities in his personal bearing—in elegance of dress (a bit on the foppish side, perhaps), grace of movement, beauty of handwriting, ease of mannerism.

5   I well remember one manifestation of this rise above the ordinary—both because we repeated the act every week and because the junction of locale and action seemed so incongruous, even to a small child of 5 or 6. Every Sunday morning, Papa Joe and I would take a stroll to the corner store on Queens Boulevard to buy the paper and a half dozen bagels. We then walked to the great world-

class tennis stadium of Forest Hills, where McEnroe and his ilk still cavort. A decrepit and disused side entrance sported a rusty staircase of three or four steps.

With his unfailing deftness, Papa Joe would take a section of the paper that we never read and neatly spread several sheets over the lowermost step (for the thought of a rust flake or speck of dust in contact with his trousers filled him with horror). We would then sit down and have the most wonderful man-to-man talk about the latest baseball scores, the rules of poker, or the results of the Friday night fights.

I retain a beautiful vision of this scene: The camera pans back and we see a tiny staircase, increasingly dwarfed by the great stadium. Two little figures sit on the bottom step—a well-dressed, elderly man gesturing earnestly; a little boy listening with adoration.

Certainty is both a blessing and a danger. Certainty provides warmth, solace, security—an anchor in the unambiguously factual events of personal observation and experience. I know that I sat on those steps with my grandfather because I was there, and no external power of suggestion has ever played havoc with this most deeply personal and private experience. But certainty is also a great danger, given the notorious fallibility—and unrivaled power—of the human mind. How often have we killed on vast scales for the "certainties" of nationhood and religion; how often have we condemned the innocent because the most prestigious form of supposed certainty — eyewitness testimony—bears all the flaws of our ordinary fallibility.

Primates are visual animals *par excellence,* and we therefore grant special status to personal observation—to being there and seeing directly. But all sights must be registered in the brain and stored somehow in its intricate memory. And the human mind is both the greatest marvel of nature and the most perverse of all tricksters; Einstein and Loge inextricably combined.

10   This special (but unwarranted) prestige accorded to direct observation has led to a serious popular misunderstanding about science. Since science is often regarded as the most objective and truth-directed of human enterprises, and since direct observation is supposed to be the favored route to factuality, many people equate respectable science with visual scrutiny—just the facts, ma'am, and palpably before my eyes.

But science is a battery of observational and inferential methods, all directed to the testing of propositions that can, in principle, be definitely proved false. A restriction of compass to matters of direct observation would stymie the profession intolerably. Science must often transcend sight to win insight. At all scales, from smallest to largest, quickest to slowest, many well-documented conclusions of science lie beyond the limited domain of direct observation. No one has ever seen an electron or a black hole, the events of picosecond or a geological eon.

One of the phoniest arguments raised for rhetorical effect by "creation scientists" tried to deny scientific status to evolution because its results take so much time to unfold and therefore can't be seen directly. But if science required such immediate vision, we could draw no conclusion about any subject that studies the past—no geology, no cosmology, no human history (including the strength and influence of religion), for that matter.

We can, after all, be reasonably sure that Henry V prevailed at Agincourt even though no photos exist and no one has survived more than 500 years to tell the tale. And dinosaurs really did snuff it tens of millions of years before any conscious observer inhabited our planet. Evolution suffers no special infirmity as a science because its grandest-scale results took so long to unfold during an unobservable past. (The small-scale results of agriculture and domestication have been recorded, and adequate evidence survives to document the broader events of a distant past.) The sciences of history rely on our ability to infer the past from signs of ancestry preserved in modern structures—as in the "panda's thumb" principle of current imperfection preserved as a legacy of ancestral inheritances originally evolved for different purposes.

Moreover, eyewitness accounts do not deserve their conventional status as ultimate arbiters even when testimony of direct observation can be marshaled in abundance. In her sobering book, *"Eyewitness Testimony"* (Harvard University Press, 1979), Elizabeth Loftus debunks, largely in a legal context, the notion that visual observation confers some special claim for veracity. She identifies three levels of potential error in supposedly direct and objective vision: misperception of the event itself and the two great tricksters of passage through memory before later disgorgement—retention and retrieval.

15   In one experiment, for example, Loftus showed forty students a three-minute videotape of a classroom lecture disrupted by eight demonstrators (a relevant subject for a study from the early 1970s!). She gave the students a questionnaire and asked half of them: "Was the leader of the twelve demonstrators . . . a male?" and the other half, "Was the leader of the four demonstrators . . . a male?" One week later, in a follow-up questionnaire, she asked all the students: "How many demonstrators did you see entering the classroom?" Those who had previously received the question about twelve demonstrators reported seeing an average of 8.9 people; those told of four demonstrators claimed an average of 6.4. All had actually seen eight, but compromised later judgment between their actual observation and the largely subliminal power of suggestion in the first questionnaire.

People can even be induced to "see" totally illusory objects. In another experiment, Loftus showed a film of an accident, followed by a misleading question: "How fast was the white sports car going when it passed the barn while traveling along the country road?" (The film showed no barn, and a control group received a more accurate question: "How fast was the white sports car going while traveling along the country road?") A week later, 17 percent of the students in the first group stated that they had seen the nonexistent barn; only 3 percent of the control group reported a barn.

Thus, we are easily fooled on all fronts of both eye and mind: seeing, storing and recalling. The eye tricks us badly enough; the mind is infinitely more perverse. What remedy can we possibly have but constant humility, and eternal vigilance and scrutiny? Trust your memory as you would your poker buddy (one of my grandfather's mottoes from the steps).

With this principle in mind, I went searching for those steps last year after more than thirty years of absence from my natal turf. I exited the subway at 67th Avenue, walked to my first apartment at 98–50, and then set off on my grandfather's route for Queens Boulevard and the tennis stadium.

I was walking in the right direction, but soon realized that I had made a serious mistake. The tennis stadium stood at least a mile down the road, too far for those short strolls with a bag of bagels in one hand and a five-year-old boy attached to the other. In increasing puzzlement, I walked down the street and, at the very next corner, saw the steps and felt the jolt and flood of memory that drives our *recherches du temps perdus.*

20   My recall of the steps was entirely accurate—three modest flagstone rungs, bordered by rusty iron railings. But the steps are not attached to the tennis stadium; they form the side entrance to a modest brick building, now crumbling, padlocked, and abandoned, but still announcing its former use with a commercial sign, painted directly on the brick in the old industrial style: "Muller Bros. Inc. Moving & Storage"—with a telephone number below from the age before all-digit dialing: Illinois 9–9200.

Obviously, I had conflated the most prominent symbol of my old neighborhood, the tennis stadium, with an important personal place—and had constructed a juxtaposed hybrid for my mental image. Yet even now, in the face of conclusive correction, my memory of the tennis stadium soaring above the steps remains strong.

I might ask indulgence on the grounds of inexperience and relative youth for my failure as an eyewitness at the Muller Bros. steps. After all, I was only an impressionable lad of five or so, when even a modest six-story warehouse might be perceived as big enough to conflate with something truly important.

But I have no excuses for a second story. Ten years later, at a trustable age of fifteen, I made a western trip by automobile with my family; I have specially vivid memories of an observation at Devils Tower, Wyoming (the volcanic plug made most famous as a landing site for aliens in "Close Encounters of the Third Kind"). We approach from the east. My father tells us to look out for the tower from tens of miles away, for he has read in a guidebook that it rises, with an awesome near-verticality, from the dead-flat Great Plains—and that pioneer families used the tower as a landmark and beacon on their westward trek.

We see the tower, first as a tiny projection, almost square in outline, at the horizon. It gets larger as we approach, assuming its distinctive form and finally revealing its structure as a conjoined mat of hexagonal basalt columns. I have never forgotten the two features that inspired my rapt attention: the maximal rise of verticality from flatness, forming a perpendicular junction; and the steady increase in size from a bump on the horizon to a looming, almost fearful giant of a rock pile.

25   Now I know, I absolutely *know,* that I saw this visual drama, as described. The picture in my mind of that distinctive profile, growing in size, is as strong as any memory I possess. I see the tower as a little dot in the distance, as a midsized monument, as a full field of view. I have told the story to scores of people, comparing this natural reality with a sight of Chartres as a tiny toy tower twenty

miles from Paris, growing to the overarching symbol and skyline of its medieval city.

In 1987, I revisited Devils Tower with my family—the only return since my first
close encounter thirty years before. I planned the trip to approach from the east,
so that they would see the awesome effect—and I told them my story, of course.

In the context of this essay, my denouement will be anticlimactic in its
predictability, however acute my personal embarrassment. The terrain
around Devils Tower is mountainous; the monument cannot be seen from
more than a few miles away in any direction. I bought a booklet on pioneer
trails westward, and none passed anywhere near Devils Tower. We enjoyed
our visit, but I felt like a perfect fool. Later, I checked my old logbook for
that high-school trip. The monument that rises from the plain, the beacon
of the pioneers, is Scotts Bluff, Nebraska—not nearly so impressive a pile of
stone as Devils Tower.

And yet I still see Devils Tower in my mind when I think of that growing dot
on the horizon. I see it as clearly and as surely as ever, although I now know
that the memory is false.

This has been a long story for a simple moral. Papa Joe, the wise old peasant
in a natty and elegant business suit, told me on those steps to be wary of all
blandishments and to trust nothing that cannot be proved. We must extend his
good counsel to our own interior certainties, particularly those we never question because we regard eyewitnessing as paramount in veracity.

30   Of course we must treat the human mind with respect—for nature has fash-
ioned no more admirable instrument. But we must also struggle to stand back
and to scrutinize our own mental certainties. This last line poses an obvious
paradox, if not an outright contradiction—and I have no solution to offer. Yes,
step back and scrutinize your own mind. But with what?

QUESTIONS FOR DISCUSSION

1. Why is *Studies in English Grammar* Gould's most valued possession? Why
   was this book also cherished by Gould's grandfather?
2. Why does Gould remember his Sunday morning breakfasts with Papa
   Joe? Why does Gould admire his grandfather?
3. Gould is skeptical of the accuracy of direct visual observation. What evidence and descriptions does he present to support his point of view?
4. Gould is also skeptical of the accuracy of memory. Why do the subjects in
   the experiments he discusses come to different conclusions about what
   they saw and what they remembered?
5. When Gould goes back after 30 years to the place where he and Papa Joe
   had breakfast, what does Gould realize about his memory? Why does he still
   value his memory, despite its distortions? How does Gould's inaccurate recall of Devil's Tower support the premise developed in his earlier example?
6. How does Gould effectively relate his personal experiences to broader
   scientific issues involving history, memory, and observation?

CONNECTION

Compare and contrast how Gould and Li-Young Lee reflect on the way that memories of family members are embodied in objects whose meaning is changed over time (see page 128).

IDEAS FOR WRITING

1. Develop your journal assignment into an essay in which you discuss how the memory you have of a relative is connected to and influenced by a physical possession that you keep to remind yourself of the relative. What feelings and values do you associate with the possession?
2. Write an essay in which you discuss the implications of the paradox Gould presents at the end of the essay: "Step back and scrutinize your own mind. But with what?" How can people become better at reflecting on and clarifying the memories and perceptions that they bring with them from their pasts?

RELATED WEB SITES

STEPHEN JAY GOULD
http://prelectur.stanford.edu/lecturers/gould/
This Stanford University web site on Stephen Gould includes biographical and bibliographical information, excerpts of various writings, reviews of Gould's works, and relevant links.

FORSYTH'S MEMORY AND COGNITION PAGE
http://www.vcu.edu/hasweb/psy/psy101/forsyth/zmemory.htm
Donelson Forsyth's web page on memory and cognition covers memory-related issues such as sensation and perception, sleep and consciousness, stress, and trauma.

Tin Le

Enter Dragon

Tin Le was born in Vietnam and has many pleasant memories of his childhood there. In 1985, his brother, mother, and Le reunited with his father in the United States after six years of separation. Le has a special love of nature and photography; he enjoys taking pictures of landscapes and animals. Le wrote the following essay in response to a question that asked him to narrate an experience similar to Maya Angelou's in "Angel of the Candy Counter," in which a childhood memory of discrimination is countered by a fantasy of power.

Have you ever been harassed or even physically abused by your schoolmates or other people you encountered just because you were different from the "average" person in your school or community? This happened to me when I came to America in 1985, an immigrant from Vietnam, and was placed in a seventh grade classroom in Redwood City. It was a small school in a quiet community, but also a place where I had a stormy life for about a year. It was the most horrible experience that I ever had in my life. Kids at that age can be very mean to each other, and I was unfortunate to be on the receiving end of the cruelty.

I went to a school that did not have a lot of Asians. Because I was Asian, my schoolmates often teased me. Some of them, influenced by Japanese ninjas and Chinese martial art fighters in movies, often challenged me to fights because they thought that I was one of "them," the Asian martial arts fighters. When I refused to fight, they taunted me, calling me chicken. They also called me weak and a nerd because I wore glasses. For a whole year in seventh grade I suffered from their harassment.

I especially remember one day when a classmate came to me on the playground and asked if I knew Karate. When I answered, "No," he acted surprised and remarked, "All Chinese know Kung Fu; aren't you one of them? You're supposed to know some Karate. Let's fight and see who is better." Although I ignored him and walked away, he followed me and started to push me around. The more I yielded, the more he attacked me, yet I could do nothing because he was so much bigger than I was. Eventually he seemed to achieve his goal because other students started to gather around us and cheer for him. He became the hero, the macho guy, and I became the laughing stock of the school. From then on, they labeled me chicken and a weak Chinese, even though I am actually Vietnamese. In my classmates' eyes, all Asians were the same; there were no distinctions.

After this episode, many students hit me or pushed me around whenever they felt like it, because they knew that I would not fight back. For example, often at lunch time, several of them would pretend that they did not see me and would walk right into me, spilling my milk or anything else on my tray; then they would say, "Sorry." However, saying sorry solved nothing and did not replace my lunch.

5   The worst part about this experience was that I did not have anyone to turn to for help. I did not have the courage to share my problem with my parents, for I was afraid that worrying about my problem would just contribute to their own burdens. My parents had to work long hours every day so they could provide a happy life for my brother and me. Once they came home, they were very tired and they needed to rest. Furthermore, I wanted them to feel proud of me as they always had.

Fortunately, like Maya Angelou in "The Angel of the Candy Counter," I found a way to resolve my problem by developing a fantasy to endure the pain. I fantasized that I had Bruce Lee's fighting skill (he was the greatest movie star martial arts fighter; his skill even surpassed that of Chuck Norris). I imagined that I fixed up a date after school to settle my unfinished business with the guy who started my nightmare. The moment for our showdown came, and with just one roundhouse kick, I knocked him down to the ground in front of hundreds of schoolmate spectators. He begged me to let him go and promised that he would not pick on anyone anymore. In my fantasy world, from that point on, my friends began to respect me and even to move aside wherever I went. I also imagined that I would disguise myself in black clothes like those of the ninjas and rescue other victims from bullies in the school, disappearing from the scene as soon as everything was over.

Even though the fantasy did not actually solve my problem, it helped me to escape and forget about the bitter reality that I was in, allowing me to enter a world of my own. The fantasy was very helpful to me because it brought joy and a feeling of victory into my harsh experience at school. As a recent immigrant, it was hard for me to try to cope with the language and cultural barriers, and, at the same time, to deal with the bullying and abuse from the students at my school. I still cannot understand how human beings could be so cruel to one another. I realize now that people use fantasies all the time as defense mechanisms to release them from the stress and abuse they must endure in daily life. I wish that people could get to a stage where they would not have to use these compensatory fantasies, a stage in which people could accept one another for who they are, despite differences in physical character, race, and culture.

QUESTIONS FOR DISCUSSION

1. The theme and structure of Le's essay are modeled after Maya Angelou's autobiographical piece included in this chapter. How are Le's experiences and the insights he draws from them similar to Angelou's experience at the dentist? How does Le's perspective differ from hers?
2. What comment does the essay make about racially motivated bullying and its influence on Asian immigrant youth? Have you witnessed behavior similar to that described in the essay? What was your response to this harassment?
3. Le's essay concludes by stating that he cannot "understand how human beings can be so cruel to one another." What would be your response to this statement? What do you believe causes human cruelty such as that described in the essay?
4. Comment on Le's use of narrative examples to support his comments on racial harassment. How does his use of narrative help to support the major points he makes in the essay?

Melissa Burns

The Best Seat in the House

Melissa Burns wrote this essay for her freshman writing class, Community Matters. As the essay suggests, Melissa is an accomplished bassoonist. Always active in dorm life and engaged in campus activities, Melissa Burns finds community life rewarding and is always willing to accept roles of leadership.

On my bookshelf at college sits a beautiful oak box, about six inches long by three inches wide and high. Its four sides, each with two triangular end pieces, are masterfully flush; they fit together so as to unfold fully into a flattened green, felt-lined surface. Well-placed brass hinges and tight fittings guarantee a smooth alignment when the box is latched shut. The top panel is stamped with a hot-iron oval and reads "PATENTED 1889 FEBRUARY." I have been told that my grandfather, Poppy, constructed this treasure box from a kit. My mother, a young girl at the time, remembers her father carefully gluing the velvet upholstery fabric, now faded and fraying, to the box's interior. For decades, it sat undisturbed on Poppy's dresser, the keeper of his rarely worn cufflinks. When Poppy passed away, my grandmother handed the box to my mother, who subsequently placed it into my hands. It is a memory of the grandfather I never knew, a man who loved me with all his heart. Today, this cherished oak box is known as the "reed graveyard," the place where good bassoon reeds go to die.

Poppy was a master craftsman, a WWII statistical officer in Italy, a peacemaker, a member of a bombardier squadron in the European Theater, a fighter pilot, a looker, a gentleman, a joke-teller. He traveled the globe, swam Lake Erie from Buffalo to Toronto, and constructed ornate and precision grandfather clocks, among numerous other works of art. Poppy fixed all things broken—electrical appliances, furniture, hearts. He was a gentle German giant: six foot four and slender, with an olive complexion and dark but graying hair. He wore a wicked grin, as if to forewarn all whom he met of his mischievous pranks, funny sayings, and unique brand of sarcasm. My grandfather awoke one freezing morning, concerned that the razor-sharp icicles dangling from the awning of his Amherst, New York, home might injure his family and friends. Instead, it was Poppy himself who succumbed to nature's wrath. While diligently chipping away at the deadly spikes, he suffered a massive coronary heart attack, dying immediately and painlessly. There were no good-byes. Poppy left my physical world on January 10, 1986, just four days after his 72nd birthday. I was two and a half years old.

My mother has shown me so many photographs of her father and me that sometimes I believe I can conjure the contours of his long, hollowed face and cheeks or his warm embrace as we snuggled in a lawn chair in the tall green grass of summertime in upstate New York. On other occasions, I realize that I possess no actual recollection of Poppy; I've simply deceived myself into believing false, picture-induced memories, all the while praying to God that I should someday reunite with my grandfather. Poppy is gone from the earth, but not from my soul. I embrace him through stories, maxims, and possessions. Over the years, I have learned to take comfort in his status as my guardian angel, protecting and sheltering me from the atrocities of this world.

Matt, my older brother and only sibling, bears an eerily striking resemblance to Poppy—he shares the height, the charm, the gait, and most of all, that devilish, cock-eyed smile. Growing up, however, it was I who captured my grandfather's precious attention. Poppy was well known to occupy our living room rocking chair, listening anxiously for the soft cries signaling that I had awoken from an afternoon nap. He would race upstairs, sweep me from my crib, and hold me soothingly against his broad chest. That was our special time together, my only grandfather and me.

5   When I was in a playful, alert mood, Poppy would lay me down on the family room floor and conduct a series of "tests." Very much the mathematician, calculating the release of bombs and their ensuing catastrophic destruction, Poppy transformed his wartime accuracy into tender, delicate, and methodical child rearing. He concealed my toys behind his back—Would I perceive their continued existence? He raided the kitchen for pots and pans and walked circles around the room, clanging them loudly in different locations while watching my tiny head move frantically from side to side. I have a vivid mental image of a photograph in which Poppy has placed colorful plastic rings around my arms to gauge my strength. Poppy's premature testing was often dismissed as playtime nonsense by the rest of the family, yet he was seriously equipping his only granddaughter with the resources necessary to grow up strong, healthy, independent, resourceful, smart, and intuitive. Poppy was preparing my two-year-old self for a life of struggles and achievements, failures and triumphs. He took great pride in his beautiful baby granddaughter, but he never felt the satisfaction or the joy of witnessing her metamorphosis into a little girl, a teenager, and now, a woman—a woman with a talent of which Poppy was entirely unaware.

I began to play the bassoon, an extremely difficult and intricate double-reed instrument, at the unprecedented age of ten. My decision to play this instrument was prompted by words of encouragement from family friends who recognized my musical aptitude for the piano, as well as the great orchestral demand for young bassoonists. This musical decision was to become perhaps the most consequential, life-altering choice of my life. My bassoon journeys have carried me from Williams College to New York City to Germany to Prague, and most recently, to Stanford University. Because of my musical performances, I have experienced the world's most amazing sights and sounds while interacting with extraordinarily talented and kindhearted members of society.

My story begins with a stroke of luck. I established contact with a renowned bassoon performer and instructor named Stephen Walt, a Williams College teacher in high demand, who had never before considered working with a beginning pupil. Instantaneously, I could tell that our personalities were well-suited, and he became my bassoon coach for the seven years I studied the instrument until moving to California. Mr. Walt is an inspiration, a musical virtuoso, and the most warm, encouraging, demanding instructor I can possibly imagine. My success as a musician is due in great part to his dedication and guidance. Every other weekend, my father drove me from Niskayuna, New York to Williamstown, Massachusetts. Mr. Walt's lessons were worth every second of the hour-and-twenty-minute car ride along oftentimes slippery, snow-covered mountain roads.

As my years of practice accumulated, I steadily increased my skill level, becoming a proficient high school bassoonist. The summer before my sophomore year, I auditioned for, and gained acceptance to, one of America's premier youth orchestras, the Empire State Youth Orchestra. Although I was at first intimidated by the phenomenally talented musicians surrounding me in the orchestra, lengthy bus rides together, nights spent in hotels in foreign countries, and a sense of mutual admiration soon created an atmosphere in which these musicians became several of my closest friends. I will never forget the day our revered and beloved conductor, Francisco Noya, stood imposingly before us at the podium and announced in a thick Venezuelan accent, "Are you prepared to work extremely hard? 'Jes or no? 'Dis year, we play Carnegie Hall." I momentarily lost my grip on reality. Life for an orchestral musician does not reach a zenith more meaningful, more overwhelming, or more spectacular, than the opportunity to perform at *Carnegie Hall.*

For months, the idea of my orchestra's concert at Carnegie Hall constantly intruded on my thoughts. When I wasn't practicing the musical selections, my hands rehearsing complicated fingering passages, I imagined the sights and the sounds of the hall, and I stared at my monthly planner, scratching off each slowly passing day. One such day a week or so before the performance, I sat in my practice chair in the den trying to relax my aching mouth muscles, and I turned to look at the reed graveyard. Every reed I had used over the years, meticulously handcrafted from raw cane by Mr. Walt, inevitably found its way to the graveyard when it was worn-down, broken, cracked, weak, or simply no longer reliable. I carefully unfolded Poppy's box to examine its contents: hundreds of reeds, varying slightly in size, shape, cane discoloration, and string color—red, green, blue, even multi-hued—stuffed the box's interior. As I carefully lifted the reeds and let them sift through my fingers, each one evoked memories of a particular concert, practice session, summer camp, quintet, lesson, rehearsal, or pit orchestra. To this day, every tiny wooden relic, unique, beautiful, and delicate, tells a different, unforgettable story. The reed graveyard, I realized, is a metaphor for Poppy's undying love; it is representative of his personal contribution to my achievements. My greatest accomplishments, I now understood, were housed in this creation, crafted by his strong but gentle hands. Feeling revived, I closed the precious box, placed it on the shelf beside me, and resumed my practice.

10   My dream, from the moment that I began my avocation as a musician, was now materializing. I was standing in the wings of Carnegie Hall, placing my black patent leather shoes where all "the greats" had placed theirs. I peered around the velvet curtain, trembling slightly and sweating profusely. Scanning the sea of faces for a few seconds, I finally located my large cohort of immediate family and close friends. I found them sitting in the upper left-hand balcony in a private box protruding far from the wall. Matt, appropriately, was directly in front and practically falling over the railing, grinning with a true pride that I'd never seen before, and have not seen since. Poppy, I'm quite certain, was witnessing the entire scene from above. He undoubtedly had the best seat in the house. As Poppy's presence filled the air above my head, he beamed his joy through Matt, who served as a surrogate physical representation for a grandfather who would have loved, more than anyone else, to hug and hold his granddaughter on that emotional afternoon.

From the time I found my seat on the stage until the concert was over, my memories are blurred. I have been told that the show ran its entirety without a single hitch; I, for one, was too nervous, excited, ecstatic, and satisfied, to have known what was going on. Thankfully, my musical bodily functions—lungs, heart, fingers, and muscles—took over for a severely wandering mind. I simply cannot describe the fantastic, all-encompassing feeling of earning and achieving one's greatest goal.

I regained mental composure after the last note of our program finished resonating in Carnegie Hall. My attention was called immediately to my support group, cheering and clapping above all others. Beneath it all was the underlying essence of my grandfather's love. I breathed a sigh of relief, took my bows, and, bassoon clutched close to my heart, walked off the stage of the world-renowned Carnegie Hall. What happens to the dreamer when her dream becomes a reality? Is a new dream born? I currently attend Stanford University in northern California, a place I consider to be an ideal launching pad for the discovery of fresh and thrilling ambitions. I am searching for my calling, yet again.

As for Poppy, he resides in the heavens, continuing to protect his baby granddaughter as she matures, becoming stronger and more independent. Late on the night of the concert, when I arrived at my home in Niskayuna, I walked into the den and cradled the reed graveyard in my hands. I opened Poppy's box and placed the most absolutely perfect reed I had ever known inside, where it would retire among the masses that had come before. I latched the box shut as I positioned it in its resting place on the shelf, thus signifying the end to one marvelous chapter of my life. With Poppy as my copilot, I flew off in search of uncharted horizons.

Questions for Discussion

1. What did Melissa learn from Poppy? In what ways was he her first "teacher"? Why has he remained such an important role model and source of support for her?
2. What personal and family qualities do you think led Melissa to become a successful bassoonist? What did playing at Carnegie Hall mean for her?
3. Why is the essay entitled "The Best Seat in the House?" How does this phrase help to clarify her ongoing relationship with "Poppy"?
4. Discuss the writer's central symbol of the reed box. Why does Melissa value her "reed grave yard"?

TOPICS FOR RESEARCH AND WRITING

1. Write an essay in which you discuss how the readings in this chapter as well as outside readings and research have affected your understanding of the importance of memories as a rich source for writing material.

2. After reading the essays by Maya Angelou and Scott Momaday in this chapter, do some further research and write an essay about the role of memories of historical exploitation and discrimination in Native American and/or African-American communities and the writing that comes out of these communities.

3. Li-Young Lee, Judith Ortiz Cofer and Tin Le explore the impact of immigrants' memories, and how these memories are often at odds with their lives in America. Do some research into an immigrant group such as Holocaust survivors or Vietnam War refugees, and write about the legacy of traumatic memories of persecution that continue to influence these immigrants and their families.

4. After examining essays in this book such as the ones by Gould and Hampl, do some reading about the quality and improvability of memory. Can we improve our memories of recent and past events, or is memory simply a "given" ability that we can do nothing about? Write an essay that presents your findings and conclusions on this topic.

5. Hampl and Gould explore the reliability of memories of the past, questioning the extent to which the past and "history" are said to truly exist outside of what we recall and re-create through memory and imagination. Do some further research into the reliability of early memories, and draw some conclusions. Is there an "objective" past, or does each person or group of people invent a version of history? If so, what are our "versions" most often based upon? Write your conclusions in an essay.

6. Write an essay that explores your family's legacy by giving an account of several memories that have been crucial to your family's sense of identity and values. If possible, interview different family members, including extended family such as grandparents, uncles, aunts, and cousins.

 7. Write about a film that focuses on the importance of memories and/or the reliability of memory, referring to elements such as dreams of characters, flashback sequences, and other cinematic devices for showing remembered scenes. Films to consider include *Wild Strawberries, Prince of Tides, Avalon, To Sleep with Anger, Stand By Me, Cinema Paradiso, The Joy Luck Club, Lone Star, Memento, The Sixth Sense, Titanic, The Piano Lesson, The Awakening,* and *Angela's Ashes.*

Dreams, Myths, and Fairy Tales

Linda Lomahaftewa (b. 1947)
Starmakers (1990)

Linda Lomahaftewa, an art instructor at the Institute of American Indian Art in Santa Fe, New Mexico, is from a Hopi/Choctaw background and is one of the leading contemporary Native American Artists. Her works, which have appeared in many exhibits around the country, often display a whimsical sensibility while exploring elements of traditional Native myth and ritual. The vibrant painting *Starmakers* depicts the Hopi myth of the creation of the evening star.

JOURNAL

Write and illustrate a whimsical creation story that explains how some natural phenomenon came into being—a certain star or constellation, the moon, the sun, the wind, fire, rain, etc.

Myths are public dreams, dreams are private myths.
                                 JOSEPH CAMPBELL
                                 Hero With a Thousand Faces

Fantasy is the core of all writing for children, as I think it is for the writing of any book, for any creative act, perhaps for the act of living.
                                 MAURICE SENDAK

COMPARING AND CONTRASTING: STRATEGIES FOR THINKING AND WRITING

The readings selected for this chapter encourage you to think comparatively. You will find that dreams are compared to myths, myths to fairy tales, and traditional tales to modern forms of literature. Also included are different versions of the same basic myths from various cultures. We have designed the chapter in this way because comparing and contrasting are related and essential aspects of reading and writing and are crucial as well to the way the mind thinks and organizes experiences.

When you compare and contrast, you explore relationships between subjects that, despite apparent distinctions, have qualities in common. In this chapter, for example, Carl Jung uses comparison and contrast to emphasize the differences between his own ideas on dream analysis. Comparative writing demands sophisticated, analytical thinking and organization of ideas. Although everyone naturally makes comparisons while thinking, the structure of comparative writing is more balanced and complex than what one normally does when making comparisons in daily life. Prewriting is especially useful for gathering insights and details to use for comparison.

Prewriting for Comparison

You can do prewriting for a comparison paper using any of the techniques discussed in Chapter 1, such as freewriting or clustering. For example, to use brainstorming begin by dividing a piece of paper down the middle and create brainstorming lists of points or qualities you perceive in the subjects of your analysis. A student who wanted to develop a comparison between fairy tales and elementary school readers took the following notes:

Fairy Tales	*Elementary School Readers*
imaginative	seem written by "formula"
engage interest and feelings	don't involve students deeply
teach living skills and heroism	teach "basic reading skills"

encourage imagination	encourage conformity
raise some disturbing issues	avoid controversial issues

You can see some striking contrasts in the lists above. After eliminating some items and grouping the related points, the student could move from the list to a general, clearly worded thesis statement such as the following: "Fairy tales engage the feelings and mind of the child, while primary school texts often fail to attract the interests of children, and thus may actually turn children off to reading." In a very short time, this student writer has found several major points of contrast for possible development and a good central idea to unify a paragraph or essay.

Outlining and Transition

Use of an outline helps to structure extended comparison/contrast papers. An outline will help you to achieve a balanced treatment of each subject and major point in your paper. In preparing an outline, consider the kind of organization you want to use. Comparisons can be structured around points of similarity or difference. Use details to clarify and add interest to the comparison. In subject-by-subject comparing, points are made about two subjects in separate paragraphs or sections of a paper and the two subjects are brought together in the conclusion for a final evaluation or summary of major points. In writing your comparison essay, make the basic points of your comparison clear to your readers through transitional statements. As you move from one comparative issue to another, use expressions such as "in comparison to," "similarly," and "likewise." If the differences between your subjects seem more striking than the similarities, use contrast as your major strategy for examining and noting distinctions, emphasizing your points with transitional expressions such as "in contrast to" and "another point of distinction." As student writer Josh Groban does in his comparison essay in this chapter between the Yao myth of creation and the story of Genesis in the Bible, order and develop your points with care, distinguishing between similarities and differences to retain a clear sense of the overall purpose of your comparison, to understand complex realities, and to evaluate.

Evaluation

Evaluating involves making a judgment based on a standard that you hold about a subject or issue. In the prewriting exercise above, the student who contrasted fairy tales with elementary school textbooks made an evaluation of each based on personal likes and dislikes: The student liked fairy tales and disliked textbooks. Although the student writer didn't discuss her standards for judging children's literature, we can assume that she likes reading that is entertaining and engaging and is bored by writing that exists simply as a tool for learning. The student might have even thought more critically about the standards that are appropriate for school readers. If she had, she might have considered the problems that schools have in selecting and judging materials for different types of learners. Regardless of your subject of comparison you can come closer to seeing whether your values are realistic guides for belief and behavior by establishing guidelines for comparing your standards with those of other people.

Logical Fallacies of Comparison and Contrast

When you think and write comparatively, you may find yourself falling into misleading patterns of thought. A common problem involving comparison and contrast is drawing rigid distinctions that force a choice between artificially opposed positions. Often a contrastive statement will imply that one position is a bad choice: "America, Love it or leave it"; "A person is either a God-fearing Christian or a sinful atheist"; "You're either a real he-man or a spineless sissy." Such statements employ both an incorrect use of contrast and an inappropriate use of evaluation by setting up an either/or dilemma. There are occasions when any comparison oriented to evaluating may seem inappropriate. In comparing and contrasting the myths from different cultures included in this chapter, you may note that each myth of creation involves very different sets of images and values relative to the act and purpose of creation. When thinking about radically different cultures and values, it is more useful simply to make relevant distinctions than to attempt to evaluate one culture as superior or inferior to another.

In the faulty analogy, another common error in comparing, a person attempts to create a connection between two subjects when there are insufficient strong points of similarity. For example, a writer could argue that because life is dreamlike in certain ways, a person should go through life passively, accepting whatever happens just as one might in a dream. Analogies and imaginative, nonliteral comparisons, known as metaphors and similes, can be useful in writing, giving a sense of unexpected and imaginative connections, making descriptions clearer, and generating new insights. On the other hand, taking a metaphorical statement, such as "Life is a dream," and applying it too literally as a standard for conduct ignores real distinctions between the waking world and the sleeping world.

The section on dialogic argument in Chapter 7 discusses ways in which flexible stances in argument can allow you to move beyond rigid, unexamined standards of comparison and evaluation. For now, you should feel ready to use the strategy of comparison more systematically and productively to help you to perceive clear relationships between the public world and your inner world.

THEMATIC INTRODUCTION: DREAMS, MYTHS AND FAIRY TALES

Once you understand how your memories of particular childhood events have shaped and continue to influence your identity and the direction of your life, you may enjoy comparing your personal history to myths and fairy tales. These universal stories have helped to connect humans to larger patterns of history, to their own cultures, and to one another, despite their historical and cultural differences. Myths are patterned stories that present the reader with ideal heroes and heroines acting through dreamlike plots and settings, representing the fundamental values of a culture and a society. Fairy tales satisfy the needs of younger people, and adults as well, for dangerous adventures where evil is ultimately banished and happiness and justice ultimately prevail. Both forms provide ethical lessons that help readers to discriminate between creative and destructive or good and evil behavior.

From Greek myths to nursery rhymes and fairy tales, from Shakespearean doubles and disguises to Gothic tales of horror and revenge, from Victorian mysteries to the modern psychological short story, images of the double have marked our developing understanding of the workings of the human mind. The fundamental adventure and quest patterns of stories and legends are continually being transformed and adapted according to the values of each new age. Today's popular myths provide readers with revised values and reflections on changing cultural norms.

This chapter begins with a poem, essays, and a story that reveal the power of myths in the lives of individuals and in communal existence. The first selection, "ego-tripping (there may be a reason why)," is a poem by the African-American writer Nikki Giovanni. In this poem the speaker imagines herself living through the myths of her heritage as she realizes that identification with these myths protects her and gives her power. The next selection, psychoanalyst Erich Fromm's "Symbolic Language," is an essay in which the writer argues the need to understand the symbolic language of myths and dreams in order to better understand ourselves. Next, Gabriel García Márquez's modern tale, "The Handsomest Drowned Man in the World: A Tale for Children," chronicles the creation of a peasant myth about the redemption brought by a drowned man in a remote seaside village. In "The Four Functions of Mythology," scholar of world mythology Joseph Campbell describes the way myths help people to reconcile awareness of good and evil, to find images of the universe that validate social order, and to reaffirm spiritual meanings.

Following these introductory readings on myth, we present a portfolio of creation myths from around the world for analysis and to provide concrete examples of imaginatively charged mythical stories. These myths celebrate the mystery of creation and embody core values and beliefs about the origins of the world, its creatures, and human beings. We have included myths from the Biblical tradition of the Book of Genesis, as well as from ancient Greek, African, Native American, and Japanese traditions.

Just as dreams and myths give us clues to our unconscious selves and our connections to universal human concerns, fairy tales, a particular class of myths that have been adapted for the entertainment of children, help to enlighten them on the darker side of human nature. In the next selection, "Fairy Tales and the Existential Predicament," Bruno Bettelheim asserts that children in our modern world need to read classic fairy tales, which present the good and the bad sides of human nature and the conscious and unconscious needs and impulses of humans. To help you understand and reflect on the different ways in which a fairy tale can be interpreted and transformed by particular cultures and historical periods, we have included four versions of the Cinderella myth: "Aschenputtel" by the Brothers Grimm; a Native American version of the tale, "The Algonquin Cinderella"; a Vietnamese Cinderella story, "Tam and Cam"; and a satirical retelling by James Finn Garner, "The Politically Correct Cinderella." Garner pokes fun at those who believe that traditional fairy tales are not suitable for young children because they support traditional gender roles.

Two student essays conclude the readings selected for this chapter. In the first, Joshua Groban compares the meanings of two creation myths to show the different values and beliefs held by the cultures that produced the myths. The next student essay focuses on the Cinderella story. In "Cinderella: Politically Incorrect?" Liz Scheps analyzes the use of language and social satire in Garner's "The Politically Correct Cinderella," comparing his modern retelling to the traditional versions of the story.

Comparing myths and fairy tales from different cultures can help you gain new insights into your own culture as you see your world in a broader perspective of diverse values, emotional needs, and spiritual concerns. Drawing comparisons between versions of myths and fairy tales will help you to see how these universal forms can change and yet endure. Perhaps they will help you make sense of your contemporary world and see its connection to the past. Reflecting on and writing about the implications of your dreams and myths as well as the dreams and myths of others is an essential path to your inward journey and a deeper appreciation of the world in which you live.

Nikki Giovanni

ego-tripping (there may be a reason why)

Nikki Giovanni (b. 1943) has written children's fiction, a memoir, and essays. She is best known for her poetry. Giovanni's poetry, which she frequently has read aloud on television and recordings, has been a significant influence on younger African-American writers and poets, especially the new rap poets and musicians. Giovanni won a Ford Foundation grant and has received awards from the National Endowment for the Arts and the Harlem Cultural Council. Her first book, Black Feeling, Black Talk, *was written in 1968. Her recent publications include* Selected Poems *(1996),* Love Poems *(1997),* Blues: For All The Changes: New Poems *(1999), and* Quilting The Black-Eyed Pea: Poems and Non Poems *(2002). Currently Giovanni teaches at Virginia Polytechnic Institute and State University. As you read her poem "ego-tripping" (there may be a reason why)" (1973), notice how she is able to capture the cultural myths and historical realities that are a source of pride for African-Americans.*

JOURNAL

Imagine yourself as related to the larger-than-life heroes and/or heroines you admire. Begin each sentence of your freewrite with "I"; exaggerate and have fun!

I was born in the congo
I walked to the fertile crescent and built
   the sphinx
I designed a pyramid so tough that a star
5   that only glows every one hundred years falls
   into the center giving divine perfect light
I am bad

I sat on the throne
   drinking nectar with allah
10 I got hot and sent an ice age to europe
   to cool my thirst
My oldest daughter is nefertiti
   the tears from my birth pains
   created the nile
15 I am a beautiful woman

I gazed on the forest and burned
   out the sahara desert
   with a packet of goat's meat
   and a change of clothes
20 I crossed it in two hours
I am a gazelle so swift
   so swift you can't catch me
For a birthday present when he was three
I gave my son hannibal an elephant
25   He gave me rome for mother's day

My strength flows ever on

My son noah built new\ark and
I stood proudly at the helm
   as we sailed on a soft summer day
30 I turned myself into myself and was
   jesus
      men intone my loving name

   All praises All praises
I am the one who would save
35 I sowed diamonds in my back yard
My bowels deliver uranium
   the filings from my fingernails are
   semi-precious jewels
   On a trip north
40 I caught a cold and blew
My nose giving oil to the arab world
I am so hip even my errors are correct
I sailed west to reach east and had to round off
   the earth as I went
45 The hair from my head thinned and gold was
   laid across three continents

I am so perfect so divine so ethereal so surreal
I cannot be comprehended
except by my permission

50 I mean . . . I . . . can fly
   like a bird in the sky . . .

QUESTIONS FOR DISCUSSION

1. To emphasize her pride in her African descent, Giovanni's narrator invokes a number of African cultures, mythologies, places, and historical figures. Identify several of the African references in the poem and explain how the narrator finds pride and power through these references and comparisons.

2. Giovanni's poem combines African references with African-American expressions. Identify slang words and phrases in the poem and explain how such expressions add to the power of the poem.

3. In addition to its references to the African-Egyptian cultural tradition, the poem also alludes to biblical characters and mythologies. Point out references to the Old or New Testament of the Bible, and discuss how you think such references and implied comparisons help to develop the poem's tone and meaning.

4. Although the poem has a boisterous, buoyant feeling, at times it seems as if Giovanni may be questioning the narrator's boastfulness. Explain how expressions such as "ego tripping" and "even my errors are correct" could be read as criticisms of the narrator. Why do you think the poet built this self-critical perspective into the poem?
5. What does this poem suggest to you about the functions and power of myth in literature as well as in the inner life of the individual?

CONNECTION

Interpret the dreams and fantasies in Giovanni's poem using some of the ideas on dreams and symbols in the essay by Eric Fromm or Joseph Campbell (see pages 195 and 200).

IDEAS FOR WRITING

1. Try developing your ego-tripping freewriting into your own "rap" or "boast" poem. Refer to myths and cultural traditions that are familiar to you.
2. The speaker in Giovanni's poem seems to gain a sense of personal empowerment through making a series of mythical comparisons. Write an essay in which you argue for or against the importance of comparing yourself to and identifying with characters and situations in myths to gain a sense of pride and self-respect. Use examples of myths you or other people you know believe in that could help to develop a sense of self-esteem.

RELATED WEB SITES

NIKKI GIOVANNI
http://www.english.vt.edu/giovanni/sitemap.htm
Information on the life and work of the African-American poet, Nikki Giovanni, can be discovered at this simple URL, which shares a long list of links entirely devoted to the author. They include audio recordings, publications, events, interviews, and articles are some of the topics that can be explored.

THE POET AND THE RAPPER
http://www.findarticles.com/cf_0/m1264/1_30/54492517/p1/article.jhtml
Read this interesting article by Evelyn C. White, based on an interview with rap singer Queen Latifah, and "author/political activist" Nikki Giovanni. The article explores the connection between "racism, rap and politics."

THE HERO-MYTH CYCLE
http://www.geocities.com/Athens/Forum/8122/hero.html
All cultures have myths, legends, and tales of heroes and their grand accomplishments. Follow the links here to get a basic introduction to the elements

of that cycle. Links to the Hero-Myth Cycle also include: epics, romances, and their hybrids, hero types, and modern movies that follow the basic Hero-Myth Cycle.

Gabriel García Márquez

The Handsomest Drowned Man in the World: A Tale for Children

Gabriel García Márquez (b. 1928) grew up in a small town in Colombia, the eldest of twelve children in a poor family. In 1947 he entered the National University in Bogota, continuing his studies at the University of Cartagena, where he wrote a daily newspaper column. His first book of stories, Leaf Storm and Other Stories *(1955), which includes "The Handsomest Drowned Man in the World," confirmed his commitment to politics and social change. From 1959 to 1961, he traveled extensively while working for a Cuban news agency. After the Cuban revolution, Márquez returned to Central America to encourage other revolutionary causes. With the publication of his novel* One Hundred Years of Solitude *(1967), he was recognized as one of the most talented writers of Latin America. Among his other widely read novels are* The Autumn of the Patriarch *(1975) and* Love in the Time of Cholera *(1988). His short story collections include* Collected Stories *(1984) and* Strange Pilgrims *(1993). He received the Nobel Prize for Literature in 1982. Most recently he has published* Love and Other Demons *(1997) and* A Country for Children *(1998). Márquez's work combines the realistic and the fantastic, and he often uses peasant fables as the basis of his stories, as in the tale that follows.*

JOURNAL

Write about a local hero in your community or neighborhood who achieved larger-than-life, "mythical" status after his or her death.

The first children who saw the dark and slinky bulge approaching through the sea let themselves think it was an empty ship. Then they saw it had no flags or masts and they thought it was a whale. But when it washed up on the beach, they removed the clumps of seaweed, the jellyfish tentacles, and the remains of fish and flotsam, and only then did they see that it was a drowned man.

They had been playing with him all afternoon, burying him in the sand and digging him up again, when someone chanced to see them and spread the alarm in the village. The men who carried him to the nearest house noticed that he weighed more than any dead man they had ever known, almost as much as a horse, and they said to each other that maybe he'd been floating too long and the water had got into his bones. When they laid him on the floor they said he'd been taller than all other men because there was barely enough room for him in the house, but they thought that maybe the ability to keep on growing after death was part of the nature of certain drowned men. He had the smell of the sea about him and only his shape gave one to suppose that it was the corpse of a human being, because the skin was covered with a crust of mud and scales.

They did not even have to clean off his face to know that the dead man was a stranger. The village was made up of only twenty-odd wooden houses that had stone courtyards with no flowers and which were spread about on the end of a desertlike cape. There was so little land that mothers always went about with the fear that the wind would carry off their children and the few dead that the years had caused among them had to be thrown off the cliffs. But the sea was calm and bountiful and all the men fit into seven boats. So when they found the drowned man they simply had to look at one another to see that they were all there.

That night they did not go out to work at sea. While the men went to find out if anyone was missing in neighboring villages, the women stayed behind to care for the drowned man. They took the mud off with grass swabs, they removed the underwater stones entangled in his hair, and they scraped the crust off with tools used for scaling fish. As they were doing that they noticed that the vegetation on him came from faraway oceans and deep water and that his clothes were in tatters, as if he had sailed through laybrinths of coral. They noticed too that he bore his death with pride, for he did not have the lonely look of other drowned men who came out of the sea or that haggard, needy look of men who drowned in rivers. But only when they finished cleaning him off did they become aware of the kind of man he was and it left them breathless. Not only was he the tallest, strongest, most virile, and best built man they had ever seen, but even though they were looking at him there was no room for him in their imagination.

5　　　They could not find a bed in the village large enough to lay him on nor was there a table solid enough to use for his wake. The tallest men's holiday pants would not fit him, nor the fattest ones' Sunday shirts, nor the shoes of the one with the biggest feet. Fascinated by his huge size and his beauty, the women then decided to make him some pants from a large piece of sail and a shirt from some bridal Brabant linen so that he could continue through his death with dignity. As they sewed, sitting in a circle and gazing at the corpse between stitches, it seemed to them that the wind had never been so steady nor the sea so restless as on that night and they supposed that the change had something to do with the dead man. They thought that if that magnificent man had lived in the village, his house would have had the widest doors, and highest ceiling, and the strongest floor; his bedstead would have been made from a midship frame held together by iron bolts, and his wife would have been the happiest woman. They thought that he would have had so much authority that he could have drawn fish out of the sea simply by calling their names and that he would have put so much work into his land that springs would have burst forth from among the rocks so that he would have been able to plant flowers on the cliffs. They secretly compared him to their own men, thinking that for all their lives theirs were incapable of doing what he could do in one night, and they ended up dismissing them deep in their hearts as the weakest, meanest, and most useless creatures on earth. They were wandering through that maze of fantasy when the oldest woman, who as the oldest had looked upon the drowned man with more compassion than passion, sighed:

"He has the face of someone called Esteban."

It was true. Most of them had only to take another look at him to see that he could not have any other name. The more stubborn among them, who were the youngest, still lived for a few hours with the illusion that when they put his clothes on and he lay among the flowers in patent leather shoes his name might be Lautaro. But it was a vain illusion. There had not been enough canvas, the poorly cut and worse sewn pants were too tight, and the hidden strength of his heart popped the buttons on his shirt. After midnight the whistling of the wind died down and the sea fell into its Wednesday drowsiness. The silence put an end to any last doubts: he was Esteban. The women who had dressed him, who had combed his hair, had cut his nails and shaved him were unable to hold back a shudder of pity when they had to resign themselves to his being dragged along the ground. It was then that they understood how unhappy he must have been with that huge body since it bothered him even after death. They could see him in life, condemned to going through doors sideways cracking his head on crossbeams, remaining on his feet during visits, not knowing what to do with his soft pink, sealion hands while the lady of the house looked for her most resistant chair and begged him, frightened to death, sit here, Esteban, please, and he, leaning against the wall, smiling, don't bother, ma'am, I'm fine where I am, his heels raw and his back roasted from having done the same thing so many times whenever he paid a visit, don't bother ma'am, I'm fine where I am to avoid the embarrassment of breaking up the chair, and never knowing perhaps that the one who said don't go, Esteban, at least wait till the coffee's ready, were the ones who later on would whisper the big boob finally left, how nice, the handsome fool has gone. That was what the women were thinking beside the body a little before dawn. Later, when they covered his face with a handkerchief so that the light would not bother him, he looked so forever dead, so defenseless, so much like their men that the first furrows of tears opened in their hearts. It was one of the younger ones who began the weeping. The others, coming to, went from sighs to wails, and the more they sobbed the more they felt like weeping, because the drowned man was becoming all the more Esteban for them, and so they wept so much, for he was the most destitute, most peaceful, and most obliging man on earth, poor Esteban. So when the men returned with the news that the drowned man was not from the neighboring villages either, the women felt an opening of jubilation in the midst of their tears.

"Praise the Lord," they sighed, "he's ours!"

The men thought the fuss was only womanish frivolity. Fatigued because of the difficult nighttime inquiries, all they wanted was to get rid of the bother of the newcomer once and for all before the sun grew strong on that arid, windless day. They improvised a litter with the remains of foremasts and gaffs, tying it together with rigging so that it would bear the weight of the body until they reached the cliffs. They wanted to tie the anchor from a cargo ship to him so that he would sink easily into the deepest waves, where the fish are blind and divers die of nostalgia, and bad currents would not bring him back to shore, as had happened with other bodies. But the more they hurried, the more the women thought of ways to waste time. They walked about like startled hens, pecking with the sea charms on their breasts, some interfering on one side to put a scapular of the good wind on the drowned man, some on the other side to put a wrist compass on him, and after a great deal of *get away from there woman, stay out of the way, look, you almost made me fall on top of the dead man,* the men began to feel mistrust in their livers and started grumbling about why so many main-altar decorations for a stranger, because no matter how many nails and holywater jars he had on him, the sharks would chew him all the same, but the women kept on piling on their junk relics, running back and forth, stumbling, while they released in sighs what they did not in tears, so that the men finally exploded with *since when has there ever been such a fuss over a drifting corpse, a drowned nobody, a piece of cold Wednesday meat.* One of the women, mortified by so much lack of care, then removed the handkerchief from the dead man's face and the men were left breathless too.

10   He was Esteban. It was not necessary to repeat it for them to recognize him. If they had been told Sir Walter Raleigh, even they might have been impressed with his gringo accent, the macaw on his shoulder, his cannibal-killing blunderbuss, but there could be only one Esteban in the world and there he was, stretched out like a sperm whale, shoeless, wearing the pants of an undersized child, and with those stony nails that had to be cut with a knife. They had only to take the handkerchief off his face to see that he was ashamed, that it was not his fault that he was so big or so heavy or so handsome, and if he had known that this was going to happen, he would have looked for a more discreet place to drown in; seriously, I even would have tied the anchor off a galleon around my neck and staggered off a cliff like someone who doesn't like things in order not to be upsetting people now with this Wednesday dead body, as you people say, in order not to be bothering anyone with this filthy piece of cold meat that doesn't have anything to do with me. There was so much truth in his manner that even the most mistrustful men, the ones who felt the bitterness of endless nights at sea fearing that their women would tire of dreaming about them and begin to dream of drowned men, even they and others who were harder still shuddered in the marrow of their bones at Esteban's sincerity.

That was how they came to hold the most splendid funeral they could conceive of for an abandoned drowned man. Some women who had gone to get flowers in the neighboring villages returned with other women who could not believe what they had been told, and those women went back for more flowers when they saw the dead man, and they brought more and more until there were so many flowers and so many people that it was hard to walk about. At the final moment it pained them to return him to the waters as an orphan and they chose a father and mother from among the best people, and aunts and uncles and cousins, so that through him all the inhabitants of the village became kinsmen. Some sailors who heard the weeping from a distance went off course, and people heard of one who had himself tied to the mainmast, remembering ancient fables about sirens. While they fought for the privilege of carrying him on their shoulders along the steep escarpment by the cliffs, men and women became aware for the first time of the desolation of their streets, the dryness of their courtyards, the narrowness of their dreams as they faced the splendor and beauty of their drowned man. They let him go without an anchor so that he could come back if he wished and whenever he wished, and they all held their breath for the fraction of centuries the body took to fall into the abyss. They did not need to look to one another to realize that they were no longer all present, that they would never be. But they also knew that everything would be different from then on, that their houses would have wider doors, higher ceilings, and stronger floors so that Esteban's memory could go everywhere without bumping into beams and so that no one in the future would dare whisper the big boob finally died, too bad, the handsome fool has finally died, because they were going to paint their house fronts gay colors to make Esteban's memory eternal and they were going to break their backs digging for springs among the stones and planting flowers on the cliffs so that in future years at dawn the passengers on great liners would awaken, suffocated by the smell of gardens on the high seas, and the captain would have to come down from the bridge in his dress uniform, with his astrolabe, his pole star, and his row of war medals and, pointing to the promontory of roses on the horizon, he would say in fourteen languages, look there, where the wind is so peaceful now that it's gone to sleep beneath the beds, over there, where the sun's so bright that the sunflowers don't know which way to turn, yes, over there, that's Esteban's village.

Translated by Gregory Rabassa

QUESTIONS FOR DISCUSSION

1. What is revealed through the initial description of the drowned man? Why was "there . . . no room for him in their [the villagers'] imagination"?
2. Why and how does the drowned man make the women happy and the sea peaceful? Why does the community of women finally agree that this man must be Esteban?
3. How did the women feel about Esteban when he was alive? How do they feel about him now that he is dead?
4. Do the men of the village change their attitude toward the drowned man once they realize he is Esteban? Why or why not? Explain your point of view.
5. What is the significance of the villagers' making their island into a beautiful shrine dedicated to Esteban's size and beauty?
6. Why is the story subtitled "A Tale for Children"? What warnings and hope does the story offer?

CONNECTION

Compare this story about the origins of a myth with Joseph Campbell's "Four Functions of Mythology." Which of the four functions would this myth fulfill (see page 200)?

IDEAS FOR WRITING

1. Write an essay that examines the way the story weaves together realistic details and fantasy. How does this style help to emphasize and build the mythical quality of the story and its central character, Esteban?
2. Write an essay that interprets the myth and moral of "The Handsomest Drowned Man in the World." What truth and values are revealed in this portrait of a society in the process of creating a new myth?

RELATED WEB SITES

http://www.themodernword.com/gabo/

Learn about the author, Gabriel García Márquez, at this web site called "The Modern World." Find many links, reviews, biographical, and bibliographical information here.

MAGICAL REALISM

http://www.angelfire.com/wa2/margin/links.html

Find a wide variety of information on the subject of Magical Realism—the genre of writing that Márquez is most famous for creating—here at this URL. Learn about other authors who write in this genre along with a special section devoted entirely to Márquez's work.

Erich Fromm

The Forgotten Language

Erich Fromm (1900–1980) was born in Frankfurt, Germany to orthodox Jewish parents. In early adulthood he became an atheistic mystic and pursued an interest in psychoanalysis. He earned a Ph.D. from the University of Heidelberg in 1922 and eventually began a psychoanalytic practice as a follower of Sigmund Freud. Fromm disagreed with Freud over the primacy of the unconscious in determining personality and came to believe that culture and society were more significant factors. Fromm moved to New York in 1933, where he was received as an established figure in psychoanalytic practice. After working at Columbia University for six years, he moved on to Bennington College, then to the National University of Mexico, and back to New York where he practiced for several years before returning again to Mexico City. Fromm published extensively, including Man for Himself *(1941),* The Sane Society

(1955), The Art of Loving *(1956), and* Beyond the Chains of Illusion *(1962).*
Although Fromm believed strongly that economic class determined personality, he also
felt that many of our deepest values come from dominant myths and ideals of our cul-
ture, as can be seen in the following selection from The Forgotten Language.

JOURNAL

Narrate a dream you have had that seemed like a myth, a story with symbolic
rather than literal meaning. What do the major symbols of the dream indicate or
reveal to you?

If it is true that the ability to be puzzled is the beginning of wisdom, then this
truth is a sad commentary on the wisdom of modern man. Whatever the merits of our high degree of literary and universal education, we have lost the gift
for being puzzled. Everything is supposed to be known—if not to ourselves
then to some specialist whose business it is to know what we do not know. In
fact, to be puzzled is embarrassing, a sign of intellectual inferiority. Even children are rarely surprised, or at least they try not to show that they are; and as
we grow older we gradually lose the ability to be surprised. To have the right
answers seems all-important; to ask the right questions is considered insignificant by comparison.

This attitude is perhaps one reason why one of the most puzzling phenomena in our lives, our dreams, gives so little cause for wonder and for raising
questions. We all dream; we do not understand our dreams, yet we act as if
nothing strange goes on in our sleep minds, strange at least by comparison
with the logical, purposeful doings of our minds when we are awake.

When we are awake, we are active, rational beings, eager to make an effort to
get what we want and prepared to defend ourselves against attack. We act and we
observe; we see things outside, perhaps not as they are, but at least in such a manner that we can use and manipulate them. But we are also rather unimaginative,
and rarely—except as children or if we are poets—does our imagination go beyond duplicating the stories and plots that are part of our actual experience. We
are effective but somewhat dull. We call the field of our daytime observation "reality" and are proud of our "realism" and our cleverness in manipulating it.

When we are asleep, we awake to another form of existence. We dream. We
invent stories which never happened and sometimes for which there is not
even any precedent in reality. Sometimes we are the hero, sometimes the vil-
lain; sometimes we see the most beautiful scenes and are happy; often we are
thrown into extreme terror. But whatever the role we play in the dream *we* are
the author, it is *our* dream, *we* have invented the plot.

5   Most of our dreams have one characteristic in common: they do not follow
the laws of logic that govern our waking thought. The categories of space and
time are neglected. People who are dead, we see alive; events which we watch
in the present, occurred many years ago. We dream of two events as occurring
simultaneously when in reality they could not possibly occur at the same time.

We pay just as little attention to the laws of space. It is simple for us to move to a distant place in an instant, to be in two places at once, to fuse two persons into one, or to have one person suddenly be changed into another. Indeed, in our dreams we are the creators of a world where time and space, which limit all the activities of our body, have no power.

Another odd thing about our dreams is that we think of events and persons we have not thought of for years, and whom, in the waking state, we would never have remembered. Suddenly they appear in the dream as acquaintances whom we had thought of many times. In our sleeping life, we seem to tap the vast store of experience and memory which in the daytime we do not know exists.

Yet, despite all these strange qualities, our dreams are real to us while we are dreaming; as real as any experience we have in our waking life. There is no "as if" in the dream. The dream is present, real experience, so much so, indeed, that it suggests two questions: What is reality? How do we know that what we dream is unreal and what we experience in our waking life is real? A Chinese poet has expressed this aptly: "I dreamt last night that I was a butterfly and now I don't know whether I am a man who dreamt he was a butterfly, or perhaps a butterfly who dreams now that he is a man."

All these exciting, vivid experiences of the night not only disappear when we wake up, but we have the greatest difficulty trying to remember them. Most of them we simply forget, so completely that we do not even remember having lived in this other world. Some we faintly remember at the moment of waking, and the next second they are beyond recall. A few we do remember, and these are the ones we speak of when we say, "I had a dream." It is as if friendly, or unfriendly, spirits had visited us and at the break of day had suddenly disappeared; we hardly remember that they had been there and how intensely we had been occupied with them.

Perhaps more puzzling than all the factors already mentioned is the similarity of the products of our creativeness during sleep with the oldest creations of man—the myths.

Actually, we are not too much puzzled by myths. If they are made respectable as part of our religion, we give them a conventional and superficial acknowledgment as part of a venerable tradition; if they do not carry such traditional authority, they are taken for the childish expression of the thoughts of man before he was enlightened by science. At any rate, whether ignored, despised, or respected, myths are felt to belong to a world completely alien to our own thinking. Yet the fact remains that many of our dreams are, in both style and content, similar to myths, and we who find them strange and remote when we are awake have the ability to create these mythlike productions when we are asleep.

In the myth, too, dramatic events happen which are impossible in a world governed by the laws of time and space: the hero leaves his home and country to save the world, or he flees from his mission and lives in the belly of a big fish; he dies and is reborn; the mythical bird is burned and emerges from the ashes more beautiful than before.

Of course, different people created different myths just as different people dream different dreams. But in spite of all these differences, all myths and all dreams have one thing in common, they are all "written" in the same language, *symbolic language.*

The myths of the Babylonians, Indians, Egyptians, Hebrews, Greeks are written in the same language as those of the Ashantis or the Trukese. The dreams of someone living today in New York or in Paris are the same as the dreams reported from people living some thousand years ago in Athens or in Jerusalem. The dreams of ancient and modern man are written in the same language as the myths whose authors lived in the dawn of history.

Symbolic language is a language in which inner experiences, feelings and thoughts are expressed as if they were sensory experiences, events in the outer world. It is a language which has a different logic from the conventional one we speak in the daytime, a logic in which not time and space are the ruling categories but intensity and association. It is the one universal language the human race has ever developed, the same for all cultures and throughout history. It is a language with its own grammar and syntax, as it were, a language one must understand if one is to understand the meaning of myths, fairy tales and dreams.

15   Yet this language has been forgotten by modern man. Not when he is asleep, but when he is awake. Is it important to understand this language also in our waking state?

For the people of the past, living in the great cultures of both East and West, there was no doubt as to the answer to this question. For them myths and dreams were among the most significant expressions of the mind, and failure to understand them would have amounted to illiteracy. It is only in the past few hundred years of Western culture that this attitude has changed. At best, myths were supposed to be naïve fabrications of the prescientific mind, created long before man had made his great discoveries about nature and had learned some of the secrets of its mastery.

Dreams fared even worse in the judgment of modern enlightenment. They were considered to be plain senseless, and unworthy of the attention of grown-up men, who were busy with such important matters as building machines and considered themselves "realistic" because they saw nothing but the reality of things they could conquer and manipulate; realists who have a special word for each type of automobile, but only the one word "love" to express the most varied kinds of affective experience.

Moreover, if all our dreams were pleasant phantasmagorias in which our hearts' wishes were fulfilled, we might feel friendlier toward them. But many of them leave us in an anxious mood; often they are nightmares from which we awake gratefully acknowledging that we only dreamed. Others, though not nightmares, are disturbing for other reasons. They do not fit the person we are sure we are during daytime. We dream of hating people whom we believe we are fond of, of loving someone whom we thought we had no interest in. We dream of being ambitious, when we are convinced of being modest; we dream of bowing down and submitting, when we are so proud of our independence. But worse than all this is the fact that we do not understand our dreams while we, the waking person, are sure we can understand anything if we put our minds to it. Rather than be confronted with such an overwhelming proof of the limitations of our understanding, we accuse the dreams of not making sense.

A profound change in the attitude toward myths and dreams has taken place in the past few decades. This change was greatly stimulated by Freud's work. After starting out with the restricted aim of helping the neurotic patient to understand the reasons for his illness, Freud proceeded to study the dream as a universal human phenomenon, the same in the sick and in the healthy person. He saw that dreams were essentially no different from myths and fairy tales and that to understand the language of the one was to understand the language of the others. And the work of anthropologists focused new attention on myths. They were collected and studied, and some few pioneers in this field, like J. J. Bachofen, succeeded in throwing new light on the prehistory of man.

20   But the study of myths and dreams is still in its infancy. It suffers from various limitations. One is a certain dogmatism and rigidity that has resulted from the claims of various psychoanalytic schools, each insisting that it has the only true understanding of symbolic language. Thus we lose sight of the many-sidedness of symbolic language and try to force it into the Procrustean bed of one, and only one, kind of meaning.

Another limitation is that interpretation of dreams is still considered legitimate only when employed by the psychiatrist in the treatment of neurotic patients. On the contrary, I believe that symbolic language is the one foreign language that each of us must learn. Its understanding brings us in touch with one of the most significant sources of wisdom, that of the myth, and it brings us in touch with the deeper layers of our own personalities. In fact, it helps us to understand a level of experience that is specifically human because it is that level which is common to all humanity, in content as well as in style.

The Talmud says, "Dreams which are not interpreted are like letters which have not been opened." Indeed, both dreams and myths are important communications from ourselves to ourselves. If we do not understand the language in which they are written, we miss a great deal of what we know and tell ourselves in those hours when we are not busy manipulating the outside world.

QUESTIONS FOR DISCUSSION

1. How does Fromm critique our contemporary approach to dreams and myths in his first paragraph about modern man's need to have the "right answers"?
2. What characteristic does Fromm believe that all dreams have in common?
3. According to Fromm, what two questions do dreams raise about "reality"? Do you agree with Fromm? Explain your point of view.
4. How are dreams similar to myths? In what sense is the language of myths from different periods and different cultures still "the same"? What exactly does Fromm mean by "a language of symbols"?
5. Why does Fromm believe that the work of Freud and anthropologists has profoundly changed the attitude toward myths and dreams in recent decades? Do you think that most people accept the new attitude Fromm discusses here?

6. If, as Fromm believes, the study of dreams and myths is "still in its infancy," how does he see the future issues with which the studies will have to grapple? According to Fromm, why is it so important that we learn the "foreign language" of dreams and mythical symbols?

CONNECTION

Compare and contrast Campbell's and Fromm's interpretations of the meaning and value of dreams (see page 195).

IDEAS FOR WRITING

1. Taking one of the creation myths in this chapter, or another myth that you value, write an essay in which you analyze the symbols in the myth to determine what the message of the myth was for its original culture as well as its more universal significance. You will have to do some research on the myth that you have chosen for the topic of your essay.
2. Write an essay in which you analyze the symbols in one of your dreams. You might start with your journal entry and develop your insights.

RELATED WEB SITES

ERICH FROMM
http://www.erichfromm.de/english/
This extensive web site from "The International Erich Fromm Society" includes information about the author's life and work, as well as online reading, upcoming events devoted to Fromm, and links to the archives of his articles and essays.

SYMBOLS AND DREAMS
http://www.stanford.edu/~dement/dreams.html
Here can be found links, information about, and research on dreams. The theme of interpreting common dream images and symbols is also explored on this web site.

Joseph Campbell

The Four Functions of Mythology

Joseph Campbell (1904–1987) was born in New York and studied Medieval Literature at Columbia University. He dropped out of his doctoral program after learning that mythology would not be an acceptable subject for his dissertation.

Campbell taught mythological studies at Sarah Lawrence College for many years before retiring to Hawaii and pursuing his interests in writing and lecturing. In later life, he became a popular figure in contemporary culture, inspiring George Lucas's "Star Wars" films and doing a number of interviews with Bill Moyers on public television. Campbell shared Carl Jung's belief in the archetypal patterns of symbolism in myths and dreams. He was author and editor of many books on world mythology, including The Hero With a Thousand Faces *(1949) and his four-volume work* The Masks of God *(1962). In the following selection from "Mythological Themes in Creative Literature and Art," an essay included in the collection* Myths, Dreams, and Religion *(1970), Campbell explores what he considers to be the major functions of mythology in the life of individuals, cultures, and societies.*

JOURNAL

Write a definition of "myth" or "mythology" based on your personal associations with the terms. List as many qualities and functions of myths or mythology that you know.

Traditional mythologies serve, normally, four functions, the first of which might be described as the reconciliation of consciousness with the preconditions of its own existence. In the long course of our biological prehistory, living creatures had been consuming each other for hundreds of millions of years before eyes opened to the terrible scene, and millions more elapsed before the level of human consciousness was attained. Analogously, as individuals, we are born, we live and grow, on the impulse of organs that are moved independently of reason to aims antecedent to thought—like beasts: until, one day, the crisis occurs that has separated mankind from the beasts: the realization of the monstrous nature of this terrible game that is life, and our consciousness recoils. In mythological terms: we have tasted the fruit of the wonder-tree of the knowledge of good and evil, and have lost our animal innocence. Schopenhauer's scorching phrase represents the motto of this fallen state: "Life is something that should not have been!" Hamlet's state of indecision is the melancholy consequence: "To be, or not to be!" And, in fact, in the long and varied course of the evolution of the mythologies of mankind, there have been many addressed to the aims of an absolute negation of the world, a condemnation of life, and a backing out. These I have termed the mythologies of "The Great Reversal." They have flourished most prominently in India, particularly since the Buddha's time (sixth century B.C.), whose First Noble Truth, "All life is sorrowful," derives from the same insight as Schopenhauer's rueful dictum. However, more general, and certainly much earlier in the great course of human history, have been the mythologies and associated rites of redemption through affirmation. Throughout the primitive world, where direct confrontations with the brutal bloody facts of life are inescapable and unremitting, the initiation ceremonies to which growing youngsters are subjected are frequently horrendous, confronting them in the most appalling, vivid terms, with experiences—both optically and otherwise—of this monstrous thing that is life: and always with the requirement of a "yea," with no sense of either personal or collective guilt, but gratitude and exhilaration.

For there have been, finally, but three attitudes taken toward the awesome mystery in the great mythological traditions; namely, the first, of a "yea"; the second, of a "nay"; and the last, of a "nay," but with a contingent "yea," as in the great complex of messianic cults of the late Levant: Zoroastrianism, Judaism, Christianity, and Islam. In these last, the well-known basic myth has been, of an originally good creation corrupted by a fall, with, however, the subsequent establishment of a supernaturally endowed society, through the ultimate world dominion of which a restoration of the pristine state of the good creation is to be attained. So that, not in nature but in the social order, and not in all societies, but in this, the one and only, is there health and truth and light, integrity and the prospect of perfection. The "yea" here is contingent therefore on the ultimate world victory of this order.

The second of the four functions served by traditional mythologies—beyond this of redeeming human consciousness from its sense of guilt in life—is that of formulating and rendering an image of the universe, a cosmological image in keeping with the science of the time and of such kind that, within its range, all things should be recognized as parts of a single great holy picture, an icon as it were: the trees, the rocks, the animals, sun, moon, and stars, all opening back to mystery, and thus serving as agents of the first function, as vehicles and messengers of the teaching.

The third traditional function, then, has been ever that of validating and maintaining some specific social order, authorizing its moral code as a construct beyond criticism or human emendation. In the Bible, for example, where the notion is of a personal god through whose act the world was created, that same god is regarded as the author of the Tablets of the Law; and in India, where the basic idea of creation is not of the act of a personal god, but rather of a universe that has been in being and will be in being forever (only waxing and waning, appearing and disappearing, in cycles ever renewed), the social order of caste has been traditionally regarded as of a piece with the order of nature. Man is not free, according to either of these mythic views, to establish for himself the social aims of his life and to work, then, toward these through institutions of his own devising; but rather, the moral, like the natural order, is fixed for all time, and if times have changed (as indeed they have, these past six hundred years), so that to live according to the ancient law and to believe according to the ancient faith have become equally impossible, so much the worse for these times.

5   The first function served by a traditional mythology, I would term, then, the mystical, or metaphysical, the second, the cosmological, and the third, the sociological. The fourth, which lies at the root of all three as their base and final support, is the psychological: that, namely, of shaping individuals to the aims and ideals of their various social groups, bearing them on from birth to death

through the course of a human life. And whereas the cosmological and socio-logical orders have varied greatly over the centuries and in various quarters of the globe, there have nevertheless been certain irreducible psychological prob-lems inherent in the very biology of our species, which have remained constant, and have, consequently, so tended to control and structure the myths and rites in their service that, in spite of all the differences that have been rec-ognized, analyzed, and stressed by sociologists and historians, there run through the myths of all mankind the common strains of a single symphony of the soul. Let us pause, therefore, to review briefly in sequence the order of these irreducible psychological problems.

The first to be faced derives from the fact that human beings are born some fourteen years too soon. No other animal endures such a long period of dependency on its parents. And then, suddenly, at a certain point in life, which varies, according to the culture, from, say, twelve to about twenty years of age, the child is expected to become an adult, and his whole psychological system, which has been tuned and trained to dependency, is now required to respond to the challenges of life in the way of responsibility. Stimuli are no longer to produce responses either of appeal for help or of submission to parental discipline, but of responsible social action appropriate to one's so-cial role. In primitive societies the function of the cruel puberty rites has been everywhere and always to effect and confirm this transformation. And glancing now at our own modern world, deprived of such initiations and be-coming yearly more and more intimidated by its own intransigent young, we may diagnose a neurotic as simply an adult who has failed to cross this thresh-old to responsibility: one whose response to every challenging situation is, first, "What would Daddy say? Where's Mother?" and only then comes to real-ize, "Why gosh! *I'm* Daddy, I'm forty years old! Mother is now my wife! It is *I* who must do this thing!" Nor have traditional societies ever exhibited much sympathy for those unable or unwilling to assume the roles required. Among the Australian aborigines, if a boy in the course of his initiation seriously mis-behaves, he is killed and eaten*—which is an efficient way, of course, to get rid of juvenile delinquents, but deprives the community, on the other hand, of the gifts of original thought. As the late Professor A. R. Radcliffe-Brown of Trinity College, Cambridge, observed in his important study of the Andaman Island pygmies: "A society depends for its existence on the presence in the minds of its members of a certain system of sentiments by which the conduct of the individual is regulated in conformity with the needs of the society . . . . The sentiments in question are not innate but are developed in the individual by the action of the society upon him."† In other words: the entrance into adulthood from the long career of infancy is not, like the opening of a blossom,

---

*Géza Róheim, *The Eternal Ones of the Dream* (New York: International Universities Press, 1945), p. 232, citing K. Langloh Parker, *The Euahlayi Tribe* (London: A. Constable & Co., 1905), pp. 72–73.
†A. R. Radcliffe-Brown, *The Andaman Islanders* (Cambridge: The University Press, 1933), pp. 233–234.

to a state of naturally unfolding potentialities, but to the assumption of a social role, a mask or "persona," with which one is to identify. In the famous lines of the poet Wordsworth:

> Shades of the prison-house begin to close
> Upon the growing Boy.‡

A second birth, as it is called, a social birth, is effected, and, as the first had been of Mother Nature, so this one is of the Fathers, Society, and the new body, the new mind, are not of mankind in general but of a tribe, a caste, a certain school, or a nation.

Whereafter, inevitably, in due time, there comes a day when the decrees of nature again break forth. That fateful moment at the noon of life arrives when, as Carl Jung reminds us, the powers that in youth were in ascent have arrived at their apogee and the return to earth begins. The claims, the aims, even the interests of society, begin to fall away and, again as in the lines of Wordsworth:

> Our noisy years seem moments in the being
> Of the eternal Silence: truths that wake,
>   To perish never:
> Which neither listlessness, nor mad endeavour,
> Nor Man nor Boy,
>   Nor all that is at enmity with joy,
> Can utterly abolish or destroy!
>
> Hence in a season of calm weather
>   Though inland far we be,
> Our Souls have sight of that immortal sea
>   Which brought us hither,
> Can in a moment travel thither,
> And see the Children sport upon the shore,
> And hear the mighty waters rolling evermore.*

Both the great and the lesser mythologies of mankind have, up to the present, always served simultaneously, both to lead the young from their estate in nature, and to bear the aging back to nature and on through the last dark door. And while doing all this, they have served, also, to render an image of the world of nature, a cosmological image as I have called it, that should seem to support the claims and aims of the local social group; so that through every feature of the experienced world the sense of an ideal harmony resting on a dark dimension of wonder should be communicated. One can only marvel at the integrating, life-structuring force of even the simplest traditional organization of mythic symbols.

---

‡William Wordsworth, *Intimations of Immortality from Recollections of Early Childhood* ll. 64–65.
*Ibid., ll. 158–171.

QUESTIONS FOR DISCUSSION

1. As the title indicates, Campbell describes four functions of mythology. What are the functions and how do they differ from one another? Do you agree with this division? Would you have included other functions?

2. Why does Campbell believe that "our consciousness recoils" at the awareness of the "terrible game" of life? What is terrible or sorrowful about life? How does this awareness involve a loss of innocence similar to the tasting of the apple in the Book of Genesis? How does Christianity offer an answer to the sorrow and loss of innocence that is the nature of life?

3. Campbell believes that traditional mythology presents "an image of the universe," a sense of the order of created things. What image of the universe does traditional Judeo-Christian religion present in the Book of Genesis, for example?

4. Why do the mythic views of both the Bible and the tradition of India tell us that humans are not free? What prevents individual freedom from occurring, according to these traditional mythological views? Can you give examples of other mythic stories and classical works that contain a moral or pattern that implies there is no individual freedom of choice and action?

5. How do traditional religions and mythological systems pattern our psychological growth and development as we move toward adulthood, reducing the kind of "neurotic" fixations at a certain maturity level that are so common in our own society? How do mythologies help one to create a "persona" as a social being and prepare us emotionally to come to terms with aging and death?

6. Although Campbell approaches his topic from a general perspective, he makes his ideas more concrete through the use of quotations and references to mythologies familiar to his readers, such as the Book of Genesis from the Bible. What other examples might he have used?

CONNECTION

Compare Campbell's ideas on the function of myths with Bruno Bettelheim's ideas on the role of fairy tales in the life of the child. What common views of myths and tales are shared by these writers (see page 214)?

IDEAS FOR WRITING

1. In the longer essay from which this selection is excerpted, Campbell states that both the cosmological and social functions of mythology have been weakened through modern advances in science and technology. Write an essay in which you present several examples that either support or refute Campbell's assertion that the reliance on science and technology have diminished the power of the human spirit that myths embody.

2. Write an essay in which you discuss a myth that you are familiar with that fulfills one of the four functions that Campbell discusses in his essay. Include a copy or detailed description of the myth with your essay. In what ways is this myth woven into the cultural and social assumptions and values that form the basis of your beliefs and lifestyle?

RELATED WEB SITE

THE JOSEPH CAMPBELL FOUNDATION

http://www.jcf.org/

This foundation is a nonprofit membership organization that presents Campbell's pioneering work through the medium of this web site. Information here includes biographical and bibliographical data, as well as projects, events, and "mythological resources."

Portfolio of Creation Myths

We have selected the following myths from cultures around the world to encourage you to compare different fundamental beliefs and assumptions about reality. Preceding each myth is a note about the culture that produced it; following the portfolio is a set of questions for thought and writing.

JOURNAL

Discuss a creation myth or an experience of creating something very special to you. Develop imaginative comparisons and vivid details.

Genesis 2:4–23 (Old Testament of the Hebrew Bible)

This is the second account of creation in the book of Genesis. Genesis 2 is thought to come from a different, less formal writing tradition (the "J," or Jehovah, tradition) from that of Genesis 1 and reveals an intimate relationship between God and his natural and human creations. The following passage portrays the God Jehovah in an agricultural role, creating and watering the Garden of Eden, then creating animals, a man to till the fields, and finally a female helper for "the man." As you read the selection, consider the impact that the Book of Genesis has had on Western cultural assumptions and traditions.

Genesis 2:4: In the day that the Lord God made the earth and the heavens, (5) when no plant of the field was yet in the earth and no herb of the field had yet sprung up—for the Lord God had not caused it to rain upon the earth, and there was no man to till the ground; (6) but a mist went up from the earth and watered the whole face of the ground—(7) then the Lord God formed man of dust from the ground, and breathed into his nostrils the breath of life; and man became a living being. (8) And the Lord God planted a garden in Eden, in the east; and there he put the man whom he had formed. (9) And out of the ground the Lord God made to grow every tree that is pleasant to the sight and good for food, the tree of life also in the midst of the garden, and the tree of the knowledge of good and evil.

(10) A river flowed out of Eden to water the garden, and there it divided and became four rivers. (11) The name of the first is Pishon; it is the one which flows around the whole land of Hav'ilah, where there is gold; (12) and the gold of that land is good; bdellium and onyx stone are there. (13) The name of the second river is Gihon; it is the one which flows around the whole land of Cush. (14) And the name of the third river is Tigris, which flows east of Assyria. And the fourth river is the Euphrates.

(15) The Lord God took the man and put him in the Garden of Eden to till it and keep it. (16) And the Lord God commanded the man, saying, "You may freely eat of every tree of the garden; (17) but of the tree of the knowledge of good and evil you shall not eat, for in the day that you eat of it you shall die."

(18) Then the Lord God said, "It is not good that the man should be alone; I will make him a helper fit for him." (19) So out of the ground the Lord God formed every beast of the field and every bird of the air, and brought them to the man to see what he would call them; and whatever the man called every living creature, that was its name. (20) The man gave names to all cattle, and to the birds of the air, and to every beast of the field; but for the man there was not found a helper fit for him. (21) So the Lord God caused a deep sleep to fall upon the man, and while he slept took one of his ribs and closed up its place with flesh; (22) and the rib which the Lord God had taken from the man he made into a woman and brought her to the man. (23) Then the man said, This at last is bone of my bones and flesh of my flesh; she shall be called Woman, because she was taken out of Man.

The Pelasgian Creation Myth (Ancient Greek)

This myth is the earliest known Greek creation myth. The Pelasgian stories were gathered in rural areas of Greece by a British scholar of mythology, Robert Graves, and published in his book The Pelasgian Myth *(1955). The following brief selection from the book describes the ritual dancing and coupling of the primal Eurynome, the "Goddess of All Things," with the snake Ophion. It is this coupling that produces the planets, the earth, life, and Pelasgus, the first man. The myth makes an interesting contrast with the Genesis story from the Old Testament.*

In the beginning, Eurynome, the Goddess of All Things, rose naked from Chaos, but found nothing substantial for her feet to rest upon, and therefore divided the sea from the sky, dancing lonely upon its waves. She danced towards the south, and the wind set in motion behind her seemed something new and apart with which to begin a work of creation.

Wheeling about, she caught hold of this north wind, rubbed it between her hands, and behold! the great serpent Ophion. Eurynome danced to warm herself, wildly and more wildly, until Ophion, grown lustful, coiled about those divine limbs and was moved to couple with her. Now, the North Wind, who is also called Boreas, fertilizes; which is why mares often turn their hind-quarters to the wind and breed foals without aid of a stallion. So Eurynome was likewise got with child.

Next, she assumed the form of a dove, brooding on the waves and, in due process of time, laid the Universal Egg. At her bidding, Ophion coiled seven times about this egg, until it hatched and split in two. Out tumbled all things that exist, her children: sun, moon, planets, stars, the earth with its mountains and rivers, its trees, herbs, and living creatures.

Eurynome and Ophion made their home upon Mount Olympus, where he vexed her by claiming to be the author of the Universe. Forthwith she bruised his head with her heel, kicked out his teeth, and banished him to the dark caves below the earth.

5   Next, the goddess created the seven planetary powers, setting a Titaness and a Titan over each. Theia and Hyperion for the Sun; Phoebe and Atlas for the Moon; Dione and Crius for the planet Mars; Metis and Coeus for the planet Mercury; Themis and Eurynmedon for the planet Jupiter; Tethys and Oceanus for Venus; Rhea and Cronus for the planet Saturn. But the first man was Pelasgus, ancestor of the Pelasgians; he sprang from the soil of Arcadia, followed by certain others, whom he taught to make huts and feed upon acorns and sew pig-skin tunics such as poor folk still wear in Euboea and Phocis.

The Chameleon Finds (Yao-Bantu, African)

"The Chameleon Finds" is a creation myth of the Yao, a Bantu tribe living by Lake Nyasa in Mozambique, Africa. Expressive of a close relationship with nature, this Yao myth, with a clever Chameleon and a helper Spider as the creator-god's assistants, takes a critical view of human beings. The unnatural and destructive culture of the humans causes the animals to flee and the gods to retreat from the earth. As you read this creation story, compare the critical view of human culture held by the Yao with that of the other myths in this section.

At first there were no people. Only Mulungu and the decent peaceful beasts were in the world. One day Chameleon sat weaving a fish-trap, and when he had finished he set it in the river. In the morning he pulled the trap and it was full of fish, which he took home and ate. He set the trap again. In the morning he pulled it out and it was empty: no fish.

"Bad luck," he said, and set the trap again.

The next morning when he pulled the trap he found a little man and woman in it. He had never seen any creatures like this.

"What can they be?" he said. "Today I behold the unknown." And he picked up the fish-trap and took the two creatures to Mulungu.

5   "Father," said Chameleon, "see what I have brought."

Mulungu looked. "Take them out of the trap," he said. "Put them down on the earth and they will grow."

Chameleon did this. And the man and woman grew. They grew until they became as tall as men and women are today.

All the animals watched to see what the people would do. They made fire. They rubbed two sticks together in a special way and thus made fire. The fire caught in the bush and roared through the forest and the animals had to run to escape the flames. The people caught a buffalo and killed it and roasted it in the fire and ate it. The next day they did the same thing. Every day they set fires and killed some animal and ate it.

"They are burning up everything!" said Mulungu. "They are killing my people!"

10   All the beasts ran into the forest as far away from mankind as they could get. Chameleon went into the high trees.

"I'm leaving!" said Mulungu. He called to Spider. "How do you climb on high?" he said.

"Very nicely," said Spider. And Spider spun a rope for Mulungu and Mulungu climbed the rope and went to live in the sky.

Thus the gods were driven off the face of the earth by the cruelty of man.

The Yauelmani Yokut Creation

The Yauelmani Yokuts were a small tribe from the southern San Joaquin Valley in California with their own unique language and customs. The following creation myth demonstrates the cooperative, nonhierarchical values of this tribal group. It is similar to many other Native American creation stories in that a group of animals and birds, as opposed to men or gods, perform the creation. The animals work together persistently despite deaths, failed efforts, and earthquakes to perform the work of creating the world from a primal ocean.

At first there was water everywhere. A tree grew up out of the water to the sky. On the tree there was a nest. Those who were inside did not see any earth. There was only water to be seen. The eagle was the chief of them. With him were the wolf, Coyote, the panther, the prairie falcon, the hawk called *po'yon,* and the condor. The eagle wanted to make the earth. He thought, "We will have to have land." Then he called *k'uik'ui,* a small duck. He said to it: "Dive down and bring up the earth." The duck dived, but did not reach the bottom. It died. The eagle called another kind of duck. He told it to dive. This duck went far down. It finally reached the bottom. Just as it touched the mud there it died. Then it came up again. Then the eagle and the other six saw a little dirt under its fingernail. When the eagle saw this he took the dirt from its nail. He mixed it with *telis* and *pele* seeds and ground them up. He put water with the mixture and made dough. This was in the morning. Then he set it in the water and it swelled and spread everywhere, going out from the middle. (These seeds when ground and mixed with water swell.) In the evening the eagle told his companions: "Take some earth." They went down and took a little earth up in the tree with them. Early in the morning, when the morning star came, the eagle said to the wolf: "Shout." The wolf shouted and the earth disappeared, and all was water again. The eagle said: "We will make it again," for it was for this purpose that they had taken some earth with them into the nest. Then they took *telis* and *pele* seeds again, and ground them with the earth, and put the mixture into the water, and it swelled out again. Then early next morning when the morning star appeared, the eagle told the wolf again: "Shout!" and he shouted three times. The earth was shaken by the earthquake, but it stood. Then Coyote said: "I must shout too." He shouted and the earth shook a very little. Now it was good. Then they came out of the tree on the ground. Close to where this tree stood there was a lake. The eagle said: "We will live here." Then they had a house there and lived there.

Spider Woman Creates the Humans (Hopi, Native American)

The Hopi, who reside in several villages in northern Arizona, have kept themselves separate from other cultures and have maintained their native traditions and myths. The following myth of creation is only a brief selection from the much longer Hopi Emergence Story that uses birth imagery to explain a complex sequence of transformations in the act of creation. In the Hopi culture, the Emergence Story is told to the tribal initiates on the last evening of the year, after which the young men ascend a ladder to emerge from the kiva (Hopi dwelling) as full-fledged adult members of the Hopi community.

"Spider Woman Creates the Humans" is unique because of its use of a female creator who functions as mother-goddess, singer, and artist, molding the original people from multicolored clay while singing them the Creation Song.

So Spider Woman gathered earth, this time of four colors, yellow, red, white, and black; mixed with tuchvala, the liquid of her mouth; molded them; and

covered them with her white-substance cape which was the creative wisdom itself. As before, she sang over them the Creation Song, and when she uncovered them these forms were human beings in the image of Sotuknang. Then
she created four other beings after her own form. They were wuti, female partners, for the first four male beings.

When Spider Woman uncovered them the forms came to life. This was at
the time of the dark purple light, Qoyangnuptu, the first phase of the dawn of
Creation, which first reveals the mystery of man's creation.

They soon awakened and began to move, but there was still a dampness on
their foreheads and a soft spot on their heads. This was at the time of the yellow light, Sikangnuqua, the second phase of the dawn of Creation, when the
breath of life entered man.

In a short time the sun appeared above the horizon, drying the dampness
on their foreheads and hardening the soft spot on their heads. This was the
time of the red light, Talawva, the third phase of the dawn of Creation, when
man, fully formed and firmed, proudly faced his Creator.

5 "That is the Sun," said Spider Woman. "You are meeting your Father the Creator for the first time. You must always remember and observe these three
phases of your Creation. The time of the three lights, the dark purple, the yellow, and the red reveal in turn the mystery, the breath of life, and warmth of
love. These comprise the Creator's plan of life for you as sung over you in the
Song of Creation."

The Beginning of the World (Japanese)

*Like the other myths in this section, this Japanese story describes the process of cre-
ation (in this selection, of the islands of Japan), but uses gentle irony as well as elements of courtly protocol and diplomatic conflict resolution around issues such as the
proper social role of the sexes. The following creation myth about the creation of the
islands of Japan is from Genji Shibukawa's* Tales from the Kojiki *(712 C.E.),
translated by Yaichiro Isobe. The* Kojiki *or* Records of Ancient Matters *is the oldest work written in the original symbols used to record the Japanese language, the
Chinese Kanji characters introduced to Japan through Korea in the sixth century.*

Before the heavens and the earth came into existence, all was a chaos,
unimaginably limitless and without definite shape or form. Eon followed
eon: then, lo! out of this boundless, shapeless mass something light and transparent rose up and formed the heaven. This was the Plain of High Heaven, in
which materialized . . . three divine beings are called the Three Creating
Deities.

In the meantime what was heavy and opaque in the void gradually precipitated
and became the earth, but it had taken an immeasurably long time before it condensed sufficiently to form solid ground. In its earliest stages, for millions and

millions of years, the earth may be said to have resembled oil floating, medusa-like, upon the face of the waters. Suddenly like the sprouting up of a reed . . . many gods were thus born in succession, and so they increased in number, but as long as the world remained in a chaotic state, there was nothing for them to do.

Whereupon, all the Heavenly deities summoned the two divine beings, Izanagi and Izanami, and bade them descend to the nebulous place, and by helping each other, to consolidate it into terra firma. "We bestow on you," they said, "this precious treasure, with which to rule the land, the creation of which we command you to perform." So saying they handed them a spear . . . embellished with costly gems. The divine couple received the sacred weapon respectfully and ceremoniously and then withdrew from the presence of the Deities, ready to perform their august commission. Proceeding forthwith to the Floating Bridge of Heaven, which lay between the heaven and the earth, they stood awhile to gaze on that which lay below. What they beheld was a world not yet condensed, but looking like a sea of filmy fog floating to and fro in the air, exhaling the while an inexpressibly fragrant odor.

They were, at first, perplexed just how and where to start, but at length Izanagi suggested to his companion that they should try the effect of stirring up the brine with their spear. So saying he pushed down the jeweled shaft and found that it touched something. Then drawing it up, he examined it and observed that the great drops which fell from it almost immediately coagulated into an island, which is, to this day, the Island of Onokoro. Delighted at the result, the two deities descended forthwith from the Floating Bridge to reach the miraculously created island. In this island they thenceforth dwelt and made it the basis of their subsequent task of creating a country. Then wishing to become espoused, they erected in the center of the island a pillar, the Heavenly August Pillar, and built around it a great palace called the Hall of Eight Fathoms.

5   Thereupon the male Deity turning to the left and the female Deity to the right, each went round the pillar in opposite directions. When they again met each other on the further side of the pillar, Izanami, the female Deity, speaking first, exclaimed: "How delightful it is to meet so handsome a youth!" To which Izanagi, the male Deity, replied: "How delightful I am to have fallen in with such a lovely maiden!" After having spoken thus, the male Deity said that it was not in order that woman should anticipate man in a greeting. Nevertheless, they fell into connubial relationship, having been instructed by two wagtails which flew to the spot. Presently the Goddess bore her divine consort a son, but the baby was weak and boneless as a leech. Disgusted with it, they abandoned it on the waters, putting it in a boat made of reeds. Their second offspring was as disappointing as the first.

The two Deities, now sorely disappointed at their failure and full of misgivings, ascended to Heaven to inquire of the Heavenly Deities the causes of their misfortunes. The latter performed the ceremony of divining and said to them: "It is the woman's fault. In turning round the Pillar, it was not right and proper that the female Deity should in speaking have taken precedence of the male. That is the reason."

The two Deities saw the truth of this divine suggestion, and made up their minds to rectify the error. So, returning to the earth again, they went once more around the Heavenly Pillar. This time Izanagi spoke first saying: "How delightful to meet so beautiful a maiden!" "How happy I am," responded Izanami, "that I should meet such a handsome youth!" This process was more appropriate and in accordance with the law of nature. After this, all the children born to them left nothing to be desired. First, the island of Awaji was born, next, Shikoku, then, the island of Oki, followed by Kyushu; after that, the island Tsushima came into being, and lastly, Honshu, the main island of Japan. The name of . . . the Country of the Eight Great Islands was given to these eight islands. After this, the two Deities became the parents of numerous smaller islands destined to surround the larger ones.

QUESTIONS FOR DISCUSSION

1. What different images of the creator gods are presented in the various myths? Is the primary god in each clearly described? What powers and limits does the god have? Does the god operate alone or with other helping beings? What conclusions about the culture that produced each myth can you draw from these differences?

2. In the myths that present a clear picture of the physical world of the creation, how is the world described? How orderly and sequential is the act of creating the different elements and beings of the world? What conclusions can you draw from the varied presentation in these creation myths about the values of the culture that produced each myth?

3. Creation myths make significant comments on the roles and status of the sexes in various cultures. Compare and contrast the roles of sex and gender in the different creation myths included.

4. Another issue presented in some creation myths is the relationship of men and women to their creator. How do the humans in the various myths relate to the creator gods? How worshipful of God are the humans in the various myths?

5. Compare the ways that the different myths show the relationship between humans and nature. How harmonious a part of nature or how much at odds with nature do humans seem in the various myths? How are animals involved in the act of creation? Does part of the natural world need to be destroyed for creation to be completed?

6. Creation myths differ in tone. They can be imaginative and dreamlike, solemn and serious, philosophical, or even comical and mocking in tone. Compare the tone and attitude toward creation presented in each of the myths; then draw some conclusions about the values of each culture.

IDEAS FOR WRITING

1. Write your own creation myth, using characters, descriptions, and narration to illustrate the relationship between different aspects of creation:

gods, animals, people, and the earth. At the end of your myth, comment on the values and ideas about the creative process and the world that your myth is designed to illustrate.

2. Develop an essay in the form of an extended comparison between two or three creation myths, each of which illustrates fundamental values and beliefs about gods, humans, and the natural world.

RELATED WEB SITES

CREATION MYTHS—"MYTHING LINKS"
http://www.mythinglinks.org/ct~creation.html
Learn about creation myths from around the world at this web site. Here you will find an annotated and illustrated collection of worldwide links to mythologies, fairy tales and folklore, sacred arts, and sacred traditions.

OLD TESTAMENT ONLINE
http://www.hope.edu/academic/religion/bandstra/BIBLE/OT.HTM
Look up a specific passage of the Old Testament online at this URL. The entire contents of the Old Testament can also be read here.

Bruno Bettelheim

Fairy Tales and the Existential Predicament

Born in Vienna and educated at the University of Vienna, Bruno Bettelheim (1903–1991) was imprisoned in a Nazi concentration camp for a time before immigrating to the United States. After settling in Chicago, he worked with autistic children, serving as Director of the University of Chicago Orthogenic School from 1944 to 1973. Bettelheim's books, such as On Learning to Read *(1981) and* A Good Enough Parent *(1987), focus on the relationships between reading, parenting, and raising emotionally healthy children. The following selection from* The Uses of Enchantment *(1976) presents a psychological perspective of the impact traditional fairy tales have on children. As you read the selection, think about whether you agree with Bettelheim's theories about the role that fairy tales play in creating healthy children.*

JOURNAL

Narrate the fairy tale that you remember most vividly from your childhood. Why do you think you remember it? Would you share (or have you shared) this tale with your own children? Why or why not?

In order to master the psychological problems of growing up—overcoming narcissistic disappointments, oedipal dilemmas, sibling rivalries; becoming able to relinquish childhood dependencies; gaining a feeling of selfhood and of self-worth, and a sense of moral obligation—a child needs to understand what is going on within his conscious self so that he can also cope with that which goes on in his unconscious. He can achieve this understanding, and with it the ability to cope, not through rational comprehension of the nature and content of his unconscious, but by becoming familiar with it through spinning out daydreams—ruminating, rearranging, and fantasizing about suitable story elements in response to unconscious pressures. By doing this, the child fits unconscious content into conscious fantasies, which then enable him to deal with that content. It is here that fairy tales have unequaled value, because they offer new dimensions to the child's imagination which would be impossible for him to discover as truly on his own. Even more important, the form and structure of fairy tales suggest images to the child by which he can structure his daydreams and with them give better direction to his life.

In child or adult, the unconscious is a powerful determinant of behavior. When the unconscious is repressed and its content denied entrance into awareness, then eventually the person's conscious mind will be partially overwhelmed by derivatives of these unconscious elements, or else he is forced to keep such rigid, compulsive control over them that his personality may become severely crippled. But when unconscious material *is* to some degree permitted to come to awareness and worked through in imagination, its potential for causing harm—to ourselves or others—is much reduced; some of its forces can then be made to serve positive purposes. However, the prevalent parental belief is that a child must be diverted from what troubles him most: his formless, nameless anxieties, and his chaotic, angry, and even violent fantasies. Many parents believe that only conscious reality or pleasant and wish-fulfilling images should be presented to the child—that he should be exposed only to the sunny side of things. But such one-sided fare nourishes the mind only in a one-sided way, and real life is not all sunny.

There is a widespread refusal to let children know that the source of much that goes wrong in life is due to our very own natures—the propensity of all men for acting aggressively, asocially, selfishly, out of anger and anxiety. Instead, we want our children to believe that, inherently, all men are good. But children know that *they* are not always good; and often, even when they are, they would prefer not to be. This contradicts what they are told by their parents, and therefore makes the child a monster in his own eyes.

The dominant culture wishes to pretend, particularly where children are concerned, that the dark side of man does not exist, and professes a belief in an optimistic meliorism. Psychoanalysis itself is viewed as having the purpose of making life easy—but this is not what its founder intended. Psychoanalysis was created to enable man to accept the problematic nature of life without being defeated by it, or giving in to escapism. Freud's prescription is that only by struggling courageously against what seem like overwhelming odds can man succeed in wringing meaning out of his existence.

5   This is exactly the message that fairy tales get across to the child in manifold form: that a struggle against severe difficulties in life is unavoidable, is an intrinsic part of human existence—but that if one does not shy away, but steadfastly meets unexpected and often unjust hardships, one masters all obstacles and at the end emerges victorious.

Modern stories written for young children mainly avoid these existential problems, although they are crucial issues for all of us. The child needs most particularly to be given suggestions in symbolic form about how he may deal with these issues and grow safely into maturity. "Safe" stories mention neither death or aging, the limits to our existence, nor the wish for eternal life. The fairy tale, by contrast, confronts the child squarely with the basic human predicaments.

For example, many fairy stories begin with the death of a mother or father; in these tales the death of the parent creates the most agonizing problems, as it (or the fear of it) does in real life. Other stories tell about an aging parent who decides that the time has come to let the new generation take over. But before this can happen, the successor has to prove himself capable and worthy. The Brothers Grimm's story "The Three Feathers" begins: "There was once upon a time a king who had three sons . . . . When the king had become old and weak, and was thinking of his end, he did not know which of his sons should inherit the kingdom after him." In order to decide, the king sets all his sons a difficult task; the son who meets it best "shall be king after my death."

It is characteristic of fairy tales to state an existential dilemma briefly and pointedly. This permits the child to come to grips with the problem in its most essential form, where a more complex plot would confuse matters for him. The fairy tale simplifies all situations. Its figures are clearly drawn; and details, unless very important, are eliminated. All characters are typical rather than unique.

Contrary to what takes place in many modern children's stories, in fairy tales evil is as omnipresent as virtue. In practically every fairy tale good and evil are given body in the form of some figures and their actions, as good and evil are omnipresent in life and the propensities for both are present in every man. It is this duality which poses the moral problem, and requires the struggle to solve it.

10   Evil is not without its attractions—symbolized by the mighty giant or dragon, the power of the witch, the cunning queen in "Snow White"—and often it is temporarily in the ascendancy. In many fairy tales a usurper succeeds for a time in seizing the place which rightfully belongs to the hero—as the wicked sisters do in "Cinderella." It is not that the evildoer is punished at the story's end which makes immersing oneself in fairy stories an experience in moral education, although this is part of it. In fairy tales, as in life, punishment or fear of it is only a limited deterrent to crime. The conviction that crime does not pay is a much more effective deterrent, and that is why in fairy tales the bad person always loses out. It is not the fact that virtue wins out at the end which promotes morality, but that the hero is most attractive to the child, who identifies with the hero in all his struggles. Because of this identification the child imagines that he suffers with the hero his trials and tribulations, and triumphs with him as virtue is victorious. The child makes such identifications all on his own, and the inner and outer struggles of the hero imprint morality on him.

The figures in fairy tales are not ambivalent—not good and bad at the same time, as we all are in reality. But since polarization dominates the child's mind, it also dominates fairy tales. A person is either good or bad, nothing in between. One brother is stupid, the other is clever. One sister is virtuous and industrious, the others are vile and lazy. One is beautiful, the others are ugly. One parent is all good, the other evil. The juxtaposition of opposite characters is not for the purpose of stressing right behavior, as would be true for cautionary tales. (There are some amoral fairy tales where goodness or badness, beauty or ugliness play no role at all.) Presenting the polarities of character permits the child to comprehend easily the difference between the two, which he could not do as readily were the figures drawn more true to life, with all the complexities that characterize real people. Ambiguities must wait until a relatively firm personality has been established on the basis of positive identifications. Then the child has a basis for understanding that there are great differences between people, and that therefore one has to make choices about who one wants to be. This basic decision, on which all later personality development will build, is facilitated by the polarizations of the fairy tale.

Furthermore, a child's choices are based, not so much on right versus wrong, as on who arouses his sympathy and who his antipathy. The more simple and straightforward a good character, the easier it is for a child to identify with it and to reject the bad other. The child identifies with the good hero not because of his goodness, but because the hero's condition makes a deep positive appeal to him. The question for the child is not "Do I want to be good?" but "Who do I want to be like?" The child decides this on the basis of projecting himself wholeheartedly into one character. If this fairy-tale figure is a very good person, then the child decides that he wants to be good, too.

Amoral fairy tales show no polarization or juxtaposition of good and bad persons; that is because these amoral stories serve an entirely different purpose. Such tales or type figures as "Puss in Boots," who arranges for the hero's success through trickery, and Jack, who steals the giant's treasure, build character not by promoting choices between good and bad, but by giving the child the hope that even the meekest can succeed in life. After all, what's the use of choosing to become a good person when one feels so insignificant that he fears he will never amount to anything? Morality is not the issue in these tales, but rather, assurance that one can succeed. Whether one meets life with a belief in the possibility of mastering its difficulties or with the expectation of defeat is also a very important existential problem.

The deep inner conflicts originating in our primitive drives and our violent emotions are all denied in much of modern children's literature, and so the child is not helped in coping with them. But the child is subject to desperate feelings of loneliness and isolation, and he often experiences mortal anxiety. More often than not, he is unable to express these feelings in words, or he can do so only by indirection: fear of the dark, of some animal, anxiety about his body. Since it creates discomfort in a parent to recognize these emotions in his child, the parent tends to overlook them, or he belittles these spoken fears out of his own anxiety, believing this will cover over the child's fears.

15   The fairy tale, by contrast, takes these existential anxieties and dilemmas very seriously and addresses itself directly to them: the need to be loved and the fear that one is thought worthless; the love of life, and the fear of death. Further, the fairy tale offers solutions in ways that the child can grasp on his level of understanding. For example, fairy tales pose the dilemma of wishing to live eternally by occasionally concluding: "If they have not died, they are still alive." The other ending—"And they lived happily ever after"—does not for a moment fool the child that eternal life is possible. But it does indicate that which alone can take the sting out of the narrow limits of our time on this earth: forming a truly satisfying bond to another. The tales teach that when one has done this, one has reached the ultimate in emotional security of existence and permanence of relation available to man; and this alone can dissipate the fear of death. If one has found true adult love, the fairy story also tells, one doesn't need to wish for eternal life. This is suggested by another ending found in fairy tales: "They lived for a long time afterward, happy and in pleasure."

An uninformed view of the fairy tale sees in this type of ending an unrealistic wish-fulfillment, missing completely the important message it conveys to the child. These tales tell him that by forming a true interpersonal relation, one escapes the separation anxiety which haunts him (and which sets the stage for many fairy tales, but it's always resolved at the story's ending). Furthermore, the story tells, this ending is not made possible, as the child wishes and believes, by holding on to his mother eternally. If we try to escape separation anxiety and death anxiety by desperately keeping our grasp on our parents, we will only be cruelly forced out, like Hansel and Gretel.

Only by going out into the world can the fairy-tale hero (child) find himself there; and as he does, he will also find the other with whom he will be able to live happily ever after; that is, without ever again having to experience separation anxiety. The fairy tale is future-oriented and guides the child—in terms he can understand in both his conscious and his unconscious mind—to relinquish his infantile dependency wishes and achieve a more satisfying independent existence.

Today children no longer grow up within the security of an extended family, or of a well-integrated community. Therefore, even more than at the times fairy tales were invented, it is important to provide the modern child with images of heroes who have to go out into the world all by themselves and who, although originally ignorant of the ultimate things, find secure places in the world by following their right way with deep inner confidence.

The fairy-tale hero proceeds for a time in isolation, as the modern child often feels isolated. The hero is helped by being in touch with primitive things—a tree, an animal, nature—as the child feels more in touch with those things than most adults do. The fate of these heroes convinces the child that, like them, he may feel outcast and abandoned in the world, groping in the dark, but, like them, in the course of his life he will be guided step by step, and given help when it is needed. Today, even more than in past times, the child needs the re-assurance offered by the image of the isolated man who nevertheless is capable of achieving meaningful and rewarding relations with the world around him.

QUESTIONS FOR DISCUSSION

1. What does Bettelheim consider to be the primary positive psychological value of fairy tales? Do you agree?
2. According to Bettelheim, how do fairy tales help children to control de-structive unconscious impulses? How does the polarization of good and evil in fairy tales help children?
3. Why does Bettelheim believe that children benefit more from reading tra-ditional versions of fairy tales than from modern stories for children?
4. How do fairy-tale endings help children to accept their isolation, their "ex-istential predicament," while at the same time encouraging them to believe in the possibility of creating meaningful relationships in their own world?
5. Why does Bettelheim believe that it is important for fairy tales to have happy endings? Do you agree with him? Why or why not?
6. What examples does Bettelheim give to support his ideas? What other ex-amples might he have provided?

CONNECTION

After reading The Brothers Grimms' version of Cinderella, included in this chap-ter, consider what place Bettelheim would see for this story within the theories he sets forth in "Fairy Tales and the Existential Predicament"(see page 214).

IDEAS FOR WRITING

1. Write a defense or refutation of Bettelheim's theory about the value of fairy tales for children. Refer specifically to both Bettelheim's ideas and to your own ideas and experiences as a child reader or as an adult parenting or teaching young children.
2. Develop your journal entry into an essay. Expand on it by showing how your interpretation of the meaning of the fairy tale has changed as you have matured.

RELATED WEB SITES

BRUNO BETTELHEIM

http://peace.saumag.edu/faculty/kardas/courses/AHG/
Bettelheim.html
Learn more about the controversial figure and work of Bruno Bettelheim at this simple but informative URL that shares many links to biographical and bibliographical information on Bettelheim.

FOLKLORE, MYTH AND LEGEND FOR CHILDREN
http://www.ucalgary.ca/~dkbrown/storfolk.html
An annotated guide to major sites dealing with traditional literature, geared
toward children will be found at this URL from "The Children's Literature
Web Guide" at the University of Calgary.

Four Versions of Cinderella

Common tales are shared throughout the world in similar yet subtly distinct
versions and are retold, generation after generation, over a period of many centuries. Following are four versions of the popular Cinderella fairy tale: the classic
Brothers Grimm fairy tale, "Aschenputtel;" the Native American "Algonquin
Cinderella"; "Tam and Cam," a Vietnamese folk version of Cinderella, and a
modern satire, James Finn Garner's "The Politically Correct Cinderella." In addition, one of the student essays in this chapter, Liz Scheps's "Cinderella: Politically
Incorrect?" responds critically to Garner's satirical story.

JOURNAL

Write down a fairy tale that you remember from your childhood. Why was this
story an important one to you when you were a child? What meaning does the
story have for you today?

The Brothers Grimm

Aschenputtel

*Jacob Grimm (1785–1863) and his brother Wilhelm Grimm (1786–1859) were
scholars of the German language and of folk culture; they collected oral narratives
that embodied the cultural values of the German peasant and reflected on universal
human concerns. The Grimms' tales have been translated into more than seventy different languages. "Aschenputtel," a version of the Cinderella story, appears here in a
version translated by Lucy Crane. As you read this tale, consider how it differs from
the less violent version more familiar to American readers through the Disney films
and picture books.*

There was once a rich man whose wife lay sick, and when she felt her end
drawing near she called to her only daughter to come near her bed, and
said, "Dear child, be pious and good, and God will always take care of you, and
I will look down upon you from heaven, and will be with you."

And then she closed her eyes and expired. The maiden went everyday to her
mother's grave and wept, and was always pious and good. When the winter

came the snow covered the grave with a white covering, and when the sun came in the early spring and melted it away, the man took to himself another wife.

The new wife brought two daughters home with her, and they were beautiful and fair in appearance, but at heart were black and ugly. And then began very evil times for the poor stepdaughter.

"Is the stupid creature to sit in the same room with us?" said they; "those who eat food must earn it. Out upon her for a kitchen-maid!"

5   They took away her pretty dresses, and put on her an old gray kirtle, and gave her wooden shoes to wear.

"Just look now at the proud princess, how she is decked out!" cried they laughing, and then they sent her into the kitchen. There she was obliged to do heavy work from morning to night, get up early in the morning, draw water, make the fires, cook, and wash. Besides that, the sisters did their utmost to torment her—mocking her, and strewing peas and lentils among the ashes, and setting her to pick them up. In the evenings, when she was quite tired out with her hard day's work, she had no bed to lie on, but was obliged to rest on the hearth among the cinders. And as she always looked dusty and dirty, they named her Aschenputtel.

It happened one day that the father went to the fair, and he asked his two stepdaughters what he should bring back for them.

"Fine clothes!" said one.

"Pearls and jewels!" said the other.

10   "But what will you have, Aschenputtel?" said he.

"The first twig, father, that strikes against your hat on the way home; that is what I should like you to bring me."

So he bought for the two stepdaughters fine clothes, pearls, and jewels, and on his way back, as he rode through a green lane, a hazel-twig struck against his hat; and he broke it off and carried it home with him. And when he reached home he gave to the stepdaughters what they had wished for, and to Aschenputtel he gave the hazel-twig. She thanked him, and went to her mother's grave, and planted this twig there, weeping so bitterly that the tears fell upon it and watered it, and it flourished and became a fine tree. Aschenputtel went to see it three times a day, and wept and prayed, and each time a white bird rose up from the tree, and if she uttered any wish the bird brought her whatever she had wished for.

Now it came to pass that the king ordained a festival that should last for three days, and to which all the beautiful young women of that country were bidden, so that the king's son might choose a bride from among them. When the two stepdaughters heard that they too were bidden to appear, they felt very pleased, and they called Aschenputtel, and said,

"Comb our hair, brush our shoes, and make our buckles fast, we are going to the wedding feast at the king's castle."

15   Aschenputtel, when she heard this, could not help crying, for she too would have liked to go to the dance, and she begged her stepmother to allow her.

"What, you Aschenputtel!" said she, "in all your dust and dirt, you want to go to the festival! you that have no dress and no shoes! you want to dance!"

But as she persisted in asking, at last the stepmother said,

"I have strewed a dish-full of lentils in the ashes, and if you can pick them all up again in two hours you may go with us."

Then the maiden went to the back-door that led into the garden, and called out,

20 "O gentle doves, O turtle-doves,
And all the birds that be,
The lentils that in ashes lie
Come and pick up for me!
The good must be put in the dish,
25 The bad you may eat if you wish."

Then there came to the kitchen-window two white doves, and after them some turtle-doves, and at last a crowd of all the birds under heaven, chirping and fluttering, and they alighted among the ashes; and the doves nodded with their heads, and began to pick, peck, pick, peck, and then all the others began to pick, peck, pick, peck, and put all the good grains into the dish. Before an hour was over all was done, and they flew away. Then the maiden brought the dish to her stepmother, feeling joyful, and thinking that now she should go to the feast; but the stepmother said,

"No, Aschenputtel, you have no proper clothes, and you do not know how to dance, and you would be laughed at!"

And when Aschenputtel cried for disappointment, she added,

"If you can pick two dishes full of lentils out of the ashes, nice and clean, you shall go with us," thinking to herself, "for that is not possible." When she had strewed two dishes full of lentils among the ashes the maiden went through the backdoor into the garden, and cried,

30 "O gentle doves, O turtle-doves,
And all the birds that be,
The lentils that in ashes lie
Come and pick up for me!
The good must be put in the dish,
35 The bad you may eat if you wish."

So there came to the kitchen-window two white doves, and then some turtle-doves, and at last a crowd of all the other birds under heaven, chirping and fluttering, and they alighted among the ashes, and the doves nodded with their heads and began to pick, peck, pick, peck, and then all the others began to pick, peck, pick, peck, and put all the good grains into the dish. And before half-an-hour was over it was all done, and they flew away. Then the maiden took the dishes to the stepmother, feeling joyful, and thinking that now she should go with them to the feast; but she said "All this is of no good to you; you cannot come with us, for you have no proper clothes, and cannot dance; you would put us to shame."

Then she turned her back on poor Aschenputtel, and made haste to set out with her two proud daughters.

And as there was no one left in the house, Aschenputtel went to her mother's grave, under the hazel bush, and cried,

"Little tree, little tree, shake over me,
40   That silver and gold may come down and cover me."

Then the bird threw down a dress of gold and silver, and a pair of slippers embroidered with silk and silver. And in all haste she put on the dress and went to the festival. But her stepmother and sisters did not know her, and thought she must be a foreign princess, she looked so beautiful in her golden dress. Of Aschenputtel they never thought at all, and supposed that she was sitting at home, and picking the lentils out of the ashes. The King's son came to meet her, and took her by the hand and danced with her, and he refused to stand up with any one else, so that he might not be obliged to let go her hand; and when any one came to claim it he answered,

"She is my partner."

And when the evening came she wanted to go home, but the prince said he would go with her to take care of her, for he wanted to see where the beautiful maiden lived. But she escaped him, and jumped up into the pigeon-house. Then the prince waited until the father came, and told him the strange maiden had jumped into the pigeon-house. The father thought to himself,

"It cannot surely be Aschenputtel," and called for axes and hatchets, and had the pigeon-house cut down, but there was no one in it. And when they entered the house there sat Aschenputtel in her dirty clothes among the cinders, and a little oil-lamp burnt dimly in the chimney; for Aschenputtel had been very quick, and had jumped out of the pigeon-house again, and had run to the hazel bush; and there she had taken off her beautiful dress and laid it on the grave, and her bird had carried it away again, and then she had put on her little gray kirtle again, and had sat down in the kitchen among the cinders.

45   The next day, when the festival began anew, and the parents and stepsisters had gone to it, Aschenputtel went to the hazel bush and cried,

"Little tree, little tree, shake over me,
That silver and gold may come down and cover me."

Then the bird cast down a still more splendid dress than on the day before. And when she appeared in it among the guests every one was astonished at her beauty. The prince had been waiting until she came, and he took her hand and danced with her alone. And when any one else came to invite her he said,

"She is my partner."

50   And when the evening came she wanted to go home, and the prince followed her, for he wanted to see to what house she belonged; but she broke away from him, and ran into the garden at the back of the house. There stood a fine large tree, bearing splendid pears; she leapt as lightly as a squirrel among the branches, and the prince did not know what had become of her. So he waited until the father came, and then he told him that the strange maiden had rushed from him, and that he thought she had gone up into the pear-tree. The father thought to himself, "It cannot surely be Aschenputtel,"

and called for an axe, and felled the tree, but there was no one in it. And when they went into the kitchen there sat Aschenputtel among the cinders, as usual, for she had got down the other side of the tree, and had taken back her beautiful clothes to the bird on the hazel bush, and had put on her old gray kirtle again.

On the third day, when the parents and the stepchildren had set off, Aschenputtel went again to her mother's grave, and said to the tree,

"Little tree, little tree, shake over me,
That silver and gold may come down and cover me."

Then the bird cast down a dress, the like of which had never been seen for splendour and brilliancy, and slippers that were of gold.

And when she appeared in this dress at the feast nobody knew what to say for wonderment. The prince danced with her alone, and if any one else asked her he answered,

"She is my partner."

And when it was evening Aschenputtel wanted to go home, and the prince was about to go with her, when she ran past him so quickly that he could not follow her. But he had laid a plan, and had caused all the steps to be spread with pitch, so that as she rushed down them the left shoe of the maiden remained sticking in it. The prince picked it up, and saw that it was of gold, and very small and slender. The next morning he went to the father and told him that none should be his bride save the one whose foot the golden shoe should fit. Then the two sisters were very glad, because they had pretty feet. The eldest went to her room to try on the shoe, and her mother stood by. But she could not get her great toe into it, for the shoe was too small; then her mother handed her a knife, and said,

"Cut the toe off, for when you are queen you will never have to go on foot." So the girl cut her toe off, squeezed her foot into the shoe, concealed the pain, and went down to the prince. Then he took her with him on his horse as his bride, and rode off. They had to pass by the grave, and there sat the two pigeons on the hazel bush, and cried,

"There they go, there they go!
There is blood on her shoe;
The shoe is too small,
—Not the right bride at all!"

Then the prince looked at her shoe, and saw the blood flowing. And he turned his horse round and took the false bride home again, saying she was not the right one, and that the other sister must try on the shoe. So she went into her room to do so, and got her toes comfortably in, but her heel was too large. Then her mother handed her the knife, saying, "Cut a piece off your heel; when you are queen you will never have to go on foot."

So the girl cut a piece off her heel, and thrust her foot into the shoe, concealed the pain, and went down to the prince, who took his bride before him on his horse and rode off. When they passed by the hazel bush the two pigeons sat there and cried,

65   "There they go, there they go!
        There is blood on her shoe;
        The shoe is too small,
        —Not the right bride at all!"

Then the prince looked at her foot, and saw how the blood was flowing from the shoe, and staining the white stocking. And he turned his horse round and brought the false bride home again.

70   "This is not the right one," said he, "have you no other daughter?"

"No," said the man, "only my dead wife left behind her a little stunted Aschenputtel; it is impossible that she can be the bride." But the King's son ordered her to be sent for, but the mother said,

"Oh no! she is much too dirty, I could not let her be seen."

But he would have her fetched, and so Aschenputtel had to appear.

First she washed her face and hands quite clean, and went in and curtseyed to the prince, who held out to her the golden shoe. Then she sat down on a stool, drew her foot out of the heavy wooden shoe, and slipped it into the golden one, which fitted it perfectly. And when she stood up, and the prince looked in her face, he knew again the beautiful maiden that had danced with him, and he cried,

75   "This is the right bride!"

The stepmother and the two sisters were thunderstruck, and grew pale with anger; but he put Aschenputtel before him on his horse and rode off. And as they passed the hazel bush, the two white pigeons cried,

        "There they go, there they go!
        No blood on her shoe;
        The shoe's not too small,
80   The right bride is she after all."

And when they had thus cried, they came flying after and perched on Aschenputtel's shoulders, one on the right, the other on the left, and so remained.

And when her wedding with the prince was appointed to be held the false sisters came, hoping to curry favour, and to take part in the festivities. So as the bridal procession went to the church, the eldest walked on the right side and the younger on the left, and the pigeons picked out an eye of each of them. And as they returned the elder was on the left side and the younger on the right, and the pigeons picked out the other eye of each of them. And so they were condemned to go blind for the rest of their days because of their wickedness and falsehood.

Related Web Sites

The Brothers Grimm
http://www.pitt.edu/~dash/grimm.html
Biographical information, studies of specific tales, electronic tales, and links to more resources on the Brothers Grimm can be found at this simple, but informative URL.

GRIMM BROTHERS @ NATIONALGEOGRAPHIC.COM
http://www.nationalgeographic.com/grimm/
This attractive and entertaining web site from National Geographic shares
texts from many of Grimms' original fairy tales. It also includes audio sam-
ples of some of the stories, beautiful images, and interactive learning tools.

The Algonquin Cinderella

*This Native American version of the Cinderella story was anthologized by Idries
Shah, a student of world folklore and Sufism, in* World Tales *(1979). As you read
the tale, notice its emphasis on the spiritual power of beauty and vision.*

There was once a large village of the MicMac Indians of the Eastern Algon-
quins, built beside a lake. At the far end of the settlement stood a lodge, and
in it lived a being who was always invisible. He had a sister who looked after him,
and everyone knew that any girl who could see him might marry him. For that
reason there were very few girls who did not try, but it was very long before anyone succeeded.

This is the way in which the test of sight was carried out: at evening-time,
when the Invisible One was due to be returning home, his sister would walk
with any girl who might come down to the lakeshore. She, of course, could see
her brother, since he was always visible to her. As soon as she saw him, she
would say to the girls:

"Do you see my brother?"

"Yes," they would generally reply—though some of them did say "No."

5   To those who said that they could indeed see him, the sister would say:

"Of what is his shoulder strap made?" Some people say that she would enquire:
"What is his moose-runner's haul?" or "With what does he draw his sled?"
And they would answer:

"A strip of rawhide" or "a green flexible branch," or something of that kind.

10   Then she, knowing that they had not told the truth, would say:

"Very well, let us return to the wigwam!"

When they had gone in, she would tell them not to sit in a certain place, because it belonged to the Invisible One. Then, after they had helped to cook the
supper, they would wait with great curiosity, to see him eat. They could be sure
that he was a real person, for when he took off his moccasins they became visible, and his sister hung them up. But beyond this they saw nothing of him, not
even when they stayed in the place all the night, as many of them did.

Now there lived in the village an old man who was a widower, and his three
daughters. The youngest girl was very small, weak and often ill: and yet her sisters, especially the elder, treated her cruelly. The second daughter was kinder,
and sometimes took her side: but the wicked sister would burn her hands and

feet with hot cinders, and she was covered with scars from this treatment. She was so marked that people called her *Oochigeaskw,* the Rough-Faced-Girl.

When her father came home and asked why she had such burns, the bad sister would at once say that it was her own fault, for she had disobeyed orders and gone near the fire and fallen into it.

15 These two elder sisters decided one day to try their luck at seeing the Invisible One. So they dressed themselves in their finest clothes, and tried to look their prettiest. They found the Invisible One's sister and took the usual walk by the water.

When he came, and when they were asked if they could see him, they answered: "Of course." And when asked about the shoulder strap or sled cord, they answered: "A piece of rawhide."

But of course they were lying like the others, and they got nothing for their pains.

The next afternoon, when the father returned home, he brought with him many of the pretty little shells from which wampum was made, and they set to work to string them.

That day, poor Little Oochigeaskw, who had always gone barefoot, got a pair of her father's moccasins, old ones, and put them into water to soften them so that she could wear them. Then she begged her sisters for a few wampum shells. The elder called her a "little pest," but the younger one gave her some. Now, with no other clothes than her usual rags, the poor little thing went into the woods and got herself some sheets of birch bark, from which she made a dress, and put marks on it for decoration, in the style of long ago. She made a petticoat and a loose gown, a cap, leggings and a handkerchief. She put on her father's large old moccasins, which were far too big for her, and went forth to try her luck. She would try, she thought, to discover whether she could see the Invisible One.

20 She did not begin very well. As she set off, her sisters shouted and hooted, hissed and yelled, and tried to make her stay. And the loafers around the village, seeing the strange little creature, called out "Shame!"

The poor little girl in her strange clothes, with her face all scarred, was an awful sight, but she was kindly received by the sister of the Invisible One. And this was, of course, because this noble lady understood far more about things than simply the mere outside which all the rest of the world knows. As the brown of the evening sky turned to black, the lady took her down to the lake.

"Do you see him?" the Invisible One's sister asked.

"I do, indeed—and he is wonderful!" said Oochigeaskw.

The sister asked:

25 "And what is his sled-string?"

The little girl said:

"It is the Rainbow."

"And, my sister, what is his bow-string?"

"It is The Spirit's Road—the Milky Way."

30 "So you *have* seen him," said his sister. She took the girl home with her and bathed her. As she did so, all the scars disappeared from her body. Her hair

grew again, as it was combed, long, like a blackbird's wing. Her eyes were now like stars: in all the world there was no other such beauty. Then, from her treasures, the lady gave her a wedding garment, and adorned her.

Then she told Oochigeaskw to take the *wife's* seat in the wigwam: the one next to where the Invisible One sat, beside the entrance. And when he came in, terrible and beautiful, he smiled and said:

"So we are found out!"

"Yes," said his sister. And so Oochigeaskw became his wife.

RELATED WEB SITE

CINDERELLA STORIES

http://www.ucalgary.ca/~dkbrown/cinderella.html

Lists of variations on the Cinderella story can be found at this URL from the University of Calgary. Links to teaching ideas, articles, and essays will also be found here.

Tam and Cam (Vietnam)

"Tam and Cam" is a Vietnamese folk-story that demonstrates how universal the Cinderella story is, as well as how unique each version is to the particular culture out of which it grew. The sensitive and resourceful Tam is similar in many ways to the Western Cinderella, yet she is very much a product of a strongly Buddhist, nature-oriented society. She is willing to use violence to attain her revenge, and she is reborn several times during the story as a different sort of being. "Tam and Cam" is retold by Vo Van Thang and Jim Larson in a bilingual version included in Vietnamese Folktales *(1993).*

There were once two stepsisters named Tam and Cam. Tam was the daughter of their father's first wife. She died when the child was young so her father took a second wife. Some years later the father died and left Tam to live with her stepmother and stepsister.

Her stepmother was most severe and treated the girl harshly. Tam had to labor all day and long into the night. When there was any daylight she had to care for the buffalo, carry water for the cooking, do the washing and pick vegetables and water-fern for the pigs to eat. At night she had to spend a lot of time husking the rice. While Tam worked hard her sister did nothing but play games. She was given pretty clothes to wear and always got the best food.

Early one morning the second-mother gave two creels to Tam and Cam and told them to go to the paddy fields to catch tiny shrimp and crab. "I will give a *yêm* of red cloth to the one who brings home a full creel," she promised.

Tam was very familiar with the task of finding shrimp and crab in the paddy fields, and by lunchtime she had filled her creel. Cam walked and waded from field to field but she could not catch anything. She looked at Tam's full creel and said to her, "Oh, my dear sister Tam, your hair is covered in mud. Get into the pond to wash it, or you will be scolded by mother when you return home."

5   Believing what her sister told her, Tam hurried to the pond to wash herself. As soon as her stepsister entered the water, Cam emptied the shrimp and crab into her own creel, and hurried home to claim the *yêm* of red cloth.

When she had finished washing and saw her empty creel Tam burst into tears.

A Buddha who was sitting on a lotus in the sky heard her sobs and came down beside her. "Why are you crying?" asked the Buddha.

Tam told him all that had happened and the Buddha comforted her. "Do not be tearful. Look into your creel and see if anything is left."

Tam looked into the creel and said to the Buddha, "There is only one tiny *bông* fish."

10   "Take the fish and put it in the pond near your home. At every meal you must save a bowl of rice with which to feed it. When you want the fish to rise to the surface to eat the rice you must call like this:

Dear *bông,* dear *bông,*
Rise only to eat my golden rice,
For that of others will not taste nice.

Goodbye child, I wish you well." After saying this the Buddha disappeared.

15   Tam put the fish in the pond as she had been bidden, and every day, after lunch and the evening meal, she took some rice to feed it. Day by day the *bông* fish grew, and the girl became great friends with it.

Seeing Tam take rice to the pond after each meal the second-mother became suspicious, and bade Cam go to spy on her stepsister. Cam hid in a bush near the pond. When Tam called the *bông* fish the hidden girl listened to the words, and rushed to her mother to tell her of the secret.

That evening, the second-mother instructed Tam that on the following day she must take the buffalo to the far field.

"It is now the season for vegetables. Buffalo cannot graze in the village. To-morrow you have to take the buffalo to the far field. If you graze in the village it will be taken by the notables."

Tam set off very early the next morning to ride the buffalo to the far field. When she was gone, Cam and her mother took rice to the pond and called the *bông* fish. It rose to the surface and the woman caught it. She then took it to the kitchen where she cooked and ate it.

20   Tam returned in the evening, and after eating her meal took rice to the pond to feed her friend. She called and called, again and again, but she saw only a drop of blood on the surface of the water. Tam knew that something terrible had happened to the *bông* fish and began to weep.

The Buddha appeared by her side again. "Why do you weep this time, my child?"

Tam sobbed out her story and the Buddha spoke. "Your fish has been caught and eaten. Now, stop crying. You must find the bones of the fish and put them in four jars. After doing this you must bury the jars. Put one under each of the legs of your bed."

Tam searched and searched for the bones of her beloved friend but could not find them anywhere. As she looked even further a rooster came and called to her.

Cock-a-doodle-do, cock-a-doodle-do,
25 A handful of rice,
And I'll find the bones for you.

Tam gave rice to the rooster, and when it had eaten it strutted into the kitchen. In no time at all the elegant fowl returned with the bones and laid them at Tam's feet. The girl placed the bones into four jars and buried one under each of the legs of her bed.

Some months later the king proclaimed that there would be a great festival. All the people of Tam's village were going to attend, and the road was thronged with well dressed people making their way to the capital. Cam and her mother put on their finest clothes in readiness to join them. When the woman saw that Tam also wanted to attend the gala day she winked at Cam. Then she mixed a basketful of unhusked rice with the basket of clean rice Tam had prepared the previous evening. "You may go to the festival when you have separated this grain. If there isn't any rice to cook when we return home you will be beaten."

With that, she and her daughter joined the happy people on their way to the festival, and left Tam to her lonely task. She started to separate the rice, but she could see that it was hopeless and she began to weep.

30 Once again the Buddha appeared by her side. "Why are there tears in your eyes?" he asked.

Tam explained about the rice grains that had to be separated, and how the festival would be over by the time she had finished.

"Bring your baskets to the yard," said the Buddha. "I will call the birds to help you."

The birds came and pecked and fluttered until, in no time at all, they had divided the rice into two baskets. Not one single grain did they eat, but when they flew away Tam began to weep again.

"Now why are you crying?" asked the Buddha.

35 "My clothes are too poor," sobbed Tam. "I thank you for your help, but I cannot go dressed like this."

"Go and dig up the four jars," ordered the Buddha. "Then you will have all you need."

Tam obeyed and opened the jars. In the first she found a beautiful silk dress, a silk *yêm* and a scarf of the same material. In the second jar she found a pair of embroidered shoes of a cunning design which fitted her perfectly. When she opened the third jar great was her surprise when she saw a miniature horse. It neighed once, and grew to become a noble steed. In the fourth jar there was a richly ornamented saddle and bridle which grew to fit the horse. She washed herself and brushed her hair until it shone. Then she put on her wonderful new clothes and rode off to the festival.

On the way she had to ride through a stream flowing over the road. As she did so, one of her embroidered shoes fell into the water and sank beneath the surface. She was in such a hurry that she could not stop to search for it, so she wrapped the other shoe in her scarf and rode on.

Shortly afterwards, the king and his entourage, led by two elephants, arrived at the same spot. The elephants refused to enter the water and lowered their tusks, bellowing and trumpeting. When no amount of goading would force them on, the king ordered his followers to search the water. One of them found the embroidered shoe and brought it to the king, who inspected it closely.

40 　Finally he said, "The girl who wore a shoe as beautiful as this must herself be very beautiful. Let us go on to the festival and find her. Whoever it fits will be my wife."

There was great excitement when all the women learned of the king's decision, and they eagerly waited for their turn to try on the shoe.

Cam and her mother struggled to make it fit, but to no avail, and when they saw Tam waiting patiently nearby the woman sneered at her. "How can someone as common as you be the owner of such a shoe? And where did you steal those fine clothes? Wait till we get home. If there isn't any rice to cook I am going to beat you severely."

Tam said nothing, but when it came her turn to try on the shoe it fitted perfectly. Then she showed the other one that was wrapped in the scarf, and everyone knew that she was the future queen.

The king ordered his servants to take Tam to the palace in a palanquin, and she rode off happily under the furious and jealous gazes of her stepsister and stepmother.

45 　Tam was very happy living in the citadel with the king, but she never forgot her father. As the anniversary of his death came nearer she asked the king if she could return to her village to prepare the offering.

When Cam and her mother saw that Tam had returned, their jealous minds formed a wicked plan. "You must make an offering of betel to your father," said the stepmother. "That areca tree over there has the best nuts. You are a good climber, so you must go to the top of the tree and get some."

Tam climbed the tree and when she was at the top her stepmother took an axe and began to chop at the trunk. The tree shivered and shook and Tam cried out in alarm. "What is happening? Why is the tree shaking so?"

"There are a lot of ants here," called her stepmother. "I am chasing them away."

She continued to chop until the tree fell. Its crown, with Tam in it, toppled into a deep pond and the beautiful young woman was drowned. The wicked murderer gathered Tam's clothes, gave them to Cam, and led her to the citadel. She explained about the terrible "accident" to the king and offered Cam as a replacement wife. The king was very unhappy, but he said nothing.

45   When Tam died she was transformed into a *vang anh* bird. The bird flew back to the palace gardens and there she saw Cam washing the king's clothes near the well. She called out to her. "Those are my husband's clothes. Dry the clothes on the pole, not on the fence, lest they be torn."

Then she flew to the window of the king's room, singing as she went. The bird followed the king everywhere and he, who was missing Tam greatly, spoke to it, "Dear bird, dear bird, if you are my wife, please come to my sleeve."

The bird sat on the king's hand and then hopped onto his sleeve. The king loved the bird so much that he often forgot to eat or sleep, and he had a golden cage made for it. He attended to it day and night and completely ignored Cam.

Cam went to her mother and told her about the bird. The woman advised that she must kill it and eat it, and make up a story to tell the king. Cam waited until the king was absent then she did, as her mother had instructed. She threw the feathers into the garden afterwards.

When the king returned he asked about the bird and Cam answered, "I had a great craving for bird meat so I had it for a meal." The king said nothing.

50   The feathers grew into a tree. Whenever the king sat beneath it the branches bent down and made a parasol to shade him. He ordered a hammock to be placed under the tree and every day he rested there.

Cam was not happy about this, and once again she sought her mother's counsel.

"You must cut down the tree in secret. Use the wood to make a loom and tell the king you will weave some cloth for him."

On a stormy day Cam had the tree felled and made into a loom. When the king asked her about it she said that the wind had blown it over, and that now she would weave cloth for him on the loom made from its timber. When she sat down at the loom it spoke to her, "Klick klack, klick klack, you took my husband. I will take your eyes."

The terrified Cam went to her mother and told her of the loom's words. "Burn the loom and take the ashes far away from the palace," she told her daughter.

55   Cam did as she was bidden and threw the ashes at the side of the road a great distance from the king's home. The ashes grew into a green *thi*, tree and when the season came it bore one piece of fruit, with a wonderful fragrance that could be smelled from far away.

An old woman, who sold drinking water at a nearby stall, was attracted by the scent and she stood beneath the tree. She looked at the fruit, opened her pocket and called longingly, "Dear *thi*, drop into my pocket. I will only smell you, never eat you."

The fruit fell into her pocket, and she loved and treasured it, keeping it in her room to look at and to smell its fragrance.

Each day, when the old woman went to her stall, a small figure stepped from the *thi* fruit and grew into the form of Tam. She cleaned the house, put things in order, cooked the rice and made soup out of vegetables from the garden. Then she became tiny again and went back inside the *thi* fruit.

The old woman was curious and decided to find out who was helping. her. One morning she pretended to go to her stall and hid behind a tree near the back door. She watched through a crack and saw Tam emerge from the *thi* fruit and grow into a beautiful girl. The old woman was very happy and rushed into the house and embraced her. She tore apart the skin of the fruit and threw it away. Tam lived happily with the old woman and helped her with the house-work every day. She also made cakes and prepared betel to sell on the stall.

60   One day the king left his citadel and rode through the countryside. When he came to the old woman's stall he saw that it was neat and clean, so he stopped. The old woman offered him water and betel, and when he accepted it he saw that the betel had been prepared to look like the wings of an eagle. He remembered that his wife had prepared betel exactly in this fashion.

"Who prepared this betel?" he asked.

"It was done by my daughter," replied the old woman.

"Where is your daughter? Let me see her."

The old woman called Tam. When she came the king recognized his beloved wife, looking even younger and more beautiful. The king was very happy, and as the old woman told him the story he sent his servants to bring a rich palanquin to carry his wife back to the citadel.

65   When Cam saw that Tam had returned she was most fearful. She did her best to ingratiate herself and asked her stepsister the secret of her great beauty

"Do you wish to be very beautiful?" asked Tam. "Come, I will show you how." Tam had her servants dig a hole and prepare a large jar of boiling water. "If you want to be beautiful you must get into this hole," Tam told her wicked stepsister.

When Cam was in the hole Tam ordered the servants to pour in the boiling water, and so her stepsister met her death. Tam had the body made into *mam*, a rich sauce, and sent it to her stepmother, saying that it was a present from her daughter.

Each day the woman ate some of the *mam* with her meals, always comment-ing how delicious it was. A crow came to her house, perched on the roof ridge and cawed, "Delicious! The mother is eating her own daughter's flesh Is there any left? Give me some."

The stepmother was very angry and chased the bird away, but, on the day when the jar of *mam* was nearly empty, she saw her daughter's skull and fell down dead.

James Finn Garner

The Politically Correct Cinderella

An author, radio personality, and improvisational theater artist, James Finn Garner (b. 1960) has lived most of his life in the Chicago area. He earned his B.A. at the University of Michigan. Garner is best known for his Politically Correct Bedtime

Stories (1994) and a sequel, Politically Correct Holiday Stories *(1995), both of which include rewritten versions of classical fairy tales. In the selection that follows, Garner satirizes the politically correct approach to reading materials that would consider the original story to be classist, sexist, and even "speciesist."*

Introduction   When they were first written, the stories on which the following tales are based certainly served their purpose—to entrench the patriarchy, to estrange people from their own natural impulses, to demonize "evil" and to "reward" an "objective" "good." However much we might like to, we cannot blame the Brothers Grimm for their insensitivity to women's issues, minority cultures, and the environment. Likewise, in the self-righteous Copenhagen of Hans Christian Andersen, the inalienable rights of mermaids were hardly given a second thought.

Today, we have the opportunity—and the obligation—to rethink these "classic" stories so they reflect more enlightened times. To that effort I submit this humble book. While its original title, *Fairy Stories for a Modern World,* was abandoned for obvious reasons (kudos to my editor for pointing out my heterosexualist bias), I think the collection stands on its own. This, however, is just a start. Certain stories, such as "The Duckling That Was Judged on Its Personal Merits and Not on Its Physical Appearance," were deleted for space reasons. I expect I have volumes left in me, and I hope this book sparks the righteous imaginations of other writers and, of course, leaves an indelible mark on our children.

If, through omission or commission, I have inadvertently displayed any sexist, racist, culturalist, nationalist, ageist, lookist, ableist, sizeist, speciesist, intellectualist, socioeconomicist, ethnocentrist, phallocentrist, heteropatriarchalist, or other type of bias as yet unnamed, I apologize and encourage your suggestions for rectification. In the quest to develop meaningful literature that is totally free from bias and purged from the influences of its flawed cultural past, I doubtless have made some mistakes.

Cinderella   There once lived a young woman named Cinderella, whose natural birthmother had died when Cinderella was but a child. A few years after, her father married a widow with two older daughters. Cinderella's mother-of-step treated her very cruelly, and her sisters-of-step made her work very hard, as if she were their own personal unpaid laborer.

5   One day an invitation arrived at their house. The prince was celebrating his exploitation of the dispossessed and marginalized peasantry by throwing a fancy dress ball. Cinderella's sisters-of-step were very excited to be invited to the palace. They began to plan the expensive clothes they would use to alter and enslave their natural body images to emulate an unrealistic standard of feminine beauty. (It was especially unrealistic in their case, as they were differently visaged enough to stop a clock.) Her mother-of-step also planned to go to the ball, so Cinderella was working harder than a dog (an appropriate if unfortunately speciesist metaphor).

When the day of the ball arrived, Cinderella helped her mother- and sisters-of-step into their ball gowns. A formidable task: It was like trying to force ten pounds of processed nonhuman animal carcasses into a five-pound skin. Next came immense cosmetic augmentation, which it would be best not to describe at all. As evening fell, her mother- and sisters-of-step left Cinderella at home to finish her housework. Cinderella was sad, but she contented herself with her Holly Near records.

Suddenly there was a flash of light, and in front of Cinderella stood a man dressed in loose-fitting, all-cotton clothes and wearing a wide-brimmed hat. At first Cinderella thought he was a Southern lawyer or a bandleader, but he soon put her straight.

"Hello, Cinderella, I am your fairy godperson, or individual deity proxy, if you prefer. So, you want to go to the ball, eh? And bind yourself into the male concept of beauty? Squeeze into some tight-fitting dress that will cut off your circulation? Jam your feet into high-heeled shoes that will ruin your bone structure? Paint your face with chemicals and makeup that have been tested on nonhuman animals?"

"Oh yes, definitely," she said in an instant. Her fairy godperson heaved a great sigh and decided to put off her political education till another day. With his magic, he enveloped her in a beautiful, bright light and whisked her away to the palace.

10   Many, many carriages were lined up outside the palace that night; apparently, no one had ever thought of carpooling. Soon, in a heavy, gilded carriage painfully pulled by a team of horse-slaves, Cinderella arrived. She was dressed in a clinging gown woven of silk stolen from unsuspecting silkworms. Her hair was festooned with pearls plundered from hard-working, defenseless oysters. And on her feet, dangerous though it may seem, she wore slippers made of finely cut crystal.

Every head in the ballroom turned as Cinderella entered. The men stared at and lusted after this wommon who had captured perfectly their Barbie-doll ideas of feminine desirability. The womyn, trained at an early age to despise their own bodies, looked at Cinderella with envy and spite. Cinderella's own mother- and sisters-of-step, consumed with jealousy, failed to recognize her.

Cinderella soon caught the roving eye of the prince, who was busy discussing jousting and bear-baiting with his cronies. Upon seeing her, the prince was struck with a fit of not being able to speak as well as the majority of the population. "Here," he thought, "is a woman that I could make my princess and impregnate with the progeny of our perfect genes, and thus make myself the envy of every other prince for miles around. And she's blond, too!"

The prince began to cross the ballroom toward his intended prey. His cronies also began to walk toward Cinderella. So did every other male in the ballroom who was younger than 70 and not serving drinks.

Cinderella was proud of the commotion she was causing. She walked with head high and carried herself like a wommon of eminent social standing. But soon it became clear that the commotion was turning into something ugly, or at least socially dysfunctional.

15   The prince had made it clear to this friends that he was intent on "possessing" the young wommon. But the prince's resoluteness angered his pals, for they too

lusted after her and wanted to own her. The men began to shout and push each other. The prince's best friend, who was a large if cerebrally constrained duke, stopped him halfway across the dance floor and insisted that *he* was going to have Cinderella. The prince's response was a swift kick to the groin, which left the duke temporarily inactive. But the prince was quickly seized by other sex-crazed males, and he disappeared into a pile of human animals.

The womyn were appalled by this vicious display of testosterone, but try as they might, they were unable to separate the combatants. To the other womyn, it seemed that Cinderella was the cause of all the trouble, so they encircled her and began to display very unsisterly hostility. She tried to escape, but her impractical glass slippers made it nearly impossible. Fortunately for her, none of the other womyn were shod any better.

The noise grew so loud that no one heard the clock in the tower chime midnight. When the bell rang the twelfth time, Cinderella's beautiful gown and slippers disappeared, and she was dressed once again in her peasant's rags. Her mother- and sisters-of-step recognized her now, but kept quiet to avoid embarrassment.

The womyn grew silent at this magical transformation. Freed from the confinements of her gown and slippers, Cinderella sighed and stretched and scratched her ribs. She smiled, closed her eyes and said, "Kill me now if you want, sisters, but at least I'll die in comfort."

The womyn around her again grew envious, but this time they took a different approach: Instead of exacting vengeance on her, they stripped off their bodices, corsets, shoes, and every other confining garment. They danced and jumped and screeched in sheer joy, comfortable at last in their shifts and bare feet.

20   Had the men looked up from their macho dance of destruction, they would have seen many desirable womyn dressed as if for the boudoir. But they never ceased pounding, punching, kicking, and clawing each other until, to the last man, they were dead.

The womyn clucked their tongues but felt no remorse. The palace and realm were theirs now. Their first official act was to dress the men in their discarded dresses and tell the media that the fight arose when someone threatened to expose the crossdressing tendencies of the prince and his cronies. Their second was to set up a clothing co-op that produced only comfortable, practical clothes for womyn. Then they hung a sign on the castle advertising CinderWear (for that was what the new clothing was called), and [through self-determination and clever marketing], they all—even the mother and sisters-of-step—lived happily ever after.

RELATED WEB SITE

JAMES FINN GARNER
http://www.jamesfinngarner.com/
"Welcome to the only official web site for the writings and activities of James Finn Garner. I intend for the stuff here to act as a bonus for my read-

ers, with extra stories, graphics, anecdotes, tidbits, trifles, and other goodies
that can't be found elsewhere."

—James Finn Garner

Questions for Discussion

1. What aspects of each tale help you to identify it as a Cinderella story?
2. How do you feel about rereading the original Grimms' tale as an adult? Does the Cinderella story hold a different meaning for you today than it did when it was first told to you? Why?
3. Contrast the tone and theme of the four versions of the story. What different attitudes toward nature and the material world are expressed in each tale?
4. Were you surprised or shocked by the violent and punitive ending of the Grimms' version? Do you think the Native American version is more suitable for children? Why do you think the popular fairy tales that most parents today read to their children are less violent than the Grimms' version?
5. Comment on the theme of alienation, exploitation, and the resolution to these issues in the various versions of Cinderella. What set of values is implied by each resolution?
6. Compare Garner in his "Politically Correct Cinderella," to the Cinderella "Aschenputtel." Does Garner's conclusion seem feasible as an alternative to the "sell-out" of the traditional Cinderella who goes to live with the prince? Which of the four versions did you prefer, and why?

Ideas for Writing

1. Write an essay that discusses how the Cinderella story helps to shape values for young women. Do you consider this story in its classic version sexist, or do you think it still has relevant meanings to convey? Explain your response.
2. Do a close comparison of any two of the Cinderella versions. You can consider such issues as nature, materialism, class dominance, and feminism.

Joshua Groban

Two Myths

Joshua Groban, who grew up in an artistic and literary family, has always been interested in mythology and issues related to creativity. In his freshman English class, Groban wrote a research paper comparing a number of different Native American accounts of the creation and was fascinated by the imagination and diversity of the visions

he encountered in his reading. The following essay is Groban's comparative response
to the two accounts of creation from the casebook of myths presented in this chapter.

An individual growing up in today's society is quickly indoctrinated into
believing the predominant myth about creation. Our church, our parents, our teachers, and the media all reinforce such concepts as Adam and
Eve and the Garden of Eden. However, every culture has its own unique myth
to explain the birth of the planet and its inhabitants. By comparing the
Bible's depiction of creation to that of the Yao myth, "The Chameleon
Finds," one is reminded of the many different and imaginative ways people
have presented such fundamental issues as gender relations, our connection
with and responsibility to the environment, and the relationship of human
beings to God.

First, we are struck by the different views of women in the two accounts of
creation, the Bible's narration of creation depicts women as secondary to and
subservient to men. In the Book of Genesis, "the cattle," "all the birds of the air,"
and "every beast of the field" are created before women. This order of creation
gives the impression that the beasts are more central to life on earth than
women, and thus are created first. But, despite the abundance of these beasts,
"there was not found a helper fit for him [man]." Genesis makes it clear that
women are given life not as man's equal, but as his "helper" or assistant. When
God finally creates females, they are divested from any sense of individuality;
they are not created in the image of God, as man is, but from the rib of man.
Thus, women are presented as owing their very existence to men. Genesis 2:4
concludes by emphasizing this idea, explaining that "she shall be called Woman,
because she was taken out of man." The Bible ties not only a woman's existence,
but even her name to men. In this way, this creation myth clearly establishes
women as subservient to men and lacking an equivalent sense of identity.

The Yao creation myth presents a different and more favorable portrayal of
women. Women are not created as an afterthought in "The Chameleon Finds,"
to function as a helper to men, as they are in the Bible. Instead, men and
women come into the world together, as companions. Males and females are
given life when The Creator plucks them from the river in his trap. The myth
says, "The next morning when he pulled the trap he found a little man and
woman in it. He had never seen any creatures like this." In this way, the two
sexes begin their existence in equality. Females do not come from males and
are not granted life after men, cattle, birds, and beasts. The myth creates men
and women together, and thus suggests that the two sexes should live their lives
in this state of equality as well.

A juxtaposition of the Genesis and Yao stories in regards to their view of nature
reveals a similar divergence. In the Bible, man dominates nature in much the same
way as he dominates women. Both the environment and females are presented in
Genesis as subservient "helpers" to man. Genesis 2:4 professes, "and out of the
ground the Lord God made to grow every tree that is pleasant to the sight and
good for food . . . ." Nature exists to serve and to help man; trees have life only to

serve mankind by being "pleasant to the sight and good for food." Like women, the role of nature is to serve man rather than exist in equality with him. The Bible reads, "The Lord God took the man and put him in the Garden of Eden to till and keep it." Man does not exist in the garden to coexist with the plants and animals of the garden. Instead, he is to "keep it," as if the earth were a possession.

5   The Yao story of creation sees humans as irresponsible and destructive in their relation to the earth. In the Yao tale, the first man and woman set fire to the vegetation and kill animals that inhabit the earth. Their creator is appalled by this behavior: "They are burning up everything," he exclaims. "They are killing my people." He is so disturbed by the way humans treat the earth that He decides to leave the planet. A spider makes him a ladder and He goes to live in the sky. The story ends, "Thus the gods were driven off the face of the earth by the cruelty of man." This myth, in contrast to the Bible, sets clear expectations about the consequences of man's mistreatment of the earth. In "The Chameleon Finds," nature, like women, has rights that should never be usurped. Genesis ignores these universal rights, affording them only to God and to man.

This contrast also exists in the way the two myths portray man's relationship to God. In Genesis, God is a distant, autocratic deity; he speaks and the act is performed. In this story, God "took" the man and "put him" in the Garden of Eden. Later, He "commands" man never to eat from the tree of good and evil. Humans are pawns controlled by this distant deity. They make no decisions in Genesis 2:4, but are instead "taken," "put," and "commanded." The Bible's God is one that controls humans and merely speaks in order to create.

The Yao Creator is an entirely different, more human sort of figure. This God is not presented as an all-powerful deity that merely speaks to create life. He unknowingly discovers humans in his trap, and no indication is given that He created them at all. This Creator does not command humans to do as He wants them to do. When humans destroy the earth, no punishment comes from a distant deity, as in the Bible. Instead, the Creator leaves the earth, leaving humans free to make their own decisions and choose their own destiny. This contrast impacts both man's relationship with God and his view of himself. In the Bible, The Creator is a force that has complete control over humans. He creates by merely speaking, commands humans, and punishes them. In contrast, the Yao Creator does not control every human action. He creates people not by speaking, but by discovering them. He does not command or punish, but leaves people to make their own choices about life on earth. This divergent approach functions to empower humans. The Yao myth enables people to feel in control of their life because no distant, supreme being controls them. Consequently, this fosters a heightened sense of morality and responsibility. "The Chameleon Finds" does not allow the individual to blame God or rely upon him. Instead, this creator diety, having set the world in motion and established His ideology, now leaves the decisions in the hands of humans, whose punishment for their crimes against nature is abandonment by the creator.

It would be misguided to contend that the discrepancy between the Bible and other myths on gender issues, the environment, and man's relationship with God proves that the Bible is responsible for the social ills of today. Religion does not create society; rather society creates religion. The Bible did not cause sexism or environmental disaster, and is not at the root of today's societal evils. However, comparing the account of The Creation in Genesis to similar myths from other cultures is of value in reminding the individual that there are no absolute truths. Every society has to define its origins and values as it sees fit. The dominance of Judeo-Christian thinking in our society does not make it more correct. There are alternative stories, such as "The Chameleon Finds," that present different visions of creation. This process of comparison can lead to an appreciation of a contrasting ideology; however, the appreciation of other religions and their view of creation comes only when someone begins to think about the validity of their own religion rather than blindly accepting it. The comparison of different creation myths is not antithetical to religion; it represents a reasoned approach to looking at God and creation and thus defines what true religious conviction really is.

QUESTIONS FOR DISCUSSION

1. What are the main points of comparison and contrast around which Groban structures his essay? Do they seem appropriate to the myths he studied, or would you have selected others?
2. How effectively does Groban use details and references to the two myths he contrasts to support his conclusions about their differences? Are there other details he might have used or different inferences he might have drawn based on the details he selects?
3. Although Groban states in some parts of his essay that all creation myths have validity, since "there are no absolute truths," he seems quite critical of the Biblical version of Creation. Do you think that some views of creation are better than others, or is each version a product of the culture that produced it?
4. What seem to be the criteria that Groban uses in his evaluation of the two myths he is comparing? Do his criteria seem appropriate, or would you substitute others? How would you set up criteria for evaluating myths of creation, if you believe that it is possible to do so?

Liz Scheps

Cinderella: Politically Incorrect?

Liz Scheps was a college senior when she wrote the following essay. She majored in linguistics and history, and her interests include popular culture, adolescent studies, earth and space science, and ice skating. The best part about writing this essay for

Scheps as a linguistic major was being given the opportunity to take an in-depth look at the language in the "Politically Correct Cinderella." In the essay that follows, Scheps critiques Garner's version of the Cinderella tale by comparing and contrasting it to the original Grimms' version.

In today's politically correct society, people may be vertically-challenged, hair-deprived, or differently-abled; they are rarely short, bald, or handicapped. While the political correctness movement is meant, in the eyes of its supporters, to remove through changes in language and ideology the prejudice towards and denigration of various types of people who do not fit the societal ideal, many critics find this social and linguistic doctoring laughable or even offensive. James Finn Garner makes hyperbolic use of the language and doctrines of the politically correct ideology in order to ridicule political correctness in his retelling of the classic Cinderella tale.

The original Cinderella story, written by the Brothers Grimm in the early nineteenth century, is not the sweet tale of fairy godmothers and singing mice that Disney has made common knowledge. The original is a darker story, in which promises are broken, deception is encouraged, and harsh revenge is exacted. The reader is instructed from the outset that Cinderella's stepsisters are "at heart black and ugly"; there is no hope for their redemption in the Grimms' tale. Similarly, it becomes clear that the stepmother is also inherently evil; she informs Cinderella that she may go to the prince's ball if she is able to pick lentils out of the ashes precisely because she believes it will be impossible for Cinderella to complete the task; when Cinderella does accomplish this feat, the stepmother simply informs her that she is too dirty and underdressed to attend. When the prince comes to their house in search of the maiden whose foot will fit the slipper, the stepmother instructs the eldest daughter to "'[c]ut the toe off, for when you are queen you will never have to go on foot.'" In the end, the stepsisters both pay for their "wickedness and falsehood" by losing their sight to the doves who are allies of Cinderella. Throughout the tale, the values of honesty, piety, goodness, resourcefulness, and closeness to nature are emphasized; the message sent is that if one is genuinely good, he or she will eventually be rewarded; if one inflicts pain on others or lies, he or she will lose out in the end.

Garner's Cinderella tale uses a parody of the myth of Cinderella to satirize politically correct language and behavior. The stepmother and stepsisters become "mother-of-step" and "sisters-of-step" respectively; this tongue in cheek labeling flouts the negative connotations that the traditional names "stepmother" and "stepsister" connote, due in large part to the legacy of the original Cinderella tale. It might also be a comment on the increasingly complex familial situations which have become common in our society; as divorce and remarriage lead to intricate webs of half-brothers, stepsisters, and so forth, the labeling patterns of these family members has become more and more nebulous in order to downplay the lack of blood relation between members of the same family. Furthermore, the multi-word label "sisters-of-step" is in keeping with the politically correct tradition of creating long convoluted names for originally blunt terms, such as hair-deprived for bald.

One of the most controversial and most publicized features of politically correct language is the movement to eliminate the word "man" from the term "woman" in order to lessen the subordinate status of the word "woman," as well as of the group that it represents. Garner plays on this notion throughout the Cinderella tale by referring to a single female as a "wommon" and a group of them as "womyn." The traditional fairy godmother is replaced, interestingly, by a man, who informs Cinderella that he is her "fairy godperson, or individual deity proxy." By replacing the fairy godmother with a male figure, Garner plays upon the challenge presented by the politically correct, particularly by feminists, to make all occupations open to both genders. Since a fairy is traditionally female in the popular conception, Garner is able to make fun of the politically correct agenda by placing a male in this fairy tale career. However, what is interesting about Garner's use of a male fairy godperson is that the role that this character plays switches as well. In the Disney-like story, the fairy godmother is a nurturing figure who aids Cinderella; in Garner's version, the godperson (who is really a godman) seems to be elevated above Cinderella; he laments her desire to conform to societal standards of beauty and finally reconciles himself to teaching her political values at a later time.

5   In addition to using politically correct language to refer to gender differences, Garner employs politically correct stereotypes and critiques of societally-determined gender roles throughout the Cinderella tale. In the Grimm original, gender is not especially important on a literal level, but many women have complained that what young girls who read fairy tales like this learn is that they should simply be good and beautiful; Cinderella gets the chance to go to the ball because she is good, but she wins the heart of the prince because she is beautiful and well-proportioned: the prince does not search for the woman who dazzled his mind, but rather for the woman who will fit a silver slipper. Garner exaggerates the politically correct critique of gender roles throughout the tale; he apparently does this to show just how much this critique ruins the charming fairy tale ideology which is a foundation of western culture. For instance, instead of having fun spending the day getting ready for the ball, the sisters-of-step "began to plan the expensive clothes they would use to alter and enslave their natural body images to emulate an unrealistic standard of feminine beauty." By thus drawing mock-critical attention to the thin supermodel look which so many feminists have attacked as being unattainable and a cause of eating disorders, low self-esteem, and other problems of women in American society, Garner ridicules the feminist position as puritanical and exaggerated: of course, he seems to say, women don't knowingly and actively enslave their bodies every time they get dressed—they just want to dress up, look good, and have some fun!

Garner portrays Cinderella as undergoing a transition not from working girl to princess, as in the original tale, but from politically incorrect to politically correct; through the course of the story she changes from a woman who wants to be beautiful and is proud of the effect her appearance has on men to a "wommon" who is independent and has no need of beauty and the attention of men; instead of tight dresses that might be bad for her health, she wears "comfortable, practical clothing" and runs her own business through "self-determination and clever marketing." Thus, Cinderella has attained the supposed goal of the politically correct and/or feminist movements, but because of Garner's sarcastic tone, she does not seem at all desirable as a heroine the way that the honest, loyal and courageous Grimms' Aschenputel is; rather she conforms to the popular media's negative stereotype of the conniving female capitalist—and she's a frump, at that! Garner holds the new, supposedly progressive Cinderella up to ridicule, reinstilling the politically incorrect notion that beauty is more important than anything else. Furthermore, the fact that "they all—even the mother- and sisters-of-step—lived happily ever after" suggests that good and evil are irrelevant in a politically correct world—no one receives their just desserts for what they have done throughout the tale. In fact, the womyn succeed because the men self-destruct sooner, forcing them to join together in bonds of feminine sisterhood, which Garner portrays as phony, just another politically correct pose.

Garner also uses his tale to ridicule the politically correct critique of men as overly competitive, drawn to women primarily for reasons of sexual conquest. In the original tale, the prince and the father are portrayed as good, civilized characters. The prince is portrayed as a young gentleman willing to do anything to find the woman who has stolen his heart. In Garner's version, the men are reduced to animalistic, sex-crazed fools. The men at the ball lust after Cinderella because she fits the Barbie-doll image which the politically correct suggest that men press onto women. The prince's first thought upon seeing her is of sex and continuing his own lineage; he ponders the idea that Cinderella "'is a wommon that I could make my princess and impregnate with the progeny of our perfect genes, and thus make myself the envy of every other prince for miles around. And she's blond too!'" These lines ridicule the guerrilla-feminist position, which claims that men simply react with the animalistic instinct to reproduce with the most fit female available, as well as the more commonly accepted female stereotype of men who revel in having sex and impregnating women and then relate their exploits to friends in order to appear super-masculine.

The original Grimm's Cinderella, like the Disney version, shows Cinderella as a character from a preindustrial, agrarian age who draws what power she has through living in harmony with nature, in touch with familiar spirits of mice, birds, and growing things. Garner seems unaware of the natural quality of the original tale, creating his Cinderella as someone who moves from a nonpolitically correct attitude towards nature to a heavily parodied kind of environmental consciousness. The environmental movement, as Garner perceives it, advocates great responsibility towards animals; thus it is politically incorrect to test cosmetics on animals, to log forests, or to wear fur or synthetic fibers which cause pollution. Garner takes this awareness to a ridiculous level, placing blame on people for every involvement they have with animals and characterizing the animals as profoundly hurt by the actions and even the casual verbal expressions of people. Thus, after Cinderella is said to be working "harder than a dog," Garner apologizes that this is "an appropriate if unfortunately speciesist metaphor." The row of carriages outside the palace is singled out as an example of the environmental irresponsibility displayed by the citizens of the kingdom in not carpooling, while everything Cinderella wears is environmentally incorrect: her dress is silk stolen from "unsuspecting" silkworms and her hair is decorated with pearls "plundered from hard-working, defenseless oysters." It is not until the end of the story, when the womyn supposedly shed the constraints of materialistic society, that they become environmentally conscious and thus politically correct. However, this development too has its ironies: they succeed not because of their social consciousness but because of their "clever marketing" of "natural" clothing—which simply reinforces materialism.

Garner clearly wishes to condemn and ridicule the politically correct agenda in his version of the Cinderella tale. By choosing to retell a classic fairy tale through the hyperbolic language of the politically correct movement, he seeks to expose the repressive, rule-bound society and overly euphemistic language usage that would result from living under a politically correct regime. His main point seems to be that the original tale and the values it connotes, no matter how old-fashioned or misogynistic they might seem, are no worse than the convoluted notions of the political correctness movement. By exaggerating the politically correct viewpoint to a laughable degree, Garner creates a tale designed to entice and entertain people of all outlooks, while at the same time providing a strong and stinging critique of political correctness, and especially of feminism.

QUESTIONS FOR DISCUSSION

1. Why does Scheps begin her essay with a summary of the original Cinderella tale? How does this help readers to better understand her critique of Garner's version?

2. What main points of contrast does Scheps make between the original story and the Garner version? How well does each of these points support her overall critique? Could she have made other points?

3. As a linguistics major, Scheps was particularly interested in the parody of "politically correct" language in the Garner version of Cinderella. How effectively does Scheps analyze the significance of made-up words and phrases in Garner's story?

4. What conclusions does Scheps draw about Garner's story in her final paragraph? Do you agree with her evaluation here?

TOPICS FOR RESEARCH AND WRITING

1 Write an essay that presents your own definition of a myth. Draw on your personal experiences and the readings in this chapter as well as outside research into the nature of myths and mythology. How does a myth differ from a lie or falsehood?

2. Write your own myth, based on your view of yourself as a hero or heroine. Then write an analysis of your myth, comparing the "ideal" self that emerges in the story you have written to your "real" self. How does your myth reflect the concerns of your generation and your own values? In what ways is your myth traditional? Make connections between your myth and other hero myths that you read about in your research.

3. Over five hundred different versions of the Cinderella tale are told in cultures around the world. Do some research to find two interesting versions from different cultures; then write a comparison paper of these two versions. What did you learn about the cultures that produced each story? See particularly *Cinderella: A Folklore Casebook* by Alan Dundes (Garland, 1992).

4. Compare and contrast a traditional myth or tale with a modern retelling of that myth, perhaps in a popular culture format such as a TV show or comic book. Reflect on how and why the original myth has been changed. Which of the two versions do you prefer and why?

5. In what important ways do you think that myths and rituals function in people's lives and in society? Write an essay in which you do some research into this issue and discuss several ways that myths serve people. Support each main point you make with an example. (See particularly the essays by Erich Fromm and Joseph Campbell in this chapter). Consider some of the problems that arise in a modern culture that has rejected many of its traditional myths and rituals.

6. Write your own modern version of a fairy tale such as Cinderella or one or the other popular Grimms' tales such as Sleeping Beauty or Hansel and Gretel, or write your own creation myth and explain your reasons for creating this tale. Refer to Bettelheim, Campbell, and Fromm when explaining your reasons for creating the tale in the particular way that you did.

 7. See one of the following films or one that you choose that explores the role of myth, either by yourself or with several of your classmates. Write an analysis of the film that discusses the ways in which the film explores the nature and meaning of myths or fairy tales and their relationship to dreams and the imagination. Choose from the following list: *Black Orpheus, The Neverending Story, Star Wars* (any episode), *The Princess Bride, The First Knight, Monty Python's Holy Grail, The Fisher King, Ever After, The Lion King, Harry Potter, Lord of the Rings, Spiderman,* and *Oh Brother Where Art Thou.*

5 Obsessions and Transformations

Vincent Van Gogh (1853–1890)
Starry Night (Saint-Remy, June 1889)

Dutch painter Vincent Van Gogh, one of the most famous modern artists, was a depressive who took his own life only one year after painting one of his greatest works, *Starry Night*. Van Gogh's expressionistic painting of a night time sky reminds us of how we transform the world as we view it through our own inner lenses of obsession, suffering, or joy.

JOURNAL

Describe a place or setting, urban or rural, interior or exterior, as you imagine a person who is emotionally distraught or disturbed might perceive it. Use figurative language and sensory appeal, but try to show how the mind distorts exterior reality according to inner pressures and concerns.

Yes indeed, I realized, looking into the mirror. There was a world in my eye. And I saw that it was possible to love it: that in fact, for all it had taught me of shame and anger and inner vision, I did love it.

ALICE WALKER
Beauty: When the Other Dancer is the Self

Even more than our experiences, our beliefs became our prisons. But we carry our healing with us even into the darkest of our inner places. A Course in Miracles says, "When I have forgiven myself and remembered who I am, I will bless everyone and everything I see." The way to freedom often lies through the open heart.

RACHEL NAOMI REMEN
Remembering

DEFINITION: WORD BOUNDARIES OF THE SELF

Definition involves clarifying a term's meaning through precise use of language and through distinguishing among several words that may be difficult to use appropriately because they have similar or overlapping meanings. Definitions, both short and expanded, can be used not only as a way of clarifying the denotative or dictionary meanings of the crucial words and abstract terminology that you use in your writing, but also as a way of exploring personal definitions of terms based on feelings, values, and language.

Public Meanings and Formal Definition

In essay writing, definition is most often used as a method for clarifying meaning for your readers. If, for example, you are writing an essay on obsessions, you would first want to define what is meant by obsession. Although you would first turn to a dictionary, an encyclopedia, or another reliable authority for a definition of this basic term, you would also need to use your own words to create your statement of meaning. Your own words will help you to develop control over the direction of your paper and capture your reader's interest. Begin by placing the term within a formal pattern. First, state the word you will be defining, in this case, "obsession;" then put the term in a larger class or group: "An obsession is a strong emotional response." Next, you will need one or more details or qualifying phrases to distinguish your term from others in the larger group of strong emotions: "An obsession is an emotional response or preoccupation that is compulsive and highly repetitive, a response over which a person often has little or no control and that can have destructive consequences." If this definition still seems inadequate, you could add more details and develop the definition further with a typical example: "Overeating can be an obsessive form of behavior."

In writing an extended definition of a key term, carefully construct the initial definition. If you place the term in too large a class, do not distinguish it from others in the class, or merely repeat your original term or a form of the term, you will have difficulty developing your ideas clearly and will confuse your reader. You also need to decide how you plan to use your definition: What will its purpose be?

Once you have created the initial definition, you can proceed to develop your paragraph or essay using other analytical writing strategies such as process analysis, discussion of cause and effect, or comparative relationships. For example, you could discuss several of the qualities of a typical obsession, provide an ordered exploration of the stages of the obsession, or examine the kinds of human growth and interactions with which the obsession can interfere, as Sharon Slayton does in her essay on the obsession with being good. For clarity, reader interest, and development, examples and illustrations can be used effectively with any of the larger analytical structures that you might wish to take advantage of in your essay: examples from personal experience, friends, or your reading of fictional or factual sources.

Stipulative and Personal Definitions

Sometimes writers decide to develop a personal definition. This form of definition, referred to as a stipulative definition, is based on the writer's personal ideals and values. In this case, you still need to be clear in making crucial distinctions. For example, if you are writing a paper on your own personal dream, you might begin with a dictionary definition of dream to contrast the qualities of your personal dream to the traditional connotations associated with the term as stated in the dictionary.

Freewriting and clustering will help you define what the term means to you and discover the term's deeper personal levels of meaning. Comparative thinking can also be useful. Write a series of sentences beginning with the words "My dream is . . ." or "My dream is like . . ." and make as many different associations with concrete objects or events as you can. Examine the associations you have made and construct a personal definition qualified with expressions such as "my," "to me," or "in my opinion," and include several personal distinguishing qualities.

A stipulative definition is often supported by personal experiences that help the reader understand the origins and basis of your views. Provide contrasts with qualities others may associate with the term. For example, other people may believe that a dream as you have defined it is just "wishful thinking," an exercise in escapism. You could argue that, to the contrary, it is necessary to have a dream as a high ideal or aspiration; otherwise, one may too readily accept a version of reality that is less than what it could be and lose faith in the imagination that is necessary to solve problems and to move confidently into the future. Thus a stipulative definition can become a type of argument, an advocacy of one's perspective on life.

Contradiction

In developing your definition, be careful not to create contradictions. Contradiction or equivocation occurs when you define a term in one way and then shift the definition to another level of meaning. To base an argument intentionally on a contradiction is at best confusing and at worst dishonest and propagandistic. For example, if you begin your paper with a definition of "myth" as the cultural and social stories that bind a people together and then shift your paper to a discussion of private dreams and personal mythology, you will confuse your reader by violating the logic of your definition, and your essay will lose much of its credibility. A better strategy for dealing with the real complexity of certain words is to concede from the start (in your thesis) that this is an expression with seemingly contradictory or ironic shades of meaning—as in the case of the word "good" in Slayton's essay in this chapter—and then spell out the complexity clearly in your definition. Read your paper carefully before turning it in, checking to see that your definition and your arguments and examples are consistent. If not, your paper needs a revision, and you may want to modify your initial definition statement.

Writing objective and personal definitions will help you clarify your thoughts, feelings, and values. As you work to find the qualities, distinctions, and personal experiences that give a complex concept a meaning that reflects your inner self as well as the consensus of the public world, you will also be moving forward on your inward journey.

THEMATIC INTRODUCTION:
OBSESSIONS AND
TRANSFORMATIONS

Dreams and fantasies can be healthy; they can serve as a means for
escape from trivial or tedious routines and demands. Popular entertainment, for example, often provides us with simple escapist fantasies
that encourage us to identify with an idealized hero or heroine. We can
become strong, beautiful, courageous, or very wise, and, for a moment,
we may be able to forget the realities of our own lives. When our minds
return from a fantasy, we may feel more refreshed, more capable of
handling daily responsibilities. Often fantasies provide more than just
possibilities of short-term escape; they can also offer insights that will lead
to deeper self-understanding as well as psychological and/or spiritual
transformation. Each individual has unique dreams and fantasies. When
these messages from our unconscious minds and from our dream worlds,
are understood and interpreted, they can help us have more fulfilling and
rewarding lives.

Some people suffer from personal obsessions and compulsions which
can lead to behavior that can be limiting and repetitive, sometimes even
destructive to self or others. In such cases, the obsession controls the
individual rather than the individual controlling the goal. Why do some
people become possessed by their fantasies and obsessions, whereas
others can maintain their psychological equilibrium and learn about themselves through their preoccupations, their unconscious dreams? How do
people's unconscious obsessions influence their day-to-day life and decision-
making processes? The essays, stories, and poem included in this chapter
provide you with a range of perspectives that will help you consider these
and other issues related to how our inner lives, our unconscious, our
dreams, nightmares, fantasies, and obsessions have a impact on political
and social life.

In this chapter's first selection, "Fog-Horn" by W. S. Merwin, the
poem's speaker reflects on the power of the forgotten, unconscious world.
The foghorn in this poem becomes a symbol of every individual's hidden
inner self, secret fears, and nightmares that may moan out in the night. The
foghorn reminds us that a part of our self exists beyond the realm of our
rational control. As you read this selection, think about the times when you
were surprised or even shocked by the power of your feelings. How do
those feelings change your waking, public, and rational life? The next two
selections show how dreams and nightmares that are analyzed, interpreted
and understood can be transformative and healing. They can change the
course of one's life in a positive and hopeful way. In "What is a Healing
Dream," Jungian analyst Mark Ian Barasch defines a healing dream while
giving many examples of how individuals have used their dreams to enrich

and improve their sense of physical and mental well being. In "Remembering," physician and psychotherapist Naomi Remen presents a case history of one of her patients who recovered and transcended her painful and dehumanizing memories of abuse and violence and of what she had to do in order to escape from Vietnam.

The next two selections explore depression, an obsessive illness. In his essay "Depression," Andrew Solomon defines and explains how "depression is the flaw in love." He argues that "To be creatures who love, we must be creatures who can despair at what we lose, and depression is the mechanism of that despair." At the same time, Solomon shows how therapy and modern medicine can help people to be transformed by their sense of deep sadness and loss to a more intense appreciation of life. Charlotte Perkins Gilman's classic short story "The Yellow Wallpaper" (1896) reveals how a character's depression leads her to obsessive hallucinations about the yellow wallpaper in her bedroom. The main character's obsessive experience can be seen as transformative. Her rebellion against the social norms and gender roles of her society shows that she may be developing a stronger sense of personal identity and self worth. Reading this story will give you insights into the destructive power of depression as well as an appreciation of the progress that has been made in helping people bring positive meaning out of their mental strife.

How many of your friends or colleagues are obsessed with their weight, their performance at a particular sport, or their appearance? The next selection shows how it is possible to transform an obsession with beauty or weight through developing a sense of self-esteem. Anne Lamott's "Hunger" shares her struggle to overcome her eating disorder. For Lamott, "learning to eat was about learning how to live—and deciding to live."

The final professional selection in this chapter, E. M. Forster's story "The Other Side of the Hedge," presents a healing fantasy. The main character escapes from his workaholic stressful daily life to a pastoral world where he learns he can be accepted as he is. For the traveler this new world initially stands in contrast to the values of progress and the work ethic that propel many of us to accept a relentless life on the road in a world where material possessions and prestige are the symbols of success, but seldom of happiness and personal fulfillment.

The two student writings that conclude this chapter also explore the power of obsession and transformation. In her essay "The Good Girl," Sharon Slayton analyses her obsession with being well-behaved and always living up to others' expectations. In her thirties, she comes to realize that doing enjoyable things for oneself is a crucial quality of a well-balanced individual. In the final essay, "Exercise and Well-being," Tiffany Castillo develops many reasons with provocative examples and evidence to help us understand why exercise is not only good for the body, but can help relieve stress and elevate one's mood as well.

The works in this chapter ask readers to look within, to listen to the questions and fears in their hearts and spirits. Through reading and reflecting on the selections in this chapter, we hope that that you can recognize obsessive types of behavior and at the same time realize that they can be potential sources of creative inspiration, transformation, and love.

W. S. Merwin

Fog-Horn

W. S. Merwin (b. 1927) was raised in Pennsylvania. After graduating from Princeton in 1947, he lived for several years in London, translating French and Spanish classics for the British Broadcasting Corporation. Merwin, who has published many collections of poems and translations, explores myths, cultural contrasts, and ecology. His style is often discontinuous, mysterious—wavering between waking and sleeping states, and creating a dialogue between the conscious and the unconscious mind. Merwin's writing often creates strong emotional responses. Some of his more widely read books include Opening the Hand *(1983),* The Vixen *(1996),* The River Sound Poems *(2000), and* The Pupil *(2001).* Fog-Horn *was included in Merwin's* The Drunk in the Furnace *(1958). As you read the poem, try to re-create the sound and image of the foghorn in your own imagination.*

JOURNAL

Write about a warning that came to you from your unconscious; a warning that might have taken the form of a dream, a fantasy, a minor accident, or a psychosomatic illness.

Surely that moan is not the thing
That men thought they were making, when they
Put it there, for their own necessities.
That throat does not call to anything human
5   But to something men had forgotten,
That stirs under fog. Who wounded that beast
Incurably, or from whose pasture
Was it lost, full grown, and time closed round it
With no way back? Who tethered its tongue
10 So that its voice could never come
To speak out in the light of clear day,
But only when the shifting blindness

Descends and is acknowledged among us,
As though from under a floor it is heard,
15 Or as though from behind a wall, always
Nearer than we had remembered? If it
Was we that gave tongue to this cry
What does it bespeak in us, repeating
And repeating, insisting on something
20 That we never meant? We only put it there
To give warning of something we dare not
Ignore, lest we should come upon it
Too suddenly, recognize it too late,
As our cries were swallowed up and all hands lost.

QUESTIONS FOR DISCUSSION

1. How does Merwin personify the foghorn making it more than just an object? Refer to specific details that you think are particularly effective.
2. What does the cry of the foghorn signify? What is its warning?
3. What words, images, and phrases make the poem seem like a dream or a nightmare?
4. Why can't the voice of the foghorn "speak out in the light of clear day"?
5. Why does the voice of the foghorn call to something "forgotten"? What parts of ourselves are we most likely to forget or ignore? What helps us to remember what we want to forget?
6. What is your interpretation of the poem? What state of mind is the poet attempting to define?

CONNECTION

Compare the foghorn as a symbol of a human obsession in Merwin's poem with the yellow wallpaper in Gilman's story. How does each symbol help to focus themes of psychic repression and denial as well as insights into the destructive consequences of obsessive behavior (see page 276)?

IDEAS FOR WRITING

1. Write an essay in which you define and clarify with examples and comparisons the positive role that you think the unconscious mind can play in helping one to create a balanced and fulfilling life. Refer to the poem in shaping your response.
2. Write a narrative or a poem in which you use an object or an animal as a comparison to or as a way of defining and understanding the unconscious mind. Try to emphasize how the unconscious mind communicates with the conscious mind.

RELATED WEB SITES

http://www.english.uiuc.edu/maps/poets/mr/merwin/merwin.htm
Poet W. S. Merwin's life and work are examined at this web site devoted to modern American poetry. Here you can also find reviews on and interviews with Merwin, as well as essays by the author.

THE ACADEMY OF AMERICAN POETS
http://www.poets.org/
Learn more about American poetry at the web site for "The Academy of American Poets." Find out about poets, poems, and events throughout the country.

Marc Ian Barasch

What Is a Healing Dream?

Marc Ian Barasch attended Yale University, where he studied literature, psychology, anthropology, and film. A long-time practitioner of Tibetan Buddhism, he was a founding member of the psychology department at Naropa University. Barasch has worked as an editor-in-chief of New Age Journal, *as a contributing editor to* Psychology Today *and* Natural Health Magazine, *and as a producer/writer for film and television. He has received the National Magazine Award and the Washington Monthly Award for Investigative Writing. His most widely read books include* The Healing Path: A Soul Approach to Illness *(1994),* Remarkable Recovery *(1995) and, most recently,* Healing Dreams: Exploring the Dreams That Can Transform Your Life *(2000), from which the following selection is excerpted.*

JOURNAL

Write about an unusual, especially memorable, or a repeated dream, one that "stopped you in your tracks" and made you think about your life from a new perspective.

I have had a most rare vision. I have had a dream, past the wit of man to say what dream it was: man is but an ass, if he go about to expound this dream. . . . The eye of man hath not heard, the ear of man hath not seen, man's hand is not able to taste, his tongue to conceive, nor his heart to report, what my dream was.
                              —*Bottom, in Shakespeare's* A Midsummer
                              Night's Dream

Most of us have had (or, inevitably, will have) at least one dream in our lives that stops us in our tracks. Such dreams tell us that we're not who we think we are. They reveal dimensions of experience beyond the everyday. They may shock us, console us, arouse us, or repulse us. But they take their place alongside our most memorable life events because they're so vivid and emblematic. Some are like parables, setting off sharp detonations of insight; others are like gripping mystery tales; still others are like mythic dramas, or horror stories, or even uproarious jokes. In our journey from childhood to age, we may count them on one hand. Yet once they have flared in the soul, they constellate there, emitting a steady, pulsarlike radiance.

The number of people I have discovered grappling with these powerful inner experiences has astounded me. In a time when the individual psyche is increasingly colonized by mass culture, when media images seem ever more intent on replacing dreams wholesale, here is an unvoiced parallel existence dreamers sometimes do not share with even their loved ones.

People often describe such striking dreams in a self-devised lexicon: "deep" dreams; "vibrational" dreams; "strong" dreams; "flash" dreams; "TV" dreams (a South African priestess); "lucky-feeling dreams" (a dog breeder in Quebec); "true" dreams (a Salish Indian healer in Oregon). A folk artist named Sultan Rogers, famous for his fancifully erotic woodcarvings, refers to his most powerful dreams as "futures," so filled are they with the urgency to be manifest in the world. (He makes a point of carving them immediately upon waking, while the sensuous images are still fresh.) Yet many I spoke with displayed a genuine reticence about discussing their dreams, as if exposing them to daylight might stunt some final germination still to come. Famed Jungian analyst Marion Woodman declined to share a dream she believed helped heal her of a serious physical illness, because, she told me, "I cannot let others into my holy of holies." Some said they feared the professional consequences of being seen as overly attentive to dreams. "I'm in the midst of putting together a multimillion-dollar deal based on a dream I had ten years ago," one man confided. His vision had become the polestar of his life. "But it wouldn't do," he said, "for my partners to think I'm relying on invisible consultants."

In the fifteen years since I began my exploration, a nascent field of research has arisen, along with a host of terms—*impactful, transformative, titanic, transcendent*—to differentiate big dreams from ordinary ones. I have coined the term *Healing Dreams*, because they seem to have a singular intensity of purpose: to lead us to embrace the contradictions between flesh and spirit, self and other, shadow and light in the name of wholeness. The very word for "dream" in Hebrew—*chalom*—derives from the verb meaning "to be made healthy or strong." With remarkable consistency, such dreams tell us that we live on the merest outer shell of our potential, and that the light we seek can be found in the darkness of a yet-unknown portion of our being.

5   Jung labeled them numinous (from the Latin *numen*, meaning "divine command"), but often just used the succinct shorthand, big. While most dreams, he wrote, were "nightly fragments of fantasy," thinly veiled commentaries on "the affairs of the everyday," these significant dreams were associated with major life passages, deep relationship issues, and spiritual turning points.

Many cultures have had a terminology for such dreams of surpassing power. The Greek New Testament seems to contain more words for inner experience than Eskimos have for snow: *onar* (a vision seen in sleep as opposed to waking); *enypnion* (a vision seen in sleep that comes by surprise); *horama* (which could refer to visions of the night, sleeping visions, or waking visions); *horasis* (a supernatural vision); *optasia* (a supernatural vision that implies the Deity revealing Himself); and so on. By and large the English language has been impoverished of a working vocabulary; we have little at hand beyond *dream* and *nightmare.* Given our cultural paucity, it can be a struggle to define these signal occurrences.

"How do you know when you've had a special dream?" I once asked a Choctaw Indian acquaintance named Preston. A humorous man with rubbery features—his role in his tribe, he told me, was as a "backwards person," a trickster and comedian—he grew uncharacteristically serious at my question.

"These vision dreams are things that you follow," he said. "Things that you do. They show you a situation that needs to be taken care of, and a way to turn it around."

"But *how* do you know?" I pressed him.

10   "It's the way you feel. That kind of dream wakes you up very sudden-like. Maybe you wake up really, really happy." He looked at me, eyebrow cocked. "Or maybe you wake up with your bed so soaking wet you'da thought you'd peed on yourself!"

His ribald comment points to a universally reported attribute of Healing Dreams—what we might call ontological weight, the heft and immediacy of lived experience. Remarks from various dreamers return often to a common theme of "realer than real." They often comment on the acuity of the senses—taste, touch, sight, smell, and hearing. I, too, can recall awakening with my ears still ringing from a dream gunshot, or waking up momentarily blinded by a dream's burst of light.

There is often a depth of emotion that beggars normal waking life. The sixteenth-century rabbi and physician Solomon Almoli wrote: "If one dreams of powerful fantasy images that cause him to be excited or to feel anger or fear during the dream itself, this is a true dream; but if the images are insipid and arouse no strong feelings, the dream is not true." Such dreams are filled not with simple anxiety, but terror; not mere pleasantness, but heart-bursting joy. People report waking up on tear-soaked pillows, or laughing in delight. (The Bantu people of Africa have a specific term for the latter—*bilita mpatshi,* or blissful dreaming.)

Healing Dreams are analogous to ancient Greek theater, where actors in colorful, oversized costumes presented stories contrived to put an audience through the emotional wringer; to make it feel, viscerally, the heroes' agonies and ecstasies. Indeed, some Healing Dreams feature larger-than-life settings and personages—palatial buildings, sweeping landscapes, beings of supernatural goodness or terrible malignancy. Healing Dreams seem designed to produce a catharsis, to lead their "audience" to a metanoia, a change of heart.

Like drama, such dreams often have an unusually coherent narrative structure. Islamic dream texts refer to the ordinary dream as *azghas*—literally, "handful of dried grass and weeds," signifying a lack of arrangement—in contrast to the more coherent messages of *akham* ("genuine inspiration from the Deity, warning from a protecting power, or revelation of coming events"). The Healing Dream's storytelling tends to be more artful, often containing a rich array of literary or cinematic devices—subplots, secondary characters, sudden reversals and surprise endings, flashbacks and flashforwards, adumbration, even voice-over narration and background music.

15   Healing Dreams often involve a sense of the uncanny or paranormal. Within the dream, one may find one has special powers to telekinetically move objects; receive information as if via telepathy; levitate; transform oneself into other creatures; visit heavens or hells. Dreamers report of out-of-body experiences; actual events foreseen; talking with the departed; having a near-identical dream to that of a friend or loved one; and other strange synchronicities. Healing Dreams hum with so much energy that, like a spark from a Van de Graaf generator, they seem to leap the gap between the visible and invisible worlds.

In such dreams, symbols tend to be extraordinarily multilayered—exaggerated cases of what Freud referred to as "over-determination," where an image seems to be "chosen" by the unconscious for its multiplicity of associations. Language itself reveals a dense richness. A key dream-word may yield half a dozen definitions, each with a different or even opposing nuance. There is often a powerful aesthetic component—such dreams may depict dances and rituals, music and song, poetry, photos, paintings, and other art forms. There is frequently a collective dimension—the dream seems to transcend the dreamer's personal concerns, reaching into the affairs of family, clan, community, or the world at large.

Such dreams also have a peculiar persistence. People report waking up with the images still before their eyes. The dream lingers in memory long after common ones fade. New meanings emerge over time. One lives, as it were, into the dream. "The *findout*," the Native American sage Lame Deer told one researcher, "has taken me all my life."

Most important, Healing Dreams, if heeded, can be transformational—creating new attitudes toward ourselves and others, magnifying our spiritual understanding, deepening the feeling side of life, producing changes in careers and relationships, even affecting society itself. After a Healing Dream, one may never be the same again.

The Dream Uses You

Many people wonder why they should bother with their dreams at all. A common answer is that they will help us with our lives, and this is certainly true. Even the most extraordinary dream, properly investigated, will have much to say about bread-and-butter issues like work, love, and health. But the Healing Dream is less a defender of our waking goals—material achievement, perfect romance, a modest niche in history—than an advocate-general for the soul, whose aims may lay athwart those of the ego. Dreams are often uninterested in the self-enhancement stratagems we mistake for progress. "It's vulgarizing to say that we can use dreams as tools—like shovels!—to get ahead, or be more assertive, like a kid who prays his little sister will drop dead so he can have her candy," a dreamworker once told me with some passion. "It's more like"—and here he seemed to fluoresce with certainty—"the dream uses *you*."

20   Such dreams "use" us only if we are willing to dwell for a time within their ambiguities without resolving them. The Jungian psychologist Robert Johnson tells of the time he had a dreamlike vision of a "spirit man" with burning orange fire coursing through his veins. The man plunged to the bottom of an indigo lake, but the fire was miraculously unquenched. Then the spirit man took Johnson by the hand and flew him to a great nebula coruscating like a diamond at the center of the universe. Standing on the very threshold of divine majesty, before vast, dazzling whorls of light eternal, Johnson tugged at the man's sleeve and asked impatiently, "This is fine, but *what is it good for?*"

"The spirit man looked at me," wrote Johnson, "in disgust: 'It isn't good for *anything*.'" Still, Johnson wondered for a long while afterward how his experience might tangibly change his life. Then he had a key insight: *He would never know.* "This magnificent power," he wrote "is transmuted into small things, day-to-day behavior, attitudes, the choices that we make in the ordinariness of daily human life."

Johnson's experience emphasizes that, contrary to a slew of popular works (starting with the dream manuals of the early Egyptians), there may be no sure-fire, direct method to utilize the power of dreams. We may be astonished by a bolt of lightning, but that doesn't mean we can harness it to flash down upon the grill to cook our steak. Healing Dreams offer few outright prescriptions. They often require us to live our questions rather than furnish instant answers.

How, then, should we see a Healing Dream? We might think of it as a window that enlarges our perspective, freeing us of a certain tunnel vision. It frames our daily concerns in a context beyond the confines of our room. The view from this dream window opens onto what we may think the exclusive province of mystics and philosophers—conundrums like the meaning of the sacred, the problem of evil, the nature of time, the quest for a true calling, the mysteries of death and love—making these issues intimately our own.

Or we might see the dream as a worthy opponent. It is often said that spiritual work is an *opus contra naturam,* going against the grain of what seems natural, normal, or even good. The unconscious is not just the repository of beauty and light, or the issuer of benign, firm-handed guidance, but the home of the trickster. The dream figure that bears the denied powers of the self often appears sinister and antithetical. Yet he may also be our secret ally: in spiritual life, what is merely pleasant can become the ego's friction-free way of sliding by without learning much of anything. By rubbing us the wrong way, the Healing Dream kindles an inner heat, forcing us to include our obstacles and adversaries in our process of growth.

25   We might regard a Healing Dream as a work of art, something that evokes a feeling of meaningfulness that cannot be put into words. Like the glowing Vermeer painting of a simple woman with a pitcher, it is the extraordinary thing that sheds light on the ordinary. Like art, dreams create a shift in perspective in

the very act of beholding them. Seeing things in a way we have not seen before—taking the stance of the appreciator rather than the analyst—changes us, as suggested by the remark by the phenomenologist Merleau-Ponty: "Rather than seeing the painting, I see according to or with it."

Healing Dreams might be conceived as visits to an otherworld with its own geography and inhabitants. From this perspective, we are explorers visiting a foreign land whose citizens have customs, beliefs, and language that are not entirely familiar. Dream images thus are experienced in their own right, not just as self-fabricated symbols. Through this sort of living encounter, dreams become the proverbial travel that broadens the mind.

Or we might regard the Healing Dream as a wise teacher, one who instructs us in the most personal way—embarrassingly so, for she knows our forbidden desires and deepest fears, our secret hopes and unexpressed gifts. This teacher tells us stories about ourselves, about our relationships to others, about our place in the larger schema. This approach may require a humility the ego finds discomforting Jung told one dreamer: "Look here, the best way to deal with a dream is to think of yourself as a sort of ignorant child, ignorant youth, and to come to the two-million-year-old man or to the old mother of days and ask, 'Now, what do you think of me?'"

What *does* the dream think? Or is a Healing Dream itself more a question posed to *us*? If so, the most reasonable-seeming answer is often the wrong one. Such dreams play by rules that confound the waking mind. But at the heart of Healing Dreams are certain consistent, if challenging, attitudes. Before we set out to understand the big dream, it would be helpful to consider some of the principles and perspectives that will recur on the journey:

- ▪ *Nonself:* Dreams show us we are not who we think we are: "We walk through ourselves," wrote James Joyce, "meeting robbers, ghosts, giants, old men, young men, wives, widows, brothers-in-love." Dreams de-center us from our everyday identity, pushing us toward a richer multiplicity of being. Thus in dreams we may be startled to find, as one dream researcher puts it, that we are "a woman and not a man, a dog not a person, a child not an adult . . . [even] two people at once." As Alice in Wonderland says: "I know who I *was* this morning, but since then I have changed several times." What Healing Dreams attempt to cure is nothing less than the ego's point of view—that habitual "I" that clings to rigid certainties of what "I want," "I fear," "I hate," "I love." What is sometimes called the ego-self or the "I" figure in our dreams may be a mere side character, reacting or observing but not in control of events. We may experience the diminution of what in waking life we most prize in ourselves, and the elevation of what we find belittling. One sign of a healthy personality is the ability to acknowledge other selfhoods and inhabit other skins.
- ▪ *Nonsense:* From the ego's standpoint, dream logic is an oxymoron. It is a sure bet that whatever we deem most ridiculous upon waking is the fulcrum point of what the dream wants to tell us. Indeed, when we find

ourselves disparaging an image as meaningless, it is a signal to retrieve it from the scrap heap and place it on the table. Like a magician, the dream may confuse us through misdirection, but only because we are paying too much attention to the right hand and not enough to the left. Like a fool in the court of a king, dreams use absurdity to tell the truth when none else dare; but the king must realize the joke is on him in order to get the punch line.

▪ *Balance:* A Healing Dream often comes to redress imbalance—something in the personality is askew, awry, not right (or perhaps, *too* right). If we have become inflated, it cuts us back down to human scale; if we wander in a dark vale, lost, it suddenly illumines the mountaintop. The psyche, Jung suggests, "is a self-regulating system that maintains its equilibrium just as the body does. Every process that goes too far immediately and inevitably calls forth compensations." The quickest way to the heart of a dream is to ask what one-sided conscious attitude it is trying to offset.

▪ *Reversal of value.* In dreams, our fixed reference points—our opinions, values, and judgments—may be revealed as mere tricks of perspective. What the conscious mind believes to be a precious gem may be a beach pebble to the spirit, while what it tosses aside may be the pearl of great price. Alice, on her journey through Wonderland's dreamscape, first drinks a potion that makes her large, and she weeps in misery. Then when another elixir makes her shrink, she finds herself literally drowning in her own tears. A few small tears, usually a matter of little import, suddenly become a matter of life or death—as indeed they may be to the dreaming soul.

▪ *Wholeness:* Healing Dreams point to the relatedness of all things, reveling in the union of opposites. They show us a vision of the divine that encompasses both growth and decay, horror and delight. We may crave a world of either\or, but the Dream says, *Both\and*. We build a wall between our social persona and our inner selves; the Dream bids us, *Demolish it*. We wish to believe we're separate from one another, but the Dream insists, *We are in this together*. We believe time to be a one-way river, flowing from past to present to future, yet the Dream reveals, *All three times at once*. We wish to be virtuous and free of taint, but the Dream insists, *The dark and the light are braided and bound*.

The Way of the Healing Dream

We live in a practical era, one that stresses the productive usage of things. Yet Healing Dreams are not easily reduced to the utilitarian. Although they may offer practical revelation, they have more in common with the realm of art, poetry, and music, where what you do with an experience is not the overriding issue. Such dreams open up a gap in the ordinary, allowing something new, and often indefinable, to enter our lives. We can work with our dreams, "unpack" them, analyze them, learn from them. But it is their residue of mystery that gives them enduring power, making them touchstones we return to again and again.

30   When we take our dreams seriously, their images and feelings subtly begin to alter our waking lives. Meaning seeps in through a kind of osmosis. We

begin to glimpse the principle that connects each to all. Any sincere attention (and commitment) to our dreams renders us spiritually combustible. What was once inert now strikes sparks.

Healing Dreams seem to *want* something of us, and often will not let go until they receive it. But few of us pay them serious mind. Their images dissipate into air, dissolve like snowflakes on water. We dive back into the slipstream of our daili-ness with something akin to relief. We sense that if we were to draw too near, the gravitational field of dreams might perturb, forever, the fixed orbit of our lives.

For this reason, I've chosen to focus as much as possible on these dreams that won't allow themselves to be tossed aside; the ones that yank off the bed-clothes, spook us, amaze us, drag us below, lift us above, damn us, save us—in terms so strong, in presence so palpable, we simply can't ignore them. *These* dreams refuse to go quietly, for they mean to change us utterly. If we look into their depths, we may behold a unique destiny struggling from its chrysalis, and watch, astonished and not a little afraid, as our unsuspected selfhood unfolds a new, wetly glistening wing.

QUESTIONS FOR DISCUSSION

1. How does Barasch use similes in the first paragraph to reinforce some of the qualities of the "healing dream"? Why would it be (as Bottom says in the quotation from *A Midsummer Night's Dream*) so difficult to "conceive" and "report" what such a dream is about?
2. Why did some of the people Barasch interviewed express "reticence" to share and discuss their healing dreams? What does this reticence, com-bined with the lack of words in our language to name such dreams, sug-gest about the value placed on dreams in our culture?
3. Why does the author compare healing dreams to Greek Theater and other dramatic forms of art?
4. In what sense are healing dreams "transformational"? How do they "use" us, changing our lives in subtle ways?
5. How do healing dreams "enlarge our perspective," serving as an oppo-nent, a teacher, or an artwork?
6. Explain the five bulleted "attitudes . . . principles and perspectives" of the healing dream. How might these five attitudes help in the healing process?

CONNECTION

Compare and contrast Fromm's views on the significance of dreams with Barasch's views (see page 195).

IDEAS FOR WRITING

1. Work with the dream you narrated in your journal entry above. Analyze it from the perspective of the five attitudes presented at the end of the essay. How did examining the dream using the attitudes delineated by Barasch help you to understand it better?

2. Write a definition of another type of dream than the healing dream, using some of the same techniques as Barasch does: listing of qualities, principles, attitudes, similes, and analogies. You can also use examples of such dreams that you have had or read about.

RELATED WEB SITES

MARC IAN BARASCH

http://www.healingdreams.com/author.htm

At this web site you will find information about author, Marc Ian Barasch, his book, *Healing Dreams,* and his work surrounding the subject of harnessing the power of dreams to heal.

DREAM LINKS

http://dir.yahoo.com/Social–Science/Psychology/Branches/Sleep–and–Dreams/

The most popular sites on dreams and their general meaning can be viewed at this URL. Information on different types of dreams, such as healing and lucid dreams, can also be found here.

Rachel Naomi Remen

Remembering

Nationally known for her leadership in the mind-body health movement, Rachel Naomi Remen, M.D. is the cofounder and medical director of the Commonweal Cancer Help Program in Bolinas, California. Formerly on the faculty of the Stanford Medical School, she is currently a clinical professor of family and community medicine at the University of California at San Francisco School of Medicine. Her books include The Masculine Principle, The Feminine Principle, *and* Humanistic Medicine *(1975),* The Human Patient *(1980),* Kitchen Table Wisdom *(1996), and* My Grandfather's Blessings *(2000). In her private practice, she has worked as a psycho-oncologist for more than 20 years. Her particular blend of caring and wisdom has developed through her professional life as a physician and her experience of living with a chronic illness for more than 40 years. In the following selection from* Kitchen Table Wisdom, *Remen reflects on the power of memory to shape identity and to heal.*

JOURNAL

Write about how and why writing or talking about resolving issues from your past helped you feel better.

What we do to survive is often different from what we may need to do in order to live. My work as a cancer therapist often means helping people to recognize this difference, to get off the treadmill of survival, and to refocus their lives. Of the many people who have confronted this issue, one of the most dramatic was an Asian woman of remarkable beauty and style. Through our work together I realized that some things which can never be fixed can still heal.

She was about to begin a year of chemotherapy for ovarian cancer, but this is not what she talked about in our first meeting. She began our work together by telling me she was a "bad" person, hard, uncaring, selfish, and unloving. She delivered this self-indictment with enormous poise and certainty. I watched the light play across her perfect skin and the polish of her long black hair and thought privately that I did not believe her. The people I had known who were truly selfish were rarely aware of it—they simply put themselves first without doubt or hesitation.

In a voice filled with shame, Ana began to tell me that she had no heart, and that her phenomenal success in business was a direct result of this ruthlessness. Most important, she felt that it was not possible for her to become well, as she had earned her cancer through her behavior. She questioned why she had come seeking help. There was a silence in which we took each other's measure. "Why not start from the beginning?" I said.

It took her more than eight months to tell her story. She had not been born here. She had come to this country at ten, as an orphan. She had been adopted by a good family, a family that knew little about her past. With their support she had built a life for herself.

5   In a voice I could barely hear, she began to speak of her experiences as a child in Vietnam during the war. She began with the death of her parents. She had been four years old the morning the Cong had come, small enough to hide in the wooden box that held the rice in the kitchen. The soldiers had not looked there after they had killed the others. When at last they had gone and she ventured from hiding she had seen that her family had been beheaded. That was the beginning. I was horrified.

She continued on. It had been a time of brutality, a world without mercy. She was alone. She had starved. She had been brutalized. Hesitantly at first, and then with growing openness, she told story after story. She had become one of a pack of homeless children. She had stolen, she had betrayed, she had hated, she had helped kill. She had seen things beyond human endurance, done things beyond imagination. Like a spore, she had become what was needed to survive.

As the weeks went by, there was little I could say. Over and over she would tell me that she was a bad person, "a person of darkness." I was filled with horror and pity, wishing to ease her anguish, to offer comfort. Yet she had done these things. I continued to listen.

Over and over a wall of silence and despair threatened to close us off from each other. Over and over I would beat it back, insisting that she tell me the worst. She would weep and say, "I do not know if I can," and hoping that I would be able to hear it, I would tell her that she must. And she would begin another story. I often found myself not knowing how to respond, unable to do anything but stand with her here, one foot in this peaceful calm office on the water, the other in a world beyond imagination. I had never been orphaned, never been hunted, never missed a meal except by choice, never violently attacked another person. But I could recognize the whisper of my darkness in hers and I stood in that place in myself to listen to her, to try to understand. I wanted to jump in, I wanted to soothe, I wanted to make sense, yet none of this was possible. Once, in despair myself, I remember thinking, "I am her first witness."

Over and over she would cry out, "I have such darkness in me." At such times it seemed to me that the cancer was actually helping her make sense of her life; offering the relief of a feared but long-awaited punishment.

10   At the close of one of her stories, I was overwhelmed by the fact that she had actually managed to live with such memories. I told her this and added, "I am in awe." We sat looking at each other. "It helps me that you say that. I feel less alone." I nodded and we sat in silence. I *was* in awe of this woman and her ability to survive. In all the years of working with people with cancer, I had never met anyone like her. I ached for her. Like an animal in a trap that gnaws off its own leg, she had survived—but only at a terrible cost.

Gradually she began to shorten the time frame of her stories, to talk of more recent events: her ruthless business practices, how she used others, always serving her own self-interest. She began to talk about her contempt, her anger, her unkindness, her distrust of people, and her competitiveness. It seemed to me that she was completely alone. "Nothing has really changed," I thought. Her whole life was still organized around her survival.

Once, at the close of a particularly painful session, I found myself reviewing my own day, noticing how much of the time I was focused on surviving and not on living. I wondered if I too had become caught in survival. How much had I put off living today in order to do or say what was expedient? To get what I thought I needed. Could survival become a habit? Was it possible to live so defensively that you never got to live at all?

"You have survived, Ana," I blurted out. "Surely you can stop now." She looked at me, puzzled. But I had nothing further to say.

One day, she walked in and said, "I have no more stories to tell."

15   "Is it a relief?" I asked her. To my surprise she answered, "No, it feels empty."

"Tell me." She looked away. "I am afraid I will not know how to survive now." Then she laughed. "But I could never forget," she said.

A few weeks after this she brought in a dream, one of the first she could remember. In the dream, she had been looking in a mirror, seeing herself reflected there to the waist. It seemed to her that she could see through her clothes, through her skin, through to the very depths of her being. She saw that she was filled with darkness and felt a familiar shame, as intense as that she had felt on the first day she had come to my office. Yet she could not look away. Then it seemed to her as if she were moving, as if she had passed through into the mirror, into her own image, and was moving deeper and deeper into her darkness. She went forward blindly for a long time. Then, just as she was certain that there was no end, no bottom, that surely this would go on and on, she seemed to see a tiny spot far ahead. As she moved closer to it, she was able to recognize what it was. It was a rose. A single, perfect rosebud on a long stem.

For the first time in eight months she began to cry softly, without pain. "It's very beautiful," she told me. "I can see it very clearly, the stem with its leaves and its thorns. It is just beginning to open. And its color is indescribable: the softest, most tender, most exquisite shade of pink."

I asked her what this dream meant to her and she began to sob. "It's mine," she said. "It is still there. All this time it is still there. It has waited for me to come back for it."

20   The rose is one of the oldest archetypical symbols for the heart. It appears in both the Christian and the Hindu traditions and in many fairy tales. It presented itself now to Ana even though she had never read these fairy tales or heard of these traditions. For most of her life, she had held her darkness close to her, had used it as her protection, had even defined herself through it. Now, finally, she had been able to remember. There was a part she had hidden even from herself. A part she had kept safe. A part that had not been touched.

Even more than our experiences, our beliefs became our prisons. But we carry our healing with us even into the darkest of our inner places. *A Course in Miracles* says, "When I have forgiven myself and remembered who I am, I will bless everyone and everything I see." The way to freedom often lies through the open heart.

QUESTIONS FOR DISCUSSION

1. Why does Ana believe that she is a bad person and that her cancer is a punishment? Do you think Ana recovers from her cancer? Why doesn't Remen tell us if Ana does or does not recover from her cancer?
2. Why do you think that Remen values memory? What is unique about her perspective on memory?
3. How and why is Remen able to help Ana? What has Remen learned from listening to Ana's struggle? What have you learned?
4. What is the significance of Ana's dream and the symbolism of the rose?
5. Why does Remen believe that "something which can never be fixed can still heal"? Explain why you agree or disagree with Remen.
6. How does Remen's discussion of Ana support her conclusion that freedom can begin only after one can forgive him or herself and have an open heart? Do you agree with Remen?

CONNECTION

Compare Remen's insights into the need to integrate traumatic memories rather than to deny their impact with Barasch's insights. Compare also the dreams that help the healing process in both essays (see page 254).

IDEAS FOR WRITING

1. Explain Remen's claim, "What we do to survive is often different from what we may need to do in order to live." Develop the idea into an essay, using examples drawn from personal experience and observation to support your main ideas.
2. Write an essay that supports or refutes Remen's implied premise that people's beliefs about themselves affect their ability to live a healthy life and recover from an illness. You can research this issue on the Internet and also include examples from your own experience and observations of others to support your main ideas.

RELATED WEB SITES

RACHEL NAOMI REMEN, MD
http://www.rachelremen.com
This web site is an excellent introduction to the work and life of Naomi Remen, a pioneer in the mind/body holistic health movement.

TRAUMA AND DISEASE: THE SIDRAN TRAUMATIC STRESS INSTITUTE
http://www.sidran.org/index.html
This organization provides online links and articles devoted to "education, advocacy and research related to the early recognition and treatment of trauma-related stress in children and the understanding and treatment of adults suffering from trauma-generated disorders."

Andrew Solomon

Depression

Andrew Solomon was born in 1963. He grew up in New York and received a B.A. from Yale University as well as a B.A. and M.A. from Cambridge University. He has written for The New Yorker, Art Forum, *and* The New York Times Magazine. *His books include* The Irony Tower: Soviet Artists in a Time of Glasnost *(1991) and the novel* A Stone Boat *(1994). The following selection is drawn from his most recent work,* The Noonday Demon: An Atlas of Depression *(2001).*

JOURNAL

Write about a time when you felt "down" or somewhat depressed. Describe your feelings and how you coped with them.

Depression is the flaw in love. To be creatures who love, we must be creatures who can despair at what we lose, and depression is the mechanism of that despair. When it comes, it degrades one's self and ultimately eclipses the capacity to give or receive affection. It is the aloneness within us made manifest, and it destroys not only connection to others but also the ability to be peacefully alone with oneself. Love, though it is no prophylactic against depression, is what cushions the mind and protects it from itself. Medications and psychotherapy can renew that protection, making it easier to love and be loved, and that is why they work. In good spirits, some love themselves and some love others and some love work and some love God: any of these passions can furnish that vital sense of purpose that is the opposite of depression. Love forsakes us from time to time, and we forsake love. In depression, the meaninglessness of every enterprise and every emotion, the meaninglessness of life itself, becomes self-evident. The only feeling left in this loveless state is insignificance.

Life is fraught with sorrows: no matter what we do, we will in the end die; we are, each of us, held in the solitude of an autonomous body; time passes, and what has been will never be again. Pain is the first experience of world-helplessness, and it never leaves us. We are angry about being ripped from the comfortable womb, and as soon as that anger fades, distress comes to take its place. Even those people whose faith promises them that this will all be different in the next world cannot help experiencing anguish in this one; Christ himself was the man of sorrows. We live, however, in a time of increasing palliatives; it is easier than ever to decide what to feel and what not to feel. There is less and less unpleasantness that is unavoidable in life, for those with the means to avoid. But despite the enthusiastic claims of pharmaceutical science, depression cannot be wiped out so long as we are creatures conscious of our own selves. It can at best be contained—and containing is all that current treatments for depression aim to do.

Highly politicized rhetoric has blurred the distinction between depression and its consequences—the distinction between how you feel and how you act in response. This is in part a social and medical phenomenon, but it is also the result of linguistic vagary attached to emotional vagary. Perhaps depression can best be described as emotional pain that forces itself on us against our will, and then breaks free of its externals. Depression is not just a lot of pain; but too much pain can compost itself into depression. Grief is depression in proportion to circumstance; depression is grief out of proportion to circumstance. It is tumbleweed distress that thrives on thin air, growing despite its detachment from the nourishing earth. It can be described only in metaphor and allegory. Saint Anthony in the desert, asked how he could differentiate between angels who came to him humble and devils who came in rich disguise, said you could tell by how you felt after they had departed. When an angel left you, you felt strengthened by his presence; when a devil left, you felt horror. Grief is a humble angel who leaves you with strong, clear thoughts and a sense of your own depth. Depression is a demon who leaves you appalled.

Depression has been roughly divided into small (mild or disthymic) and large (major) depression. Mild depression is a gradual and sometimes permanent thing that undermines people the way rust weakens iron. It is too much grief at too slight a cause, pain that takes over from the other emotions and crowds them out. Such depression takes up bodily occupancy in the eyelids and in the muscles that keep the spine erect. It hurts your heart and lungs, making the contraction of involuntary muscles harder than it needs to be. Like physical pain that becomes chronic, it is miserable not so much because it is intolerable in the moment as because it is intolerable to have known it in the moments gone and to look forward only to knowing it in the moments to come. The present tense of mild depression envisages no alleviation because it feels like knowledge.

5   Virginia Woolf has written about this state with an eerie clarity: "Jacob went to the window and stood with his hands in his pockets. There he saw three Greeks in kilts; the masts of ships; idle or busy people of the lower classes strolling or stepping out briskly, or falling into groups and gesticulating with their hands. Their lack of concern for him was not the cause of his gloom; but some more profound conviction—it was not that he himself happened to be lonely, but that all people are." In the same book, *Jacob's Room,* she describes how "There rose in her mind a curious sadness, as if time and eternity showed through skirts and waistcoats, and she saw people passing tragically to destruction. Yet, heaven knows, Julia was no fool." It is this acute awareness of transience and limitation that constitutes mild depression. Mild depression, for many years simply accommodated, is increasingly subject to treatment as doctors scrabble to address its diversity.

Large depression is the stuff of breakdowns. If one imagines a soul of iron that weathers with grief and rusts with mild depression, then major depression is the startling collapse of a whole structure. There are two models for depression: the dimensional and the categorical. The dimensional posits that depression sits on a continuum with sadness and represents an extreme version of something everyone has felt and known. The categorical describes depression as an illness totally separate from other emotions, much as a stomach virus is totally different from acid indigestion. Both are true. You go along the gradual path or the sudden trigger of emotion and then you get to a place that is genuinely different. It takes time for a rusting iron-framed building to collapse, but the rust is ceaselessly powdering the solid, thinning it, eviscerating it. The collapse, no matter how abrupt it may feel, is the cumulative consequence of decay. It is nonetheless a highly dramatic and visibly different event. It is a long time from the first rain to the point when rust has eaten through an iron girder. Sometimes the rusting is at such key points that the collapse seems total, but more often it is partial: this section collapses, knocks that section, shifts the balances in a dramatic way.

It is not pleasant to experience decay, to find yourself exposed to the ravages of an almost daily rain, and to know that you are turning into something feeble, that more and more of you will blow off with the first strong wind, making you less and less. Some people accumulate more emotional rust than others. Depression starts out insipid, fogs the days into a dull color, weakens ordinary actions until their clear shapes are obscured by the effort they require, leaves you tired and bored and self-obsessed—but you can get through all that. Not happily, perhaps, but you can get through. No one has ever been able to define the collapse point that marks major depression, but when you get there, there's not much mistaking it.

Major depression is a birth and a death: it is both the new presence of something and the total disappearance of something. Birth and death are gradual, though official documents may try to pinion natural law by creating categories such as "legally dead" and "time born." Despite nature's vagaries, there is definitely a point at which a baby who has not been in the world is in it, and a point at which a pensioner who has been in the world is no longer in it. It's true that at one stage the baby's head is here and his body not; that until the umbilical cord is severed the child is physically connected to the mother. It's true that the pensioner may close his eyes for the last time some hours before he dies, and that there is a gap between when he stops breathing and when he is declared "brain-dead." Depression exists in time. A patient may say that he has spent certain months suffering major depression, but this is a way of imposing a measurement on the immeasurable. All that one can really say for certain is that one has known major depression, and that one does or does not happen to be experiencing it at any given present moment.

The birth and death that constitute depression occur at once. I returned, not long ago, to a wood in which I had played as a child and saw an oak, a hundred years dignified, in whose shade I used to play with my brother. In twenty years, a huge vine had attached itself to this confident tree and had nearly smothered it. It was hard to say where the tree left off and the vine began. The vine had twisted itself so entirely around the scaffolding of tree branches that its leaves seemed from a distance to be the leaves of the tree; only up close could you see how few living oak branches were left, and how a few desperate little budding sticks of oak stuck like a row of thumbs up the massive trunk, their leaves continuing to photosynthesize in the ignorant way of mechanical biology.

10   Fresh from a major depression in which I had hardly been able to take on board the idea of other people's problems, I empathized with that tree. My depression had grown on me as that vine had conquered the oak; it had been a sucking thing that had wrapped itself around me, ugly and more alive than I. It had had a life of its own that bit by bit asphyxiated all of my life out of me. At the worst stage of major depression, I had moods that I knew were not my moods: they belonged to the depression, as surely as the leaves on that tree's high branches belonged to the vine. When I tried to think clearly

about this, I felt that my mind was immured, that it couldn't expand in any direction. I knew that the sun was rising and setting, but little of its light reached me. I felt myself sagging under what was much stronger than I; first I could not use my ankles, and then I could not control my knees, and then my waist began to break under the strain, and then my shoulders turned in, and in the end I was compacted and fetal, depleted by this thing that was crushing me without holding me. Its tendrils threatened to pulverize my mind and my courage and my stomach, and crack my bones and desiccate my body. It went on glutting itself on me when there seemed nothing left to feed it.

I was not strong enough to stop breathing. I knew then that I could never kill this vine of depression, and so all I wanted was for it to let me die. But it had taken from me the energy I would have needed to kill myself, and it would not kill me. If my trunk was rotting, this thing that fed on it was now too strong to let it fall; it had become an alternative support to what it had destroyed. In the tightest corner of my bed, split and racked by this thing no one else seemed to be able to see, I prayed to a God I had never entirely believed in, and I asked for deliverance. I would have been happy to die the most painful death, though I was too dumbly lethargic even to conceptualize suicide. Every second of being alive hurt me. Because this thing had drained all fluid from me, I could not even cry. My mouth was parched as well. I had thought that when you feel your worst your tears flood, but the very worst pain is the arid pain of total violation that comes after the tears are all used up, the pain that stops up every space through which you once metered the world, or the world, you. This is the presence of major depression.

I have said that depression is both a birth and a death. The vine is what is born. The death is one's own decay, the cracking of the branches that support this misery. The first thing that goes is happiness. You cannot gain pleasure from anything. That's famously the cardinal symptom of major depression. But soon other emotions follow happiness into oblivion: sadness as you had known it, the sadness that seemed to have led you here; your sense of humor; your belief in and capacity for love. Your mind is leached until you seem dim-witted even to yourself. If your hair has always been thin, it seems thinner; if you have always had bad skin, it gets worse. You smell sour even to yourself. You lose the ability to trust anyone, to be touched, to grieve. Eventually, you are simply absent from yourself.

Maybe what is present usurps what becomes absent, and maybe the absence of obfuscatory things reveals what is present. Either way, you are less than yourself and in the clutches of something alien. Too often, treatments address only half the problem: they focus only on the presence or only on the absence. It is necessary both to cut away that extra thousand pounds of the vines and to relearn a root system and the techniques of photosynthesis. Drug therapy hacks through the vines. You can feel it happening, how the medication seems to be poisoning the parasite so that bit by bit it withers away. You feel the weight going, feel the way that the branches can recover much of their natural bent. Until you have got rid of the vine, you cannot think about what has been lost.

But even with the vine gone, you may still have few leaves and shallow roots, and the rebuilding of your self cannot be achieved with any drugs that now exist. With the weight of the vine gone, little leaves scattered along the tree skeleton become viable for essential nourishment. But this is not a good way to be. It is not a strong way to be. Rebuilding of the self in and after depression requires love, insight, work, and, most of all, time.

Diagnosis is as complex as the illness. Patients ask doctors all the time, "Am I depressed?" as though the result were in a definitive blood test. The only way to find out whether you're depressed is to listen to and watch yourself, to feel your feelings and then think about them. If you feel bad without reason most of the time, you're depressed. If you feel bad most of the time with reason, you're also depressed, though changing the reasons may be a better way forward than leaving circumstance along and attacking the depression. If the depression is disabling to you, then it's major. If it's only mildly distracting, it's not major. Psychiatry's bible—the *Diagnostic and Statistical Manual,* fourth edition *(DSM-IV)*—ineptly defines depression as the presence of five or more on a list of nine symptoms. The problem with the definition is that it's entirely arbitrary. There's no particular reason to qualify five symptoms as constituting depression; four symptoms are more or less depression; and five symptoms are less severe than six. Even one symptom is unpleasant. Having slight versions of all the symptoms may be less of a problem than having severe versions of two symptoms. After enduring diagnosis, most people seek causation, despite the fact that knowing why you are sick has no immediate bearing on treating the sickness.

15   Illness of the mind is real illness. It can have severe effects on the body. People who show up at the offices of their doctors complaining about stomach cramps are frequently told, "Why, there's nothing wrong with you except that you're depressed!" Depression, if it is sufficiently severe to cause stomach cramps, is actually a really bad thing to have wrong with you, and it requires treatment. If you show up complaining that your breathing is troubled, no one says to you, "Why, there's nothing wrong with you except that you have emphysema!" To the person who is experiencing them, psychosomatic complaints are as real as the stomach cramps of someone with food poisoning. They exist in the unconscious brain, and often enough the brain is sending inappropriate messages to the stomach, so they exist there as well. The diagnosis—whether something is rotten in your stomach or your appendix or your brain—matters in determining treatment and is not trivial. As organs go, the brain is quite an important one, and its malfunctions should be addressed accordingly.

Chemistry is often called on to heal the rift between body and soul. The relief people express when a doctor says their depression is "chemical" is predicated on a belief that there is an integral self that exists across time, and on a fictional divide between the fully occasioned sorrow and the utterly random one. The word *chemical* seems to assuage the feelings of responsibility people have for the stressed-out discontent of not liking their jobs, worrying about getting old, failing at love, hating their families. There is a pleasant freedom from guilt that has been attached to *chemical.* If your brain is predisposed to depression, you need not blame yourself for it. Well, blame yourself or evolution, but remember that blame itself can be understood as a chemical process, and that happiness, too, is chemical. Chemistry and biology are not matters that impinge on the "real" self; depression cannot be separated from the person it affects. Treatment does not alleviate a disruption of identity, bringing you back to some kind of normality; it readjusts a multifarious identity, changing in some small degree who you are.

Anyone who has taken high school science classes knows that human beings are made of chemicals and that the study of those chemicals and the structures in which they are configured is called biology. Everything that happens in the brain has chemical manifestations and sources. If you close your eyes and think hard about polar bears, that has a chemical effect on your brain. If you stick to a policy of opposing tax breaks for capital gains, that has a chemical effect on your brain. When you remember some episode from your past, you do so through the complex chemistry of memory. Childhood trauma and subsequent difficulty can alter brain chemistry. Thousands of chemical reactions are involved in deciding to read this book, picking it up with your hands, looking at the shapes of the letters on the page, extracting meaning from those shapes, and having intellectual and emotional responses to what they convey. If time lets you cycle out of a depression and feel better, the chemical changes are no less particular and complex than the ones that are brought about by taking antidepressants. The external determines the internal as much as the internal invents the external. What is so unattractive is the idea that in addition to all other lines being blurred, the boundaries of what makes us ourselves are blurry. There is no essential self that lies pure as a vein of gold under the chaos of experience and chemistry. Anything can be changed, and we must understand the human organism as a sequence of selves that succumb to or choose one another. And yet the language of science, used in training doctors and, increasingly, in nonacademic writing and conversation, is strangely perverse.

The cumulative results of the brain's chemical effects are not well understood. In the 1989 edition of the standard *Comprehensive Textbook of Psychiatry*, for example, one finds this helpful formula: a depression score is equivalent to the level of 3-methoxy-4-hydroxyphenylglycol (a compound found in the urine of all people and not apparently affected by depression); minus the level of 3-methoxy-4-hydroxymandelic acid; plus the level of norepinephrine; minus the level of normetanephrine plus the level of metanepherine, the sum of those divided by the level of 3-methoxy-4-hydroxymandelic acid; plus an unspecified conversion variable; or, as *CTP* puts it: "D-type score = C_1 (MHPG) − C_2 (VMA) + C_3 (NE) − C_4 (NMN + MN)/VMA + C_0." The score should come out between one for unipolar and zero for bipolar patients, so if you come up with something else—you're doing it wrong. How much insight can such formulae offer? How can they *possibly* apply to something as nebulous as mood? To what extent specific experience has conduced to a particular depression is hard to determine; nor can we explain through what chemistry a person comes to respond to external circumstance with depression; nor can we work out what makes someone essentially depressive.

   Although depression is described by the popular press and the pharmaceutical industry as though it were a single-effect illness such as diabetes, it is not. Indeed, it is strikingly dissimilar to diabetes. Diabetics produce insufficient insulin, and diabetes is treated by increasing and stabilizing insulin in the bloodstream. Depression is *not* the consequence of a reduced level of anything we can now measure. Raising levels of serotonin in the brain triggers a process that eventually helps many depressed people to feel better, but that is *not* because they have abnormally low levels of serotonin. Furthermore, serotonin does *not* have immediate salutary effects. You could pump a gallon of serotonin into the brain of a depressed person and it would not in the instant make him feel one iota better, though a long-term sustained raise in serotonin level has some effects that ameliorate depressive symptoms. "I'm depressed but it's just chemical" is a sentence equivalent to "I'm murderous but it's just chemical'" or "I'm intelligent but it's just chemical." Everything about a person is just chemical if one wants to think in those terms. "You can say it's 'just chemistry,'" says Maggie Robbins, who suffers from manic-depressive illness. "I say there's nothing 'just' about chemistry." The sun shines brightly and that's just chemical too, and it's chemical that rocks are hard, and that the sea is salt, and that certain springtime afternoons carry in their gentle breezes a quality of nostalgia that stirs the heart to longings and imaginings kept dormant by the snows of a long winter. "This serotonin thing," says David McDowell of Columbia University, "is part of modern neuromythology." It's a potent set of stories.

20   Internal and external reality exist on a continuum. What happens and how you understand it to have happened and how you respond to its happening are usually linked, but no one is predictive of the others. If reality itself is often a relative thing, and the self is in a state of permanent flux, the passage from slight mood to extreme mood is a glissando. Illness, then, is an extreme state of emotion, and one might reasonably describe emotion as a mild form of illness. If we all felt up and great (but not delusionally manic) all the time, we could get more done and might have a happier time on earth, but that idea is creepy and terrifying (though, of course, if we felt up and great all the time we might forget all about creepiness and terror).

   Influenza is straightforward: one day you do not have the responsible virus in your system, and another day you do. HIV passes from one person to another in a definable isolated split second. Depression? It's like trying to come up with clinical parameters for hunger, which affects us all several times a day, but which in its extreme version is a tragedy that kills its victims. Some people need more food than others; some can function under circumstances of dire malnutrition; some grow weak rapidly and collapse in the streets. Similarly, depression hits different people in different ways: some are predisposed to resist or battle through it, while others are helpless in its grip. Willfulness and pride may allow one person to get through a depression that would fell another whose personality is more gentle and acquiescent.

   Depression interacts with personality. Some people are brave in the face of depression (during it and afterward) and some are weak. Since personality too has a random edge and a bewildering chemistry, one can write everything off to genetics, but that is too easy. "There is no such thing as a mood gene," says Steven Hyman, director of the National Institute of Mental Health. "It's just shorthand for very complex gene-environment interactions." If everyone has the capacity for some measure of depression under some circumstances, everyone also has the capacity to fight depression to some degree under some circumstances. Often, the fight takes the form of seeking out the treatments that will be most effective in the battle. It involves finding help while you are still strong enough to do so. It involves making the most of the life you have between your most severe episodes. Some horrendously symptom-ridden people are able to achieve real success in life; and some people are utterly destroyed by the mildest forms of the illness.

Working through a mild depression without medications has certain advantages. It gives you the sense that you can correct your own chemical imbalances through the exercise of your own chemical will. Learning to walk across hot coals is also a triumph of the brain over what appears to be the inevitable physical chemistry of pain, and it is a thrilling way to discover the sheer power of mind. Getting through a depression "on your own" allows you to avoid the social discomfort associated with psychiatric medications. It suggests that we are accepting ourselves as we were made, reconstructing ourselves only with our own interior mechanics and without help from the outside. Returning from distress by gradual degrees gives sense to affliction itself.

Interior mechanics, however, are difficult to commission and are frequently inadequate. Depression frequently destroys the power of mind over mood. Sometimes the complex chemistry of sorrow kicks in because you've lost someone you love, and the chemistry of loss and love may lead to the chemistry of depression. The chemistry of falling in love can kick in for obvious external reasons, or along lines that the heart can never tell the mind. If we wanted to treat this madness of emotion, we could perhaps do so. It is mad for adolescents to rage at parents who have done their best, but it is a conventional madness, uniform enough so that we tolerate it relatively unquestioningly. Sometimes the same chemistry kicks in for external reasons that are not sufficient, by mainstream standards, to explain the despair: someone bumps into you in a crowded bus and you want to cry, or you read about world overpopulation and find your own life intolerable. Everyone has on occasion felt disproportionate emotion over a small matter or has felt emotions whose origin is obscure or that may have no origin at all. Sometimes the chemistry kicks in for no apparent external reason at all. Most people have had moments of inexplicable despair, often in the middle of the night or in the early morning before the alarm clock sounds. If such feelings last ten minutes, they're a strange, quick mood. If they last ten hours, they're a disturbing febrility, and if they last ten years, they're a crippling illness.

25   It is too often the quality of happiness that you feel at every moment its fragility, while depression seems when you are in it to be a state that will never pass. Even if you accept that moods change, that whatever you feel today will be different tomorrow, you cannot relax into happiness as you can into sadness. For me, sadness always has been and still is a more powerful feeling; and

if that is not a universal experience, perhaps it is the base from which depression grows. I hated being depressed, but it was also in depression that I learned my own acreage, the full extent of my soul. When I am happy, I feel slightly distracted by happiness, as though it fails to use some part of my mind and brain that wants the exercise. Depression is something to do. My grasp tightens and becomes acute in moments of loss: I can see the beauty of glass objects fully at the moment when they slip from my hand toward the floor. "We find pleasure much less pleasurable, pain much more painful than we had anticipated," Schopenhauer wrote. "We require at all times a certain quantity of care or sorrow or want, as a ship requires ballast, to keep on a straight course."

There is a Russian expression: if you wake up feeling no pain, you know you're dead. While life is not only about pain, the experience of pain, which is particular in its intensity, is one of the surest signs of the life force. Schopenhauer said, "Imagine this race transported to a Utopia where everything grows of its own accord and turkeys fly around ready-roasted, where lovers find one another without any delay and keep one another without any difficulty: in such a place some men would die of boredom or hang themselves, some would fight and kill one another, and thus they would create for themselves more suffering than nature inflicts on them as it is . . . the polar opposite of suffering [is] boredom." I believe that pain needs to be transformed but not forgotten; gainsaid but not obliterated.

QUESTIONS FOR DISCUSSION

1. Solomon begins his definition of depression by claiming that "Depression is the flaw in love." What does he mean by this compelling statement, and how does he develop it further in his opening paragraphs?
2. In his third paragraph, Solomon contrasts grief with depression. What distinction does he draw, and how does this help to clarify his definition of depression?
3. How does Solomon contrast mild and major depression, and how does his example from Virginia Woolf's *Jacob's Room* help to clarify the point he is making about mild depression?
4. How does Solomon use rust as a metaphor to explain how major depression can overcome an individual? Is his metaphor effective? Explain your response.
5. How does Solomon use his personal observation of an oak tree choked by a vine to explain both depression's process and its cure through drug therapy?
6. Solomon has a complex opinion of the value of chemical therapy in treating depression. How does he explain its benefits, its limitations, and its misapplications?
7. According to Solomon, what valuable insights can grow out of depression? How do the quotations he uses from Schopenhauer help to reinforce his point at the end of the essay?

CONNECTION

Compare Solomon's and Remen's views of the therapy for the treatment of depression (see page 262).

IDEAS FOR WRITING

1. Using a series of metaphors and comparisons as Solomon does in the first part of his essay, write a definition of depression or some other type of mental or physical illness that reflects obsessive behavior.

2. Write an essay arguing for or against the concept that Solomon presents at the end of his essay: Pain and suffering are positive because they relieve complacency, help us to understand ourselves more deeply, and develop in us a stronger appreciation of beauty. According to Solomon, how is the struggle to get through a depression a form of transformation?

RELATED WEB SITES

DEPRESSION

http://www.nimh.nih.gov/publicat/depression.cfm
Information on the symptoms, biochemical makeup, and treatment, as well as the possible ramifications of depression will be found at this governmental URL. The site also offers information about medications for depression and who to contact for help or more facts on the subject.

HEALING DEPRESSION

http://www.healingdepression.com/
This site offers many resources and much useful information about clinical depression. It's purpose is "to help those whose lives have been affected by depression, including friends and family of the people who suffer from it."

Charlotte Perkins Gilman

The Yellow Wallpaper

A feminist and economist, Charlotte Perkins Gilman (1860–1935) was born in Hartford, Connecticut, and attended the Rhode Island School of Design. Her best-known work is Women and Economics *(1898); she also wrote* Herland *(1915), a feminist utopia. Gilman's "The Yellow Wallpaper" (1892), originally published as a ghost story, became popular with the rebirth of the feminist movement in the 1970s. The story is a fictionalized account of Gilman's severe depression after the birth of her daughter. While "The Yellow Wallpaper" gives us insights into the role of women at the turn of the century, many readers today can still identify with the struggles that the narrator in the story faces.*

JOURNAL

Describe a place about which you have dreamed or fantasized that embodies or symbolizes one of your fears or obsessions.

It is very seldom that mere ordinary people like John and myself secure ancestral halls for the summer.

A colonial mansion, a hereditary estate, I would say a haunted house and reach the height of romantic felicity—but that would be asking too much of fate!

Still I will proudly declare that there is something queer about it.

Else, why should it be let so cheaply? And why have stood so long untenanted?

5   John laughs at me, of course, but one expects that.

John is practical in the extreme. He has no patience with faith, an intense horror of superstition, and he scoffs openly at any talk of things not to be felt and seen and put down in figures.

John is a physician, and *perhaps*—(I would not say it to a living soul, of course, but this is dead paper and a great relief to my mind)—*perhaps* that is one reason I do not get well faster.

You see, he does not believe I am sick! And what can one do?

If a physician of high standing, and one's own husband, assures friends and relatives that there is really nothing the matter with one but temporary nervous depression—a slight hysterical tendency—what is one to do?

10   My brother is also a physician, and also of high standing, and he says the same thing.

So I take phosphates or phosphites—whichever it is—and tonics, and air and exercise, and journeys, and am absolutely forbidden to "work" until I am well again.

Personally, I disagree with their ideas.

Personally, I believe that congenial work, with excitement and change, would do me good.

But what is one to do?

15   I did write for a while in spite of them; but it *does* exhaust me a good deal—having to be so sly about it, or else meet with heavy opposition.

I sometimes fancy that in my condition, if I had less opposition and more society and stimulus—but John says the very worst thing I can do is to think about my condition, and I confess it always makes me feel bad.

So I will let it alone and talk about the house.

The most beautiful place! It is quite alone, standing well back from the road, quite three miles from the village. It makes me think of English places that you read about, for there are hedges and walls and gates that lock, and lots of separate little houses for the gardeners and people.

There is a *delicious* garden! I never saw such a garden—large and shady, full of box-bordered paths, and lined with long grape-covered arbors with seats under them.

20   There were greenhouses, but they are all broken now.

There was some legal trouble, I believe, something about the heirs and co-heirs; anyhow, the place has been empty for years.

That spoils my ghostliness, I am afraid, but I don't care—there is something strange about the house—I can feel it.

I even said so to John one moonlight evening, but he said what I felt was a draught, and shut the window.

I get unreasonably angry with John sometimes. I'm sure I never used to be so sensitive. I think it is due to this nervous condition.

25   But John says if I feel so I shall neglect proper self-control; so I take pains to control myself—before him, at least, and that makes me very tired.

I don't like our room a bit. I wanted one downstairs that opened onto the piazza and had roses all over the window, and such pretty old-fashioned chintz hangings! But John would not hear of it.

He said there was only one window and not room for two beds, and no near room for him if he took another.

He is very careful and loving, and hardly lets me stir without special direction.

I have a schedule prescription of each hour in the day; he takes all care from me, and so I feel basely ungrateful not to value it more.

30   He said he came here solely on my account, that I was to have perfect rest and all the air I could get. "Your exercise depends on your strength, my dear," said he, "and your food somewhat on your appetite; but air you can absorb all the time." So we took the nursery at the top of the house.

It is a big, airy room, the whole floor nearly, with windows that look all ways, and air and sunshine galore. It was nursery first, and then playroom and gymnasium, I should judge, for the windows are barred for little children, and there are rings and things in the walls.

The paint and paper look as if a boys' school had used it. It is stripped off—the paper—in great patches all around the head of my bed, about as far as I can reach, and in a great place on the other side of the room low down. I never saw a worse paper in my life. One of those sprawling, flamboyant patterns committing every artistic sin.

It is dull enough to confuse the eye in following, pronounced enough constantly to irritate and provoke study, and when you follow the lame uncertain curves for a little distance they suddenly commit suicide—plunge off at outrageous angles, destroy themselves in unheard-of contradictions.

The color is repellent, almost revolting: a smoldering unclean yellow, strangely faded by the slow-turning sunlight. It is a dull yet lurid orange in some places, a sickly sulphur tint in others.

35   No wonder the children hated it! I should hate it myself if I had to live in this room long.

There comes John, and I must put this away—he hates to have me write a word.

We have been here two weeks, and I haven't felt like writing before, since that first day.

I am sitting by the window now, up in this atrocious nursery, and there is nothing to hinder my writings as much as I please, save lack of strength.

John is away all day, and even some nights when his cases are serious.

40 I am glad my case is not serious!

But these nervous troubles are dreadfully depressing.

John does not know how much I really suffer. He knows there is no reason to suffer, and that satisfies him.

Of course it is only nervousness. It does weigh on me so not to do my duty in any way!

I meant to be such a help to John, such a real rest and comfort, and here I am a comparative burden already!

45 Nobody would believe what an effort it is to do what little I am able—to dress and entertain, and order things.

It is fortunate Mary is so good with the baby. Such a dear baby!

And yet I *cannot* be with him, it makes me so nervous.

I suppose John never was nervous in his life. He laughs at me so about this wallpaper!

At first he meant to repaper the room, but afterward he said that I was letting it get the better of me, and that nothing was worse for a nervous patient than to give way to such fancies.

50 He said that after the wallpaper was changed it would be the heavy bedstead, and then the barred windows, and then that gate at the head of the stairs, and so on.

"You know the place is doing you good," he said, "and really, dear, I don't care to renovate the house just for a three months' rental."

"Then do let us go downstairs," I said. "There are such pretty rooms there."

Then he took me in his arms and called me a blessed little goose, and said he would go down cellar, if I wished, and have it whitewashed into the bargain.

But he is right enough about the beds and windows and things.

55 It is as airy and comfortable a room as anyone need wish, and, of course, I would not be so silly as to make him uncomfortable just for a whim.

I'm really getting quite fond of the big room, all but that horrid paper.

Out of one window I can see the garden—those mysterious deep-shaded arbors, the riotous old-fashioned flowers, and bushes and gnarly trees.

Out of another I get a lovely view of the bay and a little private wharf belonging to the estate. There is a beautiful shaded lane that runs down there from the house. I always fancy I see people walking in these numerous paths and arbors, but John has cautioned me not to give way to fancy in the least. He says that with my imaginative power and habit of story-making, a nervous weakness like mine is sure to lead to all manner of excited fancies, and that I ought to use my will and good sense to check the tendency. So I try.

I think sometimes that if I were only well enough to write a little it would relieve the press of ideas and rest me.

60 But I find I get pretty tired when I try.

It is so discouraging not to have any advice and companionship about my work. When I get really well, John says we will ask Cousin Henry and Julia down for a long visit; but he says he would as soon put fireworks in my pillowcase as to let me have those stimulating people about now.

I wish I could get well faster.

But I must not think about that. This paper looks to me as if it *knew* what a vicious influence it had!

There is a recurrent spot where the pattern lolls like a broken neck and two bulbous eyes stare at you upside down.

65   I get positively angry with the impertinence of it and the everlastingness. Up and down and sideways they crawl, and those absurd unblinking eyes are everywhere. There is one place where two breadths didn't match, and the eyes go all up and down the line, one a little higher than the other.

I never saw so much expression in an inanimate thing before, and we all know how much expression they have! I used to lie awake as a child and get more entertainment and terror out of blank walls and plain furniture than most children could find in a toy store.

I remember what a kindly wink the knobs of our big old bureau used to have, and there was one chair that always seemed like a strong friend.

I used to feel that if any of the other things looked too fierce I could always hop into that chair and be safe.

The furniture in this room is no worse than inharmonious, however, for we had to bring it all from downstairs. I suppose when this was used as a playroom they had to take the nursery things out, and no wonder! I never saw such ravages as the children have made here.

70   The wallpaper, as I said before, is torn off in spots, and it sticketh closer than a brother—they must have had perseverance as well as hatred.

Then the floor is scratched and gouged and splintered, the plaster itself is dug out here and there, and this great heavy bed, which is all we found in the room, looks as if it had been through the wars.

But I don't mind it a bit—only the paper.

There comes John's sister. Such a dear girl as she is, and so careful of me! I must not let her find me writing.

She is a perfect and enthusiastic housekeeper, and hopes for no better profession. I verily believe she thinks it is the writing which made me sick!

75   But I can write when she is out, and see her a long way off from these windows.

There is one that commands the road, a lovely shaded winding road, and one that just looks off over the country. A lovely country, too, full of great elms and velvet meadows.

This wallpaper has a kind of subpattern in a different shade, a particularly irritating one, for you can only see it in certain lights, and not clearly then.

But in the places where it isn't faded and where the sun is just so—I can see a strange, provoking, formless sort of figure that seems to skulk about behind that silly and conspicuous front design.

There's sister on the stairs!

80   Well, the Fourth of July is over! The people are all gone, and I am tired out. John thought it might do me good to see a little company, so we just had Mother and Nellie and the children down for a week.

Of course I didn't do a thing. Jennie sees to everything now.

But it tired me all the same.

John says if I don't pick up faster he shall send me to Weir Mitchell in the fall.

But I don't want to go there at all. I had a friend who was in his hands once, and she says he is just like John and my brother, only more so!

85 Besides, it is such an undertaking to go so far.

I don't feel as if it was worthwhile to turn my hand over for anything, and I'm getting dreadfully fretful and querulous.

I cry at nothing, and cry most of the time.

Of course I don't when John is here, or anybody else, but when I am alone.

And I am alone a good deal just now. John is kept in town very often by serious cases, and Jennie is good and lets me alone when I want her to.

90 So I walk a little in the garden or down that lovely lane, sit on the porch under the roses, and lie down up here a good deal.

I'm getting really fond of the room in spite of the wallpaper. Perhaps *because* of the wallpaper.

It dwells in my mind so!

I lie here on this great immovable bed—it is nailed down, I believe—and follow that pattern about by the hour. It is as good as gymnastics, I assure you. I start, we'll say, at the bottom, down in the corner over there where it has not been touched, and I determine for the thousandth time that I *will* follow that pointless pattern to some sort of a conclusion.

I know a little of the principle of design, and I know this thing was not arranged on any laws of radiation, or alternation, or repetition, or symmetry, or anything else that I ever heard of.

95 It is repeated, of course, by the breadths, but not otherwise.

Looked at in one way, each breadth stands alone; the bloated curves and flourishes—a kind of "debased Romanesque" with delirium tremens go waddling up and down in isolated columns of fatuity.

But, on the other hand, they connect diagonally, and the sprawling outlines run off in great slanting waves of optic horror, like a lot of wallowing seaweeds in full chase.

The whole thing goes horizontally, too, at least it seems so, and I exhaust myself trying to distinguish the order of its going in that direction.

They have used a horizontal breadth for a frieze, and that adds wonderfully to the confusion.

100 There is one end of the room where it is almost intact, and there, when the crosslights fade and the low sun shines directly upon it, I can almost fancy radiation after all—the interminable grotesque seems to form around a common center and rush off in headlong plunges of equal distraction.

It makes me tired to follow it. I will take a nap, I guess.

I don't know why I should write this.

I don't want to.

I don't feel able.

105 And I know John would think it absurd. But I *must* say what I feel and think in some way—it is such a relief!

But the effort is getting to be greater than the relief.

Half the time now I am awfully lazy, and lie down ever so much. John says I mustn't lose my strength, and has me take cod liver oil and lots of tonics and things, to say nothing of ale and wines and rare meat.

Dear John! He loves me very dearly, and hates to have me sick. I tried to have a real earnest reasonable talk with him the other day, and tell him how I wish he would let me go and make a visit to Cousin Henry and Julia.

But he said I wasn't able to go, nor able to stand it after I got there; and I did not make out a very good case for myself, for I was crying before I had finished.

110 It is getting to be a great effort for me to think straight. Just this nervous weakness, I suppose.

And dear John gathered me up in his arms, and just carried me upstairs and laid me on the bed, and sat by me and read to me till it tired my head.

He said I was his darling and his comfort and all he had, and that I must take care of myself for his sake, and keep well.

He says no one but myself can help me out of it, that I must use my will and self-control and not let any silly fancies run away with me.

There's one comfort—the baby is well and happy, and does not have to occupy this nursery with the horrid wallpaper.

115 If we had not used it, that blessed child would have! What a fortunate escape! Why, I wouldn't have a child of mine, an impressionable little thing, live in such a room for worlds.

I never thought of it before, but it is lucky that John kept me here after all; I can stand it so much easier than a baby, you see.

Of course I never mention it to them any more—I am too wise—but I keep watch for it all the same.

There are things in the wallpaper that nobody knows about but me, or ever will.

Behind that outside pattern the dim shapes get clearer every day.

120 It is always the same shape, only very numerous.

And it is like a woman stooping down and creeping about behind that pattern. I don't like it a bit. I wonder—I begin to think—I wish John would take me away from here!

It is so hard to talk with John about my case, because he is so wise, and because he loves me so.

But I tried it last night.

It was moonlight. The moon shines in all around just as the sun does.

125 I hate to see it sometimes, it creeps so slowly, and always comes in by one window or another.

John was asleep and I hated to waken him, so I kept still and watched the moonlight on that undulating wallpaper till I felt creepy.

The faint figure behind seemed to shake the pattern, just as if she wanted to get out.

I got up softly and went to feel and see if the paper *did* move, and when I came back John was awake.

"What is it, little girl?" he said. "Don't go walking about like that—you'll get cold."

130   I thought it was a good time to talk, so I told him that I really was not gaining here, and that I wished he would take me away.

"Why, darling!" said he. "Our lease will be up in three weeks, and I can't see how to leave before."

"The repairs are not done at home, and I cannot possibly leave town just now. Of course, if you were in any danger, I could and would, but you really are better, dear, whether you can see it or not. I am a doctor, dear, and I know. You are gaining flesh and color, your appetite is better, I feel really much easier about you."

"I don't weigh a bit more," said I, "nor as much; and my appetite may be better in the evening when you are here but it is worse in the morning when you are away!"

"Bless her little heart!" said he with a big hug. "She shall be as sick as she pleases! But now let's improve the shining hours by going to sleep, and talk about it in the morning!"

135   "And you won't go away?" I asked gloomily.

"Why, how can I, dear? It is only three weeks more and then we will take a nice little trip for a few days while Jennie is getting the house ready. Really, dear, you are better!"

"Better in body perhaps—" I began, and stopped short, for he sat up straight and looked at me with such a stern, reproachful look that I could not say another word.

"My darling," said he, "I beg you, for my sake and for our child's sake, as well as for your own, that you will never for one instant let that idea enter your mind! There is nothing so dangerous, so fascinating, to a temperament like yours. It is a false and foolish fancy. Can you trust me as a physician when I tell you so?"

So of course, I said no more on that score, and we went to sleep before long. He thought I was asleep first, but I wasn't, and lay there for hours trying to decide whether that front pattern and the back pattern really did move together or separately.

140   On a pattern like this, by daylight, there is a lack of sequence, a defiance of law, that is a constant irritant to a normal mind.

The color is hideous enough, and unreliable enough, and infuriating enough, but the pattern is torturing.

You think you have mastered it, but just as you get well under way in following, it turns a back somersault and there you are. It slaps you in the face, knocks you down, and tramples upon you. It is like a bad dream.

The outside pattern is a florid arabesque, reminding one of a fungus. If you can imagine a toadstool in joints, an interminable string of toadstools, budding and sprouting in endless convolutions—why, that is something like it.

That is, sometimes!

145   There is one marked peculiarity about this paper, a thing nobody seems to notice but myself, and that is that it changes as the light changes.

When the sun shoots in through the east window—I always watch for that first long, straight ray—it changes so quickly that I never can quite believe it.

That is why I watch it always.

By moonlight—the moon shines in all night when there is a moon—I wouldn't know it was the same paper.

At night in any kind of light, in twilight, candlelight, lamplight, and worst of all by moonlight, it becomes bars! The outside pattern, I mean, and the woman behind it is as plain as can be.

150   I didn't realize for a long time what the thing was that showed behind, that dim subpattern, but now I am quite sure it is a woman.

By daylight she is subdued, quiet. I fancy it is the pattern that keeps her so still. It is so puzzling. It keeps me quiet by the hour.

I lie down ever so much now. John says it is good for me, and to sleep all I can.

Indeed he started the habit by making me lie down for an hour after each meal.

It is a very bad habit, I am convinced, for you see, I don't sleep.

155   And that cultivates deceit, for I don't tell them I'm awake—oh, no!

The fact is I am getting a little afraid of John.

He seems very queer sometimes, and even Jennie has an inexplicable look.

It strikes me occasionally, just as a scientific hypothesis, that perhaps it is the paper!

I have watched John when he did not know I was looking, and come into the room suddenly on the most innocent excuses, and I've caught him several times *looking at the paper!* And Jennie too. I caught Jennie with her hand on it once.

160   She didn't know I was in the room, and when I asked her in a quiet, a very quiet voice, and the most restrained manner possible, what she was doing with the paper, she turned around as if she had been caught stealing, and looked quite angry—asked me why I should frighten her so!

Then she said that the paper stained everything it touched, that she had found yellow smooches on all my clothes and John's and she wishes we would be more careful!

Did not that sound innocent? But I know she was studying that pattern, and I am determined that nobody shall find it out but myself!

Life is very much more exciting now than it used to be. You see, I have something more to expect, to look forward to, to watch. I really do eat better, and am more quiet than I was.

John is so pleased to see me improve! He laughed a little the other day, and said I seemed to be flourishing in spite of my wallpaper.

165   I turned it off with a laugh. I had no intention of telling him it was *because* of the wallpaper—he would make fun of me. He might even want to take me away.

I don't want to leave now until I have found it out. There is a week more, and I think that will be enough.

I'm feeling so much better!

I don't sleep much at night, for it is so interesting to watch developments; but I sleep a good deal during the daytime.

In the daytime it is tiresome and perplexing.

170   There are always new shoots on the fungus, and new shades of yellow all over it. I cannot keep count of them, though I have tried conscientiously.

It is the strangest yellow, that wallpaper! It makes me think of all the yellow things I ever saw—not beautiful ones like buttercups, but old, foul, bad yellow things.

But there is something else about that paper—the smell! I noticed it the moment we came into the room, but with so much air and sun it was not bad. Now we have had a week of fog and rain, and whether the windows are open or not, the smell is here.

It creeps all over the house.

I find it hovering in the dining room, skulking in the parlor, hiding in the hall, lying in wait for me on the stairs.

175   It gets into my hair.

Even when I go to ride, if I turn my head suddenly and surprise it—there is that smell!

Such a peculiar odor, too! I have spent hours in trying to analyze it, to find what it smelled like.

It is not bad—at first—and very gentle, but quite the subtlest, most enduring odor I ever met.

It used to disturb me at first. I thought seriously of burning the house—to reach the smell.

180   But now I am used to it. The only thing I can think of that it is like is the *color* of the paper! A yellow smell.

There is a very funny mark on this wall, low down, near the mopboard. A streak that runs round the room. It goes behind every piece of furniture, except the bed, a long straight, even *smooch,* as if it had been rubbed over and over.

I wonder how it was done and who did it, and what they did it for. Round and round and round—round and round and round—it makes me dizzy!

I really have discovered something at last.

Through watching so much at night, when it changes so, I have finally found out.

185   The front pattern *does* move—and no wonder! The woman behind shakes it!

Sometimes I think there are a great many women behind, and sometimes only one, and she crawls around fast, and her crawling shakes it all over.

Then in the very bright spots she keeps still, and in the very shady spots she just takes hold of the bars and shakes them hard.

And she is all the time trying to climb through. But nobody could climb through that pattern—it strangles so; I think that is why it has so many heads.

They get through and then the pattern strangles them off and turns them upside down, and makes their eyes white!

190   If those heads were covered or taken off it would not be half so bad.

I think that woman gets out in the daytime!

And I'll tell you why—privately—I've seen her!

I can see her out of every one of my windows!

It is the same woman, I know, for she is always creeping, and most women do not creep by daylight.

195   I see her in that long shaded lane, creeping up and down. I see her in those dark grape arbors, creeping all round the garden.

I see her on that long road under the trees, creeping along, and when a carriage comes she hides under the blackberry vines.

I don't blame her a bit. It must be very humiliating to be caught creeping by daylight!

I always lock the door when I creep by daylight. I can't do it at night, for I know John would suspect something at once.

And John is so queer now that I don't want to irritate him. I wish he would take another room! Besides, I don't want anybody to get that woman out at night but myself.

200   I often wonder if I could see her out of all the windows at once.

But, turn as fast as I can, I can only see out of one at one time.

And though I always see her, she *may* be able to creep faster than I can turn! I have watched her sometimes away off in the open country, creeping as fast as a cloud shadow in a wind.

If only that top pattern could be gotten off from the under one! I mean to try it, little by little.

I have found out another funny thing, but I shan't tell it this time! It does not do to trust people too much.

205   There are only two more days to get this paper off, and I believe John is beginning to notice. I don't like the look in his eyes.

And I heard him ask Jennie a lot of professional questions about me. She had a very good report to give.

She said I slept a good deal in the daytime.

John knows I don't sleep very well at night, for all I'm so quiet!

He asked me all sorts of questions too, and pretended to be very loving and kind.

210   As if I couldn't see through him!

Still, I don't wonder he acts so, sleeping under this paper for three months.

It only interests me, but I feel sure John and Jennie are affected by it.

Hurrah! This is the last day, but it is enough. John is to stay in town overnight, and won't be out until this evening.

Jennie wanted to sleep with me—the sly thing; but I told her I should undoubtedly rest better for a night all alone.

215   That was clever, for really I wasn't alone a bit! As soon as it was moonlight and that poor thing began to crawl and shake the pattern, I got up and ran to help her.

I pulled and she shook. I shook and she pulled, and before morning we had peeled off yards of that paper.

A strip about as high as my head and half around the room.

And then when the sun came and that awful pattern began to laugh at me, I declared I would finish it today!

We go away tomorrow, and they are moving all my furniture down again to leave things as they were before.

220 Jennie looked at the wall in amazement, but I told her merrily that I did it out of pure spite at the vicious thing.

She laughed and said she wouldn't mind doing it herself, but I must not get tired.

How she betrayed herself that time!

But I am here, and no person touches this paper but Me—not *alive!*

She tried to get me out of the room—it was too patent! But I said it was so quiet and empty and clean now that I believed I would lie down again and sleep all I could, and not to wake me even for dinner—I would call when I woke.

225 So now she is gone, and the servants are gone, and the things are gone, and there is nothing left but that great bedstead nailed down, with the canvas mattress we found on it.

We shall sleep downstairs tonight, and take the boat home tomorrow.

I quite enjoy the room, now it is bare again.

How those children did tear about here!

This bedstead is fairly gnawed!

230 But I must get to work.

I have locked the door and thrown the key down into the front path.

I don't want to go out, and I don't want to have anybody come in, till John comes.

I want to astonish him.

I've got a rope up here that even Jennie did not find. If that woman does get out, and tries to get away, I can tie her!

235 But I forgot I could not reach far without anything to stand on!

This bed will *not* move!

I tried to lift and push it until I was lame, and then I got so angry I bit off a little piece at one corner—but it hurt my teeth.

Then I peeled off all the paper I could reach standing on the floor. It sticks horribly and the pattern just enjoys it! All those strangled heads and bulbous eyes and waddling fungus growths just shriek with derision!

I am getting angry enough to do something desperate. To jump out of the window would be admirable exercise, but the bars are too strong even to try.

240 Besides I wouldn't do it. Of course not. I know well enough that a step like that is improper and might be misconstrued.

I don't like to *look* out of the windows even—there are so many of those creeping women, and they creep so fast.

I wonder if they all come out of that wallpaper as I did!

But I am securely fastened now by my well-hidden rope—you don't get *me* out in the road there!

I suppose I shall have to get back behind the pattern when it comes night, and that is hard!

245 It is so pleasant to be out in this great room and creep around as I please!

I don't want to go outside. I won't, even if Jennie asks me to.

For outside you have to creep on the ground, and everything is green instead of yellow.

But here I can creep smoothly on the floor, and my shoulder just fits in that long smooch around the wall, so I cannot lose my way.

Why, there's John at the door!

250   It is no use, young man, you can't open it!

How he does call and pound!

Now he's crying to Jennie for an axe.

It would be a shame to break down that beautiful door!

"John, dear!" said I in the gentlest voice. "The key is down by the front steps, under a plantain leaf!"

255   That silenced him for a few moments.

Then he said, very quietly indeed, "Open the door, my darling!"

"I can't," said I. "The key is down by the front door under a plantain leaf!" And then I said it again, several times, very gently and slowly, and said it so often that he had to go and see, and he got it of course, and came in. He stopped short by the door.

"What is the matter?" he cried. "For God's sake, what are you doing!"

I kept on creeping just the same, but I looked at him over my shoulder.

260   "I've got out at last," said I, "in spite of you and Jane. And I've pulled off most of the paper, so you can't put me back!"

Now why should that man have fainted? But he did, and right across my path by the wall, so that I had to creep over him every time!

Activity:

The drawings that follow were created by students using a computer drawing program. The students were asked to draw an image of the yellow wallpaper that for them was representative of the story's meaning. Try doing your own drawing of the wallpaper and write a paragraph explaining your response.

QUESTIONS FOR DISCUSSION

1. Why are John and the narrator spending their summer at the colonial mansion? In what ways are the room's former function, the peculiarities of its location and decoration, and the objects left behind in it significant to the story's meaning? What is causing the narrator to be sick?
2. Characterize John and then contrast him to the narrator. Who is in control? Why? How does their relationship change as the story develops?
3. Why doesn't John think that the narrator should write? Why does she want to write?
4. Describe the yellow wallpaper. Why does it fascinate the narrator? What do the wallpaper and its changes signify about the narrator?
5. Why does John faint in the final scene? Is this scene comic or tragic? Do you assume that the narrator is insane or on the verge of an important discovery? What do you think will happen to the narrator?

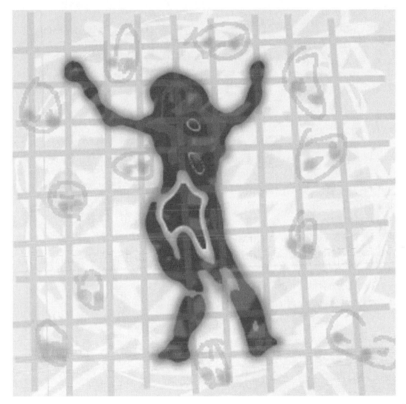

Vera Shimsky

My picture of "The Yellow Wallpaper" is a rather literal representation of the wallpaper as described in the story. The woman behind the bars is both the women imagined by the narrator and the narrator herself. She is shaking the bars, just as in the story, the narrator and the woman in the wallpaper try to free the woman from the image she has to put on for society, the bars on the wallpaper. Imagine a greenish tint to the wallpaper as the different view of it that comes with the change of the time of day. This tint is one of the things the narrator hates most about the paper. The upside-down faces with the eyes are portrayed here as circles with two glowing spots—the eyes.

Drawing this picture helped me understand even more intimately how much the narrator is the woman behind the wallpaper. In fact, the entire process of her growing more and more connected with the paper demonstrates the deterioration of her mental state. The eyes that stare at her from the wallpaper are the eyes of her husband and Jennie, as well as the rest of society who are watching her and observing whether or not she is improving. The confusing pattern of the wallpaper that the narrator cannot seem to figure out or follow all the way through represents the confusion and the struggle within her mind. The bars are what she is struggling against, both her mental condition and the pressures of the society put upon her that, instead of helping her, are making her worse. Having to visualize the wallpaper and put it into an image helped me transcend the story into a true understanding of the narrator's state of mind.

Shanney Yu

"The Yellow Wallpaper" is a story about one woman's struggle with postpartum depression. She is confined to a bedroom in order to regain her strength. The yellow wallpaper in this bedroom becomes the focal point of her attentions as its convoluted pattern slowly drives her to the brink of insanity.

The narrator describes the design of the wallpaper:

> Looked at in one way, each breadth stands alone; the bloated curves and flourishes—a kind of "debased Romanesque" with delirium tremens go waddling up and down in isolated columns of fatuity . . . they connect diagonally . . . in great slanting waves of optic horror . . . The whole thing goes horizontally, too . . . and I exhaust myself trying to distinguish the order of its going in that direction.

The narrator is also convinced that the twisted design of the wallpaper is the prison of one or more women. She feels as if the eyes of these women follow her every move. ". . . those absurd unblinking eyes are everywhere . . . I can see a strange, provoking, formless sort of figure that seems to skulk about behind that sill and conspicuous front design."

I tried to incorporate all of these elements into my drawing. I started by drawing vertical bars that run across the entire drawing, creating a sort of prison effect. In the tangled web of the pattern, I drew two "unblinking" eyes. The swirls around the eyes make up the face of a trapped woman and the swirls beneath this face are her arms. Her hands grasp the bars as she struggles to be freed. The circular swirls I drew next serve two purposes: to make the design all the more hypnotic as well as to represent the other "unblinking" eyes that taunt the narrator.

6. Do you think the story makes a feminist statement about the causes for mental illness? Why or why not?

CONNECTION

Compare the narrator's obsession with the wallpaper and the trapped women behind it to Anne Lamott's obsession with thinness and eating in "Hunger." Which work takes a more feminist position in response to the obsession and its transformation into meaningful action (see below)?

IDEAS FOR WRITING

1. Write an essay in which you discuss the relevance of the story to the ways that men and women communicate with one another or try to control one another's behavior in modern society.
2. Write an essay in which you analyze and interpret the symbol of the wallpaper in the story, taking into consideration the student drawings and interpretations on pages 289–290.

RELATED WEB SITES

CHARLOTTE PERKINS GILMAN

http://www.womenwriters.net/domesticgoddess/gilman1.html
Explaining the life and work of Charlotte Perkins Gilman, this web site provides links, criticism, and a biography of Gilman. The site also features many other women writers, from the beginning of the nineteenth century, who wrote domestic fiction.

THE YELLOW WALLPAPER SITE

http://www.cwrl.utexas.edu/~daniel/amlit/wallpaper/wallpaper.html
This student-created "Yellow Wallpaper Site" includes a discussion forum, an online version of the text of the "Yellow Wallpaper," an interactive comment site for discussion of the story's ending, and Gilman's reply to some of the responses to the story.

Anne Lamott

Hunger

Anne Lamott (b. 1954) grew up in Marin County, north of San Francisco, where she still lives. After attending two years of Goucher College from 1971–1973, Lamott began her career as a writer. To help support herself, she has also worked as an editor, a restaurant critic, a lecturer, and writing teacher. Hard Laughter *(1980), about her father's struggle with brain cancer, was her first widely acclaimed book. Her prose works include* Operating Instructions: A Journal of My Son's First Year *(1993), and* Bird by Bird *(1994) in which Lamott explores the crucial human connections between writing and life. In 1997 Lamott's novel,* Crooked Little Heart, *became a best-seller immediately after its publication. The following selection, "Hunger," about her personal obsession with food and eating, is from her most recent collection of essays,* Traveling Mercies *(1998).*

JOURNAL

Explore your thoughts and feelings about eating disorders. You might want to write about the causes or the effects of the condition or your observations of people who have or have had an eating disorder.

This is the story of how, at the age of thirty-three, I learned to feed myself. To begin with, here's what I did until then: I ate, starved, binged, purged, grew fat, grew thin, grew fat, grew thin, binged, purged, dieted, was good, was bad, grew fat, grew thin, grew thinner.

I had been a lean and energetic girl, always hungry, always eating, always thin. But I weighed 100 pounds at thirteen, 130 at fourteen. For the next ten years, I dieted. It is a long, dull story. I had lots of secrets and worries about me and food and my body. It was very scary and obsessive, the way it must feel for someone who is secretly and entirely illiterate.

One week after my father was diagnosed with brain cancer, I discovered bulimia. I felt like I'd discovered the secret to life, because you could eat yourself into a state of emotional numbness but not gain weight. Then I learned how to do it more effectively by reading articles in women's magazines on how to stop doing it. I barfed, but preferred laxatives. It was heaven: I lost weight.

5   All right, OK: there were some problems. I was scared all the time, full of self-loathing, and my heart got funky. When you've lost too much water and electrolytes, your muscular heart cramps up; it races like a sewing machine. Sometimes it would skip beats, and other times there would be a terrible feeling of vacuum, as if there were an Alhambra water tank in my heart and a big bubble had just burbled to the surface.

I would try to be good, in the puritanical sense, which meant denying my appetites. Resisting temptation meant I was good—strong, counter-animal—and I'd manage to resist fattening foods for a while. But then the jungle drums would start beating again.

I looked fine on the outside: thin, cheerful, even successful. But on the inside, I was utterly obsessed. I went into a long and deep depression after seeing some photos of people on a commune, working with their hands and primitive tools and workhorses, raising healthy food. I could see that they were really tuned to nature, to the seasons, to a direct sense of bounty, where you plant something and it grows and you cut it down or pick it and eat it, savoring it and filling up on it. But I was a spy in the world of happy eating, always hungry, or stuffed, but never full.

Luckily I was still drinking at the time.

But then all of a sudden I wasn't. When I quit in 1986, I started getting healthier in almost every way and I had all these women helping me, and I told them almost every crime and secret I had, because I believed them when they said that we are as sick as our secrets. My life got much sweeter right away, and less dramatic; the pond inside me began to settle, and I could see through the water, which was the strangest sensation because for all those years I'd been taking various sticks—desperate men, financial drama, impossible deadlines— and stirring that pond water up. So now I was noticing beautiful little fish and dreamy underwater plants, and shells lying in the sand. I started getting along with myself pretty well for the first time in my life. But I couldn't or wouldn't tell anyone that for the last ten years I had been bingeing and purging, being on a diet, being good, getting thin, being bad, getting fat.

10 I remember hanging out with these people, letting their stories wash over me, when all of a sudden the thing inside would tap me on the shoulder and whisper, "OK, honey, let's go." And I'd cry out inwardly, No! No! "Sorry," it would say, "time to go shopping." And silently I'd cry out, Please don't make me go shopping! I'm not even hungry! "Shh, shh," it would whisper, "Let's go."

I felt that when I got sober, God had saved me from drowning, but now I was going to get kicked to death on the beach. It's so much hipper to be a drunk than a bulimic. Drunks are like bikers or wrestlers; bulimics are baton twirlers, gymnasts. The voice would say how sorry it was, but then glance down at its watch, tap its foot and sigh, and I'd sigh loudly too, and get up, and trudge behind it to the store.

It was actually more painful than that. It reminded me of the scene in Kazantzakis's *The Last Temptation of Christ*, when Jesus is walking along in the desert, really wanting to spend his life in a monastery praying, secluded and alone with God. Only of course God has different plans for him and, to get his attention, sends eagles down to wrap their talons around Jesus' heart, gripping him so that he falls to the sand in pain.

I did not feel eagle talons, but I felt gripped in the heart by a presence directing me to do exactly what it said. It said it was hungry and we had to go to the store.

So that voice and I would go buy the bad things—the chocolates, the Chee•tos, the Mexican food—and big boxes of Epsom salts and laxatives. I grew weaker and more desperate until finally, one day in 1987, I called a woman named Rita Groszmann, who was listed in the Yellow Pages as a specialist in eating disorders. I told her what was going on and that I had no money, and she said to come in anyway, because she was afraid I was going to die. So I went in the next day.

15   I sat in her office and explained how I'd gotten started and that I wasn't ready to stop but that I was getting ready to be ready to stop. She said that was fine. I said that in fact I was going to go home that very night and eat chocolates and Mexican food and then purge. She said fine. I said, "Don't try to stop me." She said, "OK." I said, "There's nothing you can do to stop me, it's just the way it is," and we did this for half an hour or so, until she finally said very gently that she was not going to try to take my bulimia away from me. That she in fact was never going to take anything away from me, because I would try to get it back. But she said that I had some choices.

They were ridiculous choices. She proposed some, and I thought, This is the angriest person I've ever met. I'll give you a couple of examples. If I was feeling lonely and overwhelmed and about to binge, she said I could call someone up and ask them if they wanted to meet me for a movie. "Yeah," I said, "right." Or here's another good one: If I was feeling very *other*, sad and scared and overwhelmed, I could invite someone over for a meal, and then see if he or she felt like going for a walk. It is only because I was raised to be Politeness Person that I did not laugh at her. It was like someone detoxing off heroin, who's itching to shoot up, being told to take up macramé.

She asked if I was willing to make one phone call after I ate and buy time. I could always purge if I needed to, but she wanted me to try calling one person and see what happened. Now I'm not stupid. I knew she was up to something.

But I was really scared by the power the bad voice had over me, and I felt beaten up and out of control, scared of how sick I had somehow become, how often my pulse raced and my heart skipped beats, scared that one time when the eagle talons descended, they would grip too hard and pop me open. So I agreed. I got home, ate a more or less regular meal, called a friend, made contact, and didn't purge. The next day, I ate a light breakfast and lunch, and then a huge dinner, rooting around the fridge and cupboards like a truffle pig. But then I called my younger brother. He came over. We went for a walk.

Several weeks later, during one of our sessions, Rita asked me what I'd had for breakfast. "Cereal," I said.

20   "And were you hungry when you ate?"

"What do you mean?" I asked.

"I mean, did you experience hunger, and then make breakfast?"

"I don't really understand what you're asking," I said.

"Let me put it this way," she said. "Why did you have breakfast?"

25   "Oh! I see," I said. "I had breakfast because it was breakfast time."

"But were you hungry?"

I stared at her a moment. "Is this a trick question?" I asked.

"No," she said. "I just want to know how you know it's time to eat."

"I know it's time to eat because it's mealtime," I said. "It's morning, so I eat breakfast, or it's midday, so I eat lunch. And so on."

30   To make a long story ever so slightly shorter, she finally asked me what it felt like when I was hungry, and I could not answer. I asked her to explain what it felt like when she was hungry, and she described a sensation in her stomach of emptiness, an awareness of appetite.

So for the next week, my assignment was to notice what it felt like when I was hungry. It was so strange. I was once again the world's oldest toddler. I walked aroung peering down as if to look inside my stomach, as if it was one of those old-fashioned front-loading washing machines with a window through which you could see the soapy water swirling over your clothes. And I paid attention until I was able to isolate this feeling in my stomach, a gritchy kind of emptiness, like a rat was scratching at the door, wanting to be let in.

"Wonderful," Rita said, and then gave me my next assignment: first, to notice when I was hungry, and then—this blew my mind—to feed myself.

I practiced, and all of a sudden I was Helen Keller after she breaks the code for "water," walking around touching things, learning their names. Only in my case, I was discovering which foods I was hungry for, and what it was like to eat them. I felt a strange loneliness at first, but then came upon a great line in one of Geneen Roth's books on eating, which said that awareness was about learning to keep yourself company. So I'd feel the scratchy emptiness in my belly, and I'd mention to myself that I seemed hungry. And then I'd ask myself, in a deeply maternal way, what I felt like eating.

"Well, actually, I feel like some Chee•tos," I might say. So I'd go and buy a bag of Chee•tos, put some in a bowl, and eat them. God! It was amazing. Then I'd check in with myself: "Do you want some more?" I'd ask.

35   "No," I'd say. "But don't throw them out."

I had been throwing food out or wetting it in the sink since I was fourteen, ever since my first diet. Every time I broke down and ate forbidden foods, I would throw out or wet what I'd left uneaten, because each time I was about to start over and be good again.

"I'm hungry," I'd say to myself. "I'd like some frosting."

"OK."

"And some Chee•tos."

40   So I'd have some frosting and some Chee•tos for breakfast. I'd eat for a while. Then I'd check in with myself, kindly: "More?"

"Not now," I'd say. "But don't wet them. I might want some more later."

I ate frosting and Chee•tos for weeks. Also, cookies that a local bakery made with M&M's instead of chocolate chips. I'd buy half a dozen and keep them on the kitchen counter. It was terrifying; it was like knowing there were snakes in my kitchen. I'd eat a little, stop when I was no longer hungry. "Want one more cookie?" I'd ask.

"No, thanks," I'd say. "But maybe later. Don't wet them."

I never wet another bag of cookies. One day I woke up and discovered that I also felt like having some oranges, then rice, then sautéed bell peppers.

Maybe also some days the random pound of M&M's. But from then on I was always able at least to keep whatever I ate down—or rather, in my case, up. I went from feeling like a Diane Arbus character, viewed through the lens of her self-contempt, to someone filmed by a friendly cousin, someone who gently noted the concentration on my face as I washed a colander of tiny new potatoes.

45   Over the years, my body has not gotten firmer. Just the opposite in fact. But when I feel fattest and flabbiest and most repulsive, I try to remember that gravity speaks; also, that no one needs that plastic-body perfection from women of age and substance. Also, that I do not live in my thighs or in my droopy butt. I live in joy and motion and cover-ups. I live in the nourishment of food and the sun and the warmth of the people who love me.

It is, finally, so wonderful to have learned to eat, to taste and love what slips down my throat, padding me, filling me up, that I'm not uncomfortable calling it a small miracle. A friend who does not believe in God says, "Maybe not a miracle, but a little improvement," but to that I say, Listen! You must not have heard me right: I couldn't *feed* myself! So thanks for your input, but I know where I was, and I know where I am now, and you just can't get here from there. Something happened that I had despaired would ever happen. It was like being a woman who has despaired of ever getting to be a mother but now who cradles a baby. So it was either a miracle—Picasso said, "Everything is a miracle; it's a miracle that one does not dissolve in one's bath like a lump of sugar"—or maybe it was more of a gift, one that required some assembly. But whatever it was, learning to eat was about learning to live—and deciding to live; and it is one of the most radical things I've ever done.

QUESTIONS FOR DISCUSSION

1. Lamott writes in the first person about her own eating disorder. How does this influence the meaning of the essay for you? Do you think a more clinical or statistical approach to the subject would have been more or less effective? Explain your response.

2. After Lamott stops drinking, she says, "The pond inside me began to settle, and I could see through the water." What can she see? Why is she still unable to reveal her secret eating disorder? Why does she think it is harder to recover from alcohol addiction than from eating-disordered behavior?

3. What do the eagle talons symbolize? Why does Lamott finally call Rita Grossman to ask for help with her eating disorder? How do Rita and the choices she offers help Lamott ?

4. What does Lamott's food wetting ritual symbolize?

5. Why does she need to relearn what it feels like to be hungry and feed herself? What allows her to take this responsibility for herself? How does she accomplish this simple but challenging task?

6. Why does Lamott conclude that deciding to feed herself and live was "one of the most radical things I've ever done"?

CONNECTION

Compare Lamott's obsession with her eating disorder with the depressed state of mind described by Andrew Solomon. Does an eating disorder seem to you to be a symptom of depression (see page 266)?

IDEAS FOR WRITING

1. Write an essay in which you discuss the positive aspects of Lamott's struggle to overcome her eating disorder. Consider how her obsession and struggle transform her life.
2. Write a paper on the causes and/or effects of eating disorders.

RELATED WEB SITES

ANNE LAMOTT

http://www.barclayagency.com/lamott.html

Anne Lamott's life and work are presented at this URL through a brief text, links of interest, a schedule of her appearances, and an "Anne Lamott FAQ" section.

EATING DISORDERS AWARENESS AND PREVENTION

http://www.edap.org/

The National Eating Disorders Association hosts this web site to provide information, referrals, support, prevention, and conferences for individuals with eating disorders or people interested in learning about the issue.

E. M. Forster

The Other Side of the Hedge

E. M. Forster (1879–1970) was born in London and educated at Cambridge. Individualistic and liberal in his political views, he was a member of the Bloomsbury group, a distinguished coterie of writers and critics that included Virginia Woolf and Roger Frye. A prolific author of critical essays, stories, and social novels such as A Room with a View *(1908) and* Passage to India *(1924), Forster wrote the utopian fantasy "The Other Side of the Hedge" (1903) during a transitional period in his early life, shortly after his graduation from Cambridge and after a trip to Greece and Italy. The story presents an alternative vision to competitive, technologically oriented modern lifestyles.*

Write about an experience, fantasy, or dream you have had in which you found yourself exhausted by your current lifestyle and imagined or ventured into an alternate, more natural world where you could relax and not be pressured to compete.

My pedometer told me that I was twenty-five; and, though it is a shocking thing to stop walking, I was so tired that I sat down on a milestone to rest. People outstripped me, jeering as they did so, but I was too apathetic to feel resentful, and even when Miss Eliza Dimbleby, the great educationist, swept past, exhorting me to persevere, I only smiled and raised my hat.

At first I thought I was going to be like my brother, whom I had had to leave by the roadside a year or two round the corner. He had wasted his breath on singing, and his strength on helping others. But I had travelled more wisely, and now it was only the monotony of the highway that oppressed me—dust under foot and brown crackling hedges on either side, ever since I could remember.

And I had already dropped several things—indeed, the road behind was strewn with the things we all had dropped; and the white dust was settling down on them, so that already they looked no better than stones. My muscles were so weary that I could not even bear the weight of those things I still carried. I slid off the milestone into the road, and lay there prostrate, with my face to the great parched hedge, praying that I might give up.

A little puff of air revived me. It seemed to come from the hedge; and, when I opened my eyes, there was a glint of light through the tangle of boughs and dead leaves. The hedge could not be as thick as usual. In my weak, morbid state, I longed to force my way in, and see what was on the other side. No one was in sight, or I should not have dared to try. For we of the road do not admit in conversation that there is another side at all.

5   I yielded to the temptation, saying to myself that I would come back in a minute. The thorns scratched my face, and I had to use my arms as a shield, depending on my feet alone to push me forward. Halfway through I would have gone back, for in the passage all the things I was carrying were scraped off me, and my clothes were torn. But I was so wedged that return was impossible, and I had to wiggle blindly forward, expecting every moment that my strength would fail me, and that I should perish in the undergrowth.

Suddenly cold water closed round my head, and I seemed sinking down for ever. I had fallen out of the hedge into a deep pool. I rose to the surface at last, crying for help, and I heard someone on the opposite bank laugh and say: "Another!" And then I was twitched out and laid panting on the dry ground.

Even when the water was out of my eyes, I was still dazed, for I had never been in so large a space, nor seen such grass and sunshine. The blue sky was no longer a strip, and beneath it the earth had risen grandly into hills—clean, bare buttresses, with beech trees in their folds, and meadows and clear pools at their feet. But the hills were not high, and there was in the landscape a sense of human occupation—so that one might have called it a park, or garden, if the words did not imply a certain triviality and constraint.

As soon as I got my breath, I turned to my rescuer and said:

"Where does this place lead to?"

10 "Nowhere, thank the Lord!" said he, and laughed. He was a man of fifty or sixty—just the kind of age we mistrust on the road—but there was no anxiety in his manner, and his voice was that of a boy of eighteen.

"But it must lead somewhere!" I cried, too much surprised at his answer to thank him for saving my life.

"He wants to know where it leads!" he shouted to some men on the hill side, and they laughed back, and waved their caps.

I noticed then that the pool into which I had fallen was really a moat which bent round to the left and to the right, and that the hedge followed it continually. The hedge was green on this side—its roots showed through the clear water, and fish swam about in them—and it was wreathed over with dog-roses and Traveller's Joy. But it was a barrier, and in a moment I lost all pleasure in the grass, the sky, the trees, the happy men and women, and realized that the place was but a prison, for all its beauty and extent.

We moved away from the boundary, and then followed a path almost parallel to it, across the meadows. I found it difficult walking, for I was always trying to out-distance my companion, and there was no advantage in doing this if the place led nowhere. I had never kept step with anyone since I left my brother.

15 I amused him by stopping suddenly and saying disconsolately, "This is perfectly terrible. One cannot advance: one cannot progress. Now we of the road—"

"Yes. I know."

"I was going to say, we advance continually."

"I know."

"We are always learning, expanding, developing. Why, even in my short life I have seen a great deal of advance—the Transvaal War, the Fiscal Question, Christian Science, Radium. Here for example—"

20 I took out my pedometer, but it still marked twenty-five, not a degree more.

"Oh, it's stopped! I meant to show you. It should have registered all the time I was walking with you. But it makes me only twenty-five."

"Many things don't work in here," he said. "One day a man brought in a Lee-Metford, and that wouldn't work."

"The laws of science are universal in their application. It must be the water in the moat that has injured the machinery. In normal conditions everything works. Science and the spirit of emulation—those are the forces that have made us what we are."

I had to break off and acknowledge the pleasant greetings of people whom we passed. Some of them were singing, some talking, some engaged in gardening, hay-making, or other rudimentary industries. They all seemed happy; and I might have been happy too, if I could have forgotten that the place led nowhere.

25 I was startled by a young man who came sprinting across our path, took a little fence in fine style, and went tearing over a ploughed field till he plunged

into a lake, across which he began to swim. Here was true energy, and I exclaimed: "A cross-country race! Where are the others?"

"There are no others," my companion replied; and, later on, when we passed some long grass from which came the voice of a girl singing exquisitely to herself, he said again: "There are no others." I was bewildered at the waste in production, and murmured to myself, "What does it all mean?"

He said: "It means nothing but itself"—and he repeated the words slowly, as if I were a child.

"I understand," I said quietly, "but I do not agree. Every achievement is worthless unless it is a link in the chain of development. And I must not trespass on your kindness any longer. I must get back somehow to the road and have my pedometer mended."

"First, you must see the gates," he replied, "for we have gates, though we never use them."

30   I yielded politely, and before long we reached the moat again, at a point where it was spanned by a bridge. Over the bridge was a big gate, as white as ivory, which was fitted into a gap in the boundary hedge. The gate opened outwards, and I exclaimed in amazement, for from it ran a road—just such a road as I had left—dusty under foot, with brown crackling hedges on either side as far as the eye could reach.

"That's my road!" I cried.

He shut the gate and said: "But not your part of the road. It is through this gate that humanity went out countless ages ago, when it was first seized with the desire to walk."

I denied this, observing that the part of the road I myself had left was not more than two miles off. But with the obstinacy of his years he repeated: "It is the same road. This is the beginning, and though it seems to run straight away from us, it doubles so often, that it is never far from our boundary and sometimes touches it." He stooped down by the moat, and traced on its moist margin an absurd figure like a maze. As we walked back through the meadows, I tried to convince him of his mistake.

"The road sometimes doubles to be sure, but that is part of our discipline. Who can doubt that its general tendency is onward? To what goal we know not—it may be to some mountain where we shall touch the sky, it may be over precipices into the sea. But that it goes forward—who can doubt that? It is the thought of that that makes us strive to excel, each in his own way, and gives us an impetus which is lacking with you. Now that man who passed us—it's true that he ran well, and jumped well, and swam well; but we have men who can run better, and men who can jump better, and who can swim better. Specialization has produced results which would surprise you. Similarly, that girl—"

35   Here I interrupted myself to exclaim: "Good gracious me! I could have sworn it was Miss Eliza Dimbleby over there, with her feet in the fountain!"

He believed that it was.

"Impossible! I left her on the road, and she is due to lecture this evening at Tunbridge Wells. Why, her train leaves Cannon Street in—of course my watch has stopped like everything else. She is the last person to be here."

"People always are astonished at meeting each other. All kinds come through the hedge, and come at all times—when they are drawing ahead in the race, when they are lagging behind, when they are left for dead. I often stand near the boundary listening to the sounds of the road—you know what they are—and wonder if anyone will turn aside. It is my great happiness to help someone out of the moat, as I helped you. For our country fills up slowly, though it was meant for all mankind."

"Mankind have other aims," I said gently, for I thought him well-meaning; "and I must join them." I bade him good evening, for the sun was declining, and I wished to be on the road by nightfall. To my alarm, he caught hold of me, crying: "You are not to go yet!" I tried to shake him off, for we had no interests in common, and his civility was becoming irksome to me. But for all my struggles the tiresome old man would not let go; and, as wrestling is not my specialty, I was obliged to follow him.

40   It was true that I could have never found alone the place where I came in, and I hoped that, when I had seen the other sights about which he was worrying, he would take me back to it. But I was determined not to sleep in the country, for I mistrusted it, and the people too, for all their friendliness. Hungry though I was, I would not join them in their evening meals of milk and fruit, and, when they gave me flowers, I flung them away as soon as I could do so unobserved. Already they were lying down for the night like cattle—some out on the bare hillside, others in groups under the beeches. In the light of an orange sunset I hurried on with my unwelcome guide, dead tired, faint from want of food, but murmuring indomitably: "Give me life, with its struggles and victories, with its failures and hatreds, with its deep moral meaning and its unknown goal!"

At last we came to a place where the encircling moat was spanned by another bridge, and where another gate interrupted the line of the boundary hedge. It was different from the first gate; for it was half transparent like horn, and opened inwards. But through it, in the waning light, I saw again just such a road as I had left—monotonous, dusty, with brown crackling hedges on either side, as far as the eye could reach.

I was strangely disquieted at the sight, which seemed to deprive me of all self-control. A man was passing us, returning for the night to the hills, with a scythe over his shoulder and a can of some liquid in his hand. I forgot the destiny of our race. I forgot the road that lay before my eyes, and I sprang at him, wrenched the can out of his hand, and began to drink.

It was nothing stronger than beer, but in my exhausted state it overcome me in a moment. As in a dream, I saw the old man shut the gate, and heard him say: "This is where your road ends, and through this gate humanity—all that is left of it—will come in to us."

Though my senses were sinking into oblivion, they seemed to expand ere they reached it. They perceived the magic song of nightingales, and the odour of invisible hay, and stars piercing the fading sky. The man whose beer I had stolen lowered me down gently to sleep off its effects, and, as he did so, I saw that he was my brother.

QUESTIONS FOR DISCUSSION

1. What type of person is the narrator? Do you like him? How does he feel about competition? What is his attitude toward his brother? Does he find pleasure in his life?
2. What is the meaning of the road and the runners on it? What does the hedge suggest? What does it hide from view?
3. What is suggested by the narrator's closing his eyes just before seeing the light through the hedge? What is the significance of his difficult passage through the hedge ("all the things I was carrying were scraped off me . . . I had to wiggle blindly forward")?
4. What are the main qualities of life on "the other side of the hedge"? How is the landscape different? In what type of activities do the citizens participate? How do they feel about progress and achievement?
5. What is your response to the narrator's initial reaction to the world on the other side of the hedge? Do you agree that this world is "but a prison," that "the place led nowhere"? Are the narrator's arguments about the advantages of the road convincing? Explain your point of view.
6. Who is the man with the scythe? What choice does the narrator make at the close of the story? Why? Do you find the ending of the story hopeful or disturbing?

CONNECTION

Compare the experience of transformation in this story with Anne Lamott's (see page 291).

IDEAS FOR WRITING

1. Write an extended comparison between your own vision of a relaxed, noncompetitive lifestyle and the other side of the hedge presented in Forster's story. How is your perspective similar to and/or different from that of Forster's narrator? How much of your life do you feel should be spent in noncompetitive activities?
2. Based on evidence given in the story, write an essay in which you interpret the narrator's final gesture. Do you believe that the narrator has changed his perspective and that he will stay on the other side, or do you think he will return to life on the road? In your view, has he made the right decision?

RELATED WEB SITES

E. M. FORSTER

http://emforster.de/hypertext/template.php3?t=life

E. M. Forster's life and works are the subject of this web site entirely devoted to the author. The site also shares pictures, links and even a message board for fans of Forster's work.

Utopia
http://www.nypl.org/utopia/Pt3resources.html
Visit the New York Public Library's exhibit on "The Search for the Ideal Society in the Western World" at this URL. The exhibit offers an illustrative and narrative exploration of utopian ideologies from its origins through the ages with links, pictures, and bibliographies.

Sharon Slayton

The Good Girl

After growing up in Florida and spending several years in Denver working in the computer field, Sharon Slayton moved to California to complete her education. When she wrote this essay, she was a part-time student in psychology with plans to transfer to a four-year university and to become a lawyer. Slayton enjoys writing and has contributed several articles to small business newsletters. The following essay was written in response to a question posed in her critical thinking class that asked her to define a form of obsessive or addictive behavior about which she had personal knowledge.

Most people who meet me today see a very strong and confident individual. They see a young woman who has accomplished a great deal in a short time. They see a very responsible and reliable person who can be counted on to get a job done with skill and competency. Typically, I am spokesperson for any group of which I become part. I am looked to for leadership and guidance among my friends and colleagues. I am quite proud of my reputation; however, I wish that I had come by it through some other means. You see, all of these admirable characteristics were developed over the past 25 years through an obsession with being good.

Maybe I should rephrase that, because merely being "good" has never quite been "good" enough for me—not since I was six years old and my parents failed to believe me about the most important issue in my life. I went to them for protection against a child molester, and they refused to believe that such a thing could be happening in their world. Those things do not happen to "nice" people, to "good" people. Those things could not happen to *their* child. My parents defended themselves the only way they knew how, by denying the reality of my perceptions and telling me that I was "bad" for telling such stories. Their choice of the word "bad" affected everything I was ever to do afterwards. From that time on I understood only one thing, that I must be "good."

"Good" soon came to encompass everything in my world: school, friends, home, work, society. I had to be good; and, if at all possible, I had to be great.

Every deed at which I excelled, every recognition I received, every honor be-
stowed meant that I was one step closer to no longer being "bad." As the years
passed, I forgot why I was trying so hard and lost touch with the reasoning that
had started this quest—yet I pursued my goal with a diligence and devotion
that can only be termed as obsessive.

I knew just about everyone at school, but I never made many friends. I didn't
have time to be bothered with people, except superficially, because I was totally
preoccupied with my grades; I had to get all "A's." Nothing less would do.
When I wasn't studying, I was deeply involved in clubs and organizations. I decided, while still in elementary school, when I saw my first high school yearbook, that I would have the longest senior listing in my high school class when
I graduated. Out of a class of almost eight hundred students, I got what I
wanted. I had hoped my parents would be proud, but they hardly seemed to
notice.

5   By the time I was fifteen I was looking for more ways to show "them" that I
could do anything, and do it well. I was a junior in high school and started
working full time while attending classes all day. My day began at 7:20 a.m.
when the first bell rang and ended around 1:00 a.m. when I arrived home from
work. Neither I nor my family needed extra money, but for me, there was no
other way: I always had to do more. I kept this schedule up until I graduated.
Of course, I was an honor student; I was also a student council representative,
vice president of two clubs, treasurer of one. I attended and received top
awards in state foreign language competitions in two languages and was a
member of two choral groups which gave concerts state-wide and which participated in state-level competitions. No one ever seemed to notice or to care.

What I didn't notice was that my parents were immensely proud of me. They
often bragged about me to their friends and relatives, but I wasn't paying attention. I was after something that they could never give. My "badness" no longer
existed for them, and probably had not since about an hour after that episode
when I was six—but it was very much a part of me. I picked everything apart,
thinking that everything could always use improvement, that nothing was
"good" enough as it was. My grades were good, but some of the subjects weren't
as "easy" for me as I wished. I was popular, but there were always some people I
didn't know. I was working, but I had to be the best at my job, the fastest, the
most knowledgeable. I actually learned stock numbers and prices to over two
hundred items of inventory by heart so I could impress my manager with how
good I was.

Was I getting tired? Maybe. But I was also getting plenty of recognition for
my accomplishments. I fed off of it; I lived for it; I required it. I needed every
reward or approval I got to reinforce me in my feeling that I was on the right
track, that I was getting better and better. I was no longer consciously aware of
what I was seeking. The obsession had taken over my behavior, almost completely; being constantly challenged was now a way of life. Never resting, never
relaxing, always striving, always achieving—these things were second nature to
me by the time I was twenty.

My relationships were disastrous. My constant need for approval and recognition was very difficult for anyone to supply. Likewise, no matter how much praise I was given, I never felt like it was enough. I felt that people patronized me, so I had to prove to them that I could always do more than anyone else. I criticized anyone who was willing to settle for less than I. If someone told me that they loved me, I would pick it apart, frequently arguing with the people I was involved with: "How can you say you love me? If you loved me, then you would stop making me feel like nothing I ever do is good enough."

When I was twenty-three I started my own business, which was quite successful for a time. I had moved two thousand miles away from my family, determined that I would be a great success. I was really going to make them proud this time, but my plans went awry as moving away from my family helped dim the constant need to impress them. Because of distance, they were no longer privy to my life and to daily events. Lacking the "audience" for my constant efforts to prove myself, I began to lose the motivation to excel, to be the "good one." Slowly, I began to lose interest in my business, lacking the drive to devote myself utterly to something that was unrecognized by my family. I began to realize what I might never have discovered if I had stayed close to home. Without parental recognition and approval, my business success meant little.

10   In fact, I began to realize that I had been so damned "good" all my life that I had missed out on a great deal of fun. Suddenly my life began to change. I was involved in many things, but I derived little pleasure now from activities I had thoroughly enjoyed in the past. At twenty-seven years of age I knew nothing about myself. I had no idea what I really liked and had no concept of happiness. I only knew what I was capable of accomplishing. I set about enjoying myself with the same devotion that I had given to everything else, and for the next few years my life became a set of extremes. Struggling constantly with a desire to be good and a need to be "bad," I would go out drinking with friends and get very drunk, but I was always the one who forced myself to try to act sober. I was always the one responsible for making sure that everyone else got home. I thought I was enjoying the first freedom that I had ever experienced in my life, but I had really only broadened my obsession to include being bad as well. Whatever mood I was in, whatever my particular focus was for the hour, whether being good or being bad, I accomplished either with an abandon and passion hard to match. And I was very, very unhappy.

What was the point? Did I really enjoy anything I was doing? No. I had no idea what I wanted, yet I demanded attention and recognition. If I couldn't get enough recognition from my family, then I would get it from everyone else. But that had proved unsatisfying as well. What could I do now? What was I after and what did I want? The only thing I really knew was that I didn't want to go on living like I was anymore. With the help of one of the few friends I had managed to make along the way, I started psychiatric counseling. The results of that counseling you see in what you have just read.

So, here I am today, thirty-two years old and just beginning to discover my-self as a person who exists outside of the obsession to be good. Actually, I think I have an advantage over a lot of people my age in that I covered a lot of ground when I was young. Driven by an obsession for goodness, I tested my limits and discovered what many people never learn: that I really could accom-plish anything to which I put my mind. In going from one subject to another to prove I could do it all, I was exposed to a wide variety of experiences and activi-ties, some of which I have rejected, some of which I have made a part of my current life-style. Either way, the experiences I have picked up along the way have made my life rich and varied. My obsessive past has given me a strength with which to confront the future; I just wish I had arrived here by some other way.

QUESTIONS FOR DISCUSSION

1. Despite feeling proud of her achievements, why does Slayton now wish she "had arrived here by some other way"? Do you agree with her?
2. How did Slayton's parents respond to her story about a molestation? Does their response seem understandable? Would parents today be as likely to respond as Slayton's parents did in the early 1960s?
3. This essay is an example of what is known as an extended definition. What qualities make up Slayton's definition of the "good girl" obsession? Is her definition of the essay's key terms a clear one?
4. To develop her definition essay, Slayton uses her own case history and a number of examples from her life at different stages. What are the key in-cidents that Slayton emphasizes? Are there any that seem to need more development or detail? Do all of the incidents she mentions seem relevant to her definition?

Tiffany N. Castillo

Body and Mind: Examining the Psychological Effects of Exercise

Tiffany Castillo was born and raised in Santa Barbara, California. She wrote "Body and Mind" as a freshman at Stanford University. Having been involved in sports and karate since childhood, exercise has always been a source of happiness in her life. Yet it was not until taking a psychology course in college that she began to seriously consider how exercise could be responsible for positive psychological effects. The following is a shortened version of the research paper that she wrote for her class. In it she analyzes the complex relationships between the body and the mind.

Despite the heavy fog, with each stride that I take, I can see more and more of the gravel path that lies ahead. Then, there it is, the most grueling incline on the whole trail. It winds slowly up the hill, covered by arching oak tree branches that keep the peak hidden. I quickly exhale and start my ascent. Halfway up, I feel my quads and hamstrings burning, but I push on, knowing that each step is getting me closer. Finally I reach the top. I can see the sun rising gradually and illuminating the rolling hills below. Overwhelmed by the beauty around me and the sense of accomplishment filling my chest, I smile. This inspiring impression stays with me throughout the rest of the day.

What is it about running that makes me feel so good? Is my exercise routine really what enables me to cope with many of the stresses at college? How can physical fitness have such a positive impact on the mind and emotions? These questions inspired me to research the psychological effects of exercise. Often we are reminded that physical activity results in increased overall well being. Yet I hope to examine the specifics behind this general claim: what biological mechanisms are activated by exercise? Do certain physical activities elicit different psychological responses? Do men and women have different responses to exercise? And finally, how are scientists examining the relationship between psychology and exercise? Finding the answers to these questions will not only satisfy my personal curiosity but will hopefully provide me with evidence to convince others of the psychological benefits of exercise.

Studying the psychological effects of exercise seems like a modern concept, but the roots of exercise psychology actually extend back over one hundred years. A case study done by C. Rieger in 1884 was the first published work in exercise psychology. Inspired by simple curiosity, Rieger hypnotized one woman to examine whether persuasion of the subconscious could affect the body. His results suggested that hypnosis "greatly facilitated muscular endurance" (Seraganian 28). This was one of the first allusions to a mind body connection. Such a finding was undoubtedly controversial and widely discredited in 1884, but this type of research was essential in broadening the interest in the field of exercise psychology. The science of exercise psychology grew very slowly from 1897 to the 1970s.

Mixed attitudes towards sports and exercise, and the belief that they were separate and second to intellectual activity accounted for this slow growth. Yet in the 1970s, with the popularization of Buddhism and meditation in America, this mindset started to change. One monk commented on this change, "What American Buddhists are doing is taking a path of enlightenment into a lay culture . . . and moving it right into daily practice for everyday life. It is beneficial for all of us" (Morse 42). In this example, you can see how people began to acknowledge that the separation of mind and body was destructive. This shift continued in the 1980s as Americans started using exercise to combine the mind, body, and social aspects of their lives. The development of aerobic classes such as Jazzercise, was an example of increasing national acceptance of this lifestyle. Doctors began to notice significant overall health improvements in their patients who participated in these activities. This exciting finding then inspired a surge of scientific interest in exercise, particularly the therapeutic value of exercise in the arena of mental health. This interest has certainly continued to grow, and groundbreaking results are continuously published in magazines, on the internet, or in the news.

5   We can begin to understand how exercise impacts psychology by first examining the several hypotheses that explain the science behind their relationship. The first of these is the Endorphin Hypothesis, which states that, "acute exercise results in the release and binding of endogenous opioids (B-endorphin) to receptor sites in the brain" (Seraganian 58). This theory tries to explain scientifically the euphoric effect associated with exercise that is more commonly known as a "runner's high." The opiate-like effect of exercise is generally what causes runners to describe these feelings as a "high." Many of you, especially those who run or know runners, are probably familiar with this effect. Such familiarity often influences people to claim that the Endorphin Hypothesis is valid, yet empirical tests of this hypothesis have generally failed to support it.

The Monoamine Hypothesis is another theory that tries to attribute the positive psychological effects of exercise with chemical functions in the brain. This hypothesis claims, "The affective benefits of exercise may derive from increased levels of central monoamine neurotransmitters accompanying exercise" (Seraganian 46). One study established that a relationship exists between deficits in monoamine activity and depression. This discovery seems to prove that the prevalence of these monoamine neurotransmitters (chemical messengers) is somehow responsible for the positive psychological response to exercise; yet this hypothesis remains largely unsubstantiated. Thus we can see how the exact chemistry between the body and the brain, as initiated by exercise, remains a misunderstood and widely disputed mystery.

Our best understanding of the biology behind exercise and psychology has been achieved through the study of the sympathetic and parasympathetic nervous systems. It has been proven that the sympathetic nervous system is activated by exercise. Characteristics of an excited sympathetic nervous system include increased heart rate or sweating. After exercise, the body needs to recover and so the parasympathetic nervous system takes over to restore the body to its status quo by reducing heart rate and blood pressure. This rebound by the parasympathetic nervous system is often associated with a state of relaxation as well as many other positive emotions that people report after exercise. We can see that this theory applies to many different forms of exercise, unlike the Endorphin Hypothesis, yet it still presents a rather vague explanation for how exercise affects our mind. This inconclusiveness causes me to believe that biology cannot explain why exercise positively affects our mind. Instead of initiating a specific biological reaction, I think that exercise has its positive mental and emotional impact by triggering a psychological response.

Because of their psychological basis, I find that the last two hypotheses most successfully explain why exercise has a positive impact on our mind. First, the Distraction Hypothesis states that exercise is psychologically beneficial because of "the temporary respite from life stresses or worries that it provides" (Seraganian 69). This hypothesis makes sense. Since our minds can only physically handle a certain amount of information or thoughts at once, by focusing intensely on just one activity (exercise) we are able to experience a pleasant "release" from worries or concerns. Author and fitness expert Walt Schafer, expresses this idea in his statement, "exercise prevents and reduces bound energy, thereby preventing and reducing distress" (21). But perhaps these therapeutic benefits of exercise are best described by a depression patient (JR), "If I am truly exerting myself, it is not possible to dwell on anything outside of the present moment. It is a mental nap." (qtd. in Landers). Thus we can see how the Distraction Hypothesis is an explanation for how exercise positively affects the psyche of some people. It is important to note, however, that the effects of distraction are not the only forces at work here. A study revealed that rest was not as effective in reducing stress and anxiety as exercise was (Schafer 39). This suggests that there still must be a biological mechanism during exercise, in addition to the mere distraction, that is responsible for these positive psychological effects. Now you might be wondering: What about those who instead of needing "to get away" or "slow down", feel the need to take control or to be more authoritative?

The Mastery Hypothesis applies to these individuals. It states that, "exercise may increase people's sense of mastery or accomplishment and thereby lead to improved affect" (Seraganian 55). Like the Distraction Hypothesis, this explanation is appealing because it discusses feelings that many can relate to or understand. It has a comprehensible and practical application. Also in this theory, we can again see the therapeutic effect of exercise. A recently published article directly speaks to this relationship, "One of the positive psychological benefits of systematic exercise is the development of a sense of personal mastery and positive self regard, which we believe is likely to play some role in the depression reducing effects of exercise" (Babyak 635). Returning to the patient JR, we are provided with a real life example that contextualizes this hypothesis, "whether I go [to the gym] or not and how much energy I exert, feels good to me, because it is something that I am able to consciously control, especially when I feel that my life is out of control" (qtd. in Landers).

10   I think that the last two hypotheses most accurately describe the essence of why exercise has positive mental and emotional effects. Since they were both psychologically based hypotheses, I believe that this suggests that the best explanation for the effect of exercise on the mind is also psychological. Empirically testing and measuring psychological variables is very challenging and producing sound results is even more daunting. It is probably for these reasons that scientists have had such difficulty in explaining this relationship. Although the lack of such an explanation might logically hinder any growth or interest in this field, I find that the contrary is true. It seems that scientists have moved beyond the question of why exercise has a positive psychological effect and, instead, have become more interested in proving how it has a positive impact.

Over the past few decades, thousands of papers have been published in which numerous types of physical activities are compared to their specific mental and emotional results. One of the most common studies has been to examine whether exercise can treat depression and anxiety, which are the most widely clinically diagnosed mood disorders in America. Despite the occasional dissenting opinion, the majority of studies from the past two decades have been confirmed by <u>Research Digest</u> editor Daniel M. Landers as having "enough evidence to support the claim that exercise is related to positive mental health as indicated by relief in symptoms of depression and anxiety." The acceptance of this belief by the scientific and medical communities has been extremely important because it has allowed for a new way to treat patients. Psychotherapists can now confidently prescribe exercise as a form of therapy for patients with depression or anxiety disorders. In fact, results from various experiments have shown exercise to be more effective in treating depression than prescription drugs or no treatment at all. Michael Babyak at Duke University conducted such a study using 156 adults with major depressive disorder. The patients were divided into three groups and given either exercise therapy, no treatment, or prescribed a drug called sertraline. After a four-month treatment session, the patients who had the exercise therapy showed the greatest relief from depression. An even more convincing discovery was made in the follow-up study conducted six months after the therapy completion. The follow-up showed that the exercise therapy patients had the lowest relapse rates and that those who continued to exercise on their own had an even lower incidence of relapse (Babyak). This evidence suggests that exercise provides patients with the most effective lifelong treatment for depression and anxiety.

While I have focused on exercise as an effective form of treatment for patients diagnosed with a clinical illness, one certainly does not have to have an emotional or mood disorder to experience significant benefits from exercise. Instead, exercise is like a universal medicine that can help anyone cope with a wide range of problems. As we briefly discussed earlier, exercise helps people cope with the stressors that they encounter in daily life. It provides a way to clear one's mind and obtain a sense of control when one may feel as though everything else in life is out of control. In general, various studies have confirmed that individuals who exercise frequently are more capable of coping with stressful life events than those who are inactive. Stress in the lives of college students has been a widely investigated issue and scientists have recently looked at how exercise may impact students' lives. In 1994 Morse, Walker, and Monroe showed that, "Even a six-week combined aerobic-anaerobic exercise regimen reduced the intensity of the stress response among college students" (Morse 41). From personal experience, however, I would argue that stress-reduction from exercise can be attained almost instantaneously. For example, from instances when I have been overwhelmed by schoolwork to when my boyfriend was in the hospital, even a twenty-minute run would make me feel significantly better.

The benefits of exercise as a coping mechanism are also important because they extend beyond the alleviation of psychological issues. A highly fit individual's ability to cope with "high stress", allows he or she to experience significantly fewer physical health problems than a "low fit" individual. In addition to strengthening the immune system's response to stressors, frequent exercise has been shown to improve one's overall quality of life. Beginning with its role as a coping mechanism, we can trace the results of exercise like a positive domino effect. It has been hypothesized that the greater sense of "internal control" that one experiences from exercise leads to an increase in self-esteem, which then accounts for a decrease in emotional tension and an increase in outgoing behavior such as playfulness.

In several surveys that I conducted, I found that people consistently reported revitalization as one of the strongest feelings that they experience after exercising. I believe that this shows that the majority of people do not recognize exercise as therapeutic. This is probably because Western culture often teaches us that therapy is something that is prescribed and comes in a bottle. Such a cultural perspective tends to discourage us from acknowledging the therapeutic value of physical activity. Thus, Americans often report that they exercise simply because it makes them "feel good" and not because they think that it has therapeutic value. While it is great that people can have such a simple relationship with exercise and still experience its tremendous benefits, I wish that I could convince more people to at least give exercise a chance, because the rewards last a lifetime.

WORKS CITED

Babyak, Michael. "Exercise Treatment for Major Depression: Maintenance of Therapeutic Benefit at 10 Months." Psychosomatic Medicine 62 (2000): 633–38.

Landers, Daniel M. "The Influence of Exercise on Mental Health." PCPFS Research Digest Series 12, #10. 26 Feb. 2002 <http://www.fitness.gov/mentalhealth.htm>.

Morse, A. "The Effect of Exercise on a Psychological Measure of the Stress Response." Wellness Perspectives 11 (1994): 39–46.

Schafer, Walt. Stress Management for Wellness. 4th ed. Chicago: Harcourt, 2000.

Seranganian, Peter. Exercise Psychology: The Influence of Physical Exercise on Psychological Processes. New York: Wiley-Interscience Publication, 1993.

QUESTIONS FOR DISCUSSION

1. What various writing strategies does Tiffany Castillo use in her first two paragraphs to engage her readers' interest in her topic? Do you think her opening is effective?

2. How long has exercise psychology been a field of research? Why has there been resistance to this field of study? What happened to make people more open to the relationships between exercise and psychology?

3. What biological evidence does Castillo present to show a relationship between body chemistry and a person's sense of well being? Why does Castillo believe that the Distraction Theory and the Mastery Theory offer a better explanation of how exercise positively affects one's state of mind?

4. Why does Castillo try to persuade her readers that "exercise is like a universal medicine that can help anyone cope with a wide range of issues"? Explain why you agree or disagree with her. Refer to your own experiences and the experiences of friends and family to support your point of view.

TOPICS FOR RESEARCH AND WRITING

1. Write an extended definition of one of the following terms: *nightmare, obsession, fantasy, depression.* Provide examples from your research and contrasts to indicate how your sense of the term differs from the dictionary meaning, how readings in this text have influenced your current definition, and how your personal experiences have helped you to understand the term's meaning.

2. Using the essay by Barasch as a starting point, research the concept of lucid dreaming as an alternative to being overwhelmed by frightening nightmares. Write a paper in which you define this expression and explore the causes and effects of the lucid dreaming process. Do you consider lucid dreaming valid as a way of controlling dreams and finding a way to use their power for creative thinking?

3. As Naomi Remen does in her essay "Remembering," many psychologists have written of the importance of uncovering buried and traumatic memories of the distant past; sometimes these psychologists use controversial therapies such as hypnosis. Do some research into this issue and write an essay about the validity of the use of "buried memories" in the healing process.

4. Gilman's "The Yellow Wallpaper" concerns a nineteenth century woman's obsession and nervous breakdown after childbirth. How were young women who suffered from "nervous disorders" such as postpartum depression treated in nineteenth century medicine? Research this aspect of medical history and draw some conclusions. How do modern treatments differ?

5. Using Lamott's essay "Hunger" as a point of departure, do some research and write an essay defining the nature and origins of eating disorders such as anorexia and bulimia. What social, psychological, or chemical factors can lead to an eating disorder?

6. Marc Barasch and Naomi Remen write about escape from depression and obsession through a form of spiritual transformation that comes from a "healing dream." Do some research into ways that strongly charged dreams can lead to mental healing and draw some conclusions about the efficacy of such approaches in contrast to more traditional forms of therapy or medications.

7. See one of the following films that explores the relationship between nightmares and obsessions, either by yourself or with several of your classmates. Write an individual or collaborative analysis of the film, focusing on the definition the film provides for the type of obsession it examines and whether it regards the obsession as a primarily negative or potentially positive state of mind. Here are some choices: *Field of Dreams, The Piano, House of Games, Jacob's Ladder, Death Becomes Her, A Beautiful Mind, Tom and Viv, Moulin Rouge, Beloved, Traffic, What Dreams May Come, Insomnia, The Cell, Girl Interrupted,* and *Requiem for a Dream.*

Journeys in Sexuality
and Gender

6

Marc Chagall (1887–1985)
Birthday (1915)

Painted less than a year after Russian-born painter Marc Chagall's arrival in Paris, *Birthday* shows the romantic, bohemian influence of the artist's life in the city. This painting is typical of Chagall's work in its rejection of realism, physical laws, and visual logic for a visionary art that creates its own rules in order to reveal the reality of dreams, the passions, and the spirit.

JOURNAL

Write about a romantic relationship that made you feel the world was upside-down, with all the normal rules of logic suspended.

*No one who accepts the view that censorship is the chief reason for dream
distortion will be surprised to learn from the results of dream interpretation that
most of the dreams of adults are traced back by analysis to erotic wishes.*
                              SIGMUND FREUD
                              Erotic Wishes and Dreams

She obeyed him; she always did as she was told.
                              MAXINE HONG KINGSTON
                              No Name Woman

*No, it wasn't easy for any of us, girls and boys, as we forced our beautiful, free-
flowing child-selves into those narrow, constricting cubicles labeled female and male.*
                              JULIUS LESTER
                              Being a Boy

CAUSALITY AND THE INWARD JOURNEY

What causes people to have certain kinds of dreams or to remember a particular dream? Do people's gender concerns influence their dreams? How
do dreams and sexual fantasies influence an individual's waking life and
personal relationships? Why can certain people use their dreams to make
their lives richer while others are overwhelmed by their unconscious fears?
All of these questions, central to the issues raised in *Dreams and Inward Journeys,* are also issues of causality.

As you reflect on your dreams and emotions, working to understand
what you read and to create clear, focused arguments, causal analysis will
be a fundamental part of your thinking process. Causal analysis can help
you to understand your inner life, to interpret your relationship to the public world, and to explain how and why things happen the way they do.
Finding connections that exist between two events, understanding how one
event led to or produced another event, and speculating about the consequences of earlier events—all involve causal reasoning.

Observing and Collecting Information

People naturally search for solutions to mental dilemmas and physical problems, wanting to explain why something occurred and how they can improve the situation. In most cases, the more confident we are about our
explanations of any event, the better we feel. Observing and collecting information about both your inner and outer world will increase your chances
of making accurate causal connections and inferences about the sources
and meanings of your dreams and the public events that are influencing

PCC Bookstores - Sylvania

7094 CASH-1   4818 0001 105

978032112394 NEW
FORD/DREAMS+INWARD   MDS 1N   49.75
                     TOTAL   49.75

APPROVAL: 046555   SEQ.NUM: 0032
ACCOUNT NUMBER 4046XXXXXXXXXXXX 0505
VISA/MASTER CARD   49.75

Last Day for Returns 7/7/03 Thanks!

7/29/03 2:03 PM

you. For example, if you are keeping a dream journal, you may find that after writing down your dreams for a while, you notice repeated images or situations that may reflect your psychological concerns and may help you to draw more accurate inferences about your inner needs. Similarly, keeping a media journal of newspaper clippings or stories downloaded from the Internet will help you become more alert to issues of cause and effect in the external world: immediate and long-term causes for our country's attack on another nation, for instance, or the effects of a series of "strategic" bombing raids on the ecological system, rate of global pollution and disease, and the flow of refugees out of and into various countries in a region of the world.

Whether you are studying dreams, literature, or current events, be sure that the causal connections you make are sound ones. Observe carefully and consider all possible causes, not simply the obvious, immediate ones. For example, student writer Julie Bordner Apodaca began her preparation to write "Gay Marriage: Why the Resistance?" (included in this chapter) with her own personal observations of biased comments about gay relationships, comments that had come up in conversations she had with other students and people in her community. These comments led her to consider some of the deeper, underlying causes of homophobia. She searched for information about the causes through further conversations and interviews with students and with her own mother, who is a psychotherapist. Apodaca also read a number of books and magazine articles on the subject, some of which are referred to in the bibliography that accompanies her essay. Ultimately, she found so many causes of bias that she chose to classify them into several different categories: religious, sociopolitical, and medical.

In writing a causal analysis, whether of a dream, a short story, or a social issue, it is also essential that you provide adequate evidence, both factual and logical, for the conclusions that you draw. You may believe that you understand the causes involved quite clearly, but perceiving these connections for yourself is not enough; you must re-create for your reader, in clear and specific language, the mental process you went through to arrive at your conclusions. Methodically and carefully questioning your own thought process will help you clarify your insights, to generate new ideas and evidence that can be used to support your analysis, and avoid logical fallacies.

Causal Logical Fallacies

People create connections between events or personal issues about which they feel strongly, often rushing their thinking process to a hasty conclusion. One of the most common errors, the post hoc fallacy ("after this, therefore because of this"), mistakenly attempts to create a causal connection between unrelated events that follow each other closely in time. But a sequence in time is not necessarily a causal sequence. In fact, most magical or superstitious thinking relative to dreams and daily life is based on faulty causal analysis of sequences in time. For instance, people may carry a burden of guilt because of accidental sequential parallels between their inner thoughts and outer events, such as a dream of the death of a loved one and that person's subsequent death or injury.

Another common problem in thinking and writing about causality is causal oversimplification, in which a person argues that one thing caused something to happen, when in fact a number of different elements worked together to produce a major effect or outcome. For example, one's dream of flying may have been inspired in part by watching a television program about pilots the night before; yet other causes may also be present: one's love for performing or "showing off" or one's joy about a recent accomplishment. When trying to apply a broad theory to explain many individual cases, thinkers often become involved in causal oversimplification. We can ask, for example, if Freud's theories about the sexual content and sources of dreams really explain the entire range of dream stories and imagery. What other causes and sources might he have neglected to consider? Asking about other possible causal relations not covered by a causal thesis will help you to test the soundness of your analysis.

The "slippery slope" fallacy is also of particular relevance to the issues explored in this text. In the slippery slope fallacy, a reasoned analysis of causes and effects is replaced by a reaction of fear, in which a person might argue that if one seemingly insignificant event is allowed to happen, there will be serious consequences. Of course, in some cases this may be true: If one isn't careful about sexually transmitted diseases, there is the possibility that a person may get AIDS and eventually die. In most cases, however, theorizing about dreadful future events can become a way of validating irrational fears and can become a way of providing an excuse for maintaining the status quo. Recognizing the slippery slope fallacies both in others' thinking and within one's own thinking can help you to free yourself from irrational anxiety and develop better critical thinking skills.

Good causal reasoning can lead you closer to understanding and developing theories and explanations for the multiple causes and effects of the issues and events you encounter in your reading and in your own life. With an awareness of the complexities of causal thinking, you should be able to think and write more critically, clearly, and persuasively.

THEMATIC INTRODUCTION: SEXUALITY AND GENDER

People in all cultures define themselves in relationship to their gender role and sexuality. Individuals develop a sense of their gender role through observation and participation in the values of their family, peer group, culture, and spiritual traditions. The shifting social definitions of acceptable gender role behavior have led many people to feel confused about their gender identity and about what constitutes appropriate behavior toward the opposite sex. Each culture is continually modifying appropriate public gender roles for men and women. While people often rebel consciously against their culture's gender roles, a person's sexuality is a much more intimate and unconscious aspect of her or his personality. Psychologists have a wide range of opinions about the relationships among sexuality, dreams, and gender roles, but one can reasonably conclude that dreams often manifest sexual content. In our world there is growing acceptance of nontraditional sexual orientations. The acceptance or rejection of a person's sexual orientation by family and peers plays a major role in an individual's ability to find peace and contentment. Each of the readings selected for this chapter relates to a particular issue of controversy related to sexuality and/or gender roles.

We begin with a poem, "Nargis' Toilette" by Chitra Divakaruni, which provides insights into traditional forms of Muslim wedding preparations, a traditional ritual designed to channel sexuality and gender identity along socially and religiously sanctioned lines. The poem seems to pose the question of what we gain and lose when we discard such rituals. The next reading, "No Name Woman" by Maxine Hong Kingston, portrays a traditional Chinese village culture where women are subordinate to men. The memoir demonstrates how a woman in that culture could easily be destroyed by rigid expectations of gender role and conduct as it condemns the repression and the impact of psychologically controlling erotic feelings through rigid social codes. The next essay by Sigmund Freud, "Erotic Wishes and Dreams" presents the theories of the founder of modern psychiatry based on dream symbol interpretation. Freud claims that the deeper content of many of our dreams reflects sexual desire and erotic wish fulfillment.

The next two selections are stories that explore the intense conflicts that the main characters, both unmarried couples, have about the consequences of their sexuality and gender roles. Ernest Hemingway's "Hills Like White Elephants," a dialogue between a young couple having drinks at a train station, reveals that the man and the woman have different, conflicting, but representative expectations about relationships and love. In "The Two," Gloria Naylor shows how partners in a stable lesbian relationship have conflicts that are similar to those experienced in a traditional marriage, while experiencing the added stress caused by the gossip and hostility in their immediate community because of the nontraditional nature of their sexual relationship.

David Sedaris, in "I Like Guys," presents a tragic-comic memoir of growing up gay in the late 1950s, pointing out how school integration did little to alleviate the sexual oppression experienced by gay youth of the period. In fact, at Sedaris's school, teachers of all races joined forces in ridiculing gay mannerisms and perpetuating stereotypes. Cooper Thompson, the author of our next selection, visited public schools a generation after David Sedaris's graduation, only to find that the worst insult a young man could experience was still that of being a called a "fag." In his essay, "A New Vision of Masculinity," Thompson argues for gender relations based on respect and consideration rather than "mutual fear and distrust."

The two student essays that close this chapter also present points of view on current gender issues. In "On Not Being a Girl," Rosa Contreras, discusses the difficulties she faced growing up in a Mexican-American family that expected her to follow the gender roles of her traditional-culture immigrant family while also expecting her to attend college. In "Gay Marriage: Why the Resistance?," Julie Bordner Apodaca writes about the political and social struggles for gay relationships to be recognized as legitimate family units and considers some of the reasons why it is difficult for such relationships to gain acceptance.

As we enter the new millennium, the issues of gender identity and sexuality only promise to become more complex. We think that the readings in this chapter will give you some insights into the customs of the past as well as provocative points of view about changing gender roles and nontraditional sexual orientation.

Chitra Divakaruni

Nargis' Toilette

Born in Calcutta, India, Chitra Divakaruni received a B.A. from the University of Calcutta and a Ph.D. in English Literature from the University of California at Berkeley in 1985. Divakaruni has taught English and creative writing at Foothill College in California and at the University of Houston, Texas. She has had poetry and stories published in literary magazines in both India and the United States. Her poetry collections include The Reason for Nasturtiums *(1990) and* Leaving Yuba City *(1997). Divakaruni has written two collections of short stories,* Arranged Marriages *(1995) and* The Unknown Errors of Our Lives *(2000), as well as three novels:* Mistress of Spices *(1997),* Sister of My Heart *(1999), and* Vine of Desire *(2002). In the poem "Nargis' Toilette," from* The Black Candle *(1991), Divakaruni explores the world of a veiled Muslim woman.*

JOURNAL

Write about a marriage ritual that you feel is erotic and dreamlike.

The uncovered face of a woman
is as a firebrand, inflaming men's
desires and reducing to ashes
the honor of her family.
5   —Muslim saying—

Powder to whiten skin
unsnagged as a just-ripe peach.
Kohl to underline the eye's mute deeps.
Attar of rose touched to the dip
10   behind the earlobe,
the shadow between the breasts,
the silk creases
of the crimson *kameez*.

In the women's courtyard
15   it is always quiet,
the carved iron gates locked.
The palm shivers by the marble fountain.
The *bulbul* sings to its crimson double
in the mirrored cage.

20   Satin *dupattas* rustle.

The women put henna
on Nargis' hands. They braid,
down her back,
the forest's long shadows,
25   their laughter like the silver anklets
they are tying to her feet.

Today the women will take Nargis
to visit the women of the Amin family.
They will drink chilled pomegranate juice,
30   nibble pistachio *burfis* green as ice.
The grandmothers will chew
betel leaves and discuss the heat.

Nargis will sit, eyes down,
tracing the peacock pattern

35 on the mosaic floor.
    If Allah wills, a marriage
    will be arranged
    with the Amins' second son
    whose face Nargis will see
40 for the first time
    in the square wedding mirror
    placed in the bride's lap.

    It is time to go.
    They bring her *burkha*,
45 slip it over her head.
    Someone adjusts the lace slits to her eyes.
    The *burkha* spills silk-black to her feet
    and spreads, spreads,
    over the land, dark wave
50 breaking over the women, quenching
    their light.

    Now all is ready.
    Like a black candle
    Nargis walks to the gate.

QUESTIONS FOR DISCUSSION

1. Why do you think the poem begins with an epigram from a Muslim saying? What is the relationship between the meaning of the saying and the meaning of the poem?
2. From reading and thinking about the poem, explain your understanding of Muslim marriage traditions. What impact do you think such traditions may have on the individual and on married couples?
3. Discuss several of the images and rituals in the poem that create the sense of sensuality woven into Nargis' preparation to meet the man selected to be her husband. What makes the preparation seem dreamlike?
4. Why is Nargis compared to a "black candle" as she walks to the gate to meet the man who may choose her to be his wife?
5. Although Nargis is the one chosen and not the one who makes the choice, she does have power. What is her power? Why is she dangerous? How does her veiled presence emphasize the theme of danger?

CONNECTION

Compare the function of the traditional marriage ritual in this poem with the comments made on the function of mythic patterns and ritual in Joseph Campbell's "Four Functions of Mythology" in Chapter 4 (see page 200).

IDEAS FOR WRITING

1. Write an essay in which you compare and contrast the role and power of a wife in a traditional culture such as Pakistan or India to the role and power of a wife in a modern, less traditional culture such as modern America. What are the advantages and disadvantages of being a wife in each culture?

2. Develop your journal entry into an essay in which you discuss how marriage and sexuality are enhanced through traditional rituals that engage the imagination and the senses. Refer to literature and the popular media as well as to personal experience to support your main points.

RELATED WEB SITES

CHITRA BANERJEE DIVAKARUNI

http://www.umiacs.umd.edu/users/sawweb/sawnet/books/chitra_divakaruni.html

This web site includes an author profile of Chitra Divakaruni, articles by and about the author, book reviews, upcoming readings, and links to other sites related to Divakaruni's works.

MUSLIM AND INDIAN WEDDING RITUALS

http://www.netguruindia.com/matri/muslim.asp

This Indian web site shares information on many important Muslim and Indian wedding rituals. The site also gives summaries of other culture's marriage rituals such as Christian and Sikh.

Maxine Hong Kingston

No Name Woman

Maxine Hong Kingston (b. 1940) is from Stockton, California, where she grew up listening to the stories her mother would tell about Chinese village life. Hong Kingston graduated from the University of California at Berkeley and taught high school and college English in Hawaii for a number of years before returning to the San Francisco Bay Area to write and teach at U.C. Berkeley. Books by Hong Kingston include a personal memoir, The Woman Warrior: Memories of a Childhood among Ghosts *(1976), a historical account of Chinese-American life,* China Men *(1980); and a novel,* Tripmaster Monkey: His Fake Book *(1989). Her most recent book is* To Be the Poet *(2002), in the Harvard Press series* The William E. Massey, Sr. Lectures in the History of American Civilization. *The following selection from* The Woman Warrior *reflects on one of the stories Hong Kingston's mother told her about an aunt in China whose sexual indiscretion leads her to become a "no name woman" and to lose her place in the life of the community.*

Retell a story that you heard from a family member when you were a child that warned you of the dangers of adult life and sexuality.

"You must not tell anyone," my mother said, "what I am about to tell you. In China your father had a sister who killed herself. She jumped into the family well. We say that your father has all brothers because it is as if she had never been born.

"In 1924 just a few days after our village celebrated seventeen hurry-up weddings—to make sure that every young man who went 'out on the road' would responsibly come home—your father and his brothers and your grandfather and his brothers and your aunt's new husband sailed for America, the Gold Mountain. It was your grandfather's last trip. Those lucky enough to get contracts waved good-bye from the decks. They fed and guarded the stowaways and helped them off in Cuba, New York, Bali, Hawaii. 'We'll meet in California next year,' they said. All of them sent money home.

"I remember looking at your aunt one day when she and I were dressing; I had not noticed before that she had such a protruding melon of a stomach. But I did not think, 'She's pregnant,' until she began to look like other pregnant women, her shirt pulling and the white tops of her black pants showing. She could not have been pregnant, you see, because her husband had been gone for years. No one said anything. We did not discuss it. In early summer she was ready to have the child, long after the time when it could have been possible.

"The village had also been counting. On the night the baby was to be born the villagers raided our house. Some were crying. Like a great saw, teeth strung with lights, files of people walked zigzag across our land, tearing the rice. Their lanterns doubled in the disturbed black water, which drained away through the broken bunds. As the villagers closed in, we could see that some of them, probably men and women we knew well, wore white masks. The people with long hair hung it over their faces. Women with short hair made it stand up on end. Some had tied white bands around their foreheads, arms, and legs.

5   "At first they threw mud and rocks at the house. Then they threw eggs and began slaughtering our stock. We could hear the animals scream their deaths—the roosters, the pigs, a last great roar from the ox. Familiar wild heads flared in our night windows; the villagers encircled us. Some of the faces stopped to peer at us, their eyes rushing like searchlights. The hands flattened against the panes, framed heads, and left red prints.

"The villagers broke in the front and the back doors at the same time, even though we had not locked the doors against them. Their knives dripped with the blood of our animals. They smeared blood on the doors and walls. One woman swung a chicken, whose throat she had slit, splattering blood in red arcs about her. We stood together in the middle of our house, in the family hall with the pictures and tables of the ancestors around us, and looked straight ahead.

"At that time the house had only two wings. When the men came back, we would build two more to enclose our courtyard and a third one to begin a second courtyard. The villagers rushed through both wings, even your grandparents' rooms, to find your aunt's, which was also mine until the men returned. From this room a new wing for one of the younger families would grow. They ripped up her clothes and shoes and broke her combs, grinding them underfoot. They tore her work from the loom. They scattered the cooking fire and rolled the new weaving in it. We could hear them in the kitchen breaking our bowls and banging the pots. They overturned the great waist-high earthenware jugs; duck eggs, pickled fruits, vegetables burst out and mixed in acrid torrents. The old woman from the next field swept a broom through the air and loosed the spirits-of-the-broom over our heads. 'Pig.' 'Ghost.' 'Pig,' they sobbed and scolded while they ruined our house.

"When they left, they took sugar and oranges to bless themselves. They cut pieces from the dead animals. Some of them took bowls that were not broken and clothes that were not torn. Afterward we swept up the rice and sewed it back up into sacks. But the smells from the spilled preserves lasted. Your aunt gave birth in the pigsty that night. The next morning when I went for the water, I found her and the baby plugging up the family well.

"Don't let your father know that I told you. He denies her. Now that you have started to menstruate, what happened to her could happen to you. Don't humiliate us. You wouldn't like to be forgotten as if you had never been born. The villagers are watchful."

10   Whenever she had to warn us about life, my mother told stories that ran like this one, a story to grow up on. She tested our strength to establish realities. Those in the emigrant generations who could not reassert brute survival died young and far from home. Those of us in the first American generations have had to figure out how the invisible world that the emigrants built around our childhoods fit in solid America.

The emigrants confused the gods by diverting their curses, misleading them with crooked streets and false names. They must try to confuse their offspring as well, who, I suppose, threaten them in similar ways—always trying to get things straight, always trying to name the unspeakable. The Chinese I know hide their names; sojourners take new names when their lives change and guard their real names with silence.

Chinese-Americans, when you try to understand what things in you are Chinese, how do you separate what is peculiar to childhood, to poverty, insanities, one family, your mother who marked your growing with stories from what is Chinese? What is Chinese tradition and what is the movies?

If I want to learn what clothes my aunt wore, whether flashy or ordinary, I would have to begin, "Remember Father's drowned-in-the-well sister?" I cannot ask that. My mother has told me once and for all the useful parts. She will add nothing unless powered by Necessity, a riverbank that guides her life. She plants vegetable gardens rather than lawns; she carries the odd-shaped tomatoes home from the fields and eats food left for the gods.

Whenever we did frivolous things, we used up energy; we flew high kites. We children came up off the ground over the melting cones our parents brought home from work and the American movie on New Year's Day—*Oh, You Beautiful Doll* with Betty Grable one year, and *She Wore a Yellow Ribbon* with John Wayne another year. After the one carnival ride each, we paid in guilt; our tired father counted his change on the dark walk home.

15   Adultery is extravagance. Could people who hatch their own chicks and eat the embryos and the heads for delicacies and boil the feet in vinegar for party food, leaving only the gravel, eating even the gizzard lining—could such people engender a prodigal aunt? To be a woman, to have a daughter in starvation time was a waste enough. My aunt could not have been the lone romantic who gave up everything for sex. Women in the old China did not choose. Some man had commanded her to lie with him and be his secret evil. I wonder whether he masked himself when he joined the raid on her family.

Perhaps she encountered him in the fields or on the mountain where the daughters-in-law collected fuel. Or perhaps he first noticed her in the marketplace. He was not a stranger because the village housed no strangers. She had to have dealings with him other than sex. Perhaps he worked an adjoining field, or he sold her the cloth for the dress she sewed and wore. His demand must have surprised, then terrified her. She obeyed him; she always did as she was told.

When the family found a young man in the next village to be her husband, she stood tractably beside the best rooster, his proxy, and promised before they met that she would be his forever. She was lucky that he was her age and she would be the first wife, an advantage secure now. The night she first saw him, he had sex with her. Then he left for America. She had almost forgotten what he looked like. When she tried to envision him, she only saw the black and white face in the group photograph the men had had taken before leaving.

The other man was not, after all, much different from her husband. They both gave orders: she followed. "If you tell your family, I'll beat you. I'll kill you. Be here again next week." No one talked sex, ever. And she might have separated the rapes from the rest of living if only she did not have to buy her oil from him or gather wood in the same forest. I want her fear to have lasted just as long as rape lasted so that the fear could have been contained. No drawn-out fear. But women at sex hazarded birth and hence lifetimes. The fear did not stop but permeated everywhere. She told the man, "I think I'm pregnant." He organized the raid against her.

On nights when my mother and father talked about their life back home, sometimes they mentioned an "outcast table" whose business they still seemed to be settling, their voices tight. In a communal tradition, where food is precious, the powerful older people made wrongdoers eat alone. Instead of letting them start separate new lives like the Japanese, who could become samurais and geishas, the Chinese family, faces averted but eyes glowering sideways, hung on to the offenders and fed them leftovers. My aunt must have lived in the same house as my parents and eaten at an outcast table. My mother spoke about the raid as if she had seen it, when she and my aunt, a daughter-in-law to a different household, should not have been living together at all. Daughters-in-law lived with their husbands' parents, not their own; a synonym for marriage in Chinese is "taking a daughter-in-law." Her husband's parents could have sold her, mortgaged her, stoned her. But they had sent her back to her own mother and father, a mysterious act hinting at disgraces not told me. Perhaps they had thrown her out to deflect the avengers.

20   She was the only daughter; her four brothers went with her father, husband and uncles "out on the road" and for some years became western men. When the goods were divided among the family, three of the brothers took land, and the youngest, my father, chose an education. After my grandparents gave their daughter away to her husband's family, they had dispensed all the adventure and all the property. They expected her alone to keep the traditional ways, which her brothers, now among the barbarians, could tumble without detection. The heavy, deep-rooted women were to maintain the past against the flood, safe for returning. But the rare urge west had fixed upon our family, and so my aunt crossed boundaries not delineated in space.

The work of preservation demands that the feelings playing about in one's guts not be turned into action. Just watch their passing like cherry blossoms. But perhaps my aunt, my forerunner, caught in a slow life, let dreams grow and fade and after some months or years went toward what persisted. Fear at the enormities of the forbidden kept her desires delicate, wire and bone. She looked at a man because she liked the way the hair was tucked behind his ears, or she liked the question-mark line of a long torso curving at the shoulder and straight at the hip. For warm eyes or a soft voice or a slow walk—that's all—a few hairs, a line, brightness, a sound, a pace, she gave up family. She offered us up for a charm that vanished with tiredness, a pigtail that didn't toss when the wind died. Why, the wrong lighting could erase the dearest thing about him.

It could very well have been, however, that my aunt did not take subtle enjoyment of her friend, but, a wild woman, kept rollicking company. Imagining her free with sex doesn't fit, though. I don't know any women like that, or men either. Unless I see her life branching into mine, she gives me no ancestral help.

To sustain her being in love, she often worked at herself in the mirror, guessing at the colors and shapes that would interest him, changing them frequently in order to hit on the right combination. She wanted him to look back.

On a farm near the sea, a woman who tended her appearance reaped a reputation for eccentricity. All the married women blunt-cut their hair in flaps about their ears or pulled it back in tight buns. No nonsense. Neither style blew easily into heart-catching tangles. And at their weddings they displayed themselves in their long hair for the last time. "It brushed the backs of my knees," my mother tells me. "It was braided, and even so, it brushed the backs of my knees."

25   At the mirror my aunt combed individuality into her bob. A bun could have been contrived to escape into black streamers blowing in the wind or in quiet

wisps about her face, but only the older women in our picture album wear buns. She brushed her hair back from her forehead, tucking the flaps behind her ears. She looped a piece of thread, knotted into a circle between her index fingers and thumbs, and ran the double strand across her forehead. When she closed her fingers as if she were making a pair of shadow geese bite, the string twisted together catching the little hairs. Then she pulled the thread away from her skin, ripping the hairs out neatly, her eyes watering from the needles of pain. Opening her fingers, she cleaned the thread, then rolled it along her hairline and the tops of her eyebrows. My mother did the same to me and my sisters and herself. I used to believe that the expression "caught by the short hairs" meant a captive held with a depilatory string. It especially hurt at the temples, but my mother said we were lucky we didn't have to have our feet bound when we were seven. Sisters used to sit on their beds and cry together, she said, as their mothers or their slave removed the bandages for a few minutes each night and let the blood gush back into their veins. I hope that the man my aunt loved appreciated a smooth brow, that he wasn't just a tits-and-ass man.

Once my aunt found a freckle on her chin, at a spot that the almanac said predestined her for unhappiness. She dug it out with a hot needle and washed the wound with peroxide.

More attention to her looks than these pullings of hairs and pickings at spots would have caused gossip among the villagers. They owned work clothes and good clothes, and they wore good clothes for feasting the new seasons. But since a woman combing her hair hexes beginnings, my aunt rarely found an occasion to look her best. Women looked like great sea snails—the corded wood, babies, and laundry they carried were the whorls on their backs. The Chinese did not admire a bent back; goddesses and warriors stood straight. Still there must have been a marvelous freeing of beauty when a worker laid down her burden and stretched and arched.

Such commonplace loveliness, however, was not enough for my aunt. She dreamed of a lover for the fifteen days of New Year's, the time for families to exchange visits, money, and food. She plied her secret comb. And sure enough she cursed the year, the family, the village, and herself.

Even as her hair lured her imminent lover, many other men looked at her. Uncles, cousins, nephews, brothers would have looked, too, had they been home between journeys. Perhaps they had already been restraining their curiosity, and they left, fearful that their glances, like a field of nesting birds, might be startled and caught. Poverty hurt, and that was their first reason for leaving. But another, final reason for leaving the crowded house was the never-said.

30   She may have been unusually beloved, the precious only daughter, spoiled and mirror gazing because of the affection the family lavished on her. When her husband left, they welcomed the chance to take her back from the in-laws; she could live like the little daughter for just a while longer. There are stories that my grandfather was different from other people, "crazy ever since the little Jap bayoneted him in the head." He used to put his naked penis on the dinner

table, laughing. And one day he brought home a baby girl, wrapped up inside his brown western-style greatcoat. He had traded one of his sons, probably my father, the youngest, for her. My grandmother made him trade back. When he finally got a daughter of his own, he doted on her. They must have all loved her, except perhaps my father, the only brother who never went back to China, having once been traded for a girl.

Brothers and sisters, newly men and women, had to efface their sexual color and present plain miens. Disturbing hair and eyes, a smile like no other, threatened the ideal of five generations living under one roof. To focus blurs, people shouted face to face and yelled from room to room. The immigrants I know have loud voices, unmodulated to American tones even after years away from the village where they called their friendships out across the fields. I have not been able to stop mother's screams in public libraries or over telephones. Walking erect (knees straight, toes pointed forward, not pigeon-toed, which is Chinese-feminine) and speaking in an inaudible voice, I have tried to turn myself American-feminine. Chinese communication was loud, public. Only sick people had to whisper. But at the dinner table, where the family members came nearest one another, no one could talk, not the outcasts nor any eaters. Every word that falls from the mouth is a coin lost. Silently they gave and accepted food with both hands. A preoccupied child who took his bowl with one hand got a sideways glare. A complete moment of total attention is due everyone alike. Children and lovers have no singularity here, but my aunt used a secret voice, a separate attentiveness.

She kept the man's name to herself throughout her labor and dying; she did not accuse him that he be punished with her. To save her inseminator's name she gave silent birth.

He may have been somebody in her own household, but intercourse with a man outside the family would have been no less abhorrent. All the village were kinsmen, and the titles shouted in loud country voices never let kinship be forgotten. Any man within visiting distance would have been neutralized as a lover—"brother," "younger brother," "older brother"—one hundred and fifteen relationship titles. Parents researched birth charts probably not so much to assure good fortune as to circumvent incest in a population that has but one hundred surnames. Everybody has eight million relatives. How useless then sexual mannerisms, how dangerous.

As if it came from an atavism deeper than fear, I used to add "brother" silently to boys' names. It hexed the boys, who would or would not ask me to dance, and made them less scary and as familiar and deserving of benevolence as girls.

35   But, of course, I hexed myself also—no dates. I should have stood up, both arms waving, and shouted out across libraries, "Hey, you! Love me back." I had no idea, though, how to make attraction selective, how to control its direction and magnitude. If I made myself American-pretty so that the five or six Chinese boys in the class fell in love with me, everyone else—the Caucasian, Negro, and Japanese boys—would too. Sisterliness, dignified and honorable, made much more sense.

Attraction eludes control so stubbornly that whole societies designed to organize relationships among people cannot keep order, not even when they bind people to one another from childhood and raise them together. Among the very poor and the wealthy, brothers married their adopted sisters, like doves. Our family provided some romance, paying adult brides' prices and providing dowries so that their sons and daughters could marry strangers. Marriage promises to turn strangers into friendly relatives—a nation of siblings.

In the village structure, spirits shimmered among the live creatures, balanced and held in equilibrium by time and land. But one human being flaring up into violence could open up a black hole, a maelstrom that pulled in the sky. The frightened villagers, who depended on one another to maintain the real, went to my aunt to show her a personal, physical representation of the break she had made in the "roundness." Misallying couples snapped off the future, which was to be embodied in true offspring. The villagers punished her for acting as if she could have a private life, secret and apart from them.

If my aunt had betrayed the family at a time of large grain yields and peace, when many boys were born, the wings were being built on many houses, perhaps she might have escaped such severe punishment. But the men—hungry, greedy, tired of planting in dry soil, cuckolded—had had to leave the village in order to send food-money home. There were ghost plagues, bandit plagues, wars with the Japanese, floods. My Chinese brother and sister had died of an unknown sickness. Adultery, perhaps only a mistake during good times, became a crime when the village needed food.

The round moon cakes and round doorways, the round tables of graduated size that fit one roundness inside another, round windows and rice bowls— these talismans had lost their power to warn this family of the law: a family must be whole, faithfully keep the descent line by having sons to feed the old and the dead, who in turn look after the family. The villagers came to show my aunt and her lover-in-hiding a broken house. The villagers were speeding up the circling of events because she was too short-sighted to see that her infidelity had already harmed the village, that waves of consequences would return unpredictably, sometimes in disguise, as now, to hurt her. This roundness had to be made coin-sized so that she would see its circumference: punish her at the birth of her baby. Awaken her to the inexorable. People who refused fatalism because they could invent small resources insisted on culpability. Deny accidents and wrest fault from the stars.

40   After the villagers left, their lanterns now scattering in various directions toward home, the family broke their silence and cursed her. "Aiaa, we're going to die. Death is coming. Death is coming. Look what you've done. You've killed us. Ghost! Dead ghost! Ghost! You've never been born." She ran out into the fields, far enough from the house so that she could no longer hear their voices, and pressed herself against the earth, her own land no more. When she felt the birth coming, she thought that she had been hurt. Her body seized together.

"They've hurt me too much," she thought. "This is gall, and it will kill me." With forehead and knees against the earth, her body convulsed and then relaxed. She turned on her back, lay on the ground. The black well of sky and stars went out and out and out forever; her body and her complexity seemed to disappear, without home, without a companion, in eternal cold and silence. An agoraphobia rose in her, speeding higher and higher, bigger and bigger; she would not be able to contain it; there would be no end to fear.

Flayed, unprotected against space, she felt pain return, focusing her body. This pain chilled her—a cold, steady kind of surface pain. Inside, spasmodically, the other pain, the pain of the child, heated her. For hours she lay on the ground, alternately body and space. Sometimes a vision of normal comfort obliterated reality: she saw the family in the evening gambling at the dinner table, the young people massaging their elder's backs. She saw them congratulating one another, high joy on the mornings the rice shoots came up. When these pictures burst, the stars drew yet further apart. Black space opened.

She got to her feet to fight better and remembered that old-fashioned women gave birth in their pigsties to fool the jealous, pain-dealing gods, who do not snatch piglets. Before the next spasms could stop her, she ran to the pigsty, each step a rushing out into emptiness. She climbed over the fence and knelt in the dirt. It was good to have a fence enclosing her, a tribal person alone.

Laboring, this woman who had carried her child as a foreign growth that sickened her every day, expelled it at last. She reached down to touch the hot, wet, moving mass, surely smaller than anything human, and could feel that it was human after all—fingers, toes, nails, nose. She pulled it up on to her belly, and it lay curled there, butt in the air, feet precisely tucked one under the other. She opened her loose shirt and buttoned the child inside. After resting, it squirmed and thrashed and she pushed it up to her breast. It turned its head this way and that until it found her nipple. There, it made little snuffling noises. She clenched her teeth at its preciousness, lovely as a young calf, a piglet, a little dog.

She may have gone to the pigsty as a last act of responsibility: she would protect this child as she had protected its father. It would look after her soul, leaving supplies on her grave. But how would this tiny child without family find her grave when there would be no marker for her anywhere, neither in the earth nor the family hall? No one would give her a family hall name. She had taken the child with her into the wastes. At its birth the two of them had felt the same raw pain of separation, a wound that only the family pressing tight could close. A child with no descent line would not soften her life but only trail after her, ghost-like, begging her to give it purpose. At dawn the villagers on their way to the fields would stand around the fence and look.

45   Full of milk, the little ghost slept. When it awoke, she hardened her breasts against the milk that crying loosens. Toward morning she picked up the baby and walked to the well.

Carrying the baby to the well shows loving. Otherwise abandon it. Turn its face into the mud. Mothers who love their children take them along. It was probably a girl; there is some hope of forgiveness for boys.

"Don't tell anyone you had an aunt. Your father does not want to hear her name. She has never been born." I have believed that sex was unspeakable and words so strong and fathers so frail that "aunt" would do my father mysterious harm. I have thought that my family, having settled among immigrants who had also been their neighbors in the ancestral land, needed to clean their name, and a wrong word would incite the kinspeople even here. But there is more to this silence: they want me to participate in her punishment. And I have.

In the twenty years since I heard this story I have not asked for details nor said my aunt's name; I do not know it. People who can comfort the dead can also chase after them to hurt them further—a reverse ancestor worship. The real punishment was not the raid swiftly inflicted by the villagers, but the family's deliberately forgetting her. Her betrayal so maddened them, they saw to it that she would suffer forever, even after death. Always hungry, always needing, she would have to beg food from other ghosts, snatch and steal it from those whose living descendants give them gifts. She would have to fight the ghosts massed at crossroads for the buns a few thoughtful citizens leave to decoy her away from village and home so that the ancestral spirits could feast unharassed. At peace, they could act like gods, not ghosts, their descent lines providing them with paper suits and dresses, spirit money, paper houses, paper automobiles, chicken, meat, and rice into eternity—essences delivered up in smoke and flames, steam and incense rising from each rice bowl. In an attempt to make the Chinese care for people outside the family, Chairman Mao encourages us now to give our paper replicas to the spirits of outstanding soldiers and workers, no matter whose ancestors they may be. My aunt remains forever hungry. Goods are not distributed evenly among the dead.

My aunt haunts me—her ghost drawn to me because now, after fifty years of neglect, I alone devote pages of paper to her, though not origamied into houses and clothes. I do not think she always means me well. I am telling on her, and she was a spite suicide, drowning herself in the drinking water. The Chinese are always very frightened of the drowned one, whose weeping ghost, wet hair hanging and skin bloated, waits silently by the water to pull down a substitute.

QUESTIONS FOR DISCUSSION

1. Why is this a "story to grow on"? What lesson is it designed to teach? Does the daughter, Maxine, accept her mother's purpose in telling the story, or does she interpret the story to create a new meaning from it?

2. What possible reasons for the aunt's pregnancy and suicide does the narrator propose? What do these different reasons suggest about the status of women in the Chinese family and about the double standard for male and female behavior in Chinese culture prior to World War II? Do you

think that in today's Chinese families men and women are treated equally?

3. Why was it so important for Chinese family members to "efface their sexual color" and to remain silent at meals? How is this ritual reflective of their culture's values?

4. What relationship exists between the individual and the community in the Chinese village of the "No Name Woman"? How is this relationship between the individual and the community different from the one in your neighborhood?

5. Why did the aunt's killing of her infant, combined with her suicide, reflect "signs of loving"? Why was the infant "probably a girl"?

6. Why does the aunt's ghost continue to haunt the narrator? What perspective on gender roles do they seem to share? In what ways are the two women different from one another?

CONNECTION

Compare the traditional status of women as seen in "No Name Woman" with that of the Muslim bride in "Nargis' Toilette" (see page 318).

IDEAS FOR WRITING

1. Write about a relative who continues to haunt your family or a relative about whom there is a family legend because of his or her sexual life. What does the legacy of this ghostlike figure reflect about your family's values? What impact has it had on your own values?

2. Write about a value or tradition related to gender role or sexuality that your grandparents or parents accepted and that you have rebelled against. What do you think influenced you to believe in values different from those that were accepted by your parents and grandparents? How does this generation gap influence the functioning of your family?

RELATED WEB SITES

MAXINE HONG KINGSTON
http://voices.cla.umn.edu/authors/MaxineHongKingston.html
At this informative web site on Maxine Hong Kingston you will find extensive biographical and bibliographical writings on the Chinese-American author. Links to other related web sites are also included.

THE ASIAN-AMERICAN EXPERIENCE
http://www.lib.uci.edu/rrsc/asiamer.html
Created by the University of California at Irvine, this web site provides several links to various URLs devoted to understanding the Asian-American experience and Asian culture.

Sigmund Freud

Erotic Wishes and Dreams

> *Known as the founder of the psychoanalytic method and of concepts such as the un-*
> *conscious mind and the Oedipus complex, Sigmund Freud (1856–1939) was also a*
> *pioneer in the scientific study of dreams and human sexuality. Freud spent most of his*
> *life in Vienna, where he practiced psychoanalysis and published many important stud-*
> *ies on psychology and dream interpretation as well as cultural studies that focus on*
> *psychological interpretations of art and history. His works include* Interpretation of
> Dreams *(1900),* Totem and Taboo, *and* Leonardo da Vinci: A Study in Psycho-
> sexuality. *In "Erotic Wishes and Dreams," from his explanation of dream theory,*
> On Dreams *(1901), Freud presents his ideas on dream symbolism and expresses his*
> *conviction that dreams focus on erotic wishes and fantasies, although sometimes in a*
> *disguised form.*

JOURNAL

Write about a dream you have had that you consider explicitly or implicitly sexual
in its content. Did you consider the dream to be a form of wish fulfillment, or
could there have been some other explanation for the dream and its images?

No one who accepts the view that the censorship is the chief reason for
dream distortion will be surprised to learn from the results of dream interpretation that most of the dreams of adults are traced back by analysis to *erotic
wishes.* This assertion is not aimed at dreams with an *undisguised* sexual content,
which are no doubt familiar to all dreamers from their own experience and are
as a rule the only ones to be described as "sexual dreams." Even dreams of this
latter kind offer enough surprises in their choice of the people whom they
make into sexual objects, in their disregard of all the limitations which the
dreamer imposes in his waking life upon his sexual desires, and by their many
strange details, hinting at what are commonly known as "perversions." A great
many other dreams, however, which show no sign of being erotic in their manifest content, are revealed by the work of interpretation in analysis as sexual
wish fulfillments; and, on the other hand, analysis proves that a great many of
the thoughts left over from the activity of waking life as "residues of the previous day" only find their way to representation in dreams through the assistance
of repressed erotic wishes.

There is no theoretical necessity why this should be so; but to explain the
fact it may be pointed out that no other group of instincts has been submitted
to such far-reaching suppression by the demands of cultural education, while
at the same time the sexual instincts are also the ones which, in most people,
find it easiest to escape from the control of the highest mental agencies. Since

we have become acquainted with infantile sexuality, which is often so unobtrusive in its manifestations and is always overlooked and misunderstood, we are justified in saying that almost every civilized man retains the infantile forms of sexual life in some respect or other. We can thus understand how it is that repressed infantile sexual wishes provide the most frequent and strongest motive forces for the construction of dreams.*

There is only one method by which a dream which expresses erotic wishes can succeed in appearing innocently nonsexual in its manifest content. The material of the sexual ideas must not be represented as such, but must be replaced in the content of the dream by hints, allusions and similar forms of indirect representation. But, unlike other forms of indirect representation, that which is employed in dreams must not be immediately intelligible. The modes of representation which fulfill these conditions are usually described as "symbols" of the things which they represent. Particular interest has been directed to them since it has been noticed that dreamers speaking the same language make use of the same symbols, and that in some cases, indeed, the use of the same symbols extends beyond the use of the same language. Since dreamers themselves are unaware of the meaning of the symbols they use, it is difficult at first sight to discover the source of the connection between the symbols and what they replace and represent. The fact itself, however, is beyond doubt, and it is important for the technique of dream interpretation. For, with the help of a knowledge of dream symbolism, it is possible to understand the meaning of separate elements of the content of a dream or separate pieces of a dream or in some cases even whole dreams, without having to ask the dreamer for his associations. Here we are approaching the popular ideal of translating dreams and on the other hand are returning to the technique of interpretation used by the ancients, to whom dream interpretation was identical with interpretation by means of symbols.

Although the study of dream symbols is far from being complete, we are in a position to lay down with certainty a number of general statements and a quantity of special information on the subject. There are some symbols which bear a single meaning almost universally: thus the Emperor and Empress (or the King and Queen) stand for the parents, rooms represent women and their entrances and exits the openings of the body. The majority of dream symbols serve to represent persons, parts of the body and activities invested with erotic interest; in particular, the genitals are represented by a number of often very surprising symbols, and the greatest variety of objects are employed to denote them symbolically. Sharp weapons, long and stiff objects, such as tree trunks and sticks, stand for the male genital; while cupboards, boxes, carriages or ovens may represent the uterus. In such cases as these the *tertium comparationis*, the common element in these substitutions, is immediately intelligible; but

---

*See my *Three Essays on the Theory of Sexuality* (1905) [Author's note].

there are other symbols in which it is not so easy to grasp the connection. Symbols such as a staircase or going upstairs, representing sexual intercourse, a tie or cravat for the male organ, or wood for the female one, provoke our unbelief until we can arrive at an understanding of the symbolic relation underlying them by some other means. Moreover a whole number of dream symbols are bisexual and can relate to the male or female genitals according to the context.

5   Some symbols are universally disseminated and can be met with in all dreamers belonging to a single linguistic or cultural group; there are others which occur only within the most restricted and individual limits, symbols constructed by an individual out of his own ideational material. Of the former class we can distinguish some whose claim to represent sexual ideas is immediately justified by linguistic usage (such, for instance, as those derived from agriculture, e.g., "fertilization" or "seed") and others whose relation to sexual ideas appears to reach back into the very earliest ages and to the most obscure depths of our conceptual functioning. The power of constructing symbols has not been exhausted in our own days in the case of either of the two sorts of symbols which I have distinguished at the beginning of this paragraph. Newly discovered objects (such as airships) are, as we may observe, at once adopted as universally available sexual symbols.

It would, incidentally, be a mistake to expect that if we had a still profounder knowledge of dream symbolism (of the "language of dreams") we could do without asking the dreamer for his associations to the dream and go back entirely to the technique of dream interpretation of antiquity. Quite apart from individual symbols and oscillations in the use of universal ones, one can never tell whether any particular element in the content of a dream is to be interpreted symbolically or in its proper sense, and one can be certain that the *whole* content of a dream is not to be interpreted symbolically. A knowledge of dream symbolism will never do more than enable us to translate certain constituents of the dream content, and will not relieve us of the necessity for applying the technical rules which I gave earlier. It will, however, afford the most valuable assistance to interpretation precisely at points at which the dreamer's associations are insufficient or fail altogether.

Dream symbolism is also indispensable to an understanding of what are known as "typical" dreams, which are common to everyone, and of "recurrent" dreams in individuals.

If the account I have given in this short discussion of the symbolic mode of expression in dreams appears incomplete, I can justify my neglect by drawing attention to one of the most important pieces of knowledge that we possess on this subject. Dream symbolism extends far beyond dreams: it is not peculiar to dreams, but exercises a similar dominating influence on representation in fairy tales, myths and legends, in jokes and in folklore. It enables us to trace the intimate connections between dreams and these latter productions. We must not suppose that dream symbolism is a creation of the dream work; it is in all probability a characteristic of the unconscious thinking which provides the dream work with the material for condensation, displacement and dramatization.

QUESTIONS FOR DISCUSSION

1. Why does Freud believe that "repressed infantile sexual wishes" are the strongest motivation behind dreams and their primary content? Does he provide convincing evidence for this belief?
2. How might a dream express erotic wishes and at the same time appear innocent of sexual content? What might cause this apparent contradiction?
3. How does Freud define "symbols" as they appear in dreams? What examples does he provide? Do these seem like sexual symbols to you?
4. How does Freud compare traditional, culturally universal dream symbols with more modern symbols based on technological inventions? Can you think of modern dream symbols that have sexual implications?
5. According to Freud, why is it always a mistake to create dream interpretations without investigating the dreamer's own associations with the symbols from his or her dreams? Do you agree with Freud that popular books which list the meanings of dream symbols are basically worthless? Explain your position.
6. What is the relationship between dream symbolism, the unconscious mind, and more literary works such as fairy tales, myths, and legends? Do you agree with Freud's comparison and analysis?

CONNECTION

Compare Freud's view of sexuality, gender, dreams, and fantasy to Maxine Hong Kingston's observations in "No Name Woman." How would Freud respond (see page 321)?

IDEAS FOR WRITING

1. Apply Freud's theory about the content and symbolism of dreams to a dream you have had. Write an interpretive essay about your dream. Did Freud's ideas help you to understand your dream and its causes more clearly? What else might have influenced the imagery and events in your dream?
2. Because Freud's theories about the repressed erotic content and symbolism in dreams can also be applied to fantasy literature such as myths and fairy tales, many critics have attempted "Freudian" analyses of imaginative literature. Using a "Freudian" or sexual-symbol approach, try to interpret the characters, symbolism, and events of one of the stories or myths in this text. Did you find this approach satisfactory? Why or why not?

RELATED WEB SITES

SIGMUND FREUD
http://www.freudfile.org/
This web site is dedicated to the life and work of Sigmund Freud. It offers information about his biography, self-analysis and work, as well as about the

personalities who interacted with his ideas and with the development of psychoanalysis. Bibliographical notes, quotations, and references concerning Freud and his activity in the psychoanalysis field will also be found here.

THE AMERICAN PSYCHOANALYTIC ASSOCIATION
http://www.apsa.org

Learn about psychoanalysis at this large web site devoted to the subject. It also includes many relevant links, essays, news, and information on upcoming conferences.

Ernest Hemingway

Hills Like White Elephants

Ernest Hemingway (1899–1961) is remembered for his adventurous life as well as for his novels and stories. Born in Oak Park, Illinois, as a boy he often went hunting and fishing with his father. After he finished high school, Hemingway began to work as a newspaper reporter for the Kansas City Star and the Toronto Star. He went on to be a foreign correspondent, meeting expatriate writers in Paris and covering World War I. His war experiences and contacts with the expatriate community formed the basis for much of his early fiction, as well as the novels The Sun Also Rises (1926) and A Farewell to Arms (1929). He was awarded the Nobel Prize in 1954. Influenced by his journalistic experience, Hemingway saw himself primarily as a realist whose seemingly simple style was designed to strip away inauthentic language: "When you have read something by me you actually experience the thing." "Hills Like White Elephants," a story about a conflict between lovers, appeared in his collection In Our Time (1925).

JOURNAL

Describe a verbal conflict you had with a member of the opposite gender. In what ways was your conflict related to your different values, especially those connected to your gender identity? Explain why you think the two of you were unable to communicate with one another.

The hills across the valley of the Ebro were long and white. On this side there was no shade and no trees and the station was between two lines of rails in the sun. Close against the side of the station there was the warm shadow of the building and a curtain, made of strings of bamboo beads, hung across the open door into the bar, to keep out flies. The American and the girl with him sat at a table in the shade, outside the building. It was very hot and the express from Barcelona would come in forty minutes. It stopped at this junction for two minutes and went on to Madrid.

"What should we drink?" the girl asked. She had taken off her hat and put it on the table.

"It's pretty hot," the man said.

"Let's drink beer."

5   "*Dos cervezas,*" the man said into the curtain.

"Big ones?" a woman asked from the doorway.

"Yes. Two big ones."

The woman brought two glasses of beer and two felt pads. She put the felt pads and the beer glasses on the table and looked at the man and the girl. The girl was looking off at the line of hills. They were white in the sun and the country was brown and dry.

"They look like white elephants," she said.

10   "I've never seen one," the man drank his beer.

"No, you wouldn't have."

"I might have," the man said. "Just because you say I wouldn't have doesn't prove anything."

The girl looked at the bead curtain. "They've painted something on it," she said. "What does it say?"

"Anis del Toro. It's a drink."

15   "Could we try it?"

The man called "Listen" through the curtain. The woman came out from the bar.

"Four reales."

"We want two Anis del Toro."

"With water?"

20   "Do you want it with water?"

"I don't know," the girl said. "Is it good with water?"

"It's all right."

"You want them with water?" asked the woman.

"Yes, with water."

25   "It tastes like licorice," the girl said and put the glass down.

"That's the way with everything."

"Yes," said the girl. "Everything tastes of licorice. Especially all the things you've waited so long for, like absinthe."

"Oh, cut it out."

"You started it," the girl said. "I was being amused. I was having a fine time."

30   "Well, let's try and have a fine time."

"All right. I was trying. I said the mountains looked like white elephants. Wasn't that bright?"

"That was bright."

"I wanted to try this new drink: That's all we do, isn't it—look at things and try new drinks?"

"I guess so."

35   The girl looked across at the hills.

"They're lovely hills," she said. "They don't really look like white elephants. I just meant the coloring of their skin through the trees."

"Should we have another drink?"

"All right."

The warm wind blew the bead curtain against the table.

40   "The beer's nice and cool," the man said.

"It's lovely," the girl said.

"It's really an awfully simple operation, Jig," the man said. "It's not really an operation at all."

The girl looked at the ground the table legs rested on.

"I know you wouldn't mind it, Jig. It's really not anything. It's just to let the air in."

45   The girl did not say anything.

"I'll go with you and I'll stay with you all the time. They just let the air in and then it's all perfectly natural."

"Then what will we do afterward?"

"We'll be fine afterward. Just like we were before."

"What makes you think so?"

50   "That's the only thing that bothers us. It's the only thing that's made us unhappy."

The girl looked at the bead curtain, put her hand out, and took hold of two of the strings of beads.

"And you think then we'll be all right and be happy."

"I know we will. You don't have to be afraid. I've known lots of people that have done it."

"So have I," said the girl. "And afterward they were all so happy."

55   "Well," the man said, "if you don't want to you don't have to. I wouldn't have you do it if you didn't want to. But I know it's perfectly simple."

"And you really want to?"

"I think it's the best thing to do. But I don't want you to do it if you don't really want to."

"And if I do it you'll be happy and things will be like they were and you'll love me?"

"I love you now. You know I love you."

60   "I know. But if I do it, then it will be nice again if I say things are like white elephants, and you'll like it?"

"I'll love it. I love it now but I just can't think about it. You know how I get when I worry."

"If I do it you won't ever worry?"

"I won't worry about that because it's perfectly simple."

"Then I'll do it. Because I don't care about me."

65   "What do you mean?"

"I don't care about me."

"Well, I care about you."

"Oh, yes. But I don't care about me. And I'll do it and then everything will be fine."

"I don't want you to do it if you feel that way."

70 The girl stood up and walked to the end of the station. Across, on the other side, were fields of grain and trees along the banks of the Ebro. Far away, beyond the river, were mountains. The shadow of a cloud moved across the field of grain and she saw the river through the trees.

"And we could have all this," she said. "And we could have everything and every day we make it more impossible."

"What did you say?"

"I said we could have everything."

"We can have everything."

75 "No, we can't."

"We can have the whole world."

"No, we can't."

"We can go everywhere."

"No, we can't. It isn't ours any more."

80 "It's ours."

"No, it isn't. And once they take it away, you never get it back."

"But they haven't taken it away."

"We'll wait and see."

"Come on back in the shade," he said. "You mustn't feel that way."

85 "I don't feel any way," the girl said. "I just know things."

"I don't want you to do anything that you don't want to do—"

"Nor that isn't good for me," she said. "I know. Could we have another beer?"

"All right. But you've got to realize—"

"I realize," the girl said. "Can't we maybe stop talking?"

90 They sat down at the table and the girl looked across at the hills on the dry side of the valley and the man looked at her and at the table.

"You've got to realize," he said, "that I don't want you to do it if you don't want to. I'm perfectly willing to go through with it if it means anything to you."

"Doesn't it mean anything to you? We could get along."

"Of course it does. But I don't want anybody but you. I don't want any one else. And I know it's perfectly simple."

"Yes, you know it's perfectly simple."

95 "It's all right for you to say that, but I do know it."

"Would you do something for me now?"

"I'd do anything for you."

"Would you please please please please please please please stop talking?"

He did not say anything but looked at the bags against the wall of the station. There were labels on them from all the hotels where they had spent nights.

100 "But I don't want you to," he said, "I don't care anything about it."

"I'll scream," the girl said.

The woman came out through the curtains with two glasses of beer and put them down on the damp felt pads. "The train comes in five minutes," she said.

"What did she say?" asked the girl.

"That the train is coming in five minutes."

105   The girl smiled brightly at the woman, to thank her.

"I'd better take the bags over to the other side of the station," the man said. She smiled at him.

"All right. Then come back and we'll finish the beer."

He picked up the two heavy bags and carried them around the station to the other tracks. He looked up the tracks but could not see the train. Coming back, he walked through the barroom, where people waiting for the train were drinking. He drank an Anis at the bar and looked at the people. They were all waiting reasonably for the train. He went out through the bead curtain. She was sitting at the table and smiled at him.

"Do you feel better?" he asked.

110   "I feel fine," she said. "There's nothing wrong with me. I feel fine."

QUESTIONS FOR DISCUSSION

1. What mood is created through setting the story in a train station bar in a foreign country with a view of the "long and white" hills across the Ebro River valley? Why does Jig admire the view of the mountains, the field of grain, and the river?

2. Why does Jig remark that the hills remind her of "white elephants"? What symbolism is suggested by the expression "a white elephant"?

3. What is the subject of the disagreement between the American and Jig? How are their personalities and outlooks on life contrasted through their positions in the disagreement?

4. Point out lines in the dialogue that seem to have a double or oblique meaning. For example, when Jig remarks, "Everything tastes of licorice. Especially the things you've waited so long for, like absinthe," what motivates her remark and to what is she actually referring? What does she mean when she says "It isn't ours any more"?

5. What is ironic about the American's line, "They just let the air in and then it's perfectly natural"? Give other examples of irony in the American's comments. Do you think the American intends to be ironic?

6. Do you think that the characters' attitudes about what is important in a relationship are typical of male/female conflicts? Could you identify with one of the characters' points of view, or were you sympathetic to both?

CONNECTION

Compare and contrast the conflicts about the nature and problems of love in "Hills Like White Elephants" and "The Two" (see page 341).

IDEAS FOR WRITING

1. Based on evidence from the conversation between the couple earlier in the story, write an essay in which you interpret the meaning of Jig's final remark in the story, "I feel fine."
2. Write a story involving a conflict between two characters using the type of brief dialogue and simple, unadorned description that characterizes Hemingway's "Hills Like White Elephants."

RELATED WEB SITES

ERNEST HEMINGWAY

http://www.lostgeneration.com/hrc.htm

"The Hemingway Resource Center" hosts this extensive web site devoted to the life and works of Ernest Hemmingway. It includes biographical and bibliographical information, articles, interviews, audio clips, a FAQ section, a site search engine, and even a story writing contest section.

FACTS ABOUT ABORTION

http://www.abortionfacts.com/

Created to inform the public about the many issues surrounding abortion, this web site is intended to provide factual articles on the controversial subject. It includes many essays, links, and extensive information about abortion and other related topics.

Gloria Naylor

The Two

Gloria Naylor (b. 1950) was raised in New York City; her parents were originally from Mississippi. After high school she spent seven years as a missionary for the Jehovah's Witnesses but then turned from religion to a strong belief in feminism. Naylor attended Brooklyn College of the City University of New York where she earned a B.A. in 1981. She went on to study at Yale and completed her M.A. in African-American studies in 1983. Naylor has taught at a number of universities, including Princeton, New York University, Boston University, and the University of Pennsylvania. Her novel, The Women of Brewster Place: A Novel in Seven Stories *(1982), in which "The Two" appears, won the American Book Award for the best first novel and was later made into a television mini-series. Naylor won a National Endowment for the Arts Fellowship in 1985 and a Guggenheim Fellowship in 1988. Her subsequent novels, such as* Mama Day *(1988),* Children of the Night *(1985), and* The Men of Brewster Place *(1998), reflect Naylor's belief in the importance of courage, community, and cultural identity.*

JOURNAL

Write about a person who was judged differently once people learned that he or she did not follow traditional sex roles.

At first they seemed like such nice girls. No one could remember exactly when they had moved into Brewster. It was earlier in the year before Ben was killed—of course, it had to be before Ben's death. But no one remembered if it was in the winter or spring of that year that the two had come. People often came and went on Brewster Place like a restless night's dream, moving in and out in the dark to avoid eviction notices or neighborhood bulletins about the dilapidated condition of their furnishings. So it wasn't until the two were clocked leaving in the mornings and returning in the evenings at regular intervals that it was quietly absorbed that they now claimed Brewster as home. And Brewster waited, cautiously prepared to claim them, because you never knew about young women, and obviously single at that. But when no wild music or drunken friends careened out of the corner building on weekends, and especially, when no slightly eager husbands were encouraged to linger around that first-floor apartment and run errands for them, a suspended sigh of relief floated around the two when they dumped their garbage, did their shopping, and headed for the morning bus.

The women of Brewster had readily accepted the lighter, skinny one. There wasn't much threat in her timid mincing walk and the slightly protruding teeth she seemed so eager to show everyone in her bell-like good mornings and evenings. Breaths were held a little longer in the direction of the short dark one—too pretty, and too much behind. And she insisted on wearing those thin Qiana dresses that the summer breeze molded against the maddening rhythm of the twenty pounds of rounded flesh that she swung steadily down the street. Through slitted eyes, the women watched their men watching her pass, knowing the bastards were praying for a wind. But since she seemed oblivious to whether these supplications went answered, their sighs settled around her shoulders too. Nice girls.

And so no one even cared to remember exactly when they had moved into Brewster Place, until the rumor started. It had first spread through the block like a sour odor that's only faintly perceptible and easily ignored until it starts growing in strength from the dozen mouths it had been lying in, among clammy gums and scum-coated teeth. And then it was everywhere—lining the mouths and whitening the lips of everyone as they wrinkled up their noses at its pervading smell, unable to pinpoint the source or time of its initial arrival. Sophie could—she had been there.

It wasn't that the rumor had actually begun with Sophie. A rumor needs no true parent. It only needs a willing carrier, and it found one in Sophie. She had been there—on one of those August evenings when the sun's absence is a mockery because the heat leaves the air so heavy it presses the naked skin down on your body, to the point that a sheet becomes unbearable and sleep impossible. So most of Brewster was outside that night when the two had come in together, probably from one of those air-conditioned movies downtown, and had greeted the ones who were loitering around their building. And they had started up the steps when the skinny one tripped over a child's ball and the darker one had grabbed her by the arm and around the waist to break her fall. "Careful, don't wanna lose you now." And the two of them had laughed into each other's eyes and went into the building.

5   The smell had begun there. It outlined the image of the stumbling woman and the one who had broken her fall. Sophie and a few other women sniffed at the spot and then, perplexed, silently looked at each other. Where had they seen that before? They had often laughed and touched each other—held each other in joy or its dark twin—but where had they seen *that* before? It came to them as the scent drifted down the steps and entered their nostrils on the way to their inner mouths. They had seen that—done that—with their men. That shared moment of invisible communion reserved for two and hidden from the rest of the world behind laughter or tears or a touch. In the days before babies, miscarriages, and other broken dreams, after stolen caresses in barn stalls and cotton houses, after intimate walks from church and secret kisses with boys who were now long forgotten or permanently fixed in their lives—that was where. They could almost feel the odor moving about in their mouths, and they slowly knitted themselves together and let it out into the air like a yellow mist that began to cling to the bricks on Brewster.

So it got around that the two in 312 were *that* way. And they had seemed like such nice girls. Their regular exits and entrances to the block were viewed with a jaundiced eye. The quiet that rested around their door on the weekends hinted of all sorts of secret rituals, and their friendly indifference to the men on the street was an insult to the women as a brazen flaunting of unnatural ways.

Since Sophie's apartment windows faced theirs from across the air shaft, she became the official watchman for the block, and her opinions were deferred to whenever the two came up in conversation. Sophie took her position seriously and was constantly alert for any telltale signs that might creep out around their drawn shades, across from which she kept a religious vigil. An entire week of drawn shades was evidence enough to send her flying around with reports that as soon as it got dark they pulled their shades down and put on the lights. Heads nodded in knowing unison—a definite sign. If doubt was voiced with a "But I pull my shades down at night too," a whispered "Yeah, but you're not *that* way" was argument enough to win them over.

Sophie watched the lighter one dumping their garbage, and she went outside and opened the lid. Her eyes darted over the crushed tin cans, vegetable peelings, and empty chocolate chip cookie boxes. What do they do with all them chocolate chip cookies? It was surely a sign, but it would take some time to figure that one out. She saw Ben go into their apartment, and she waited and blocked his path as he came out, carrying his toolbox.

"What ya see?" She grabbed his arm and whispered wetly in his face.

10   Ben stared at her squinted eyes and drooping lips and shook his head slowly. "Uh, uh, uh, it was terrible."

"Yeah?" She moved in a little closer.

"Worst busted faucet I seen in my whole life." He shook her hand off his arm and left her standing in the middle of the block.

"You old sop bucket," she muttered, as she went back up on her stoop. A broken faucet, huh? Why did they need to use so much water?

Sophie had plenty to report that day. Ben had said it was terrible in there. No, she didn't know exactly what he had seen, but you can imagine—and they did. Confronted with the difference that had been thrust into their predictable world, they reached into their imaginations and, using an ancient pattern, weaved themselves a reason for its existence. Out of necessity they stitched all of their secret fears and lingering childhood nightmares into this existence, because even though it was deceptive enough to try and look as they looked, talk as they talked, and do as they did, it had to have some hidden stain to invalidate it—it was impossible for them both to be right. So they leaned back, supported by the sheer weight of their numbers and comforted by the woven barrier that kept them protected from the yellow mist that enshrouded the two as they came and went on Brewster Place.

15   Lorraine was the first to notice the change in the people on Brewster Place. She was a shy but naturally friendly woman who got up early, and had read the morning paper and done fifty sit-ups before it was time to leave for work. She came out of her apartment eager to start her day by greeting any of her neighbors who were outside. But she noticed that some of the people who had spoken to her before made a point of having something else to do with their eyes when she passed, although she could almost feel them staring at her back as she moved on. The ones who still spoke only did so after an uncomfortable pause, in which they seemed to be peering through her before they begrudged her a good morning or evening. She wondered if it was all in her mind and she thought about mentioning it to Theresa, but she didn't want to be accused of being too sensitive again. And how would Tee even notice anything like that anyway? She had a lousy attitude and hardly ever spoke to people. She stayed in that bed until the last moment and rushed out of the house fogged-up and grumpy, and she was used to being stared at—by men at least—because of her body.

Lorraine thought about these things as she came up the block from work, carrying a large paper bag. The group of women on her stoop parted silently and let her pass.

"Good evening," she said, as she climbed the steps.

Sophie was standing on the top step and tried to peek into the bag. "You been shopping, huh? What ya buy?" It was almost an accusation.

"Groceries." Lorraine shielded the top of the bag from view and squeezed past her with a confused frown. She saw Sophie throw a knowing glance to the others at the bottom of the stoop. What was wrong with this old woman? Was she crazy or something?

20   Lorraine went into her apartment. Theresa was sitting by the window, reading a copy of *Mademoiselle*. She glanced up from her magazine. "Did you get my
chocolate chip cookies?"

"Why good evening to you, too, Tee. And how was my day? Just wonderful."
She sat the bag down on the couch. "That little Baxter boy brought in a puppy
for show-and-tell, and the damn thing pissed all over the floor and then proceeded to chew the heel off my shoe, but, yes, I managed to hobble to the store
and bring you your chocolate chip cookies."

Oh, Jesus, Theresa thought, she's got a bug up her ass tonight.

"Well, you should speak to Mrs. Baxter. She ought to train her kid better
than that." She didn't wait for Lorraine to stop laughing before she tried to
stretch her good mood. "Here, I'll put those things away. Want me to make
dinner so you can rest? I only worked half a day, and the most tragic thing that
went down was a broken fingernail and that got caught in my typewriter."

Lorraine followed Theresa into the kitchen. "No, I'm not really tired, and fair's
fair, you cooked last night. I didn't mean to tick off like that; it's just that . . . well,
Tee, have you noticed that people aren't as nice as they used to be?"

25   Theresa stiffened. Oh, God, here she goes again. "What people, Lorraine?
Nice in what way?"

"Well, the people in this building and on the street. No one hardly speaks
anymore. I mean, I'll come in and say good evening—and just silence. It wasn't
like that when we first moved in. I don't know, it just makes you wonder; that's
all. What are they thinking?"

"I personally don't give a shit what they're thinking. And their good evenings
don't put any bread on my table."

"Yeah, but you didn't see the way that woman looked at me out there. They
must feel something or know something. They probably—"

"They, they, they!" Theresa exploded. "You know, I'm not starting up with
this again, Lorraine. Who in the hell are they? And where in the hell are we?
Living in some dump of a building in this God-forsaken part of town around a
bunch of ignorant niggers with the cotton still under their fingernails because
of you and your theys. They knew something in Linden Hills, so I gave up an
apartment for you that I'd been in for the last four years. And then they knew
in Park Heights, and you made me so miserable there we had to leave. Now
these mysterious theys are on Brewster Place. Well, look out the window, kid.
There's a big wall down that block, and this is the end of the line for me. I'm
not moving anymore, so if that's what you're working yourself up to—save it!"

30   When Theresa became angry she was like a lump of smoldering coal, and
her fierce bursts of temper always unsettled Lorraine.

"You see, that's why I didn't want to mention it." Lorraine began to pull at
her fingers nervously. "You're always flying up and jumping to conclusions—no
one said anything about moving. And I didn't know your life has been so miserable since you met me. I'm sorry about that," she finished tearfully.

Theresa looked at Lorraine, standing in the kitchen door like a wilted leaf,
and she wanted to throw something at her. Why didn't she ever fight back? The

very softness that had first attracted her to Lorraine was now a frequent cause for irritation. Smoked honey. That's what Lorraine had reminded her of, sitting in her office clutching that application. Dry autumn days in Georgia woods, thick bloated smoke under a beehive, and the first glimpse of amber honey just faintly darkened about the edges by the burning twigs. She had flowed just that heavily into Theresa's mind and had stuck there with a persistent sweetness.

But Theresa hadn't known then that this softness filled Lorraine up to the very middle and that she would bend at the slightest pressure, would be constantly seeking to surround herself with the comfort of everyone's goodwill, and would shrivel up at the least touch of disapproval. It was becoming a drain to be continually called upon for this nurturing and support that she just didn't understand. She had supplied it at first out of love for Lorraine, hoping that she would harden eventually, even as honey does when exposed to the cold. Theresa was growing tired of being clung to—of being the one who was leaned on. She didn't want a child—she wanted someone who could stand toe to toe with her and be willing to slug it out at times. If they practiced that way with each other, then they could turn back to back and beat the hell out of the world for trying to invade their territory. But she had found no such sparring partner in Lorraine, and the strain of fighting alone was beginning to show on her.

"Well, if it was that miserable, I would have been gone a long time ago," she said, watching her words refresh Lorraine like a gentle shower.

35   "I guess you think I'm some sort of a sick paranoid, but I can't afford to have people calling my job or writing letters to my principal. You know I've already lost a position like that in Detroit. And teaching is my whole life, Tee."

"I know," she sighed, not really knowing at all. There was no danger of that ever happening on Brewster Place. Lorraine taught too far from this neighborhood for anyone here to recognize her in that school. No, it wasn't her job she feared losing this time, but their approval. She wanted to stand out there and chat and trade makeup secrets and cake recipes. She wanted to be secretary of their block association and be asked to mind their kids while they ran to the store. And none of that was going to happen if they couldn't even bring themselves to accept her good evenings.

Theresa silently finished unpacking the groceries. "Why did you buy cottage cheese? Who eats this stuff?"

"Well, I thought we should go on a diet."

"If *we* go on a diet, then you'll disappear. You've got nothing to lose but your hair."

40   "Oh, I don't know. I thought that we might want to try and reduce our hips or something." Lorraine shrugged playfully.

"No, thank you. We are very happy with our hips the way they are," Theresa said, as she shoved the cottage cheese to the back of the refrigerator. "And even when I lose weight, it never comes off there. My chest and arms just get smaller, and I start looking like a bottle of salad dressing."

The two women laughed, and Theresa sat down to watch Lorraine fix dinner. "You know, this behind has always been my downfall. When I was coming up in Georgia with my grandmother, the boys used to promise me penny candy if I would let them pat my behind. And I used to love those jawbreakers—you know, the kind that lasted all day and kept changing colors in your mouth. So I was glad to oblige them, because in one afternoon I could collect a whole week's worth of jawbreakers."

"Really. That's funny to you? Having some boy feeling all over you."

Theresa sucked her teeth. "We were only kids, Lorraine. You know, you remind me of my grandmother. That was one straight-laced old lady. She had a fit when my brother told her what I was doing. She called me into the smokehouse and told me in this real scary whisper that I could get pregnant from letting little boys pat my butt and that I'd end up like my cousin Willa. But Willa and I had been thick as fleas, and she had already given me a step-by-step summary of how she'd gotten into her predicament. But I sneaked around to her house that night just to double check her story, since that old lady had seemed so earnest. 'Willa, are you sure?' I whispered through her bedroom window. 'I'm tellin' ya, Tee,' she said. 'Just keep both feet on the ground and you home free.' Much later I learned that advice wasn't too biologically sound, but it worked in Georgia because those country boys didn't have much imagination."

45   Theresa's laughter bounced off of Lorraine's silent, rigid back and died in her throat. She angrily tore open a pack of the chocolate chip cookies. "Yeah," she said, staring at Lorraine's back and biting down hard into the cookie, "it wasn't until I came up north to college that I found out there's a whole lot of things that a dude with a little imagination can do to you even with both feet on the ground. You see, Willa forgot to tell me not to bend over or squat or—"

"Must you!" Lorraine turned around from the stove with her teeth clenched tightly together.

"Must I what, Lorraine? Must I talk about things that are as much a part of my life as eating or breathing or growing old? Why are you always so uptight about sex or men?"

"I'm not uptight about anything. I just think it's disgusting when you go on and on about—"

"There's nothing disgusting about it, Lorraine. You've never been with a man, but I've been with quite a few—some better than others. There were a couple who I still hope to this day will die a slow, painful death, but then there were some who were good to me—in and out of bed."

50   "If they were so great, then why are you with me?" Lorraine's lips were trembling.

"Because—" Theresa looked steadily into her eyes and then down at the cookie she was twirling on the table. "Because," she continued slowly, "you can take a chocolate chip cookie and put holes in it and attach it to your ears and call it an earring, or hang it around your neck on a silver chain and pretend it's a necklace—but it's still a cookie. See—you can toss it in the air and call it a

Frisbee or even a flying saucer, if the mood hits you, and it's still just a cookie. Send it spinning on a table—like this—until it's a wonderful blur of amber and brown light that you can imagine to be a topaz or rusted gold or old crystal, but the law of gravity has got to come into play, sometime, and it's got to come to rest—sometime. Then all the spinning and pretending and hoopla is over with. And you know what you got?"

"A chocolate chip cookie," Lorraine said.

"Uh-huh." Theresa put the cookie in her mouth and winked. "A lesbian." She got up from the table. "Call me when dinner's ready, I'm going back to read." She stopped at the kitchen door. "Now, why are you putting gravy on that chicken, Lorraine? You know it's fattening."

QUESTIONS FOR DISCUSSION

1. How does the sentence, "They seemed like such nice girls," set the tone for the story? How often is this phrase repeated? When does it become ironic?
2. Describe Brewster Place and the people who live there. Why are the residents such gossips and rumor spreaders? What is their first impression of Lorraine and Theresa? Why does their attitude toward the women change?
3. What is the connection between the story's theme and the shift in point of view midway through the story? Why does the author wait to present the women's perspective and names?
4. Contrast Lorraine and Theresa's attitudes about their neighbors. How do their different attitudes reflect deeper differences in their personalities and within their relationship?
5. In what ways does the chocolate chip cookie symbolize and clarify Theresa's point about her sexual orientation? Does Lorraine see the cookie in the same way as does Theresa? How do you think their relationship will develop? Will it survive the social pressures the couple will have to endure?
6. With which of the main characters were you most sympathetic? Why?

CONNECTION

Compare the attitude of the tenants toward "The Two" with the villagers' response to the pregnant woman in "No Name Woman" (see page 321).

IDEAS FOR WRITING

1. Write an essay that compares the two sections of the story, the first part that reflects the perspective of the neighbors and the second part that involves a dialogue between Lorraine and Theresa. How does this contrasting structure help to emphasize the values reflected in the story?
2. Write an essay in which you analyze the story in terms of what it reveals about popular attitudes that are based on a lack of knowledge and understanding of lesbians or women who live together in nontraditional relationships.

RELATED WEB SITES

GLORIA NAYLOR
http://voices.cla.umn.edu/authors/GloriaNaylor.html
Discover who author Gloria Naylor is at this literary web site. A biography and a selected bibliography, as well as other relevant links will be found at the URL.

PARENTS, FAMILIES & FRIENDS OF LESBIANS & GAYS (PFLAG)
http://www.pflag.org
Learn about PFLAG at this URL. PFLAG is a national nonprofit organization devoted to providing ways to have dialogues about sexual orientation and gender identity, and acts to create a society that is healthy and respectful of human diversity.

David Sedaris

I Like Guys

David Sedaris was born in 1957 in Raleigh, North Carolina. He completed his degree from the Art Institute of Chicago in 1987. Sedaris has worked as a radio commentator and diarist for the National Public Radio (NPR); has written short stories; and has worked as apartment cleaner, moving company worker, and an office worker. In 2000 Sedaris won the Lambda Literary Award in the humor category. Sedaris's most widely read work includes Barrel Fever: Stories and Essays *(1994),* Naked *(1997),* Holidays on Ice *(short stories, 1997), and* Me Talk Pretty One Day *(2000).*

JOURNAL

How were homosexual students treated at the high school that you attended?

Shortly before I graduated from eighth grade, it was announced that, come fall, our county school system would adopt a policy of racial integration by way of forced busing. My Spanish teacher broke the news in a way she hoped might lead us to a greater understanding of her beauty and generosity.

"I remember the time I was at the state fair, standing in line for a Sno-Kone," she said, fingering the kiss curls that framed her squat, compact face. "And a little colored girl ran up and tugged at my skirt, asking if she could touch my hair. 'Just once,' she said. 'Just one time for good luck.'

"Now, I don't know about the rest of you, but my hair means a lot to me." The members of my class nodded to signify that their hair meant a lot to them as well. They inched forward in their seats, eager to know where this story might be going. Perhaps the little Negro girl was holding a concealed razor blade. Maybe she was one of the troublemakers out for a fresh white scalp.

I sat marveling at their naiveté…. Like all her previous anecdotes, this woman's story was headed straight up her ass.

5   "I checked to make sure she didn't have any candy on her hands, and then I bent down and let this little colored girl touch my hair." The teacher's eyes assumed the dewy, faraway look she reserved for such Hallmark moments. "Then this little fudge-colored girl put her hand on my cheek and said, 'Oh,' she said, 'I wish I could be white and pretty like you.'" She paused, positioning herself on the edge of the desk as though she were posing for a portrait the federal government might use on a stamp commemorating gallantry. "The thing to remember," she said, "is that more than anything in this world, those colored people wish they were white."

I wasn't buying it. This was the same teacher who when announcing her pregnancy said, "I just pray that my firstborn is a boy. I'll have a boy and then maybe later I'll have a girl, because when you do it the other way round, there's a good chance the boy will turn out to be funny."

"'Funny,' as in having no arms and legs?" I asked.

"That," the teacher said, "is far from funny. That is tragic, and you, sir, should have your lips sewn shut for saying such a cruel and ugly thing. When I say 'funny,' I mean funny as in …" She relaxed her wrist, allowing her hand to dangle and flop. "I mean 'funny' as in *that* kind of funny." She minced across the room, but it failed to illustrate her point, as this was more or less her natural walk, a series of gamboling little steps, her back held straight, giving the impression she was balancing something of value atop her empty head. My seventh-period math teacher did a much better version. Snatching a purse off the back of a student's chair, he would prance about the room, batting his eyes and blowing kisses at the boys seated in the front row. "So fairy nice to meet you," he'd say.

Fearful of drawing any attention to myself, I hooted and squawked along with the rest of the class, all the while thinking, *That's me he's talking about.* If I was going to make fun of people, I had to expect a little something in return, that seemed only fair. Still, though, it bothered me that they'd found such an easy way to get a laugh. As entertainers, these teachers were nothing, zero. They could barely impersonate themselves. "Look at you!" my second-period gym teacher would shout, his sneakers squealing against the basketball court. "You're a group of ladies, a pack of tap-dancing queers."

10   The other boys shrugged their shoulders or smiled down at their shoes. They reacted as if they had been called Buddhists or vampires; sure, it was an insult, but no one would ever mistake them for the real thing. Had they ever chanted in the privacy of their backyard temple or slept in a coffin, they would have felt the sting of recognition and shared my fear of discovery.

I had never done anything with another guy and literally prayed that I never would. As much as I fantasized about it, I understood that there could be nothing worse than making it official. You'd seen them on television from time to time, the homosexuals, maybe on one of the afternoon talk shows. No one ever came out and called them a queer, but you could just tell by their voices as they flattered the host and proclaimed great respect for their fellow guests. These were the celebrities never asked about their home life, the comedians running scarves beneath their toupees or framing their puffy faces with their open palms in an effort to eliminate the circles beneath their eyes. "The poor man's face lift," my mother called it. Regardless of their natty attire, these men appeared sweaty and desperate, willing to play the fool in exchange for the studio applause they seemed to mistake for love and acceptance. I saw something of myself in their mock weary delivery, in the way they crossed their legs and laughed at their own jokes. I pictured their homes: the finicky placement of their throw rugs and sectional sofas, the magazines carefully fanned just so upon the coffee tables with no wives or children to disturb their order. I imagined the pornography hidden in their closets and envisioned them powerless and sobbing as the police led them away in shackles, past the teenage boy who stood bathed in the light of the television news camera and shouted, "That's him! He's the one who touched my hair!"

It was my hope to win a contest, cash in the prizes, and use the money to visit a psychiatrist who might cure me of having homosexual thoughts. Electroshock, brain surgery, hypnotism—I was willing to try anything. Under a doctor's supervision, I would buckle down and really change, I swore I would.

My parents knew a couple whose son had killed a Presbyterian minister while driving drunk. They had friends whose eldest daughter had sprinkled a Bundt cake with Comet, and knew of a child who, high on spray paint, had set fire to the family's cocker spaniel. Yet, they spoke of no one whose son was a homosexual. The odds struck me as bizarre, but the message was the same: this was clearly the worst thing that could happen to a person. The day-to-day anxiety was bad enough without my instructors taking their feeble little potshots. If my math teacher were able to subtract the alcohol from his diet, he'd still be on the football field where he belonged; and my Spanish teacher's credentials were based on nothing more than a long weekend in Tijuana, as far as I could tell. I quit taking their tests and completing their homework assignments, accepting Fs rather than delivering the grades I thought might promote their reputations as good teachers. It was a strategy that hurt only me, but I thought it cunning. We each had our self-defeating schemes, all the boys I had come to identify as homosexuals. Except for a few transfer students, I had known most of them since the third grade. We'd spent years gathered together in cinderblock offices as one speech therapist after another tried to cure us of our lisps. Had there been a walking specialist, we probably would have met there, too. These were the same boys who carried poorly forged notes to gym class and were the first to raise their hands when the English teacher asked for a volunteer to read aloud from *The Yearling* or *Lord of the Flies*. We had long ago identified one another and understood that because of everything we had in common, we could never be friends. To socialize would have drawn too much attention to ourselves. We were members of a secret society founded on self-loathing. When a teacher or classmate made fun of a real homosexual, I made certain my laugh was louder than anyone else's. When a club member's cloth-ing was thrown into the locker-room toilet, I was always the first to cheer. When it was my clothing, I watched as the faces of my fellows broke into recognizable expressions of relief. *Faggots,* I thought. *This should have been you.*

Several of my teachers, when discussing the upcoming school integration, would scratch at the damp stains beneath their arms, pulling back their lips to reveal every bit of tooth and gum. They made monkey noises, a manic succes-sion of ohhs and ahhs meant to suggest that soon our school would be no dif-ferent than a jungle. Had a genuine ape been seated in the room, I guessed he might have identified their calls as a cry of panic. Anything that caused them suffering brought me joy, but I doubted they would talk this way come fall. From everything I'd seen on television, the Negros would never stand for such foolishness. As a people, they seemed to stick together. They knew how to fight, and I hoped that once they arrived, the battle might come down to the gladia-tors, leaving the rest of us alone.

15   At the end of the school year, my sister Lisa and I were excused from our vol-unteer jobs and sent to Greece to attend a month-long summer camp adver-tised as "the Crown Jewel of the Ionian Sea." The camp was reserved exclusively for Greek Americans and featured instruction in such topics as folk singing and something called "religious prayer and flag." I despised the idea of sum-mer camp but longed to boast that I had been to Europe. "It changes people!" our neighbor had said. Following a visit to Saint-Tropez, she had marked her garden with a series of tissue-sized international flags. A once discreet and modest woman, she now paraded about her yard wearing nothing but clogs and a flame-stitched bikini. "Europe is the best thing that can happen to a per-son, especially if you like wine!"

I saw Europe as an opportunity to re-invent myself. I might still look and speak the same way, but having walked those cobblestoned streets, I would be identified as Continental. "He has a passport," my classmates would whisper. "Quick, let's run before he judges us!"

I told myself that I would find a girlfriend in Greece. She would be a French tourist wandering the beach with a loaf of bread beneath her arm. Lisette would prove that I wasn't a homosexual, but a man with refined tastes. I saw us holding hands against the silhouette of the Acropolis, the girl begging me to take her accordion as a memento of our love. "Silly you," I would say, brushing the tears from her eyes, "just give me the beret, that will be enough to hold you in my heart until the end of time."

In case no one believed me, I would have my sister as a witness. Lisa and I weren't getting along very well, but I hoped that the warm Mediterranean waters might melt the icicle she seemed to have mistaken for a rectal thermometer. Faced with a country of strangers, she would have no choice but to appreciate my company.

Our father accompanied us to New York, where we met our fellow campers for the charter flight to Athens. There were hundreds of them, each one confi-dent and celebratory. They tossed their complimentary Aegean Airlines tote bags across the room, shouting and jostling one another. This would be the way I'd act once we'd finally returned from camp, but not one moment before. Were it an all-girl's camp, I would have been able to work up some enthusiasm. Had they sent me alone to pry leeches off the backs of blood-thirsty Pygmies, I might have gone bravely—but spending a month in a dormitory full of boys, that was asking too much. I'd tried to put it out of my mind, but faced with their boisterous presence, I found myself growing progressively more hysterical. My nervous tics shifted into their highest gear, and a small crowd gathered to watch what they believed to be an exotic folk dance. If my sister was anxious about our trip, she certainly didn't show it. Prying my fingers off her wrist, she crossed the room and introduced herself to a girl who stood picking salvageable butts out of the standing ashtray. This was a tough-looking Queens native named Stefani Heartattackus or Testicockules. I recall only that her last name had granted her a lifelong supply of resentment. Stefani wore mirrored aviator sunglasses and carried an oversized comb in the back pocket of her hiphugger jeans. Of all the girls in the room, she seemed the least likely candidate for my sister's friendship. They sat beside each other on the plane, and by the time we disembarked in Athens, Lisa was speaking in a very bad Queens accent. During the long flight, while I sat cowering beside a boy named Seamen, my sister had undergone a complete physical and cultural transformation. Her shoulder-length hair was now parted on the side, covering the left half of her face as if to conceal a nasty scar. She cursed and spat, scowling out the window of the chartered bus as if she'd come to Greece with the sole intention of kicking its dusty ass. "What a shithole," she yelled. "Jeez, if I'd knowed it was gonna be dis hot, I woulda stayed home wit my headdin da oven, right, girls!"

20   It shamed me to hear my sister struggle so hard with an accent that did nothing but demean her, yet I silently congratulated her on the attempt. I approached her once we reached the camp, a cluster of whitewashed buildings hugging the desolate coast, far from any neighboring village.

"Listen, asshole," she said, "as far as this place is concerned, I don't know you and you sure as shit don't know me, you got that?" She spoke as if she were auditioning for a touring company of *West Side Story*, one hand on her hip and the other fingering her pocket comb as if it were a switchblade.

"Hey, Carolina!" one of her new friends called.

"A righta ready," she brayed. "I'm comin', I'm comin'."

That was the last time we spoke before returning home. Lisa had adjusted with remarkable ease, but something deep in my stomach suggested I wouldn't thrive nearly as well. Camp lasted a month, during which time I never once had a bowel movement. I was used to having a semiprivate bathroom and could not bring myself to occupy one of the men's room stalls, fearful that someone might recognize my shoes or, even worse, not see my shoes at all and walk in on me. Sitting down three times a day for a heavy Greek meal became an exercise akin to packing a musket. I told myself I'd sneak off during one of our field trips, but those toilets were nothing more than a hole in the floor, a hole I could have filled with no problem whatsoever. I considered using the Ionian

Sea, but for some unexplained reason, we were not allowed to swim in those waters. The camp had an Olympic-size pool that was fed from the sea and soon grew murky with stray bits of jellyfish that had been pulverized by the pump. The tiny tentacles raised welts on campers' skin, so shortly after arriving, it was announced that we could photograph both the pool *and* the ocean but could swim in neither. The Greeks had invented democracy, built the Acropolis, and then called it a day. Our swimming period was converted into "contemplation hour" for the girls and an extended soccer practice for the boys.

25   "I really think I'd be better off contemplating," I told the coach, massaging my distended stomach. "I've got a personal problem that's sort of weighing me down."

Because we were first and foremost Americans, the camp was basically an extension of junior high school except that here everyone had an excess of moles or a single eyebrow. The attractive sports minded boys ran the show, currying favor from the staff and ruining our weekly outdoor movie with their inane heckling. From time to time the rented tour buses would carry us to view one of the country's many splendors, and we would raid the gift shops, stealing anything that wasn't chained to the shelf or locked in a guarded case. These were cheap, plated puzzle rings and pint-size vases, little pompommed shoes, and coffee mugs reading SPARTA IS FOR A LOVER. My shoplifting experience was the only thing that gave me an edge over the popular boys. "Hold it like this," I'd whisper. "Then swivel around and slip the statue of Diana down the back of your shorts, covering it with your T-shirt. Remember to back out the door while leaving and never forget to wave good-bye."

There was one boy at camp I felt I might get along with, a Detroit native named Jason who slept on the bunk beneath mine. Jason tended to look away when talking to the other boys, shifting his eyes as though he were studying the weather conditions. Like me, he used his free time to curl into a fetal position, staring at the bedside calendar upon which he'd x-ed out all the days he had endured so far. We were finishing our 7:15 to 7:45 wash-and-rinse segment one morning when our dormitory counselor arrived for inspection shouting, "What are you, a bunch of goddamned faggots who can't make your beds?"

I giggled out loud at his stupidity. If anyone knew how to make a bed, it was a faggot. It was the others he needed to worry about. I saw Jason laughing, too, and soon we took to mocking this counselor, referring to each other first as "faggots" and then as "stinking faggots." We were "lazy faggots" and "sunburned faggots" before we eventually became "faggoty faggots." We couldn't protest the word, as that would have meant acknowledging the truth of it. The most we could do was embrace it as a joke. Embodying the term in all its clichéd glory, we minced and pranced about the room for each other's entertainment when the others weren't looking. I found myself easily out-performing my teachers, who had failed to capture the proper spirit of loopy bravado inherent in the role. *Faggot*, as a word, was always delivered in a harsh, unforgiving tone befitting those weak or stupid enough to act upon their impulses. We used it as a joke, an accusation, and finally as a dare. Late at night I'd feel my bunk buck and sway, knowing that Jason was either masturbating or beating eggs for an omelette. *Is it me he's thinking about?* I'd follow his lead and wake the next morning to find our entire iron-frame unit had wandered a good eighteen inches away from the wall. Our love had the power to move bunks.

Having no willpower, we depended on circumstances to keep us apart. *This cannot happen* was accompanied by the sound of bedsprings whining, *Oh, but maybe just this once.* There came an afternoon when, running late for flag worship, we found ourselves alone in the dormitory. What started off as name-calling escalated into a series of mock angry slaps. We wrestled each other onto one of the lower bunks, both of us longing to be pinned. "You kids think you invented sex," my mother was fond of saying. But hadn't we? With no instruction manual or federally enforced training period, didn't we all come away feeling we'd discovered something unspeakably modern? What produced in others a feeling of exhilaration left Jason and me with a mortifying sense of guilt. We fled the room as if, in our fumblings, we had uncapped some virus we still might escape if we ran fast enough. Had one of the counselors not caught me scaling the fence, I felt certain I could have made it back to Raleigh by morning, skittering across the surface of the ocean like one of those lizards often featured on television wildlife programs.

30   When discovered making out with one of the Greek bus drivers, a sixteen-year-old camper was forced to stand beside the flagpole dressed in long pants and thick sweaters. We watched her cook in the hot sun until, fully roasted, she crumpled to the pavement and passed out.

"That," the chief counselor said, "is what happens to people who play around."

If this was the punishment for a boy and a girl, I felt certain the penalty for two boys somehow involved barbed wire, a team of donkeys, and the nearest volcano. Nothing, however, could match the cruelty and humiliation Jason and I soon practiced upon each other. He started a rumor that I had stolen an athletic supporter from another camper and secretly wore it over my mouth like a surgical mask. I retaliated, claiming he had expressed a desire to become a dancer. "That's nothing," he said to the assembled crowd, "take a look at what I found on David's bed!" He reached into the pocket of his tennis shorts and withdrew a sheet of notebook paper upon which were written the words I LIKE GUYS. Presented as an indictment, the document was both pathetic and comic. Would I supposedly have written the note to remind myself of that fact, lest I forget? Had I intended to wear it taped to my back, advertising my preference the next time our rented buses carried us off to yet another swinging sexual playground?

I LIKE GUYS. He held the paper above his head, turning a slow circle so that everyone might get a chance to see. I supposed he had originally intended to plant the paper on my bunk for one of the counselors to find. Presenting it himself had foiled the note's intended effect. Rather than beating me with sticks and heavy shoes, the other boys simply groaned and looked away, wondering why he'd picked the thing up and carried it around in his pants pocket. He might as well have hoisted a glistening turd, shouting, "Look what

he did!" Touching such a foul document made him suspect and guilty by association. In attempting to discredit each other, we wound up alienating ourselves even further.

Jason—even his name seemed affected. During meals I studied him from
across the room. Here I was, sweating onto my plate, my stomach knotted
and cramped, when *he* was the one full of shit. Clearly he had tricked me,
cast a spell or slipped something into my food. I watched as he befriended
a girl named Theodora and held her hand during a screening of *A Lovely
Way to Die,* one of the cave paintings the head counselor offered as a weekly
movie.

35   She wasn't a bad person, Theodora. Someday the doctors might find a way
to transplant a calf's brain into a human skull, and then she'd be just as lively
and intelligent as he was. I tried to find a girlfriend of my own, but my one possible candidate was sent back home when she tumbled down the steps of the
Parthenon, causing serious damage to her leg brace.

Jason looked convincing enough in the company of his girlfriend. They
scrambled about the various ruins, snapping each other's pictures while I hung
back fuming, watching them nuzzle and coo. My jealousy stemmed from the
belief that he had been cured. One fistful of my flesh and he had lost all symptoms of the disease.

Camp ended and I flew home with my legs crossed, dropping my bag of
stolen souvenirs and racing to the bathroom, where I spent the next several
days sitting on the toilet and studying my face in a hand mirror. *I like guys.* The
words had settled themselves into my features. I was a professional now, and it
showed.

I returned to my volunteer job at the mental hospital, carrying harsh Greek
cigarettes as an incentive to some of the more difficult patients.

"Faggot!" a woman shouted, stooping to protect her collection of pinecones.
"Get your faggoty hands away from my radio transmitters."

40   "Don't mind Mary Elizabeth," the orderly said. "She's crazy."

Maybe not, I thought, holding a pinecone up against my ear. She's gotten
the faggot part right, so maybe she was onto something.

The moment we boarded our return flight from Kennedy to Raleigh, Lisa re-
arranged her hair, dropped her accent, and turned to me saying, "Well, I thought
that was very nice, how about you?" Over the course of five minutes, she had eliminated all traces of her reckless European self. Why couldn't I do the same?

In late August my class schedule arrived along with the news that I would not
be bused. There had been violence in other towns and counties, trouble as far
away as Boston; but in Raleigh the transition was peaceful. Not only students
but many of the teachers had been shifted from one school to another. My new
science teacher was a black man very adept at swishing his way across the room,
mocking everyone from Albert Einstein to the dweebish host of a popular children's television program. Black and white, the teachers offered their ridicule
as though it were an olive branch. "Here," they said, "this is something we each
have in common, proof that we're all brothers under the skin."

QUESTIONS FOR DISCUSSION

1. Why does Sedaris introduce his selection with the fact that the school district will implement racial integration with forced busing? What does the Spanish teacher's anecdote about the "colored girl" at the state fair who wanted to touch the teacher's hair reflect about common attitudes of the time regarding racial integration in the schools?
2. Why is Sedaris critical of his teachers and especially their sense of humor? What does Sedaris fear? Why does Sedaris believe that he is a member of a secret society founded on self-loathing?
3. How and why does Sedaris identify with the African-American students who will be coming to his school in the fall? Why does he welcome their arrival and feel that they have more power than he does?
4. Why is Sedaris anxious about his one-month trip to summer camp in Greece? Why is it easier for his sister Lisa to adjust to camp, have a good time there, and leave her experiences of the summer behind her?
5. Why are Jason and Sedaris frightened by their sexual experience? Why does Sedaris become jealous of Jason? What did you learn about the fears of a junior high school boy who realizes that he is a homosexual from reading this narrative?
6. Why does Sedaris end the essay with the fact that the enforced busing doesn't take place and the observation of his new science teacher as, "a black man very adept at swishing his way across the room, mocking everyone from Albert Einstein to the dweebish host of a popular children's television program"? What does he mean when he says, "Black and white, the teachers offered their ridicule as through it were an olive branch."?

CONNECTION

Compare Sedaris's recollections of attitudes toward homosexuality in school with those encountered by Cooper Thompson in his essay "A New Vision of Masculinity" (see page 358).

IDEAS FOR WRITING

1. What purpose do you think that Sedaris had in mind when writing and publishing this selection? Write an essay in which you discuss his most important points. Do you think he is successful at what he set out to achieve?
2. Write an essay that compares the way students and teachers dealt with the issue of homosexuality at your own high school with Sedaris's experiences and insights. How were the comments and activities sanctioned at Sedaris's junior high both similar and different from what was happening at your high school? How do you feel about the way homosexuals were treated at your high school?

RELATED WEB SITES

DAVID SEDARIS

http://home.pacifier.com/~paddockt/sedaris.html

Learn about David Sedaris at this web site dedicated to the author and comedian. Read articles about Sedaris, read or listen to his work and interviews, view his bibliography, talk to other fans, and find out where the author will speak next.

GAY LITERATURE

http://www.gayliterature.com/biblios.htm

This web site is devoted to sharing the works of the world's gay writers. One can also find several relevant links to other sites that discuss gay literature and its influence on society.

Cooper Thompson

A New Vision of Masculinity

Cooper Thompson, M.S. (b. 1950) is a consultant, writer, and teacher. He has been the Education Coordinator of the Campaign to End Homophobia and is currently an author and independent trainer in the areas of awareness of racism and gender bias. His current project involves traveling across the country to interview white men who, like himself, are dedicated to challenging racism and sexism. Thompson has served on numerous committees devoted to achieving community accord through eradicating racism and gender bias and has written a number of essays, pamphlets and brochures on these subjects, including White Men and the Denial of Racism *(1997) and* Coming Out to Your Parents *(1998). The essay included here first appeared in* Changing Men *(1985).*

JOURNAL

Write about a time in high school or middle school when you experienced pressure to prove yourself either highly masculine or highly feminine.

I was once asked by a teacher in a suburban high school to give a guest presentation on male roles. She hoped that I might help her deal with four boys who exercised extraordinary control over the other boys in the class. Using ridicule and their status as physically imposing athletes, these four wrestlers had succeeded in stifling the participation of the other boys, who were reluctant to make comments in class discussions.

As a class we talked about the ways in which boys got status in that school and how they got put down by others. I was told that the most humiliating put-down was being called a "fag." The list of behaviors which could elicit ridicule filled two large chalkboards, and it was detailed and comprehensive; I got the sense that a boy in this school had to conform to rigid, narrow standards of masculinity to avoid being called a fag. I, too, felt this pressure and became very conscious of my mannerisms in front of the group. Partly from exasperation, I decided to test the seriousness of these assertions. Since one of the four boys had some streaks of pink in his shirt, and since he had told me that wearing pink was grounds for being called a fag, I told him that I thought he was a fag. Instead of laughing, he said, "I'm going to kill you."

Such is the stereotypic definition of strength that is associated with masculinity. But it is a very limited definition of strength, one based on dominance and control and acquired through the humiliation and degradation of others.

Contrast this with a view of strength offered by Pam McAllister in her introduction to *Reweaving the Web of Life:*

> The "Strength" card in my Tarot deck depicts, not a warrior going off to battle with his armor and his mighty sword, but a woman stroking a lion. The woman has not slain the lion nor maced it, not netted it, nor has she put on it a muzzle or a leash. And though the lion clearly has teeth and long sharp claws, the woman is not hiding, nor has she sought a protector, nor has she grown muscles. She doesn't appear to be talking to the lion, nor flattering it, nor tossing it fresh meat to distract its hungry jaws.
>
> The woman on the "Strength" card wears a flowing white dress and a garland of flowers. With one hand she cups the lion's jaws, with the other she caresses its nose. The lion on the card has big yellow eyes and a long red tongue curling out of its mouth. One paw is lifted and the mane falls in thick red curls across its broad torso. The woman. The lion. Together they depict strength.

5   This image of strength stands in direct contrast to the strength embodied in the actions of the four wrestlers. The collective strength of the woman and the lion is a strength unknown in a system of traditional male values. Other human qualities are equally foreign to a traditional conception of masculinity. In workshops I've offered on the male role stereotype, teachers and other school personnel easily generate lists of attitudes and behaviors which boys typically seem to not learn. Included in this list are being supportive and nurturant, accepting one's vulnerability and being able to ask for help, valuing women and "women's work," understanding and expressing emotions (except for anger), the ability to empathize with and empower other people, and learning to resolve conflict in nonaggressive, noncompetitive ways.

All of this should come as no surprise. Traditional definitions of masculinity include attributes such as independence, pride, resiliency, self-control, and physical strength. This is precisely the image of the Marlboro man, and to some extent, these are desirable attributes for boys and girls. But masculinity goes beyond these qualities to stress competitiveness, toughness, aggressiveness, and power. In this context, threats to one's status, however small, cannot be avoided or taken lightly. If a boy is called a fag, it means that he is perceived as weak or timid—and therefore not masculine enough for his peers. There is enormous pressure for him to fight back. Not being tough at these moments only proves the allegation.

Violence is learned not just as a way for boys to defend allegations that they are feminized, but as an effective, appropriate way for them to normally behave. In "The Civic Advocacy of Violence" Wayne Ewing clearly states:

> I used to think that we simply tolerated and permitted male abusiveness in our society. I have now come to understand rather, that we *advocate* physical violence. Violence is presented as effective. Violence is taught as the normal, appropriate and necessary behavior of power and control. Analyses which interweave advocacy of male violence with "Super Bowl Culture" have never been refuted. Civic expectations—translated into professionalism, financial commitments, city planning for recreational space, the raising of male children for competitive sport, the corporate ethics of business ownership of athletic teams, profiteering on entertainment—all result in the monument of the National Football League, symbol and reality at once of the advocacy of violence.

Ultimately, violence is the tool which maintains what I believe are the two most critical socializing forces in a boy's life: *homophobia*, the hatred of gay men (who are stereotyped as feminine) or those men believed to be gay, as well as the fear of being perceived as gay; and *misogyny*, the hatred of women. The two forces are targeted at different classes of victims, but they are really just the flip sides of the same coin. Homophobia is the hatred of feminine qualities in men while misogyny is the hatred of feminine qualities in women. The boy who is called a fag is the target of other boys' homophobia as well as the victim of his own homophobia. While the overt message is the absolute need to avoid being feminized, the implication is that females—and all that they traditionally represent—are contemptible. The United States Marines have a philosophy which conveniently combines homophobia and misogyny in the belief that "When you want to create a group of male killers, you kill 'the woman' in them."

The pressures of homophobia and misogyny in boys' lives have been poignantly demonstrated to me each time that I have repeated a simple yet provocative activity with students. I ask them to answer the question, "If you woke up tomorrow and discovered that you were the opposite sex from the one you are now, how would you and your life be different?" Girls consistently indicate that there are clear advantages to being a boy—from increased independence and career opportunities to decreased risks of physical and sexual assault—and eagerly answer the question. But boys often express disgust at this possibility and even refuse sometimes to answer the question. In her reports of a broadbased survey using this question, Alice Baumgartner reports the following responses as typical of boys: "If I were a girl, I'd be stupid and weak as a string;" "I would have to wear make-up, cook, be a mother, and yuckky stuff like that;" "I would have to hate snakes. Everything would be miserable;" "If I were a girl, I'd kill myself."

10   The costs associated with a traditional view of masculinity are enormous, and the damage occurs at both personal and societal levels. The belief that a boy should be tough (aggressive, competitive, and daring) can create emo-

tional pain for him. While a few boys experience short-term success for their toughness, there is little security in the long run. Instead, it leads to a series of challenges which few, if any, boys ultimately win. There is no security in being at the top when so many other boys are competing for the same status. Toughness also leads to increased chances of stress, physical injury, and even early death. It is considered manly to take extreme physical risks and voluntarily engage in combative, hostile activities.

The flip side of toughness—nurturance—is not a quality perceived as masculine and thus not valued. Because of this, boys and men experience a greater emotional distance from other people and fewer opportunities to participate in meaningful interpersonal relationships. Studies consistently show that fathers spend very small amounts of time interacting with their children. In addition, men report that they seldom have intimate relationships with other men, reflecting their homophobia. They are afraid of getting too close and don't know how to take down the walls that they have built between themselves.

As boys grow older and accept adult roles, the larger social costs of masculinity clearly emerge. Most women experience male resistance to an expansion of women's roles; one of the assumptions of traditional masculinity is the belief that women should be subordinate to men. The consequence is that men are often not willing to accept females as equal, competent partners in personal and professional settings. Whether the setting is a sexual relationship, the family, the streets, or the battlefield, men are continuously engaged in efforts to dominate. Statistics on child abuse consistently indicate that the vast majority of abusers are men, and that there is no "typical" abuser. Rape may be the fastest growing crime in the United States. And it is men, regardless of nationality, who provoke and sustain war. In short, traditional masculinity is life threatening.

Masculinity, like many other human traits, is determined by both biological and environmental factors. While some believe that biological factors are significant in shaping some masculine behavior, there is undeniable evidence that cultural and environmental factors are strong enough to override biological impulses. What is it, then, that we should be teaching boys about being a man in a modern world?

- Boys must learn to accept their vulnerability, learn to express a range of emotions such as fear and sadness, and learn to ask for help and support in appropriate situations.
- Boys must learn to be gentle, nurturant, cooperative, and communicative, and in particular, learn nonviolent means of resolving conflicts.
- Boys must learn to accept those attitudes and behaviors which have traditionally been labeled feminine as necessary for full human development—thereby reducing homophobia and misogyny. This is tantamount to teaching boys to love other boys and girls.

Certain qualities like courage, physical strength, and independence, which are traditionally associated with masculinity, are indeed positive qualities for males, provided that they are not manifested in obsessive ways nor used to exploit or dominate others. It is not necessary to completely disregard or unlearn what is traditionally called masculine. I believe, however, that the three areas above are crucial for developing a broader view of masculinity, one which is healthier for all life.

15   These three areas are equally crucial for reducing aggressive, violent behavior among boys and men. Males must learn to cherish life for the sake of their *own* wholeness as human beings, not just *for* their children, friends, and lovers. If males were more nurturant, they would be less likely to hurt those they love.

Leonard Eron, writing in the *American Psychologist,* puts the issue of unlearning aggression and learning nurturance in clear-cut terms:

> Socialization is crucial in determining levels of aggression. No matter how aggression is measured or observed, as a group males always score higher than females. But this is not true for all girls. There are some girls who seem to have been socialized like boys who are just as aggressive as boys. Just as some females can learn to be aggressive, so males can learn *not* to be aggressive. If we want to reduce the level of aggression in society, we should also discourage boys from aggression very early on in life and reward them too for other behaviors; in other words, we should socialize boys more like girls, and they should be encouraged to develop socially positive qualities such as tenderness, cooperation, and aesthetic appreciation. The level of individual aggression in society will be reduced only when male adolescents and young adults, as a result of socialization, subscribe to the same standards of behavior as have been traditionally encouraged for women.

Where will this change in socialization occur? In his first few years, much of a boy's learning about masculinity comes from the influences of parents, siblings, and images of masculinity such as those found on television. Massive efforts will be needed to make changes here. But at older ages, school curriculum and the school environment provide powerful reinforcing images of traditional masculinity. This reinforcement occurs through a variety of channels, including curriculum content, role modeling, and extracurricular activities, especially competitive sports.

School athletics are a microcosm of the socialization of male values. While participation in competitive activities can be enjoyable and healthy, it too easily becomes a lesson in the need for toughness, invulnerability, and dominance. Athletes learn to ignore their own injuries and pain and instead try to injure and inflict pain on others in their attempts to win, regardless of the cost to themselves or their opponents. Yet the lessons learned in athletics are believed to be vital for full and complete masculine development, and as a model for problem-solving in other areas of life.

In addition to encouraging traditional male values, schools provide too few experiences in nurturance, cooperation, negotiation, nonviolent conflict resolution, and strategies for empathizing with and empowering others. Schools should become places where boys have the opportunity to learn these skills; clearly, they won't learn them on the street, from peers, or on television.

20   Despite the pressure on men to display their masculinity in traditional ways, there are examples of men and boys who are changing. "Fathering" is one example of a positive change. In recent years, there has been a popular emphasis on child-care activities, with men becoming more involved in providing care to children, both professionally and as fathers. This is a clear shift from the more traditional view that child rearing should be delegated to women and is not an appropriate activity for men.

For all the male resistance it has generated, the Women's Liberation Movement has at least provided a stimulus for some men to accept women as equal partners in most areas of life. These are the men who have chosen to learn and grow from women's experiences and together with women are creating new norms for relationships. Popular literature and research on male sex roles are expanding, reflecting a wider interest in masculinity. Weekly news magazines such as *Time* and *Newsweek* have run major stories on the "new masculinity," suggesting that positive changes are taking place in the home and in the workplace. Small groups of men scattered around the country have organized against pornography, battering and sexual assault. Finally, there is the National Organization for Changing Men which has a pro-feminist, pro-gay, pro-"new man" agenda, and its ranks are slowly growing.

In schools where I have worked with teachers, they report that years of efforts to enhance educational opportunities for girls have also had some positive effects on boys. The boys seem more tolerant of girls' participation in co-ed sports activities and in traditionally male shops and courses. They seem to have a greater respect for the accomplishments of women through women's contributions to literature and history. Among elementary school-aged males, the expression of vulnerable feelings is gaining acceptance. In general, however, there has been far too little attention paid to redirecting male role development.

I think back to the four wrestlers and the stifling culture of masculinity in which they live. If schools were to radically alter this culture and substitute for it a new vision of masculinity, what would that look like? In this environment, boys would express a full range of behaviors and emotions without fear of being chastised. They would be permitted and encouraged to cry, to be afraid, to show joy, and to express love in a gentle fashion. Extreme concern for career goals would be replaced by a consideration of one's need for recreation, health, and meaningful work. Older boys would be encouraged to tutor and play with younger students. Moreover, boys would receive as much recognition for artistic talents as they do for athletics, and, in general, they would value leisure-time, recreational activities as highly as competitive sports.

In a system where maleness and femaleness were equally valued, boys might no longer feel that they have to "prove" themselves to other boys; they would simply accept the worth of each person and value those differences. Boys would realize that it is permissible to admit failure. In addition, they would seek out opportunities to learn from girls and women. Emotional support would become commonplace, and it would no longer be seen as just the role of the female to provide the support. Relationships between boys and girls would no longer be based on limited roles, but instead would become expressions of two individuals learning from and supporting one another. Relationships between boys would reflect their care for one another rather than their mutual fear and distrust.

25   Aggressive styles of resolving conflicts would be the exception rather than the norm. Girls would feel welcome in activities dominated by boys, knowing that they were safe from the threat of being sexually harassed. Boys would no longer boast of beating up another boy or of how much they "got off" of a girl the night before. In fact, the boys would be as outraged as the girls at rape or other violent crimes in the community. Finally, boys would become active in efforts to stop nuclear proliferation and all other forms of military violence, following the examples set by activist women.

The development of a new conception of masculinity based on this vision is an ambitious task, but one which is essential for the health and safety of both men and women. The survival of our society may rest on the degree to which we are able to teach men to cherish life.

Questions for Discussion

1. How does Thompson test the comment that in a high school he observed in 1985, "The most humiliating put down [for a male] was being called a 'fag'"? What masculine characteristics brought status to the boys in the class that Thompson is visiting? What traditional description of masculinity does Thompson establish?

2. Why does Thompson argue that there is a civic advocacy of violence in our culture? What examples does he present through his reference to Wayne Ewing's article? Do you agree or disagree with Thompson? Explain your point of view.

3. Why does Thompson argue that support of masculine violence within a culture helps to maintain homophobia and misogyny? Explain why you agree or disagree with Thompson's analysis.

4. According to Thompson, how are men diminished by the traditional view of masculinity? Provide examples of the negative consequences of this traditional masculine definition from your own experiences or from experiences that you have observed.

5. What three areas does Thompson believe that men must work on to expand and humanize the meaning of masculinity? What qualities do they need to develop?

6. How does Thompson see our culture changing to support more feminine and less aggressive roles for men through different forms of "socialization" for boys and girls? What is Thompson's new vision of masculinity? Based on your own experiences and reflections, how much progress has our society made in attaining his vision?

CONNECTION

How do you think that Thompson would explain the teenage anguish that Sedaris expresses in "I Like Guys"? Do you think that he could have offered Sedaris any helpful advice? What might it be (see page 349)?

IDEAS FOR WRITING

1. Thompson often visits classrooms and asks students, "If you woke up tomorrow and discovered that you were the opposite sex how would you and your life be different?" Write an essay and develop a response to this question. Explain the positive and negative consequences of the change as you imagine them. Conclude with a paragraph that discusses how you felt about writing this speculative discussion.
2. An underlying assumption of Thompson's essay is that masculine and feminine identities are largely created by society or "nurture" as opposed to being "nature" or genetically based. What is your position on this issue? You might do some research on the subject to see what evidence there is for both points of view.

RELATED WEB SITES

MEN'S ISSUES PAGE
http://www.vix.com/pub/men/index.html
Visit this URL of links, hosted by "The World Wide Web Virtual Library," to find out about several U.S. men's movements and issues, as well as to see comprehensive reference lists of men's movement around the world.

GENDER ISSUES RESEARCH CENTER
http://www.gendercenter.org
The goal of this web site from the Gender Issues Research Center is "to provide resources [about gender issues] without the conflict and frustration brought by special interest groups and politicians." The material on this web site is compiled from nonpartisan departments of the U.S. government and research organizations.

Rosa Contreras

On Not Being a Girl

Rosa Contreras was born in Jalisco, Mexico, and raised in Half Moon Bay, California. She majored in Latin American studies and anthropology. Writing the following essay— a response to Julius Lester's essay "On Being a Boy"—helped Contreras to think more analytically about the expectations that her family had for her when she was a young girl and about how both her expectations and those of her family changed as she prepared herself for college.

JOURNAL

Write about an experience during your teenage years in which you disagreed with your family over what your role or responsibilities should be as a girl or a boy.

As I grew into adolescence, I experienced constant conflict between being a girl and having what have been traditionally considered "masculine" qualities. At the same time that I wanted to be contemplative and artful, I also wanted to take the initiative and all the responsibility which is typically a male role. I envied the opposite sex and their advantages and often found myself frustrated by my culture's traditional views of gender roles; I tried actively to break away from the typical role of a girl as defined in the Mexican family. In fact, growing up in a Mexican household with strong cultural values while also experiencing American culture with its less clearly defined gender roles allowed me to criticize both cultures from different perspectives. This allowed me to take the ideals that I liked from both and reject those that I did not agree with. In this manner, I was able to build my own set of values, and naturally, I have tried to inculcate them into my family.

As the oldest child in my family, I was given by my parents responsibilities fit for an adult, while they insisted that I remain a little girl, innocent and oblivious to boys and sex. I, in turn, rebelled; I did not want to be seen as an obedient, subservient girl, with all the qualities that make for a good Mexican wife. Every day I pushed to assert myself as strong, able to take on anything and succeed. I wanted to show my father and every other male in my life that I could do everything a boy could, if not more.

By the time I was twelve, I was tired of being a girl, sick of girls' activities. By this time I had accumulated five baby dolls, fourteen Barbie dolls, three Ken dolls, and four younger siblings. The fact that I was a girl, and the oldest one at that, burdened me with the responsibility of watching over my sisters and brother. If they hurt themselves, or strayed away from home, no one was blamed except me. I still remember one day when my little brother ran into the house, crying because he had slipped on the gravel while running. Upon hearing my brother's shrill cries, my father became irritated and turned toward me: "Look what happened! You're supposed to watch them!" I became angry. Why was I being blamed? Why did I have to watch them all the time?

One day I finally yelled out to my parents what I had been feeling for a while: "Why do I always get yelled at for the things they do? It's not my fault!—I can't always be watching THEM. THEY'RE your kids; you chose to have them! I wasn't even asked! I never asked to be born, much less asked to be born first!"

5   Looking back, I realize that those were extremely cruel and ungrateful words. Nevertheless, with this outcry, I opened my parents' eyes, and they saw that they were, in fact, being unreasonable when they expected me to watch four children all the time. Maybe they had already realized the unfairness of the situation I was in, because they did not protest or reprimand me for telling them how I felt. Afterwards, I was no longer blamed for my siblings' actions, and was given more independence from caring for them.

Along with protesting against the rules of watchdog and disciplinarian, which, in Mexican culture, are commonly reserved for girls, I did not like it that my family members disapproved of my love of reading. Nobody in my immediate or extended family gives books the importance that I do. Maybe the fact that I am a girl meant that books should not be very important to me. In old Mexican tradition, there exists the idea that it is not good for women to know too much. Not good for whom? For their husbands. A man was not a "real" man if his wife knew more than he did. However, I suspect that the main problem my family had with my reading books was that I often neglected my household chores because I would, literally, spend all day submerged in learning about other people, other worlds.

By the time I was twelve, I had disappointed my parents in their quest to make me a productive and useful young lady, according to what Mexican custom decrees. While the rest of the house was clean, my room was a mess. I had other things to do, like homework, studying for tests, reading, and playing basketball. And horror of horrors! I couldn't even cook a pot of beans. My mother was often distressed at my inability (and lack of desire) to cook and do housework, which simply did not interest me. I felt housework was a waste of time, and I'd rather be doing something else. More importantly, though, I hated it because I associated it with the oppression and subservience of Latina women, including those in my family.

The different roles of men and women in Mexican society are clearly marked and instilled in children from a very young age. While in first and third grade, I went to elementary school in Mexico. While the boys were encouraged to excel in athletics and academics, the girls competed in crocheting and embroidering. At the end of the year, there was a contest to see whose work was the most beautiful. Approximately once every two weeks, each girl had to help in either mopping, cleaning windows, or sweeping her classroom. Therefore, at a very young age, girls were taught to do housework and feminine things, like embroidery. My mother, all my aunts, and most Mexican women that I know were taught that the value of a woman consisted in keeping her family well-fed and a squeaky-clean house.

I realize that it was complicated for my mother to pass on these same values to me because we were no longer living in Mexico. But possibly because we were so far away from Mexico, it became very important for her to make this new home like her old one. Therefore, she tried to make sure that, although her daughters were being raised in a foreign country, we were still raised as she was taught. So when I refused to agree with the traditional Mexican ideals for raising a girl, she probably felt as though she had somehow failed. But I could not go along with what I truly felt was wrong. I could not please my older relatives in the way I was expected to because living in the United States, where the issue of women's rights is more openly debated, had opened my eyes to new and better possibilities for women.

10   From elementary school to high school, I went to school with a predominantly white population and came home to a Mexican household. At school I was taught what I liked. The teachers encouraged and praised me for my love of reading. Boys and girls were equally expected to do well in both sports and academics. Boys even took home economics! But often, when I brought home these ideas and chose to read rather than do housework or wait on my father and siblings, I was scolded. I was in a new environment that my parents had never experienced, so they did not understand why I felt so strongly about the way of life women had always led in Latin-American cultures.

From reading, which allowed me to learn a lot about other people, other life-styles, and achieving excellent grades in school, I often felt that I knew it all. I became very outspoken. At first, I scolded my mother privately when I saw her being subservient to my father. When she waited up for him, I would become angry and tell her: "Why are you doing this? I can't believe you're waiting up for him to feed him dinner! It's not like he can't get it himself!" Later, I became bolder. For example, when I'd hear my dad ask my mother for tortillas, I would say: "They're on the stove. You can get them." By the time I was twelve, I had my future laid out for me. I would always say that when I got older, I would have a career and my husband would share in the household responsibilities. I was not about to go out and work and then come home to do even more work. I understood that the status of my mother as a housewife required that she do this kind of work, but I felt it was unfair that she had to work all day, while my father could come home and not do anything for the rest of the evening.

I know that the many outbursts and arguments I have had (and still do, although less often now than before) concerning women's equality were the cause for much conflict in my household. However, I realize today that because of my efforts, my parents have changed their ideas about what women can accomplish. As a young girl, I refused to mold myself to be good and docile, with traditional moral values and knowledge. I understand that these ideas are very ingrained in Mexican society and they will be hard to change, but I cannot stand by and watch the oppression of these women and keep myself quiet. Now, as a young woman, I'm on my way to defying the role traditionally designated for women. During my high school days, my mother often encouraged me to study hard so that I could have a career. She would tell me: "Study, so that you can have a better life." She wanted me to have the option of being someone else rather than a full-time housewife, who always depends on her husband. I believe I have shown my father that I am capable of succeeding, just like all men and women can if given the opportunity. He has grown to accept me as I am and to understand my way of thinking. I have earned my parents' respect, and today they are extremely proud of all that I have achieved.

QUESTIONS FOR DISCUSSION

1. What aspects of Mexican-American culture made it difficult for Contreras to feel comfortable in her family role?
2. What might have contributed to Contreras's mother's tendency to reinforce the old ways? How were her family's values influenced by living in the United States? How did her family respond to her rebellion?
3. How does Contreras use examples of her family's interactions and her responsibilities in the home to illustrate her thesis about not fitting into the mold of "proper" female behavior?
4. Why do you think that Contreras's parents finally supported her desire to become independent?

Julie Bordner Apodaca

Gay Marriage: Why the Resistance?

Julie Bordner Apodaca was a student at the College of Alameda in California when she wrote the following essay. She is a native of Alameda and an aspiring writer who returned to college part-time after ten years out of school, while also working and starting a family. Ever since her elementary school days, Apodaca has enjoyed argumentation and has tried to encourage her fellow students and co-workers to see beyond biases and misconceptions about people whom society has labeled as "different." Thus when she was assigned to write a paper on a controversial issue for her critical thinking course, she chose to write on the subject of gay marriages and to examine the underlying causes for bias against such relationships.

JOURNAL

What are your feelings about gay marriage? Why is it such a controversial issue?

It has been over twenty years since the Stonewall riot triggered the civil rights movement in the gay and lesbian community. In the past two years, a good portion of the movement's focus has been on the issue of legalized marriage for homosexual couples, a move which many leaders in the gay community see as essentially conservative, as a sign that gays are opting for more traditional, stable life-styles and desire recognition as committed couples. Thus American society has been asked to expand the traditionally heterosexual institution of marriage to include gay and lesbian couples. The response from mainstream America has been largely negative, due in part to the homophobic attitudes that permeate our society.

To understand why society continues to have a negative reaction to the idea of legalizing gay marriage, we must first understand homophobia. Webster's defines homophobia as "hatred or fear of homosexuals or homosexuality." Homophobic attitudes, which are generally emotional and lacking in factual foundation, have many origins, some of which are religious, some political and sociological, some psychological, some even medical in nature. In a general sense, it can be argued that the roots of homophobia in America can be found in the institutions and philosophy that are at the heart of our culture: our dominant religious tradition, our political and class systems, our moral perspective, and our psychological makeup.

Some of the most passionate arguments against legalization of gay and lesbian marriages stem from the Judaic and Christian fundamentalist religions in our society. A common belief is that homosexuality is a sin; not only is it morally wrong, but it mocks natural laws and the will of God. Marriage is a sanctified privilege of heterosexual union that constructs a foundation for the procreation and nurture of children. Despite the fact that many gays have dependent children from previous heterosexual unions, homosexuals are not seen by the religious fundamentalist as having the capacity for procreation within their relationships; thus sexual relations between homosexuals are viewed by many religious people as sinful and mocking, a way of undermining the essential meaning of marriage.

Some social thinkers hold views against homosexual marriage which coincide in some ways with those of the religious fundamentalists. Such individuals resist the legalization or wide acceptance of gay relationships, fearing the repercussions to the already threatened traditional family. With the stigma against homosexuality relaxed, perhaps the 20 percent of closeted homosexuals who marry heterosexual partners may instead choose gay partners. This could lead to a decline in the numbers of heterosexual marriages and even to the rise of other unusual social arrangements thought of as destabilizing to our society, such as polygamy or group marriage (Hartinger 682). The traditional two-partner heterosexual marriage, already on the decline, could become a rarity, and our basic social structure, which historically was designed around this form of relationship, may crumble. The weakness of this type of causal reasoning is that it is based upon an assumption that it is somehow unhealthy for a society to change and evolve, as well as upon a view of the "stable nuclear family unit" that denies historical realities such as abusive families, alcoholism in the nuclear family, and other causes for the decline of the nuclear family, such as the high cost of maintaining a home, the high divorce rate, and the trend towards dual career families.

5   Despite the weaknesses in the reasoning, arguments against gay marriages as contributors towards the undermining of traditional families often have been used by politicians in order to win the support of the populace who feel that family values are endangered. Vice President Dan Quayle's attacks on the "cultural elite" during the 1992 presidential campaign could be seen as a veiled attack on

homosexuals and their relationships. According to Quayle, the cultural elite are those who "respect neither tradition or standards. They believe that moral truths are relative and all 'life styles' are equal" (qtd. in Salter A15). Quayle's comments stirred both praise and rage throughout America in the summer of 1992; his ideas touched a sympathetic chord for many who are painfully aware of the increased fragility of the traditional nuclear, heterosexual family unit.

However, it is not only religious, conservative sociologists, and aspiring politicians who promote homophobia; our government and its official branches play a key role as well. For instance, the United States military continues to resist fully accepting homosexuals in the armed forces, despite any evidence that would suggest that these individuals generally are unfit for duty, disruptive, or that they pose a security threat. The discrimination against homosexual relationships in the military is instrumental in fostering and maintaining the psychological fears and stereotypes associated with homosexuals: that they are unstable, immoral, and, in some vague sense, a threat to the security of our nation.

The AMA does not classify homosexuality as a disease or a disorder, due to scientific experiments done in the 1950s that discredited the notion of the homosexual as any more neurotic or maladjusted than any other group in society. However, many people continue to cling to the outmoded belief that homosexuality is a psychological disorder. Some, including a minority in the psychiatric profession, believe that homosexuality should be therapeutically treated, rather than sanctioned by recognition of homosexual unions as the equivalent to "normal" married relationships. However, psychologist Richard Isay does not believe that the fear of homosexuality is simply a reaction to the idea of a "deviant" sex act; Isay considers that the fear and hatred for homosexuality is related intimately to "the fear and hatred of what is perceived as being 'feminine' in other men and in oneself" (qtd. in Alter 27). Thus, for some people, insecurity and mistrust of one's own sexuality may cause irrational anxiety about or contempt towards the homosexual. If homosexual marriages were legal, gay couples might feel free publicly and physically to express their affections. This possibility of overt display of homosexuality in turn adds to the homophobic individual's fantasies that, rather than witnessing such encounters with "natural" revulsion, he or she could possibly experience an unwanted arousal.

Another common psychological concern about homosexual marriages, despite evidence that points to homosexuality as a quasi-biological sexual orientation rather than a learned or conditioned sexual response, is that legally sanctioned gay relationships will somehow influence children to become homosexual. The reasoning goes that adolescents and even younger children are often confused by the intense and unfamiliar sexual feelings stirring inside them; thus the adolescent confronted with the "normality" of homosexual relationships, in or out of their own family circle, might tend to gravitate toward this kind of sexual outlook. Furthermore, part of the stereotype of the homosexual as sexual deviant is that gays enjoy the company of young children and might, if not sufficiently isolated from mainstream society, take advantage of the vulnerability of naive and confused adolescents, encouraging such children to engage in gay sex.

A more recent fear that fuels the hostility to gay marriages is medically-based, but, as so many of the fears discussed above, based upon causal oversimplification. Consider AIDS; this disease is really a nightmare for our entire society, not just confined to the gay community, and it can be spread by both heterosexual sexual conduct and drug-related activity. Yet the fearful stereotype persists that AIDS is somehow a "gay" disease; in fact, some religious zealots have even spoken of AIDS as God's "divine retribution" against gays for their blasphemous behavior, despite the reality that gays didn't originate the disease and in spite of the fact that the gay community has made enormous progress in educating itself about AIDS and in discontinuing the unsafe sexual practices of the past. The legalization of homosexual marriage elicits the fear among those with a deep fear of both AIDS and homosexuality, that, along with the resulting increase in the numbers of homosexuals, such legalization will somehow cause the AIDS epidemic to become even more severe. This is truly an ironic misconception, when we consider that monogamous marriage, gay or heterosexual, is one of the most conservative sexual practices, one of the least likely to lead to a spread of disease beyond the bounds of matrimony.

10   As we have seen, there are many causes for the fear that surrounds the legalization of homosexual marriages. The cumulative effect of these causes has prevented legislation supporting such relationships in almost all parts of the country. Although some of the arguments against homosexual marriages may seem on the surface to have some justification, most are based on ignorance, irrationality, and fear. Perhaps, as Ernest Van Den Haag puts it, "nothing will persuade heterosexuals to believe that homosexuality is psychologically or morally as legitimate as their own heterosexuality" (38); however, despite the resistance that is likely to occur, it seems to me that a national effort should be made to dispel the misconceptions regarding homosexuality. What benefit is there in hiding behind irrational fears? Homosexuality is not going to disappear; history has proven that. Society would benefit from a better understanding of homosexuality, for if people were able to think more critically about the myths and the issues surrounding homosexuality, perhaps there would be a decrease in the nation's homophobia and an increased understanding from which all people, gay and heterosexual alike, would benefit. We cannot expect a change overnight, but we can begin to educate the ignorant and break down some of the prejudice. As Martin Luther King, Jr., once said, "Take the first step in faith. You don't have to see the whole staircase, just take the first step."

WORKS CITED

Alter, Jonathan. "Degrees of Discomfort." <u>Newsweek</u> 12 March 1992: 27.

Hartinger, Brent. "A Case for Gay Marriage." <u>Commonweal</u> 22 Nov. 1991: 681–683.

Salter, Stephanie. "The 'Cultural Elite' and the Rest of Us." San Francisco <u>Chronicle</u> 14 June 1992: A15.

Van Den Haag, Ernest. "Sodom and Begorrah." <u>National Review</u> 29 April 1991: 35–38.

Questions for Discussion

1. What are the major causes of the resistance to gay marriage as explored in the essay? Could the student have discussed other causes? Which ones?
2. Apodaca refutes the reasoning that underlies most of the "fears" she discusses. Is her refutation effective and fair?
3. What factual evidence does Apodaca use to support her general statements and conclusions? What additional evidence might she have used?
4. This essay includes some quotations from authorities or spokespersons to support some of the writer's ideas and conclusions about social attitudes. Were such citations of authorities handled appropriately, or would you have liked to see either more or less reliance on citation of authority?

TOPICS FOR RESEARCH AND WRITING

1. Develop an extended definition of masculinity. When relevant show how it relates to the ideas presented by Thompson, Sedaris, and Hemingway. To what extent is masculinity primarily a cultural concept and to what extent is it a biological reality or a product of evolution? Do some research to help find some answers to these questions.

2. After reading the selections by Divakaruni and Hong Kingston, review what you have learned about the limits, challenges, or advantages of being born female in a traditional society; consider also your own experiences and outside readings in this area. Write your findings in a documented essay.

3. Write an essay based on readings from the text, research, as well as your own thoughts and feelings about the role that sex plays in an individual's life, health, and sense of well-being. Consider if sex is primarily a procreative act, an expression of love, an erotic experience, or a combination of experiences. Does the importance of sex and the sexual act vary significantly from culture to culture?

4. Reread the selection by Freud in this chapter that reflects on the relationships among dreams, the unconscious, and sexuality, and do some further reading in this area. Write your conclusions in the form of a documented essay. To what extent are dreams the product of the unconscious repression of sexual desires, and to what extent are they related more to issues in waking life?

5. How are definitions of male and female identity continuing to change in the era of cyberspace? In addition to doing some outside reading, you might interview some people you know who spend a lot of time in chat rooms and/or visit some chat rooms where gender identity role-playing is common.

6. The works in this chapter by Sedaris, Thompson, and Naylor explore societal fears and rejection of gays. Do some research into these fears and their origins, and write an essay about the causes and effects of homophobia.

7. Write about a film that portrays an issue of sexuality or gender. How does the film comment on certain issues raised in the readings in this chapter? You can select a film from the following list or one of your own choosing: *Incredible Adventure of Two Girls in Love*, *Oleanna*, *Fried Green Tomatoes*, *The Crying Game*, *The Wedding Banquet*, *Orlando*, *Oscar Wilde*, *Shakespeare in Love*, *Boys Don't Cry*, *Chasing Amy*, *Legally Blonde*, and *Waiting To Exhale*.

The Double/The Other

Pablo Picasso (1881–1973)
Girl Before a Mirror (1932)

Created at the height of Picasso's artistic power, *Girl Before a Mirror* incorporates what he had learned through the great twentieth-century art movements to which he contributed—Expressionism, Primitivism, Cubism, Classicism, and Surrealism. The painting portrays a woman whose beautiful, masklike classical profile seems to reflect in her mirror an image of her inner self.

JOURNAL

Write about what you see when you look at yourself in a mirror. Does the image you see look like the self you know, or does it seem like someone else, not entirely familiar or acceptable to you?

Within each one of us there is another whom we do not know. He speaks to us in dreams and tells us how differently he sees us from how we see ourselves.

CARL JUNG

Our challenge is to call forth the humanity within each adversary, while preparing for the full range of possible responses. Our challenge is to find a path between cynicism and naiveté.

FRAN PEAVEY
Us and Them

ARGUMENT AND DIALOGUE

Traditional Argument

Traditional argument begins by defining a problem or issue, then taking a position or stance. In this form of argument the advocate develops a clear thesis and demonstrates its validity through a series of convincing logical arguments, factual supports, and references to authority. Often the major aim of argument is seen as an attack on the ideas and positions of an opponent with the goal of persuading the audience of the correctness of the proponent's position. Arguments that don't quite fit into the debater's viewpoint are sometimes ignored or are introduced as refutation of the principal argument. Such traditional debate is frequently linked to political rhetoric, where only one candidate can be elected. A fundamental part of public life, oppositional argument at its best can be a powerful method of presenting one's own position and beliefs. At its worst, traditional argument can be manipulative and one-sided, leading people to believe that debate is a matter of verbal warfare, that every decision implies an either/or choice rather than an attempt at genuine communication. For examples of oppositional argument that lead to verbal warfare, visit some politically-oriented web sites on the Internet—or read the editorial page of your daily newspaper.

Dialogic Argument

Dialogic Argument is a form of argument based on thoroughly presenting facts and reasons for supporting a position. This type of argument acknowledges the importance of creating a bridge between opposing viewpoints that are often rigidly separated in a traditional argument. It may remind you of the literary dialogue between opposites that we see at work in some of this chapter's stories and poems; it is best exemplified in expository form here in Fran Peavey's essay, "Us and Them." The dialogic argument emphasizes the need for discussion and a genuine exchange of ideas, while making a conscious effort to bring together seemingly irreconcilable viewpoints in order to arrive at a synthesis of opposing perspectives and allow the writer and the audience to learn more about themselves. Through the dialogic approach you can come to a new awareness of positions you may not have understood or considered. Working to understand these opposite positions does not necessarily imply that you totally accept them, or that you abandon your own ideas and viewpoints. What it does suggest is that you consider the possibilities of strong arguments, positions, and value systems that are different from your own, and that you make a real attempt to integrate these positions into your thinking.

Dialogue and Prewriting

An effective prewriting strategy for a balanced argument paper involves engaging your opponent in a dialogue. Begin by creating a dialogue that explores different positions relative to your subject, your thesis, and your supporting points. Following is an example of an excerpt from student dialogue on the subject of reading fairy tales to small children. We have labeled the two sides in the dialogue "I" and "Me." "I" stands for the position that the student really wants to present, while "Me" represents the side of the argument, perhaps a side of the self that the writer doesn't want to acknowledge and perceives as the opponent.

> I: I think all children should read fairy tales. I always loved hearing them as a kid; I liked the scary parts and the adventures. Fairy tales are so much more engrossing than the trash on the boob tube.

> ME: I can see that you really like fairy tales. But wouldn't a lot of kids who get upset easily be frightened by reading stories about mean stepmothers and wicked witches, like in "Hansel and Gretel"?

> I: I understand what you're saying; fairy tales might frighten some children, especially if they were very young or if they had had some really horrible things happen in their own lives that the stories reminded them of. Still, I think I can handle your objections. Kids should be read fairy tales by an adult who makes time to explain the issues in the story and who can reassure them if they think the story is too scary; after all, a fairy tale is "only a story."

> ME: Well, I can see the point in having adults read the stories and explain them, but you're wrong about TV. There are some great programs for kids, like *Sesame Street* and *Barney*, that teach children to have positive values. And what about the values in those fairy tales? *Sesame Street* teaches you to love everyone and to give girls equal opportunities to succeed! Fairy tales are so old-fashioned and sexist, with all those beautiful sleeping princesses waiting around for Prince Charming.

> I: I know what you mean. The values in fairy tales aren't always very modern. That's why it's really important that the adult who reads the stories

> to the kids discusses the old-fashioned way of life that is being presented
> and compares the world of the tale with our own values and life-styles. I
> can see letting kids watch TV, too. Fairy tales are only a part of the imag-
> inative experience of childhood, but they're still a very important part!

In this short dialogue, you see the "I" and "Me" positions being brought
closer together. "I"'s initial position is now more clearly stated, with some
important, common sense qualifications brought in through the interaction
with the "Me."

Prewriting and the Audience

Before you write your essay, try to establish a similar kind of dialogue with
your imaginary audience as you did with yourself. As in traditional argument or in any type of writing, this involves trying to determine the interests and values of your audience. For example, the student writing about
fairy tales would have to decide if the audience includes cautious parents of
school age children or liberal educators with a progressive philosophy of
child rearing. Creating a clear mental image of the audience is essential before appropriate arguments can be selected. Once you have a clear image of
the audience in mind, approach your readers directly and respectfully.
Make the audience an integral part of your arguments. Do not try to manipulate or dazzle them with your facts and figures; instead, establish a
common ground and state the positions you hold in common with them
while designating areas of mutual agreement or possible compromise. This
approach will remind you to keep your audience's point of view in mind and
will facilitate meaningful communication.

Defining Key Terms

As in traditional argument, it is important for dialogic arguers to define
their terms. Definitions support clear communication and help develop rap-
port in an argument. People feel more comfortable in a discussion when
they understand what key terms mean. For example, if I am arguing for
reading fairy tales to young children and am referring to fairy tales such as
those of Hans Christian Andersen, while my audience thinks I am discussing modern fantasy children's stories such as those by Maurice Sendak,
then we are really thinking about different definitions of a fairy tale and will
be unlikely to come to a mutual understanding. When defining your terms,
use simple, straightforward definitions; avoid connotative language designed to manipulate or trick your audience.

Evaluating Facts

If you have taken a statistics course or read articles in journals, you know
that facts and statistics can be interpreted in a variety of ways. When reading the factual studies that will form an important part of the support in
any argument paper, you need to consider a number of questions. Have the

results of the social scientists or psychologists you are studying been confirmed by other researchers? Are the data current? Was it collected by qualified researchers using thorough and objective methods? Are the results expressed in clear and unambiguous language? These and other questions should be asked about your sources of information so that you can create a sound factual base for the arguments you use in your paper. In doing research for your argument, you might look at web sites, even extremist ones, to get the feeling for some of the strong sentiments that different groups have about your issue—but don't rely on these partisan, advocacy sites to provide objective information. On the other hand, you do need to mention both widely believed facts and popular misconceptions that may *oppose* the argument you are making. You will need to respectfully show your audience how some of these beliefs are not factual, how others are not relevant, and concede that some are relevant and either can be dealt with by your proposed argument, or cannot within the practical limits of the situation at hand. Present your supporting facts clearly; avoid overstating your conclusions in absolute, unqualified terms or over generalizing from limited data.

Feelings in Argument

Emotions play such a significant role in our lives that any argument that tried to be totally rational, pretending that emotional concerns were unimportant and that only facts have significance would be unrealistic and ineffective. Emotions, both your own and those of your audience, are a central concern in argument. Although you need to present your ideas in ways that won't offend your readers, when feelings are a central issue in the argument itself, emotional issues do need to be directly confronted. For example, it would be impossible to discuss a subject such as abortion without acknowledging your own feelings and those of the audience. In this case, sharing such feelings will help to create an open and trusting relationship with your audience.

However, an important distinction must be made between acknowledging your feelings and exploiting them to manipulate your readers. Often, strong arguments are based on emotions, which can be exaggerated in an attempt to strengthen your position and cause you to overlook important issues. Avoid language that could ignite emotional fireworks in a discussion. Bringing in irrelevant appeals for pity or fear can obscure the real issues involved in a discussion. Try to use language that is emotionally neutral in describing the positions and ideas taken by the opposition. By doing so, you are more likely to keep the confidence of readers who might otherwise be offended by an adversarial position and manipulative language.

Argument can be one of the most satisfying forms of writing, but it can be one of the most difficult. To satisfy both the factual, logical, and emotional demands of shaping an effective argument, you can:

- Use the inner dialogue as an aid to prewriting and exploring different positions.
- Empathize with and acknowledge the assumptions and needs of your audience.
- Define key terms.
- Evaluate and use relevant factual supports.
- Be honest and direct in your treatment of the emotional aspects of an issue.

All of these strategies will be of use to you in your efforts to find a stance in argument that allows you to build bridges between your inner world and the worlds of others. This type of argument, when thoughtfully developed with an audience in mind, can be one of the most effective means of communication that a writer can draw upon, both in academic discourse and in private and community life.

THEMATIC INTRODUCTION: THE DOUBLE/THE OTHER

Many of us are conscious of having an alternate self that, for whatever reasons, we do not make public. We sometimes see glimpses of an alternative or underground personality in a family member, friend, supervisor, colleague, or even in a media figure. From Greek myths to nursery rhymes and fairy tales, from Shakespearean doubles and disguises to Gothic tales of horror and revenge, from Victorian mysteries to the modern psychological short story, images of the double, of twins in spirit or twins in reality, have marked our developing understanding of the workings of the human mind.

The frequent recurrence and popularity of the double in mythology and literature is often attributed to the human need to explore, understand, and perhaps conquer divided feelings that individuals have about the parts of themselves that are in conflict. These conflicts are revealed in many forms: the good versus the evil self, the rational versus the irrational, the civilized versus the antisocial or criminal self, the masculine self versus the feminine self, the physical self versus the spiritual self, the controlled, conventional versus the wild self, the practical versus the dreamy self.

Although literature and human experiences suggest that inward journeys into the mind's dual nature can lead to confusion, even neurosis or psychosis, there is the possibility of integrating and balancing the opposing parts through developing an increased awareness of the inner self. In this way, through the main character of a poem or story, the writer or a reader can experience a form of rebirth, emerging with a more balanced and confident sense of self and purpose. Your journey through this chapter will provide you with new insights into the dualities within the human personality.

The chapter opens with two selections that explore the double nature of the self. First, in Judith Ortiz Cofer's poem, "The Other," the Hispanic-American speaker acknowledges the power of her "other," who is sensual, uninhibited, even dangerous, and more in touch with her cultural roots than her well-behaved public self. Similarly, in "Updike and I," novelist John Updike explores the duality of his nature in the contrast between his social self and his writer self.

The next two readings will help you to think about the importance of getting the oppositional sides of your mind and psyche to work together productively. Jungian therapist Robert Johnson in his essay, "Owning Your Own Shadow," explores the dangerous consequences, both to individuals and to their societies, of failing to recognize and heal inner divisions within the human mind. In a selection from his classic double novella, *The Strange Case of Dr. Jekyll and Mr Hyde* ("Henry Jekyll's Full Statement of the Case"), Robert Louis Stevenson illustrates through the voice of the doomed Dr. Jekyll the negative consequences of trying to separate the good or civilized side of the human character from its sensual and irrational side.

The next three selections discuss the crucial impact of citizens' inner conflict on political and social stances and decisions. In "Being Black and Feeling Blue," Shelby Steele discusses the ways in which an African-American's negative self-concept, or internalized "anti-self," can make his or her personal and public success difficult. Next, in her essay "Ideologies of Madness," Susan Griffin explains the origins of dualistic thinking and the mind-body split in Western thought while looking at the consequences of this split in terms of war and the nuclear struggle and race and gender conflicts. In an effort to find some way out of the dilemma of the other in society, in her essay "Us and Them," longtime peace activist Fran Peavey suggests a new approach to community organization and political action that avoids dehumanizing and dismissing the opposition. Instead, Peavy encourages a balanced response to problem solving.

The two student essays that conclude the chapter offer new ways of thinking about how the double-sided nature of social issues can be internalized and affect the development of an individual's self-concept. In the first student essay, "Mixed-Up," by Susan Voyticky, the daughter of an African-American mother and a white father, discusses some of the difficult decisions she had to make to create an identity that she could call her own. Jill Ho in "Affirmative Action: Perspectives From A Model Minority" reflects on how Asian-Americans face a glass ceiling, a double-sided reward, after gaining entry to main-stream jobs through affirmative action.

Exploring the duality of the human mind and spirit as reflected in the essays, stories, and poems included in this chapter should prove to be provocative and enlightening. Becoming aware of the voices that exist within you in addition to your dominant voice or persona can help you understand yourself more fully and can provide you with additional resources to draw upon in your writing.

Judith Ortiz Cofer

The Other

(See headnote on Judith Ortiz Cofer in Chapter 3). As a poet, Cofer often explores issues of cultural identity and heritage. In the following poem, notice how Cofer presents the inner conflict of identity experienced by the speaker through a series of progressively disturbing images.

JOURNAL

Write about a part of yourself that you have difficulty accepting because the "other" in you seems too unconventional, too wild or irresponsible.

A sloe-eyed dark woman shadows me.
In the morning she sings
Spanish love songs in a high
falsetto filling my shower stall
5   with echoes.
She is by my side
in front of the mirror as I slip
into my tailored skirt and she
into her red cotton dress.
10 She shakes out her black mane as I
run a comb through my close-cropped cap.
Her mouth is like a red bull's eye
daring me.
Everywhere I go I must
15 make room for her: she crowds me
in elevators where others wonder
at all the space I need.
At night her weight tips my bed, and
it is her wild dreams that run rampant
20 through my head exhausting me. Her heartbeats,
like dozens of spiders carrying the poison
of her restlessness over the small
distance that separates us,
drag their countless legs
25 over my bare flesh.

QUESTIONS FOR DISCUSSION

1. How would you characterize the "other" that Cofer creates in this poem? Is it anything like your own "other"?
2. Describe the speaker's main self. How does her main self differ from that of the "other"?
3. Which part of the speaker is dominant? Which side do you think will eventually win out in the struggle?
4. Why do you think the two sides of the speaker's personality are in conflict? What different cultural and gender roles does each side reflect?
5. What images help to vividly portray the "other" and to contrast her with the speaker's main self?
6. What dreams and nocturnal fantasies of the speaker help to convey the struggle between the two sides of her personality? What do you think is meant by the fantasy image, "Her heartbeats,/like dozens of spiders carrying the poison/of her restlessness . . ."? In what sense is the restlessness a poison?

CONNECTION

Analyze this poem as a statement of the shadow as defined in the selection by Robert Johnson (see page 387).

IDEAS FOR WRITING

1. Write an essay about an inner struggle you have experienced that reflects a cultural conflict between two of the following: the culture of your parents, your friends, your school, your workplace, or of your church. Include examples of ways that your inner conflict is reflected in your dreams and fantasies.

2. Write an essay that could take the form of a dialogue in which you explore inner conflicts that you have about making an important decision in your life. You might want to discuss whether to change your position on political or social issues, on ways of relating to a marriage partner, friend, parent, supervisor at work, or teacher. After exploring your options, which choice seems preferable?

RELATED WEB SITES

ILLUMINATING THE SHADOW: AN INTERVIEW WITH CONNIE ZWEIG
http://www.scottlondon.com/insight/scripts/zweig.html
This online interview with author and psychotherapist Connie Zweig, from a weekly radio series called "Insight & Outlook" defines the Jungian concept of the shadow and discusses celebrity and public fascination with the idea of the shadow-self. The interview also raises the question of how to best integrate the shadow and the self.

TWINS IN LITERATURE
http://www.modcult.brown.edu/students/angell/twinslit.html
This site provides historical background on the roles that twins and the theme of the double have played in both literature and film.

John Updike

Updike and I

John Updike (b. 1932) was raised in Shillington, Pennsylvania, and completed his B.A. at Harvard in 1954. After studying art at the Ruskin School in Oxford, England, he returned to New York where he joined the staff of the New Yorker. In 1959, Updike published his first novel, The Poorhouse Fair. At this time he moved with his family to Ipswich, Massachusetts, and made writing his full-time career. Updike is best known for his sequence of novels about Harry "Rabbit" Angstrom, who lives in suburbia and continually thinks back to his life as a high school athlete: Rabbit Run (1960); Rabbit Redux (1971); Rabbit Is Rich (1981); and Rabbit at Rest (1990), which won the Pulitzer Prize in 1991. Updike has written a number of other best-selling novels. The Witches of Eastwick (1984) was made into a

*popular film starring Jack Nicholson. Some of Updike's short story collections in-
clude* Problems *(1979),* Trust Me *(1987), and* The Afterlife and Other Stories
(1994). His recent novels include Toward the End of Time *(1997), and* Seek My
Face *(2002). In the brief fantasy "Updike and I" (1995), Updike reflects playfully
on his creation of a literary "persona," a public double that sometimes gets confused
with the "real" Updike.*

JOURNAL

Write about the persona or self that is projected by your writing. How is the self
that emerges in your writing different from your conversational everyday self?

I created Updike out of the sticks and mud of my Pennsylvania boyhood, so I
can scarcely resent it when people, mistaking me for him, stop me on the
street and ask me for his autograph. I am always surprised that I resemble him
so closely that we can be confused. Meeting strangers, I must cope with an extra brightness in their faces, an expectancy that I will say something worthy of
him; they do not realize that he works only in the medium of the written word,
where other principles apply, and hours of time can be devoted to a moment's
effect. Thrust into "real" time, he can scarcely function, and his awkward pleasantries and anxious stutter emerge through my lips. Myself, I am rather suave. I
think fast, on my feet, and have no use for the olfactory complexities and
lame double entendres and pained exactions of language in which he is cus-
tomarily mired. I move swiftly and rather blindly through life, spending the
money he earns.

I early committed him to a search for significance, to philosophical issues
that give direction and point to his verbal inventions, but I am not myself aware
of much point or meaning to things. Things are, rather unsayably, and when I
force myself to peruse his elaborate scrims of words I wonder where he gets it
all—not from me, I am sure. The distance between us is so great that the bad
reviews he receives do not touch me, though I treasure his few prizes and
mount them on the walls and shelves of my house, where they instantly yellow
and tarnish. That he takes up so much of my time, answering his cloying mail
and reading his incessant proofs, I resent. I feel that the fractional time of day
he spends away from being Updike is what feeds and inspires him, and yet, per-
versely, he spends more and more time being Updike, that monster of whom
my boyhood dreamed.

Each morning I awake from my dreams, which as I age leave an ever
more sour taste. Men once thought dreams to be messages from the gods,
and then from something called the subconscious, as it sought a salubrious
rearrangement of the contents of the day past; but now it becomes hard to
believe that they partake of any economy. Instead, a basic chaos seems
expressed: a random play of electricity generates images of inexplicable
specificity.

I brush my teeth, I dress and descend to the kitchen, where I eat and read the newspaper, which has been dreaming its own dreams in the night. Postponing the moment, savoring every small news item and vitamin pill and sip of unconcentrated orange juice, I at last return to the upstairs and face the rooms that Updike has filled with his books, his papers, his trophies, his projects. The abundant clutter stifles me, yet I am helpless to clear away much of it. It would be a blasphemy. He has become a sacred reality to me. I gaze at his worn wooden desk, his boxes of dull pencils, his blank-faced word processor, with a religious fear. Suppose, some day, he fails to show up? I would attempt to do his work, but no one would be fooled.

QUESTIONS FOR DISCUSSION

1. From what materials has Updike created the persona "Updike"? Why does Updike not feel resentment about being mistaken for "Updike"? Why is he surprised?
2. Why does "Updike" have difficulty functioning in real time? How and why does he differ from his creator in terms of social skills?
3. How are "Updike" and Updike's values and beliefs different? Why does Updike refer to the persona "Updike" as a monster? Does he seem genuinely monstrous to you?
4. What view of dreams does Updike present? How does the emphasis on the dream state in "Updike and I" help you to understand the relationship between "Updike" and the "I" in the narrative?
5. The essay includes descriptions of the objects related to "Updike" and his career world. How do these objects help define the persona of "Updike," and why does the narrator, Updike, feel these objects constitute a "sacred reality"?

CONNECTION

Compare John Updike's story of his other self with Judith Ortiz Cofer's expression of her speaker's other self (see page 382).

IDEAS FOR WRITING

1. Write an essay similar to "Updike and I" that explores the differences that exist between the part of yourself that writes and the part that exists in the everyday world. What have you learned about yourself from thinking about these differences?
2. Take an inventory of the objects you have accumulated in your home or room. How do these objects support and validate different selves within you? Write an essay that takes this inventory into account and explains how the different aspects of your personality and character developed and how these different personality traits support one another.

RELATED WEB SITE

JOHN UPDIKE—"THE CENTAURIAN SITE"
http://userpages.prexar.com/joyerkes/
This extensive web site is designed to provide information and promote discussion about writer John Updike's life and work. Many relevant links can be found about the author such as interviews and essays discussing his fiction.

Robert Johnson

Owning Your Own Shadow

Distinguished Jungian therapist Robert Johnson has written extensively on personality archetypes, healing and integration, and human relationships. His works include Inner Work: Using Dreams and Active Imagination for Personal Growth *(1989),* Lying With the Heavenly Woman: Understanding and Integrating the Feminine Archetypes in Men's Lives *(1995),* Balancing Heaven and Earth: A Memoir *(1998), and* Owning Your Own Shadow: Understanding the Dark Side of the Psyche *(1993), from which the following selection is excerpted.*

JOURNAL

Write about a dream in which you felt as if a character in the dream seemed to represent an aspect of yourself. Describe the character in as much detail as you can. Then explain when and why you think that you are like this dream character.

The shadow: What is this curious dark element that follows us like a saurian tail and pursues us so relentlessly in our psychological world? What role does it occupy in the modern psyche?

The persona is what we would like to be and how we wish to be seen by the world. It is our psychological clothing and it mediates between our true selves and our environment just as our physical clothing presents an image to those we meet. The ego is what we are and know about consciously. The shadow is that part of us we fail to see or know.*

---

*Jung used the term *shadow* in this general sense early in his formulation. Later the term indicated those characteristics of our own sex that have been lost to us. We are using the term in its general meaning in this book.

How the Shadow Originates

We all are born whole and, let us hope, will die whole. But somewhere early on our way, we eat one of the wonderful fruits of the tree of knowledge, things separate into good and evil, and we begin the shadow-making process; we divide our lives. In the cultural process we sort out our God-given characteristics into those that are acceptable to our society and those that have to be put away. This is wonderful and necessary, and there would be no civilized behavior without this sorting out of good and evil. But the refused and unacceptable characteristics do not go away; they only collect in the dark corners of our personality. When they have been hidden long enough, they take on a life of their own— the shadow life. The shadow is that which has not entered adequately into consciousness. It is the despised quarter of our being. It often has an energy potential nearly as great as that of our ego. If it accumulates more energy than our ego, it erupts as an overpowering rage or some indiscretion that slips past us; or we have a depression or an accident that seems to have its own purpose. The shadow gone autonomous is a terrible monster in our psychic house.

The civilizing process, which is the brightest achievement of humankind, consists of culling out those characteristics that are dangerous to the smooth functioning of our ideals. Anyone who does not go through this process remains a "primitive" and can have no place in a cultivated society. We all are born whole but somehow the culture demands that we live out only part of our nature and refuse other parts of our inheritance. We divide the self into an ego and a shadow because our culture insists that we behave in a particular manner. This is our legacy from having eaten of the fruit of the tree of knowledge in the Garden of Eden. Culture takes away the simple human in us, but gives us more complex and sophisticated power. One can make a forceful argument that children should not be subjected to this division too soon or they will be robbed of childhood; they should be allowed to remain in the Garden of Eden until they are strong enough to stand the cultural process without being broken by it. This strength comes at different ages for different individuals and it requires a keen eye to know when children are ready to adapt to the collective life of a society.

5   It is interesting to travel about the world and see which characteristics various cultures affix to the ego and which to the shadow. It becomes clear that culture is an artificially imposed structure, but an absolutely necessary one. We find that in one country we drive on the right side of the road; in another, the left. In the West a man may hold hands with a woman on the street but not with another man; in India he may hold hands with a male friend but not with a woman. In the West one shows respect by wearing shoes in formal or religious places; in the East it a sign of disrespect to wear shoes when one is in a temple or house. If you go into a temple in India with your shoes on you will be put out and told not to come back until you learn some manners. In the Middle East one burps at the end of a meal to show pleasure; in the West this would be very bad manners.

The sorting process is quite arbitrary. Individuality, for instance, is a great virtue in some societies and the greatest sin in others. In the Middle East it is a virtue to be selfless. Students of a great master of painting or poetry will often sign their work with the name of their master rather than their own. In our culture, one brings to his or her own name the highest publicity possible. The clash of these opposing points of view is dangerous as the rapidly expanding communication network of the modern world brings us closer together. The shadow of one culture is a tinderbox of trouble for another.

It is also astonishing to find that some very good characteristics turn up in the shadow. Generally, the ordinary, mundane characteristics are the norm. Anything less than this goes into the shadow. But anything better also goes into the shadow! Some of the pure gold of our personality is relegated to the shadow because it can find no place in that great leveling process that is culture.

Curiously, people resist the noble aspects of their shadow more strenuously than they hide the dark sides. To draw the skeletons out of the closet is relatively easy, but to own the gold in the shadow is terrifying. It is more disrupting to find that you have a profound nobility of character than to find out you are a bum. Of course you are both; but one does not discover these two elements at the same time. The gold is related to our higher calling, and this can be hard to accept at certain stages of life. Ignoring the gold can be as damaging as ignoring the dark side of the psyche, and some people may suffer a severe shock or illness before they learn how to let the gold out. Indeed, this kind of intense experience may be necessary to show us that an important part of us is lying dormant or unused. In tribal cultures, shamans or healers often experience an illness that gives them the insight they need to heal themselves and then bring wisdom to their people. This is often the case for us today. We are still operating with the archetype of the wounded healer who has learned to cure himself and find the gold in his experience.

Wherever we start and whatever culture we spring from, we will arrive at adulthood with a clearly defined ego and shadow, a system of right and wrong, a teeter-totter with two sides.* The religious process consists of restoring the wholeness of the personality. The word religion means to re-relate, to put back together again, to heal the wounds of separation. It is absolutely necessary to engage in the cultural process to redeem ourselves from our animal state; it is equally necessary to accomplish the spiritual task of putting our fractured, alienated world back together again. One must break away from the Garden of Eden but one must also restore the heavenly Jerusalem.

10   Thus it is clear that we must make a shadow, or there would be no culture; then we must restore the wholeness of the personality that was lost in the cultural

---

*Ego and *right* are thought to be synonymous in all cultures, while *shadow* and *wrong* are also to be paired. There is great cultural strength in knowing exactly what is right and what is wrong and to ally oneself appropriately. This is cultural "rightness," highly effective but very clumsy. When the Inquisition of the Middle Ages judged someone and often condemned him or her to be burned at the stake, there had to be an unquestioned basis for such a decision. The fact that individuality and the freedom of belief was evolving in the Western psyche added fuel to this one-sided attitude. Fanaticism always indicates unconscious uncertainty not yet registering in consciousness.

ideals, or we will live in a state of dividedness that grows more and more painful throughout our evolution. Generally, the first half of life is devoted to the cultural process—gaining one's skills, raising a family, disciplining one's self in a hundred different ways; the second half of life is devoted to restoring the wholeness (making holy) of life. One might complain that this is a senseless round trip except that the wholeness at the end is conscious while it was unconscious and childlike at the beginning. This evolution, though it seems gratuitous, is worth all the pain and suffering that it costs. The only disaster would be getting lost halfway through the process and not finding our completion. Unfortunately, many Westerners are caught in just this difficult place.

Balancing Culture and Shadow

It is useful to think of the personality as a teeter-totter or seesaw. Our acculturation consists of sorting out our God-given characteristics and putting the acceptable ones on the right side of the seesaw and the ones that do not conform on the left. It is an inexorable law that no characteristic can be discarded; it can only be moved to a different point on the seesaw. A cultured person is one who has the desired characteristics visible on the right (the righteous side) and the forbidden ones hidden on the left. All our characteristics must appear somewhere in this inventory. Nothing may be left out.

A terrible law prevails that few people understand and that our culture chooses to ignore almost completely. That is, the seesaw must be balanced if one is to remain in equilibrium. If one indulges characteristics on the right side, they must be balanced by an equal weight on the left side. The reverse is equally true. If this law is broken, then the seesaw flips and we lose our balance. This is how people flip into the opposite of their usual behavior. The alcoholic who suddenly becomes fanatical in his temperance, or the conservative who suddenly throws all caution to the wind, has made such a flip. He has only substituted one side of his seesaw for the other and made no lasting gain.

The seesaw may also break at the fulcrum point if it is too heavily loaded. This is a psychosis or breakdown. Slang terms are exact in describing these experiences. One must keep the balance intact, though this often requires a very great expenditure of energy.

The psyche keeps its equilibrium as accurately as the body balances its temperature, its acid-alkaline ratio, and the many other fine polarities. We take these physical balances for granted but rarely do we recognize their psychological parallels.

15   To refuse the dark side of one's nature is to store up or accumulate the darkness; this is later expressed as a black mood, psychosomatic illness, or unconsciously inspired accidents. We are presently dealing with the accumulation of a whole society that has worshiped its light side and refused the dark, and this residue appears as war, economic chaos, strikes, racial intolerance. The front page of any newspaper hurls the collective shadow at us. We must be whole whether we like it or not; the only choice is whether we will incorporate the shadow consciously and with some dignity or do it through some neurotic be-

havior. George Bernard Shaw said that the only alternative to torture is art. This means we will engage in our creativity (in the ceremonial or symbolic world) or have to face its alternative, brutality.

Any repair of our fractured world must start with individuals who have the insight and courage to own their own shadow. Nothing "out there" will help if the interior projecting mechanism of humankind is operating strongly. The tendency to see one's shadow "out there" in one's neighbor or in another race or culture is the most dangerous aspect of the modern psyche. It has created two devastating wars in this century and threatens the destruction of all the fine achievements of our modern world. We all decry war but collectively we move toward it. It is not the monsters of the world who make such chaos but the collective shadow to which every one of us has contributed. World War II gave us endless examples of shadow projection. One of the most highly civilized nations on earth, Germany, fell into the idiocy of projecting its virulent shadow on the Jewish people. The world had never seen the equal of this kind of destruction and yet we naively think we have overcome it. At the beginning of the 1990s, with the collapse of the Berlin Wall and a new relationship with the Soviet Union, we entered a brief period of euphoria and were convinced that we had left the dark days behind. It seemed nothing less than a miracle that the shadow projection between the United States and the Soviet Union had subsided, after years of the Cold War. Yet here is an example of what human creativity can do: we unconsciously picked up the energy released from this relationship and put the shadow in another place!

Only months later, we were engaged in another struggle, with terrifying technological power behind it. When the United States went to war in the Persian Gulf, once again we saw the rise of primitive psychology—with both sides projecting devils and demons onto their opponents. This kind of behavior, backed up by nuclear arms, is more than the world can bear. Is there a way to prevent these catastrophic wars, which pit shadow against shadow?

Our Western tradition promises that if even a few people find wholeness, the whole world will be saved. God promised that if just one righteous man could be found in Sodom and Gomorrah, those cities would be spared. We can take this out of its historical context and apply it to our own inner city. Shadow work is probably the only way of aiding the outer city—and creating a more balanced world.

A horrible proverb states that every generation must have its war so that young men can taste the blood and chaos of the battlefield. Our armies and navies have a high place in our society and any parade or military band starts hot blood flowing in the veins of men, young and old. Though I consciously question warfare and its place in an intelligent society, I was not immune to that hot blood when I was in Strasbourg one cold evening. I saw a detachment of the French foreign legion marching down the street with their colorful uniforms, their comraderie, and their jaunty song, and I would have given anything to join them. My own shadow had surfaced and for a moment hot blood completely overruled intelligence and thought.

20   A whole generation can live a modern, civilized life without ever touching much of its shadow nature. Then predictably—twenty years is the alloted time—that unlived shadow will erupt and a war will burst forth that no one wanted but to which everyone—both men and women—has contributed. Apparently, the collective need for shadow expression supersedes the individual determination to contain the dark. And so it happens that an era of disciplined creativity is always followed by an astounding display of annihilation. There are better ways of coping with the shadow, but until they are common knowledge we will continue to have these outbursts in their most destructive form.

Dr. Jung has pointed out that it requires a sophisticated and disciplined society to fight a war as long and complicated as World Wars I and II. He said that primitive people would have tired of their war in a few weeks and gone home. They would not have had a great accumulation of shadow since they live more balanced lives and never venture as far from the center as we do. It was for us civilized people to bring warfare to its high development. And so the greater the civilization, the more intent it is upon its own destruction. God grant that evolution may proceed quickly enough for each of us to pick up our own dark side, combine it with our hard-earned light, and make something better of it all than the opposition of the two. This would be true holiness.

QUESTIONS FOR DISCUSSION

1. In his opening paragraphs, how does Johnson differentiate between the persona, the ego, and the shadow? If any of these terms are unclear to you, look them up in a dictionary of psychological terms or in an unabridged dictionary.

2. Why does Johnson believe that the shadow originated in the sorting of good/bad values within the cultural or civilizing process? What problems does he see developing from this arbitrary sorting process in terms both of modern, multi-cultural society, and within the individual?

3. Why does Johnson believe the religious process can help us heal ourselves and integrate ego with shadow? How does he contrast the religious process with the cultural process and at what periods of life is each dominant?

4. Why does Johnson believe the two world wars were created by "the tendency to see one's shadow 'out there' in one's neighbor or in another race or culture"? Is his reasoning convincing here? Explain your point of view.

5. How does Johnson describe the way our country has tended to "put the shadow in another place" as soon as one enemy or crisis has subsided? What does this suggest to you about the power and persistence of shadow projections?

6. Why does Johnson believe that after 20 years of peace "an era of disciplined creativity is always followed by an astounding display of annihilation"? Does he present a viable alternative to this tendency? Do you think that there is a positive alternative to this phenomenon? What is it?

CONNECTION

Compare and contrast the way that Johnson and Griffin explore the relationships between war and the shadow (see page 418).

IDEAS FOR WRITING

1. Write an essay about a current international conflict or pattern of prejudice that may come from an outward projection of our inner shadow of undesirable qualities onto our enemies. Discuss some of the ways that political propaganda heightens the attachment of shadow qualities to the enemy in the particular conflict that you are analyzing. How do you feel about the conflict and what impact you can have on its outcome?
2. Narrate a dream or an experience in which you felt menaced by a person or symbolic representation that seemed to you to embody your shadow. Did you try to create some balance in yourself after this experience, to become more accepting of the shadow within you? What did you do? Were you successful?

RELATED WEB SITES

SHADOW DANCING

http://www.cgjungpage.org/articles/shadow.html

Read the article, "Meeting Your Secret Self" and Becoming Whole," by Robin Robertson at this web site devoted to Jungian psychology. The essay provides the reader with a Jungian approach to finding "unity with your shadow side."

PRACTICE SHADOW

http://www.spiritualityhealth.com/newsh/items/blank/item_205.html

"By *owning your shadow*, you embrace your full humanity," claims the web site "Spirituality and Health." This URL offers books, articles, and relevant links on how "to make peace with those parts of ourselves that we find to be despicable."

Robert Louis Stevenson

Henry Jekyll's Full Statement of the Case from *The Strange Case of Dr. Jekyll and Mr. Hyde*

Scottish author Robert Louis Stevenson (1850–1894) wrote the short novel The Strange Case of Dr. Jekyll and Mr. Hyde *(1886) at a time when he was very ill with tuberculosis. In the following selection, the conclusion to Stevenson's classic tale*

of good and evil, the character Henry Jekyll, a highly respected London physician, has chemically altered his own inner nature, constructing a morally depraved "second self," Mr. Hyde. The following statement of Dr. Jekyll, written just before his death, sets forth his reasons for and the fatal consequences of tampering with his inner world. The letter was found by his friends who discovered only the body of Mr. Hyde with a crushed phial of cyanide poison in his hand.

JOURNAL

Write about experiencing your "other" or anti-self, through some change in your normal mental state, perhaps from an emotional crisis, chemical stimulation, an illness, or extreme fatigue.

I was born in the year 18_ to a large fortune, endowed besides with excellent parts, inclined by nature to industry, fond of the respect of the wise and good among my fellow-men, and thus, as might have been supposed, with every guarantee of an honourable and distinguished future. And indeed the worst of my faults was a certain impatient gaiety of disposition, such as has made the happiness of many, but such as I found it hard to reconcile with my imperious desire to carry my head high, and wear a more than commonly grave countenance before the public. Hence it came about that I concealed my pleasures; and that when I reached years of reflection, and began to look round me and take stock of my progress and position in the world, I stood already committed to a profound duplicity of life. Many a man would have even blazoned such irregularities as I was guilty of; but from the high views that I had set before me, I regarded and hid them with an almost morbid sense of shame. It was thus rather the exacting nature of my aspirations than any particular degradation in my faults, that made me what I was, and, with even a deeper trench than in the majority of men, severed in me those provinces of good and ill which divide and compound man's dual nature. In this case, I was driven to reflect deeply and inveterately on that hard law of life, which lies at the root of religion and is one of the most plentiful springs of distress. Though so profound a double-dealer, I was in no sense a hypocrite; both sides of me were in dead earnest; I was no more myself when I laid aside restraint and plunged in shame, than when I laboured, in the eye of day, at the furtherance of knowledge or the relief of sorrow and suffering. And it chanced that the direction of my scientific studies, which led wholly towards the mystic and the transcendental, reacted and shed a strong light on this consciousness of the perennial war among my members. With every day, and from both sides of my intelligence, the moral and the intellectual, I thus drew steadily nearer to that truth, by whose partial discovery I have been doomed to such a dreadful shipwreck: that man is not truly one, but truly two. I say two, because the state of my own knowledge does not pass beyond that point. Others will follow, others will outstrip me on the same lines; and I hazard the guess that man will be ultimately known for a mere polity of multifarious, incongruous and independent denizens. I, for my part, from the nature of my life, advanced infallibly in one direction and in one direction only. It was on the moral side, and in my own person, that I learned to recognise the thorough and primitive duality of man; I saw that, of the two natures that contended in the field of my consciousness, even if I could rightly be said to be either, it was only because I was radically both; and from an early date, even before the course of my scientific discoveries had begun to suggest the most naked possibility of such a miracle, I had learned to dwell with pleasure, as a beloved daydream, on the thought of the separation of these elements. If each, I told myself, could be housed in separate identities, life would be relieved of all that was unbearable; the unjust might go his way, delivered from the aspirations and remorse of his more upright twin; and the just could walk steadfastly and securely on his upward path, doing the good things in which he found his pleasure, and no longer exposed to disgrace and penitence by the hands of his extraneous evil. It was the curse of mankind that these incongruous faggots were thus bound together—that in the agonized womb of consciousness, these polar twins should be continuously struggling. How, then, were they dissociated?

I was so far in my reflections when, as I have said, a side light began to shine upon the subject from the laboratory table. I began to perceive more deeply than it has ever yet been stated, the trembling immateriality, the mist-like transience, of this seemingly so solid body in which we walk attired. Certain agents I found to have the power to shake and pluck back that fleshy vestment, even as a wind might toss the curtains of a pavilion. For two good reasons, I will not enter deeply into this scientific branch of my confession. First, because I have been made to learn that the doom and burden of our life is bound for ever on man's shoulders, and when the attempt is made to cast it off, it but returns upon us with more unfamiliar and more awful pressure. Second, because, as my narrative will make, alas! too evident, my discoveries were incomplete. Enough, then, that I not only recognised my natural body from the mere aura and effulgence of certain of the powers that make up my spirit, but managed to compound a drug by which these powers should be dethroned from their supremacy, and a second form and countenance substituted, none the less natural to me because they were the expression, and bore the stamp of lower elements in my soul.

I hesitated long before I put this theory to the test of practice. I knew well that I risked death; for any drug that so potently controlled and shook the very fortress of identity, might, by the least scruple of an overdose or at the least inopportunity in the moment of exhibition, utterly blot out that immaterial tabernacle which I looked to it to change. But the temptation of a discovery so singular and profound at last overcame the suggestions of alarm. I had long since prepared my tincture; I purchased at once, from a firm of wholesale chemists, a large quantity of a particular salt which I knew, from my experiments, to be the last ingredient required; and late one accursed night, I compounded the elements, watched them boil and smoke together in the glass, and when the ebullition had subsided, with a strong glow of courage, drank off the potion.

The most racking pangs succeeded: a grinding in the bones, deadly nausea, and a horror of the spirit that cannot be exceeded at the hour of birth or death. Then these agonies began swiftly to subside, and I came to myself as if out of a great sickness. There was something strange in my sensations, something indescribably new and, from its very novelty, incredibly sweet. I felt younger, lighter, happier in body; within I was conscious of a heady recklessness, a current of disordered sensual images running like a millrace in my fancy, a dissolution of the bonds of obligation, an unknown but not an innocent freedom of the soul. I knew myself, at the first breath of this new life, to be more wicked, tenfold more wicked, sold a slave to my original evil; and the thought, in that moment, braced and delighted me like wine. I stretched out my hands, exulting in the freshness of these sensations; and in the act, I was suddenly aware that I had lost in stature.

5   There was no mirror, at that date, in my room; that which stands beside me as I write, was brought there later on and for the very purpose of these transformations. That night, however, was far gone into the morning—the morning, black as it was, was nearly ripe for the conception of the day—the inmates of my house were locked in the most rigorous hours of slumber, and I determined, flushed as I was with hope and triumph, to venture in my new shape as far as to my bedroom. I crossed the yard, wherein the constellations looked down upon me, I could have thought, with wonder, the first creature of that sort that their unsleeping vigilance had yet disclosed to them; I stole through the corridors, a stranger in my own house; and coming to my room, I saw for the first time the appearance of Edward Hyde.

I must here speak by theory alone, saying not that which I know, but that which I suppose to be most probable. The evil side of my nature, to which I had now transferred the stamping efficacy, was less robust and less developed than the good which I had just deposed. Again, in the course of my life, which had been, after all, nine tenths a life of effort, virtue and control, it had been much less exercised and much less exhausted. And hence, as I think, it came about that Edward Hyde was so much smaller, slighter and younger than Henry Jekyll. Even as good shone upon the countenance of the one, evil was written broadly and plainly on the face of the other. Evil besides (which I must still believe to be the lethal side of man) had left on that body an imprint of deformity and decay. And yet when I looked upon that ugly idol in the glass, I was conscious of no repugnance, rather of a leap of welcome. This, too, was myself. It seemed natural and human. In my eyes it bore a livelier image of the spirit, it seemed more express and single, than the imperfect and divided countenance I had been hitherto accustomed to call mine. And in so far I was doubtless right. I have observed that when I wore the semblance of Edward Hyde, none could come near to me at first without a visible misgiving of the flesh. This, as I take it, was because all human beings, as we meet them, are commingled out of good and evil: and Edward Hyde, alone in the ranks of mankind, was pure evil.

I lingered but a moment at the mirror: the second and conclusive experiment had yet to be attempted; it yet remained to be seen if I had lost my identity beyond redemption and must flee before daylight from a house that was no longer mine; and hurrying back to my cabinet, I once more prepared and drank the cup, once more suffered the pangs of dissolution, and came to myself once more with the character, the stature and the face of Henry Jekyll.

That night I had come to the fatal crossroads. Had I approached my discovery in a more noble spirit, had I risked the experiment while under the empire of generous or pious aspirations, all must have been otherwise, and from these agonies of death and birth, I had come forth an angel instead of a fiend. The drug had no discriminating action; it was neither diabolical nor divine; it but shook the doors of the prisonhouse of my disposition; and like the captives of Phillipi, that which stood within ran forth. At that time my virtue slumbered; my evil, kept awake by ambition, was alert and swift to seize the occasion; and the thing that was projected was Edward Hyde. Hence, although I had now two characters as well as two appearances, one was wholly evil, and the other was still the old Henry Jekyll, that incongruous compound of whose reformation and improvement I had already learned to despair. The movement was thus wholly toward the worse.

Even at that time, I had not conquered my aversion to the dryness of a life of study. I would still be merrily disposed at times; and as my pleasures were (to say the least) undignified, and I was not only well known and highly considered, but growing toward the elderly man, this incoherency of my life was daily growing more unwelcome. It was on this side that my new power tempted me until I fell in slavery. I had but to drink the cup, to doff at once the body of the noted professor, and to assume, like a thick cloak, that of Edward Hyde. I smiled at the notion; it seemed to me at the time to be humorous; and I made my preparations with the most studious care. I took and furnished that house in Soho, to which Hyde was tracked by the police; and engaged as a housekeeper a creature whom I knew well to be silent and unscrupulous. On the other side, I announced to my servants that a Mr. Hyde (whom I described) was to have full liberty and power about my house in the square; and to parry mishaps, I even called and made myself a familiar object, in my second character. I next drew up that will to which you so much objected; so that if anything befell me in the person of Dr. Jekyll, I could enter on that of Edward Hyde without pecuniary loss. And thus fortified, as I supposed, on every side, I began to profit by the strange immunities of my position.

10   Men have before hired bravoes to transact their crimes, while their own person and reputation sat under shelter. I was the first that ever did so for his pleasures. I was the first that could plod in the public eye with a load of genial respectability, and in a moment, like a schoolboy, strip off these lendings and spring headlong into the sea of liberty. But for me, in my impenetrable mantle, the safety was complete. Think of it—I did not even exist! Let me but escape into my laboratory door, give me but a second or two to mix and swallow the draught that I had always standing ready; and whatever he had done, Edward

Hyde would pass away like the stain of breath upon a mirror; and there in his stead, quietly at home, trimming the midnight lamp in his study, a man who could afford to laugh at suspicion, would be Henry Jekyll.

The pleasures which I made haste to seek in my disguise were, as I have said, undignified; I would scarce use a harder term. But in the hands of Edward Hyde, they soon began to turn toward the monstrous. When I would come back from these excursions, I was often plunged into a kind of wonder at my vicarious depravity. This familiar that I called out of my own soul, and sent forth alone to do his good pleasure, was a being inherently malign and villainous; his every act and thought centered on self; drinking pleasure with bestial avidity from any degree of torture to another; relentless like a man of stone. Henry Jekyll stood at times aghast before the acts of Edward Hyde; but the situation was apart from ordinary laws, and insidiously relaxed the grasp of conscience. It was Hyde, after all, and Hyde alone, that was guilty. Jekyll was no worse; he woke again to his good qualities seemingly unimpaired; he would even make haste, where it was possible, to undo the evil done by Hyde. And thus his conscience slumbered.

Into the details of the infamy at which I thus connived (for even now I can scarce grant that I committed it) I have no design of entering; I mean but to point out the warnings and the successive steps with which my chastisement approached. I met with one accident which, as it brought on no consequence, I shall no more than mention. An act of cruelty to a child aroused against me the anger of a passerby, whom I recognised the other day in the person of your kinsman; the doctor and the child's family joined him; there were moments when I feared for my life; and at last, in order to pacify their too just resentment, Edward Hyde had to bring them to the door, and pay them in a cheque drawn in the name of Henry Jekyll. But this danger was easily eliminated from the future, by opening an account at another bank in the name of Edward Hyde himself; and when, by sloping my own hand backward, I had supplied my double with a signature, I thought I sat beyond the reach of fate.

Some two months before the murder of Sir Danvers, I had been out for one of my adventures, had returned at a late hour, and woke the next day in bed with somewhat odd sensations. It was in vain I looked about me; in vain I saw the decent furniture and tall proportions of my room in the square; in vain that I recognised the pattern of the bed curtains and the design of the mahogany frame; something still kept insisting that I was not where I was, that I had not wakened where I seemed to be, but in the little room in Soho where I was accustomed to sleep in the body of Edward Hyde. I smiled to myself, and, in my psychological way, began lazily to inquire into the elements of this illusion, occasionally, even as I did so, dropping back into a comfortable morning doze. I was still so engaged when, in one of my more wakeful moments, my eyes fell upon my hand. Now the hand of Henry Jekyll (as you have often remarked) was professional in shape and size: it was large, firm, white and comely. But the hand which I now saw, clearly enough, in the yellow light of a mid-London morning, lying half shut on the bedclothes, was lean, corded, knuckly, of a dusky pallor and thickly shaded with a swart growth of hair. It was the hand of Edward Hyde.

I must have stared upon it for near half a minute, sunk as I was in the mere stupidity of wonder, before terror woke up in my breast as sudden and startling as the crash of cymbals; and bounding from my bed, I rushed to the mirror. At the sight that met my eyes, my blood was changed into something exquisitely thin and icy. Yes, I had gone to bed Henry Jekyll, I had awakened Edward Hyde. How was this to be explained? I asked myself; and then, with another bound of terror—how was it to be remedied? It was well on in the morning; the servants were up; all my drugs were in the cabinet—a long journey down two pairs of stairs, through the back passage, across the open court and through the anatomical theatre, from where I was then standing horror-struck. It might indeed be possible to cover my face; but of what use was that, when I was unable to conceal the alteration in my stature? And then with an overpowering sweetness of relief, it came back upon my mind that the servants were already used to the coming and going of my second self. I had soon dressed, as well as I was able, in clothes of my own size; had soon passed through the house, where Bradshaw stared and drew back at seeing Mr. Hyde at such an hour and in such a strange array; and ten minutes later, Dr. Jekyll had returned to his own shape and was sitting down, with a darkened brow, to make a feint of breakfasting.

15 Small indeed was my appetite. This inexplicable incident, this reversal of my previous experience, seemed, like the Babylonian finger on the wall, to be spelling out the letters of my judgment; and I began to reflect more seriously than ever before on the issues and possibilities of my double existence. That part of me which I had the power of projecting, had lately been much exercised and nourished; it had seemed to me of late as though the body of Edward Hyde had grown in stature, as though (when I wore that form) I were conscious of a more generous tide of blood, and I began to spy a danger that, if this were much prolonged, the balance of my nature might be permanently overthrown, the power of voluntary change be forfeited, and the character of Edward Hyde become irrevocably mine. The power of the drug had not been always equally displayed. Once, very early in my career, it had totally failed me; since then I had been obliged on more than one occasion to double, and once, with infinite risk of death, to treble the amount; and these rare uncertainties had cast hitherto the sole shadow on my contentment. Now, however, and in the light of that morning's accident, I was led to remark that whereas, in the beginning, the difficulty had been to throw off the body of Jekyll, it had of late gradually but decidedly transferred itself to the other side. All things therefore seemed to point to this: that I was slowly losing hold of my original and better self, and becoming slowly incorporated with my second and worse.

Between these two, I now felt I had to choose. My two natures had memory in common, but all other faculties were most unequally shared between them. Jekyll (who was composite) now with the most sensitive apprehensions, now with a greedy gusto, projected and shared in the pleasures and adventures of

Hyde; but Hyde was indifferent to Jekyll, or but remembered him as the mountain bandit remembers the cavern in which he conceals himself from pursuit. Jekyll had more than a father's interest; Hyde had more than a son's indifference. To cast in my lot with Jekyll, was to die to those appetites which I had long secretly indulged and had of late begun to pamper. To cast it in with Hyde, was to die to a thousand interests and aspirations, and to become, at a blow and forever, despised and friendless. The bargain might appear unequal; but there was still another consideration in the scales; for while Jekyll would suffer smartingly in the fires of abstinence, Hyde would be not even conscious of all that he had lost. Strange as my circumstances were, the terms of this debate are as old and commonplace as man; much the same inducements and alarms cast the die for any tempted and trembling sinner; and it fell out with me, as it falls with so vast a majority of my fellows, that I chose the better part and was found wanting in the strength to keep to it.

Yes, I preferred the elderly and discontented doctor, surrounded by friends and cherishing honest hopes; and bade a resolute farewell to the liberty, the comparative youth, the light step, leaping impulses and secret pleasures, that I had enjoyed in the disguise of Hyde. I made this choice perhaps with some unconscious reservation, for I neither gave up the house in Soho, nor destroyed the clothes of Edward Hyde, which still lay ready in my cabinet. For two months, however, I was true to my determination; for two months, I led a life of such severity as I had never before attained to, and enjoyed the compensations of an approving conscience. But time began at last to obliterate the freshness of my alarm; the praises of conscience began to grow into a thing of course; I began to be tortured with throes and longings, as of Hyde struggling after freedom; and at last, in an hour of moral weakness, I once again compounded and swallowed the transforming draught.

I do not suppose that, when a drunkard reasons with himself upon his vice, he is once out of five hundred times affected by the dangers that he runs through his brutish, physical insensibility; neither had I, long as I had considered my position, made enough allowance for the complete moral insensibility and insensate readiness to evil, which were the leading characters of Edward Hyde. Yet it was by these that I was punished. My devil had been long caged, he came out roaring. I was conscious, even when I took the draught, of a more unbridled, a more furious propensity to ill. It must have been this, I suppose, that stirred in my soul that tempest of impatience with which I listened to the civilities of my unhappy victim; I declare, at least, before God, no man morally sane could have been guilty of that crime upon so pitiful a provocation; and that I struck in no more reasonable spirit than that in which a sick child may break a plaything. But I had voluntarily stripped myself of all those balancing instincts by which even the worst of us continues to walk with some degree of steadiness among temptations and in my case, to be tempted, however slightly, was to fall.

Instantly the spirit of hell awoke in me and raged. With a transport of glee, I mauled the unresisting body, tasting delight from every blow; and it was not till weariness had begun to succeed, that I was suddenly, in the top fit of my delirium, struck through the heart by a cold thrill of terror. A mist dispersed; I saw my life to be forfeit; and fled from the scene of these excesses, at once glorying and trembling, my lust of evil gratified and stimulated, my love of life screwed to the topmost peg. I ran to the house in Soho, and (to make assurance doubly sure) destroyed my papers; thence I set out through the lamplit streets, in the same divided ecstasy of mind, gloating on my crime, light-headedly devising others in the future, and yet still hastening and still hearkening in my wake for the steps of the avenger. Hyde had a song upon his lips as he compounded the draught, and as he drank it, pledged the dead man. The pangs of transformation had not done tearing him, before Henry Jekyll, with streaming tears of gratitude and remorse, had fallen upon his knees and lifted his clasped hands to God. The veil of self-indulgence was rent from head to foot. I saw my life as a whole: I followed it up from the days of childhood, when I had walked with my father's hand, and through the self-denying toils of my professional life, to arrive again and again, with the same sense of unreality, at the damned horrors of the evening. I could have screamed aloud, I sought with tears and prayers to smother down the crowd of hideous images and sounds with which my memory swarmed against me; and still, between the petitions, the ugly face of my iniquity stared into my soul. As the acuteness of this remorse began to die away, it was succeeded by a sense of joy. The problem of my conduct was solved. Hyde was thenceforth impossible; whether I would or not, I was now confined to the better part of my existence; and O, how I rejoiced to think of it! with what willing humility I embraced anew the restrictions of natural life! with what sincere renunciation I locked the door by which I had so often gone and come, and ground the key under my heel!

20   The next day, came the news that the murder had been overlooked, that the guilt of Hyde was patent to the world, and that the victim was a man high in public estimation. It was not only a crime, it had been a tragic folly. I think I was glad to know it; I think I was glad to have my better impulses thus buttressed and guarded by the terrors of the scaffold. Jekyll was now my city of refuge; let but Hyde peep out an instant, and the hands of all men would be raised to take and slay him.

I resolved in my future conduct to redeem the past; and I can say with honesty that my resolve was fruitful of some good. You know yourself how earnestly, in the last months of the last year, I laboured to relieve suffering; you know that much was done for others, and that the days passed quietly, almost happily for myself. Nor can I truly say that I wearied of this beneficent and innocent life; I think instead that I daily enjoyed it more completely; but I was still cursed with my duality of purpose; and as the first edge of my penitence wore off, the lower side of me, so long indulged, so recently chained down, began to growl for licence. Not that I dreamed of resuscitating Hyde; the bare idea of that would startle me to frenzy; no, it was in my own person that I was once more tempted to trifle with my conscience; and it was as an ordinary secret sinner that I at last fell before the assaults of temptation.

There comes an end to all things; the most capacious measure is filled at last; and this brief condescension to my evil finally destroyed the balance of my soul. And yet I was not alarmed; the fall seemed natural, like a return to the old days before I had made my discovery. It was a fine, clear, January day, wet under foot where the frost had melted, but cloudless overhead; and the Regent's Park was full of winter chirrupings and sweet with spring odours. I sat in the sun on a bench; the animal within me licking the chops of memory; the spiritual side a little drowsed, promising subsequent penitence, but not yet moved to begin. After all, I reflected, I was like my neighbours; and then I smiled, comparing myself with other men, comparing my active goodwill with the lazy cruelty of their neglect. And at the very moment of that vainglorious thought, a qualm came over me, a horrid nausea and the most deadly shuddering. These passed away, and left me faint; and then, as in its turn faintness subsided, I began to be aware of a change in the temper of my thoughts, a greater boldness, a contempt of danger, a solution of the bonds of obligation. I looked down; my clothes hung formlessly on my shrunken limbs; the hand that lay on my knee was corded and hairy. I was once more Edward Hyde. A moment before I had been safe of all men's respect, wealthy, beloved—the cloth laying for me in the dining-room at home; and now I was the common quarry of mankind, hunted, house-less, a known murderer, thrall to the gallows.

My reason wavered, but it did not fail me utterly. I have more than once observed that, in my second character, my faculties seemed sharpened to a point and my spirits more tensely elastic; thus it came about that, where Jekyll perhaps might have succumbed, Hyde rose to the importance of the moment. My drugs were in one of the presses of my cabinet; how was I to reach them? That was the problem that (crushing my temples in my hands) I set to myself to solve. The laboratory door I had closed. If I sought to enter by the house, my own servants would consign me to the gallows. I saw I must employ another hand, and thought of Lanyon. How was he to be reached? how persuaded? Suppose that I escaped capture in the streets, how was I to make my way into his presence? and how should I, an unknown and displeasing visitor, prevail on the famous physician to rifle the study of his colleague, Dr. Jekyll? Then I remembered that of my original character, one part remained to me: I could write my own hand; and once I had conceived that kindling spark, the way that I must follow became lighted up from end to end.

Thereupon, I arranged my clothes as best I could, and summoning a passing hansom, drove to an hotel in Portland Street, the name of which I chanced to remember. At my appearance (which was indeed comical enough, however tragic a fate these garments covered) the driver could not conceal his mirth. I gnashed my teeth upon him with a gust of devilish fury; and the smile withered from his face—happily for him—yet more happily for myself, for in another instant I had certainly dragged him from his perch. At the inn, as I entered, I looked about me with so black a countenance as made the attendants tremble, not a look did they exchange in my presence; but obsequiously took my orders, led me to a private room, and brought me wherewithal to write. Hyde in danger of his life was a creature new to me; shaken with inordinate anger, strung to the pitch of murder, lusting to inflict pain. Yet the creature was astute; mastered his fury with a great effort of the will; composed his two important letters, one to Lanyon and one to Poole; and that he might receive actual evidence of their being posted, sent them out with directions that they should be registered. Thenceforward, he sat all day over the fire in the private room, gnawing his nails; there he dined, sitting alone with his fears, the waiter visibly quailing before his eye; and thence, when the night was fully come, he set forth in the corner of a closed cab, and was driven to and fro about the streets of the city. He, I say—I cannot say, I. That child of Hell had nothing human; nothing lived in him but fear and hatred. And when at last, thinking the driver had begun to grow suspicious, he discharged the cab and ventured on foot, attired in his misfitting clothes, an object marked out for observation, into the midst of the nocturnal passengers, these two base passions raged within him like a tempest. He walked fast, hunted by his fears, chattering to himself, skulking through the less frequented thoroughfares, counting the minutes that still divided him from midnight. Once a woman spoke to him, offering, I think, a box of lights. He smote her in the face, and she fled.

25   When I came to myself at Lanyon's, the horror of my old friend perhaps affected me somewhat: I do not know; it was at least but a drop in the sea to the abhorrence with which I looked back upon these hours. A change had come over me. It was no longer the fear of the gallows, it was the horror of being Hyde that racked me. I received Lanyon's condemnation partly in a dream; it was partly in a dream that I came home to my own house and got into bed. I slept after the prostration of the day, with a stringent and profound slumber which not even in the nightmares that wrung me could avail to break. I awoke in the morning shaken, weakened, but refreshed. I still hated and feared the thought of the brute that slept within me, and I had not of course forgotten the appalling dangers of the day before; but I was once more at home, in my own house and close to my drugs; and gratitude for my escape shone so strong in my soul that it almost rivalled the brightness of hope.

I was stepping leisurely across the court after breakfast, drinking the chill of the air with pleasure, when I was seized again with those indescribable sensations that heralded the change; and I had but the time to gain the shelter of my cabinet, before I was once again raging and freezing with the passions of Hyde. It took on this occasion a double dose to recall me to myself; and alas! six hours after, as I sat looking sadly in the fire, the pangs returned, and the drug had to be re-administered. In short, from that day forth it seemed only by a great effort as of gymnastics, and only under the immediate stimulation of the drug, that I was able to wear the countenance of Jekyll. At all hours of the day and night, I would be taken with the premonitory shudder; above all, if I slept, or even dozed for a moment in my chair, it was always as Hyde that I awakened. Under the strain of this continually impending doom and by the sleeplessness to which I now condemned myself, ay, even beyond what I had thought possible to man, I became, in my own person, a creature eaten up and emptied by fever, languidly weak both in body and mind, and solely occupied by one thought: the horror of my other self. But when I slept, or when the virtue of the medicine wore off, I would leap almost without transition (for the pangs of transformation grew daily less marked) into the possession of a fancy brimming with images of terror, a soul boiling with causeless hatreds, and a body that seemed not strong enough to contain the raging energies of life. The powers of Hyde seemed to have grown with the sickliness of Jekyll. And certainly the hate that now divided them was equal on each side. With Jekyll, it was a thing of vital instinct. He had now seen the full deformity of that creature that shared with him some of the phenomena of consciousness, and was co-heir with him to death: and beyond these links of community, which in themselves made the most poignant part of his distress, he thought of Hyde, for all his energy of life, as of something not only hellish but inorganic. This was the shocking thing; that the slime of the pit seemed to utter cries and voices; that the amorphous dust gesticulated and sinned; that what was dead, and had no shape, should usurp the offices of life. And this again, that that insurgent horror was knit to him closer than a wife, closer than an eye; lay caged in his flesh, where he heard it mutter and felt it struggle to be born; and at every hour of weakness, and in the confidence of slumber, prevailed against him, and deposed him out of life. The hatred of Hyde for Jekyll was of a different order. His terror of the gallows drove him continually to commit temporary suicide, and return to his subordinate station of a part instead of a person; but he loathed the necessity, he loathed the despondency into which Jekyll was now fallen, and he resented the dislike with which he was himself regarded. Hence the apelike tricks that he would play me, scrawling in my own hand blasphemies on the pages of my books, burning the letters and destroying the portrait of my father; and indeed, had it not been for his fear of death, he would long ago have ruined himself in order to involve me in the ruin. But his love of life is wonderful; I go further: I, who sicken and freeze at the mere thought of him, when I recall the abjection and passion of this attachment, and when I know how he fears my power to cut him off by suicide, I find it in my heart to pity him.

It is useless, and the time awfully fails me, to prolong this description; no one has ever suffered such torments, let that suffice; and yet even to these, habit brought—no, not alleviation—but a certain callousness of soul, a certain acquiescence of despair; and my punishment might have gone on for years, but for the last calamity which has now fallen, and which has finally severed me from my own face and nature. My provision of the salt, which had never been renewed since the date of the first experiment, began to run low. I sent out for a fresh supply and mixed the draught; the ebullition followed, and the first change of colour, not the second; I drank it and it was without efficacy. You will learn from Poole how I have had London ransacked; it was in vain; and I am now persuaded that my first supply was impure, and that it was that unknown impurity which lent efficacy to the draught.

About a week has passed, and I am now finishing this statement under the influence of the last of the old powders. This, then, is the last time, short of a miracle, that Henry Jekyll can think his own thoughts or see his own face (now how sadly altered!) in the glass. Nor must I delay too long to bring my writing to an end; for if my narrative has hitherto escaped destruction, it has been by a combination of great prudence and great good luck. Should the throes of change take me in the act of writing it, Hyde will tear it in pieces; but if some time shall have elapsed after I have laid it by, his wonderful selfishness and circumscription to the moment will probably save it once again from the action of his ape-like spite. And indeed the doom that is closing on us both has already changed and crushed him. Half an hour from now, when I shall again and forever reindue that hated personality, I know how I shall sit shuddering and weeping in my chair, or continue, with the most strained and fearstruck ecstasy of listening, to pace up and down this room (my last earthly refuge) and give ear to every sound of menace. Will Hyde die upon the scaffold? or will he find courage to release himself at the last moment? God knows; I am careless; this is my true hour of death, and what is to follow concerns another than myself. Here then, as I lay down the pen and proceed to seal up my confession, I bring the life of that unhappy Henry Jekyll to an end.

QUESTIONS FOR DISCUSSION

1. What strengths, faults, and inner divisions of character does Jekyll describe in the first paragraph of the narrative? Why does he feel a need to conceal his pleasures?

2. Upon what fantasy or "beloved daydream" does Jekyll come to dwell? Why does he become so obsessed with this fantasy? What does he invent to make his fantasy a reality? Is his invention a success?

3. What are the differences in appearance, stature, power, and age between Dr. Jekyll and Mr. Hyde? How do these physical distinctions underscore symbolically the differences in their characters as well as the flaws in Dr. Jekyll's original character and the folly of artificially separating the two parts of the self?

4. How does Jekyll first respond to the changes in his character? How does his response and the nature of the control over the double personality gradually change? What difficulty does he experience in deciding which of his sides to finally repress?

5. Why is Jekyll unable to stick with his decision to refrain from doubling his personality? When he again reverts to Hyde, how has Hyde changed? What crime does Hyde perform, and how does Jekyll react to the crime? How does he attempt to reform himself? Under what circumstances does Hyde emerge a final time? How would you explain the mutual loathing that each side now feels for the other?

6. From the evidence in the letter, which side of the personality do you think killed Mr. Hyde: Hyde himself, in an act of suicide, or Jekyll, in an act of combined murder/suicide of both sides of his personality? Explain your response using references to the text.

CONNECTION

Analyze this story in light of Susan Griffin's ideas about the relationship between people's belief in a double-sided nature and the mind-body split (see
page 418).

IDEAS FOR WRITING

1. After reading the entire text of *The Strange Case of Doctor Jekyll and Mr. Hyde*,
   write an essay in which you interpret the story as a criticism of rigid social
   conventions and moral standards of acceptable or unacceptable, good or
   bad behavior. In what ways does the story suggest that such strict standards can heighten the division between an individual's good and bad side,
   the main self and the double or shadow self?

2. This story concerns the dual nature of the human psyche, the struggle between our good side and our bad side, between the conscious mind and
   the unthinking appetites of the body. What do you think can be done to
   ease such a struggle? Write a paper in which you argue for an approach to
   life that would help to heal the split between potential Jekyll and Hyde
   personalities within the human psyche.

RELATED WEB SITES

THE ROBERT LOUIS STEVENSON WEBSITE

http://www.esterni.unibg.it/siti_esterni/rls/rls.htm

A biography, bibliography, texts, images, associations, derivative works, mu-
seums, and events on Robert Louis Stevenson can all be found at this extensive web site devoted to the author.

DOCTOR JEKYLL AND MR. HYDE

http://www.novelguide.com/dr.jekyllandmr.hyde/

This useful web site provides a chapter-by-chapter book analysis, character pro-
files, theme analysis, an author biography, and even a "Top Ten Quotes" section.

Shelby Steele

Being Black and Feeling Blue

*Shelby Steele was born in Chicago in 1946. His parents were active in the civil rights
movement, and Steele grew up with a keen sense of the realities of racial conflict and
injustice. He received a Ph.D. in English at the University of Utah in 1974, and is a
professor of English at San Jose State University in California. His essays on self-*

esteem and social status among African-Americans have appeared in many magazines and newspapers. His first book The Content of Our Character: A New Vision of Race in America *(1990) has been a controversial best-seller because of its focus on what Steele perceives as a sort of victim complex, based on past racism, that makes it more difficult for African-Americans to achieve success. Steele's most recent book,* A Dream Deferred: The Second Betrayal of Black Freedom in America *(1998), continues and updates his critique of contemporary race relations in America. The following excerpt from* The Content of Our Character *explores how many African-Americans experience an "anti-self" as a result of generations of racial oppression.*

JOURNAL

Steele develops the concept of an "anti-self" in his selection. Before reading it, think about whether you feel you have an anti-self. Present an example to illustrate the power of that side of your personality.

In the early seventies when I was in graduate school, I went out for a beer late one afternoon with another black graduate student whom I'd only known casually before. This student was older than I—a stint in the army had interrupted his education—and he had the reputation of being bright and savvy, of having applied street smarts to the business of getting through graduate school. I suppose I was hoping for what would be called today a little mentoring. But it is probably not wise to drink with someone when you are enamored of his reputation, and it was not long before we stumbled into a moment that seemed to transform him before my very eyes. I asked him what he planned to do when he finished his Ph.D., fully expecting to hear of high aspirations matched with shrewd perceptions on how to reach them. But before he could think, he said with a kind of exhausted sincerity, "Man, I just want to hold on, get a job that doesn't work me too hard, and do a lot of fishing." Was he joking, I asked. "Hell, no," he said with exaggerated umbrage. "I'm not into it like the white boys. I don't need what they need."

I will call this man Henry and report that, until five or six years ago when I lost track of him, he was doing exactly as he said he would do. With much guile and little ambition he had moved through a succession of low-level administrative and teaching jobs, mainly in black studies programs. Of course, it is no crime to just "hold on," and it is hardly a practice limited to blacks. Still, in Henry's case there was truly a troubling discrepancy between his ambition and a fine intelligence recognized by all who knew him. But in an odd way this intelligence was more lateral than vertical, and I would say that it was rechanneled by a certain unseen fear into the business of merely holding on. It would be easy to say that Henry had simply decided on life in a slower lane than he was capable of traveling in, or that he was that rare person who had achieved ambitionless contentment. But if this was so, Henry would have had wisdom rather than savvy, and he would not have felt the need to carry himself with more self-importance than his station justified. I don't think Henry was uninterested in ambition; I think he was afraid of it.

It is certainly true that there is a little of Henry in most people. My own compulsion to understand him informs me that I must have seen many elements of myself in him. And though I'm sure he stands for a universal human blockage, I also believe that there is something in the condition of being black in America that makes the kind of hesitancy he represents one of black America's most serious and debilitating problems. As Henry reached the very brink of expanded opportunity, with Ph.D. in hand, he diminished his ambition almost as though his degree delivered him to a kind of semiretirement. I don't think blacks in general have any illusions about semiretirement, but I do think that, as a group, we have hesitated on the brink of new opportunities that we made enormous sacrifices to win for ourselves. The evidence of this lies in one of the most tragic social ironies of late twentieth-century American life: as black Americans have gained in equality and opportunity, we have also declined in relation to whites, so that by many socioeconomic measures we are further behind whites today than before the great victories of the civil rights movement. By one report, even the black middle class, which had made great gains in the seventies, began to lose ground to its white counterpart in the eighties. Most distressing of all, the black underclass continues to expand rather than shrink.

Of course, I don't suggest that Henry's peculiar inertia singularly explains social phenomena so complex and tragic. I do believe, however, that blacks in general are susceptible to the same web of attitudes and fears that kept Henry beneath his potential, and that our ineffectiveness in taking better advantage of our greater opportunity has much to do with this. I think there is a specific form of racial anxiety that all blacks are vulnerable to that can, in situations where we must engage the mainstream society, increase our self-doubt and undermine our confidence so that we often back away from the challenges that, if taken, would advance us. I believe this hidden racial anxiety may well now be the strongest barrier to our full participation in the American mainstream; that it is as strong or stronger even than the discrimination we still face. To examine this racial anxiety, allow me first to look at how the Henry was born in me.

5   Until the sixth grade, I attended a segregated school in a small working-class black suburb of Chicago. The school was a dumping ground for teachers with too little competence or mental stability to teach in the white school in our district. In 1956, when I entered the sixth grade, I encountered a new addition to the menagerie of misfits that was our faculty—an ex-Marine whose cruelty was suggested during our first lunch hour when he bit the cap off his Coke bottle and spit it into the wastebasket. Looking back I can see that there was no interesting depth to the cruelty he began to show us almost immediately—no consumptive hatred, no intelligent malevolence. Although we were all black and he was white, I don't think he was even particularly racist. He had obviously needed us to like him though he had no faith that we would. He ran the class like a gang leader, picking favorites one day and banishing them the next. And then there was a permanent pool of outsiders, myself among them,

who were made to carry the specific sins that he must have feared most in himself.

The sin I was made to carry was the sin of stupidity. I misread a sentence on the first day of school, and my fate was sealed. He made my stupidity a part of the classroom lore, and very quickly I in fact became stupid. I all but lost the ability to read and found the simplest math beyond me. His punishments for my errors rose in meanness until one day he ordered me to pick up all of the broken glass on the playground with my bare hands. Of course, this would have to be the age of the pop bottle, and there were sections of this playground that glared like a mirror in sunlight. After half an hour's labor I sat down on strike, more out of despair than rebellion.

Again, cruelty was no more than a vibration in this man, and so without even a show of anger he commandeered a bicycle, handed it to an eighth-grader— one of his lieutenants—and told the boy to run me around the school grounds "until he passes out." The boy was also given a baseball bat to "use on him when he slows down." I ran two laps, about a mile, and then pretended to pass out. The eighth-grader knew I was playing possum but could not bring himself to hit me and finally rode off. I exited the school yard through an adjoining corn-field and never returned.

I mention this experience as an example of how one's innate capacity for in-security is expanded and deepened, of how a disbelieving part of the self is brought to life and forever joined to the believing self. As children we are all wounded in some way and to some degree by the wild world we encounter. From these wounds a disbelieving *anti-self* is born, an internal antagonist and saboteur that embraces the world's negative view of us, that believes our wounds are justified by our own unworthiness, and that entrenches itself as a lifelong voice of doubt. This anti-self is a hidden aggressive force that scours the world for fresh evidence of our unworthiness. When the believing self announces its aspirations, the anti-self always argues against them, but never on their merits (this is a healthy function of the believing self). It argues instead against our worthiness to pursue these aspirations and, by its lights, we are never worthy of even our smallest dreams. The mission of the anti-self is to deflate the believing self and, thus, draw it down into inertia, passivity, and faithlessness.

The anti-self is the unseen agent of low self-esteem; it is a catalytic energy that tries to induce low self-esteem in the believing self as though it were the complete truth of the personality. The anti-self can only be contained by the strength of the believing self, and this is where one's early environment be-comes crucial. If the childhood environment is stable and positive, the family whole and loving, the schools good, the community safe, then the believing self will be reinforced and made strong. If the family is shattered, the schools indif-ferent, the neighborhood a mine field of dangers, the anti-self will find evi-dence everywhere with which to deflate the believing self.

10   This does not mean that a bad childhood cannot be overcome. But it does mean—as I have experienced and observed—that one's *capacity* for self-doubt and self-belief are roughly the same from childhood on, so that years later

when the believing self may have strengthened enough to control the anti-self, one will still have the same capacity for doubt whether or not one has the *actual* doubt. I think it is this struggle between our capacities for doubt and belief that gives our personalities one of their peculiar tensions and, in this way, marks our character.

My own anti-self was given new scope and power by this teacher's persecution, and it was so successful in deflating my believing self that I secretly vowed never to tell my parents what was happening to me. The anti-self had all but sold my believing self on the idea that I was stupid, and I did not want to feel that shame before my parents. It was my brother who finally told them, and his disclosure led to a boycott that closed the school and eventually won the dismissal of my teacher and several others. But my anti-self transformed even this act of rescue into a cause of shame—if there wasn't something wrong with me, why did I have to be rescued? The anti-self follows only the logic of self-condemnation.

But there was another dimension to this experience that my anti-self was only too happy to seize upon. It was my race that landed me in this segregated school and, as many adults made clear to me, my persecution followed a timeless pattern of racial persecution. The implications of this were rich food for the anti-self—my race was so despised that it had to be segregated; as a black my education was so unimportant that even unbalanced teachers without college degrees were adequate; ignorance and cruelty that would be intolerable in a classroom of whites was perfectly all right in a classroom of blacks. The anti-self saw no injustice in any of this, but instead took it all as confirmation of a racial inferiority that it could now add to the well of personal doubt I already had. When the adults thought they were consoling me—*"Don't worry. They treat all blacks this way"*—they were also deepening the wound and expanding my capacity for doubt.

And this is the point. The condition of being black in America means that one will likely endure more wounds to one's self-esteem than others and that the capacity for self-doubt born of these wounds will be compounded and expanded by the black race's reputation of inferiority. The anti-self will most likely have more ammunition with which to deflate the believing self and its aspirations. And the universal human struggle to have belief win out over doubt will be more difficult.

More than difficult, it is also made inescapable by the fact of skin color, which, in America, works as a visual invocation of the problem. Black skin has more dehumanizing stereotypes associated with it than any other skin color in America, if not the world. When a black presents himself in an integrated situation, he knows that his skin alone may bring these stereotypes to life in the minds of those he meets and that he, as an individual, may be diminished by his race before he has a chance to reveal a single aspect of his personality. By the symbology of color that operates in our culture, black skin accuses him of inferiority. Under the weight of this accusation, a black will almost certainly doubt himself on some level and to some degree. The ever-vigilant anti-self will grab this racial doubt and mix it into the pool of personal doubt, so that when a black walks into an integrated situation—a largely white college campus, an employment office, a business lunch—he will be vulnerable to the entire realm of his self-doubt before a single word is spoken.

15   This constitutes an intense and lifelong racial vulnerability and anxiety for blacks. Even though a white American may have been wounded more than a given black, and therefore have a larger realm of inner doubt, his white skin, with its connotations of privilege and superiority, will actually help protect him from that doubt and from the undermining power of his anti-self, at least in relations with blacks. In fact, the larger the realm of doubt, the more he may be tempted to rely on his white skin for protection from it. Certainly in every self-avowed white racist, whether businessman or member of the Klan, there is a huge realm of self-contempt and doubt that hides behind the mythology of white skin. The mere need to pursue self-esteem through skin color suggests there is no faith that it can be pursued any other way. But if skin color offers whites a certain false esteem and impunity, it offers blacks vulnerability.

This vulnerability begins for blacks with the recognition that we belong, quite simply, to the most despised race in the human community of races. To be a member of such a group in a society where all others gain an impunity by merely standing in relation to us is to live with a relentless openness to diminishment and shame. By the devious logic of the anti-self, one cannot be open to such diminishment without in fact being inferior and therefore deserving of diminishment. For the anti-self, the charge verifies the crime, so that racial vulnerability itself is evidence of inferiority. In this sense, the anti-self is an internalized racist, our own subconscious bigot, that conspires with society to diminish us.

So when blacks enter the mainstream, they are not only vulnerable to society's racism but also to the racist within. This internal racist is not restricted by law, morality, or social decorum. It cares nothing about civil rights and equal opportunity. It is the self-doubt born of the original wound of racial oppression, and its mission is to establish the justice of that wound and shackle us with doubt.

Of course, the common response to racial vulnerability, as to most vulnerabilities, is denial—the mind's mechanism for ridding itself of intolerable possibilities. For blacks to acknowledge a vulnerability to inferiority anxiety, in the mist of a society that has endlessly accused us of being inferior, feels nothing less than intolerable—as if we were agreeing with the indictment against us. But denial is not the same as eradication, since it only gives unconscious life to what is intolerable to our consciousness. Denial reassigns rather than vanquishes the terror of racial vulnerability. This reassignment only makes the terror stronger by making it unknown. When we deny, we always create a dangerous area of self-ignorance, an entire territory of the self that we cannot afford to know. Without realizing it, we begin to circumscribe our lives by avoiding those people and situations that might breach our denial and force us to see consciously what we fear. Though the denial of racial vulnerability is a human enough response, I think it also makes our public discourse on race circumspect and unproductive, since we cannot talk meaningfully about problems we are afraid to name.

Denial is a refusal of painful self-knowledge. When someone or something threatens to breach this refusal, we receive an unconscious shock of the very vulnerability we have denied—a shock that often makes us retreat and more often makes us intensify our denial. When blacks move into integrated situations or face challenges that are new for blacks, the myth of black inferiority is always present as a *condition* of the situation, and as such it always threatens to breach our denial of racial vulnerability. It also threatens to make us realize consciously what is intolerable to us—that we have some anxiety about inferiority. We feel this threat unconsciously as a shock of racial doubt delivered by the racist anti-self (always the inner voice of the myth of black inferiority). Consciously, we feel this shock as a sharp discomfort or a desire to retreat from the situation. Almost always we will want to intensify our denial.

20   I will call this *integration shock,* since it occurs most powerfully when blacks leave their familiar world and enter the mainstream. Integration shock and denial are mutual intensifiers. The stab of racial doubt that integration shock delivers is a pressure to intensify denial, and a more rigid denial means the next stab of doubt will be more threatening and therefore more intense. The symbiosis of these two forces is, I believe, one of the reasons black Americans have become preoccupied with racial pride, almost to the point of obsession over the past twenty-five or so years. With more exposure to the mainstream, we have endured more integration shock, more jolts of inferiority anxiety. And, I think, we have often responded with rather hyperbolic claims of black pride by which we deny that anxiety. In this sense, our self-consciousness around pride, our need to make a point of it, is, to a degree, a form of denial. Pride becomes denial when it ceases to reflect self-esteem quietly and begins to compensate loudly for unacknowledged inner doubt. Here it also becomes dangerous since it prevents us from confronting and overcoming that doubt.

I think the most recent example of black pride-as-denial is the campaign (which seems to have been launched by a committee) to add yet another name to the litany of names that blacks have given themselves over the past century. Now we are to be African-Americans instead of, or in conjunction with, being black Americans. This self-conscious reaching for pride through nomenclature suggests nothing so much as a despair over the possibility of gaining the less conspicuous pride that follows real advancement. In its invocation of the glories of a remote African past and its wistful suggestion of homeland, this name denies the doubt black Americans have about their contemporary situation in America. There is no element of self-confrontation in it, no facing of real racial vulnerabilities, as there was with the name "black." I think "black" easily became the name of preference in the sixties, precisely because it was not a denial but a confrontation of inferiority anxiety, with the shame associated with the color black. There was honest self-acceptance in this name, and I think it diffused much of our vulnerability to the shame of color. Even between blacks, "black" is hardly the drop-dead fighting word it was when I was a child. Possibly we are ready now for a new name, but I think "black" has been our most powerful name yet because it so frankly called out our shame and doubt and helped us (and others) to accept ourselves. In the name "African-American" there is too much false neutralization of doubt, too much looking away from the caldron of our own experience. It is a euphemistic name that hides us even from ourselves.

I think blacks have been more preoccupied with pride over the past twenty-five years because we have been more exposed to integration shock since the 1964 Civil Rights Act made equal opportunity the law of the land (if not quite the full reality of the land). Ironically, it was the inequality of opportunity and all the other repressions of legal segregation that buffered us from our racial vulnerability. In a segregated society we did not have the same accountability to the charge of racial inferiority since we were given little opportunity to disprove the charge. It was the opening up of opportunity—anti-discrimination laws, the social programs of the Great Society, equal opportunity guidelines and mandates, fair housing laws, affirmative action, and so on—that made us individually and collectively more accountable to the myth of black inferiority and therefore more racially vulnerable.

This vulnerability has increased in the same proportion that our freedom and opportunity have increased. The exhilaration of new freedom is always followed by a shock of accountability. Whatever unresolved doubt follows the oppressed into greater freedom will be inflamed since freedom always carries a burden of proof, always throws us back on ourselves. And freedom, even imperfect freedom, makes blacks a brutal proposition: if you're not inferior, prove it. This is the proposition that shocks us and makes us vulnerable to our underworld of doubt. The whispers of the racist anti-self are far louder in the harsh accountability of freedom than in subjugation, where the oppressor is so entirely to blame. The bitter irony of all this is that our doubt and the hesitancy it breeds now help limit our progress in America almost as systematically as segregation once did. Integration shock gives the old boundaries of legal segregation a regenerative power. To avoid the shocks of doubt that come from entering the mainstream, or plunging more deeply into it, we often pull back at precisely those junctures where segregation once pushed us back. In this way we duplicate the conditions of our oppression and reenact our role as victims even in the midst of far greater freedom and far less victimization. Certainly there is still racial discrimination in America, but I believe that the unconscious replaying of our oppression is now the greatest barrier to our full equality.

The way in which integration shock regenerates the old boundaries of segregation for blacks is most evident in three tendencies—the tendency to minimalize or avoid real opportunities, to withhold effort in areas where few blacks have achieved, and to self-segregate in integrated situations.

25   If anything, it is the presence of new opportunities in society that triggers integration shock. If opportunity is a chance to succeed, it is also a chance to fail. The vulnerability of blacks to hidden inferiority anxiety makes failure a much

more forbidding prospect. If a black pursues an opportunity in the mainstream—opens a business, goes up for a challenging job or difficult promotion—and fails, that failure can be used by the anti-self to confirm both personal and racial inferiority. The diminishment and shame will tap an impersonal, as well as personal, source of doubt. When a white fails, he alone fails. His doubt is strictly personal, which gives him more control over the failure. He can discover *his* mistakes, learn the reasons *he* made them, and try again. But the black, laboring under the myth of inferiority, will have this impersonal, culturally determined doubt with which to contend. This form of doubt robs him of a degree of control over his failure since he alone cannot eradicate the cultural myth that stings him. There will be a degree of impenetrability to his failure that will constitute an added weight of doubt.

The effect of this is to make mainstream opportunity more intimidating and risky for blacks. This is made worse in that blacks, owing to past and present deprivations, may come to the mainstream in the first place with a lower stock of self-esteem. High risk and low self-esteem is hardly the best combination with which to tackle the challenges of a highly advanced society in which others have been blessed by history with very clear advantages. Under these circumstances, opportunity can seem more like a chance to fail than a chance to succeed. All this makes for a kind of opportunity aversion that I think was behind the hesitancy I saw in Henry, in myself, and in other blacks of all class backgrounds. It is also, I believe, one of the reasons for the sharp decline in the number of black students entering college, even as many colleges launch recruiting drives to attract more black students.

This aversion to opportunity generates a way of seeing that minimalizes opportunity to the point where it can be ignored. In black communities the most obvious entrepreneurial opportunities are routinely ignored. It is often outsiders or the latest wave of immigrants who own the shops, restaurants, cleaners, gas stations, and even the homes and apartments. Education is a troubled area in black communities for numerous reasons, but certainly one of them is that many black children are not truly imbued with the idea that learning is virtually the same as opportunity. Schools—even bad schools—were the opportunity that so many immigrant groups used to learn the workings and the spirit of American society. In the very worst inner-city schools there are accredited teachers who teach the basics, but too often to students who shun those among them who do well, who see studying as a sucker's game and school itself as a waste of time. One sees in many of these children almost a determination not to learn, a suppression of the natural impulse to understand, which cannot be entirely explained by the determinism of poverty. Out of school, in the neighborhood, these same children learn everything. I think it is the meeting with the mainstream that school symbolizes that clicks them off. In the cultural ethos from which they come, it is always these meetings that trigger the aversion to opportunity, behind which lies inferiority anxiety. Their parents and their culture send them a double message: go to school but don't really apply yourself. The risk is too high.

This same pattern of avoidance, this unconscious circumvention of possibility, is also evident in our commitment to effort—the catalyst of opportunity. Difficult, sustained effort—in school, career, or family life—will be riddled with setbacks, losses, and frustrations. Racial vulnerability erodes effort for blacks by exaggerating the importance of these setbacks, by recasting them as confirmation of racial inferiority rather than the normal pitfalls of sustained effort. The racist anti-self greets these normal difficulties with an I-told-you-so attitude, and the believing self, unwilling to risk seeing that the anti-self is right, may grow timid and pull back from the effort. As with opportunity, racial vulnerability makes hard effort in the mainstream a high-risk activity for blacks.

But this is not the case in those areas where blacks have traditionally excelled. In sports and music, for example, the threat of integration shock is effectively removed. Because so many blacks have succeeded in these areas, a black can enter them without being racially vulnerable. Failure carries no implication of racial inferiority, so the activity itself is far less risky than those in which blacks have no record of special achievement. Certainly, in sports and music one sees blacks sustain the most creative and disciplined effort and then seize opportunities where one would have thought there were none. But all of this changes the instant racial vulnerability becomes a factor. Across the country thousands of young black males take every opportunity and make every effort to reach the elite ranks of the NBA or NFL. But in the classroom, where racial vulnerability is a hidden terror, they and many of their classmates put forth the meagerest effort and show a virtual indifference to the genuine opportunity that is education.

30   But the most visible circumvention that results from integration shock is the tendency toward self-segregation that, if anything, seems to have increased over the last twenty years. Along with opportunity and effort, it is also white people themselves who are often avoided. I hear young black professionals say they do not socialize with whites after work unless at some "command performance" that comes with the territory of their career. On largely white university campuses where integration shock is particularly intense, black students often try to enforce a kind of neo-separatism that includes black "theme" dorms, black student unions, Afro-houses, black cultural centers, black student lounges, and so on. There is a geopolitics involved in this activity, where race is tied to territory in a way that mimics the whites only\colored only designations of the past. Only now these race spaces are staked out in the name of pride.

I think this impulse to self-segregate, to avoid whites, has to do with the way white people are received by the black anti-self. Even if the believing self wants to see racial difference as essentially meaningless, the anti-self, that hidden perpetrator of racist doubt, sees white people as better than black people. Its mission is to confirm black inferiority, and so it looks closely at whites, watches the way they walk, talk, and negotiate the world, and then grants these styles of being and acting superiority. Somewhere inside every black is a certain awe at the power and achievement of the white race. In every barbershop gripe session where whites are put through the grinder of black anger, there will be a kind of

backhanded respect—"Well, he might be evil, but that white boy is smart."
True or not, the anti-self organizes its campaign against the believing self's
faith in black equality around this supposition. And so, for blacks (as is true for
whites in another way), white people in the generic sense have no neutrality. In
themselves, they are stimulants to the black anti-self, deliverers of doubt. Their
color slips around the deepest need of blacks to believe in their own im-
mutable equality and communes directly with their self-suspicion.

So it is not surprising to hear black students on largely white campuses say
that they are simply more comfortable with other blacks. Nor is it surprising to
see them caught up in absurd contradictions—demanding separate facilities
for themselves even as they protest apartheid in South Africa. Racial vulnerability is a species of fear and, as such, it is the progenitor of countless ironies.
More freedom makes us more vulnerable so that in the midst of freedom we
feel the impulse to carve our segregated comfort zones that protect us more
from our own doubt than from whites. We balk before opportunity and pull
back from effort just as these things would bear fruit. We reconstitute the
boundaries of segregation just as they become illegal. By averting opportunity
and curbing effort for fear of awakening a sense of inferiority, we make inevitable the very failure that shows us inferior.

One of the worst aspects of oppression is that it never ends when the oppressor begins to repent. There is a legacy of doubt in the oppressed that follows long after the cleanest repentance by the oppressor, just as guilt trails the
oppressor and makes his redemption incomplete. These themes of doubt and
guilt fill in like fresh replacements and work to duplicate the oppression. I
think black Americans are today more oppressed by doubt than by racism and
that the second phase of our struggle for freedom must be a confrontation
with that doubt. Unexamined, this doubt leads us back into the tunnel of our
oppression where we reenact our victimization just as society struggles to end
its victimization of us. We are not a people formed in freedom. Freedom is always a call to possibility that demands an overcoming of doubt. We are still new
to freedom, new to its challenges, new even to the notion that self-doubt can be
the slyest enemy of freedom. For us freedom has so long meant the absence of
oppression that we have not yet realized it also means the conquering of doubt.

Of course, this does not mean that doubt should become a lake we swim in,
but it does mean that we should begin our campaign against doubt by acknowledging it, by outlining the contours of the black anti-self so that we can know
and accept exactly what it is that we are afraid of. This is knowledge that can be
worked with, knowledge that can point with great precision to the actions
through which we can best mitigate doubt and advance ourselves. This is the
sort of knowledge that gives the believing self a degree of immunity against the
anti-self and that enables it to pile up little victories that, in sum, grant even
more immunity.

35   Certainly inferiority has long been the main theme of the black anti-self, its
most lethal weapon against our capacity for self-belief. And so, in a general
way, the acceptance of this piece of knowledge implies a mission: to show

ourselves and (only indirectly) the larger society that we are not inferior in any dimension. That this should already be assumed goes without saying. But what "should be" falls within the province of the believing self, where it has no solidity until the doubt of the anti-self is called out and shown false by demonstrable action in the real world. This is the proof that grants the "should" its rightful solidity, that transforms it from a well-intentioned claim into a certainty.

The temptation is to avoid so severe a challenge, to maintain a black identity, painted in the colors of pride and culture, that provides us with a way of seeing ourselves apart from this challenge. It is easier to be "African-American" than to organize oneself on one's own terms and around one's own aspirations and then, through sustained effort and difficult achievement, put one's insidious anti-self quietly to rest. No black identity, however beautifully conjured, will spare blacks this challenge that, despite its fairness or unfairness, is simply in the nature of things. But then I have faith that in time we will meet this challenge since this, too, is in the nature of things.

QUESTIONS FOR DISCUSSION

1. Explain Steele's concept of the anti-self. What are its origins and what type of wounds contribute to it? What does the anti-self argue for and against?
2. Steele begins his essay with his friend Henry's decision not to choose an ambitious career. How does Steele's next example about his own elementary school days reveal "how the Henry was born in me"? Are these two examples convincing? Why or why not? Explain.
3. How do black adults who tell their children, "Don't worry. They treat all blacks that way," contribute to the anti-self? Do you agree that this contributes to the anti-self?
4. Steele claims that the anti-self is "an internalized racist, our own unconscious bigot, that conspires with society to diminish us," and that, in today's world, "the unconscious replaying of our oppression is now the greatest barrier to our full equality." What evidence does Steele present to back up these assertions? Is his evidence convincing?
5. What does Steele mean by "integration shock," "self-segregation," and "black pride as denial"? How does the anti-self lead to these responses?
6. What methods does Steele use to argue for his perspective on black culture and identity? Does his argument seem to be "dialogic," that is, does he take the arguments and feelings of his opposition into account? Is his approach effective? Explain your point of view.

CONNECTION

Compare Steele's idea of the shadowy anti-self that holds back one's potential with the struggle and the shadow as described by Robert Johnson (see page 387).

IDEAS FOR WRITING

1. Steele argues against the "self-segregation" of blacks. What is your response to the new black separatist movement? Do you agree with Steele that it is a sign of "integration shock" and self-doubt? Do you see it as a genuine cultural affirmation, a positive step forward for African-Americans? Write an essay in which you take a position on this issue.

2. Steele's argument rests on a consideration of the psychological responses of blacks to the injustices of the past. Write an essay in support of his position or refute it.

RELATED WEB SITE

SHELBY STEELE: "THE NEW BETRAYAL OF BLACK FREEDOM IN AMERICA"
http://www.independent.org/tii/forums/990224ipfTrans.html#0
Read the transcript of author Shelby Steele's address to the Independent Policy Forum to commemorate Black History Month.

Susan Griffin

Ideologies of Madness

Susan Griffin was born in 1943 in Los Angeles, California. She attended the University of California, Berkeley from 1960–1963, and finished her B.A. and M.A. at San Francisco State University. Susan Griffin has worked as an assistant editor, an instructor in English and Women's studies at University of California at Berkeley, and has taught in the Poetry in the Schools program. Griffin is known for her nonfiction writings on women's studies and cultural issues as well as for her poetry, for which she has won many awards, including the Ina Coolbrith Prize in Poetry (1963), The National Endowment for the Arts grant (1976), and the Commonwealth Club Silver Medal (1988). Her most widely read works are Woman and Nature *(1978),* Pornography and Silence: Culture's Revolt against Nature *(1981), and* A Chorus of Stones *(1992). Griffin's most recent collections of poetry include* Bending Home: Selected and New Poems *(1998) and* What Her Body Thought: A Journey into the Shadows *(1999). The selection that follows brings together many of Griffin's social and psychological interests with a focus on nuclear conflict and the cultural consequences of the mind-body split in Western culture.*

JOURNAL

Write about a time when you chose not to think about an unpleasant political or international reality.

Nuclear war has been described as a form of madness. Yet rarely does one take this insight seriously when contemplating the dilemma of war and peace. I wish to describe here the state of mind that has produced nuclear weaponry as a species of socially accepted insanity. This is a state of mind born of that philosophical assumption of our civilization which attempts to divide human consciousness from nature. Exploring the terrain of this state of mind, one will find in this geography, in the subterranean and unseen region that is part of its foundation and history, the hatred of the other in the quite literal forms of misogyny (the hatred of women), racism and anti-Semitism.

If one approaches the explosion of a nuclear weapon as if this were symptomatic of an underlying mental condition, certain facets begin to take on metaphorical meaning. Even the simplest physical aspects of a nuclear chain reaction carry a psychological significance. In order for a chain reaction to be created, the atom must be split apart. The fabric of matter has to be torn asunder. In a different vein, it is important to realize that the first atomic weapons were dropped over a people regarded in the demonology of our civilization as racially inferior. Tangentially, and carrying a similar significance, the first nuclear device exploded over Bikini atoll had a pinup of Rita Hayworth pasted to its surface. And then, speaking of a history that has largely been forgotten or ignored, the prototype of the first missiles capable of carrying nuclear warheads was invented and designed in the Third Reich. And those first rockets, the German V-2 rockets, were produced in underground tunnels by prisoners of concentration camps who were worked to death in this production.

These facets of the existence of nuclear weaponry can lead us to a deeper understanding of the troubled mind that has created our current nuclear crisis. To begin at one particular kind of beginning, with the history of thought, one can see the philosophical roots of our current crisis in the splitting of the atom. In the most basic terms, what occurs when the atom is split is a division between energy and matter. Until this century, modern science assumed matter and energy to be separate. This assumption began not with scientific observation but out of a religious bias. Examining the early history of science, one discovers that the first scientists were associated with and supported by the Church (as was most scholarship at that time) and that they asked questions derived from Christian theology. "What is the nature of light?" A question intimately bound up with the theory of relativity and quantum physics began as a religious question. And the guiding paradigm of the religion that posed this question has been a fundamental dualism between matter and spirit. Matter, or body and earth, were the degraded regions, belonging to the devil and corruption. Spirit, or the realm of pure intellect and heavenly influence, belonged to God, and was, in human experience, won only at the expense of flesh.

Of course, science does not recognize the categories of spirit and matter any longer, except through a process of translation. In the new vocabulary, though, the old dualism has been preserved. Now, matter was conceived of as earth-bound and thus subject to gravity, and energy, the equivalent of spirit, was described as a free agent, inspiring and enlivening. Newtonian physics continued the old dualism, but Einsteinian physics does not.

5   When Einstein discovered the formula that eventually led to the development of the atomic bomb, what he saw was a continuum between matter and energy, instead of a separation. What we call solid matter is not solid, nor is it static. Matter is, instead, a process of continual change. There is no way to divide the energy of this motion from the physical property of matter. What is more, energy has mass. And not only is there no division between matter and energy as such, but to divide any single entity from any other single entity becomes an impossibility. No particular point exists where my skin definitely ends and the air in the atmosphere begins and this atmosphere ends and your skin begins. We are all in a kind of field together. And finally, with the new physics, the old line between subject and object has also disappeared. According to Heisenberg's Principle of Uncertainty, whatever we observe we change through our participation. Objectivity with its implied superiority and control has also vanished.

One might imagine that, with the disappearance of a scientific basis for dualism and the appearance of a physical view that is unified and whole, a different philosophy might arise, one which might help us make peace with nature. But instead what this civilization chose to do with this new insight was to find a way to separate matter from energy (it is spoken of as "liberating" the energy from the atom). And this separation has in turn produced a technology of violence which has divided the world into two separate camps who regard each other as enemies.

The real enemy, however, in dualistic thinking, is hidden: the real enemy is ourselves. The same dualism which imagines matter and energy to be separate also divides human nature, separating what we call our material existence from consciousness. This dualism is difficult to describe without using dualistic language. Actually, the mind cannot be separated from the body. The brain is part of the body and is affected by blood flow, temperature, nourishment, muscular movement. The order and rhythm of the body, bodily metaphors, are reflected in the medium of thought, in our patterns of speech. Yet we conceive of the mind as separate from and above the body. And through a subtle process of socialization since birth, we learn to regard the body and our natural existence as something inferior and without intelligence. Most of the rules of polite behavior are designed to conceal the demands of the body. We excuse ourselves, and refer to our bodily functions through euphemism.

From this dualistic frame of mind two selves are born: one acknowledged and one hidden. The acknowledged self identifies with spirit, with intellect, with what we imagine is free of the influence of natural law. The hidden self is part of nature, earth-bound, inextricable from the matrix of physical existence. We have become very seriously alienated from this denied self. So seriously that our alienation has become a kind of self-hatred, and this self-hatred is leading us today toward the suicidal notion of nuclear combat.

Of course, the body and mind are not separate. And, ironically, the warfare incipient between our ideas of who we are and who we really are is made more intense through this unity. Consciousness cannot exclude bodily knowledge. We are inseparable from nature, dependent on the biosphere, vulnerable to the processes of natural law. We cannot destroy the air we breathe without destroying ourselves. We are reliant on one another for our survival. We are all mortal. And this knowledge comes to us, whether we want to receive it or not, with every breath.

10   The dominant philosophies of this civilization have attempted to posit a different order of being over and against this bodily knowledge. According to this order of being, we are separate from nature and hence above natural process. In the logic of this order, we are meant to dominate nature, control life, and, in some sense felt largely unconsciously, avoid the natural event of death.

    Yet in order to maintain a belief in this hierarchy one must repress bodily knowledge. And this is no easy task. Our own knowledge of our own natural existence comes to us not only with every breath but with hunger, with intimacy, with dreams, with all the unpredictable eventualities of life. Our imagined superiority over nature is constantly challenged by consciousness itself. Consciousness emerges from and is immersed in material experience. Consciousness is not separable from perception, which is to say sensuality, and as such cannot be separated from matter. Even through the process of the most abstract thought we cannot entirely forget that we are part of nature. In the biosphere nothing is ever entirely lost. Death itself is not an absolute end but rather a transformation. What appears to be lost in a fire becomes heat and ash. So, too, no knowledge can ever really be lost to consciousness. It must remain, even if disguised as a mere symbol of itself.

    If I choose to bury a part of myself, what I bury will come back to haunt me in another form, as dream, or fear, or projection. This civilization, which has buried part of the human self, has created many projections. Out of the material of self-hatred several categories of otherness have been fashioned. Existing on a mass scale and by social agreement, these categories form a repository for our hidden selves.

    The misogynist's idea of women is a fundamental category of otherness for this civilization. In the ideology of misogyny, a woman is a lesser being than a man. And the root cause of her inferiority is that she is closer to the earth, more animal, and hence material in her nature. She is thus described as more susceptible to temptations of the flesh (or devils, or serpents), more emotional and hence less capable of abstract thought than a man. Similarly, in the ideology of racism, those who are perceived as other are, at one and the same time, more sensual and erotic and less intelligent.

    During the rise of fascism in Europe a fictitious document was created called the *Protocols of the Elders of Zion*. In this "document" Jewish elders plan to corrupt and eventually seize Aryan bloodlines through the rape and seduction of Aryan women. If one has projected a part of the self upon another, one must always be afraid that this self will return, perhaps even entering one's own bloodstream. But what is equally significant about this myth, and the symbolic life of the racist and anti-Semitic imagination, is that a sexual act, and especially rape, lies at the heart of its mythos.

15   It was in writing a book on pornography that I first began to understand the ideology of misogynist projection. Since so much in pornography is violent, I began to ask myself why sexual experience is associated with violence. This is a

question which poses itself again in the context of nuclear weaponry, not only because Rita Hayworth's image happened to adorn an experimental nuclear bomb, nor simply because of the phallic shape of the missile, nor the language employed to describe the weapons—the first atomic bomb called "little boy," the next "big boy"—but also because of the sexualization of warfare itself, the eroticization of violence in war, the supposed virility of the soldier, the test of virility which is supposed to take place on the battlefield, and the general equivalency between masculine virtues and prowess in battle.

Over time in my study of pornography I began to understand pornographic imagery as an expression of the fear of sexual experience itself. Sexual experience takes one back to a direct knowledge of nature, including mortality, and of one's own body before culture has intervened to create the delusion of dominance. It is part of the nature of sexual pleasure and of orgasm to lose control. And finally the feel of a woman's breast, or of human skin against bare skin at all, must recall infancy and the powerlessness of infancy.

As infants we all experience an understanding of dependence and vulnerability. Our first experience of a natural, material power outside ourselves was through the bodies of our mothers. In this way we have all come to associate nature with the body of a woman. It was our mother who could feed us, give us warmth and comfort, or withhold these things. She had the power of life and death over us as natural process does now.

It was also as infants that we confronted what we have come to know as death. What we call death—coldness, isolation, fear, darkness, despair, trembling—is really the experience of an infant. What death really is lies in the dimension of the unknown. But, from the infantile experience of what we call death, one can see the psychological derivation of civilization's association between women and death. (One sees this clearly in the creation myth from Genesis, as Eve the seductress brings death into the world.) In this sense, too, sexual experience returns one to a primal fear of death. And through this understanding one can begin to see that at the center of the impulse to rape is the desire to dominate the power of sexual experience itself and to deny the power of nature, including mortality, as this is felt through sexual experience.

The connection between sexuality and violence exists as a kind of subterranean theme in the fascist and authoritarian mentality. In several places in Jacobo Timerman's book, *Prisoner Without a Name, Cell Without a Number,* he points out a relationship between the violence of the dictator and a pornographic attitude toward sexuality. Imprisoned and tortured himself, he recalls that those who did not do "a good scrubbing job" when ordered to clean the prison floors were forced to "undress, lean over with their index finger on the ground and have them rotate round and round dragging their finger on the ground without lifting it. You felt," he writes, "as if your kidneys were bursting." Another punishment was to force prisoners to run naked along the passageway, "reciting aloud sayings dictated" to them, such as "My mother is a whore, I masturbate, I respect the guard, the police love me."

20   That, to the fascist mind, "the other" represents a denied part of the self becomes clear in the following story about Adolf Hitler. In a famous passage in

Mein Kampf he describes the moment when he decided to devote his life's work to anti-Semitism. He recounts that while walking through the streets of Vienna he happened to see an old man dressed in the traditional clothes of Jewish men in that city at that time, i.e., in a caftan. The first question he asked was, "Is this man Jewish?" and then he corrected himself and replaced that question with another, "Is this man German?"

If one is to project a denied self onto another, one must first establish that this other is different from oneself. Were one to notice any similarity, one would be endangered by the perception that what one projects may belong to oneself. The question that Hitler asked himself became a standard part of German textbooks in the Third Reich. A stereotypical portrait of a Jewish man's face was shown under the question, "Is this man German?" and the correct answer the students were taught was, of course, "No." In fact, Germany became a nation rather late. For centuries it existed as a collection of separate tribes, and one of the oldest tribes in that nation was Jewish.

Hitler's story of the man in the caftan became a standard part of his orations. He would become nearly hysterical at times telling the story, and is said to have even vomited once. In the light of this history, a seemingly trivial story from Hitler's early life becomes significant. As a young art student he bought his clothes secondhand because, like many students, he was poor. In this period most of those selling secondhand clothing were Jewish and Hitler bought from a Jewish clothes seller one item of clothing that he wore so often that he began to be identified with this apparel. And that was a caftan.

What is also interesting historically is that the caftan was a form of medieval German dress. Exiled from Germany during a period of persecution, many Jews, who then lived in ghettos, continued to wear this traditional German dress and were still wearing it when they returned to Germany centuries later. Not only did Hitler fail to recognize an image of himself encountered in the streets of Vienna, but so did an entire generation of Germans. And an entire civilization, that to which we all belong, is in conflict with a part of human nature, which we try to bury and eventually even destroy.

The weapons that now threaten to destroy the earth and life as we know it were developed because the Allied nations feared that the fascist powers were making them. And the missiles which are now part and parcel of nuclear weaponry were first developed in the Third Reich. It is crucial now in our understanding of ourselves and what it is in us that has led to the nuclear crisis that we begin to look at the Nazi Holocaust as a mirror, finding a self-portrait in "the other" who is persecuted and denied, and seeing a part of ourselves too in the fascist dictator who would destroy that denied self.

25   The illusion this civilization retains, that we are somehow above nature, is so severe that in a sense we have come to believe that we can end material existence without dying. The absurdity of nuclear weaponry as a strategy for defense, when the use of those weapons would annihilate us, would in itself argue this. But if you look closely at the particulars of certain strategies within the overall nuclear strategy you encounter again the same estranged relationship with reality.

An official who was part of Reagan's administration, T. K. Jones, actually proposed that a viable method of civil defense would be to issue each citizen a shovel. It took an eight-year-old boy to point out that this plan cannot work because, after you dig a hole and get into it for protection, someone else must stand outside the hole and shovel dirt on top. The Pentagon refers to its strategies for waging nuclear war as SIOP.* One year the Pentagon actually went through the paces of an SIOP plan. As a literary scholar I found the scenario which the Pentagon wrote for this dramatization very disturbing. The Pentagon was free to write this play in any way that they wished; yet they wrote that the President was killed with a direct hit to Washington, D.C. Any student of tragic drama will tell you that what happens to the king, or the President, is symbolic of what happens to the self. But symbolically this death is not treated as real. Though the earthly self dies, in the Pentagon's version the sky self does not die: the Vice-President goes up in an airplane fully equipped to wage nuclear war by computer. There is such a plane flying above us now, and at every hour of the day and night.

The division that we experience from the natural self, the self that is material and embedded in nature, impairs our perceptions of reality. As Timerman writes:

> The devices are recurrent in all totalitarian ideology, to ignore the complexities of reality, or even eliminate reality, and instead establish a simple goal and a simple means of attaining that goal.

Through maintaining the supremacy of the idea, one creates a delusion of a supernatural power over nature. Proceeding from an alienation from nature and an estrangement from the natural self, our civilization has replaced reality with an idea of reality.

In the development of this alienation as a state of mind, the delusion of well-being and safety eventually becomes more important than the realistic considerations which will actually effect well-being or safety. Hannah Arendt writes of an illusionary world created by totalitarian movements ". . . in which through sheer imagination uprooted masses can feel at home, and are spared the never-ending shocks which real life and real experience deal to human beings. . . ." Later, in *The Origins of Totalitarianism,* she speaks of the state of mass mind under the Third Reich in which people ceased to believe in what they perceived with their own eyes and ears, preferring the conflicting reports issued by the Führer.

One encounters the same failure to confront reality in Stalin's psychology as it is described by Isaac Deutscher in his biography:

> He [Stalin] was now completely possessed by the idea that he could achieve a miraculous transformation of the whole of Russia by a single *tour de force.* He seemed to live in a half-real and half-dreamy world of statistical figures and in-

---

SIOP: Acronym for Strategic Integrated Operational Plan.

dices of industrial orders and instructions, a world in which no target and no objective seemed beyond his and the party's grasp.*

During the period of forced collectivization of farms, Stalin destroyed actual farms before the collectivized farms were created. As Deutscher writes, it was as if a whole nation destroyed its real houses and moved "lock, stock and barrel into some illusory buildings."

30 We are, in fact, now living in such an illusory building. The entire manner in which plans for a nuclear war are discussed, rehearsed, and envisioned partakes of a kind of unreality, an anesthetized and nearly automatic functioning, in which cerebration is strangely unrelated to experience or feeling. The generals imagine themselves conducting nuclear war from a room without windows, with no natural light, choosing strategies and targets by looking at enormous computerized maps. The language they use to communicate their decisions is all in code. No one uses the word "war," the word "bomb," the word "death," or the words "blood," "pain," "loss," "grief," "shock," or "horror." In Siegfried Sassoon's** recollection of World War I, he remembers encountering a man, a soldier like himself, who has just learned that his brother was killed. The man is half crazy, tearing his clothes off and cursing at war. As Sassoon passed beyond this man into the dark of the war, he could still hear "his uncouth howlings." It is those "uncouth howlings" that those who are planning nuclear war have managed to mute in their imagination.

But of course that howling is not entirely lost. In the shared imagination of our civilization, it is the "other" who carries emotion, the women who howl. And, far from wishing to protect the vulnerable and the innocent, it is the secret desire of this civilization to destroy those who feel, and to silence feeling. This hidden desire becomes apparent in pornography where women are pictured in a traditional way as weaker than men and needing protection, and yet where erotic feeling is freely mixed with the desire to brutalize and even murder women.

One can find a grim picture of the insane logic of the alienated mind of our civilization in the pornographic film *Peeping Tom*. The hero of this movie is a pornographic film maker. He has a camera armed with a spear. As he photographs a woman's naked body the camera releases the weapon and makes a record of her death agonies. The final victory of the alienated mind over reality is to destroy that reality (and one's experience of it) and replace reality with a record of that destruction. One finds the same pattern in the history of actual atrocities. In California a man lured women into the desert with a promise of work as pornographic models. There, while he tortured and murdered them, he made a photographic record of the event. The Nazis themselves kept the best documentation of atrocities committed in the concentration camps. And

---

*Isaac Deutscher, *Stalin: A Political Biography* (Oxford, 1961).
**Siegfried Sassoon, "The Complete Memoirs of George Sherston," as collected in *Sassoon's Long Journey*, ed. Paul Fussell (London, 1983).

the most complete records of the destruction of Native Americans have been kept by the United States military.

Now, the state of conflict in which this civilization finds itself has worsened. The enemy is not simply "the other" but life itself. And it is in keeping with the insane logic of alienation that the Pentagon has found a way that it believes we can win nuclear war. We have situated satellites in space that will record the process of annihilation of life. The Pentagon counts as a future victor that nation which has gathered the best documentation of the destruction.

There is, however, another form of reflection available to us by virtue of our human nature. We are our own witnesses. We can see ourselves. We are part of nature. And nature is not divided. Matter is intelligent. Feeling, sense, the needs of the body, all that has been consigned to the "other," made the province of women, of darkness, contains a deeper and a sustaining wisdom. It remains for us to empower that knowledge and carry it into the world. In insanity and madness, one is lost to oneself. It is only by coming home to ourselves that we can survive.

QUESTIONS FOR DISCUSSION

1. Why does Griffin use the word "madness" in her essay to describe nuclear war? What does she mean by "ideologies of madness," and what examples does she give to clarify her definition?
2. Why does Griffin believe that a series of traditional divisions or dualisms have contributed to the type of nuclear madness she discusses in her essay? What are some of these divisions and how do they relate to a particular deep division in Western culture and philosophy?
3. According to Griffin, what are the two selves that are born through dualistic thinking? Why does Griffin believe that the hidden enemy is "ourselves"? What is the relationship between our hidden inner enemies and our real enemies?
4. Why does Griffin come to see the misogynist's idea of women, the violent sexual imagery of pornography, authoritarianism, and racial hatred all as related projections of a destructive dualism? Do you agree with Griffin? Do you think that her analysis is overly simplified? Explain your point of view.
5. Why does Griffin believe that most people live today in an illusory building, in a state of denial of the reality of genocide and the nuclear age? What examples does she provide of this denial?
6. What two kinds of reflection does Griffin recommend as possible first steps toward a solution to our current crisis? In these types of reflection, what does she recommend that we see and recognize, both within and without? What deeper connections do we need to perceive?

CONNECTION

Consider the problem of dualism as presented in Griffin's essay in contrast to Peavey's solutions to dualism. Which writer's position makes the most sense to you? Explain your point of view (see page 427).

IDEAS FOR WRITING

1. Write an essay in which you discuss Griffin's observations about the way people tend to deny or avoid thinking about the precarious, violent nature of national and international events in modern times. Give examples of ways in which either you or the people you know manage to live in "an illusory building" in which unpleasant sociopolitical realities are tuned out.
2. Write a research essay in which you examine Griffin's analysis of the popularity and impact of violent pornography and discuss alternative perspectives on the causes and effects of pornographic obsession. How convincing is her view of pornography in comparison to alternative explanations that you have found in your research?

RELATED WEB SITES

SUSAN GRIFFIN

http://www.depts.drew.edu/wmst/corecourses/wmst111/
timeline_bios/SGriffin.htm

Learn about author Susan Griffin at this URL via information on her publications, quotes, and links. Also, see a transcript of a radio interview in which Griffin speaks about her book, *Pornography and Silence.*

WOMEN'S STUDIES RESOURCES: FEMINIST THEORY

http://bailiwick.lib.uiowa.edu/wstudies/theory.html

You will find links to several articles and web sites on issues relating to feminist theories, compiled by the University of Iowa, at this extensive URL. The many topics range from woman in philosophy to gender and race.

Fran Peavey (with Myrna Levy and Charles Varon)

Us and Them

Fran Peavey is a long time California peace activist, ecologist, and community organizer. Peavey's books include Heart Politics *(1984),* A Shallow Pool of Time: One Woman Grapples with the Aids Epidemic *(1989)* By Life's Grace: Musings on the Essence of Social Change *(1994) (with Radmila Manojlovic Zarkovic), the anthology* I Remember: Writings by Bosnian Women Refugees *(1996), and* Heart Politics Revisited *(2000). Peavey has also written articles for a number of alternative-press publications, and has served as a long time observer of the Balkans struggle and the war in Kosovo. As you read her essay "Us and Them," from* Heart Politics, *consider how the people whom we feel are different from us politically or socially can be mistakenly perceived as alien beings with whom we have nothing in common, and how accepting the "other" outside of ourselves is something like accepting the rejected parts of our own identity.*

JOURNAL

Write about someone with whom you have trouble communicating because this individual is different from you in some way. What do you have in common with this person that could form the basis for better communication?

Time was when I knew that the racists were the lunch-counter owners who refused to serve blacks, the warmongers were the generals who planned wars and ordered the killing of innocent people, and the polluters were the industrialists whose factories fouled the air, water and land. I could be a good guy by boycotting, marching, and sitting in to protest the actions of the bad guys.

But no matter how much I protest, an honest look at myself and my relationship with the rest of the world reveals ways that I too am part of the problem. I notice that on initial contact I am more suspicious of Mexicans than of whites. I see that I'm addicted to a standard of living maintained at the expense of poorer people around the world—a situation that can only be perpetuated through military force. And the problem of pollution seems to include my consumption of resources and creation of waste. The line that separates me from the bad guys is blurred.

When I was working to stop the Vietnam War, I'd feel uneasy seeing people in military uniform. I remember thinking, "How could that guy be so dumb as to have gotten into that uniform? How could he be so acquiescent, so credulous as to have fallen for the government's story in Vietnam?" I'd get furious inside when I imagined the horrible things he'd probably done in the war.

Several years after the end of the war, a small group of Vietnam veterans wanted to hold a retreat at our farm in Watsonville. I consented, although I felt ambivalent about hosting them. That weekend, I listened to a dozen men and women who had served in Vietnam. Having returned home only to face ostracism for their involvement in the war, they were struggling to come to terms with their experiences.

5   They spoke of some of the awful things they'd done and seen, as well as some things they were proud of. They told why they had enlisted in the army or cooperated with the draft: their love of the United States, their eagerness to serve, their wish to be brave and heroic. They felt their noble motives had been betrayed, leaving them with little confidence in their own judgment. Some questioned their own manhood or womanhood and even their basic humanity. They wondered whether they had been a positive force or a negative one overall, and what their buddies' sacrifices meant. Their anguish disarmed me, and I could no longer view them simply as perpetrators of evil.

How had I come to view military people as my enemies? Did vilifying soldiers serve to get me off the hook and allow me to divorce myself from responsibility for what my country was doing in Vietnam? Did my own anger and righteousness keep me from seeing the situation in its full complexity? How had this limited view affected my work against the war?

When my youngest sister and her husband, a young career military man, visited me several years ago, I was again challenged to see the human being within the soldier. I learned that as a farm boy in Utah, he'd been recruited to be a sniper.

One night toward the end of their visit, we got to talking about his work. Though he had also been trained as a medical corpsman, he could still be called on at any time to work as a sniper. He couldn't tell me much about this part of his career—he'd been sworn to secrecy. I'm not sure he would have wanted to tell me even if he could. But he did say that a sniper's work involved going abroad, "bumping off" a leader, and disappearing into a crowd.

When you're given an order, he said, you're not supposed to think about it. You feel alone and helpless. Rather than take on the Army and maybe the whole country himself, he chose not to consider the possibility that certain orders shouldn't be carried out.

10   I could see that feeling isolated can make it seem impossible to follow one's own moral standards and disobey an order. I leaned toward him and said, "If you're ever ordered to do something that you know you shouldn't do, call me immediately and I'll find a way to help. I know a lot of people would support your stand. You're not alone." He and my sister looked at each other and their eyes filled with tears.

How do we learn whom to hate and fear? During my short lifetime, the national enemies of the United States have changed several times. Our World War II foes, the Japanese and the Germans, have become our allies. The Russians have been in vogue as our enemy for some time, although during a few periods relations improved somewhat. The North Vietnamese, Cubans, and Chinese have done stints as our enemy. So many countries seem capable of incurring our national wrath—how do we choose among them?

As individuals, do we choose our enemies based on cues from national leaders? From our schoolteachers and religious leaders? From newspapers and TV? Do we hate and fear our parents' enemies as part of our family identity? Or those of our culture, subculture, or peer group?

Whose economic and political interests does our enemy mentality serve?

At a conference on holocaust and genocide I met someone who showed me that it is not necessary to hate our opponents, even under the most extreme circumstances. While sitting in the hotel lobby after a session on the German holocaust, I struck up a conversation with a woman named Helen Waterford. When I learned she was a Jewish survivor of Auschwitz, I told her how angry I was at the Nazis. (I guess I was trying to prove to her that I was one of the good guys.)

15   "You know," she said, "I don't hate the Nazis." This took me aback. How could anyone who had lived through a concentration camp not hate the Nazis?

Then I learned that Helen does public speaking engagements with a former leader of the Hitler Youth movement: they talk about how terrible facism is as viewed from both sides. Fascinated, I arranged to spend more time with Helen and learn as much as I could from her.

In 1980, Helen read an intriguing newspaper article in which a man named Alfons Heck described his experiences growing up in Nazi Germany. When he was a young boy in Catholic school, the priest would come in every morning and say, "Heil Hitler," and then "Good Morning," and finally, "In the name of the Father and the Son and the Holy Spirit . . ." In Heck's mind, Hitler came before God. At ten, he volunteered for the Hitler Youth, and he loved it. It was in 1944, when he was sixteen, that Heck first learned that the Nazis were systematically killing the Jews. He thought, "This can't be true." But gradually he came to believe that he had served a mass murderer.

Heck's frankness impressed Helen, and she thought, "I want to meet that man." She found him soft-spoken, intelligent and pleasant. Helen had already been speaking publicly about her own experiences of the holocaust, and she asked Heck to share a podium with her at an upcoming engagement with a group of four-hundred schoolteachers. They spoke in chronological format, taking turns telling their own stories of the Nazi period. Helen told of leaving Frankfurt in 1934 at age twenty-five.

She and her husband, an accountant who had lost his job when the Nazis came to power, escaped to Holland. There they worked with the underground Resistance, and Helen gave birth to a daughter. In 1940 the Nazis invaded Holland. Helen and her husband went into hiding in 1942. Two years later, they were discovered and sent to Auschwitz. Their daughter was hidden by friends in the Resistance. Helen's husband died in the concentration camp.

20   Heck and Waterford's first joint presentation went well, and they decided to continue working as a team. Once, at an assembly of eight-hundred high school students, Heck was asked, "If you had been ordered to shoot some Jews, maybe Mrs. Waterford, would you have shot them?" The audience gasped. Heck swallowed and said, "Yes. I obeyed orders. I would have." Afterward he apologized to Helen, saying he hadn't wanted to upset her. She told him, "I'm glad you answered the way you did. Otherwise, I would never again believe a word you said."

Heck is often faced with the "once a Nazi, always a Nazi" attitude. "You may give a good speech," people will say, "but I don't believe any of it. Once you have believed something, you don't throw it away." Again and again, he patiently explains that it took years before he could accept the fact that he'd been brought up believing falsehoods. Heck is also harassed by neo-Nazis, who call him in the middle of the night and threaten: "We haven't gotten you yet, but we'll kill you, you traitor."

How did Helen feel about the Nazis in Auschwitz? "I disliked them. I cannot say that I wished I could kick them to death—I never did. I guess that I am just not a vengeful person." She is often denounced by Jews for having no hate, for not wanting revenge. "It is impossible that you don't hate," people tell her.

At the conference on the holocaust and genocide and in subsequent conversations with Helen, I have tried to understand what has enabled her to remain so objective and to avoid blaming individual Germans for the holocaust, for her suffering and for her husband's death. I have found a clue in her passionate study of history.

For many people, the only explanation of the holocaust is that it was the creation of a madman. But Helen believes that such an analysis only serves to shield people from believing that a holocaust could happen to them. An appraisal of Hitler's mental health, she says, is less important than an examination of the historical forces at play and the ways Hitler was able to manipulate them.

25   "As soon as the war was over," Helen told me, "I began to read about what had happened since 1933, when my world closed. I read and read. How did the 'S.S. State' develop? What was the role of Britain, Hungary, Yugoslavia, the United States, France? How can it be possible that the holocaust really happened? What is the first step, the second step? What are people searching for when they join fanatical movements? I guess I will be asking these questions until my last days."

Those of us working for social change tend to view our adversaries as enemies, to consider them unreliable, suspect, and generally of lower moral character. Saul Alinsky, a brilliant community organizer, explained the rationale for polarization this way:

> One acts decisively only in the conviction that all the angels are on one side and all the devils are on the other. A leader may struggle toward a decision and weigh the merits and demerits of a situation which is 52 percent positive and 48 percent negative, but once the decision is reached he must assume that his cause is 100 percent positive and the opposition 100 percent negative. . . . Many liberals, during our attack on the then-school superintendent [in Chicago], were pointing out that after all he wasn't a 100-percent devil, he was a regular churchgoer, he was a good family man, and he was generous in his contributions to charity. Can you imagine in the arena of conflict charging that so-and-so is a racist bastard and then diluting the impact of the attack with qualifying remarks? This becomes political idiocy.

But demonizing one's adversaries has great costs. It is a strategy that tacitly accepts and helps perpetuate our dangerous enemy mentality.

Instead of focusing on the 52-percent "devil" in my adversary, I choose to look at the other 48 percent, to start from the premise that within each adversary I have an ally. That ally may be silent, faltering, or hidden from my view. It may be only the person's sense of ambivalence about morally questionable parts of his or her job. Such doubts rarely have a chance to flower because of the overwhelming power of the social context to which the person is accountable. *My* ability to be *their* ally also suffers from such pressures. In 1970, while the Vietnam War was still going on, a group of us spent the summer in Long Beach, California, organizing against a napalm factory there. It was a small factory that mixed the chemicals and put the napalm in canisters. An accidental explosion a few months before had spewed hunks of napalm gel onto nearby homes and lawns. The incident had, in a real sense, brought the war home. It spurred local residents who opposed the war to recognize their community's connection with one of its most despicable elements. At their request, we worked with and strengthened their local group. Together we presented a slide show and tour of the local military-industrial complex for community leaders, and we picketed the napalm factory. We also met with the president of the conglomerate that owned the factory.

We spent three weeks preparing for this meeting, studying the company's holdings and financial picture and investigating whether there were any lawsuits filed against the president or his corporation. And we found out as much as we could about his personal life: his family, his church, his country club, his hobbies. We studied his photograph, thinking of the people who loved him and the people he loved, trying to get a sense of his worldview and the context to which he was accountable.

30   We also talked a lot about how angry we were at him for the part he played in killing and maiming children in Vietnam. But though our anger fueled our determination, we decided that venting it at him would make him defensive and reduce our effectiveness.

When three of us met with him, he was not a stranger to us. Without blaming him personally or attacking his corporation, we asked him to close the plant, not to bid for the contract when it came up for renewal that year, and to think about the consequences of his company's operations. We told him we knew where his corporation was vulnerable (it owned a chain of motels that could be boycotted), and said we intended to continue working strategically to force his company out of the business of burning people. We also discussed the company's other war-related contracts, because changing just a small part of his corporation's function was not enough; we wanted to raise the issue of economic dependence on munitions and war.

Above all, we wanted him to see us as real people, not so different from himself. If we had seemed like flaming radicals, he would have been likely to dismiss our concerns. We assumed he was already carrying doubts inside himself, and we saw our role as giving voice to those doubts. Our goal was to introduce ourselves and our perspective into his context, so he would remember us and consider our position when making decisions.

When the contract came up for renewal two months later, his company did not bid for it.

Working for social change without relying on the concept of enemies raises some practical difficulties. For example, what do we do with all the anger that we're accustomed to unleashing against an enemy? Is it possible to hate actions and policies without hating the people who are implementing them? Does empathizing with those whose actions we oppose create a dissonance that undermines our determination?

35   I don't delude myself into believing that everything will work out for the best if we make friends with our adversaries. I recognize that certain military strategists are making decisions that raise the risks for us all. I know that some police officers will rough up demonstrators when arresting them. Treating our adversaries as potential allies need not entail unthinking acceptance of their actions. Our challenge is to call forth the humanity within each adversary, while preparing for the full range of possible responses. Our challenge is to find a path between cynicism and naiveté.

QUESTIONS FOR DISCUSSION

1. Why does Peavey no longer find it easy to feel clear about the distinctions between the good guys and the bad guys? What elements of the bad guys does she now perceive in herself?

2. What was Peavey's rationale for being angry at soldiers? What did Peavey learn from her experience hosting a group of Vietnam veterans on her farm?
3. What did Peavey learn from the visit with her sister and her sister's husband, a military sniper? Does Peavey feel that the husband should be forgiven? Do you agree?
4. How does Peavey's friendship with Helen Waterford break down preconceptions Peavey holds about Nazis and concentration camp survivors? Do you agree with Waterford and Peavey's new perspective on Nazis?
5. Through providing an example of her own successful organizing technique against a napalm factory, Peavey attempts to refute an argument by organizer Saul Alinsky against the folly of qualifying our attacks on our enemies. Is Peavey's argument a convincing one?
6. How effective is Peavey's conclusion in anticipating and resolving objections readers might have to her position? What point does she concede? Does her concession weaken or strengthen her argument?

CONNECTION

Compare Peavey's view on effective activism which works toward accepting the socially defined "other" or antagonist with the views of Susan Griffin in "Ideologies of Madness" (see page 418).

IDEAS FOR WRITING

1. After reading Peavey's essay and the discussion by the editors at the beginning of this chapter on the dialogic argument, write an essay where you argue either for or against Peavey's approach to resolving political differences. If you see her approach as working better in some situations than in others, provide examples of areas of conflict where the approach might or might not work.
2. One of Peavey's points relates to how anger and righteousness sometimes prevent us from seeing the perspective of our opponents, or from seeing them as human, like ourselves. Write an essay about an experience in which you separated yourself from another person or an opposed group of people because of your anger or righteousness but later were able to understand and identify with their behavior and accept their differences.

RELATED WEB SITES

INTERVIEW WITH FRAN PEAVEY
http://www.jobsletter.org.nz/hpx/fran98.htm

STRATEGIC QUESTIONING
http://www.context.org/ICLIB/IC40/Peavey.htm
This web site provides guidelines for strategic questioning.

CRABGRASS
http://www.crabgrass.org/
Crabgrass is a small Non–Governmental Organization based in San Francisco that works globally and locally, on environmental, social justice and human rights issues. The site features articles by Fran Peavey.

Susan Voyticky

Mixed-Up

Susan Voyticky grew up in Brooklyn, New York. She enjoys traveling, studying genetics, and writing poetry. The following essay was written for her freshman English class in response to a question that asked students to reflect on an aspect of their ethnic heritage about which they have conflicting feelings.

Having parents from different ethnic groups and growing up mixed is not easy in this country; in fact, it can really mix a person up, culturally as well as socially. Often, mixed children are confused about the cultural group to which they belong, and sometimes these children are alienated from half or even all of their cultural background. Other times children exposed to two distinct cultures feel pressured by society to choose one culture and social group to fit into and to define themselves through. However, as a person of mixed background, I try, despite the pressures that society puts on me, to relate to both my European and to my African heritage. I realize that I have a unique and independent cultural identity.

My lack of wanting to identify with a particular culture defines who I am. For instance, I remember going shopping in a store when I was ten years old that had black and white floor tiles. I decided to play with two children, a boy and a girl who were my age. After a while the girl said, "We'll [she and the boy] step on the white tiles, and you [pointing to me] step on the black tiles 'cause you're black." I couldn't believe what she had said. Even at that age, I found the idea insulting to my existence—she was ignoring half of me. I replied indignantly, "You two can step on the white tiles, I'll step anywhere I want because I'm both." Then I quickly returned to my mother.

As a child, I quickly grew to realize that I was not ethnically "identifiable." During recess at my elementary school I often would try to play with the few African-American girls at my school. Usually the game was double-dutch, but I didn't know how to play, and the African-American kids said I turned the rope "like a white girl." To whites, I was black, and to blacks, I was less than black. I refused to be either; my ethnicity is an entirely different color—gray. If my mother is black and my father is white, then I most certainly must be gray. What else does one get by mixing black and white? Some would consider gray a "drab" color, but often one forgets gray comes in an infinite number of shades.

Because I have not chosen to identify with only one of my parents' cultures, I'll never know the comfort of belonging to a specific group of people with ancient customs and rituals. This society does not recognize my unique cross-cultural heritage of African-American, Irish, Russian, Polish, and Czechoslovakian. Few people choose to be mixed, to accept everything about themselves, and sometimes they are not given the choice. I have lost something in not being "white"; I also have lost something in not being "black." However, I have gained something important: my cultural independence. My brother puts it best when he says, "God was making a bunch of cookies. The white people he took out of the oven too soon. The black people he took out too late. We are the perfect cookies. One day everyone will be perfect, like us."

5   I struggle to be accepted in this society for what I am and not for what others would make of me. The longer I live, the more I feel pressured by society to "label" myself. When standardized forms were handed out in school, I would ask the teachers, "What should I fill out?" Most replied that I could fill whichever I wished. Most of the time that's what I did. One year I was black, the next year I was white, the next year I'd fill out two ovals. In high school, I was told I was black, because the federal government has a rule that if one is one fourth black, one is black. I ignored this and continued to fill out forms in my usual way.

Finally the true test of my "grayness" arrived—college applications. My mother said that I should fill out African-American, for the ethnic question, considering that it would improve my chances of being accepted. I didn't listen to her, for it's not in my nature to lie. How could I not be honest about who I was? On half of my applications I wrote "Black-Caucasian"; on the other half I wrote, "White African-American." My mother was not amused by what seemed to her a completely inane act. She didn't understand that I can't be told what I am, because I know who I am. In my blood run the tears of slaves torn from their homeland and the sweat of poor farmers looking for a better life. Their struggle is part of my identity.

A large part of one's culture is internal and cannot be represented simply by the color of one's skin. In this society it is difficult to be accepted for anything more than face value, but each person must try to be who he or she is within, not simply in the eyes of society. I am proud of my choice of identity with both of my ethnic backgrounds. Although being mixed often means being "mixed–up," being mistaken for something you are not by people too ignorant to care. Identity is more than skin deep.

QUESTIONS FOR DISCUSSION

1. What aspects of her mixed ethnic background cause Voyticky the most difficulty? How has she tried to resolve her problem of identity?
2. Compare Voyticky's view of the consequences of a mixed cultural and ethnic background with that presented in the poem by Judith Ortiz Cofer, "The Other."
3. Do you agree with Voyticky's approach to choosing an ethnicity for her college applications, or do you think that she should have taken fuller advantage of the opportunities afforded her?

4. Voyticky illustrates her essay with several examples drawn from her experience of being of mixed heritage at different stages of her life. What does each example add to her essay's persuasiveness and its portrait of the dilemmas faced in our society by individuals from backgrounds similar to Voyticky's? What other kinds of evidence or examples would have helped to persuade you?

Jill Ho

Affirmative Action: Perspectives from a Model Minority

Born in Taipei, Taiwan in 1979, Jill Ho immigrated to the United States with her family and was educated in this country. In high school she was involved in many student organizations and was the cofounder of the first Asian-American Student Organization in Wichita, Kansas. She plans to complete a biology major and to pursue a career in medicine. In her spare time, she enjoys rollerblading, doing crossword puzzles, keeping up with current events, and designing web pages. Ho wrote the following essay as a response to a professional essay by Dinesh D'Souza that criticized affirmative action and hiring quotas.

Intelligent. Hardworking. Compliant. These three words are used frequently to describe Asian-Americans who succeed in educational and occupational spheres. When I hear these words, they make me cringe because they mask my individuality and define my identity according to stereotypical expectations. A widespread belief referred to by Asian-American scholars as the Model Minority Myth holds that Asian-Americans are more successful than other minority groups. This stereotype has led to the distorted perspective that Asian-Americans do not really need affirmative action and racial preference programs for education and employment; thus, in practice, such programs for the most part do not benefit and often completely ignore Asians.

Being Asian was just a minor part of my identity until high school, when I realized that my "Asianness" affected how people perceived me, regardless of how I perceived myself. Since ninth grade, I have chosen to leave the racial background bubble blank on my standardized tests, because I strongly believe that my identity cannot be summarized in the three short words *Asian/Pacific Islander.* I am proud of my cultural background, which is similar to that of many other Asians who have grown up in the United States and who experience their culture not as all-Asian or all-American, nor as a combination of "partly Asian" and "partly American," but rather as something unique.

Despite my pride in my identity, being Asian-American has forced me to deal with situations which have made me feel excluded from both Asian *and* American cultures through pervasive stereotyping. For example, I am currently enrolled in a first year Chinese language class because my relatives tease me for not being able to speak my native tongue. On the first day of class, a student who apparently assumed I was already fluent in Chinese asked me why I was enrolled in the introductory class. It was strange that my relatives would think I wasn't "Asian enough" until I had learned how to speak Chinese while my classmate thought I was "too Asian" to be in the beginners class. My classmate's harmless question suggested that she thought most Asian-Americans were bilingual. Other common misperceptions include the stereotypes of Asians as hardworking, highly intelligent, socially awkward or even "nerdy," modest and passive, interested in math and science, and deficient in their command of spoken English (Cheng 278). While many traits associated with the Model Minority are positive, the myth supports a powerful stereotype that many Asians feel pressured to fit.

Not only does the Model Minority Myth tell Asians how they should behave, it also silences the unique experiences of Asian Americans. Dinesh D'Souza points out how ludicrous it would be to "abolish racial preferences for all groups except African Americans" (28). In a country as multi-ethnic as the United States, it would seem extremely unfair to propose affirmative action plans, which only focus on one minority group; yet Asians are already invisible minorities, excluded by most if not all racial preference programs, even though they are the fastest growing minority group in the United States. In 1980, 3.5 million Asian Americans were living in the United States; by 1990 that figure had doubled to 7.3 million and numbers are still increasing (Cheng and Thatchenkery 270). Part of the reason Asians are frequently not considered as minorities for preferences is the widespread belief that Asians are successful without benefiting from racial preferences; therefore they aren't disadvantaged enough. While Asian-Americans include the same spectrum of demographic diversity as any other minority group, the Model Minority Myth leads people to believe that most Asians are Ivy League overachievers, despite the fact that many live in poverty in the inner city.

5   Because people generally refuse to acknowledge their minority status, Asian-Americans are often unfairly treated in the workplace. The Model Minority Myth frequently appears to give Asians an initial advantage in getting hired when compared to other groups; however, Asians are actually at a disadvantage if we consider their job-related qualifications. Even when more educated than white applicants, Asians are often underpaid and occupy positions lower than would be expected for their level of education and training. Because people generally believe Asians are intelligent and industrious, many Asians feel they have to prove they are extra qualified to be considered for a position; once hired, they have to be exceptional to be promoted. When education and experience are accounted for, Asian-American high school graduates "earn 26 percent less than comparably educated white high school graduates, and Asian-American college graduates earn 11 percent less than white college graduates" (Narasaki 5). While other applicants need only prove they are well-qualified, Asians are forced to prove they are qualified above and beyond the already high expectations the Model Minority Myth sets for them.

However, despite the problems Asian-Americans have in the workplace, I agree with D'Souza that forcing companies to meet racial quotas may unfairly

result in consideration of issues entirely unrelated to who is most qualified. Selecting the less competent over better qualified applicants who do not benefit
from racial preference programs is not only unfair towards qualified candidates denied positions at that company, but also unfair for the companies
forced to absorb the economic costs of rejecting the best applicants (D'Souza
30). Furthermore, as D'Souza explains, companies would be unlikely to reject a
highly qualified minority applicant for racial reasons because it would make no
economic sense to do so; in fact, it would only hurt companies trying to compete in the market-place to ignore talented minority applicants (30).

At the same time, affirmative action programs are essential to help minorities combat promotion discrimination. While it is reasonable to assume that
companies are unlikely to discriminate blatantly against minorities in the hiring process, D'Souza fails to recognize that minority employees are far less
likely to receive promotions or pay increases. This glass ceiling effect is common for all members of minority groups, but especially so for Asian-Americans,
who are victims of the Model Minority Myth. Since the stereotype portrays
Asians as diligent, hardworking, and compliant, many employers believe that
Asians are ideal employees because they are non-confrontational. After his
1992 interviews with human resource managers in the Silicon Valley, Edward
Park concluded that "Asian-Americans are seen as expendable workers who
may be hired and fired at will because they will take what is offered and are too
passive to complain, let alone file wrongful termination lawsuits" (163).

The same notion that Asians are unlikely to complain makes it more difficult for Asians to receive promotions or pay raises. The glass ceiling which prevents minority members from advancing to upper management positions
especially affects Asian-Americans. In top management fewer than 1 percent
are minority members and even in companies where there are numerous
overqualified Asian employees in lower positions, fewer than .3 percent of senior level positions are held by Asian-Americans (Cheng 285). One possible explanation is that the same passive nature thought to prevent Asians from
complaining if not promoted would also make them ineffective managers. Additionally, another aspect of the Model Minority Myth, poor English skills, may
lead employers to believe that Asian supervisors would be unable to communicate clearly to employees. For many minorities, especially Asian-Americans, discrimination within companies for promotions is a bigger problem than
possible discrimination in initial hiring.

Eric Foner points out that we cannot pretend that "eliminating affirmative
action will produce a society in which rewards are based on merit" because race
is still an issue (925). Although few companies today would openly refuse to
hire minority employees, the unusually low number of minorities with equal se-
niority and\or equal pay in companies still reflects the effects of promotion discrimination. To remedy this situation, racial preference programs should strive
to create equal access to higher education for all minorities so anyone can have
the training to be well qualified for the workplace. Furthermore, employers
need to focus on breaking down barriers that limit opportunities for minority

promotion to senior-level positions so anyone can break through the glass ceiling. All people, regardless of race, gender, religion, or sexual orientation should be accepted in the workplace for who they are and rewarded for their competency and hard work on the job.

WORKS CITED

Cheng, Cliff. "Are Asian American Employees a Model Minority or Just a Minority?" Journal of Applied Behavioral Sciences Sep. 1997: 277–90.

Cheng, Cliff and Tojo Joseph Thatchenkery. "Why is There a Lack of Workplace Diversity Research on Asian Americans?" Journal of Applied Behavioral Sciences Sep. 1997: 270–76.

D'Souza, Dinesh. "Beyond Affirmative Action." National Review 9 Dec. 1996: 26–30.

Foner, Eric. "Hiring Quotas for White Males Only." The Nation 26 June 1995: 924–95.

Narasaki, K.K. "Separate But Equal? Discrimination and the Need for Affirmative Action Legislation." Perspectives on Affirmative Action. Los Angeles: Asian Pacific American Public Policy Institute, 1995. 5–8.

Park, Edward. "Asians Matter: Asian American Entrepreneurs in the Silicon Valley High Technology Industry." Reframing the Immigration Debate. B. Hing and R. Lee, Eds. Los Angeles: UCLA Asian American Studies Center, 1996. 155–77

QUESTIONS FOR DISCUSSION

1. What is the Model Minority Myth? How do the traits of the model influence the lives of Asian-Americans?
2. What examples from her own experiences does Ho provide? Are they effective?
3. What position does this essay take on Dinesh D'Souza's "Beyond Affirmative Action"? How does Ho both agree and disagree with D'Souza?
4. What solutions does Ho offer for improving work opportunities for Asian-Americans? Do you think her solutions are clearly stated and adequate?

Topics for Research and Writing

1. Do some research into the use of the double in Stevenson's *Dr. Jekyll and Mr. Hyde*. You should read the complete text, preferably an annotated version, and find some biographical information about Stevenson's life and the values of the time when he lived in order to see how the values of his society played a role in his creation of Jekyll and Hyde. How does the double of Jekyll/Hyde reveal typical preoccupations of Victorian England such as sexual repression and the hypocrisy of maintaining the façade of proper behavior in a society whose moral standards ignored the realities of violence, illegitimacy, drug use, and rampant prostitution? In what ways does the struggle Stevenson portrays seem relevant to the struggles people go through today?

2. Before Stevenson wrote *Jekyll and Hyde*, the double had had a long history as a literary subject, particularly in the Romantic era (late 18th and early 19th Centuries). Do some research into classic doubles stories by writers like Hoffmann, Mary Shelley, and Poe. Try to formulate some conclusions about the enduring popularity of this theme in literature.

3. At its most extreme, inability to incorporate the shadow self into one's dominant personality reveals itself in mental illness and breakdown. Do some research into a type of mental illness such as schizophrenia or multiple personality disorder in which the individual's personality tends to fragment into portions which cannot acknowledge one another or function together as a unified self. What are the causes of the particular disorder you have chosen to study? What treatments have been tried in the past and which ones are currently available?

4. Although the double is often seen as having a primarily psychological origin, there are often social and practical reasons why someone may choose to lead a literal "double life." Do some research into those who have chosen to pass as the "other," such as women who choose to disguise themselves as men, blacks who choose to pass for white, gays who are "closeted" or pass for "straight," etc. What are the social causes of this type of self-concealment? What are the psychological effects of having to conceal one's true self in society?

5. Shelby Steele's "Being Black and Feeling Blue" examines the way our society fails to acknowledge the contributions of ethnic and cultural minorities in America, despite the fact that this is in theory a multicultural society. Do some research into the psychological impact of being perceived by the dominant society as the "other," as a sort of shadowy outsider, less than a "real" American.

6. People have long been fascinated by identical twins as literal doubles. Do some research on the inner world of identical twins; consider some of the following issues: In what ways does each twin see himself/herself in the other? How are twins bonded with one another for life? What happens when identical twins are reared apart and later reunited? How does a surviving twin respond psychologically to the death of her or his sibling? Why and how does one twin often see his/her other as a shadow self?

7. Write an analysis of a film that dramatically portrays the double or divided personality. How does this film echo insights provided by one or more of the authors in this chapter? You might consider a film such as one of the following: *Three Faces of Eve*, *Dr. Jekyll and Mr. Hyde* (several versions of this film exist, each with a different view of the double), *Mary Reilly* (still another perspective on Jekyll and Hyde), *Dead Ringers*, *The Double Life of Veronique*, *True Lies*, *Sliding Doors*, *Ringers*, *Multiplicity*, *Adaptation*.

8 Society's Dreams

Roy Lichtenstein (1923–1997)
Hopeless (1963)

Roy Lichtenstein, one of the leading members of the American pop-art movement of the 1960s, devoted many of his paintings to enlargements of frames from comic books, as can be seen in *Hopeless*, based on a woman depicted in D.C. Comics' *Girls' Romances*. Lichtenstein's large, striking paintings question the relationship between commercial and fine art while looking beneath the surface of popular arts like the comic strip to reflect on the sexism, dehumanization, and mechanization revealed in the mass media.

JOURNAL

Find an interesting frame from a comic book or comic strip and write an analysis of what the image reveals about popular culture's perspective on gender, romance, violence, or some other social issue.

When we wake
the news of the world embraces us . . .

STEPHEN DUNN
Middle Class Poem

We would not have to insist that images reflect life, except that all too often we ask
life to reflect images.

GISH JEN
Challenging the Asian Illusion

RESEARCH WRITING

More so than any other type of writing, the research paper is a journey outward, into the worlds of many other writers past and present who have articulated their thoughts and views on a subject of public interest. The challenge in developing a research paper is in the synthesizing and harmonizing of diverse voices that you encounter and respond to in the course of your research. At the same time, you need to intersperse your own perspective, arguments, and conclusions. This writing process, if successful, can lead to a document that is clearly your own yet properly introduces and fairly credits the ideas and language of your sources.

The new skills needed to integrate and document facts and a variety of intellectual perspectives often overwhelm students as they begin a research paper. To minimize your anxiety, try to maintain a balance between your curious and creative self and your logical and rational self. The steps that follow will provide your rational side with a map to keep you on the main trail, but you should also allow your curious and creative mind to explore the many side paths and research possibilities that you will discover as you compose your paper. Above all, start early and pace yourself. A research paper needs to be completed in stages; it takes time to gather, to absorb, and to develop a response to the materials that will be incorporated into your paper.

For many students, being assigned a research paper raises a number of practical questions and issues: "How many sources will I be expected to use?" "What procedure should I follow in taking notes and doing a bibliography?" "How does the computer in the library catalog information?" "How can I access and evaluate information on the World Wide Web?" While these concerns are essential parts of the research paper writing process, we do not discuss specific techniques of finding, quoting, and documenting source information in the library or on the World Wide Web because these issues are thoroughly covered in most standard writing handbooks. Librarians are also available and willing to help you with your research. We will discuss the process involved in producing a research paper and the importance of maintaining a sense of voice and control over the information and point of view that you are presenting.

Research is more than a catalog of interesting facts and quotations; it also helps writers understand and evaluate their own perspectives and see their topic in relationship to their personal values and to broader issues. Professional writers naturally turn to outside sources to deepen their own personal perspective and to better inform and engage their readers. Because their writing is thoughtfully constructed and thoroughly revised, their source material becomes an integral part of their writer's voice and stance. What was originally research doesn't sound strained, dry, or tacked on, even though they may have used numerous brief quotations and paraphrases of their source material.

While it is natural to think about how your paper will be evaluated, it is more important to remain curious and to have fun discovering your sources and learning about your subject. It is helpful to keep a regular log of your process, making journal entries as you move through each stage, gather new insights, and new understanding about how your mind works under the pressure of research paper deadlines.

Finding a Topic

Spend some time exploring possible topics for your paper. Writing brief summaries of several different topics may help you to decide on the topic that interests you most. The best research papers are produced by students who are thoroughly engaged in their topic and in communicating what they have learned. Their enthusiasm and intellectual curiosity help them to work through the inevitable frustrations associated with learning how to use a library and tracking down information that may not be easily available.

After you complete some preliminary research, reevaluate and narrow your general topic further, if necessary, so that it can be covered within the scope and limits of the assignment. Notice, for instance, how Jason Glickman in his essay "Technology and the Future of American Wilderness" in this chapter has narrowed the focus of his essay from the general topic of wilderness to American wilderness. He further narrows the scope of his research by choosing to focus only on the impact of digital technology—cellular telephones and laptop computers—on the wilderness experience. He made his pager more manageable by focusing on a particular topic—one that he was concerned and knowledgeable about.

Timetable and Process

Make a timetable for your project and follow it. For example, you might allow yourself two to three weeks to do research and to establish a working bibliography. Then schedule several work sessions to write the first draft, and several more days to complete your research and revise the draft, to complete the final draft, check your documentation, and do the final proofreading. At every stage in this process you should seek out as much useful feedback and advice as you possibly can. Tell your family and friends about your topic; they may have ideas about where to find sources. Read your first draft to your friends and give your teacher a copy. Make sure that your readers clearly understand your paper's purpose and that your writing holds their interest. Don't feel discouraged if you find that you need to do several revisions to clarify your ideas. This is a natural part of the research paper writing process.

Your Voice and the Voices of Your Sources

Practice careful reading and accurate note taking as you prepare to write your paper. To avoid becoming bored or overwhelmed by the sources you are working with, treat them as outside voices, as people you want to have a dialogue with. Take every quotation you intend to use in your paper and paraphrase it carefully into your own language to make sure that you really understand it. If you feel confused or intimidated by a source, freewriting may help you to get in touch with your feelings and responses to the authority. Are the assertions of this authority correct, or do your experiences suggest that some comments are questionable? In our study questions throughout this text we've created models of questions you can ask as you analyze a text. Now it is time for you to begin posing and answering your own questions about your text sources. Undigested sources often produce a glorified book report, a rehash of ideas that you have not fully absorbed and integrated with your own point of view. For further information on evaluating sources and the facts they present, both from print and electronic media such as web sites, newsgroups, and listservs, see the section on argument in Chapter 7 of *Dreams and Inward Journeys* and any of a number of recent texts such as *Researching Online* (Longman 1999).

Purpose and Structure

Always keep focused on the purpose and structure in your essay. Your research paper should express an original central purpose and have a compelling thesis. Each major idea must be introduced by a clear topic sentence and supported by evidence and examples. While using an outline is very helpful, feel free to revise the outline as you do further research and make changes in your original perspective. A research paper brings together many different ideas into a unified, original vision of a subject that, as the writer, only you can provide.

Language and Style

As you write your first draft, and particularly as you work through later stages of the paper, continue to express your own writer's voice. Your point of view should be communicated in language with which you are comfortable. Your voice should always be your paper's guide. Read your paper aloud periodically. Is it tedious to listen to? Is it interesting? Do you sound like yourself in this essay? Check your vocabulary and compare it with the sense of language in your previous papers. Are you using more multisyllabic words than usual or a specialized jargon that even you can hardly understand, one that is too derivative of your sources? Are your sentences more convoluted than usual? Have you lost touch with your own personal voice? Consider the answer to all of these questions. Make sure that your paper reflects your point of view. Remember that your sources are supporting what you think and believe.

The Computer as a Research Partner

Whether you work on a computer at home or use the computers in your library's resource center, please consider the advantage of using a computer at all stages of your research writing process. The Internet can help you to identify and refine topics; you also should keep a record of your writing timetable and progress on your computer files. It is helpful to gather and store information from different sources on the computer to save the time of copying information. When it comes time to draft your research paper, you can just start writing and integrating the information you have already saved, moving major portions of the paper around. Fine editing is done more efficiently with the use of a computer. There are even computer programs such as *Endnote* (Niles software, Berkeley, Ca. http://www.niles.com), that allow you to search hundreds of libraries and databases and to automatically format your data into different bibliographic formats, including the MLA Works Cited format required for most English classes.

Writing a research paper is a challenge that provides you with the opportunity to develop, to utilize, and to integrate your research and writing skills as well as your creativity. A well written research paper is a genuine accomplishment, a milestone on your inward journey.

THEMATIC INTRODUCTION: SOCIETY'S DREAMS

Who creates and monitors the dreams of our society and our own dreams? The readings in this chapter suggest different ways that social customs; mass media such as film, television, advertising, and political ideology influence our dreams and self-concepts. Although it would be naive to imagine that we could have total control over our own dreams, creating them without being influenced by our culture, family, and friends, many of us aspire to be individualistic, first valuing our inner feelings and thoughts while forming impressions and evaluations of our social and political worlds. In modern society, however, individualism is often undermined and threatened by social forces that seek to mold us into loyal citizens, passive consumers, productive and compliant workers. Eager to escape temporarily from our immediate problems or to conform to our social world, we allow ourselves to deny the impact that overexposure to the mass media and the steady barrage of consumerist and political propaganda can have on the development and integrity of our private selves as well as on our sense of its power to shape us.

One of the most common ways that society enters our minds and creates distorted pictures of the external world and its values is through the news. Television newscasts, radio talk shows, and newspaper stories select and present reports of human events and natural disasters that are terribly disturbing: full of uncontrollable dangers, disasters, and violence. These reports, while sometimes accurate, often intensify the negative, especially in contrast to what occurs in day-to-day life. To the extent that we internalize these nightmarish pictures of the world, our inner lives and private dream worlds are affected.

Our first two selections explore different ways that we process what we learn from the media. In Louise Erdrich's poem "Dear John Wayne," we learn about the impact that film images of the settling of the West and the conquest of the "redskins" continue to have on Native Americans. In "Pictures in Our Heads," Anthony Pratkanis and Elliot Aronson examine the exaggerated impressions held by heavy television viewers of the level of violence and risk in society. This selection asks us to question why we allow the news media to define the questions and issues that concern us. The article urges media consumers and media outlets to take more responsibility in selecting what is newsworthy and true.

We already know that many commentators have argued that the media and political propaganda have a significant impact on the choices we make. Eric Schlosser in his essay "McTeachers and Coke Dudes" exposes the way that the media have even infiltrated the elementary grades of the public schools. The school curriculum now includes commercials for fast foods and soft drinks. Because of the sheer intensity and multifaceted nature of the barrage of media information, some radical media critics provide counter cultural alternatives to media-driven culture. Kalle Lasn, author of the essay "The Ecology of Mind," argues that the media is making us physically and mentally ill.

Many of us lack a clear perspective on the impact of the media because a society seeped in media images is all that we have ever known. Helena Norberg-Hodge, a critic of the impact of global media images on people from Third World countries, presents in her essay, "The Pressure to Modernize," a disturbing case history of the introduction of global trade and international media in Tibet. The impact on the customs, beliefs, and self-esteem of this small, isolated culture in the Tibetan plateau region in the north of India is shocking and encourages us to think more about how easily we accept what the media feed us. Addressing a related issue that is both local and global in scope, philosopher Sissela Bok, in "Aggression: The Impact of Media Violence" examines the impact of the violence in television and films on children's abilities to control their own aggression.

The next essay critiques the entertainment media that give Americans as well as the world audience for U.S. produced media, powerful images of what it is like to be American. Todd Gitlin's "Three Formulas" examines three types of film formulas—the Western, the action film, and the cartoon—that have spread a distorted view of American values.

The final selection in the chapter explores the ways that our relationship to the wilderness and our ability to find solace there has been affected by the medium of portable technology. In his research essay, "Technology and the Future of the American Wilderness," student writer Jason Glickman examines the historic concept of the wilderness in American culture and explores the impact of digital technology on the contemporary wilderness experience.

We hope by reading the selections in this chapter you will think more deeply and more critically about the ways that your dreams and beliefs are being shaped by the mass media, social conventions, and political ideology. An important part of a writer's inward journey involves clarification of your values. Unraveling your own genuine dreams and values from those that are artificial and mass-produced can be both liberating and life affirming.

Louise Erdrich

Dear John Wayne

Louise Erdrich (b. 1954) was raised in Wahpeton, North Dakota, as a member of the Turtle Mountain Chippewa tribe and her parents encouraged her to write. Her culture valued story telling and Erdrich attended Dartmouth College where she studied with Michael Dorris, who she later married. She earned a B.A. from Dartmouth in 1976

*and an M.F.A. in creative writing from Johns Hopkins University several years
later. Her first novel* Love Medicine *(1984, expanded edition 1993), which won the
National Book Critics Circle Award, introduces many of the characters and clan histories that are developed in her novels,* The Beet Queen *(1986),* Tracks *(1988),
and* The Bingo Palace *(1994). Her recent work includes* Antelope Woman
(1998), The Last Report on the Miracles at Little No Horse *(2001), and* The
Birchbark House *(2002) . The poem that follows, "Dear John Wayne," is included
in her first book of poetry,* Jacklight *(1984).*

JOURNAL

Write about a film that influenced your view of a particular cultural, ethnic, or national group.

August and the drive-in picture is packed.
We lounge on the hood of the Pontiac
surrounded by the slow-burning spirals they sell
at the window, to vanquish the hordes of mosquitoes.
5 Nothing works. They break through the smoke-screen
for blood.

Always the look-out spots the Indians first,
spread north to south, barring progress.
The Sioux, or Cheyenne, or some bunch
10 in spectacular columns, arranged like SAC missiles,
their feathers bristling in the meaningful sunset.

The drum breaks. There will be no parlance.
Only the arrows whining, a death-cloud of nerves
swarming down on the settlers
15 who die beautifully, tumbling like dust weeds
into the history that brought us all here
together: this wide screen beneath the sign of the bear.

The sky fills, acres of blue squint and eye
that the crowd cheers. His face moves over us,
20 a thick cloud of vengeance, pitted
like the land that was once flesh. Each rut,
each scar makes a promise: *It is
not over, this fight, not as long as you resist.
Everything we see belongs to us.*

25 A few laughing Indians fall over the hood
slipping in the hot spilled butter.

The eye sees a lot, John, but the heart is so blind.
How will you know what you own?
He smiles, a horizon of teeth
30   the credits reel over, and then the white fields
again blowing in the true-to-life dark.
The dark films over everything.
We get into the car
scratching our mosquito bites, speechless and small
35   as people are when the movie is done.
We are back in ourselves.

How can we help but keep hearing his voice,
the flip side of the sound-track, still playing:
Come on, boys, we've got them
40   *where we want them, drunk, running.*
They will give us what we want, what we need:
The heart is a strange wood inside of everything
we see, burning, doubling, splitting out of its skin.

QUESTIONS FOR DISCUSSION

1. What is the ironic significance of the setting of the poem: a drive-in movie
    in August, where "hordes of mosquitoes" attack Indian patrons?
2. How are the Native Americans characterized in the second stanza? How
    does Erdrich use ironic images and details to critique the stereotypical at-
    titudes of Native Americans that the film reflects? Are Native Americans
    characterized differently in contemporary films?
3. What image of the "history that brought us all here together" is presented
    in the poem? How do you think the Native Americans would have told
    the film's story?
4. What is the impact of the huge close-up face and eye of John Wayne de-
    scribed in the fourth stanza? What attitude toward Native Americans
    does Wayne's face portray? Why is the poem addressed to Wayne?
5. What criticisms of Wayne's values and the values of the Western film
    genre are made through the italicized lines in stanzas five and six? Who is
    speaking in these lines?
6. Who is describing the heart in these lines: "the heart is so blind. . . ." and
    "The heart is a strange wood. . . ."? Interpret the meaning of these lines.

CONNECTION

Compare Erdrich's poem to Todd Gitlin's observations on the distorted images that American History gives of the place and contribution of minorities
to American culture (see page 493).

IDEAS FOR WRITING

1. Write a critique of a particular film that you believe exploits racist stereotypes and could possibly influence the public negatively against a particular group of people.
2. Write about a film that you believe challenges stereotypes and presents a positive or original, revealing view of a group of people who have been stereotyped negatively.

RELATED WEB SITES

LOUISE ERDRICH

http://voices.cla.umn.edu/authors/LouiseErdrich.html
From the "Voice from the Gaps" web site, this URL features author Louise Erdrich. It includes a biography, a selected bibliography, and related links for understanding Erdrich's life and contribution to American literature.

INTERNET RESOURCES ON NATIVE AMERICANS

http://falcon.jmu.edu/~ramseyil/native.htm
This is the Internet School Library Media Center [ISLMC] Native American page. Find bibliographies, directories to pages of individual tribes, history and historical documents, periodicals and general links.

UNITED NATIVE AMERICA MEDIA LINKS

http://www.unitednativeamerica.com/media.html#Media
This site provides an extensive collection of links to community-based, national and international media sites and political organizations dedicated to spreading information about and improving social and economic status of Native Americans.

Anthony Pratkanis and Elliot Aronson

Pictures in Our Heads

Anthony Pratkanis and Elliot Aronson are professors of psychology at the University of California, Santa Cruz. Pratkanis has taught courses in consumerism and advertising at Carnegie Mellon. He has written many articles for both popular and scholarly journals and is an editor of Attitude Structure and Function *(1989) and, with Aronson,* Social Psychology *(1993). Aronson is one of the world's most highly regarded social psychologists. He is the author of many books, including* The Social Animal *(1972, 7th ed. 1995) and* The Jigsaw Classroom *(1978, 1997). The following article is from Pratkanis's and Aronson's* The Age of Propaganda *(1992), a book that focuses on the ways people's views of the world are influenced and molded by the constant barrage of media propaganda.*

JOURNAL

Write about an attitude you have toward a certain political or social issue, an attitude that you believe was influenced by the images from television news.

In *Public Opinion*, the distinguished political analyst Walter Lippmann tells the story of a young girl, brought up in a small mining town, who one day went from cheerfulness into a deep spasm of grief.[1] A gust of wind had suddenly cracked a kitchen windowpane. The young girl was inconsolable and spoke incomprehensibly for hours. When she finally was able to speak intelligibly, she explained that a broken pane of glass meant that a close relative had died. She was therefore mourning her father, whom she felt certain had just passed away. The young girl remained disconsolate until, days later, a telegram arrived verifying that her father was still alive. It appears that the girl had constructed a complete fiction based on a simple external fact (a broken window), a superstition (broken window means death), fear, and love for her father.

The point of Lippmann's story was not to explore the inner workings of abnormal personality, but to ask a question about ourselves: To what extent do we, like the young girl, let our fictions guide our thoughts and actions? Lippmann believed that we are much more similar to that young girl than we might readily admit. He contended that the mass media paint an imagined world and that the "pictures in our heads" derived from the media influence what men and women will do and say at any particular moment. Lippmann made these observations in 1922. Seven decades later, we can ask: What is the evidence for his claim? To what extent do the pictures we see on television and in other mass media influence how we see the world and set the agenda for what we view as most important in our lives?

Let's look at the world we see on television. George Gerbner and his associates have conducted the most extensive analysis of television to date.[2] Since the late 1960s, these researchers have been videotaping and carefully analyzing thousands of prime-time television programs and characters. Their findings, taken as a whole, indicate that the world portrayed on television is grossly misleading as a representation of reality. Their research further suggests that, to a surprising extent, we take what we see on television as a reflection of reality.

In prime-time programming, males outnumber females by 3 to 1, and the women portrayed are younger than the men they encounter. Nonwhites (especially Hispanics), young children, and the elderly are underrepresented; and members of minority groups are disproportionately cast in minor roles. Moreover, most prime-time characters are portrayed as professional and managerial workers: Although 67 percent of the work force in the United States are employed in blue-collar or service jobs, only 25 percent of TV characters hold such jobs. Finally, crime on television is ten times more prevalent than it is in real life. The average 15-year-old has viewed more than 13,000 TV killings. Over half of TV's characters are involved in a violent confrontation each week; in reality, fewer than 1 percent of people in the nation are victims of criminal violence in any given year, according to FBI statistics. David Rintels, a television writer and former president of the Writers' Guild of America, summed it up best when he said, "From 8 to 11 o'clock each night, television is one long lie."[3]

5   To gain an understanding of the relationship between watching television and the pictures in our heads, Gerbner and his colleagues compared the attitudes and beliefs of heavy viewers (those who watch more than four hours a day) and light viewers (those who watch less than two hours a day). They found that heavy viewers (1) express more racially prejudiced attitudes; (2) overestimate the number of people employed as physicians, lawyers, and athletes; (3) perceive women as having more limited abilities and interests than men; (4) hold exaggerated views of the prevalence of violence in society; and (5) believe old people are fewer in number and less healthy today than they were twenty years ago, even though the opposite is true. What is more, heavy viewers tend to see the world as a more sinister place than do light viewers; they are more likely to agree that most people are just looking out for themselves and would take advantage of you if they had a chance. Gerbner and his colleagues conclude that these attitudes and beliefs reflect the inaccurate portrayals of American life provided to us by television.

Let's look at the relationship between watching television and images of the world by looking more closely at how we picture criminal activity. In an analysis of "television criminology," Craig Haney and John Manzolati point out that crime shows dispense remarkably consistent images of both the police and criminals.[4] For example, they found that television policemen are amazingly effective, solving almost every crime, and are absolutely infallible in one regard: The wrong person is never in jail at the end of a show. Television fosters an illusion of certainty in crimefighting. Television criminals generally turn to crime because of psychopathology or insatiable (and unnecessary) greed. Television emphasizes criminals' personal responsibility for their actions and largely ignores situational pressures correlated with crime, such as poverty and unemployment.

Haney and Manzolati go on to suggest that this portrayal has important social consequences. People who watch a lot of television tend to share this belief system, which affects their expectations and can cause them to take a hard-line stance when serving on juries. Heavy viewers are likely to reverse the presumption of innocence, believing that defendants must be guilty of something, otherwise they wouldn't be brought to trial.

A similar tale can be told about other "pictures painted in our heads." For example, heavy readers of newspaper accounts of sensational and random crimes report higher levels of fear of crime. Repeated viewing of R-rated violent "slasher" films is associated with less sympathy and empathy for victims of rape. When television is introduced into an area, the incidence of theft increases, perhaps due partly to television's promotion of consumerism, which may frustrate and anger economically deprived viewers who compare their life-styles with those portrayed on television.[5]

It should be noted, however, that the research just described—that done by Gerbner and colleagues and by others—is correlational; that is, it shows merely an association, not a causal relation, between television viewing and beliefs. It is therefore impossible to determine from this research whether heavy viewing actually causes prejudiced attitudes and inaccurate beliefs or whether people already holding such attitudes and beliefs simply tend to watch more television. In order to be certain that watching TV causes such attitudes and beliefs, it would be necessary to perform a controlled experiment in which people are randomly assigned to conditions. Fortunately, some recent experiments do allow us to be fairly certain that heavy viewing does indeed determine the pictures we form of the world.

10   In a set of ingenious experiments, the political psychologists Shanto Iyengar and Donald Kinder varied the contents of evening news shows watched by their research participants.[6] In their studies, Iyengar and Kinder edited the evening news so that participants received a steady dose of news about a specific problem facing the United States. For example, in one of their experiments, some participants heard about the weaknesses of U.S. defense capabilities; a second group watched shows emphasizing pollution concerns; a third group heard about inflation and economic matters.

The results were clear. After a week of viewing the specially edited programs, participants emerged from the study more convinced than they were before viewing the shows that the target problem—the one receiving extensive coverage in the shows they had watched—was a more important one for the country to solve. What is more, the participants acted on their newfound perceptions, evaluating the current president's performance on the basis of how he handled the target issue and evaluating more positively than their competitors those candidates who took strong positions on those problems.

Iyengar and Kinder's findings are not a fluke. Communications researchers repeatedly find a link between what stories the mass media cover and what viewers consider to be the most important issues of the day.[7] The content of the mass media sets the public's political and social agenda. As just one example, in a pioneering study of an election in North Carolina, researchers found that the issues that voters came to consider to be most important in the campaign coincided with the amount of coverage those issues received in the local media.[8] Similarly, the problems of drug abuse, NASA incompetence, and nuclear energy were catapulted into the nation's consciousness by the coverage of dramatic events such as the drug-related death of basketball star Len Bias, the *Challenger* explosion, and the nuclear-reactor accidents at Three Mile Island and Chernobyl. Former Secretary of State Henry Kissinger clearly understood the power of the news media in setting agendas. He once noted that he never watched the content of the evening news but was only interested in "what they covered and for what length of time, to learn what the country was getting."[9]

Of course, each of us has had extensive personal contact with many people in a myriad of social contexts; the media are just one source of our knowledge about political affairs and different ethnic, gender, and occupational groups. The information and impressions we receive through the media are relatively less influential when we can also rely on firsthand experience. Thus those of us who have been in close contact with several women who work outside the home are probably less susceptible to the stereotypes of women portrayed on television. On the other hand, regarding issues with which most of us have had limited or no personal experience, such as crime and violence, television and the other mass media are virtually the only vivid source of information for constructing our image of the world.

The propaganda value of the mass media in painting a picture of the world has not been overlooked by would-be leaders. Such social policy as a "get tough on crime" program, for example, can be easily sold by relating it to the prime-time picture of crime as acts committed by the psychopathic and the greedy, rather than dealing with situational determinants such as poverty and unemployment. In a similar vein, it is easier to sell a "war on drugs" after the drug-related death of a prominent basketball star or to promote an end to nuclear power after a fatal tragedy at a nuclear reactor.

15   It is even more important for a would-be leader to propagate his or her own picture of the world. The political scientist Roderick Hart notes that since the early 1960s, U.S. presidents have averaged over twenty-five speeches per month—a large amount of public speaking.[10] Indeed, during 1976, Gerald Ford spoke in public once every six hours, on average. By speaking frequently on certain issues (and gaining access to the nightly news), a president can create a political agenda—a picture of the world that is favorable to his or her social policies. Indeed, one of President Bush's key advisors is Robert Teeter, a pollster who informs the president on what Americans think and what issues should be the topic of his speeches. This can be of great importance in maintaining power. According to Jeffery Pfeffer, an expert on business organizations, one of the most important sources of power for a chief executive officer is the ability to set the organization's agenda by determining what issues will be discussed and when, what criteria will be used to resolve disputes, who will sit on what committees, and, perhaps most importantly, which information will be widely disseminated and which will be selectively ignored.[11]

Why are the pictures of the world painted by the mass media so persuasive? For one thing, we rarely question the picture that is shown. We seldom ask ourselves, for example, "Why are they showing me this story on the evening news rather than some other one? Do the police really operate in this manner? Is the world really this violent and crime-ridden?" The pictures that television beams into our homes are almost always simply taken for granted as representing reality.

Once accepted, the pictures we form in our heads serve as fictions to guide our thoughts and actions. The images serve as primitive social theories— providing us with the "facts" of the matter, determining which issues are most pressing, and decreeing the terms in which we think about our social world. As the political scientist Bernard Cohen observed,

[The mass media] may not be successful much of the time in telling people *what to think,* but it is stunningly successful in telling its readers *what to think about* . . . The world will look different to different people, depending . . . on the map that is drawn for them by writers, editors, and publishers of the papers they read.[12]

END NOTES

1. Lippmann, W. (1922). *Public opinion.* New York: Harcourt, Brace.
2. Gerbner, G., Gross, L., Morgan, M., & Signorielli, N. (1986). "Living with television: The dynamics of the cultivation process." In J. Bryant & D. Zillman (Eds.), *Perspectives on media effects* (pp. 17–40). Hillsdale, NJ: Erlbaum.
3. Quoted in *Newsweek,* December 6, 1982, p. 40.
4. Haney, C., & Manzolati, J. (1981). "Television criminology: Network illusions on criminal justice realities." In E. Aronson (Ed.), *Readings about the social animal* (3rd ed.; pp. 125–136). New York: W. H. Freeman.
5. See Heath, L. (1984). "Impact of newspaper crime reports on fear of crime: Multimethodological investigation." *Journal of Personality and Social Psychology,* 47, 263–276; Linz, D. G., Donnerstein, E., & Penrod, S. (1988). "Effects of long-term exposure to violent and sexually degrading depictions of women." *Journal of Personality and Social Psychology,* 55, 758–768; Henningan, K., Heath, L., Wharton, J. D., Del Rosario, M., Cook, T. D., & Calder, B. (1982). "Impact of the introduction of television on crime in the United States: Empirical findings and theoretical implications." *Journal of Personality and Social Psychology,* 42, 461–477.
6. Iyengar, S., & Kinder, D. R. (1987). *News that matters.* Chicago: University of Chicago Press.
7. Rogers, E. M., & Dearing, J. W. (1988). "Agenda-setting research: Where has it been, Where is it going?" In J. A. Anderson (Ed.), *Communication Yearbook* 11 (pp. 555–594). Beverly Hills, CA: Sage.
8. McCombs, M. E., & Shaw, D. L. (1972). "The agenda setting function of mass media." *Public Opinion Quarterly,* 36, 176–187.
9. Dilenschneider, R. L. (1990). *Power and influence.* New York: Prentice-Hall.
10. Hart, R. P. (1987). *The sound of leadership.* Chicago: University of Chicago Press.
11. Pfeffer, J. (1981). *Power in organizations.* Cambridge, MA: Ballinger.
12. Cited in Rogers and Dearing (1988). See note 7.

QUESTIONS FOR DISCUSSION

1. What is the point of Walter Lippmann's story of the young girl who superstitiously mourned her father? Why is this an effective way to begin the essay?

2. What are the "pictures in our heads" that Lippmann and the authors of the essay comment on? How do these pictures both resemble and differ from dreams and fantasies?

3. What conclusions can be drawn from George Gerbner's television program analysis? What comparisons did Gerbner and his associates make between different kinds of viewers and their beliefs?

4. How are criminals usually portrayed on television? What impact does this portrayal have on our attitudes and beliefs? How have politicians used stereotypical portrayals of criminals and crime to sell their programs to the public?

5. What flaw can be found in Gerbner's research? How have the experiments of Iyengar and Kinder on evening news shows and their viewers helped to correct and support Gerbner's research?

6. Explain Bernard Cohen's distinction between the media's telling us what to think as opposed to telling us "what to think about." What does Cohen consider the media's most stunning success? What examples does he provide?

CONNECTION

Compare and contrast Pratkanis's and Lasn's evaulation of the impact of television news, media images, and information overload (see page 464).

IDEAS FOR WRITING

1. Do some research into recent intensive media coverage of a political event or a controversial issue. Discuss the media's impact on the public's perceptions of the reality of the situation. You might take a look at some public opinion polls that were taken during the period you are discussing and examine typical stories aired on television and in the newspapers.
2. Write about your attitudes toward a political issue covered extensively by the mass media. Explain to what degree your political views and social outlook were influenced by the media in contrast to your direct experience and/or conversations about the event.

RELATED WEB SITES

ELLIOT ARONSON AND SOCIAL PSYCHOLOGY
http://aronson.socialpsychology.org/
Social psychologist Elliot Aronson's biography and work are featured at this web site entitled the "Social Psychology Network." The site claims to have the largest social psychology database on the Internet, with over 5000 links to psychology-related resources.

PROPAGANDA
http://carmen.artsci.washington.edu/propaganda/intro.htm
Learn about the common techniques of propaganda at this web site devoted to the subject. Also find out about examples of, and references to logical fallacies in this age-old ploy to shape the masses.

Eric Schlosser

McTeachers and Coke Dudes

Eric Schlosser is an investigative journalist currently working for the Atlantic Monthly. *He won the National Magazine Award for reporting in 1994 for a series of articles in the* Atlantic *about the marijuana enforcement laws, and also received the Sidney Hillman Foundation award in 1995 for his reportage on California's strawberry industry. His first book,* Fast Food Nation *(2000) is an exposé of the impact of the fast food industry on public health in the United States and abroad. He is currently working on an expanded version of an article he wrote for the* Atlantic *entitled "The Prison Industrial Complex." The following selection is from* Fast Food Nation.

Do you remember advertisements for soda and fast-food products as a part of your
high school culture? What kind of impact did these ads have on you?

Not satisfied with marketing to children through playgrounds, toys, cartoons, movies, videos, charities, and amusement parks, through contests,
sweepstakes, games, and clubs, via television, radio, magazines, and the Internet, fast food chains are now gaining access to the last advertising-free outposts
of American life. In 1993 District 11 in Colorado Springs started a nationwide
trend, becoming the first public school district in the United States to place ads
for Burger King in its hallways and on the sides of its school buses. Like other
school systems in Colorado, District 11 faced revenue shortfalls, thanks to growing enrollments and voter hostility to tax increases for education. The initial
Burger King and King Sooper ad contracts were a disappointment for the district, gaining it just $37,500 a year—little more than $1 per student. In 1996,
school administrators decided to seek negotiating help from a professional,
hiring Dan DeRose, president of DD Marketing, Inc., of Pueblo, Colorado.
DeRose assembled special advertising packages for corporate sponsors. For
$12,000, a company got five school-bus ads, hallway ads in all fifty-two of the
district's schools, ads in their school newspapers, a stadium banner, ads over
the stadium's public-address system during games, and free tickets to high
school sporting events.

Within a year, DeRose had nearly tripled District 11's ad revenues. But his
greatest success was still to come. In August of 1997, DeRose brokered a ten-
year deal that made Coca-Cola the district's exclusive beverage supplier, bringing the schools up to $11 million during the life of the contract (minus DD
Marketing's fee). The deal also provided free use of a 1998 Chevy Cavalier to a
District 11 high school senior, chosen by lottery, who had good grades and a
perfect attendance record.

District 11's marketing efforts were soon imitated by other school districts in
Colorado, by districts in Pueblo, Fort Collins, Denver, and Cherry Creek. Administrators in Colorado Springs did not come up with the idea of using corporate sponsorship to cover shortfalls in a school district's budget. But they took it
to a whole new level, packaging it, systematizing it, leading the way. Hundreds of
public school districts across the United States are now adopting or considering
similar arrangements. Children spend about seven hours a day, one hundred
and fifty days a year, in school. Those hours have in the past been largely free of
advertising, promotion, and market research—a source of frustration to many
companies. Today the nation's fast food chains are marketing their products in
public schools through conventional ad campaigns, classroom teaching materials, and lunch-room franchises, as well as a number of unorthodox means.

The proponents of advertising in the schools argue that it is necessary to
prevent further cutbacks; opponents contend that schoolchildren are becoming a captive audience for marketers, compelled by law to attend school and

then forced to look at ads as a means of paying for their own education. America's schools now loom as a potential gold mine for companies in search of young customers. "Discover your own river of revenue at the schoolhouse gates," urged a brochure at the 1997 Kids Power Marketing Conference. "Whether it's first-graders learning to read or teenagers shopping for their first car, we can guarantee an introduction of your product and your company to these students in the traditional setting of the classroom."

5   DD Marketing, with offices in Colorado Springs and Pueblo, has emerged as perhaps the nation's foremost negotiator of ad contracts for schools. Dan DeRose began his career as the founder of the Minor League Football System, serving in the late 1980s as both a team owner and a player. In 1991, he became athletic director at the University of Southern Colorado in Pueblo. During his first year, he raised $250,000 from corporate sponsors for the school's teams. Before long he was raising millions of dollars to build campus sports facilities. He was good at getting money out of big corporations, and formed DD Marketing to use this skill on behalf of schools and nonprofits. Beverage companies and athletic shoe companies had long supported college sports programs, and during the 1980s began to put up the money for new high school scoreboards. Dan DeRose saw marketing opportunities that were still untapped. After negotiating his first Colorado Springs package deal in 1996, he went to work for the Grapevine-Colleyville School District in Texas. The district would never have sought advertising, its deputy superintendent told the *Houston Chronicle*, "if it weren't for the acute need for funds." DeRose started to solicit ads not only for the district's hallways, stadiums, and buses, but also for its rooftops—so that passengers flying in or out of the nearby Dallas–Forth Worth airport could see them—and for its voice-mail systems. "You've reached Grapevine-Colleyville school district, proud partner of Dr Pepper," was a message that DeRose proposed. Although some people in the district were skeptical about the wild ideas of this marketer from Colorado, DeRose negotiated a $3.4 million dollar exclusive deal between the Grapevine-Colleyville School District and Dr Pepper in June of 1997. And Dr Pepper ads soon appeared on school rooftops.

Dan DeRose tells reporters that his work brings money to school districts that badly need it. By pitting one beverage company against another in bidding wars for exclusive deals, he's raised the prices being offered to schools. "In Kansas City they were getting 67 cents a kid before," he told one reporter, "and now they're getting $27." The major beverage companies do not like DeRose and prefer not to deal with him. He views their hostility as a mark of success. He doesn't think that advertising in the schools will corrupt the nation's children and has little tolerance for critics of the trend. "There are critics to penicillin," he told the *Fresno Bee*. In the three years following his groundbreaking contract for School District 11 in Colorado Springs, Dan DeRose negotiated agreements for seventeen universities and sixty public school systems across the United States, everywhere from Greenville, North Carolina, to Newark, New Jersey. His 1997 deal with a school district in Derby, Kansas, included the commitment to open a Pepsi GeneratioNext Resource Center at an elementary school. Thus far, DeRose has been responsible for school and university beverage deals worth more than $200 million. He typically accepts no money up front, then charges schools a commission that takes between 25 and 35 percent of the deal's total revenues.

The nation's three major beverage manufacturers are now spending large sums to increase the amount of soda that American children consume. Coca-Cola, Pepsi, and Cadbury-Schweppes (the maker of Dr Pepper) control 90.3 percent of the U.S. market, but have been hurt by declining sales in Asia. Americans already drink soda at an annual rate of about fifty-six gallons per person— that's nearly six hundred twelve-ounce cans of soda per person. Coca-Cola has set itself the goal of raising consumption of its products in the United States by at least 25 percent a year. The adult market is stagnant; selling more soda to kids has become one of the easiest ways to meet sales projections. "Influencing elementary school students is very important to soft drink marketers," an article in the January 1999 issue of *Beverage Industry* explained, "because children are still establishing their tastes and habits." Eight-year-olds are considered ideal customers; they have about sixty-five years of purchasing in front of them. "Entering the schools makes perfect sense," the trade journal concluded.

The fast food chains also benefit enormously when children drink more soda. The chicken nuggets, hamburgers, and other main courses sold at fast food restaurants usually have the lowest profit margins. Soda has by far the highest. "We at McDonald's are thankful," a top executive once told the *New York Times*, "that people like drinks with their sandwiches." Today McDonald's sells more Coca-Cola than anyone else in the world. The fast food chains purchase Coca-Cola syrup for about $4.25 a gallon. A medium Coke that sells for $1.29 contains roughly 9 cents' worth of syrup. Buying a large Coke for $1.49 instead, as the cute girl behind the counter always suggests, will add another 3 cents' worth of syrup—and another 17 cents in pure profit for McDonald's.

"Liquid Candy," a 1999 study by the Center for Science in the Public Interest, describes who is not benefiting from the beverage industry's latest marketing efforts: the nation's children. In 1978, the typical teenage boy in the United States drank about seven ounces of soda every day; today he drinks nearly three times that amount, deriving 9 percent of his daily caloric intake from soft drinks. Soda consumption among teenaged girls has doubled within the same period, reaching an average of twelve ounces a day. A significant number of teenage boys are now drinking five or more cans of soda every day. Each can contains the equivalent of about ten teaspoons of sugar. Coke, Pepsi, Mountain Dew, and Dr Pepper also contain caffeine. These sodas provide empty calories and have replaced far more nutritious beverages in the American diet. Excessive soda consumption in childhood can lead to calcium deficiencies and a greater likelihood of bone fractures. Twenty years ago, teenage boys in the United States drank twice as much milk as soda; now they drink twice as much soda as milk. Softdrink consumption has also become commonplace among American toddlers. About one-fifth of the nation's one- and two-year-olds now drink soda. "In one of the most despicable marketing gambits," Michael Jacobson, the author of "Liquid Candy" reports, "Pepsi, Dr Pepper and Seven-Up encourage feeding soft drinks to babies by licensing their logos to a major maker of baby bottles, Munchkin Bottling, Inc." A 1997 study published in the *Journal of Dentistry for Children* found that many infants were indeed being fed soda in those bottles.

10   The school marketing efforts of the large soda companies have not gone entirely unopposed. Administrators in San Francisco and Seattle have refused to allow any advertising in their schools. "It's our responsibility to make it clear that schools are here to serve children, not commercial interests," declared a member of the San Francisco Board of Education. Individual protests have occurred as well. In March of 1998, 1,200 students at Greenbrier High School in Evans, Georgia, assembled in the school parking lot, many of them wearing red and white clothing, to spell out the word "Coke." It was Coke in Education Day at the school, and a dozen Coca-Cola executives had come for the occasion. Greenbrier High was hoping for a $500 prize, which had been offered to the local high school that came up with the best marketing plan for Coca-Cola discount cards. As part of the festivities, Coke executives had lectured the students on economics and helped them bake a Coca-Cola cake. A photographer was hoisted above the parking lot by a crane, ready to record the human C-O-K-E for posterity. When the photographer started to take pictures, Mike Cameron— a Greenbrier senior, standing amid the letter *C*—suddenly revealed a T-shirt that said "Pepsi." His act of defiance soon received nationwide publicity, as did the fact that he was immediately suspended from school. The principal said Cameron could have been suspended for a week for the prank, but removed him from classes for just a day. "I don't consider this a prank," Mike Cameron told the *Washington Post.* "I like to be an individual. That's the way I am."

Most school advertising campaigns are more subtle than Greenbrier High's Coke in Education Day. The spiraling cost of textbooks has led thousands of American school districts to use corporate-sponsored teaching materials. A 1998 study of these teaching materials by the Consumers Union found that 80 percent were biased, providing students with incomplete or slanted information that favored the sponsor's products and views. Procter & Gamble's *Decision Earth* program taught that clear-cut logging was actually good for the environment; teaching aids distributed by the Exxon Education Foundation said that fossil fuels created few environmental problems and that alternative sources of energy were too expensive; a study guide sponsored by the American Coal Foundation dismissed fears of a greenhouse effect, claiming that "the earth could benefit rather than be harmed from increased carbon dioxide." The Consumers Union found Pizza Hut's Book It! Program—which awards a free Personal Pan Pizza to children who reach targeted reading levels—to be "highly commercial." About twenty million elementary school students participated in Book It! during the 1999–2000 school year; Pizza Hut recently expanded the program to include a million preschoolers.

Lifetime Learning Systems is the nation's largest marketer and producer of corporate-sponsored teaching aids. The group claims that its publications are

used by more than 60 million students every year. "Now you can enter the classroom through custom-made learning materials created with your specific marketing objectives in mind," Lifetime Learning said in one of its pitches to
corporate sponsors. "Through these materials, your product or point of view
becomes the focus of discussions in the classroom," it said in another, ". . . the
centerpiece in a dynamic process that generates long-term awareness and lasting attitudinal change." The tax cuts that are hampering America's schools
have proved to be a marketing bonanza for companies like Exxon, Pizza Hut,
and McDonald's. The money that these corporations spend on their "educational" materials is fully tax-deductible.

The fast food chains run ads on Channel One, the commercial television
network whose programming is now shown in classrooms, almost every school
day, to eight million of the nation's middle, junior, and high school students—
a teen audience fifty times larger than that of MTV. The fast food chains place
ads with Star Broadcasting, a Minnesota company that pipes Top 40 radio into
school hallways, lounges, and cafeterias. And the chains now promote their
food by selling school lunches, accepting a lower profit margin in order to create brand loyalty. At least twenty school districts in the United States have their
own Subway franchises; an additional fifteen hundred districts have Subway delivery contracts; and nine operate Subway sandwich carts. Taco Bell products
are sold in about forty-five hundred school cafeterias. Pizza Hut, Domino's,
and McDonald's are now selling food in the nation's schools. The American
School Food Service Association estimates that about 30 percent of the public
high schools in the United States offer branded fast food. Elementary schools
in Fort Collins, Colorado, now serve food from Pizza Hut, McDonald's, and
Subway on special lunch days. "We try to be more like the fast food places
where these kids are hanging out," a Colorado school administrator told the
Denver Post. "We want kids to think school lunch is a cool thing, the cafeteria a
cool place, that we're 'with it,' that we're not institutional . . ."

The new corporate partnerships often put school officials in an awkward position. The Coca-Cola deal that DD Marketing negotiated for Colorado Springs
School District 11 was not as lucrative as it first seemed. The contract specified
annual sales quotas. School District 11 was obligated to sell at least seventy
thousand cases of Coca-Cola products a year, within the first three years of the
contract, or it would face reduced payments by Coke. During the 1997–98
school year, the district's elementary, middle, and high schools sold only
twenty-one thousand cases of Coca-Cola products. Cara DeGette, the news editor of the *Colorado Springs Independent,* a weekly newspaper, obtained a memo-
randum sent to school principals by John Bushey, a District 11 administrator.
On September 28, 1998, at the start of the new school year, Bushey warned the
principals that beverage sales were falling short of projections and that as a result school revenues might be affected. Allow students to bring Coke products
into the classrooms, he suggested; move Coke machines to places where they
would be accessible to students all day. "Research shows that vendor purchases
are closely linked to availability," Bushey wrote. "Location, location, location is

the key." If the principals felt uncomfortable allowing kids to drink Coca-Cola during class, he recommended letting them drink the fruit juices, teas, and bottled waters also sold in the Coke machines. At the end of the memo, John Bushey signed his name and then identified himself as "the Coke dude."

15   Bushey left Colorado Springs in 2000 and moved to Florida. He is now the principal of the high school in Celebration, a planned community run by The Celebration Company, a subsidiary of Disney.

QUESTIONS FOR DISCUSSION

1. What moved District 11 in Colorado Springs and many other school districts to accept ads for fast-food restaurants and other corporate sponsors? What was the criticism of the campaign? Do the arguments against in-school advertising seem justified? Explain your point of view.

2. Why is it so important for soft-drink manufacturers to increase sales to school children and youth? Does their need for sales justify the huge ad campaigns they have embarked upon? Why isn't the health of school children a concern for the manufacturers?

3. What impact on children's health do soda sales have? What evidence does the essay provide to support its conclusions on this issue?

4. What protests, at an institutional and individual level, have been launched against the in-school advertising and promotional campaigns? Have these protests been successful? Why or why not?

5. How have corporate campaigns transformed the physical environment, the curriculum, and the study materials of many school districts?

6. Who is the "Coke dude" and what positions has he held in schools? Do you think his approach to corporate advertising is effective? Is it ethical? Explain your point of view.

CONNECTION

How does Schlosser's critique of the fast food media advertising help you to understand why Lasn believes that advertisements are the most dangerous of the media pollutants (see page 464)?

IDEAS FOR WRITING

1. Although "McTeachers and Coke Dudes" lacks a direct argumentative thesis and may seem like a piece of reporting, it is intended as a piece of research-based argumentation. Write an analysis of the essay, pointing out places where the language chosen reveals the author's position on in-school advertising, and discuss the use of sometimes shocking facts and statistics that help Schlosser to make his critical points. Then explain why you agree or disagree with Schlosser's point of view. Use examples from your own experiences to support your position.

2. Write a research essay that explains how corporations captured the school lunch market. Why do you think that parents failed to protest against fast food lunches and soft drinks at school sooner? Propose some ways that the current situation can be changed so that school children can have healthier food for lunches and snacks.

RELATED WEB SITES

ERIC SCHLOSSER AND *FAST FOOD NATION*
http://www.powells.com/authors/schlosser.html
Read an informative interview with author Eric Schlosser at this web site, which is focused on the ideas in Schlosser's book, *Fast Food Nation*.

ADVERTISING IN SCHOOLS
http://www.commercialfree.org/commercialismtext.html
Many educators, parents, and students worry about advertising in schools. Learn about commercialism in schools at this URL—why it can be a problem and how people can get involved to help improve the situation.

Kalle Lasn

The Ecology of Mind

Kalle Lasn, who was born in 1942 in Tallinn, Estonia, a republic of the former Soviet Union, spent his childhood in German camps for displaced persons. In 1944 his family fled to Australia, where he later earned his B.S. in pure and applied mathematics from the University of Adelaide. In the 1960s, Lasn worked for a time as an advertising executive in Japan, and then immigrated to British Columbia where he took up documentary filmmaking. Lasn currently lives and works in Vancouver, Canada, with his family. Having received more than 15 international awards, Lasn's documentaries have been broadcast on PBS, CBC, and around the world. Lasn is the founder of Adbusters *magazine (1989), Adbusters Media Foundation, and Powershift Advertising Agency. He also founded Culture Jammers, an organization that seeks to topple advertising powerhouses. The selection that follows is excerpted from his latest book,* Culture Jam *(2000).*

JOURNAL

Describe how the media affect your mood and mental state, or the mental states of people you know. Do you think the media help to make people neurotic?

"Is everybody crazy?" Writer Jim Windolf posed the question in an October 1997 issue of *The New York Observer*, and then answered it himself with numbers.

If you add up all the psychological ailments Americans complain of, the portrait that emerges is of a nation of basket-cases. Ten million suffer from Seasonal Affective Disorder. Fourteen million are alcoholics. Fifteen million are pathologically socially anxious. Fifteen million are depressed. Three million suffer panic attacks. Ten million have Borderline Personality Disorder. Twelve million have "restless legs." Five million are obsessive\compulsive. Two million are manic-depressive. Ten million are addicted to sex. Factoring in wild-card afflictions like Chronic Fatigue Syndrome and multiple chemical sensitivity, and allowing for overlap (folks suffering from more than one problem), Windolf concluded that "77 percent of the adult population is a mess." With a couple of new quantifiable disorders, "everybody in the country will be officially nuts."

His cheeky point is that Americans are turning into annoyingly self-absorbed hypochondriacs. Why? Because they can. Go ahead and cry, says the prevailing psychological wisdom. Any trifling discomfort you might feel has been legitimized. Your pain is valid. If you think you're sick, you are.

There may be a grain of truth to this. People who live in a time relatively free of crises, amidst widespread peace and a galloping economy, will sometimes manufacture crises, inflating minor irritants into major traumas. But surely there's more to the story than that. I think what we have here is a labeling problem. An awful lot of people are feeling down and they don't know why. Something is draining their energy, addling their brains—but they don't know what.

5   Fact: Worldwide rates of major depression in every age group have risen steadily since the 1940s. Rates of suicide, unipolar disorder, bipolar disorder and alcoholism have all climbed significantly. The U.S. has a higher rate of depression than almost every other country, and cross-cultural data show that as Asian countries Americanize, their rates of depression increase accordingly. Moreover, recent research by the American National Institute of Mental Health confirms that "mood disorders" have increased in each successive generation throughout the twentieth century. I don't usually trust such statistics, but casual observation seems to bear the trend out. Is it just me or is every parent now weighing the merits of Ritalin? Their kids are hyper, unfocused, inattentive. They cannot stay "on task." Mom and Dad aren't faring much better. Tempers are short, attentions wander. Many people—and I include myself in this group—seem to be experiencing higher highs and lower lows these days. We soar the skies one moment, then feel slack and depressed the next.

Why might this be happening? Some researchers blame environmental pollutants: chemical agents in the air, water or food. Others point to cultural and economic factors that are increasing the stress in our everyday lives. No one knows for sure.

But it's tantalizing to guess. In Saul Bellow's novel *Humboldt's Gift*, the narrator wonders how it is that Americans can unashamedly claim to be "suffering," when compared to the rest of the world they are immensely blessed. His answer

is that while most people tend to associate suffering with scarcity and depriva-
tion, there's a very different kind of suffering that's caused by *plenitude.*

Plenitude is American culture's perverse burden. Most Americans have
everything they could possibly want, and they still don't think it's nearly
enough. When everything is at hand, nothing is ever hard-won, and when nothing is hard-won, nothing really satisfies. Without satisfaction, our lives become
shallow and meaningless. In this era of gigantism—corporate megamergers,
billion-dollar-grossing films and grande lattes—we embrace the value of More
to compensate for lives that seem, somehow, Less. Eat the instant you're hungry and, as the Buddhist master put it, "You will never find out what your
hunger is for." Plenitude feeds the malaise as it fills the stomach.

In the last quarter century the insatiable craving for the consumer culture's
big, big show has only grown stronger. To meet the demand, media spectacles
have colonized our mental environment, crowding out history and context. In
their place there is now only a flood of disconnected information: The market
is soaring, the planet is warming, this fall's hemlines are knee-high, there's a
famine in East Africa.

10   Could it be that all of these things together—the curse of plenitude, the image explosion, the data overload, the hum of the media that, like Denny's, are
always awake and bustling—are driving us crazy? I lay my money here. More
than anything else, it is our mediated, consumption-driven culture that's making us sick.

Look at the way most of us relax. We come home after work, exhausted. We
turn on the TV—a reflex. (If we live alone, we may simply be craving the simu-
lacrum of another human presence.) We sit there passively hour after hour,
barely moving except to eat. We receive but we do not transmit. Identical images flow into our brains, homogenizing our perspectives, knowledge, tastes
and desires. We watch nature shows instead of venturing out into nature. We
laugh at sitcom jokes but not at our spouse's. We spend more evenings enjoying video sex than making love ourselves. And this media-fed fantasy changes
us. (Remember the hoodlum Alex in *A Clockwork Orange*, undergoing behavior-
modifying aversion therapy via hours and hours of graphic sex and violence on
TV? For him the boundaries blurred. "The colors of the real world only become real," he noticed, "when you viddy them in a film.") Layer upon layer of
mediated artifice come between us and the world until we are mummified. The
commercial mass media are rearranging our neurons, manipulating our emotions, making powerful new connections between deep immaterial needs and
material products. So virtual is the hypodermic needle that we don't feel it. So
gradually is the dosage increased that we're not aware of the toxicity.

Relatively speaking, this is all very new—too new for its effect on the species
to be fully known. We're still adjusting to the all-pervasive media. We are the
first two or three generations in history to grow up in a predominantly electronic environment. It took humans thousands of generations to adapt to living
on the land (our "natural environment") so it's reasonable to assume it will take
dozens of generations to adapt to the new electronic mass media environment

that's rapidly replacing the "natural" one. The wild mood swings and the barely repressed anger may simply be symptoms of a shock our systems are experiencing. We are new evolutionary beings, panting for breath on an electronic beach.

We still haven't answered the most basic questions—such as how media violence affects children—let alone the big-picture issues, such as what happens to a whole culture when its citizens start spending half their waking lives in virtual environments. We know there's a correlation between TV viewing and voter apathy (the more TV you watch, the less likely you are to participate in the direct democratic process). We know that TV viewing is linked to childhood obesity (and to the extent that body image erodes self-esteem, we can get an idea of the degree to which TV addiction is harmful to the average child). Beyond that, we're largely guessing. We don't really know what psychological or physiological mechanisms are at work. And because we don't know, to a great extent—and this is the truly odd and scary part—we don't worry much about it.

Ten years ago we didn't think twice about the chemicals in our food or the toxins generated by industry; we thought they were "well within acceptable limits." We were dead wrong about that and today we may be repeating the same mistake with "mental pollution"—nonchalantly absorbing massive daily doses of it without a second thought. Our mental environment is a common-property resource like the air or the water. We need to protect ourselves from unwanted incursions into it, much the same way we lobbied for nonsmoking areas ten years ago.

15   The antismoking lobby succeeded because people knew without being told that cigarettes were killing their friends and families. They demanded hard data about the risks of breathing in secondhand smoke. They disbelieved glib assurances that cigarettes were safe and that the right to smoke superseded the right to breathe clean air. They trusted their passion and their rage.

More important, antismoking activists changed our idea of what smoking is all about. They uncooled the cigarette companies and their brands, forever connecting smoking and death in all of our minds. It was, perhaps, the first victory in the fight for our mental environment—an ecology as rife with pollutants as any befouled river or cloud or smog. We long ago learned to watch what we dump into nature or absorb into our bodies; now we need to be equally careful about what we take into our minds.

What follows is just a beginning, an introduction to some of the mental pollutants and information viruses we deal with daily—a survey of the threats to our "ecology of mind."

Noise

In 1996, the World Health Organization declared noise to be a significant health problem, one that causes physiological changes in sleep, blood pressure and digestion. It's now understood that noise doesn't have to be loud to do damage.

For thousands of generations, the ambient noise was rain and wind and people talking. Now the sound track of the world is vastly different. Today's noise is all-spectrum, undecodable. More and more people suffer the perpetual buzz of tinnitus—a ringing in the ears caused by exposure to a loud noise (or in some cases, just by aging). One of the treatments for tinnitus is to fit sufferers with a hearing aid that broadcasts white noise. The brain learns to interpret white noise as a background distraction, like traffic sounds, and filters it out along with the tinnitus. The brain works that way for the rest of us as well. The "whiter" the sound in our environment gets, the more we dismiss it as background and stop hearing it. Ultimately, *everything* becomes background noise and we hear almost nothing.

20   Noise is probably the best understood of the mental pollutants. It's really the only one to which the term "mental pollution" has already been applied. From the dull roar of rush-hour traffic to the drone of your fridge to the buzz coming out of your computer, various kinds of noise (blue, white, pink, black) are perpetually seeping into our mental environment. To make matters worse, the volume is constantly being cranked up. Two, perhaps three generations have already become stimulation addicted. Can't work without background music. Can't jog without a Discman. Can't study without the TV on. Our neurons are continuously massaged by Muzak and the hum of monitors. The essence of our postmodern age may be found in that kind of urban score. Trying to make sense of the world above the din of our wired world is like living next to a freeway—you get used to it, but at a much diminished level of mindfulness and well-being.

Quiet feels foreign now, but quiet may be just what we need. Quiet may be to a healthy mind what clean air and water and a chemical-free diet are to a healthy body. In a clean mental environment, we may find our mood disorders subsiding. It's no longer easy to manufacture quietude, nor is it always practical to do so. But there are ways to pick up the trash in your mindscape: Switch off the TV set in your dentist's waiting room. Lose that noisy fridge. Turn off the stereo. Put your computer under the table. Poet Marianne Moore contends that the deepest feeling always shows itself in silence. I think she's got it right.

Jolts

A noise is a jolt, but a jolt isn't necessarily a noise. In broadcasting terms, a jolt is any "technical event" that interrupts the flow of sound or thought or imagery—a shift in camera angle, a gunshot, a cut to a commercial. A jolt forces your mind to pump for meaning.

In 1978, when Jerry Mander first defined "technical events" in his classic book *Four Arguments for the Elimination of Television*, regular TV programming averaged ten technical events per minute and commercials twenty (public television averaged three to four). Twenty years later these figures have doubled. MTV delivers sixty events per minute, and some viewers, still insufficiently jolted, seek more action by roaming the channels. (Channel-surfers, ironically, are both the cause and the effect of jolt hyperinflation. The more frequently viewers surf, the more broadcasters are inclined to fill their programming with jolts to hold the attention of surfers. And surfers, conditioned to expect ever-quicker jolts, become more inclined to surf.)

Why are jolts so inherently interesting? The behavioral psychologist Ivan Pavlov was among the first to try to explain this. Any stimulus change—any jolt—releases hormones that trigger the biologically encoded fight-or-flight response, vestigial from a time when survival depended on being alert to anything in the environment that happened at faster than normal or "natural" speed. The response was designed to keep us from being eaten by cave bears. It was not designed to keep us glued to our TV sets.

25   However, most TV programs do just that. They are scripted to deliver the maximum number of jolts per minute (and keep viewers suspended through the breaks). When you watch MTV, you are in fight-or-flight mode practically the whole time. Random violence and meaningless sex drop in out of the blue and without context. "Unlike news reports or thematic TV programs, which usually prepare the viewer for violent scenes," concluded a 1995 study on the psychological aspects of MTV viewing, "the abruptness of music-video cuts tends to have greater shock effect . . . and may have more detrimental influence on the viewer." Much has been made of the way toddlers will sit mesmerized before shows like *Teletubbies*, but put a baby in front of MTV and you'll see the same level of rapture. It's an innate response, one that the industry has been quick to exploit.

In the early 1980s, technological advances changed the way films were made. Up to that point, filmmaking was a painstaking process of finding the organic shape of the story, then developing the narrative by weaving together the components, literally splicing strips of 16mm or 35mm film together by hand. National Film Board of Canada founder John Grierson's adage "Everything is beautiful if you get it in the right order" was understood to be a kind of occupational law. Today, new video-editing techniques allow filmmakers to take shortcuts. If there is a structural problem in your story, well, you can just mask it with a jolt. You can solve a continuity problem by simply bamboozling the audience, briefly scrambling their brains. Story editing has become more and more a process of "jolt management." If you can create enough jolts, you have an engaging film.

That's the premise the commercial media operate on today. Keep the jolts coming. Keep audiences on the edge and sell their attention spans to the advertiser before they regain their bearings. What's a postmodern spectacle after all, if not an array of carefully orchestrated jolts?

Is it possible to have too many jolts? Yes. When the levels rise above a certain threshold, the viewer\listener stops pumping for meaning and just surrenders to the flow, to being both entertained and paralyzed. The narrative of actual life is suspended for the duration of the show.

Perhaps the time has come to quantify the consequences of such mental pollution. If psychologists studied the impact of noise and jolt levels in our mental environment the way biologists research the effects of chemicals in our air, water and food, perhaps we could determine how much our brains can safely absorb. We could then compare the risks posed by different mental environments. We could compare living in Los Angeles with living in Portland, or growing up in North America with growing up in Australia. We could create a "livability" index more accurate than the ones that simply measure greenspace, minimum wage and the number of schools.

30   With reliable mental-environment indexes, we could rate TV programs and stations by how many jolts per hour they manufacture, how much clutter they dump into the public mind and how this may be affecting our mental health. We could then set new agendas: to reduce, not increase, the number of jolts our brains absorb.

Shock

The average North American witnesses five acts of violence (killings, gunshots, assaults, car chases, rapes) per hour of prime time network TV watched. Such statistics are now more likely to prompt yawns than gasps. They don't mean much if we don't distinguish between types of violence—pro wrestling versus *Goodfellas* versus Indonesian cops clubbing student demonstrators on the evening news. Experts can't even seem to agree on whether violence on TV is increasing. Two recent studies turned up conflicting results, and the head of one research team, by way of explanation, mumbled something about flawed methodology.

So the stats are confusing. That hardly means harm is not being done.

The first agenda of the commercial media is, I believe, to sell fear. What the "news" story of a busload of tourists gunned down in Egypt and the cop show about widespread corruption on the force have in common is that they contribute to the sense that the world is a menacing, inhospitable, untrustworthy place. Fear breeds insecurity—and then consumer culture offers us a variety of ways to buy our way back to security.

As for sex in the media, there seems—surprise—to be as big a bull market as ever. TV programmers know what stops us from zapping the channels: pouting lips, pert breasts, buns of steel, pneumatic superyouth.

35   TV sexuality is a campaign of disinformation, much like TV news. The truth is stretched, the story is hyped. *If you look like a TV star or a model, a desirable mate will be available to you; if you don't, it won't.* Try telling me that living with that message your whole life hasn't changed the way you feel about yourself.

Growing up in an erotically charged media environment alters the very foundations of our personalities. I think it distorts our sexuality. It changes the way you feel when someone suddenly puts their hand on your shoulder, hugs you, or flirts with you through the car window. I think the constant flow of commercially scripted pseudosex, rape and pornography makes us more voyeuristic, insatiable and aggressive—even though I can't prove it with hard facts.

Similarly, I have no hard proof that daily exposure to media violence shapes the way you feel about crime and punishment, or affects the way you feel about that guy standing next to you at the bus stop. What I do know is that my natural instinct for spontaneity, camaraderie and trust has been blunted. I used to pick up hitchhikers; now I hardly ever do. I rarely speak to strangers anymore.

TV programming is inundated by sex and violence because the networks have determined they are an efficient way to produce audiences. The commercial media are to the mental environment what factories are to the physical environment. A factory dumps pollutants into the water or air because that's the most efficient way to produce plastic or wood pulp or steel. A TV or radio station "pollutes" the cultural environment because that's the most efficient way to produce audiences. It pays to pollute. The psychic fallout is just the cost of putting on the show.

Hype

Advertisements are the most prevalent and toxic of the mental pollutants. From the moment your radio alarm sounds in the morning to the wee hours of late-night TV, microjolts of commercial pollution flood into your brain at the rate of about three thousand marketing messages per day. Every day, an estimated 12 billion display ads, 3 million radio commercials, and more than 200,000 TV commercials are dumped into North America's collective unconscious.

40   Corporate advertising (or is it the commercial media?) is the largest single psychological project ever undertaken by the human race. Yet for all of that, its impact on us remains unknown and largely ignored. When I think of the media's influence over years, over decades, I think of those brainwashing experiments conducted by Dr. Ewen Cameron in a Montreal psychiatric hospital in the 1950s. The idea of the CIA-sponsored "depatterning" experiments was to outfit conscious, unconscious or semiconscious subjects with headphones, and flood their brains with thousands of repetitive "driving" messages that would alter their behavior over time. Sound familiar? Advertising aims to do the same thing. Dr. Cameron's guinea pigs emerged from the Montreal trials with serious psychological damage. It was a great scandal. But no one is saying boo about the ongoing experiment of mass media advertising. In fact, new guinea pigs voluntarily come on board every day.

The proliferation of commercial messages has happened so steadily and relentlessly that we haven't quite woken up to the absurdity of it all. No longer are ads confined to the usual places: buses, billboards, stadiums. Anywhere your eyes can possibly come to rest is now a place that, in corporate America's view, can and ought to be filled with a logo or product message.

You reach down to pull your golf ball out of the hole and there, at the bottom of the cup, is an ad for a brokerage firm. You fill your car with gas, there's an ad on the nozzle. You wait for your bank machine to spit out money and an ad pushing GICs scrolls by in the little window. You drive through the heartland and the view of the wheatfields is broken at intervals by enormous billboards. Your kids watch Pepsi and Snickers ads in the classroom. (The school has made the devil's bargain of accepting free audiovisual equipment in exchange for airing these ads on "Channel One.") You think you've seen it all, but you haven't. An Atlanta-based marketing firm announces plans to send an inflatable billboard filled with corporate logos into geostationary orbit viewable every night like a second moon. British sprinter Linford Christie appears at a press conference with little panthers replacing the pupils of his eyes, where his sponsor's logo has been imprinted on specially made contact lenses. New York software engineers demonstrate a program that turns your cursor into a corporate icon whenever you visit a commercial site. A Japanese schoolboy becomes a neon sign during his daily two-hour subway commute by wearing a battery-powered vest promoting an electronics giant. Administrators in a Texas school district announce plans to boost revenues by selling ad space on the roofs of the district's seventeen schools—arresting the attention of the fifty-eight million commercial jet passengers who fly into Dallas each year. Kids tattoo their calves with swooshes. Other kids, at raves, begin wearing actual bar codes that other kids can scan, revealing messages such as "I'd like to sleep with you." A boy named David Bentley in Sydney, Australia, literally rents his head to corporate clients, shaving a new ad into his hair every few weeks. ("I know for sure that at least two thousand teenagers at my high school will read my head every day to see what it says," says the young entrepreneur. "I just wish I had a bigger head.") You pick up a banana in the supermarket and there, on a little sticker, is an ad for the new summer blockbuster at the multiplex. ("It's interactive because you have to peel them off," says one ad executive of this new delivery system. "And people look at ten pieces of fruit before they pick one, so we get multiple impressions.") Boy Scouts in the U.K. sell corporate ad space on their merit badges. An Australian radio station dyes its logo on two million eggs. IBM beams its logo onto clouds above San Francisco with a scanning electron microscope and a laser—the millennial equivalent of Commissioner Gordon summoning Batman to the Batcave. (The image is visible from ten miles away.) Bestfoods unveils plans to stamp its Skippy brand of peanut butter onto the crisp tabula rasa of a New Jersey beach each morning at low tide, where it will push peanut butter for a few hours before being washed away by the waves. (The company is widely commended for its environmental responsibility.) Coca-Cola strikes a six-month deal with the Australian postal service for the right to cancel stamps with a Coke ad. A company called VideoCarte installs interactive screens on supermarket carts so that you can see ads while you shop. (A company executive calls the little monitors "the most powerful micromarketing medium available today.")

A few years ago, marketers began installing ad boards in men's washrooms on college campuses, at eye level above the urinals. From their perspective, it was a brilliant coup: Where else is a guy going to look? But when I first heard this was being done, I was incensed. One of the last private acts was being co-opted. "What's been the reaction on campus?" I asked the reporter who told me the story. "Not much reaction," he said. It became apparent, as these ad boards began springing up in bars and restaurants, and just about anywhere men stand to pee, that not only did guys not share my outrage, they actually welcomed a little diversion while nature took its course.

This flood of psycho-effluent is spreading all around us, and we love every minute of it. The adspeak means nothing. It means worse than nothing. It is "anti-language" that, whenever it runs into truth and meaning, annihilates it.

45   There is nowhere to run. No one is exempt and no one will be spared. In the silent moments of my life, I often used to hear the opening movement of Beethoven's Ninth Symphony play in my head. Now I hear that kid singing the Oscar Meyer Wiener song.

Unreality

At a recent Adbusters Media Foundation office party, two young guys walked in the door, grabbed a beer and went straight to the computers, where they surfed the Net for two hours. Except for a few minutes here and there when people came up behind them and commented on something, they had no social interaction whatsoever. I know these guys. They are both very bright. They'd score well up there on IQ tests. But I wondered how they'd score on a "reality index"— which I define as the ratio of time spent in a virtual versus a "real" environment. The measurement is easy enough to calculate. Jot down in a notebook the number of times a day you laugh at real jokes with real people in real situations against the number of times you laugh at media-generated jokes, the amount of sex you have against the amount of sex you watch, and so on.

As psychoenvironmental indexes go, it might be quite revealing.

We face more and more opportunities and incentives to spend time in cyberspace or to let the TV do the thinking. This is "unreality": a mediated world so womblike and seductive, it's hard not to conclude it's a pretty nice place to be. In that world of unreality, it's easy to forget you're a citizen and that the actual world is an interactive place. The other day as I sat staring at my toaster, waiting for a bagel to pop up, I suddenly felt as if I was about to receive a jolt. There's kind of internal "clock" that people who work with computers develop. There's a finite amount of time you're allowed to be still and silent (before, for example, the screensaver kicks in), so you develop a sixth sense that tells you when that time is up. It occurred to me, looking at the toaster, that I had not moved a mouse or a cursor for about a minute, and I had the distinct feeling I was about to be "dumped" off-line. I was going to lose my connection. Then the bagel popped up, jarring me back to the sensory world. The smell reached my nose and I thought of the old Woody Allen line, in a paraphrase: Whatever you think of reality, it's still the only place to get a good toasted bagel.

Erosion of Empathy

A wave of shock is striking society that is so new we don't yet have a name for it. It was concocted by advertisers who saw that consumers had become too jaded and media-savvy to respond to mere sexual titillation or intellectual games. The new shock ads go straight to the soul. They aren't clever or coy so much as deeply, morbidly unsettling. *Advertising Age* columnist Bob Garfield calls them "advertrocities." Benetton's dying AIDS patients and dead Bosnian soldiers. Calvin Klein models drowsing in shooting galleries with hunted, heroin-hollowed eyes. Diesel jeans' cryptic "ads within ads," set in North Korea, featuring images of skinny models on the side of a bus packed with (presumably) starving, suffering locals. ("There's no limit to how thin you can get," says the ad on the bus.)

50   I think these ads are operating on a deeper level than even the advertisers themselves know or understand. Their cumulative effect is to erode our ability to empathize, to take social issues seriously, to be moved by atrocity. They inure us to the suffering (or joy) of other people. They engender an attitude of malaise toward the things that make us most human. We pretend not to care as advertisers excavate the most sacred parts of ourselves, and we end up actually not caring.

The first time we saw a starving child on a late-night TV ad, we were appalled. Maybe we sent money. As these images became more familiar though, our compassion evaporated. Eventually, these ads started to repulse us. Now we never want to see another starving child again. Our sensitivity to violence has been eroded by the same process of attrition; likewise our sexual responsiveness.

There was a time when Claudia Schiffer in her Guess? jeans got our attention. Now she and her supermodel ilk hardly raise an eyebrow, and real people look downright asexual. The motherboard of our libido has been reseeded.

This blunting of our emotions is a self-perpetuating process. The more our psyches are corroded, the more desensitized we become to the corrosive. The more indifferent we become, the more voltage it takes to shock us. On it goes, until our minds become a theater of the absurd, and we become shockproof.

Information Overload

There is more information in the Sunday *New York Times* than the average person living during the Renaissance would have absorbed in a lifetime. The information glut, the so-called data smog hanging low in the valleys, calls to mind the bewildered student's lament: "I don't need to know any more—I already know more than I can understand." Information overload gave William Gibson's Johnny Mnemonic something called the "back shakes." That's a science fiction conceit, but anyone who ever bought a satellite dish or logged onto the Lexis\Nexis database can surely identify.

55   "Most information has long stopped being useful for us," wrote Neil Postman, the author of *Amusing Ourselves to Death*. "Information has become a form of garbage. It comes indiscriminately—directed at no one in particular, disconnected from usefulness; we are swamped by information, have no control over it and do not know what to do with it. And the reason we don't is that we no longer have a coherent conception of ourselves, our universe and our relation to one another and our world. We do not know where we came from, where we are going or why we are going there. We have no coherent framework to direct our definition of our problems or our search for their solutions. Therefore, we have no criteria for judging what is meaningful, useful, or relevant information. Our defenses against the information glut have broken down; our information immune system is inoperable."

Infotoxins

If we now absorb a surreal quantity of information, then the *quality* of that information is even more disturbing. The reality presented to us by the media always has a spin on it. Ads stretch the truth, news bites give only part of the story, and White House press releases are carefully tailored to make the president look good. We are constantly being hyped, suckered and lied to.

The marketers, spin doctors and PR agents who produce this propaganda realize what we as a society hate to admit: Disinformation works.

Do an overwhelming number of respected scientists believe that human actions are changing the Earth's climate? Yes. OK, that being the case, let's undermine that by finding and funding those few contrarians who believe otherwise. Promote their message widely and it will accumulate in the mental environment, just as toxic mercury accumulates in a biological ecosystem. Once enough of the toxin has been dispersed, the balance of public understanding will shift. Fund a low-level campaign to suggest that any threat to the car is an attack on personal freedoms. Create a "grassroots" group to defend the right to drive. Portray anticar activists as prudes who long for the days of the horse and buggy. Then sit back, watch your infotoxins spread—and get ready to sell bigger, better cars for years and years to come.

Can we come up with antidotes to these infoviruses that infect our minds? The answer may depend on how much we've ingested of the most powerful and persistent infotoxin of them all: cynicism.

Loss of Infodiversity

60 Information diversity is as critical to our long-term survival as biodiversity. Both are parts of the bedrock of human existence. And so, when one man gains control of more than half a country's daily newspapers (as is the case with Conrad Black in Canada), or amasses a global media empire the size of Rupert Murdoch's, it's a serious problem; the scope of public discourse shrinks. When a handful of media megacorporations control not only the daily newspapers and TV airwaves but the magazine, book publishing, motion picture, home video and music industries as well, information and cultural diversity both plummet.

A 1998 survey of eleven- to fifteen-year-old boys and girls in a school in Kathmandu revealed that their favorite TV program was MTV and the most popular radio station was Hits FM, a western music channel. Few of the students ever watched Nepal Television or India's *Doordarshan*. In a dozen Asia-Pacific countries surveyed by the A. C. Nielsen company the same year, Coke was the favorite drink in eleven (in Thailand, the favorite drink was Pepsi). In downtown London, Bangkok, Tokyo or Los Angeles, you will invariably see a McDonald's restaurant on one corner, a Benetton store on the other and a bunch of transnational corporate logos across the street.

Cultural homogenization has graver consequences than the same hairstyles, catchphrases, music and action-hero antics perpetrated *ad nauseam* around the

world. In all systems, homogenization is poison. Lack of diversity leads to ineffi-
ciency and failure. The loss of a language, tradition or heritage—or the forgetting of *one good idea*—is as big a loss to future generations as a biological species
going extinct.

An Environmental Movement of the Mind

"There was once a town in the heart of America where all life seemed to live in
harmony with its surroundings . . . Then a strange blight crept over the area
and everything began to change."

The fictitious town that fell prey to this "strange illness" in Rachel Carson's
famous environmental manifesto *Silent Spring* is a kind of Everytown, U.S.A.
Once there was fecundity and the happy buzz of diverse life. Then human intervention caught up with nature. In this quiet season, no chicks hatched. The
cattle and sheep sickened and died. No birds returned; the farmers spoke of
much illness in their families. "It was," Carson says, "a spring without voices."

65   No witchcraft, no enemy action or natural catastrophe silenced the rebirth
of new life in this stricken world. The people did it themselves—with chemicals
and pesticides.

The language and the metaphors Carson used thirty years ago apply equally
well to the mental environment we have created for ourselves today. A single
voice fills Everytown now; at its say-so, all the sheep lie down in sync. Life in this
stricken, alien world has not so much been silenced as reengineered.

We cannot continue polluting our minds. We cannot allow advertisers to
continue preying on our emotions. We cannot allow a handful of media con-
glomerates to seize control of the global communications superstructure.
Silent Spring and other books and documentaries of its time shocked us into
realizing that our natural environment was dying, and catalyzed a wave of activism that changed the world. Now it's time to do the same for our mental
environment.

QUESTIONS FOR DISCUSSION

1. Discuss the essay's title. How does Lasn believe that the media upset the
   "ecology of mind"? Does he make his causal relations clear? How?
2. According to Lasn, what is the suffering caused by plenitude? How does
   Lasn see the media as contributing too much plenitude, too much data,
   noise, and jolts? How have the media made it hard for us to relax?
3. In what ways do the media shock viewers and distort our sense of sexuality? Why do the media want to play on viewers' fears? According to
   Lasn, why are advertisements the "most prevalent and toxic of the mental
   pollutants"?
4. Lasn describes erosion of empathy, information overload, infotoxins, and
   loss of infodiversity. How well does he define each of these phenomena

and its effect on people's lives? What did you learn from his discussion of this erosion?

5. In a broader sense, what are the consequences to human development and socialization of these mental pollutants?

6. In thinking about Lasn's argument, how do you see these mental pollutants changing your life and mental health? In what ways have you been aware of how the media's mental pollutants have affected our culture?

CONNECTION

Compare and contrast Lasn's and Aronson's critiques of the media (see page 451).

IDEAS FOR WRITING

1. Lasn concludes his essay, "*Silent Spring* and other books and documentaries of its time shocked us into realizing that our natural environment was dying, and catalyzed a wave of activism that changed the world. Now it's time to do the same for our mental environment." Write an essay in support of Lasn's call to action. Develop a plan to change some of the negative qualities of the media in order to improve the mental health of our culture, our mental health as individuals.

2. Write an essay that focuses on one experience or a series of experiences that convinced you that the media was undermining your mental health. Be as specific as possible: Discuss the negative mental impact of the coverage of particular new events, television programs, music, or the Internet. What do you do to protect your mental health in the face of the overwhelming amounts of negative media events?

RELATED WEB SITES

KALLE LASN AT ADBUSTERS

http://adbusters.org/magazine/28/usa.html

Read an article by author and activist Kalle Lasn concerning the historical roots of America in relationship to the corporation. Other essays and information can be read in response to the commercialization of the world at this web site by "Adbusters," a nonprofit organization edited by Lasn.

THE CENTER FOR A NEW AMERICAN DREAM

http://www.newdream.org/bulletin/Lasn.html

The Center for a New American Dream helps Americans consume responsibly to protect the environment, enhance quality of life and promote social justice. Visit the organizations web site to find out how to help. Also, read an interview with Kalle Lasn at the above URL.

Helena Norberg-Hodge

The Pressure to Modernize and Globalize

A Swedish philosopher, linguist, teacher, and activist fighting against the excesses of economic development and its impact on the cultures of traditional societies and local culture, Helena Norberg Hodge has lived in Ladakh (Kashmir) in the Himalayas for more than 30 years. She learned the language and became the first foreigner to be accepted into this isolated community. She has helped the Kadakhis to understand the negative effects of modernization on their culture. Norberg-Hodge is the author of Ancient Futures: Learning from Ladakh *(1991), a film of the same name based on her book, as well as coauthor of* From the Ground Up *(1993). She currently serves as President of the Ladakh Project for Counter Development on the Tibetan Plateau as well as President of the International Society of Ecology and Culture. In 1986 she received the Right Livelihood Award, also known as the "Alternative Nobel Prize."*

JOURNAL

Write about what you think might be the advantages or disadvantages for an isolated people to be introduced to modern economic methods, culture, and technology.

Ladakh is a high-altitude desert on the Tibetan Plateau in northern-most India. To all outward appearances, it is a wild and inhospitable place. In summer the land is parched and dry; in winter it is frozen solid by a fierce, un-relenting cold. Harsh and barren, Ladakh's land forms have often been described as a "moonscape."

Almost nothing grows wild—not the smallest shrub, hardly a blade of grass. Even time seems to stand still, suspended on the thin air. Yet here, in one of the highest, driest, and coldest inhabited places on Earth, the Ladakhis have for a thousand years not only survived but prospered. Out of barren desert they have carved verdant oases—terraced fields of barley, wheat, apples, apricots, and vegetables, irrigated with glacial meltwater brought many miles through stone-lined channels. Using little more than stone-age technologies and the scant resources at hand, the Ladakhis established a remarkably rich culture, one that met not only their material wants but their psychological and spiritual needs as well.

Until 1962, Ladakh, or "Little Tibet," remained almost totally isolated from the forces of modernization. In that year, however, in response to the conflict in Tibet, the Indian Army built a road to link the region with the rest of the country. With the road came not only new consumer items and a government bureaucracy but, as I shall show, a first misleading impression of the world outside. Then, in 1975, the region was opened up to foreign tourists, and the process of "development" began in earnest.

Based on my ability to speak the language fluently from my first year in Ladakh, and based on almost two decades of close contact with the Ladakhi people, I have been able to observe almost as an insider the effect of these changes on the Ladakhis' perception of themselves. Within the space of little more than a decade, feelings of pride gave way to what can best be described as a cultural inferiority complex. In the modern sector today, most young Ladakhis—the teenage boys in particular—are ashamed of their cultural roots and desperate to appear modern.

Tourism

5   When tourism first began in Ladakh, it was as though people from another planet suddenly descended on the region. Looking at the modern world from something of a Ladakhi perspective, I became aware of how much more successful our culture looks from the outside than we experience it on the inside.

Each day many tourists would spend as much as $100—an amount roughly equivalent to someone spending $50,000 per day in America. In the traditional subsistence economy, money played a minor role and was used primarily for luxuries—jewelry, silver, and gold. Basic needs—food, clothing, and shelter— were provided for without money. The labor one needed was free of charge, part of an intricate web of human relationships.

Ladakhis did not realize that money meant something very different for the foreigners; that back home they needed it to survive; that food, clothing, and shelter all cost money—a lot of money. Compared to these strangers, the Ladakhis suddenly felt poor.

This new attitude contrasted dramatically with the Ladakhis' earlier self-confidence. In 1975, I was shown around the remote village of Hemis Shukpachan by a young Ladakhi named Tsewang. It seemed to me that all the houses we saw were especially large and beautiful. I asked Tsewang to show me the houses where the poor people lived. Tsewang looked perplexed a moment, then responded, "We don't have any poor people here."

Eight years later I overheard Tsewang talking to some tourists. "If you could only help us Ladakhis," he was saying, "we're so poor."

10   Besides giving the illusion that all Westerners are multimillionaires, tourism and Western media images also help perpetuate another myth about modern life—that we never work. It looks as though our technologies do the work for us. In industrial society today, we actually spend more hours working than people in rural, agrarian economies, but that is not how it looks to the Ladakhis. For them, work is physical work: ploughing, walking, carrying things. A person sitting behind the wheel of a car or pushing buttons on a typewriter doesn't appear to be working.

Media Images

Development has brought not only tourism but also Western and Indian films and, more recently, television. Together they provide overwhelming images of luxury and power. There are countless tools, magical gadgets, and machines— machines to take pictures, machines to tell the time, machines to make fire, to travel from one place to another, to talk with someone far away. Machines can do everything; it's no wonder the tourists look so clean and have such soft, white hands.

Media images focus on the rich, the beautiful, and the mobile, whose lives are endless action and glamour. For young Ladakhis, the picture is irresistible. It is an overwhelmingly exciting version of an urban American Dream, with an emphasis on speed, youthfulness, super-cleanliness, beauty, fashion, and competitiveness. "Progress" is also stressed: Humans dominate nature, while technological change is embraced at all costs.

In contrast to these utopian images from another culture, village life seems primitive, silly, and inefficient. The one-dimensional view of modern life becomes a slap in the face. Young Ladakhis—whose parents ask them to choose a way of life that involves working in the fields and getting their hands dirty for very little or no money—feel ashamed of their own culture. Traditional Ladakh seems absurd compared with the world of the tourists and film heroes.

This same pattern is being repeated in rural areas all over the South, where millions of young people believe contemporary Western culture to be far superior to their own. This is not surprising: looking as they do from the outside, all they can see is the material side of the modern world—the side in which Western culture excels. They cannot so readily see the social or psychological dimensions: the stress, the loneliness, the fear of growing old. Nor can they see environmental decay, inflation, or unemployment. This leads young Ladakhis to develop feelings of inferiority, to reject their own culture wholesale, and at the same time to eagerly embrace the global monoculture. They rush after the sunglasses, walkmans, and blue jeans—not because they find those jeans more attractive or comfortable but because they are symbols of modern life.

15   Modern symbols have also contributed to an increase in aggression in Ladakh. Young boys now see violence glamorized on the screen. From Western-style films, they can easily get the impression that if they want to be modern, they should smoke one cigarette after another, get a fast car, and race through the countryside shooting people left and right.

Western-Style Education

No one can deny the value of real education—the widening and enrichment of knowledge. But today in the Third World, education has become something quite different. It isolates children from their culture and from nature, training them instead to become narrow specialists in a Westernized urban environment. This process has been particularly striking in Ladakh, where modern schooling acts almost as a blindfold, preventing children from seeing the very context in which they live. They leave school unable to use their own resources, unable to function in their own world.

With the exception of religious training in the monasteries, Ladakh's traditional culture had no separate process called education. Education was the product of a person's intimate relationship with the community and the ecosystem.

Children learned from grandparents, family, and friends and from the natural world.

Helping with the sowing, for instance, they would learn that on one side of the village it was a little warmer, on the other side a little colder. From their own experience children would come to distinguish different strains of barley and the specific growing conditions each strain preferred. They learned how to recognize and use even the tiniest wild plant, and how to pick out a particular animal on a faraway mountain slope. They learned about connection, process, and change, about the intricate web of fluctuating relationships in the natural world around them.

For generation after generation, Ladakhis grew up learning how to provide themselves with clothing and shelter: how to make shoes out of yak skin and robes from the wool of sheep; how to build houses out of mud and stone. Education was location-specific and nurtured an intimate relationship with the living world. It gave children an intuitive awareness that allowed them, as they grew older, to use resources in an effective and sustainable way.

20   None of that knowledge is provided in the modern school. Children are trained to become specialists in a technological rather than an ecological society. School is a place to forget traditional skills and, worse, to look down on them.

Western education first came to Ladakhi villages in the 1970s. Today there are about two hundred schools. The basic curriculum is a poor imitation of that taught in other parts of India, which itself is an imitation of British education. There is almost nothing Ladakhi about it.

Once, while visiting a classroom in Leh, the capital, I saw a drawing in a textbook of a child's bedroom that could have been in London or New York. It showed a pile of neatly folded handkerchiefs on a four-poster bed and gave instructions as to which drawer of the vanity unit to keep them in. Many other schoolbooks were equally absurd and inappropriate. For homework in one class, pupils were supposed to figure out the angle of incidence that the Leaning Tower of Pisa makes with the ground. Another time they were struggling with an English translation of *The Iliad*.

Most of the skills Ladakhi children learn in school will never be of real use to them. In essence, they receive an inferior version of an education appropriate for a New Yorker, a Parisian, or a Berliner. They learn from books written by people who have never set foot in Ladakh, who know nothing about growing barley at 12,000 feet or about making houses out of sun-dried bricks.

This situation is not unique to Ladakh. In every corner of the world today, the process called *education* is based on the same assumptions and the same Eurocentric model. The focus is on faraway facts and figures, on "universal" knowledge. The books propagate information that is believed to be appropriate for the entire planet. But since the only knowledge that can be universally applicable is far removed from specific ecosystems and cultures, what children learn is essentially synthetic, divorced from its living context. If they go on to higher education, they may learn about building houses, but these "houses" will be the universal boxes of concrete and steel. So too, if they study agriculture, they will learn about industrial farming: chemical fertilizers and pesticides; large machinery and hybrid seeds. The Western educational system is making us all poorer by teaching people around the world to use the same global resources, ignoring those that the environment naturally provides. In this way, Western-style education creates artificial scarcity and induces competition.

25   In Ladakh and elsewhere, modern education not only ignores local resources but, worse still, robs children of their self-esteem. Everything in school promotes the Western model and, as a direct consequence, makes children think of themselves and their traditions as inferior.

Western-style education pulls people away from agriculture and into the city, where they become dependent on the money economy. Traditionally there was no such thing as unemployment. But in the modern sector there is now intense competition for a very limited number of paying jobs, principally in the government. As a result, unemployment is already a serious problem.

Modern education has brought some obvious benefits, such as improvement in the literacy rate. It has also enabled the Ladakhis to be more informed about the forces at play in the world outside. In so doing, however, it has divided Ladakhis from each other and the land and put them on the lowest rung of the global economic ladder.

Local Economy Versus Global Economy

When I first came to Ladakh the Western macroeconomy had not yet arrived, and the local economy was still rooted in its own soils. Producers and consumers were closely linked in a community-based economy. Two decades of development in Ladakh, however, have led to a number of fundamental changes, the most important of which is perhaps the new dependence on food and energy from thousands of miles away.

The path toward globalization depends upon continuous government investments. It requires the buildup of a large-scale industrial infrastructure that includes roads, mass communications facilities, energy installations, and schools for specialized education. Among other things, this heavily subsidized infrastructure allows goods produced on a large scale and transported long distances to be sold at artificially low prices—in many cases at lower prices than goods produced locally. In Ladakh, the Indian government is not only paying for roads, schools, and energy installations but is also bringing in subsidized food from India's breadbasket, the Punjab. Ladakh's local economy—which has provided enough food for its people for two thousand years—is now being invaded by produce from industrial farms located on the other side of the Himalayas. The food arriving in lorries by the ton is cheaper in the local bazaar than food grown a five-minute walk away. For many Ladakhis, it is no longer worthwhile to continue farming.

30   In Ladakh this same process affects not just food but a whole range of goods, from clothes to household utensils to building materials. Imports from distant parts of India can often be produced and distributed at lower prices than goods produced locally—again, because of a heavily subsidized

industrial infrastructure. The end result of the long-distance transport of sub-sidized goods is that Ladakh's local economy is being steadily dismantled, and with it goes the local community that was once tied together by bonds of interdependence.

Conventional economists, of course, would dismiss these negative impacts, which cannot be quantified as easily as the monetary transactions that are the goal of economic development. They would also say that regions such as the Punjab enjoy a "comparative advantage" over Ladakh in food production, and it therefore makes economic sense for the Punjab to specialize in growing food, while Ladakh specializes in some other product, and that each trade with the other. But when distantly produced goods are heavily subsidized, often in hidden ways, one cannot really talk about comparative advantage or, for that matter, "free markets," "open competition in the setting of prices," or any of the other principles by which economists and planners rationalize the changes they advocate. In fact, one should instead talk about the unfair advantage that industrial producers enjoy, thanks to a heavily subsidized infrastructure geared toward large-scale, centralized production.

In the past, individual Ladakhis had real power, since political and eco-nomic units were small, and each person was able to deal directly with the other members of the community. Today, "development" is hooking people into ever-larger political and economic units. In political terms, each Ladakhi has become one of a national economy of eight hundred million, and, as part of the global economy, one of about six billion.

In the traditional economy, everyone knew they had to depend directly on family, friends, and neighbors. But in the new economic system, political and eco-nomic interactions take a detour via an anonymous bureaucracy. The fabric of lo-cal interdependence is disintegrating as the distance between people increases. So too are traditional levels of tolerance and cooperation. This is particularly true in the villages near Leh, where disputes and acrimony within close-knit commu-nities and even families have dramatically increased in the last few years. I have even seen heated arguments over the allocation of irrigation water, a procedure that had previously been managed smoothly within a cooperative framework.

As mutual aid is replaced by dependence on faraway forces, people begin to feel powerless to make decisions over their own lives. At all levels, passivity, even apathy, is setting in; people are abdicating personal responsibility. In the traditional village, for example, repairing irrigation canals was a task shared by the whole community. As soon as a channel developed a leak, groups of people would start shoveling away to patch it up. Now people see this work as the gov-ernment's responsibility and will let a channel go on leaking until the job is done for them. The more the government does for the villagers, the less the vil-lagers feel inclined to help themselves.

35   In the process, Ladakhis are starting to change their perception of the past. In my early days in Ladakh, people would tell me there had never been hunger. I kept hearing the expression *tungbos zabos*: "enough to drink, enough to eat." Now, particularly in the modern sector, people can be heard saying, "Develop-ment is essential; in the past we couldn't manage, we didn't have enough."

The cultural centralization that occurs through the media is also contributing both to this passivity and to a growing insecurity. Traditionally, village life included lots of dancing, singing, and theater. People of all ages joined in. In a group sitting around a fire, even toddlers would dance, with the help of older siblings or friends. Everyone knew how to sing, to act, to play music. Now that the radio has come to Ladakh, people do not need to sing their own songs or tell their own stories. Instead, they can sit and listen to the *best* singer, the *best* storyteller. As a result, people become inhibited and self-conscious. They are no longer comparing themselves to neighbors and friends, who are real people—some better at singing but perhaps not so good at dancing—and they never feel themselves to be as good as the stars on the radio. Community ties are also broken when people sit passively listening to the very best rather than making music or dancing together.

Artificial Needs

Before the changes brought by tourism and modernization, the Ladakhis were self-sufficient, both psychologically and materially. There was no desire for the sort of development that later came to be seen as a "need." Time and again, when I asked people about the changes that were coming, they showed no great interest in being modernized; sometimes they were even suspicious. In remote areas, when a road was about to be built, people felt, at best, ambivalent about the prospect. The same was true of electricity. I remember distinctly how, in 1975, people in Stagmo village laughed about the fuss that was being made to bring electric lights to neighboring villages. They thought it was a joke that so much effort and money was spent on what they took to be a ludicrous gain: "Is it worth all that bother just to have that thing dangling from your ceiling?"

More recently, when I returned to the same village to meet the council, the first thing they said to me was, "Why do you bother to come to our backward village where we live in the dark?" They said it jokingly, but it was obvious they were ashamed of the fact they did not have electricity.

Before people's sense of self-respect and self-worth had been shaken, they did not need electricity to prove they were civilized. But within a short period the forces of development so undermined people's self-esteem that not only electricity but Punjabi rice and plastic have become needs. I have seen people proudly wear wristwatches they cannot read and for which they have no use. And as the desire to appear modern grows, people are rejecting their own culture. Even the traditional foods are no longer a source of pride. Now when I'm a guest in a village, people apologize if they serve the traditional roasted barley, *ngamphe*, instead of instant noodles.

40   Surprisingly, perhaps, modernization in Ladakh is also leading to a loss of individuality. As people become self-conscious and insecure, they feel pressure to conform, to live up to the idealized images—to the American Dream. By contrast, in the traditional village, where everyone wears the same clothes and

looks the same to the casual observer, there seems to be more freedom to relax, and villagers can be who they really are. As part of a close-knit community, people feel secure enough to be themselves.

QUESTIONS FOR DISCUSSION

1. How did Ladakhis survive in their barren land, being totally isolated from modern life? Why were the forces of modernization introduced into Ladakh in 1962? What increased the acceleration of modernization in 1975?
2. How does knowing that the author of this article learned the native language of Ladakh and lived there for 30 years affect your interpretation and evaluation of the conclusions that she draws about the effects of modernization on the traditional culture of Ladakh?
3. Contrast the value that the people of Ladakh placed on money before and after tourists began to come to Ladakh. How did the introduction of large amounts of money impact the way that the Ladakhians viewed themselves and their culture?
4. How has the introduction of media images including, Western and Indian films as well as television, affect the character and quality of life in Ladakh?
5. The author points out that the people in Ladakh only see the material prosperity of Western culture but are not exposed to the psychological and social problems that develop in a materialistic culture. What problems does the author discuss?
6. What are the positive and negative effects of bringing Western Education to Third World Countries such as Ladakh?

CONNECTION

Compare and contrast Gitlin's and Norberg-Hodge's perspectives on the impact of the media on Third World Countries (see page 493).

IDEAS FOR WRITING

1. Do some research into the positive and negative impact of Western education on Third World Countries. If you prefer, focus on one particular Third World Country. Write an essay that presents what you have learned as well as your perspective on the impact of Western education. What solutions do you have for the new problems that these traditional countries are now facing?
2. Research the impact of the modern media on Third World Countries. If you prefer, focus on one particular Third World Country. Write an essay that presents what you have learned as well as your perspective on the impact of the modern media on traditional culture. What solutions do you have for the new problems that these traditional countries are now facing?

RELATED WEB SITES

HELENA NORBERG-HODGE

http://www.unitedearth.com.au/HNHinterview.html

Look at an interview with Helena Norberg-Hodge at this URL. You will also find links to more articles about the author and activist and find some suggestions to help her cause to promote locally based alternatives to our world's global consumer culture.

THE INTERNATIONAL SOCIETY FOR ECOLOGY & CULTURE (ISEC)

http://www.isec.org.uk/

The International Society for Ecology & Culture (ISEC) was founded by Helena Norberg-Hodge and is a nonprofit organization concerned with the protection of both biological and cultural diversity. Visit the ISEC's web site, which emphasizes education for action, to find out programs, events, relevant links, and other ways to get involved.

Sissela Bok

Aggression: The Impact of Media Violence

Sissela Bok has made a major contribution to the contemporary debate over values and ethical issues in society. Born in Sweden to liberal economists and peace activists Alva and Gunnar Myrdal, Bok was influenced by her parents' devotion to public causes. In 1992 she wrote a biography of her mother, Alva Myrdal: A Daughter's Memoir. *Bok left Sweden at an early age to study abroad; she received her Ph.D. in philosophy from Harvard University in 1970. She has been a Professor of Philosophy at Brandeis University and is currently a Distinguished Fellow at the Harvard Center for Population and Development Studies. Bok's writings on ethical issues include* Lying: Moral Choice in Public and Private Life *(1978),* Secrets: On the Ethics of Concealment and Revelation *(1983),* A Strategy for Peace: Human Values and the Threat of War *(1989),* Common Values *(1995), and, most recently,* Mayhem: Violence as Public Entertainment *(1998), that contains the following essay on the relationship between media and aggression.*

JOURNAL

Do you believe that media violence can cause a significant amount of actual violence in children? How could you prove your belief to be a fact?

E ven if media violence were linked to no other debilitating effects, it would remain at the center of public debate so long as the widespread belief persists that it glamorizes aggressive conduct, removes inhibitions toward such conduct, arouses viewers, and invites imitation. It is only natural that the links of media violence to aggression should be of special concern to families and communities. Whereas increased fear, desensitization, and appetite primarily affect the viewers themselves, aggression directly injures others and represents a more clear-cut violation of standards of behavior. From the point of view of public policy, therefore, curbing aggression, has priority over alleviating subtler psychological and moral damage.

Public concern about a possible link between media violence and societal violence has further intensified in the past decade, as violent crime reached a peak in the early 1990s, yet has shown no sign of downturn, even after crime rates began dropping in 1992. Media coverage of violence, far from declining, has escalated since then, devoting ever more attention to celebrity homicides and copycat crimes. The latter, explicitly modeled on videos or films and sometimes carried out with meticulous fidelity to detail, are never more relentlessly covered in the media than when they are committed by children and adolescents. Undocumented claims that violent copycat crimes are mounting in number contribute further to the ominous sense of threat that these crimes generate. Their dramatic nature drains away the public's attention from other, more mundane forms of aggression that are much more commonplace, and from . . . other . . . harmful effects of media violence.

Media analyst Ken Auletta reports that, in 1992, a mother in France sued the head of a state TV channel that carried the American series *MacGyver,* claiming that her son was accidentally injured as a result of having copied MacGyver's recipe for making a bomb. At the time, Auletta predicted that similar lawsuits were bound to become a weapon against media violence in America's litigious culture. By 1996, novelist John Grisham had sparked a debate about director Oliver Stone's film *Natural Born Killers,* which is reputedly linked to more copycat assaults and murders than any other movie to date. Grisham wrote in protest against the film after learning that a friend of his, Bill Savage, had been killed by nineteen-year-old Sarah Edmondson and her boyfriend Benjamin Darras, eighteen: after repeated viewings of Stone's film on video, the two had gone on a killing spree with the film's murderous, gleeful heroes expressly in mind. Characterizing the film as "a horrific movie that glamorized casual mayhem and bloodlust," Grisham proposed legal action:

> Think of a film as a product, something created and brought to market, not too dissimilar from breast implants. Though the law has yet to declare movies to be products, it is only a small step away. If something goes wrong with the product, either by design or defect, and injury ensues, then its makers are held responsible. . . . It will take only one large verdict against the like of Oliver Stone, and his production company, and perhaps the screenwriter, and the studio itself, and then the party will be over. The verdict will come from the heartland, far away from Southern California, in some small courtroom with no cameras. A jury will finally say enough is enough; that the demons placed in Sarah Edmondson's mind were not solely of her own making.

As a producer of books made into lucrative movies—themselves hardly devoid of violence—and as a veteran of contract negotiations within the entertainment industry, Grisham may have become accustomed to thinking of films in industry terms as "products." As a seasoned courtroom lawyer, he may have found the analogy between such products and breast implants useful for invoking product liability to pin personal responsibility on movie producers and directors for the lethal consequences that their work might help unleash.

5   Oliver Stone retorted that Grisham was drawing "upon the superstition about the magical power of pictures to conjure up the undead spectre of censorship." In dismissing concerns about the "magical power of pictures" as merely superstitious, Stone sidestepped the larger question of responsibility fully as much as Grisham had sidestepped that of causation when he attributed liability to filmmakers for anything that "goes wrong" with their products so that "injury ensues."

Because aggression is the most prominent effect associated with media violence in the public's mind, it is natural that it should also remain the primary focus of scholars in the field. The "aggressor effect" has been studied both to identify the short-term, immediate impact on viewers after exposure to TV violence, and the long-term influences. . . . There is near-unanimity by now among investigators that exposure to media violence contributes to lowering barriers to aggression among some viewers. This lowering of barriers may be assisted by the failure of empathy that comes with growing desensitization, and intensified to the extent that viewers develop an appetite for violence—something that may lead to still greater desire for violent programs and, in turn, even greater desensitization.

When it comes to viewing violent pornography, levels of aggression toward women have been shown to go up among male subjects who view sexualized violence against women. "In explicit depictions of sexual violence," a report by the American Psychological Association's Commission on Youth and Violence concludes after surveying available research data, "it is the message about violence more than the sexual nature of the materials that appears to affect the attitudes of adolescents about rape and violence toward women." Psychologist Edward Donnerstein and colleagues have shown that if investigators tell subjects that aggression is legitimate, then show them violent pornography, their aggression toward women increases. In slasher films, the speed and ease with which "one's feelings can be transformed from sensuality into viciousness may surprise even those quite conversant with the links between sexual and violent urges."

Viewers who become accustomed to seeing violence as an acceptable, common, attractive way of dealing with problems find it easier to identify with aggressors and to suppress any sense of pity or respect for victims of violence. Media violence has been found to have stronger effects of this kind when carried out by heroic, impressive, or otherwise exciting figures, especially when they are shown as invulnerable and are rewarded or not punished for what they do. The same is true when the violence is shown as justifiable, when viewers identify with the aggressors rather than with their victims, when violence is routinely resorted to, and when the programs have links to how viewers perceive their own environment.

While the consensus that such influences exist grows among investigators as research accumulates, there is no consensus whatsoever about the size of the correlations involved. Most investigators agree that it will always be difficult to disentangle the precise effects of exposure to media violence from the many other factors contributing to societal violence. No reputable scholar accepts the view expressed by 21 percent of the American public in 1995, blaming television more than any other factor for teenage violence. Such tentative estimates as have been made suggest that the media account for between 5 and 15 percent of societal violence. Even these estimates are rarely specific enough to indicate whether what is at issue is all violent crime, or such crimes along with bullying and aggression more generally.

10   One frequently cited investigator proposes a dramatically higher and more specific estimate than others. Psychiatrist Brandon S. Centerwall has concluded from large-scale epidemiological studies of "white homicide" in the United States, Canada, and South Africa in the period from 1945 to 1974, that it escalated in these societies within ten to fifteen years of the introduction of television, and that one can therefore deduce that television has brought a doubling of violent societal crime:

> Of course, there are many factors other than television that influence the amount of violent crime. Every violent act is the result of a variety of forces coming together—poverty, crime, alcohol and drug abuse, stress—of which childhood TV exposure is just one. Nevertheless, the evidence indicates that if hypothetically, television technology had never been developed, there would today be 10,000 fewer homicides each year in the United States, 70,000 fewer rapes, and 700,000 fewer injurious assaults. Violent crime would be half of what it now is.

Centerwall's study, published in 1989, includes controls for such variables as firearm possession and economic growth. But his conclusions have been criticized for not taking into account other factors, such as population changes during the time period studied, that might also play a role in changing crime rates. Shifts in policy and length of prison terms clearly affect these levels as well. By now, the decline in levels of violent crime in the United States since Centerwall's study was conducted, even though television viewing did not decline ten to fifteen years before, does not square with his extrapolations. As for "white homicide" in South Africa under apartheid, each year brings more severe challenges to official statistics from that period.

Even the lower estimates, however, of around 5 to 10 percent of violence as correlated with television exposure, point to substantial numbers of violent crimes in a population as large as America's. But if such estimates are to be used in discussions of policy decisions, more research will be needed to distinguish between the effects of television in general and those of particular types of violent programming, and to indicate specifically what sorts of images increase the aggressor effect and by what means; and throughout to be clearer about the nature of the aggressive acts studied.

Media representatives naturally request proof of such effects before they are asked to undertake substantial changes in programming. In considering possible remedies for a problem, inquiring into the reasons for claims about risks is entirely appropriate. It is clearly valid to scrutinize the research designs, sampling methods, and possible biases of studies supporting such claims, and to ask about the reasoning leading from particular research findings to conclusions. But to ask for some demonstrable pinpointing of just when and how exposure to media violence affects levels of aggression sets a dangerously high threshold for establishing risk factors.

We may never be able to trace, retrospectively, the specific set of television programs that contributed to a particular person's aggressive conduct. The same is true when it comes to the links between tobacco smoking and cancer, between drunk driving and automobile accidents, and many other risk factors presenting public health hazards. Only recently have scientists identified the specific channels through which tobacco generates its carcinogenic effects. Both precise causative mechanisms and documented occurrences in individuals remain elusive. Too often, media representatives formulate their requests in what appear to be strictly polemical terms, raising dismissive questions familiar from debates over the effects of tobacco: "How can anyone definitively pinpoint the link between media violence and acts of real-life violence? If not, how can we know if exposure to media violence constitutes a risk factor in the first place?"

15   Yet the difficulty in carrying out such pinpointing has not stood in the way of discussing and promoting efforts to curtail cigarette smoking and drunk driving. It is not clear, therefore, why a similar difficulty should block such efforts when it comes to media violence. The perspective of "probabilistic causation" . . . is crucial to public debate about the risk factors in media violence. The television industry has already been persuaded to curtail the glamorization of smoking and drunk driving on its programs, despite the lack of conclusive documentation of the correlation between TV viewing and higher incidence of such conduct. Why should the industry not take analogous precautions with respect to violent programming?

Americans have special reasons to inquire into the causes of societal violence. While we are in no sense uniquely violent, we need to ask about all possible reasons why our levels of violent crime are higher than in all other stable industrialized democracies. Our homicide rate would be higher still if we did not imprison more of our citizens than any society in the world, and if emergency medical care had not improved so greatly in recent decades that a larger proportion of shooting victims survive than in the past. Even so, we have seen an unprecedented rise not only in child and adolescent violence, but in levels of rape, child abuse, domestic violence, and every other form of assault.

Although America's homicide rate has declined in the 1990s, the rates for suicide, rape, and murder involving children and adolescents in many regions have too rarely followed suit. For Americans aged fifteen to thirty-five years, homicide is the second leading cause of death, and for young African Americans, fifteen to twenty-four years, it is *the* leading cause of death. In the decade following the mid-1980s, the rate of murder committed by teenagers fourteen to seventeen more than doubled. The rates of injury suffered by small children are skyrocketing, with the number of seriously injured children nearly quadrupling from 1986 to 1993; and a proportion of these injuries are inflicted by children upon one another. Even homicides by children, once next to unknown, have escalated in recent decades.

America may be the only society on earth to have experienced what has been called an "epidemic of children killing children," which is ravaging some of its communities today. As in any epidemic, it is urgent to ask what it is that makes so many capable of such violence, victimizes so many others, and causes countless more to live in fear. Whatever role the media are found to play in this respect, to be sure, is but part of the problem. Obviously, not even the total elimination of media violence would wipe out the problem of violence in the United States or any other society. The same can be said for the proliferation and easy access to guns, or for poverty, drug addiction, and other risk factors. As Dr. Deborah Prothrow-Stith puts it, "It's not an either or. It's not guns or media or parents or poverty."

We have all witnessed the four effects that I have discussed . . . —fearfulness, numbing, appetite, and aggressive impulses—in the context of many influences apart from the media. Maturing involves learning to resist the dominion that these effects can gain over us; and to strive, instead, for greater resilience, empathy, self-control, and respect for self and others. The process of maturation and growth in these respects is never completed for any of us; but it is most easily thwarted in childhood, before it has had chance to take root. Such learning calls for nurturing and education at first; then for increasing autonomy in making personal decisions about how best to confront the realities of violence.

20   Today, the sights and sounds of violence on the screen affect this learning process from infancy on, in many homes. The television screen is the lens through which most children learn about violence. Through the magnifying power of this lens, their everyday life becomes suffused by images of shootings, family violence, gang warfare, kidnappings, and everything else that contributes to violence in our society. It shapes their experiences long before they have had the opportunity to consent to such shaping or developed the ability to cope adequately with this knowledge. The basic nurturing and protection to prevent the impairment of this ability ought to be the birthright of every child.

QUESTIONS FOR DISCUSSION

1. What question does Bok believe John Grisham and Oliver Stone avoid in their debate over the impact of films on "copycat" violent crimes? Do their arguments seem reasonable to you, as she presents them here?
2. According to the research that Bok discusses, what circumstances tend to have the greatest impact on viewers' tendency to find violence acceptable?

3. According to Bok, what further research remains to be done before we can draw more definitive conclusions about the impact of such violence on actual patterns of aggression?
4. Bok points out the difficulty in making a clear-cut connection between smoking and cancer, even though we presume there is a cause. How effective is her analogy with media violence as a presumed cause of actual violence among heavy viewers? Do her conclusions here seem clear and reasonable?
5. What does Dr. Deborah Prothrow-Stith mean when she states, "It's not an either or. It's not guns or media or parents or poverty"? What conclusions does Bok suggest can be drawn from this statement about causes and solutions for the "problem" of media violence?
6. How, according to Bok, might excessive exposure to media violence thwart a child's ability to learn to resist aggression and to acquire such traits as empathy, respect, and self-control? Do you agree?

CONNECTION

Compare the way Bok tries to demonstrate a connection between TV violence and violence in the life of children with the efforts of Anthony Pratkanis and Elliot Aronson to show a relationship between viewing of violence in the media and beliefs about violence in society. Which seems to make the most convincing connection (see page 451)?

IDEAS FOR WRITING

1. Write an essay in which you consider some alternative causes for the current outbreak of youth violence. For instance, what about parental neglect and abuse, the decay of our educational system, or the violence of war?
2. If you accept Bok's argument that there is too much media violence and that this can lead to more youth aggression, how do we cut back on the media violence to which young people are currently being exposed? Write an essay in the form of a proposal for change, considering some ideas that have been suggested and that are currently being tried on a limited basis.

RELATED WEB SITES: SISSELA BOK

SISSELA BOK, "RESISTING POLARIZATION"
http://www.globalethics.org/interviews/bok_10-02-2001.html
Following the terrorist attacks of September 11th, 2001 the Institute for Global Ethics began conversations with thought-leaders here and abroad about the way the world is changing. This URL provides an interview with author Sissela Bok that gives her thoughts on the post-9/11 world and links to many other thinkers' views.

FIGHTING VIOLENCE
http://www.news.harvard.edu/gazette/1998/03.05/
FightingViolenc.html
Visit Harvard Univerisity's "Gazette," a web based newspaper that shares an article about fighting violence and the media at this URL. The article is based on the ideas of Sissela Bok.

Todd Gitlin

Three Formulas

Todd Gitlin was born in 1943 and raised in New York. He earned his B.A. at Harvard University, in 1963, his M.A. at the University of Michigan in 1966, and his Ph.D. at the University of California at Berkeley in 1977. Gitlin is currently a Professor of Culture, Sociology, and Journalism at New York University. He has won many grants and awards; the most prestigious include a MacArthur Foundation Award, a Rockefeller Foundation Grant, and a National Endowment for the Humanities Grant. He is a regular contributor to New York Times, Harper's, The Nation, Washington Post, Yale Review, and many other publications. His works include The Twilight of Common Dreams: Why America Is Wracked by Culture Wars *(1996),* Sacrifice *(1999),* Inside Prime Time *(revised ed., 1999), and* Media Unlimited *(2001), from which the selection that follows is excerpted.*

JOURNAL

Write about a type of American "formula" film that is popular today around the world. What image of America might this type of film portray to foreign viewers?

In a world of image-choked markets, sellers signal buyers what to expect. Formula and style are the two principal signals. Three now-global formulas are especially formidable: the Western (with a variant, the road movie); the "action movie," and the cartoon. These hardly exhaust the sum of American products. Among Hollywood's most successful exports are cop stories, horror and caper films, ensemble melodramas (from *Dallas* to *Friends*), fun-in-the-sun frolics (from *How to Stuff a Wild Bikini* to *Baywatch*), and easily diagrammed romantic comedies (*Pretty Woman, What Women Want*). Hollywood also produces less easily exportable genres, like the courtroom drama. But Westerns, action movies, and cartoons are at the core of Hollywood's global appeal. They can be bent, spliced, and blended (recombination being a distinctly American talent). Even cop and spy sagas, science fiction, soap operas, and beach extravaganzas are essentially variations on the three essential types.

The Western tradition that the literary historian Richard Slotkin calls "regeneration through violence" has been a staple of American popular culture since the hunter-hero myths and captivity narratives of the seventeenth century, mixing primitivism and romance, individualism and patriotism, moral purity and conservative restoration. The Virginian, John Wayne in his cowboy incarnations, Gary Cooper in *High Noon*, the Lone Ranger—each rugged everyman served the community without being roped into it. Each was an outsider without a past, a plainspoken skeptic, a straight shooter who saw through pretense, a friend of the downtrodden—and at the same time, a violent servant of law and order. On the frontier between civilization and wilderness, where the stagecoach ran into raiding Indians or highwaymen, good and evil collided. The avatar of a moral community of equal citizens invariably overcame both Indian barbarism and the unbridled rapacity of railroads and big ranchers. He was a laconic Emerson in buckskins—an American Adam.

The stylized melodrama of civilization taming the wilderness predates the movies, weaving in and out of the actual westward expansion, the legend inseparable from the events. (You did not have to be an American to get behind this iconography. The romantic Western novels of the German Karl May were hugely popular throughout Europe.) The army scout and hunter William Cody rode in celebrity buffalo hunts, appeared in dime novels, starred in plays (during the winters, going back to scouting in the summers), lent his name to his "own" novels, and published a self-mythologizing *Autobiography*. In 1883, he launched his outdoor Wild West show, complete with sharpshooters and animals, promoted as "America's National Entertainment"—a spectacle that in some fashion or other he performed for the next three decades. The Wild West was a stunning success throughout Europe, including France (Cody played for five months at the Exposition Universelle in Paris), Spain, Italy (where he was received by the pope), Austria, Germany, Holland, and Belgium. Among the 2.5 million people estimated to have attended the show during Cody's six months in London in 1887 was Queen Victoria, who arranged for a command performance and marveled in her journal: "All the different people, wild, painted Red Indians from America, on their wild bare backed horses, of different tribes,—cow boys, Mexicans, &c., all came tearing round at full speed, shrieking & screaming, which had the weirdest effect." In 1912, Cody carried his epic into the movies with a one-reeler, *The Life of Buffalo Bill*, followed by a series of reenactments of *Indian War Pictures*.

From the movies' earliest days, Westerns were central. The first big commercial hit was *The Great Train Robbery* (1903). In 1910, more than 20 percent of American movies were Westerns; in 1931–35, about 17 percent. Between 1939 and 1969, Richard Slotkin writes, the Western was "the most consistently popular and most widely produced form of action film." This popularity carried into television. In 1955–57, Westerns accounted for nearly 15 percent of all prime-time network hours; in 1959, more than 24 percent. They were "consistently among the top-rated TV shows for most of the 1955–70 period." Between the 1957–58 and 1960–61 seasons, prime-time Westerns attracted roughly a third of the entire viewing audience. Westerns weathered urbanization and suburbanization alike. The wide-open range with its rough-hewn towns certified enduring value for people who drove station wagons and lived in split-level, ranch-style houses.

5   The Western outlasted the frontier by more than seven decades and continues to be relocated and re-created in various formats and incarnations. We are familiar with the gunfighter-type cop who annoys the brass (*Dirty Harry*), the space jockey who freelances (*Star Wars*), and the future cop who revolts (*Blade Runner*). The TV series *60 Minutes* and its investigative offshoots are the Westerns of journalism: every week, the good guy breezes into town, a town where he or she does not belong, uncovers evil, and defends the community. In the movies, the city became the frontier. Steve McQueen moved off the range and morphed into *Bullitt*; Clint Eastwood, *Dirty Harry*. Harrison Ford's Indiana Jones, roving scourge of Indian surrogates, had license to roam anywhere. Television acquired the cop show, and the wilderness moved to the ghetto.

During the late days of Communism, the most popular television shows in Hungary were two American police dramas, *Kojak* and *The Streets of San Francisco*. I once asked a Hungarian media researcher for an explanation. The regime would not permit careful research, but he thought Hungarians found the casual, informal, approachable American cops much preferable to the regime's.

The Western, in short, is the drama of the most rugged individualist in the service of the community—admirably suited to flatter the hopes of all who yearn to reinvent themselves, to master some social or psychic wilderness and emerge with a satisfied mind.

Apparently opposite but closely related is the road movie, where the hero flees the community not on a horse but in a car, a modern gunfighter testing himself in a mechanized wilderness. Roots are traps. The goal may be as straightforward as escaping the law or as ambitious as "finding yourself," but either way, you cast loose and make yourself up as you go along, refusing to play by the rules. The protagonists may be innocents falsely accused (*I Was a Fugitive from a Chain Gang*, *The Fugitive*), criminals in full criminality (*Bonnie and Clyde*, *Badlands*, *Natural Born Killers*), seekers (*Easy Rider*), or runaways (*The Defiant Ones*, *O Brother, Where Art Thou?*). They may be male-bonded or coupled, even female (*Thelma and Louise*). From Walt Whitman through Woody Guthrie, Bob Dylan, and Bruce Springsteen, the road has drawn the lyricist, too. The hero may have been "born to be wild" or may desperately discover that "freedom's just another word for nothing left to lose." The road can be an ocean, a desert, a river. But ultimately, the setting matters less than the yearning. In 1989, an East German student told historian Paul Buhle that the night the Berlin Wall came down she dreamed of Route 66. Of course, the Route 66 she dreamed of no longer existed, having been bypassed by Interstate 40. She was dreaming of the American TV series of the early 1960s.

Action Movies: Soft-Core Apocalypse

The so-called action movie displays a harsher, more cynical attitude. Dependent on technical advances in computerization, cinematography, and makeup, its ballet of destruction represents a breakdown of the Western's melodramatic clarity. In a world so indiscriminately brutal that weathering its assaults and

frictions, or even feeling fright, is an achievement, it offers the pleasure of ni-
hilistic transcendence. Action movies come in many varieties: rogue cop adventure, Vietnam vet revenge, futurist hot pursuit, Eastern martial arts, and battle
epic, among others. What they have in common is kinetic shock.

10   Delivering the disposable sensation, the jolt of fear, the rageful satisfaction
of revenge, the action movie is the quintessential *now* phenomenon. The im-
perative is to jab, startle, and batter a spectator who has become used to being
jabbed, startled, battered. This need to raise the stakes explains the remarkable
casualness of the action movie's gory images. Spasms of graphic mayhem litter
the screen like punctuation marks. Motives and moral consequences are likely
to be dispensable fluff, the plot a sprint from one bloodbath to the next. When
Hollywood censorship lifted and Sam Peckinpah made screen blood spurt in
slow motion in *The Wild Bunch* (1969), he was subverting the tidy ritualistic
shoot-out of the conventional Western. But out of last year's formalist departure Hollywood brews next year's formula. With *The Godfather* (1972), gruesome slaughter was on its way to becoming ritualized choreography.

One generation later, even directors lionized for *auteurist* excellence take
pride in performing assault and battery on the human image, topping each
other in maimings and disfigurements. Grisliness and offhand apocalypse
abound. If Martin Scorsese made blood flow with shootings and stabbings in
GoodFellas (1990), by 1995, in *Casino*, he was forcing a character's head into a
vise and squeezing it until his eye started to pop out. But all the grotesquerie
cannot be traced simply to improvements, if that's the right word, in special
effects; neither is it simply a product of the lifting of movie censorship—which
by itself explains why gore is permitted, but not why there is so much of it. If
everything can be shown, still, why bother showing it? Nor can violence in the
real world account for the violence of the media, for movies and videos are far
more hideous than the streets. Facing a jaded audience, the filmmakers up
the dosage.

The gory, explosive, and slasher styles draw to the cineplex the demographic
segment most eager to get out of their houses: teenagers. These films are box-
office successes virtually everywhere they show. Four films produced by one
man (*Die Hard* 1 and 2, *Lethal Weapon* 1 and 2) grossed a total of $1 billion
worldwide. *Rambo* was a success in places where the American war in Vietnam
was far from popular—Vietnam, for example. John Rambo was not simply a
reincarnation of the Western hero, not just character, not just redemption, not
John Wayne; he was vengeance, a human wrecking ball, a destroyer of worlds.
The teenage soldiers-cum-murderers who dressed up in Rambo regalia from
Afghanistan to Bosnia knew which Rambo it was they wanted to emulate: the
no-nonsense killer. The *Rambo* grunt, the Schwarzenegger one-liner, the *Die
Hard* machinegun burst evidently speak to a take-no-prisoners sensibility that
appeals to adolescent boys everywhere.

Around the world, these films and the comparable video games and heavy
metal music domesticate brutality. Unable to name modern dangers exactly,
young people—males, especially—don't know whether to crave or fear the end

of days. Often they feel their masculinity is wounded. Aggression comes easily to them. Action movies and their equivalents in video games and sound are rehearsals. They are the Dolbys of emotional noise amid the mess and inconclusiveness of everyday life. To lead the audience to feel intensely without risk, they administer homeopathic doses of shock. A pile of bodies is no longer shocking. You go to test your toughness and feel the thrill of momentarily losing it—in a comfortable seat, with popcorn. The butcher knives, blood spatters, tire squeals, and humdrum executions are neither exactly realistic nor tragic. The beings who die never really lived. They can be "blown away" so painlessly because they were cartoons in the first place. Life is fluff; such is the way of the world. Move on.

Entertainment certainly has as one of its purposes the muffling of the knowledge of mortality, and the paradox is that this knowledge can be muffled by blowing life away close-up. Action movies, heavy metal, gangsta rap, violent video games, and the other forms of mortality kitsch express a giddy sense of the weightlessness of existence. To behold human images casually "taken out" is to become inured to a world of casual violence and murky threat. During these artificially darkened moments, we know we are all foam on the torrent. The notion of sensitivity training gives rise to worldly mirth, except among the people who practice it, but a strong strain in popular culture amounts to insensitivity training. Few viewers maim or kill because of what they find at the movies, but they do learn to tolerate a world that maims and kills. The relentless cuts, the gruesomeness, and the one-liners offer the experience of the kinetic sublime—a cutting loose from the terrestrial gravity of everyday life into a stratosphere of pure motion, suspense, and release. Whoever gets snuffed, however many bodies pile up, the spectator always survives. Censors like to speak of gratuitous violence, but the adjective misses the point. Violence is the purpose of the show. As cigarettes are instruments for the delivery of nicotine, an "action movie" or violent video game is an occasion for the delivery of controlled bursts of adrenaline. No wonder they are reviewed as if they were pharmaceuticals.

15   The purveyors of casual violence, gore, and threat, when pressed, take a walk on the demand side and offer a predictable alibi: suppliers deliver only the goods demanded. They claim that their products provide catharsis. But these overnight Aristotelians are as foolish as they are self-serving. The action spectator feels neither pity nor terror for the victims. If the movies were cathartic, violent crime ought to have declined steadily over recent decades as gory movies multiplied. Until the recent downturn (probably caused by an aging population, a strong economy, more imprisonment, better police work, and early deaths of young criminals), that didn't happen.

But if the industry is disingenuous, the Puritans who fight media violence are no closer to the truth. The would-be censors generally do not wonder why the media are saturated with casual aggression—what's in it for the customers. The censorious impulse is not known for its curiosity. It does not wonder what the noise is silencing, why so many people—not only Americans, not only teenagers—might take pleasure in skimming the surface of death. The campaigners believe they know what screen violence does: it invites imitation in the real world. But brutality plays on-screen virtually everywhere on earth without generating epidemics of copy-cat carnage. Demonic Hollywood is a handy issue for politicians who prefer to avoid palpable social failure: poverty, inequality, guns. To blame human wickedness on images is the moralistic recourse of a society that is unwilling to condemn trash on aesthetic grounds. Since the market expresses the only value worth valuing, moral condemnation is untenable unless junk entertainment is believed to have murderous consequences. It isn't bad enough that the movies are ugly. To be judged bad, they have to do bad. The campaign against virtual violence is as shallow as the images it condemns.

Cartoons: Ceremonies of Innocent Wackiness

Next to the not-so-noble savagery of the terrorist and the slasher, Hollywood offers packaged innocence. The Disney-based cartoon and the various Disneylands are in the business of producing adorableness. In movies, comic books, television shows, theme parks, stories, musical theater, and their many accoutrements, Disney assembles smoothness. At the turn of 2001, the corporation bearing the founder's name was bringing in $22 billion in annual sales; its market value was some $52 billion. *Toy Story* had broken movie records in Shanghai, packing in 1 million customers in a city of 13 million. According to Disney CEO Michael Eisner, per capita spending on Disney products in the United States was $65. In Japan, where Disney artifacts are for sale at tourist shrines, it was $45. In denunciatory France, the figure was equally $45. The Disney style of cheery, chirpy fun is arguably America's most potent export in popular culture.

Walt Disney built an empire of pleasantries. He was ruthless—willing to break unions and lead an anti-Communist panic—but not least, he was talented. He was not the first movie cartoonist or best draftsman, but he was the first with a musical soundtrack, first to add voices and sound effects (*yelp! squeal! smack!*), first with Technicolor, and first to produce a full-length animated feature. As critic Richard Schickel has pointed out, he was jokey and an efficient story editor. Efficiency was essential to his success. The Henry Ford of cartoons, he achieved productivity by assembly-line methods, dividing the labor among several teams of animators. Like General Motors, he improved his product with regular model changes.

Disney knew about *synergy* before it became a corporate cliché. As early as 1927, he understood cross-promotion, licensing a chocolate-coated marshmallow candy bar featuring his cartoon character Oswald the Lucky Rabbit. In the 1950s, he was the first Hollywood chief to jump into the small screen and produce a weekly television show. His ABC *Disneyland* series was essentially a stupendously successful, ongoing ad for his new theme park in Anaheim, California. Later, the company Mickey Mouse spawned bought its own cable network and then ABC. Walt Disney was early to grasp the saturation principle. No one better understood how to pump product at high volume and speed into the growing media stream. A classic monopolist, wherever possible he built his own conduits, filled them with Disneyness, and excluded the competition. His little world promoted his little world.

20 But again, no supply-side advantages fully explain the demand side. Surely it matters that Disney was (and as a company remains) relentlessly upbeat, offering cozy feeling—not ecstatic but family-friendly. The enterprises are deeply shallow and shallowly clean. The parks are fenced-in, centrally cast utopias, flawed by neither conflict nor challenge. Everywhere, the cartoons are not only accessible but dubbed into local languages for local convenience. But there must be more to the demand side.

In the early 1970s, during Salvador Allende's socialist regime, Chilean writer Ariel Dorfman and his Belgian collaborator Armand Mattelart published *How to Read Donald Duck*, a pamphlet charging Disney with propaganda—justifying capitalist greed, displaying smugness toward backward savages, and so on. In Europe, the pamphlet became sufficiently renowned that the Disney corporation charged copyright violation and the U.S. Customs impounded imports. A decade later, in exile in the United States, Dorfman felt compelled to ask what *bound* people to Disney. Why did they enjoy what they were not compelled to enjoy? Surely not because the cartoons fronted for American imperialism. He recalled meeting a slum dweller in Chile who, having heard that Dorfman was crusading against comic books, photo novels, sitcoms, and the rest of industrialized fiction, pleaded: "Don't take my dreams away from me."

In his sequel, *The Empire's Old Clothes* (1983), Dorfman delivered one of the most striking passages in the whole bulky history of ruminations on popular culture. What, he asked, explained the *hold* of cartoonish fiction, especially the products of America's culture industry, even among people battered by American power? Here he came to a conclusion so unexpected (for a man of the left) that he interrupted his own writing to ask, "Did I write that?"

> American mass culture appealed to the child the audience would like to be, the child they remembered, the child they still felt themselves at times to be. . . . In spite of resistance from national cultures and diverse subcultures which have rejected homogenization, in spite of overwhelming elite and intellectual criticism of these works of fiction, the infantilization that seems to be such an essential centerpiece of mass media culture may be grounded in a certain form of human nature that goes beyond historical circumstances. The way in which American mass culture reaches out to people may touch upon mechanisms embedded in our innermost being.

"*Human nature . . . beyond historical circumstances . . . innermost being*"—strong claims, but Dorfman was undoubtedly right. Different societies treat childhood differently, but what is universal is the child's biological dependency, playfulness, and naïveté. America, child of the West, youngest of civilizations, is singular in its affirmation of childishness, and is both cherished and despised for it, but the appeal of its cartoon childishness is undeniable. Cartoon characters are incarnations of an innocence that can never be dispelled. Their large heads are the heads of newborns, their smooth faces signs of perpetual immaturity. Life has not yet weathered them or bent their bodies. Cartoons, offering vaguely adult activities in the trappings of childish bodies, appeal to the universal experience of having been a child in a world run by adults. Moreover, as Dorfman wrote, Mickey Mouse "joins power and infantilization." He "lords it over everybody" while his smile "disarms all criticism." The innocent mouse, "like the mass culture into which he was born, automatically reconciles the adult and the child by appealing to" our fundamental biology—"the fact that humans are instinctually conditioned to protect their young and are prepared by nature to react well to anything that resembles juvenility." So Mickey Mouse appeals to minds and hearts everywhere by "addressing our most tender feelings for our progeny and for the future."

Disney's harmless hijinks also play on the pleasure that a democratic age finds in twitting authority. Disney's adults, like Scrooge McDuck, are pleasingly foolish, foils for fun-loving disobedience. The forces of badness get their lumps—there is always the prospect of justice—yet no one gets punished severely. Disney enshrines the little guy who thumbs his nose at power, the little gal who gets the glass slipper. Rebellion amounts to growing pains, inevitable, painless, and harmless—that is to say, fun.

25   Then why *shouldn't* people everywhere revel in Disney's animated innocence? Or George Lucas's cartoonish space fables? Why shouldn't live action physical comedy appeal as well? From Chaplin and Laurel and Hardy to Jerry Lewis and Jim Carrey, clowning combines childish insouciance and wildness, suggesting the joys of surmounting social convention—for a while. I once asked a Chinese student what Chinese viewers think when they watch the Academy Award ceremonies. "We think Americans are wild and crazy people," she said. Years later, during the popular National Basketball Association broadcast in China, a Beijing university student wearing jeans and a T-shirt said on the subject of Dennis Rodman: "I couldn't accept this from a Chinese player, but he's an American, so we expect it." Americans may look like cartoon savages, "wild and crazy people," but they are not only cast as the world's pleasure principle; they are its projective screen, its global outlaw, buffoon, and marshal wrapped up in one.

QUESTIONS FOR DISCUSSION

1. What are the three principal Hollywood entertainment formulas that have captured the national and global markets? Do you agree that other formulas, such as science fiction, soap operas, and "beach extravaganzas" are really just "variations on the three essential types"?

2. What, according to Gitlin and Slotkin, are the characteristics of the Western drama, and what is the source of its lasting popularity? What values and ideals does this type of film portray? What are some of its modern variations, both in film and TV programming?

3. What are the characteristic attitudes and values of action movies? How does the action film represent a "breakdown" of the Western's clear-cut values?

4. Why is the action film so popular with male teenagers? Why is Gitlin critical of the alibi of filmmakers who justify the violence in these films, while

at the same time being critical of those who campaign against the violence in the action movies? Do you think his position is logical or consistent?

5. What are the values and appeals inherent in cartoons? How does Ariel Dorfman's analysis of "infantilization" help to explain their appeals? Why does Gitlin believe these films are about a certain kind of rebellion?

6. Discuss the final sentence in the essay in terms of the overall effect on the worldwide image of Americans in the films that Gitlin has discussed. In what sense are Americans seen through these films as "the world's pleasure principle; . . . its projective screen, its global outlaw, buffoon, and marshal wrapped into one"?

CONNECTION

Compare Gitlin's views on the causes of media violence and the need for censorship to those of Sissela Bok. With which writer do you most agree and why (see page 486)?

IDEAS FOR WRITING

1. Pick one of the three types of formula films Gitlin discusses and apply his analysis of the typical values and attitudes such films project to a particular film you have seen. Use a film that is available on video, so you can watch it again and replay crucial scenes and interactions. How does the film embody and project the values Gitlin believes such films contain, and what other, perhaps contrary values it might also exhibit?

2. Write an essay in which you explain Gitlin's criticism of the film industry's alibi about the cathartic nature of the violence in action films. Indicate whether you agree or disagree with his views and why.

RELATED WEB SITES

ONLINE STUDY GUIDE: THE MASS MEDIA
http://www.personal.kent.edu/~glhanson/studyguides/sg-ma
ssmedia.htm
View this web site from Kent University's School of Journalism and Mass communication devoted to understanding the relationship between media, power, and culture. At the above URL, you can look at the school's "online study guide" of mass media, which mentions author Todd Gitlin.

THE MEDIA RESOURCE CENTRE
http://www.mediademocracy.net/nobody.htm
This Canada based web site and organization, "The Media Resource Centre," shares many links dedicated to bringing "alternative media on the net, media that tells it the way it is, plus some research-organization websites that do the same." The organization and links concern the issues of democratizing the mass media, control of the mass media, media bias, and media commercialization.

Jason Glickman

Technology and the Future of the American Wilderness

> *Jason Glickman, who enjoys working with computers as well as canoeing, hiking, and backpacking in wilderness areas, wrote the following research paper for his introductory writing course. Glickman critiques the dependence on communication technology such as cell phones and lap-tops because this "portable" communications technology makes it difficult for people to experience the quiet and solitude of the wilderness. Notice how Glickman uses extensive historical and contemporary research to build his case for a wilderness experience free of technological and media intrusion.*

> *When one finally arrives at the point where schedules are forgotten, and becomes immersed in ancient rhythms, one begins to live.*
> SIGURD OLSON

In Olson's home—the vast lakeland wilderness of northern Minnesota— schedules are forgotten with ease. Air and water engage in a fanciful dance tenderly embraced by lush forest. A canoe glides through the water with the slice of a razor, yet disturbs nothing. It has no motor; this vessel is propelled by the paddle's whisper.

In the wilderness I am at home. In the wilderness America is at home; since its birth, the nation's identity has been deeply rooted in its wilderness. First formulated by Henry David Thoreau and popularized by John Muir, the *wilderness experience* has become classically American. The Wilderness Act, which outlawed motor vehicles in designated backcountry areas, validated Muir's efforts. In the thirty-five years since its passage, the Act has been very effective in fostering wilderness appreciation. But will this success continue into the twenty-first century?

Today, the wilderness experience is again threatened by technology. Devices like global positioning system (GPS) receivers, cellular phones, and palmtop computers deaden the wilderness experience. If the traditional wilderness experience is defined by a disconnection from society, how can America reconcile the growing use of information technology in the outdoors? How can America reconcile the potential loss of the wilderness experience, heretofore crucial to its identity? Legislation will not suffice, for it cannot evolve as rapidly as information technology does. To ensure the wilderness experience's long-term viability, backcountry users must champion a new outdoor ethics. Developing a technology-directed clone of Leave No Trace (the most successful minimum impact program to date) is the best way to preserve the wilderness experience.

In contrast to contemporary concerns, America's earliest colonists thought little of preserving wilderness. They imported a utilitarian view of wilderness, measuring its value in economic terms. The wilderness was not to be enjoyed, but subjugated in the name of human progress. As poet and naturalist Gary Snyder observes, in early America, "wild is associated with unruliness," and represented a disorder that ought to be controlled (5). The driving vision of pioneer ideology was the taming of Western wilderness for human benefit.

5   In the nineteenth century, however, a new attitude emerged that wilderness could be enjoyed for its mere existence (Nash 67). Thinkers like Ralph Waldo Emerson initiated a gradual appreciation of the beauty and solitude of the backcountry. As Emerson noted, "[T]he sky, the mountain, the tree, the animal, give us a delight in and for themselves" (531). In a statement that would become a mantra for wilderness advocates, Emerson's friend and fellow transcendenalist, Henry David Thoreau, decreed that "in wildness is the preservation of the world" (qtd. in Nash 84). In attaching this degree of divinity to wilderness, Emerson and Thoreau hoped to remove its stigma.

Thoreau's influence upon the popular conception of "wilderness" cannot be overlooked. His quest for refuge from the stress of industrial society led him deep into the Canadian backcountry, yet he still clung to the threads of civilization. Hoping to strike a balance, Thoreau authored a vision of the wilderness as a refresher—a sort of spiritual vacation. His idea was deeply influential, as he "led the intellectual revolution that was beginning to invest wilderness with attractive rather than repulsive qualities" (Nash 95).

Thoreau's view of wilderness as an idyllic respite from industrial civilization soon bore a new idea: *the wilderness experience*. Central to the wilderness experience was one's willingness to blend into the landscape rather than dominate it. Though Thoreau first conceived these ideals, John Muir is credited with entering "the wilderness experience" into the national lexicon. In his <u>Wilderness and The American Mind</u>, Roderick Nash writes, " Wild country needed a champion, and in . . . John Muir it found one" (122). Muir's ideals borrowed heavily from transcendentalism, but diverged in their unabashed enthusiasm. This zeal propagated itself in his writing, which enjoyed a greater audience than any wilderness or conservation issues had ever before (Nash 131). Muir's notion of walking into the high Sierra with only what he could carry on his back and emerging at his fancy " . . . demanded dependency on self rather than on society" (Nash 253). Others would soon adopt this notion, crafting it into the archetypal wilderness experience.

In Muir's lifetime, straddling the turn of the century, it was possible for one to simply "run away" from industrial society into the wilderness. This was ensured by the remoteness, harshness, and sheer scale of much of the American landscape. Nash notes, "For a time in the history of the West, lack of technology held in check human desire to modify the land" (276). Without efficient transportation, it would be impossible for industrial society to encroach upon the deepest wilderness. However, in the twentieth century, all but the most unforgiving wilderness was threatened by the advent of the automobile. The question,

"What is technology's place in the wilderness?" moved into the foreground. Here, more philosophical questions at the root of the issue emerge. At what level are beauty, solitude, independence, and oneness with nature jeopardized? When does the progress of man directly encroach upon the wilderness experience? Can we let the wilderness experience change, or must we preserve it as Thoreau and Muir envisioned it?

Early twentieth century conservationists, in the mold of Thoreau and Muir, argued for the maintenance of the traditional wilderness experience through the protection of land. Aldo Leopold, borrowing from Thoreau, developed a "land ethic," which "changes the role of Homo sapiens from conqueror of the land-community to plain member and citizen of it" (qtd. in Watkins 3). In this decree, Leopold reinforced the foundation for the traditional wilderness experience. For if man could adopt such a land ethic, he could ensure that the solitude and beauty of the wilderness would remain intact for ages.

10   Strong efforts to legislate Leopold's vision took root after World War II. In September 1964, the U.S. Congress passed "The Wilderness Act," designating some 9 million acres as "wilderness areas." The Act stipulated that ". . . there shall be no commercial enterprise and no permanent road within any wilderness area . . . there shall be no temporary road, no use of motor vehicles, motorized equipment or motorboats, no landing of aircraft, no other form of mechanical transport, and no structure or installation within any such area" (Section 4c). For both wilderness advocates and opponents, this was a striking measure. In anointing a wilderness area as land free of the combustion engine—arguably the foremost symbol of post-Industrial Revolution progress—the Wilderness Act offered a barrier to the relentless onslaught of progress (Borrie and Friemund 1).

Preserving the land so that future generations could enjoy it in its original state was the Wilderness Act's central concern. It specified that wilderness areas "shall be administered for the use and enjoyment of the American people in such manner as will leave them unimpaired for future use and enjoyment as wilderness" (Sec. 2a). In theory, the Act allowed one to experience the Sierra Nevada exactly as Muir had done seventy-five years earlier. Muir's exploration of the Sierra was at its time unmatched in scope; he pioneered first ascents on many of the range's most forbidding peaks. The illusion that one is the *first* to climb a distant peak or paddle a raging river is key to the wilderness experience. Whether or not others have done so is mostly irrelevant; the beauty of the moment comes in that one is able to share it with nature alone. The degree of importance the Wilderness Act attached to such a feat was a major victory for backcountry enthusiasts, for it validated the intangible value of the wilderness experience.

However, because of its position in technological history, the Wilderness Act was ill-suited to be the wilderness experience's ultimate protector. Its passage stood at a pivotal point: after the close of the Industrial Revolution, but at the brink of the computer age. In 1965, few could have fathomed the potential for information technology. Especially in the last decade, computing has become smaller, faster, and cheaper. Powerful laptop computers can now be had in packages well under five pounds. Cellular towers dot the landscape, allowing one to place a call from nearly anywhere. Satellite phones allow one to literally talk to *anyone* on the globe from *anywhere* on the globe. GPS units permit one to pinpoint their location to within 100 yards—*anywhere on earth*. While contemporary society lauds these technological miracles, they also pose a direct threat to the wilderness experience.

The wilderness experience hinges on a *disconnection* from society—the lack of dependency that Nash cites. Information technology works directly against this ideal. In theory, one might stay connected to the Internet for the entire duration of a backcountry stay. This, of course, is currently impossible due to battery limitations, but, with solar energy and superior batteries, can it be long before it is a reality? The traditional wilderness experience minimizes the gap between man and nature. Modern information technology just does the opposite; it erects a barrier between humans and the wilderness. Man is shielded from nature's vitality by his technology, precluding one from becoming "immersed in ancient rhythms," as Olson wrote. It follows that successive generations of technology will further this trend, further numbing the reality of a backcountry trip.

With every new device will come "more shallow contact and superficial understandings," writes David Strong in Crazy Mountains: Using Wilderness to Weigh Technology (163). For an experience whose meaning lay in its spiritual depth, Strong's contention is ominous. Traveling in the wilderness is a relatively simple affair—technology brings unnecessary complexity to the wilderness. "The beauty of backpacking is its simplicity," I was once told, "it's nothing more than walking." Not having anything to focus on but *walking* facilitates incredible self-reflection and natural appreciation. The spirituality of the wilderness experience is marred by the presence of technology. Recognizing and dispatching technology's imposition has become a focal point for wilderness advocates in the last half-decade.

15   Accordingly, a wealth of discussion has sprung up to find an appropriate role for information technology in the wilderness. In an article entitled "Tech overload victims, unite!," Dan McMillan argues that modern computing devices have no place in the wilderness:

> I read about this wondrous little [cellular phone and e-mail] device the morning after returning from a week-long backpacking trip in Idaho's Seven Devils Wilderness Area. The entire point of said trip being to get away from anything more technologically advanced than a water filter. (1)

McMillan's objection is shared by a variety of wilderness users. In an interview of six Stanford students (whose trail time ranged from one to over one hundred nights) about technology's impact upon the wilderness, information technology was unanimously stigmatized. Galen Weston, a freshman with extensive experience in the Sierra backcountry, laments, "The more you bring, it cheapens [the experience]." Wary of this type of reaction, magazines like Backpacker and Outside have been reluctant to take a stance on the use of information technology in the wilderness.

In this fashion, the March 1999 issue of <u>Outside</u> reviewed cellular phones, handheld computers, and satellite phones in an aptly named article: "Always in Touch (If, That is, You Want to Be)." The title's qualification lends credence to the argument that information technology's role in the wilderness ought to be determined by the individual user. However, the <u>Outside</u> article also included a sidebar reviewing a protective case for cell phones, noting that it " . . . is lined with enough padding to take a good licking but not so much that you won't hear an incoming call" (Hurtig 1).

Receiving a call in the backcountry clearly violates the wilderness experience—it's an obvious connection to society. But, some might argue, isn't it an individual's *right* to receive a call? If one wishes *not* to have a traditional wilderness experience, isn't that permissible? Absolutely. But a cell-phone-toting visitor's right to receive calls should not infringe upon others' right to the magnificently rich silence of a backcountry jaunt. In nature's comparatively quiet sound-scape, a cell phone's digital whine carries much farther than in an urban environment. Many wilderness users consider it a disappointment to see any other humans while in the backcountry—how will they react when they hear or see a cellular phone in use? For wilderness advocates, the chief virtue of the wilderness experience—the enjoyment of nature's unbridled power—is threatened by information technology. How, then, to guarantee that the traditional wilderness experience remains intact? The Wilderness Act, while safeguarding against the technology of yesteryear, lacks provisions for the technology of tomorrow. An act whose basis is the outlaw of specific technologies cannot protect the wilderness experience in an ever-advancing society. Will the Act's failure mark the end of the wilderness experience as we know it? To address this question, one must further examine the character of the wilderness experience.

The wilderness experience is fundamentally aesthetic; it is highly dependent on sensory impulse: the bite of an alpine breeze; the smell of a pine forest; the soft lapping of water against a canoe. Therefore, this aesthetic must be the standard for the maintenance of the wilderness experience. In the two decades following the Wilderness Act, this aesthetic was threatened by the rapidly growing ranks of wilderness users. To combat this trend, wilderness advocates initiated "minimum impact" movements. Leave No Trace (LNT), begun in the early '80s, is one such program. Originally conceived by a Forest Service ranger, LNT is today spearheaded by the National Outdoor Leadership School (NOLS). While some of LNT's guidelines directly protect the *wilderness* itself (i.e. depositing human waste away from water sources), others are aesthetically-oriented—designed solely to preserve the *wilderness experience*. The NOLS <u>Wilderness Guide</u> offers this snippet:

> NOLS issues tents and backpacks in earth tones of blue, brown, and green, rather than bright Day-Glo colors, to help ensure that we fade into beauty and solitude which our students, instructors, and other backpackers are in the wilderness to enjoy. (Simer and Sullivan 24)

20   Such a guideline is wholly visual; the physical impact of a bright orange parka upon the land is nonexistent. LNT's success in this sort of outdoor ethic has garnered it a wide network of support: four federal partnerships, heavy corporate backing, and NOLS' influence as the leading outdoor education program in the world ("Leave No Trace: Questions and Answers"). Much of LNT's success may be attributable to the fact that it is not legislation and is thus endlessly adaptable. As new threats to the wilderness experience have emerged, LNT has been able to compensate appropriately.

Such a revision occurred on February 24th as LNT added a new principle to the six it had already established. The seventh, "Be Considerate of Other Visitors," is necessarily broad to reflect LNT's overall mission ("Principles of Leave No Trace"). But this principle may also be applied to the role of information technology in the wilderness. Implicit in the principle is the assurance that visitors may have a traditional wilderness experience; it could be amended to read "Be Considerate of Other Visitors *so as Not to Disturb Their Wilderness Experience*" without betraying its original meaning. The added clause is actually a concise statement of LNT's true purpose: maintaining the viability of the wilderness so that the wilderness experience remains intact.

LNT has demonstrated an ability to successfully engender respect for the wilderness and its occupants. If articulated properly, a new outdoor ethics in the mold of LNT would effectively counter high-tech's threat to the wilderness experience. As LNT does, such a program would *educate* rather than *regulate*. In lieu of declaring a role for information technology in the wilderness, it would inform people as to *why* technology threatens the wilderness experience. Appreciation for the wilderness experience would grow in turn; once something is threatened—e.g. an endangered species—it draws more attention.

This new ethics might even be designed as a subset of LNT so as to use the latter's name recognition. Wilderness and technology advocates alike are desperately looking for ways to make these two American fixtures coexist; a tech-directed outdoor ethics would encourage the productive dialogue that's just beginning. As technology becomes more and more advanced, this exchange of ideas will become increasingly crucial. Wilderness advocates must voice their displeasure with technology that infringes upon the wilderness experience.

To be sure, the American wilderness is at a crossroads. The looming technological threat will continue to mount; how does America respond? Does she place a higher valuation on her wilderness, or does she let the Wilderness Act become just another wayward roadblock in the progress of man? The goal for wilderness users must not be the condemnation of technology, but finding a way to blend the traditional wilderness experience with new technology. This synergy will become even more critical for America's identity in the years ahead. In an increasingly tech-driven society, Americans will need a way to escape. Hopefully, that way will continue to be among the snow-capped peaks, cold mountain streams, and sheer magnificence of *their wilderness*.

WORKS CITED

Borrie, William T. and Wayne A. Friemund. <u>Wilderness in the 21st Century: Are There Technical Solutions to our Technical Solutions?</u> University of Montana, Oct. 1997. 2 Feb. 1999 <http://www.forestry.umt.edu/ people/borrie/papers/techno>.

Daniel, John. "Toward Wild Heartlands." <u>Audubon</u> Sep.–Oct. 1994: 38–47.

Emerson, Ralph Waldo. <u>The Works of Ralph Waldo Emerson</u>. New York: Black Reader's Service, 1929.

Hurtig, Brent. "Review: Always in Touch (If, That Is, You Want to Be)." <u>Outside.</u> Mar. 1999. 28 Feb. 1999 <http://outside.starwave.com:80/magazine/0399/9903review.html>.

"Leave No Trace: Questions and Answers." <u>Leave No Trace Home Page</u>. 1998. 1 Mar. 1999 <http://www.lnt.org/LNT_FAQ.html>.

McMillan, Dan. "Tech Overload Victims, Unite!" <u>The Business Journal of Portland</u> 12 Oct. 1998. 1 Feb. 1999 <http://www.amcity.com/portland/stories/101298/editorial2.html>.

Nash, Roderick. <u>Wilderness and the American Mind</u>. New Haven, Connecticut: Yale University Press, 1982.

"Principles of Leave No Trace." <u>Leave No Trace Home Page</u>. 1998. 1 Mar. 1999 <http://www. lnt.org/ LNTPrinciples/LNTPrinciples.update.html>.

Simer, Peter and John Sullivan. <u>The National Outdoor Leadership School's Wilderness Guide</u>. New York: Simon and Schuster, 1983.

Snyder, Gary. <u>The Practice of the Wild</u>. San Francisco: North Point Press, 1990.

Strong, David. <u>Crazy Mountains: Learning From Wilderness to Weigh Technology</u>. Albany, New York: State University of New York Press, 1995.

Watkins, T.H. "The Hundred-Million-Acre Understanding." <u>Audubon</u>. Sep.–Oct. 1994: 36–39.

Weston, Galen. <u>Interview on Technology</u>. Stanford, California. 19 Feb. 1999.

QUESTIONS FOR DISCUSSION

1. Why does Glickman begin his essay with the quotation and introductory paragraph on Sigurd Olson?

2. How does Glickman define both the wilderness experience and the Wilderness Act ? How do these two definitions help prepare us for the contemporary problem he wants to discuss?

3. How have technological advances affected the wilderness experience? Why is the Wilderness Act unable to cope with current technology?

4. What solution does Glickman present for the problems related to technology that he explores in his essay? Does his solution seem adequate? Is a solution to this problem possible?

TOPICS FOR RESEARCH AND WRITING

1. Many critics have commented that mass communications media often portray a biased or stereotyped image of minority groups, sometimes excluding certain groups altogether. After reading the essay by Pratkanis and Aronson and doing further research into the media coverage of one ethnic group, write your conclusions in the form of a documented research essay.

2. After reading the essay by Pratkanis and Aronson and doing further research into media bias and selective reporting, write a research paper that discusses the media's coverage and influence on the outcome of a significant event in your community, city, or state.

3. After doing some outside reading and Internet research, write an essay that focuses on the ways that computers and the electronic environment have influenced modern life and perceptions of reality. Consider whether communication through computers and the World Wide Web is more positive than negative or more negative than positive.

4. Examine the current television schedule (cable as well as network TV) for programs that you think encourage imagination, creativity, and a concern for the inner life; then read some media reviews of these programs in print media or the Internet. After considering the media critiques made by Lasn, write an evaluative review of several such programs, trying to draw some conclusions about the potential the television medium has for improving the quality of modern life, as well as the ways it often fails to achieve its potential.

5. Considering the ideas of writers such as Lasn, Bok, and others in this chapter, write a research paper that addresses the negative impact of a particular mass medium or aspect of a medium on the self-concept and mental health of citizens in our society. Define and present examples of the problem; then suggest solutions such as legislation or citizen action. You could discuss issues such as children's TV programs, MTV, subliminal persuasion, or other forms of manipulative advertising, or excessive sex and violence in the media.

6. Write a research essay that discusses the way that images of roles and behavior for people in other societies are created and/or reinforced by American mass media broadcast and other various forms available abroad. Consider the ideas of Gitlin and Hodge in your essay.

7. Write about a film that examines issues of advertising, propaganda, or mass media on society, politics, and the inner life of the individual. Watch the film and take notes on the dialogue and any other details that can be used to support the conclusions you draw; also read some critical responses to the film, both in popular journals and in specialized magazines that critique films. You might select a film from the following list: *Day of the Locust, Network, Broadcast News, 1984, The Kiss of the Spider Woman, The Celluloid Closet, Hoop Dreams, Pulp Fiction, To Die For, The Matrix, The Truman Show, Wag the Dog, Pleasantville,* or *American Beauty.*

9 Visions of Spirituality

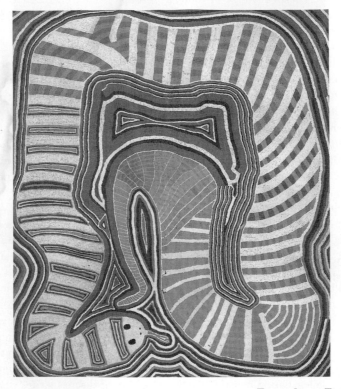

Tommy Lowry Tjapaltjarri
Warrmala the Serpent (1986)

This Aboriginal painting depicts Warrmala, a Rainbow Serpent, resting at Patjar-rnga, a deep desert waterhole in western Australia. Both waterholes and serpents are sacred in Aboriginal culture and religious art. The waterhole represents the place where life is nurtured in times of drought and in "dreamings," while the Rainbow Serpent is a creator god associated with the coming of the rainy season and with rebirth and spiritual renewal.

JOURNAL

Write about a natural creature that represents to you some important spiritual quality or power. What is the source of its power?

Holiness is a force, and like the others can be resisted. It was given but I didn't want to see it, God or no God.
                                                ANNIE DILLARD

With this faith we will be able to hew out of the mountain of despair a stone of hope. With this faith we will be able to transform the jangling discords of our nation into a beautiful symphony of brotherhood.
                                                MARTIN LUTHER KING, JR.

There is no phenomenon in the universe that does not intimately concern us, from a pebble resting at the bottom of the ocean, to the movement of a galaxy millions of light years away.
                                                THICH NHAT HANH

CREATIVITY, PROBLEM SOLVING, AND SYNTHESIS

Creativity and spirituality have many similar qualities. Both involve a new way of seeing—going beyond the surface appearance of things to find deeper and more complex meanings. These new insights may include a combination of information and experience into a new synthesis that solves problems and/or produces something that a person can value and respect. In the case of writing, that new thing may be a poem, story, or nonfiction work that is humanely and aesthetically satisfying, both to you and to others. While many people are inspired by the examples of creative visionaries in different fields and can learn from studying their techniques, creativity is in large part a generative rather than an imitative and technical process, a process of discovery that often originates in the unconscious mind, sometimes without a clear goal or defined product in mind—at least at the beginning. An open, receptive mental attitude encourages the initiation of the creative process.

Everyone is potentially creative; in fact, all people are creative when they dream, whether or not they are consciously aware of the process. As author John Steinbeck noted, a problem is often "resolved in the morning after the committee of sleep has worked it out." In waking life people are creative in a more conscious, directed manner, seeking solutions to problems in order to survive and to make their lives more comfortable and rewarding. For example, when you redecorate your room, look for a better job, or select a new course of study in school, you are working on creative solutions for the problems that you have recognized in your life, just as you are when you write a proposal for your job or for one of your classes at school. You may see what you are doing at work or school as competing for a raise or completing a course requirement—but there is also an element of creativity in every new solution, and it is usually the creative ideas that get the most attention.

Although it is true that everyone exercises some degree of creativity, it is equally true that most people have the potential to be far more creative in many aspects of their lives than they are. Writers, psychologists, and social scientists have identified patterns of behavior that are likely to block an individual's creativity. Understanding how these mental traps work may help you find a way to release yourself from nonproductive behavior and to become more creative.

Habit Versus Risk

Habit and self-image can be major blocks to creativity. If your inner self-image is that of a person stuck in a round of repetitive daily tasks and rituals, it is unlikely that you will feel that you have the capacity to be creative. You may have come to believe that you really need to follow a ritualized pattern in performing your job, relating to people, or writing. This type of thinking also protects you from taking risks: the risk of an original expression of a feeling or situation, the risk of a controversial solution to a problem, the risk of not being understood by others.

Furthermore, creative risk-taking approaches to problem solving can be quite time-consuming. Many people convince themselves that they don't have the time to explore a new and creative approach, that it is more efficient to follow a method that has worked (or sort of worked) in the past. This inclination to play it safe and to be overly concerned with time management is typical of workers, managers, students, teachers, and writers who fear change and are wary of embarking on a new direction in their lives. Even if you see yourself as a non-risk-taking person, it is never too late to change. Fantasizing about new approaches and thinking about alternatives is a positive first step toward finding creative solutions. Try to develop your alternative fantasies, as do many of the writers in this chapter.

Reason Versus Intuition

You may be building another obstacle to uncovering your creativity if you value a linear, rational approach to handling problems to the extent that you ignore the imaginative, emotional, and intuitive side of the mind and the solutions that your imagination might suggest. Did you know that many landmark solutions to creative problems, both in the arts and in the sciences, were born in the unconscious mind and some specifically in dreams: Descartes' philosophical system, the invention of the sewing machine needle, the pattern of the benzene ring, as well as the basic concepts for classic works of literature such as Mary Shelley's *Frankenstein*, Samuel Taylor

Coleridge's "Kubla Khan," and Robert Louis Stevenson's *The Strange Case of Dr. Jekyll and Mr. Hyde.*

We do not want you to think that all you have to do is to take a nap and allow your problems to solve themselves, or that if you sleep long enough, you will discover the seeds of great art and great ideas. We do encourage you to look to your dream mind for ideas and feelings and to allow your unconscious mind to have time to process and integrate ideas that are being developed by your rational mind. For example, after you have finished the first draft of a paper, go for a walk, or a swim, or listen to some music, or take a nap. Let your unconscious mind have a chance to think about what you have written. When you return to your first draft, you may find that your unconscious mind has sent you new ideas to work with or that you have a solution to a problem in your paper that was frustrating you.

Developing Self-Confidence: Learning to Trust Your Own Processes

Another barrier to the creative process can come from trying too hard to please an authority such as a teacher or employer. If you focus your energy on trying to please your teacher at the expense of what you think or believe, an inner conflict may keep you from writing your paper altogether. If you become too reliant on your instructor's assignment and approval, you will not be developing your own working style and sense of independence, which every writer must possess. Finally, if you rush to produce a finished paper in one draft, you will miss the excitement of discovery, the potential for personal involvement that is an essential part of the writing process; it is always preferable to relax and work within a writing project rather than to become too concerned with what it is supposed to be.

Evaluation and Application

The creative problem-solving process does include evaluation and application—but only after you give free expression to a range of imaginative solutions and ideas. Once you have finished the creative or generative part of your writing project, you will want to think about whether or not you have accomplished your goals. To evaluate your work, you need to establish clear standards so that you can compare your work with that of others. Always try to formulate standards that are challenging and yet realistic.

Peer sharing can be a useful comparative and evaluative process that will help you to create realistic standards for assessing your own writing in relationship to that of your classmates. Through sharing your work as well as reading and editing the work of your classmates, you will begin to develop realistic standards for the style, structure, and content of your writing. Learn to ask questions of yourself and of your peers. Develop criteria for evaluating papers as you go along. Soon you will find that you have established a vocabulary that allows you to talk about one another's papers and that you have defined some standards for effective writing.

Synthesis

Synthesis, the final step in the creative process, involves bringing a number of different ideas or solutions, which you may have considered separately, together to form an integrated solution. For example, if you are trying to decide on a method for presenting an essay on "How to Make Your Dreams Work for You," you will need to evaluate and then synthesize or integrate the different points of view of experts as well as your own on the subject of dream power. Synthesis is an excellent metaphor for the gathering and unifying of information from diverse sources that can produce a lively research proposal. In a sense, synthesis also defines the writing process itself, as writing involves bringing together a number of different skills to solve a variety of problems: engaging your reader's interest, persuading your reader, developing an overall structure and pattern, supporting your main ideas, and using language that is both appropriate and creative. The student essay in this chapter by Josh Styles, "Knowing Spirituality," contains examples of synthesis writing in his development of a complex philosophical definition that mediates between ideas and quotations from different writers while also employing strategies of illustration, contrast, and classification to build and support his argument.

Writing is a rewarding activity that can help you discover your thoughts and feelings and combine them in new ways. In any type of writing, you work through the stages and difficulties inherent in the creative process as a whole.

THEMATIC INTRODUCTION:
VISIONS OF SPIRITUALITY

Prophetic dreams and visions can provide valuable insights into the human spirit in its most creative, courageous, and hopeful state. From ancient times to the present, people have discovered solutions to personal aesthetic, social and scientific problems through interpreting the messages brought to them from their dreams and intuitions. People have used their dreams and intuitions in another perspective, finding insight and spiritual healing through analysis of their dreams. The selections in this chapter reflect the experiences of people from different cultures, generations, and social classes. They present a range of issues and experiences, all of which speak about a unique quality of spirituality. While many people connect their spirituality to a particular religion, in this chapter we are presenting spirituality more broadly, as being capable of embracing all religions and including all people who have nonreligious spiritual experiences.

We open our chapter with Emily Dickinson's poem, "This World is not Conclusion." Her cogent questioning of traditional religious piety and her continued feeling of being drawn to the world of the spirit will help you to think about the reasons why people continue to struggle with spiritual questions in an age of reason and science. The two essays that follow are narratives of spiritual doubt and discovery. In Annie Dillard's "A Field of Silence," the author experiences a moment of intense spiritual illumination while living a life of solitude on an isolated farm, even though she admits to having difficulty accepting or making sense of her experience. In "Santa Teresa" Terry Tempest Williams tells about her visit to the ancient city of Avila in the central plateau of Spain, where the mystic nun and poet Santa Teresa lived in the early sixteenth century. Through her dreams and experiences on her pilgrimage to Santa Teresa's village, Williams discovers the depth of her own spiritual thirst.

In the next selection, "Neither Here Nor There," psychotherapist Thomas Moore writes about the importance of finding meditative spaces, threshold places where spiritual illumination can be welcomed: "they are not the place of life and not the place of death." Moore believes that these are the places where "the deep soul prospers." "In the Forests of Gombe" tells of Jane Goodall's mystical experience after the death of her husband while she is sitting by a lake in Tanganyika, which has been her home with the chimpanzees that she came to study—and grew to know and love. From her experience in the forests of Gombe, Goodall comes to realize that scientific and mystical knowledge can be interconnected.

Our next two selections discuss ways that spiritual beliefs and social activism can be joined. In his powerful speech, "I Have a Dream," Martin Luther King, Jr. develops a politically charged vision that uses both modern and biblical language to create a plea for a future free of racial injustice and exploitation. King's speech, originally delivered at a huge civil rights rally in Washington, D.C., had a great impact on his audience, making it more possible for brotherhood and spirituality to become integrated into the daily lives of many Americans. Our final professional selection is taken from the work of the world renowned Vietnamese Buddhist monk and peace activist, Thich Nhat Hanh, whom Martin Luther King nominated for a Nobel Prize. In his essay, "Love in Action," Hanh presents many reasons and examples to convince us why environmentalists, psychotherapists, and those whom they can influence must try to heal themselves and others through meditating on the connections between the mind, the spirit, and nature.

The two student essays that conclude this chapter each capture a sense of what they believe is the meaning and importance of spirituality. Josh Spires in "Knowing Spirituality" structures his definition essay to include everyday and religious spiritual experiences only to conclude: "Spirituality cannot be pinned to a specific form, duration or effect, yet we still need to try to understand its meaning in our lives." Elizabeth Matchett writes of her new understanding of the essence of spirituality in her essay "The Gift." It is her experience of being with her father, who has been a primary source of security in her life, in his hospital room when he dies from an unexpected heart attack that brings Matchett to realize that death is not the ending of her relationship with her father. She feels the presence of his spirit comforting her, bringing her peace and a sense of strength and security.

We hope that the readings in this chapter will encourage you to think and reflect more deeply on the enduring qualities of spiritual life. While spirituality has an individual meaning for each person, we can strive to nourish our spiritual lives, both in the public world and in our inner worlds of dreams. Our visions will create the future.

Emily Dickinson

501, *This World Is not Conclusion*

Emily Dickinson (1830–1886) lived nearly her entire life in her parents' home in Amherst, Massachusetts. Although Dickinson attended the nearby Amherst Academy, she was mostly self-educated. She came from a family who traced their lineage back to the Puritans. Her father, Edward Dickinson, was a prominent lawyer and community leader. Dickinson focused her energies on a few intense friendships, her family, her household obligations, and her writing. She wrote more than seventeen hundred poems, although only ten appeared in print during her lifetime. All of her other work was published after her death, and her complete poems appear in The Poems of Emily Dickinson, *edited by Thomas H. Johnson (1955). Dickinson's approach to poetry was radical both in form and content. Her work was more concentrated and emotionally powerful than most nineteenth-century poetry; and it has had a strong influence on modern writers with its highly compressed quality, ambiguousness of language, irregular verse forms and expressive punctuation. Her critical stance on accepted nineteenth-century views of society, spirituality, nature, and love also anticipate modern poetry. In many of her poems Dickinson comments on spiritual issues with questioning, irony, and mixed emotions.*

JOURNAL

Write about a time when you were confused about a matter of religious faith or belief. Was your confusion ever resolved?

This World is not Conclusion.
A Species stands beyond—
Invisible, as Music—
But positive, as Sound—
5   It beckons, and it baffles—
Philosophy—don't know—
And through a Riddle, at the last—
Sagacity, must go—
To guess it, puzzles scholars—
10 To gain it Men have borne
Contempt of Generations
And Crucifixion, shown—
Faith slips—and laughs, and rallies—
Blushes, if any see—
15 Plucks at a twig of Evidence—
And asks a Vane, the way—
Much Gesture, from the Pulpit—
Strong Hallelujahs roll—
Narcotics cannot still the Tooth
20 That nibbles at the soul—

Questions for Writing

1. By making the first line of the poem a clear declarative statement, what initial sense of the narrator's religious faith is given?

2. According to the narrator, what qualities of the "Species" that "stands beyond" make it difficult to define or to hold a common belief about? How do these same qualities make it desirable, alluring?

3. Give one or more examples of the type of questions, the riddle or paradoxes offered by the concept of the world "beyond" and its "Species." Why do you think these questions are intriguing to so many, and why would people risk contempt and even martyrdom for them?

4. Starting on line 12, six verbs are used to describe religious faith. What overall commentary on faith do these verbs make?

5. Lines 15–16 seem to make a comment on organized religion. What is the connotation here of the words "Much Gesture" combined with the "Strong Hallelujahs" that "roll"? Does the narrator seem to take the revivalist church service seriously, to join in the praising, or to take a more critical stance?

6. Examine the metaphor of a toothache in the final lines. What is the source of the toothache, what are the "narcotics" the narrator refers to?

CONNECTION

Compare and contrast the value that Emily Dickinson and Annie Dillard find in religion and/or spirituality (see page 519).

IDEAS FOR WRITING

1. Develop your journal entry into a reflective essay about your religious confusion and its resolution or aftermath.

2. After looking at the interpretive questions above, state what you believe to be the poet's view of religious speculation, faith, and organized religion. Then write an essay in which you state whether you agree or disagree with the poet's ideas on religion. Include reasons and examples to support your ideas.

RELATED WEB SITES

EMILY DICKINSON
http://www.poets.org/academy/news/edick
Visit this web site on poets to learn about the life and work of author Emily Dickinson. Here you will also find relevant links on Dickinson, as well as links to the writers that she admired.

THE AGNOSTIC CHURCH
http://www.agnostic.org/httoc.htm
This URL, entitled the "Agnostic Bible Table of Contents," shares information on agnosticism and agnostic viewpoints on many topics such as the bible, God's existence, western civilization, and even family values.

Annie Dillard

A Field of Silence

Poet, essayist, and naturalist Annie Dillard (b. 1945) was raised in Pittsburgh, Pennsylvania. She received an M.A. in 1968 from Hollins College in Virginia. Dillard has worked as an editor and college teacher and has written many essays and books, including Pilgrim at Tinker Creek *(1974) (for which she received a Pulitzer Prize),* An American Childhood *(1987),* The Writing Life *(1989),* The Living: A Novel *(1992),* Mornings Like These: Found Poems *(1995), and* For the Time Being *(1999). In her essay "A Field of Silence" (1978), Dillard explores a powerful vision she once had on a remote farm and reflects on the difficulty she has in accepting and sharing this kind of experience in a world that values rationality and scientific progress.*

JOURNAL

Write about a time when you were alone in nature and felt you made an abrupt break from your familiar perception of reality and began to experience the world from a new perspective.

There is a place called "the farm" where I lived once, in a time that was very lonely. Fortunately I was unconscious of my loneliness then, and felt it only deeply, bewildered, in the half-bright way that a puppy feels pain.

I loved the place, and still do. It was an ordinary farm, a calf-raising, haymaking farm, and very beautiful. Its flat, messy pastures ran along one side of the central portion of a quarter-mile road in the central part of an island, an island in Puget Sound, so that from the high end of the road you could look west toward the Pacific, to the Sound and its hundred islands, and from the other end—and from the farm—you could see east to the water between you and the mainland, and beyond it the mainland's mountains slicked smooth with snow.

I liked the clutter about the place, the way everything blossomed or seeded or rusted; I liked the hundred half-finished projects, the smells, and the way the animals always broke loose. It is calming to herd animals. Often a regular rodeo breaks out—two people and a clever cow can kill a morning—but still, it is calming. You laugh for a while, exhausted, and silence is restored; the beasts are back in their pastures, the fences not fixed but disguised as if they were fixed, ensuring the animals' temporary resignation; and a great calm descends, a lack of urgency, a sense of having to invent something to do until the next time you must run and chase cattle.

The farm seemed eternal in the crude way the earth does—extending, that is, a very long time. The farm was as old as earth, always there, as old as the island, the Platonic form of "farm," of human society itself and at large, a piece of land eaten and replenished a billion summers, a piece of land worked on, lived on, grown over, plowed under, and stitched again and again, with fingers or with leaves, in and out and into human life's thin weave. I lived there once.

5   I lived there once and I have seen, from behind the barn, the long roadside pastures heaped with silence. Behind the rooster, suddenly, I saw the silence heaped on the fields like trays. That day the green hayfields supported silence evenly sown; the fields bent just so under the even pressure of silence, bearing it, even, palming it aloft: cleared fields, part of a land, a planet, they did not buckle beneath the heel of silence, nor split up scattered to bits, but instead lay secret, disguised as time and matter as though that were nothing, ordinary— disguised as fields like those which bear the silence only because they are spread, and the silence spreads over them, great in size.

I do not want, I think, ever to see such a sight again. That there is loneliness here I had granted, in the abstract—but not, I thought, inside the light of God's presence, inside his sanction, and signed by his name.

I lived alone in the farmhouse and rented; the owners, Angus and Lynn, in their twenties, lived in another building just over the yard. I had been reading and restless for two or three days. It was morning. I had just read at breakfast an Updike story, "Packed Dirt, Churchgoing, A Dying Cat, A Traded Car," which moved me. I heard our own farmyard rooster and two or three roosters across the street screeching. I quit the house, hoping at heart to see Lynn or Angus, but immediately to watch our rooster as he crowed.

It was Saturday morning late in the summer, in early September, clear-aired and still. I climbed the barnyard fence between the poultry and the pastures; I watched the red rooster, and the rooster, reptilian, kept one alert and alien eye on me. He pulled his extravagant neck to its maximum length, hauled himself high on his legs, stretched his beak as if he were gagging, screamed, and blinked. It was a ruckus. The din came from everywhere, and only the most rigorous application of reason could persuade me that it proceeded in its entirety from this lone and maniac bird.

After a pause, the roosters across the street would start, answering the proclamation, or cranking out another round, arrhythmically, interrupting. In the same way there is no pattern nor sense to the massed stridulations of cicadas; their skipped beats, enjambments, and failed alterations jangle your spirits, as though each of those thousand insects, each with identical feelings, were stubbornly deaf to the others, and loudly alone.

10   I shifted along the fence to see if Lynn or Angus was coming or going. To the rooster I said nothing, but only stared. And he stared at me: we were both careful to keep the wooden fence slat from our line of sight, so that this profiled eye and my two eyes could meet. From time to time I looked beyond the pastures to learn if anyone might be seen on the road.

When I was turned away in this manner, the silence gathered and struck me. It bashed me broadside from nowhere, as if I'd been hit by a plank. It dropped from the heavens above me like yard goods; ten acres of fallen, invisible sky choked the fields. The pastures on either side of the road turned green in a surrealistic fashion, monstrous, impeccable, as if they were holding their breath. The roosters stopped. All the things of the world—the fields and the fencing, the road, a parked orange truck—were stricken and self-conscious. A world pressed down on their surfaces, a world battered just within their surfaces, and that real world, so near to emerging, had got struck.

There was only silence. It was the silence of matter caught in the act and embarrassed. There were no cells moving, and yet there were cells. I could see the shape of the land, how it lay holding silence. Its poise and its stillness were unendurable, like the ring of the silence you hear in your skull when you're little and notice you're living, the ring which resumes later in life when you're sick.

There were flies buzzing over the dirt by the henhouse, moving in circles and buzzing, black dreams in chips off the one long dream, the dream of the regular world. But the silent fields were the real world, eternity's outpost in time, whose look I remembered but never like this, this God-blasted, paralyzed day. I felt myself tall and vertical, in a blue shirt, self-conscious, and wishing to die. I heard the flies again; I looked at the rooster who was frozen looking at me.

Then at last I heard whistling, human whistling far on the air, and I was not able to bear it. I looked around, heartbroken; only at the big yellow Charolais farm far up the road was there motion—a woman, I think, dressed in pink, and pushing a wheelbarrow easily over the grass. It must have been she who was whistling and heaping on top of the silence those hollow notes of song. But the slow sound of the music—the beautiful sound of the music ringing the air like a stone bell—was isolated and detached. The notes spread into the general air and became the weightier part of silence, silence's last straw. The distant woman and her wheelbarrow were flat and detached, like mechanized and pink-painted properties for a stage. I stood in pieces, afraid I was unable to move. Something had unhinged the world. The houses and roadsides and pastures were buckling under the silence. Then a Labrador, black, loped up the distant driveway, fluid and cartoonlike, toward the pink woman. I had to try to turn away. Holiness is a force, and like the others can be resisted. It was given, but I didn't want to see it, God or no God. It was as if God had said, "I am here, but not as you have known me. This is the look of silence, and of loneliness unendurable: it too has always been mine, and now will be yours." I was not ready for a life of sorrow, sorrow deriving from knowledge I could just as well stop at the gate.

15   I turned away, willful, and the whole show vanished. The realness of things disassembled. The whistling became ordinary, familiar; the air above the fields released its pressure and the fields lay hooded as before. I myself could act. Looking to the rooster I whistled to him myself, softly, and some hens appeared at the chicken house window, greeted the day, and fluttered down.

Several months later, walking past the farm on the way to a volleyball game, I remarked to a friend, by way of information, "There are angels in those fields." Angels! That silence so grave and so stricken, that choked and unbearable green! I have rarely been so surprised at something I've said. Angels! What are angels! I had never thought of angels, in any way at all.

From that time I began to think of angels. I considered that sights such as I had seen of the silence must have been shared by the people who said they saw angels. I began to review the thing I had seen that morning. My impression now of those fields is of thousands of spirits—spirits trapped, perhaps, by my refusal to call them more fully, or by the paralysis of my own spirit at that time— thousands of spirits, angels in fact, almost discernible to the eye, and whirling. If pressed I would say they were three or four feet from the ground. Only their motion was clear (clockwise, if you insist); that, and their beauty unspeakable.

There are angels in those fields, and I presume, in all fields, and everywhere else. I would go to the lions for this conviction, to witness this fact. What all this means about perception, or language, or angels, or my own sanity, I have no idea.

QUESTIONS FOR DISCUSSION

1. How does the loneliness Dillard experiences on the farm help to set the stage for her vision?
2. What causes Dillard's vision? Why does her vision end?
3. How does Dillard make the abstract notion of absolute silence concrete, vibrant, and alive? How do you respond to her image?
4. Why is the stillness unendurable? What similes does Dillard use to express her concept? Why does she try to turn away from her vision? Why is her vision one of sorrow?
5. Why does Dillard reverse an accepted assumption by referring to the regular world as a dream? What does she mean by regular and dream in the context of her essay?
6. After having time to reflect, Dillard decides, "There are angels in those fields." How do you imagine the angels? Why is it significant that Dillard, usually so precise and perceptive, has no idea about the meaning of her vision and has difficulty talking about it? How do you interpret her vision of spirituality?

CONNECTION

Compare and contrast Annie Dillard's and Terry Tempest Williams's visions. What different values and conclusions does each come to based upon their experiences (see page 523)?

IDEAS FOR WRITING

1. Write a reflective essay on a vision or an intense moment of natural insight you have had. Why was it difficult for you to share this experience? Were you able to do so? In what form?
2. Write an essay in which you attempt to interpret Dillard's vision, based on what you know about her from reading this essay. What does Dillard's vision reveal about her personality, values, and response to the natural world?

RELATED WEB SITES

ANNIE DILLARD

http://www.well.com/user/elliotts/smse_dillard.html

Read the essay called "The Mysticism of Annie Dillard's Pilgrim at Tinker Creek," by Sandra Elliott, at this URL and also find out about the life and works of Dillard. The article focuses on the writer as a modern-day mystic and on her ideas about our relationship with the Divine.

THE ECOTHEOLOGY OF ANNIE DILLARD: A STUDY IN AMBIVALENCE

http://www.crosscurrents.org/dillard.htm

Go to the "Cross Currents" web site from the Association for Religion and Intellectual Live and read Pamela A. Smith's article "The Ecotheology Of Annie Dillard: A Study In Ambivalence." In this essay you will learn about Dillard's unique brand of "ecotheology" and her resistance to any labels at all.

Terry Tempest Williams

Santa Teresa

Terry Tempest Williams was born in 1959 and was raised in Nevada in a family who were members of the Church of Jesus Christ of Latter-Day Saints. She attended the Teton Science School where she earned a B.A. in English and an M.A. in environmental education. She has worked as a naturalist for the Utah Museum of Natural History and lives with her husband in the mountains outside of Salt Lake City, Utah. She is a well-respected nature writer; some of her better known published works include Pieces of White Shell *(1984),* Coyote's Canyon *(1989),* Desert Quartet *(1995), and* A Love that is Wild *(1998). Her most recent book,* Red: Patience and Passion in the Desert *(2001), traces her long-term commitment to preserving the power and spiritual allure of the desert environment. Recently Williams has turned to a deeper study of spiritual issues in her book* Leap *(2000) a study of Hieronymus Bosch's medieval masterpiece* The Garden of Delights. *In this book, as in the essay below on Spanish mystic Santa Teresa, Williams sees intense relations between the spiritual thirst of the past and the needs of the contemporary world.*

JOURNAL

Write about the meaning prayer has for you or for someone close to you who prays on a regular basis.

On the train to Avila, tamarisks are in bloom. Pines. Junipers. Arid shrub country pocketed with boulders. Magpies. Poppies. The *meseta* or plateau country of central Spain looks much like my home in the American southwest. Little excess. Nothing wasted.

The medieval walls surrounding the *ciudad antigua,* the old city, of Avila are the threshold to the world of Santa Teresa in the early sixteenth century. Even though the walls were built miraculously five hundred years earlier by 1,900 men in nine years after the town had been reclaimed from the Moors, it is her presence that lingers.

Hundreds of swifts circle her city; pink, white, and yellow roses flourish against the stone wall. Bouquets of wildflowers are left in her honor. Overhead three storks fly toward the bell tower of Carmen, where they nest. Did Santa Teresa know these birds, these mediators between heaven and earth? These swifts and storks must have swayed her thinking. Surely the Holy Spirit appears in more incarnations than doves.

To whom do I pray?

5   A Spanish woman sits in the row across from me in the Iglesia de Santa Teresa, reciting her prayers in whispers as she rotates each bead of her rosary through her fingers. Her hands are folded beneath her chin. She alternates her prayers with the reading of the scriptures.

To whom do I pray?

I kneel before the statue of Santa Teresa, gilded and animated by the soft light in this small dark alcove. Her right hand is outstretched as though she were about to touch Spirit, her left hand covers her heart.

I close my eyes and listen.

After many minutes of silence, what comes into my mind is the phrase, "wet not dry."

10   I close my eyes and concentrate more deeply, let these words simply pass through as one does with distractions in meditation. Again, the words, "wet not dry." The woman across the aisle from me is weeping. Her private utterings, *para ti,* for you, for you, are audible. I open my eyes feeling little emotion and look down at the worn tiles beneath my feet. The Spanish woman faces the saint, bows, crosses herself, and leaves.

Wondering if I should be here at all, I try once again to pray. In the stillness, the phrase returns.

All I can hear in the sanctity of this chapel is what sounds at best like a cheap antiperspirant jingle. I do not feel my heart. Filled with shame, I look up at Santa Teresa's face.

Later that afternoon, I steady myself by sitting beneath an old cottonwood tree, similar to the ones I have sat under a hundred times in the desert. I open Santa Teresa's autobiography, *The Life of Saint Teresa Avila by Herself* and randomly turn to a page: ". . . and God converted the dryness of my soul into a great tenderness."

I turn another page: "Only once in my life do I remember asking Him for consolation and that was when I was very dry. . . ."

15 And another: "It is my opinion that though a soul may seem to be deriving some immediate benefit when it does anything to further itself in this prayer of union, it will in fact very quickly fall again, like buildings without foundations. . . . Remain calm in times of dryness."

Santa Teresa's book articulates "the Four Waters of Prayer." She says simply that wetness brings us "to a recollected state." A well. A spring. A fountain. To drink deeply from the Spirit and quench the aridity of the soul to retrieve, revive, and renew our relationship with God.

Where are my tears? Where is the rain? I ask myself. "I am now speaking of that rain that comes down abundantly from heaven to soak and saturate the whole garden."

The leaves of the cottonwood tree shield me from the heat as I read her *Confessions* slowly: "Who is this whom all my faculties thus obey? Who is it that in a moment sheds light amidst such great darkness, who softens a heart that seemed to be of stone and sheds the water of gentle tears where for so long it had seemed to be dry? Who gives these desires? Who gives this courage? What have I been thinking of? What am I afraid of?"

The smells of lavender and rosemary collide in the garden. Something breaks open in me. My soul is brittle, my body a desert. What might it mean to honor thirst before hunger and joy before obligation?

20 *Un botella de agua. Necesito un botella de agua.* These are the first words out of my mouth this morning as I awaken from a dream.

The Monasterio de Encarnación, a dignified granite fortress north of the wall, is not far from the *parador* where I am staying. In 1534, Santa Teresa walked through these doors when she was twenty years old. It is closed. I sit on the stone steps outside the corridor. *Hace calor.* I settle in the shade and read some more of Santa Teresa's words: "All its joys came in little sips."

The mystic writes about women and the importance of discretion in speaking of one's spiritual experiences, the need to share with others of like mind for solace and safety, reflection and inspiration.

Joseph Smith believed so full in Santa Teresa's visions that he had himself sealed to the Carmelite nun in "the everlasting covenant of marriage," not uncommon to the "spiritual wife doctrine" he initiated through the revelation and practice of polygamy. He recognized her as a spiritual soulmate, trusting that revelations from God have been and will be continuous through time, that the truth is soul-wrenching, having said himself that he shared only a hundredth of what he saw when the heavens opened up to him. Schooled in the hermetic traditions of Santa Teresa's time, he might have felt as though they were contemporaries, sympathetic to her roving states of being.

I am weak, light-headed, perhaps because of the heat, perhaps because of the intensity of Santa Teresa's story: a child who at the age of ten vowed to be a nun but at age fourteen blossomed into a vibrant young woman enraptured by the sensory pleasures of the world, gifted in poetry and literature.

25   She fell tumultuously in love and was so frightened by her own sexuality that she confessed to her father, who immediately sent her to the convent; there, struggling with the disciplined life set by the nuns against her own instinctive nature, she succumbed to violent seizures and bouts of hysteria that eventually left her paralyzed for years, seized by the darkest of visions. Unable to move, her pain barely tolerable, she renounced all medical treatments and relied solely on prayer, never giving up hope of being healed. At one point, when she was deep in a coma mistaken for death, the nuns dug a grave for her. And then the miraculous day arrived. In 1540, she awoke to find her arms and legs no longer paralyzed. She had successfully passed through her journey through hell. Teresa de Avila stood up and walked. It was proclaimed a miracle, a cure that reached the masses, whereupon people from surrounding villages came to see the nun whom God had healed.

Her life from that point forward was a testament of austere devotion and simplicity, but she never gave up her pen.

Inside the *monasterio,* there are relics: a wooden log that Santa Teresa used as a pillow; a small statue of Christ "covered with wounds," which is said to have been very important to her spiritual awakening of great compassion and sorrow; a statue of Saint Joseph, who taught her how to pray. The nuns have passed down the story that this statue used to talk to Santa Teresa. When she left on her travels she would leave him on the prioress's chair. Upon her return, he would tell her everything that had gone on in her absence.

The key to her cell where she lived for twenty-seven years begs to be turned. Turn the key. Santa Teresa's hand opens the door.

Stillness.

30   Downstairs, there is a tiny revolving door made of oak. It was the only access the nuns had to the outside world, sending messages out with one turn and receiving them with another in silence.

I descend further into the stark parlor where San Juan de la Cruz and Santa Teresa were *suspendidos en éxtasis,* lifted in ecstasy. Once again, I sit quietly. The word *casado* comes to into my mind—married, a prayer of union, a state of oneness with God and with whom we confide our bodies. The Divine Lover. In these moments of pure union, body, soul, and spirit are fused.

Ecstasy. Elevation. Suspension.

The bells of Monasterio de la Encarnación begin ringing. In the courtyard, two young girls are singing; one is playing the guitar, the other is clapping with her eyes closed. I walk down the road to the plaza, where there is a fountain bubbling up from a stone basin, and sit down.

Teenagers play in the pool below the fountain. They flirt and splash each other, then the young men and women, soaked, hoist each other up and over the stone wall and disappear. A man interrupts their frolicking to fill two jugs tied together by a rope that he swings over his neck.

35   The small plaza is quiet. I walk to the fountain and wash my face and hands and arms. The water is cold and invigorating.

An old man in a black beret comes to the fountain carrying a plastic sack with two one-gallon water jugs. He is wearing blue canvas slippers.

I learn he is from one of the outlying *pueblos* in the mountains, that he makes this journey once a week to collect water for his wife from this particular fountain. His wife is especially devoted to Santa Teresa de Avila. She believes this water restores the spirit and all manner of ailments. He invites me to drink the water with him.

I watch him walk carefully over the uneven cobbles and cannot guess his age. He is a small and handsomely weathered man. He lifts his weary legs over the steps of the fountain, stoops down, and then with great deliberation begins to fill each bottle. He fills one with about an inch of water, shakes the bottle, then pours it out, filling it the second time as he sits down on the stone ledge above the spout. The old man enjoys several sips, wipes his mouth with the back of his hand, and fills it again.

Joining him from below, I cup my hands below the running water and drink.

40   The old man gestures to one of the two bottles he has just painstakingly filled. It rests on the ledge like a prism separating light as the sun shines through.

At first, I do not understand. Perhaps he is offering me another drink?

Gracias, pero no.

He persists.

Para mí?

45   He nods. He hands me one of his bottles. I hardly know what to do. The old man had walked so far for this water. What will his wife say when he returns home to the mountains with only one bottle? How to receive this gift? What can I give him in return? I hold the jug of water close and feel its refreshment even against my skin.

Gracias, señor, para tu regalo.

De nada.

The old man nods and smiles and slowly shifts his weight on his right hand to ease himself up. He bends down and puts the other bottle in his bag.

After he is gone, I look back toward the fountain. "For tears gain everything; and one kind of water attracts another. . . ."

QUESTIONS FOR DISCUSSION

1. What is it about Avila that reminds Williams of her homeland, the American Southwest? How does this similarity help to set a tone for the narrative of Santa Teresa that follows?

2. Why does the sight of the swifts above Avila remind Williams of Santa Teresa's visions of the Holy Spirit?

3. Williams asks the question "To whom do I pray?" What answer is implied in the paragraphs that follow, particularly by the jingle, "wet not dry"?

4. How does Santa Teresa continue the spiritual metaphor of wetness and dryness in her "Four Waters of Prayer"? What is the significance of Williams's dream phrase, *"Necesito un botella de agua"*?

5. How is the metaphor of marriage (*casado* in Spanish) used to describe both the faith of Joseph Smith and that of Santa Teresa and San Juan de La Cruz?

6. How does the narrative of the fountain and the gift to Williams of water from the fountain outside the Monasterio de la Encarnación provide an effective ending for the essay? How does the final quotation help tie the essay together and emphasize what Williams has learned from her experience?

CONNECTION

Compare Williams's mystical realization with Annie Dillard's (see page 519).

IDEAS FOR WRITING

1. Write an essay in which you analyze the meaning of the metaphors of water, wetness, and dryness. What does Williams seem to be saying about the path from spiritual dryness to wetness (spiritual nourishment)?

2. Do some reading about the mystic thinking of Santa Teresa and San Juan de La Cruz. Citing their poems and other writings, explain what they seemed to mean when referring to being *casado* with "the Divine Lover." How do their views on the subject seem similar to or different from those of Joseph Smith, first spiritual leader of the Church of Jesus Christ of Latter-Day Saints (Mormon Church)?

RELATED WEB SITES

TERRY TEMPEST WILLIAMS
http://www.coyoteclan.com/
This site is a resource for information related to the life and work of Terry Tempest Williams, author, naturalist, and environmental activist. Articles, a biography, a bibliography, and a community section will also be found at this web site.

SAINT TERESA
http://www.karmel.at/eng/teresa.htm
Learn about St. Teresa of Avila at this informational URL. Here, you will find a picture and essay on the life and the historical background of the famous saint.

Thomas Moore

Neither Here Nor There

Thomas Moore is a best-selling author and lecturer on various aspects of spirituality in everyday life; he specializes in helping people find ways to cultivate their "soul," which he perceives not in a specific theological sense but as "the source of creativity and wisdom in human beings." Moore served as a Catholic monk for 12 years before leaving monastic life to marry and pursue an academic career. He received four degrees in nine years of study, a B.A. and M.A. in music, an M.S. in theology, and finally a Ph.D. in religion and psychology from Syracuse University. After completing his education, he taught at the university level for ten years before beginning to write, lecture, and practice psychotherapy. Moore's books include Care of the Soul *(1992),* Soul Mates *(1994),* Original Self: Living with Paradox and Originality *(2000), and* The Soul's Religion: Cultivating a Profoundly Spiritual Way of Life *(2002). The essay that follows first appeared in* Parabola.

JOURNAL

Describe a time when you found yourself in a state of mind that was "neither here nor there," a place between normal states of being, a twilight zone. What did you learn from being in that state of mind?

There are places in this world that are neither here nor there, neither up nor down, neither real nor imaginary. These are the inbetween places, difficult to find and even more challenging to sustain. Yet they are the most fruitful places of all. For in these liminal narrows a kind of life takes place that is out of the ordinary, creative, and once in a while genuinely magical. We tend to divide life between mind and matter and to assume that we must be in one or the other or both. But religion and folklore tell of another place that is often found by accident, where strange events take place, and where we learn things that can't be discovered in any other way.

Sometimes the transitional places are physical and fairly obvious. An elevator, for instance, is a peculiar place where speech can be difficult and social posture odd. An escalator offers several moments of interstitial existence, when you can see everything but can do nothing. As a writer, I search for the liminal places where ideas, words, and images are stored and ready for use. For many, the shower seems to be such a place, but it doesn't work for me. There I am all sensation and no reverie. Playing the piano places me on a threshold where thoughts multiply and come to life. But a dull lecture is best of all, even one that I am giving.

Emotion is a good vehicle to the places in between. People tell stories of discovering unknown strength when they are trying to save a child. I have stepped beyond the ordinary in times of depression, when I was so withdrawn that an unfamiliar sense of self suddenly arose as from the shadows. Christmas and Halloween, when they really work, can cast a spell that makes ordinary awareness recede into the background on behalf of momentary magic. I believe that the fantasy exuberance in these two festivals, apart from their religious meanings, keeps our overly rational society sane.

A mode of entrance is crucial. A door. A window. We need a chink in the otherwise unbroken surface of what we consider real and proper. Recently a woman wrote to tell me her dream. She was in a garden, holding a child's hand and moving toward a break in the hedge, when a butterfly landed on her nose and covered over her face. There is step one: we need something serendipitous to veil our usual identity. The Greeks thought that the soul was a butterfly—a perfect covering.

5   The break in the hedge opened to a central area where the sun shone brilliantly. The gap need not be physical, but it is required. In the dark wood at the beginning of his journey, Dante says, "I don't know how to describe my entering there, I was so sleepy at that point that I lost track of the actual path." Before I go to sleep, ideas come out, and I wonder sometimes if the drug problems in our society are nothing more than a quest for Dante's somnambulance.

Religion is in the business of finding and constructing methods of getting sleepy, feeling lost, arriving and departing: pilgrimage, procession, fasting, incense, chanting, illuminated books. Psychoanalysis similarly makes use of transference, which means "to carry across," a word easily linked to a bridge, which Sandor Ferenczi interpreted as the movement from what is to what will be. In ordinary life we need methods tailored to our temperaments that effectively take us off the treadmill and the beaten path.

On the same day I got the hedge dream letter, I heard from a man who was deciding whether to quit his law practice and become an art historian. He was on an elevator of sorts and didn't feel comfortable being between places. But there lies yet another aspect of thresholds—insecurity seems to be the emotion proper to the place. I wrote back saying that I felt both envy and relief not to be in his place.

I think that the curse of liminality asks for treatment in kind. We need to enter more fully and more willingly into that realm under the rocks and behind the mirror. We are too sincere, too productive, and too realistic. In his aptly named little book *A Celtic Twilight*, W. B. Yeats tells many disorienting stories about figures who are neither faeries nor human, or who are both, and who would make good role models for us all:

> By the Hospital Lane goes the "Faeries" Path. Every evening they travel from the hill to the sea, from the sea to the hill. At the sea end of their path stands a cottage. One night Mrs. Arbunathy, who lived there, left her door open, as she was expecting her son. Her husband was asleep by the fire; a tall man came in and sat beside him. After he had been sitting there for a while, the woman said, "In the name of

God, who are you?" He got up and went out, saying, "Never leave the door open at this hour, or evil may come to you." She woke her husband and told him. "One of the Good People has been with us," said he.

During hours of psychotherapy, I have heard several dreams of doors left ajar and windows cracked open. The dreamer was deathly afraid of who or what might come in because of this negligence, and of course as therapist I suspected that whoever it was, it was probably someone useful and necessary. Often we attain thresholds best through inadvertence. If we want their benefits, we might not always aim for consciousness and awareness but rather a gap in our attention. In my view, the emphasis in some spiritual communities on continuing consciousness defeats the purpose.

10   I have a fascination for doors, doorways, and vestibules. In another life I'd like to be a maker of extraordinary doors. They are actual thresholds and at the same time images for the deep transitional passages. Standing in a doorway, you are forced into the imagination, wondering what you will find on the other side. It is a place full of expectant fantasy. Gaston Bachelard said, "If one were to give an account of all the doors one has closed and opened, of all the doors one would like to reopen, one would have to tell the story of one's entire life." William Blake made an etching of death's door, showing an old man about to walk under the lintel, with the subscript: "The Door of Death is made of Gold, the Immortal eyes cannot behold."

The foyer of a building is another place of special liminal appeal and magic. It brings you in from the heat or cold and prepares you for a human climate and interaction. In a theater it is also a place of conviviality during the intermission—liminal itself—of a play or performance of music, where you can once again talk and eat and move your body around. It is delicious, restorative time-out.

Some reckless etymologizing discovers that *foyer* is the same word as *focus*, which means hearth or fireplace and is closely connected to the goddess Hestia, who is emotional warmth deified. Interestingly, Kepler used the word *focus* for the center spot of a magnifying glass, probably because it is the place where you can burn a leaf or a bug, as I confess I used to do when I was a boy. The foyer is therefore the hot spot, the alchemical athanor where things happen, the oven or grill of transformation.

This is the key point about thresholds: they are not the place of life and not the place of death. In their narrow confines you may find fantasy, memory, dream, anxiety, miracle, intuition, and magic. These are the means by which the deep soul prospers—neither in life nor entirely out of life. This is a good place from which to make a decision and get a hunch. It is the true home of creativity. It is also the claustrophobic place of greatest fear. Anything of moment takes place in these interstices—in the tunnels and passages and waiting periods. They are indispensable and yet must be kept tangential.

It takes considerable courage to stay as long as needed in a place between, and it requires a degree of holy foolishness to seek one out. We may need a threshold experience just to find the needed threshold. My personal favorites are a piano, a Gothic cathedral, a megalith, dessert, a forest path, an Irish pub, a dark bedroom, Guillaume Dufay, a candlelit bathtub, Lord Peter Wimsey, aftershave, the moors, and honeysuckle. Each of these stands to the side of life's central concerns, and yet each makes life worth living.

QUESTIONS FOR DISCUSSION

1. In his first paragraph, how does Moore establish his definition of the state of being "Neither here nor there"? What does he mean when he refers to this place as a "liminal narrows," and what does he believe we can learn in this place?

2. What specific examples of the kind of neither here nor there places defined in the essay does Moore present in the four paragraphs that follow the introduction? Can you think of other examples?

3. In Moore's view, how do dreams and emotions help us find the places in between? Have you had experiences like the ones Moore describes here?

4. According to Moore, how does religion, as well as the transference that takes place in psychotherapy, help us to enter the neither here nor there state of being?

5. Why does Moore, a psychotherapist, believe that "the emphasis in some spiritual communities on continuing consciousness defeats its purpose"? Explain why you agree or disagree with his point.

6. Why is Moore fascinated by doors, vestibules, foyers, and thresholds? What do these spaces represent for him? Why are such places "the means by which the deep soul prospers"? Have you had experiences similar to the ones described by Moore?

CONNECTION

Compare Moore's idea of the importance of placing oneself in a place "neither here nor there" with Terry Tempest Williams's realizations about "wetness and dryness" during her time in Avila (see page 523).

IDEAS FOR WRITING

1. Develop your journal entry above into a longer essay in which you describe more fully how you entered into the place that was "neither here nor there" and how you were able to make some sense of what you learned there.

2. Write a fantasy story similar to E. M. Forster's "The Other Side of the Hedge" (Chapter 5) in which a character enters into a world outside or in between the more ordinary states of being and awareness we usually occupy. Describe the threshold world carefully and explain what the central character in the story learned in that world.

RELATED WEB SITES

THOMAS MOORE
http://www.annonline.com/interviews/960812/
Visit this URL for an audio interview with psychotherapist, writer, and lecturer Thomas Moore. Here you will also find links to a biography on Moore and other web sites related to the author.

RELIGION AND SPIRITUALITY
http://www.about.com/religion/
Learn about virtually any religion, alternative form of spirituality, or holistic healing tradition at this URL. This page consists of many links to several different religions and spiritual categories.

Jane Goodall

In the Forests of Gombe

Jane Goodall was born in London, England in 1934. She traveled to Kenya by boat at the age of 23, where she met Dr. Louis Leakey, a paleontologist and anthropologist who chose Goodall to begin a study of wild chimpanzees on the shore of Lake Tanganyika. In 1960 she observed a chimpanzee using and making tools to fish for termites. This discovery challenged the view of humans as being the only toolmakers in the animal kingdom. Research at Gombe continues to this day. Although Jane Goodall had no formal education, she was awarded a Ph.D. at Cambridge University. She is currently an honorary professor at the University of Dar es Salaam in Tanzania, East Africa. In recent years Jane Goodall has become an advocate and spokesperson for the conservation of chimpanzee habitats and for the humane treatment of captive primates. Her most recent books include Great Apes and Humans: The Ethics of Coexistence *(2001) and* The Ten Trusts: What We Must Do To Care for the Animals We Love *(2002). In the following selection from her memoir,* A Reason for Hope *(1999), Goodall writes about her mystical experience in the forest of Gombe that helped her to recover from the death of her husband and gave her life a new perspective.*

JOURNAL

Discuss a time that you spent in a forest, at the seashore—any natural setting. Did the time you spent in this natural setting rejuvenate your mind and spirit? How?

I was taught, as a scientist, to think logically and empirically, rather than intuitively or spiritually. When I was at Cambridge University in the early 1960s most of the scientists and science students working in the Department of

Zoology, so far as I could tell, were agnostic or even atheist. Those who believed in a god kept it hidden from their peers.

Fortunately, by the time I got to Cambridge I was twenty-seven years old and my beliefs had already been molded so that I was not influenced by these opinions. I believed in the spiritual power that, as a Christian, I called God. But as I grew older and learned about different faiths I came to believe that there was, after all, but One God with different names: Allah, Tao, the Creator, and so our God, for me, was the Great Spirit in Whom "we live and move and have our being." There have been times during my life when this belief wavered, when I questioned—even denied—the existence of God. At such times I felt there can be no underlying meaning to the emergence of life on earth.

Still, for me those periods have been relatively rare, triggered by a variety of circumstances. One was when my second husband died of cancer. I was grieving, suffering, and angry. Angry at God, at fate—the unjustness of it all. For a time I rejected God, and the world seemed a bleak place.

It was in the forests of Gombe that I sought healing after Derek's death. Gradually during my visits, my bruised and battered spirit found solace. In the forest, death is not hidden—or only accidentally, by the fallen leaves. It is all around you all the time, a part of the endless cycle of life. Chimpanzees are born, they grow older, they get sick, and they die. And always there are the young ones to carry on the life of the species. Time spent in the forest, following and watching and simply being with the chimpanzees, has always sustained the inner core of my being. And it did not fail me then.

5   One day, among all the days, I remember most of all. It was May 1981 and I had finally made it to Gombe after a six-week tour in America—six weeks of fund-raising dinners, conferences, meetings, and lobbying for various chimpanzee issues. I was exhausted and longed for the peace of the forest. I wanted nothing more than to be with the chimpanzees, renewing my acquaintance with my old friends, getting my climbing legs back again, relishing the sights, sounds, and smells of the forest. I was glad to be away from Dar es Salaam, with all its sad associations—the house that Derek and I had shared, the palm trees we had bought and planted together, the rooms we had lived in together, the Indian Ocean in which Derek, handicapped on land, had found freedom swimming among his beloved coral reefs.

Back in Gombe. It was early in the morning and I sat on the steps of my house by the lakeshore. It was very still. Suspended over the horizon, where the mountains of the Congo fringed Lake Tanganyika, was the last quarter of the waning moon and her path danced and sparkled toward me across the gently moving water. After enjoying a banana and a cup of coffee, I was off, climbing up the steep slopes behind my house.

In the faint light from the moon reflected by the dew-laden grass, it was not difficult to find my way up the mountain. It was quiet, utterly peaceful. Five minutes later I heard the rustlings of leaves overhead. I looked up and saw the branches moving against the lightening sky. The chimps had awakened. It was Fifi and her offspring, Freud, Frodo, and little Fanni. I followed when they moved off up the slope, Fanni riding on her mother's back like a diminutive jockey. Presently they climbed into a tall fig tree and began to feed. I heard the occasional soft thuds as skins and seeds of figs fell to the ground.

For several hours we moved leisurely from one food tree to the next, gradually climbing higher and higher. On an open grassy ridge the chimps climbed into a massive mbula tree, where Fifi, replete from the morning's feasting, made a large comfortable nest high above me. She dozed through a midday siesta, little Fanni asleep in her arms, Frodo and Freud playing nearby. I felt very much in tune with the chimpanzees, for I was spending time with them not to observe, but simply because I needed their company, undemanding and free of pity. From where I sat I could look out over the Kasakela Valley. Just below me to the west was the peak. From that same vantage point I had learned so much in the early days, sitting and watching while, gradually, the chimpanzees had lost their fear of the strange white ape who had invaded their world. I recaptured some of my long-ago feelings—the excitement of discovering, of seeing things unknown to Western eyes, and the serenity that had come from living, day after day, as a part of the natural world. A world that dwarfs yet somehow enhances human emotions.

As I reflected on these things I had been only partly conscious of the approach of a storm. Suddenly, I realized that it was no longer growling in the distance but was right above. The sky was dark, almost black, and the rain clouds had obliterated the higher peaks. With the growing darkness came the stillness, the hush, that so often precedes a tropical downpour. Only the rumbling of the thunder, moving closer and closer, broke this stillness; the thunder and the rustling movements of the chimpanzees. All at once came a blinding flash of lightning, followed, a split second later, by an incredibly loud clap of thunder that seemed almost to shake the solid rock before it rumbled on, bouncing from peak to peak. Then the dark and heavy clouds let loose such torrential rain that sky and earth seemed joined by moving water. I sat under a palm whose fronds, for a while, provided some shelter. Fifi sat hunched over, protecting her infant; Frodo pressed close against them in the nest; Freud sat with rounded back on a nearby branch. As the rain poured endlessly down, my palm fronds no longer provided shelter and I got wetter and wetter. I began to feel first chilly, and then, as a cold wind sprang up, freezing; soon, turned in on myself, I lost all track of time. I and the chimpanzees formed a unit of silent, patient, and uncomplaining endurance.

10   It must have been an hour or more before the rain began to ease as the heart of the storm swept away to the south. At four-thirty the chimps climbed down, and we moved off through the dripping vegetation, back down the mountainside. Presently we arrived on a grassy ridge overlooking the lake. I heard sounds of greeting as Fifi and her family joined Melissa and hers. They all climbed into a low tree to feed on fresh young leaves. I moved to a place where I could stand and watch as they enjoyed their last meal of the day. Down below, the lake was still dark and angry with white flecks where the waves broke, and rain clouds remained black in the south. To the north the sky was

clear with only wisps of gray clouds still lingering. In the soft sunlight, the chimpanzees' black coats were shot with coppery brown, the branches on which they sat were wet and dark as ebony, the young leaves a pale but brilliant green. And behind was the backcloth of the indigo sky where lightning flickered and distant thunder growled and rumbled.

Lost in awe at the beauty around me, I must have slipped into a state of heightened awareness. It is hard—impossible, really—to put into words the moment of truth that suddenly came upon me then. It seemed to me, as I struggled afterward to recall the experience, that *self* was utterly absent: I and the chimpanzees, the earth and trees and air, seemed to merge, to become one with the spirit power of life itself. The air was filled with a feathered symphony, the evensong of birds. I heard new frequencies in their music and also in the singing insects' voices—notes so high and sweet I was amazed. Never had I been so intensely aware of the shape, the color of the individual leaves, the varied patterns of the veins that made each one unique. Scents were clear as well, easily identifiable: fermenting overripe fruit; waterlogged earth; cold, wet bark; the damp odor of chimpanzee hair and, yes, my own too. I sensed a new presence, then saw a bushbuck, quietly browsing upwind, his spiraled horns gleaming and chestnut coat dark with rain.

Suddenly a distant chorus of pant-hoots elicited a reply from Fifi. As though wakening from some vivid dream I was back in the everyday world, cold, yet intensely alive. When the chimpanzees left, I stayed in that place—it seemed a most sacred place—scribbling some notes, trying to describe what, so briefly, I had experienced.

Eventually I wandered back along the forest trail and scrambled down behind my house to the beach. Later, as I sat by my little fire, cooking my dinner of beans, tomatoes, and an egg, I was still lost in the wonder of my experience. Yes, I thought, there are many windows through which we humans, searching for meaning, can look out into the world around us. There are those carved out by Western science, their panes polished by a succession of brilliant minds. Through them we can see ever farther, ever more clearly, into areas which until recently were beyond human knowledge. Through such a scientific window I had been taught to observe the chimpanzees. For more than twenty-five years I had sought, through careful recording and critical analysis, to piece together their complex social behavior, to understand the workings of their minds. And this had not only helped us to better understand their place in nature but also helped us to understand a little better some aspects of our own human behavior, our own place in the natural world.

Yet there are other windows through which we humans can look out into the world around us, windows through which the mystics and the holy men of the East, and the founders of the great world religions, have gazed as they searched for the meaning and purpose of our life on earth, not only in the wondrous beauty of the world, but also in its darkness and ugliness. And those Masters contemplated the truths that they saw, not with their minds only but with their hearts and souls also. From those revelations came the spiritual essence of the great scriptures, the holy books, and the most beautiful mystic poems and writings. That afternoon it had been as though an unseen hand had drawn back a curtain and, for the briefest moment, I had seen through such a window.

15   How sad that so many people seem to think that science and religion are mutually exclusive. Science has used modern technology and modern techniques to uncover so much about the formation and the development of life forms on Planet Earth and about the solar system of which our little world is but a minute part. Alas, all of these amazing discoveries have led to a belief that every wonder of the natural world and of the universe—indeed, of infinity and time—can, in the end, be understood through the logic and the reasoning of a finite mind. And so, for many, science has taken the place of religion. It was not some intangible God who created the universe, they argue, it was the big bang. Physics, chemistry, and evolutionary biology can explain the start of the universe and the appearance and progress of life on earth, they say. To believe in God, in the human soul, and in life after death is simply a desperate and foolish attempt to give meaning to our lives.

But not all scientists believe thus. There are quantum physicists who have concluded that the concept of God is not, after all, merely wishful thinking. There are those exploring the human brain who feel that no matter how much they discover about this extraordinary structure it will never add up to a complete understanding of the human mind—that the whole is, after all, greater than the sum of its parts. The big bang theory is yet another example of the incredible, the awe-inspiring ability of the human mind to learn about seemingly unknowable phenomena in the beginning of time. Time as we know it, or think we know it. But what about before time? And what about beyond space? I remember so well how those questions had driven me to distraction when I was a child.

I lay flat on my back and looked up into the darkening sky. I thought about the young man I had met during the six-week tour I had finished before my return to Gombe. He had a holiday job working as a bellhop in the big hotel where I was staying in Dallas, Texas. It was prom night, and I wandered down to watch the young girls in their beautiful evening gowns, their escorts elegant in their tuxedos. As I stood there, thinking about the future—theirs, mine, the world's—I heard a diffident voice:

"Excuse me, Doctor—aren't you Jane Goodall?" The bellhop was very young, very fresh-faced. But he looked worried—partly because he felt that he should not be disturbing me, but partly, it transpired, because his mind was indeed troubled. He had a question to ask me. So we went and sat on some back stairs, away from the glittering groups and hand-holding couples.

He had watched all my documentaries, read my books. He was fascinated, and he thought that what I did was great. But I talked about evolution. Did I believe in God? If so, how did that square with evolution? Had we really descended from chimpanzees?

20   And so I tried to answer him as truthfully as I could, to explain my own beliefs. I told him that no one thought humans had descended from chimpanzees. I

explained that I did believe in Darwinian evolution and told him of my time at Olduvai, when I had held the remains of extinct creatures in my hands. That I had traced, in the museum, the various stages of the evolution of, say, a horse: from a rabbit-sized creature that gradually, over thousands of years, changed, became better and better adapted to its environment, and eventually was transformed into the modern horse. I told him I believed that millions of years ago there had been a primitive, apelike, humanlike creature, one branch of which had gone on to become the chimpanzee, another branch of which had eventually led to us.

"But that doesn't mean I don't believe in God," I said. And I told him something of my beliefs, and those of my family. I told him that I had always thought that the biblical description of God creating the world in seven days might well have been an attempt to explain evolution in a parable. In that case, each of the days would have been several million years.

"And then, perhaps, God saw that a living being had evolved that was suitable for His purpose. *Homo sapiens* had the brain, the mind, the potential. Perhaps," I said, "that was when God breathed the Spirit into the first Man and the first Woman and filled them with the Holy Ghost."

The bellhop was looking considerably less worried. "Yes, I see," he said. "That could be right. That does seem to make sense."

I ended by telling him that it honestly didn't matter how we humans got to be the way we are, whether evolution or special creation was responsible. What mattered and mattered desperately was our future development. How should the mind that can contemplate God relate to our fellow beings, the other life forms of the world? What is our human responsibility? And what, ultimately, is our human destiny? Were we going to go on destroying God's creation, fighting each other, hurting the other creatures of His planet? Or were we going to find ways to live in greater harmony with each other and with the natural world? That, I told him, was what was important. Not only for the future of the human species, but also for him, personally. When we finally parted his eyes were clear and untroubled, and he was smiling.

25   Thinking about that brief encounter, I smiled too, there on the beach at Gombe. A wind sprang up and it grew chilly. I left the bright stars and went inside to bed. I knew that while I would always grieve Derek's passing, I could cope with my grieving. That afternoon, in a flash of "outsight" I had known timelessness and quiet ecstasy, sensed a truth of which mainstream science is merely a small fraction. And I knew that the revelation would be with me for the rest of my life, imperfectly remembered yet always within. A source of strength on which I could draw when life seemed harsh or cruel or desperate. The forest, and the spiritual power that was so real in it, had given me the "peace that passeth understanding."

QUESTIONS FOR DISCUSSION

1. Why did Goodall return to the forest?

2. Goodall says that living in the natural world "dwarfs yet somehow enhances human emotions." Explain her assertion within the context of her experience in the forest.

3. What precipitates Goodall's mystical experience? Why and how is her sense of reality altered? When does her mystical experience end? What insights does Goodall take away from this moment?

4. Describe Goodall's writing style. Does her style help to engage you in her experiences and beliefs? Give examples of effective use of time and unusual shifts of perspective in the essay.

5. How and why does Goodall contrast her Eastern mystical experience to her Western scientific and analytical study of the complex social behaviors of chimpanzees? What conclusions does she make?

6. How does Goodall help the bellhop and her readers to understand how both scientific and religious thinking can help us to find meaning in life? Do you agree or disagree with Goodall's perspective? Explain.

CONNECTION

Compare and contrast Jane Goodall's mystical experience in nature with Terry Tempest Williams's (see page 523).

IDEAS FOR WRITING

1. After the rainstorm Goodall looks over a ridge to see the lake in a new way: "A pale watery sun had appeared and its light caught the raindrops so that the world seemed hung with diamonds, sparkling on every leaf, every blade of grass." Write a descriptive narrative about an event you witnessed in the natural world. How was the experience spiritual for you?

2. "The forest, and the spiritual power that was so real in it, had given me the 'peace that passeth understanding.'" Write an essay that explains why you think Goodall was healed by her experience in the forest and why her experience has particular meaning for you.

RELATED WEB SITES

THE JANE GOODALL INSTITUTE
http://www.janegoodall.org
The mission of the Jane Goodall Institute is to advance the power of individuals to take informed and compassionate action to improve the environment. Find out more about the institute, Jane Goodall's life and work, and how to get involved at this web site.

GOMBE NATIONAL PARK, TANZANIA
http://weber.ucsd.edu/~jmoore/apesites/Gombe/Gombe.html

Learn about Gombe National Park, the place where Jane Goodall began her research on the chimpanzees, at this web site from the University of California at San Diego. The site also features a link to UCSD's "African Ape Study Site."

Martin Luther King, Jr.

I Have a Dream

Martin Luther King, Jr. (1928–1968), who came from a family of ministers, graduated from Morehouse University and received a Ph.D. in theology from Boston University. After graduation, King became a pastor and founded the Southern Christian Leadership Conference, developing the concept, derived from the teachings of Thoreau and Gandhi, that nonviolent civil disobedience resistance is the best way to obtain civil rights and to end segregation. King won the Nobel Peace Prize in 1964. Although his life ended in a tragic assassination, King wrote many speeches and essays on race and civil rights, which are collected in books such as I Have A Dream: Writings and Speeches That Changed the World *(1992) and* The Papers of Martin Luther King, Jr. *(1992). "I Have a Dream," King's most famous speech, was originally delivered in 1963 in front of the Lincoln Memorial in Washington, D.C., before a crowd estimated at 300,000. Notice how King uses powerful language, images, and comparisons to move his massive, diverse audience and to express his idealistic dream for America's future.*

JOURNAL

Write about a time when you found yourself moved by a minister or persuasive public speaker, either in a speech you heard live or saw on television. What skills of rhetoric and\or delivery do you remember as contributing to your strong feelings in response to this speech? If you saw it on television, what elements of video editing and soundtrack (music, applause, etc.) contributed to your response?

I am happy to join with you today in what will go down in history as the greatest demonstration for freedom in the history of our nation.

Five score years ago, a great American, in whose symbolic shadow we stand today, signed the Emancipation Proclamation. This momentous decree came as a great beacon light of hope to millions of Negro slaves who had been seared in the flames of withering injustice. It came as a joyous daybreak to end the long night of their captivity.

But one hundred years later, the Negro still is not free; one hundred years later, the life of the Negro is still sadly crippled by the manacles of segregation and the chains of discrimination; one hundred years later, the Negro lives on a lonely island of poverty in the midst of a vast ocean of material prosperity; one hundred years later, the Negro is still languished in the corners of American society and finds himself in exile in his own land.

So we've come here today to dramatize a shameful condition. In a sense we've come to our nation's capital to cash a check. When the architects of our republic wrote the magnificent words of the Constitution and the Declaration of Independence, they were signing a promissory note to which every American was to fall heir. This note was the promise that all men, yes, black men as well as white men, would be guaranteed the unalienable rights of life, liberty, and the pursuit of happiness.

5   It is obvious today that America has defaulted on this promissory note in so far as her citizens of color are concerned. Instead of honoring this sacred obligation, America has given the Negro people a bad check, a check which has come back marked "insufficient funds." But we refuse to believe that the bank of justice is bankrupt. We refuse to believe that there are insufficient funds in the great vaults of opportunity of this nation. And so we've come to cash this check, a check that will give us upon demand the riches of freedom and the security of justice.

We have also come to this hallowed spot to remind America of the fierce urgency of now. This is no time to engage in the luxury of cooling off or to take the tranquilizing drug of gradualism. Now is the time to make real the promises of democracy; now is the time to rise from the dark and desolate valley of segregation to the sunlit path of racial justice; now is the time to lift our nation from the quicksands of racial injustice to the solid rock of brotherhood; now is the time to make justice a reality for all of God's children. It would be fatal for the nation to overlook the urgency of the moment. This sweltering summer of the Negro's legitimate discontent will not pass until there is an invigorating autumn of freedom and equality.

Nineteen sixty-three is not an end, but a beginning. And those who hope that the Negro needed to blow off steam and will now be content, will have a rude awakening if the nation returns to business as usual. There will be neither rest nor tranquility in America until the Negro is granted his citizenship rights. The whirlwinds of revolt will continue to shake the foundations of our nation until the bright day of justice emerges.

But there is something that I must say to my people, who stand on the worn threshold which leads into the palace of justice. In the process of gaining our rightful place, we must not be guilty of wrongful deeds. Let us not seek to satisfy our thirst for freedom by drinking from the cup of bitterness and hatred. We must forever conduct our struggle on the high plain of dignity and discipline. We must not allow our creative protests to degenerate into physical violence. Again and again we must rise to the majestic heights of meeting physical force with soul force. The marvelous new militancy, which has engulfed the Negro community, must not lead us to a distrust of all white people. For many of our white brothers, as evidenced by their presence here today, have come to realize that their destiny is tied up with our destiny. And they have come to realize that their freedom is inextricably bound to our freedom. We cannot walk alone. And as we walk, we must make the pledge that we shall always march ahead. We cannot turn back.

There are those who are asking the devotees of Civil Rights, "When will you be satisfied?" We can never be satisfied as long as the Negro is the victim of the unspeakable horrors of police brutality; we can never be satisfied as long as our bodies, heavy with the fatigue of travel, cannot gain lodging in the motels of the highways and the hotels of the cities; we cannot be satisfied as long as the Negro's basic mobility is from a smaller ghetto to a larger one; we can never be satisfied as long as our children are stripped of their selfhood and robbed of their dignity by signs stating "For Whites Only"; we cannot be satisfied as long as the Negro in Mississippi cannot vote and a Negro in New York believes he has nothing for which to vote. No! No, we are not satisfied, and we will not be satisfied until "justice rolls down like waters and righteousness like a mighty stream."

10   I am not unmindful that some of you have come here out of great trials and tribulations. Some of you have come fresh from narrow jail cells. Some of you have come from areas where your quest for freedom left you battered by the storms of persecution and staggered by the winds of police brutality. You have been the veterans of creative suffering. Continue to work with the faith that un-earned suffering is redemptive. Go back to Mississippi. Go back to Alabama. Go back to South Carolina. Go back to Georgia. Go back to Louisiana. Go back to the slums and ghettos of our Northern cities, knowing that somehow this situa-tion can and will be changed. Let us not wallow in the valley of despair.

I say to you today, my friends, so even though we face the difficulties of today and tomorrow, I still have a dream. It is a dream deeply rooted in the American dream. I have a dream that one day this nation will rise up and live out the true meaning of its creed, "We hold these truths to be self-evident, that all men are created equal." I have a dream that one day on the red hills of Georgia, sons of former slaves and the sons of former slaves owners will be able to sit down to-gether at the table of brotherhood. I have a dream that one day even the state of Mississippi, a state sweltering with the heat of injustice, sweltering with the heat of oppression, will be transformed into an oasis of freedom and justice. I have a dream that my four little children will one day live in a nation where they will not be judged by the color of their skin, but by the content of their character.

I HAVE A DREAM TODAY!

I have a dream that one day down in Alabama—with its vicious racists, with its Governor having his lips dripping with the words of interposition and nullification—one day right there in Alabama, little black boys and black girls will be able to join hands with little white boys and white girls as sisters and brothers.

I HAVE A DREAM TODAY!

15   I have a dream today that one day every valley shall be exalted, and every hill and mountain shall be made low. The rough places will be plain and the crooked places will be made straight, "and the glory of the Lord shall be re-vealed, and all flesh shall see it together."

This is our hope. This is the faith that I go back to the South with. With this faith we will be able to hew out of the mountain of despair a stone of hope. With this faith we will be able to transform the jangling discords of our nation into a beautiful symphony of brotherhood. With this faith we will be able to work together, to pray together, to struggle together, to go to jail together, to stand up for freedom together, knowing that we will be free one day. And this will be the day. This will be the day when all of God's children will be able to sing with new meaning, "My country 'tis of thee, sweet land of liberty, of thee I sing. Land where my fathers died, land of the pilgrims' pride, from every mountainside, let freedom ring." And if America is to be a great nation, this must become true.

So let freedom ring from the prodigious hilltops of New Hampshire; let freedom ring from the mighty mountains of New York; let freedom ring from the heightening Alleghenies of Pennsylvania; let freedom ring from the snow-capped Rockies of Colorado; let freedom ring from the curvaceous slopes of California. But not only that. Let freedom ring from Stone Mountain of Georgia; let freedom ring from Lookout Mountain of Tennessee; let freedom ring from every hill and mole hill of Mississippi. "From every mountainside, let freedom ring." And when this happens, and when we allow freedom to ring, when we let it ring from every village and every hamlet, from every state and every city, we will be able to speed up that day when all of God's children, black men and white men, Jews and Gentiles, Protestants and Catholics, will be able to join hands and sing in the words of the old Negro spiritual: "Free at last. Free at last. Thank God Almighty, we are free at last."

QUESTIONS FOR DISCUSSION

1. What is the dream to which the title of the essay refers? What techniques or strategies does King use to define his dream? Is his definition effective? Why or why not? Explain.

2. What does King mean by his analogy of a "promissory note"? Is this an effective metaphor? Why?

3. Who is the primary audience of King's speech, the we to whom he refers in paragraph 4, the you in paragraph 10? How does King try to appeal to the needs and concerns of this audience?

4. Who is the secondary audience for the speech, other than those to whom he refers as having "come to our nation's capital to cash a check"? What rhetorical strategies in the speech are designed to stretch its message beyond the immediate needs and expectations of the present audience and to appeal to other audiences, including those who might see the speech on television or hear it on radio?

5. What does King mean by "creative suffering" in paragraph 10? How does this expression reflect different aspects of his spiritual vision of nonviolent resistance?

6. How does King use repetition of images, phrases, and entire sentences to help convey his dream to his audience? Refer to specific examples in his speech.

CONNECTION

Compare King's dream of wanting people to be judged by the "content of their character" rather than skin color with Shelby Steele's views in "Being Black and Feeling Blue" (Chapter 7). Would he agree with Steele's critique of the "anti-self"?

IDEAS FOR WRITING

1. Write a speech in the form of an essay and/or multi-media presentation that discusses a dream that you have for our society. Express your dream in emotional and persuasive language and imagery including, slides, audio clips, or other multi-media features in order to appeal to a specific audience. Indicate your intended audience.

2. Based on your understanding and reading about the current state of civil rights in America, write an essay in which you reflect on whether King, if he were alive today, would feel that his dream for African-Americans had come true. What aspects of his dream might King feel still remain to be accomplished?

RELATED WEB SITES

THE MARTIN LUTHER KING, JR. PAPERS PROJECT

http://www-leland.stanford.edu/group/King/

Created by "The King Papers Project" at Stanford University, this web site offers a major research effort to assemble and disseminate historical information concerning Martin Luther King, Jr. and the social movements in which he participated.

THE KING CENTER

http://www.thekingcenter.org

In these web pages, you will find valuable resources and information about Dr. King and the ongoing efforts to fulfill his great dream of "the Beloved Community for America and the World."

Thich Nhat Hanh

Love in Action

Teacher, writer, spiritual leader, and political activist, Thich Nhat Hanh (b. 1926) was born in Vietnam and became a Buddhist monk at the age of sixteen. Later he studied in the United States and attended Princeton University. Hanh was exiled from Vietnam because of his nonviolent resistance against the war; he then began publishing his writing about the Vietnam conflict and was nominated for the Nobel Peace Prize in 1967. Hanh participated in the Paris peace talks that brought about the end of American involvement in Vietnam and helped refuges and dissenters after the war. He helped to found the mindfulness community of Plum Village in southwestern France for activists, artists, and Vietnam veterans, and continues to give public lectures and participate in retreats. Many of Hanh's books are published by the Community of Mindful Living in Berkeley, California, one of numerous nonprofit organizations based on his teachings. His works include Call Me by My True Names: The Collected Poems of Thich Nhat Hanh *(1993),* Love in Action: Writings on Nonviolent Social Change *(1993),* Moment by Moment: The Art and Practice of Mindfulness *(1997), and* A Buddhist Life in America *(1998). The following selection is excerpted from* Love in Action.

JOURNAL

Write about a quiet time in nature that you spent in thought and meditation. How did your perceptions of yourself and of nature change through this experience?

In 1951, I went with a few brother monks to a remote mountain in the Dai Lao region of Vietnam to build a meditation center. We asked some native mountain people for their help, and two Montagnards from the Jarai tribe joined us in clearing the forest, cutting trees into lumber, and gathering other materials for construction. They were hard workers, and we were grateful for their assistance. But after working with us only three days, they stopped coming. Without their help, we had many difficulties, as we were not familiar with the ways of the forest. So we walked to their village and asked what had happened. They said, "Why should we return so soon? You already paid us enough to live for a month! We will come again when we run out of rice." At the time, it was a common practice to underpay the Montagnards, to avoid just this kind of thing. We had paid them properly, and, surely enough, they stopped coming.

Many people criticized the Montagnards for this ethic. They said that this laziness could only lead to trouble, and they listed four reasons to support their claim: (1) The Montagnards would be happier and more comfortable if they would work harder. (2) They would earn more money, which they could save for difficult periods. (3) The Montagnards should work harder in order to help others. (4) If they would work harder, they would have the means to defend themselves from invasions and the exploitation of others. There may be some validity to each of these points, but if we look closely at the lives of the Montagnards, we will come to understand them, and ourselves, better.

1. *The Montagnards would be happier and more comfortable if they would work harder.* The Montagnards lived simply. They did not store much food at all. They had no bank accounts. But they were much more serene and at peace with themselves, nature, and other people, than almost anyone in the world. I

am not suggesting that we all return to primitive lifestyles, but it is important that we see and appreciate the wisdom contained in a lifestyle like this, a wisdom that those of us immersed in modernization and economic growth have lost.

How much stuff do we need to be happy and comfortable? Happiness and comfort vary according to taste. Some people think they need three or four houses—one on the Riviera, one in New York, one in Tokyo, and perhaps one in Fiji. Others find that a two or three-room hut is quite enough. In fact, if you own a dozen luxurious houses, you may rarely have time to enjoy them. Even when you have the time, you may not know how to sit peacefully in one place. Always seeking distraction—going to restaurants, the theater, or dinner parties, or taking vacations that exhaust you even more, you can't stand being alone and facing yourself directly.

In former times, people spent hours drinking one cup of tea with dear friends. A cup of tea does not cost much, but today, we go to a cafe and take less than five minutes to drink our tea or coffee, and even during that short time, we are mostly thinking and talking about other things, and we never even notice our tea. We who own just one house barely have the time to live in it. We leave home early in the morning after a quick breakfast and go off to work, spending an hour in the car or the train and the rest of the day in the office. Then we return home exhausted, eat dinner, watch TV, and collapse so we can get up early for work. Is this "progress"?

The Montagnards were quite content to live in simple bamboo and palm-leaf huts and wash their clothes by hand. They refused to be slaves to economic pressures. Content with just a few possessions, they rarely needed to spend their time or money seeing doctors or psychotherapists for stress-related ailments

2. *They would earn more money, which they could save for difficult periods.*
    How much do we need to save? We do not save air, because we trust that it will be available to us when we need it. Why must we stockpile food, money, or other things for our own private use, while so many others are hungry?

    People who accumulate a house, a car, a position, and so forth, identify themselves with what they own, and they think that if they lose their house, their car, or their position, they would not be themselves. To me, they are already lost. By accumulating and saving, they have constructed a false self, and in the process they have forgotten their truest and deepest self. Psychotherapists can try to help, but the cause of this illness is in their way of life. One way to help such a person would be to place him in an "underdeveloped" country where he could grow his own food and make his own clothes. Sharing the fate and simple life of peasants might help him heal quickly.

    We have enough resources and know-how to assure every human being of adequate shelter and food every day. If we don't help others live, we ourselves are not going to be able to live either. We are all in the same boat—the planet earth. Why not put our efforts into trying to help each other and save our boat instead of accumulating savings only for ourselves and our own children?

3. *The Montagnards should work harder in order to help others.*

Of course, the Montagnards could have spent more time working in order to send aid to people who were starving in other parts of the world. If they did not do so, it was because they didn't know much about the existence of other nations. They certainly did help their own tribal members whenever they got sick or when a crop was destroyed by some natural disaster. But let us reflect for a moment on what the Montagnard people did not do.

They did not harm or exploit others. They grew their own food and exchanged some of their products with other people. They did not do violence to nature. They cut only enough wood to build their houses. They cleared only enough land to plant their crops. Because of their simple lifestyle, they did not overconsume natural resources. They did not pollute the air, water, or soil. They used very little fuel and no electricity. They did not own private cars, dishwashers, or electric razors. The way they lived enabled natural resources to continually renew themselves. A lifestyle like theirs demonstrates that a future for humankind is possible, and this is the most helpful thing anyone can do to help others.

4. *If they would work harder, they would have the means to defend themselves from invasion and the exploitation of others.*

It is true that the Montagnards were exploited by others and were often victims of social injustice. They lived in remote mountain areas. If others settled nearby, they risked losing land due to a lack of means with which to defend themselves.

People said that if the rest of us in Vietnam worked as little as they did, our country would never be able to resist foreign intervention and exploitation. It seems clear that the Montagnards and others like them had to do something more. But what? If the Montagnards would have moved down to the more populated areas, they would have seen men and women working extremely hard and getting poorer. They would have seen how expensive food, lodging, electricity, water, clothing, and transportation were. Their civilized countrymen were working all day long and could barely pay for the most basic items they consumed. The Montagnards in the forest did not need to spend any money. If they would have lived and worked in the cities, how would that have helped Vietnam resist foreign intervention? All they would have learned is that in the so-called developed nations, resources are used to make bombs and other elaborate weapons, while many citizens live in misery. The Montagnards might well need nuclear weapons to resist foreign intervention if they were to catch up with their more "developed" brothers and sisters. Will social injustice ever be abolished before all people wake up and realize that unless we let others live, we ourselves will not be able to live?

Economic growth may be necessary for the welfare of people, but the present rate of economic growth is destroying humanity and nature. Injustice is rampant. We humans are part of nature, and doing harm to nature only harms us. It is not just the poor and oppressed who are victims of environmental damage. The affluent are just as much victims of pollution and the exploitation of resources. We must look at the whole picture and ask, "Does our way of life harm nature? Does our way of life harm our fellow humans? Do we live at the expense of others, at the expense of the present, and at the expense of the future?" If we answer truthfully, we will know how to orient our lives and our actions. We have much to learn from the Montagnards and others like them. We must learn to live in a way that makes a future possible.

The Human Family   Although human beings are a part of nature, we single ourselves out and classify other animals and living beings as "nature," while acting as if we were somehow separate from it. Then we ask, "How should we deal with nature?" We should deal with nature the way we should deal with ourselves! Nonviolently. We should not harm ourselves, and we should not harm nature. To harm nature is to harm ourselves, and vice versa. If we knew how to deal with ourselves and our fellow human beings, we would know how to deal with nature. Human beings and nature are inseparable. By not caring properly for either, we harm both.

We can only be happy when we accept ourselves as we are. We must first be aware of all the elements within us, and then we must bring them into harmony. Our physical and mental well-being are the result of understanding what is going on in ourselves. This understanding helps us respect nature in ourselves and also helps us bring about healing.

5   If we harm another human being, we harm ourselves. To accumulate wealth and our own excessive portions of the world's natural resources is to deprive our fellow humans of the chance to live. To participate in oppressive and unjust social systems is to widen the gap between rich and poor and thereby aggravate the situation of social injustice. Yet we tolerate excess, injustice, and war, while remaining unaware that the human race as a family is suffering. While some members of the human family are suffering and starving, for us to enjoy false security and wealth is a sign of insanity.

The fate of each individual is inextricably linked to the fate of the whole human race. We must let others live if we ourselves want to live. The only alternative to coexistence is co-nonexistence. A civilization in which we kill and exploit others for our own aggrandizement is sick. For us to have a healthy civilization, everyone must be born with an equal right to education, work, food, shelter, world citizenship, and the ability to circulate freely and settle on any part of the earth. Political and economic systems that deny one person these rights harm the whole human family. We must begin by becoming aware of what is happening to every member of the human family if we want to repair the damages already done.

To bring about peace, we must work for harmonious coexistence. If we continue to shut ourselves off from the rest of the world, imprisoning ourselves in our narrow concerns and immediate problems, we are not likely to make peace or to survive. It is difficult for one individual to preserve harmony among the elements within himself, and it is even more difficult to preserve harmony among the members of the human family. We have to understand the human race to bring it into harmony. Cruelty and disruption destroy the harmony of the family. We need legislation that keeps us from doing violence to ourselves or nature, and prevents us from being disruptive and cruel.

We have created a system that we cannot control. This system imposes itself on us, and we have become its slaves. Most of us, in order to have a house, a car, a refrigerator, a TV, and so on, must sacrifice our time and our lives in exchange. We are constantly under the pressure of time. In former times, we could afford three hours for one cup of tea, enjoying the company of our friends in a serene and spiritual atmosphere. We could organize a party to celebrate the blossoming of one orchid in our garden. But today we can no longer afford these things. We say that time is money. We have created a society in which the rich become richer and the poor become poorer, and in which we are so caught up in our own immediate problems that we cannot afford to be aware of what is going on with the rest of the human family. We see images on TV, but we do not really understand our Third World brothers and sisters.

The individual and all humanity are both a part of nature and should be able to live in harmony with nature. Nature can be cruel and disruptive and therefore, at times, needs to be controlled. To control is not to dominate or oppress but to harmonize and equilibrate. We must be deep friends with nature in order to control certain aspects of it. This requires a full understanding of nature. Typhoons, tornadoes, droughts, floods, volcanic eruptions, and proliferations of harmful insects all constitute danger and destruction to life. Although parts of nature, these things disrupt the harmony of nature. We should be able to prevent to a large degree the destruction that natural disasters cause, but we must do it in a way that preserves life and encourages harmony.

10   The excessive use of pesticides that kill all kinds of insects and upset the ecological balance is an example of our lack of wisdom in trying to control nature.

The harmony and equilibrium in the individual, society, and nature are being destroyed. Individuals are sick, society is sick, and nature is sick. We must reestablish harmony and equilibrium, but how? Where can we begin the work of healing? Would we begin with the individual, society, or the environment? We must work in all three domains. People of different disciplines tend to stress their particular areas. For example, politicians consider an effective rearrangement of society necessary for the salvation of humans and nature, and therefore urge that everyone engage in the struggle to change political systems.

We Buddhist monks are like psychotherapists in that we tend to look at the problem from the viewpoint of mental health. Meditation aims at creating harmony and equilibrium in the life of the individual. Buddhist mediation uses the breath as a tool to calm and harmonize the whole human being. As in any therapeutic practice, the patient is placed in an environment that favors the restoration of harmony. Usually psychotherapists spend their time observing and then advising their patients. I know of some, however, who, like monks, observe themselves first, recognizing the need to free their own selves from the fears, anxieties, and despair that exist in each of us. Many therapists seem to think that they themselves have no mental problems, but the monk recognizes in himself the susceptibility to fears and anxieties, and to the mental illness that is caused by the inhuman social and economic systems that prevail in today's world.

Buddhists believe that the reality of the individual, society, and nature's integral being will reveal itself to us as we recover, gradually ceasing to be possessed by anxiety, fear, and the dispersion of mind. Among the three—individual, society, and nature—it is the individual who begins to effect change. But in order to effect change, he or she must have personally recovered, must be whole. Since this requires an environment favorable to healing, he or she must seek the kind of lifestyle that is free from destructiveness. Efforts to change the environment and to change the individual are both necessary, but it is difficult to change the environment if individuals are not in a state of equilibrium. From the mental health point of view, efforts for us to recover our humanness should be given priority.

Restoring mental health does not mean simply helping individuals adjust to the modern world of rapid economic growth. The world is sick, and adapting to an unwell environment will not bring real health. Many people who seek the help of a psychotherapist are really victims of modern life, which separates human beings from the rest of nature. One way to help such a person may be to move him or her to a rural area where he can cultivate the land, grow his own food, wash his clothes in a clear river, and live simply, sharing the same life as millions of peasants around the world. For psychotherapy to be effective, we need environmental change, and psychotherapists must participate in efforts to change the environment. But that is only half their task. The other half is to help individuals be themselves, not by helping them adapt to an ill environment, but by providing them with the strength to change it. To tranquilize them is not the way. The explosion of bombs, the burning of napalm, the violent deaths of relatives and neighbors, the pressures of time, noise, and pollution, the lonely crowds have all been created by the disruptive course of our economic growth. They are all sources of mental illness, and they must end. Anything we can do to bring them to an end is preventive medicine. Political activities are not the only means to this end.

15   While helping their particular patients, psychotherapists must, at the same time, recognize their responsibility to the whole human family. Their work must also prevent others from becoming ill. They are challenged to safeguard their own humanness. Like others, psychotherapists and monks need to observe first themselves and their own ways of life. If they do, I believe they will seek ways to disengage themselves from the present economic systems in order to help reestablish harmony and balance in life. Monks and psychotherapists are human beings. We cannot escape mental illness if we do not apply our dis-

ciplines to ourselves. Caught in forgetfulness and acquiescence to the status quo, we will gradually become victims of fear, anxiety, and egotism of all kinds. But if psychotherapists and monks, through mutual sharing, help each other apply our disciplines to our own lives, we will rediscover the harmony in ourselves and thereby help the whole human family.

A tree reveals itself to an artist when he or she can establish a genuine relationship with it. If a human is not a real human being, he may look at his fellow humans and not see them; he may look at a tree and not see it. Many of us cannot see things because we are not wholly ourselves. When we are wholly ourselves, we can see how one person by living fully demonstrates to all of us that life is possible, that a future is possible. But the question, "Is a future possible?" is meaningless without seeing the millions of our fellow humans who suffer, live, and die around us. Only when we really see them will we be able to see ourselves and see nature.

The Sun My Heart When I first left Vietnam, I had a dream in which I was a young boy, smiling and at ease, in my own land, surrounded by my own people, in a time of peace. There was a beautiful hillside, lush with trees and flowers, and on it was a little house. But each time I approached the hillside, obstacles prevented me from climbing it, and then I woke up.

The dream recurred many times. I continued to do my work and to practice mindfulness, trying to be in touch with the beautiful trees, people, flowers, and sunshine that surrounded me in Europe and North America. I looked deeply at these things, and I played under the trees with the children exactly as I had in Vietnam. After a year, the dream stopped. Seeds of acceptance and joy had been planted in me, and I began to look at Europe, America, and other countries in Asia as also my home. I realized that my home is the earth. Whenever I felt homesick for Vietnam, I went outside into a backyard or a park, and found a place to practice breathing, walking, and smiling among the trees.

But some cities had very few trees, even then. I can imagine someday soon a city with no trees in it at all. Imagine a city that has only one tree left. People there are mentally disturbed, because they are so alienated from nature. Then one doctor in the city sees why people are getting sick, and he offers each person who comes to him the prescription: "You are sick because you are cut off from Mother Nature. Every morning, take a bus, go to the tree in the center of the city, and hug it for fifteen minutes. Look at the beautiful green tree and smell its fragrant bark."

20 After three months of practicing this, the patient will feel much better. But because many people suffer from the same malady and the doctor always gives the same prescription, after a short time, the line of people waiting their turn to embrace the tree gets to be very long, more than a mile, and people begin to get impatient. Fifteen minutes is now too long for each person to hug the tree, so the city council legislates a five-minute maximum. Then they have to shorten it to one minute, and then only a few seconds. Finally there is no remedy at all for the sickness.

If we are not mindful, we might be in that situation soon. We have to remember that our body is not limited to what lies within the boundary of our skin. Our body is much more immense. We know that if our heart stops beating, the flow of our life will stop, but we do not take the time to notice the many things outside of our bodies that are equally essential for our survival. If the ozone layer around our earth were to disappear for even an instant, we would die. If the sun were to stop shining, the flow of our life would stop. The sun is our second heart, our heart outside of our body. It gives all life on earth the warmth necessary for existence. Plants live thanks to the sun. Their leaves absorb the sun's energy, along with carbon dioxide from the air, to produce food for the tree, the flower, the plankton. And thanks to plants, we and other animals can live. All of us—people, animals, plants, and minerals—"consume" the sun, directly and indirectly. We cannot begin to describe all the effects of the sun, that great heart outside of our body.

When we look at green vegetables, we should know that it is the sun that is green and not just the vegetables. The green color in the leaves of the vegetables is due to the presence of the sun. Without the sun, no living being could survive. Without sun, water, air, and soil, there would be no vegetables. The vegetables are the coming-together or many conditions near and far.

There is no phenomenon in the universe that does not intimately concern us, from a pebble resting at the bottom of the ocean, to the movement of a galaxy millions of light years away. Walt Whitman said, "I believe a blade of grass is no less than the journey-work of the stars. . . ." These words are not philosophy. They come from the depths of his soul. He also said, "I am large, I contain multitudes."

This might be called a meditation on "interbeing endlessly interwoven." All phenomena are interdependent. When we think of a speck of dust, a flower, or a human being, our thinking cannot break loose from the idea of unity, of one, of calculation. We see a line drawn between one and many, one and not one. But if we truly realize the interdependent nature of the dust, the flower, and the human being, we see that unity cannot exist without diversity. Unity and diversity interpenetrate each other freely. Unity is diversity, and diversity is unity. This is the principle of interbeing.

25   If you are a mountain climber or someone who enjoys the countryside or the forest, you know that forests are our lungs outside of our bodies. Yet we have been acting in a way that has allowed millions of square miles of land to be deforested, and we have also destroyed the air, the rivers, and parts of the ozone layer. We are imprisoned in our small selves, thinking only of some comfortable conditions for this small self, while we destroy our large self. If we want to change the situation, we must begin by being our true selves. To be our true selves means we have to *be* the forest, the river, and the ozone layer. If we visualize ourselves as the forest, we will experience the hopes and fears of the trees. If we don't do this, the forests will die, and we will lose our chance for peace. When we understand that we inter-are with the trees, we will know that it is up to us to make an effort to keep the trees alive. In the last twenty years, our automobiles and factories have created acid rain that has destroyed so many trees. Because we inter-are with the trees, we know that if they do not live, we too will disappear very soon.

We humans think we are smart, but an orchid, for example, knows how to produce noble, symmetrical flowers, and a snail knows how to make a beautiful, well-proportioned shell. Compared with their knowledge, ours is not worth much at all. We should bow deeply before the orchid and the snail and join our palms reverently before the monarch butterfly and the magnolia tree. The feeling of respect for all species will help us recognize the noblest nature in ourselves.

An oak tree is an oak tree. That is all an oak tree needs to do. If an oak tree is less than an oak tree, we will all be in trouble. In our former lives, we were rocks, clouds, and trees. We have also been an oak tree. This is not just Buddhist; it is scientific. We humans are a young species. We were plants, we were trees, and now we have become humans. We have to remember our past existences and be humble. We can learn a lot from an oak tree.

All life is impermanent. We are all children of the earth, and, at some time, she will take us back to herself again. We are continually arising from Mother Earth, being nurtured by her, and then returning to her. Like us, plants are born, live for a period of time, and then return to the earth. When they decompose, they fertilize our gardens. Living vegetables and decomposing vegetables are part of the same reality. Without one, the other cannot be. After six months, compost becomes fresh vegetables again. Plants and the earth rely on each other. Whether the earth is fresh, beautiful, and green, or arid and parched depends on the plants.

It also depends on us. Our way of walking on the earth has a great influence on animals and plants. We have killed so many animals and plants and destroyed their environments. Many are now extinct. In turn, our environment is now harming us. We are like sleepwalkers, not knowing what we are doing or where we are heading. Whether we can wake up or not depends on whether we can walk mindfully on our Mother Earth. The future of all life, including our own, depends on our mindful steps.

30 Birds' songs express joy, beauty, and purity, and evoke in us vitality and love. So many beings in the universe love us unconditionally. The trees, the water, and the air don't ask anything of us; they just love us. Even though we need this kind of love, we continue to destroy them. By destroying the animals, the air, and the trees, we are destroying ourselves. We must learn to practice unconditional love for all.

Our earth, our green beautiful earth is in danger, and all of us know it. Yet we act as if our daily lives have nothing to do with the situation of the world. If the earth were your body, you would be able to feel many areas where she is suffering. Many people are aware of the world's suffering, and their hearts are filled with compassion. They know what needs to be done, and they engage in political, social, and environmental work to try to change things. But after a period of intense involvement, they become discouraged, because they lack the strength needed to sustain a life of action. Real strength is not in power, money, or weapons, but in deep, inner peace.

If we change our daily lives—the way we think, speak, and act—we change the world. The best way to take care of the environment is to take care of the environmentalist.

Many Buddhist teachings help us understand our interconnectedness with our mother, the earth. One of the deepest is the Diamond Sutra, which is written in the form of a dialogue between the Buddha and his senior disciple, Subhuti. It begins with this question by Subhuti: "If daughters and sons of good families wish to give rise to the highest, most fulfilled, awakened mind, what should they rely on and what should they do to master their thinking?" This is the same as asking, "If I want to use my whole being to protect life, what methods and principles should I use?"

The Buddha answers, "We have to do our best to help every living being cross the ocean of suffering. But after all beings have arrived at the shore of liberation, no being at all has been carried to the other shore. If you are still caught up in the idea of a self, a person, a living being, or a life span, you are not an authentic bodhisattva." Self, person, living being, and life span are four notions that prevent us from seeing reality.

35   Life is one. We do not need to slice it into pieces and call this or that piece a "self." What we call a self is made only of non-self elements. When we look at a flower, for example, we may think that it is different from "non-flower" things. But when we look more deeply, we see that everything in the cosmos is in that flower. Without all of the non-flower elements—sunshine, clouds, earth, minerals, heat, rivers, and consciousness—a flower cannot be. That is why the Buddha teaches that the self does not exist. We have to discard all distinctions between self and non-self. How can anyone work to protect the environment without this insight?

The second notion that prevents us from seeing reality is the notion of a person, a human being. We usually discriminate between humans and non-humans, thinking that we are more important than other species. But since we humans are made of non-human elements, to protect ourselves we have to protect all of the non-human elements. There is no other way. If you think, "God created man in His own image and He created other things for man to use," you are already making the discrimination that man is more important than other things. When we see that humans have no self, we see that to take care of the environment (the non-human elements) is to take care of humanity. The best way to take good care of men and women so that they can be truly healthy and happy is to take care of the environment.

I know ecologists who are not happy in their families. They worked hard to improve the environment, partly to escape family life. If someone is not happy within himself, how can he help the environment? That is why the Buddha teaches that to protect the non-human elements is to protect humans, and to protect humans is to protect non-human elements.

The third notion we have to break through is the notion of a living being. We think that we living beings are different from inanimate objects, but according to the principle of interbeing, living beings are comprised of non-living-being elements. When we look into ourselves, we see minerals and all other non-living-being elements. Why discriminate against what we call inanimate? To protect living beings, we must protect the stones, the soil, and the oceans. Before the atomic bomb was dropped on Hiroshima, there were many beautiful stone benches in the parks. As the Japanese were rebuilding their city, they discovered that these stones were dead, so they carried them away and buried them. Then they brought in live stones. Do not think these things are not alive. Atoms are always moving. Electrons move at nearly the speed of light. According to the teaching of Buddhism, these atoms and stones are consciousness itself. That is why discrimination by living beings against non-living beings should be discarded.

The last notion is that of a life span. We think that we have been alive since a certain point in time and that prior to that moment, our life did not exist. This distinction between life and non-life is not correct. Life is made of death, and death is made of life. We have to accept death; it makes life possible. The cells in our body are dying every day, but we never think to organize funerals for them. The death of one cell allows for the birth of another. Life and death are two aspects of the same reality. We must learn to die peacefully so that others may live. This deep meditation brings forth non-fear, non-anger, and non-despair, the strengths we need for our work. With non-fear, even when we see that a problem is huge, we will not burn out. We will know how to make small, steady steps. If those who work to protect the environment contemplate these four notions, they will know how to be and how to act.

40   In another Buddhist text, the Avatamsaka (Adoring the Buddha with Flowers) Sutra, the Buddha further elaborates his insights concerning our "interpenetration" with our environment. Please meditate with me on the "Ten Penetrations":

The first is, "All worlds penetrate a single pore. A single pore penetrates all worlds." Look deeply at a flower. It may be tiny, but the sun, the clouds, and everything else in the cosmos penetrates it. Nuclear physicists say very much the same thing: one electron is made by all electrons; one electron is in all electrons.

The second penetration is, "All living beings penetrate one body. One body penetrates all living beings." When you kill a living being, you kill yourself and everyone else as well.

The third is, "Infinite time penetrates one second. One second penetrates infinite time." A *ksana* is the shortest period of time, actually much shorter than a second.

The fourth penetration is, "All Buddhist teachings penetrate one teaching. One teaching penetrates all Buddhist teaching." As a young monk, I had the opportunity to learn that Buddhism is made of non-Buddhist elements. So, whenever I study Christianity or Judaism, I find the Buddhist elements in them, and vice versa. I always respect non-Buddhist teachings. All Buddhist teachings penetrate one teaching, and one teaching penetrates all Buddhist teachings. We are free.

45   The fifth penetration is, "Innumerable spheres enter one sphere. One sphere enters innumerable spheres." A sphere is a geographical space. Innumerable spheres penetrate into one particular area, and one particular area enters into innumerable spheres. It means that when you destroy one area, you destroy every

area. When you save one area, you save all areas. A student asked me, "Thây, there are so many urgent problems, what should I do?" I said, "Take one thing and do it very deeply and carefully, and you will be doing everything at the same time."

The sixth penetration is, "All sense organs penetrate one organ. One organ penetrates all sense organs"—eye, ear, nose, tongue, body, and mind. To take care of one means to take care of many. To take care of your eyes means to take care of the eyes of innumerable living beings.

QUESTIONS FOR DISCUSSION

1. Why does Hanh begin with the example of the Montagnards' work ethic? Do you agree with his views on the Montagnards?

2. Why does Hanh believe that when we harm nature we harm ourselves both physically and psychologically? Explain why you agree or disagree with his point of view.

3. Explain why you agree or disagree with Hanh's claim, "While some members of the human family are suffering and starving, for us to enjoy false security and wealth is a sign of insanity."

4. What is the meaning of the dream that Hanh had when he first left Vietnam: What helped him to resolve the dream and his feelings of homesickness?

5. How does Hanh think that monks and psychotherapists can help their patients and the human family to establish a genuine relationship with nature and with other human beings? How can therapists and environmentalists help themselves to better mental health?

6. In the latter part of his essay, Hanh provides contemporary examples and explanation of the Buddha's "four notions that prevent us from seeing reality: the notions of self, person, living being, and life span." How does he clarify the importance of seeing beyond these deceptive notions in order to attain happiness and harmony with the environment?

CONNECTION

Compare Peter Steinhart's ideas in Chapter 2 with Hanh's ideas on improving the relationship of humans to nature (see page 75).

IDEAS FOR WRITING

1. Write an essay in response to Hanh's discussion of the importance of seeing beyond the four notions mentioned above. Do you agree or disagree that these notions damage our relationship with the environment, with the human family, and with ourselves?

2. Although Hanh believes in political action to improve our relationship with nature and the human family, his emphasis in this essay is on mindful meditation, particularly the meditation on "interbeing endlessly interwoven." Explain what Hanh means by mindful meditation of this type (you might do some outside reading on the concept of "mindfulness"); then

write an essay in which you discuss the advantages and/or disadvantages of this approach to psychological, social, ecological problems.

RELATED WEB SITES

THICH NHAT HANH

http://www.seaox.com/thich.html

You can learn about Thich Nhat Hanh, the famous Vietnamese Buddhist monk and writer, at this web site. It includes a biography, Real Audio excerpts of Thich Nhat Hanh's teachings, and a link to Hanh's book list.

BUDDHIST STUDIES VIRTUAL LIBRARY

http://www.ciolek.com/WWWVL-Buddhism.html

Visit this virtual library devoted to the study of Buddhism at this meta-web site. There are many excellent links and a search engine for specific facts surrounding the subject of Buddhism.

Josh Spires

Knowing Spirituality

Josh Spires wrote "Knowing Spirituality" for his Writing and Critical Thinking course. In this essay Spires attempts to explore the idea of spirituality through a series of examples from experience and readings such as "In the Forests of Gombe" (included in this chapter).

A spirited debate, the spirit of competition, a spiritual man—we use spirituality to describe events, ideas and people, yet the notion itself is widely misunderstood. Perhaps this is because of the unique nature of the concept. In contrast to physical objects and scientific concepts, we cannot precisely define or describe spirituality. In a way, spirituality is that which is not definable: it cannot be explained by scientific analysis or rational thought. More precisely, spirituality is at once a unique state, a sense of selflessness and unity, a process, and a way of life, which in every manifestation emphasizes the sensible over the tangible. In short, we feel spirituality—we know spirituality.

This definition is most easily applied when spirituality is viewed as a temporary state. A spiritual event, also known as an epiphany, occurs when a person enters into a state where he or she experiences outside stimuli beyond normal sensory capabilities. In this state, people do not see or hear things—stimuli instead trigger an emotional and often profound response. In this state, physical objects are relatively unimportant compared to the emotional experience. This is what makes the event spiritual. Jane Goodall presents a vivid description of a spiritual event in her essay, "In the Forests of Gombe," when she writes, "I must have slipped into a state of heightened awareness. . . . It seemed to me, as I struggled afterward to recall the experience, that *self* was utterly absent: I and the chimpanzees, the earth and the trees and air, seemed to merge, to become one with the spirit power of life itself." Goodall's experience was unique, but uniqueness alone does not make an event spiritual. It is the event's intangible quality, the heightened awareness, the loss of self, and the fact that her experience was one of oneness with a higher power that make the event spiritual.

While the timing of Goodall's experience seems random, like a sudden flash of lightning, spirituality can be a regular activity. This type of spiritual process is known as ritual. Most often encountered in religious ceremonies, ritual spirituality can take many forms, challenging our assumptions of what is or is not spiritual. For example, most people would not find their morning shower to be a spiritual experience, yet cleansing rituals are practiced around the world. What makes this type of bathing spiritual is the fact that animate objects are unimportant—the soap and water are mere props. The actual cleansing takes place within the mind, in a way that science could never describe. This quality of intangibility links the cleansing ritual with Goodall's epiphany as another spiritual experience. But cleansing rituals are only one example of spiritual processes. Ritual meals, such as Holy Communion or Passover Seder, also have profound meanings that transcend the actual objects (food and drink); similarly, the repeated ritual of meditation exercises can often trigger intense emotional responses. In all, the diversity and abundance of rituals can serve to remind us that there are many paths to spiritual goals.

A third type of spirituality demands constant self discipline through which a person chooses to live in a way that suppresses the importance of material goods and logical analysis in favor of that which only the truly devout can experience. This is the life that monks and nuns, among others, adopt. They choose to value spiritual ritual and experience above ordinary possessions and the power derived from manipulating ideas in the secular world. For example, author bell hooks chooses to live a spiritual life, although not in the confines of a convent. For her, "Living life in touch with divine spirit lets us see the light of love in all things." In her essay "Spirituality: Divine Love," hooks mentions the fundamental attribute linking all spiritual events—a separation from material objects and materialism. In fact, hooks goes so far as to indict consumerism as incompatible with spirituality, quoting Erich Fromm as saying ". . . the principle underlying capitalistic society [consumerism] and the principle of love [spirituality] are incompatible." We can conclude that the spiritual life is a life unconcerned with property. In contrast, it is a life of reflection, as well as a life of love, of unity (as seen in Goodall's vision), of connectedness. As hooks puts it, "Everyone needs to be in touch with the needs of their spirit. This interconnectedness calls us to spiritual awakening—to love. Considering the preceding discussion of spirituality, a question might arise as to whether emotion is the key to spirituality? The existence of an emotional component to the types of spirituality described might make it seem as if spirituality is just another emotion. However, it is important to remember that emotion is a larger phenomena that biological science can study physically and define, while spirituality cannot be scientifically understood. To equate "spiritual" with "emotive" is to try to define rationally a concept that is based on the irrational. So while spirituality can be emotional, emotions are not necessarily spiritual. We must remember that spiritual events are by their nature undecipherable, and that we make a terrible error when we attempt to equate them to any rational phenomenon. In reality, spirituality is only comparable with emotion in that both take place in the present. However, spiritual events are more completely fused to their moment than any emotion can be. In fact, for many, time mysteriously seems to stop during a spiritual experience.

5   Irrational, mysterious, an experience of intense unity and love—this is the closest we can come to a definition of spirituality. Spirituality cannot be pinned to a specific form, duration or effect, yet we still need to try to understand its meaning in our lives. To ignore that which we cannot explain is to choose ignorance over wonder. And wonder is a miraculous thing.

QUESTIONS FOR DISCUSSION

1. How does Josh Spires attempt to define spirituality? How does he use various writing strategies such as classification, examples, and synthesis of ideas from other writers to develop his definition?
2. What topic idea does Spires develop in paragraph 2? Did his reference to Jane Goodall's experience help you to understand his point? Explain your response.
3. Explain why you agree or disagree with Spires when he claims, "Rituals can serve to remind us that there are many paths to spiritual goals." What other examples could he have used to support his point?
4. Why does bell hooks indict consumerism as being incompatible with spirituality? Explain why you agree or disagree with hooks and Spires on this point.
5. Why does Spires argue that "while spirituality can be emotional, emotions are not necessarily spiritual?" Do you believe that this is an important distinction? Explain your response.

Elizabeth Matchett

The Gift

A returning student and teacher-trainer, Elizabeth Matchett wrote the essay that follows for a class at Stanford University in Writing and Yoga. She lives in the San Francisco Bay Area with her husband and two daughters. The idea for "The Gift" grew out of her response to the death of her father and began with a journal entry contained in the essay that follows.

Ibelieve that when God takes something away from you, you get something in return. I developed this idea as a defense mechanism over the course of my life because I was never allowed to feel sorry for myself when something I wanted didn't come through, or when the circumstances of my life seemed beyond endurance. My father was an advocate of tough love: No embraces or soft words of comfort from him. He never got any from his family, so I guess he didn't know how. His remedy was to verbally kick you in the behind by saying: "Stop feeling sorry for yourself. There is no one to blame. What happened happened. All I want to know from you is what you intend to do about it." Thus, I was forced to act, at least mentally, to resolve my problems on my own. And, more often that not, I was able to find a reasonable and logical solution or plan in order to set myself back on the road to my goal. Without my realizing it, my father was the basis of my security. He gave me the tools to cope, and, subconsciously, knowing he was there gave me a great strength and independence of will.

I lost my father recently to heart failure. His heart simply stopped beating and he fell immediately into a coma. He and my mother live 3000 miles away, in Massachusetts. At the time this was occurring, I was in Stanford Memorial Church at a dress rehearsal, singing the opening chords of the Berlioz Requiem. As I began to sing that night, I felt a severe dizziness; the church and my music began to spin before me, and I had to concentrate on staying upright for a few minutes until the spell passed. I continued singing, feeling somewhat lightheaded when my husband and two children burst into the church, frantically trying to find me on the stage. As I left the dress rehearsal, I left behind any semblance of inner life as I had known it.

I went to bed that night and did not sleep. In my heart, I knew that I had to grow up and accept this: that I would never be the same, that my life would be different now, that I had to summon the courage to face this. I did not want to find that courage. I wanted to deny it, to deny the reality. I do not know how, in the half light of dawn, I discovered the strength to drag myself from the wrinkled sheets and face the day. I awoke my husband, told him of my resolve, and cried. These tears were for myself; I was mourning the passing of my childhood. A part of me knew instinctively that a certain feeling of security was now gone forever.

Bleary-eyed yet stoic, I got up and took the first plane to Boston. There would be no tears now for awhile. Incredibly, I met a friend and colleague in the airport who was on her way to a professional conference. She greeted me cheerfully, but her cheer turned to concern when I reported the errand I was on. In fact, I realize now, it *was* an errand. I had something I needed to accomplish, but I did not realize what it was then.

5   The thing I most vividly remember as I first walked into intensive care was the smell. There is a sickly odor of medicine, sweat, and body fluids that em-

anates from a person who is living on a machine. For me, it is a gruesome smell, and I felt revolted, even though it was coming from a person I love. As I stopped in the doorway and looked at my father, I saw the strange yawn of his mouth with the tube taped to the side, the rhythmic rise and fall of his belly and chest, perfectly coordinated by the respirator. There were tubes of all sizes in his arms, nose, and slithering out at various parts of his body from under the blanket. Around his head were arranged various machines and monitors in a sort of macabre vigil. I noticed that his feet had fallen open, hanging off of the bed in a perfectly relaxed pose that I had never seen him in.

I can only call it a vision: I knew with certainty, as I have never known any-thing in my life that the essence of my father was not in that body. As that cer-tainty came upon me, I felt a *presence* around my head and shoulders that embraced me. As I leaned backward into the embrace, a further serenity came over me, and a knowledge that all was well. Without thought as to what I was doing, I went up and stroked my father's hair, which was silky. I had never stroked my father's hair before, and I was surprised at the texture. I had sup-posed that it would feel rough since his hair was so wavy—I guess I just thought it would feel like it looked. Nothing in that room felt like it looked.

His hair was soft, and his *presence* was not in his body, but physically wrapped around my shoulders and head. As I stroked his hair, the presence made me understand that all was well with him. That which had made him George Matchett was already out of his body. A small part of me rebelled against this realization: maybe he would wake up, maybe he would recover. I knew my brother thought that would happen—he had told me so on the way to the hospital—so I got up and squeezed my father's hand. His hands were large and callused—one of my earliest memories is walking with my tiny hand in his. However, *this* hand was very warm, too warm, without any feeling of life. This was not the hand of my father. I decided to check his eyes, my father's beautiful hazel eyes. When I opened the lid with my finger, his pupil stared back at me, a fixed dark orb with no glint, no spark. And *the presence* wrapped itself around me just a little bit more, as if to say "You see? It's true. But it's OK, be open to this. Let it come into you, don't be afraid."

Suddenly, a sense of peace, of complete knowing, of being filled with grace filled me. I was thoroughly unafraid for my father and for myself; I realized that, in fact, I did not have to do anything. In his passage, my father had been able to enter my soul and communicate, to tell me that all was *peaceful,* a term no one would ever use to describe my father, even on his most pacific day. In that sterile, florescent, buzzing room, where not the tiniest bit of nature's heal-ing energy could exist, I had been blessed with a moment of insight—of one-ness with myself, my father, and with all that is calm and serene.

On the third day, we did it: My brother and mother and I agreed to let them stop all life support. We came into the room after all the tubes had been re-moved to stand with him and wait. The first breath we heard him take on his own was awful—a gasping, gurgling rattle that sent my mother flying from the room. How I stood there and held his hand I can only speculate. I think it was because his presence was around me. Suddenly, a picture of myself at the dinner table as a young girl flashed into my mind. I spoke out loud of the doll house my father built for me and let me paint and of his requirement of saying the pledge of allegiance each night before eating dinner. My mother, my brother and I spent that next hour and a half reminiscing, crying a little and even laughing, as my father's breaths came harder and farther apart. This vigil was proof of my family's strength, of a bond we discovered, and I was exceedingly proud of us as we stood around him and waited. I held his hand all along.

10   Presently, there was a lull, and I was staring past the bed at the wall, lost in thought and in my childhood. Suddenly, my father's hand, which had been flaccid in my own, opened with force and then relaxed. It then clenched up and pulled toward him. I looked down at his feet and watched a sort of wave pass through his body. It moved up, passing through each part, until it finally got to his head, where it was released from his mouth in a final sucking gurgle, as though the last bit of life force was being forcibly drawn out of him by an unseen hand. I knew that was all.

I wrote in my journal that night: "I held my father's hand at the last and was overwhelmed at the memories that flooded through me. All of the hundreds of times that my tiny hand was wrapped in his and the incredible security that had brought me coursed through me. I knew, and I know, that that security is with me, that that part of my father is with me and always will be. He walks with me. I am blessed to be here and to experience this. It is a transition, not an end and not a beginning—just a transition to another part of the cycle of my soul."

My father's death allowed me to experience grace, a certainty. I am able to feel him with me all the time, helping me hold tight to my own beliefs and integrity. I can see myself looking back to now and remembering it with nostalgia. I wonder if in that time my life will be even more complicated than it is now, and if I will yearn for these simpler times, as I now yearn for my childhood on certain days. The other day my oldest daughter took my hand and put it to her cheek. She told me that she loved me and gave me a look of complete security and faith. I am in charge now, and I think I am ready.

QUESTIONS FOR DISCUSSION

1. How does Matchett's opening paragraph set the scene for the events to follow and for her final realization? What is revealed in this paragraph about her father's character and influence on her?

2. What does the description of her father's body reveal about Matchett's feelings toward him? How does the look of his comatose body contrast with the feeling of his presence in the room?

3. Describe the impact of her father's spiritual presence on Matchett. How does this presence help her to adjust to and accept his physical passing?

4. What does the final paragraph of the essay indicate about Matchett's growth through experiencing and accepting her father's death? Why is her daughter introduced in the final sentences?

TOPICS FOR RESEARCH AND WRITING

1. Emily Dickinson and Annie Dillard both indicate a conflicting desire for authentic religious experience combined with doubt and perhaps embarrassment with some of the more traditional forms of religious belief and practice. Do some further research into the place of religion in modern life. Do other writers whom you encountered express similar views of doubt and confusion about religion?

2. Jane Goodall addresses the relationship between science and religious practices such as meditation. Do some further research into modern relations between science and religion and write an essay in which you discuss ways that science and religion can reinforce and shed light on one another.

3. Terry Tempest Williams speaks of the power of prayer in her life. Do some further research into the use of prayer in religious and secular devotion. Why do people pray, and what do they derive from this practice?

4. Rituals are an important aspect in religious practice, as can be seen in the essays by Terry Tempest Williams and Thomas Moore in this chapter, as well as the essay by Campbell in Chapter 4. Do some further research on the importance of ritual observances in both religious and secular life, and write an essay in which you consider what purpose such observances serve for people and for society.

5. Annie Dillard, Terry Tempest Williams, and Jane Goodall all describe religious experiences that could be described as mystical. After doing some further research into this subject, write an essay in which you define and discuss what it means to have a mystical experience, and what the positive effects of such experiences might be.

6. Thich Nhat Hanh and King both discuss the idea of "love in action," or ways that spiritual love can be used to affect social change. Do some further research into spiritual social activism such as that and practiced by King and Hanh. What is particularly effective about social activist movements that use love and kindness as their source of energy?

 7. The following films portray spiritual leaders, positive and negative, and elements of spirituality in action. Pick one of these films, *Little Buddha, The Last Temptation of Christ, Seven Years in Tibet, Kundun, Ghandhi, The Last Wave,* or *The Third Miracle,* and write an essay in which you analyze the film and its spiritual message. What makes this film memorable, more than just a "preachy" experience?

Credits

Text Credits

The Revised Standard Version of the Bible. Copyright © 1946, 1952, 1971 by the Division of Christian Education of the National Council of Churches of Christ in the USA. Used by permission.

Maya Angelou, "The Angel of the Candy Counter" from *I Know Why the Caged Bird Sings.* Copyright © 1969 by Maya Angelou. Reprinted by permission of Random House, Inc.

Julie Apodaca, "Gay Marriage: Why the Resistance?" Reprinted by permission of the author.

Marc Ian Barasch, "What Is a Healing Dream?" from *Healing Dreams* by Marc Ian Barasch. Copyright © 2000 by Marc Ian Barasch. Used by permission of Riverhead Books, an imprint of Penguin Putnam Inc.

Bruno Bettelheim, "Fairy Tales and the Existential Predicament" from *The Uses of Enchantment.* Copyright © 1975, 1976 by Bruno Bettelheim. Reprinted by permission of Alfred A. Knopf, Inc., a division of Random House, Inc.

Sissela Bok. from *Mayhem: Violence as Public Entertainment* by Sissela Bok. Copyright © 1998 by Sissela Bok. Reprinted by permission of Perseus Books Publishers, a member of Perseus Books, L.L.C.

Mel Burns, "Memories of my Grandfather." Reprinted by permission of the author.

Joseph Campbell, "Four Functions of Mythology" from *Myths, Dreams, and Religion,* edited by Joseph Campbell. Copyright © 1970 by the Society for the Arts, Religion, and Contemporary Culture. Used by permission of Dutton, a division of Penguin Putnam, Inc.

Tiffany Castillo, "Exercise and Well-being." Reprinted by permission of the author.

"Emplumada" from *Emplumada,* by Lorna Dee Cervantes. Copyright © 1981. Reprinted by permission of the University of Pittsburgh Press.

Joyce Chang, "Drive Becarefully." Reprinted by permission of the author.

Rose Contreras, "On Not Being a Girl." Reprinted by permission of the author.

Emily Dickinson, reprinted by permission of the publishers and the Trustees of Amherst College from *The Poems of Emily Dickinson,* Thomas H. Johnson, ed., Cambridge, Mass.: The Belknap Press of Harvard University Press. Copyright © 1951, 1955, 1979 by the President and Fellows of Harvard College.

Annie Dillard, "A Field of Silence" from *Teaching a Stone to Talk: Expeditions and Encounters* by Annie Dillard. Copyright © 1982 by Annie Dillard. Reprinted by permission of HarperCollins Publishers, Inc.

Chitra Divakaruni, "Nargis' Toilette" from *The Black Candle.* Copyright © 1990 CALYX Books. Reprinted by permission of the publisher.

Loren Eiseley, from *The Immense Journey* by Loren Eiseley. Used by permission of Random House, Inc.

Peter Elbow, from *Embracing Contraries* by Peter Elbow. Copyright © 1976 By Peter Elbow. Used by permission of Oxford University Press, Inc.

Louise Erdrich, "Dear John Wayne" from *Jacklight* by Louise Erdrich. Copyright © 1984 by Louise Erdrich. Reprinted by permission of Henry Holt and Company, LLC.

James Finn Garner, from "Politically Correct Bedtime Stories." Copyright © 1994 James Finn Garner. All rights reserved. Reproduced here by permission of Wiley Publishing, Inc.

E. M. Forster, "The Other Side of the Hedge" from *Collected Tales*. Published 1947 by Alfred A. Knopf, Inc. Reprinted by permission of Alfred Knopf, Inc., a division of Random House, Inc.

Dian Fossey, "Dian Fossey and Me" by Lindsey Munro. Reprinted by permission of *The Stanford Daily Newspaper*.

Sigmund Freud. © Copyrights, The Institute of Psycho-Analysis and The Hogarth Press for permission to quote from *The Standard Edition of the Complete Psychological Works of Sigmund Freud* translated and edited by James Strachey. Reprinted by permission of The Random House Group Ltd.

Erich Fromm, *Symbolic Language: The Forgotten Language* essay by Erich Fromm. Reprinted by permission of Henry Holt and Co.

Nikki Giovanni, "Ego Tripping" from *The Women and the Men* by Nikki Giovanni. Copyright © 1970, 74, 75 by Nikki Giovanni. Reprinted by permission of HarperCollins Publishers Inc. William Morrow.

Todd Gitlin, "Three Formulas" from *Media Unlimited: How the Torrent of Images and Sounds Overwhelms Our Lives* by Todd Gitlin. Copyright © 2001 by Todd Gitlin. Reprinted by permission of Henry Holt and Company, L.L.C.

Jason Glickman, "Technology and the Future of the American Wilderness." Reprinted by permission of the author.

Jane Goodall from *Reason for Hope* by Jane Goodall. Copyright © 1999 by Soko Publications Ltd. and Phillip Berman. By permission of Warner Books, Inc.

Stephen Jay Gould, "Muller Bros. Moving & Storage." Copyright © 1990 American Museum of Natural History. Reprinted with permission from *Natural History*, September 2002.

"The Pelasgian Creation Myth" 1955 excerpt from *Ancient Greek: retold by Robert Graves*. Reprinted by permission of George Braziller Inc.

Susan Griffin, *Heros of Everyday Life*. Copyright © 1995 by Susan Griffin. Used by permission of Doubleday, a division of Random House, Inc.

Josh Groban, "Two Myths" is reprinted by permission of the author.

Thich Nhat Hanh, reprinted from *Love in Action: Writings on Nonviolent Social Change*. Copyright © 1993 by Thich Nhat Hanh. With permission of Paralax Press, Berkeley, California.

Patricia Hampl, from *I Could Tell You Stories: Sojourns in the Land of Memory* by Patricia Hampl. W. W. Norton 1999 ISBN: 0-393-32031-6.

Ernest Hemingway, reprinted with permission of Scribner, an imprint of Simon & Schuster Adult Publishing Group, from *Men Without Women* by Ernest Hemingway. Copyright © 1927 by Charles Scribner's Sons. Copyright renewed 1955, Ernest Hemingway.

Hill Ho, "Affirmative Action: Perspectives from a Model Minority." Reprinted by permission of the author.

Linda Hogan, "Walking." Copyright © 1990 by Linda Hogan, from *Dwellings: A Spiritual History of the Living World* by Linda Hogan. Used by permission of W. W. Norton & Company, Inc.

Steven Holtzman, reprinted with permission of Simon & Schuster Adult Publishing Group from *Digital Mosaics* by Steven Holtzman.

bell hooks, "Writing Autobiography" from *Talking Back: Thinking Feminist, Thinking Black*. With permission from the publisher, South End Press.

Robert Johnson, Chapter "The Shadow" from *Owning Your Own Shadow* by Robert Johnson. Copyright © 1991 by Robert A. Johnson. Reprinted by permission of HarperCollins Publishers Inc.

Steven King, "The Symbolic Language of Dreams" from *Writer's Dreaming* by Naomi Epel. Copyright © 1993 by Naomi Epel. Reprinted by permission of Carol Southern Books, a division of Crown Publishers, Inc.

Martin Luther King, Jr., "I Have A Dream." Copyright © 1963 by Martin Luther King, Jr., copyright renewed 1991 by Coretta Scott King. Reprinted by arrangement with the heirs to the Estate of Martin Luther King, Jr., c/o Writer's House, Inc. as agent for the proprietor.

Maxine Hong Kingston, "No Name Woman" from *The Woman Warrior*. Copyright © 1975, 1976, by Maxine Hong Kingston. Reprinted by permission of Alfred A. Knopf, Inc.

Jon Krakauer, from *Into Thin Air* by Jon Krakauer. Copyright © 1997 by Jon Krakauer. Used by permission of Villard Books, a division of Random House, Inc.

Anne Lamott, "Hunger" from *Travelling Mercies*. Copyright © 1999 by Anne Lamott. Reprinted by permission of Pantheon Books, a division of Random House, Inc.

Kalle Lasn, pp. 0–26 from *Culture Jam: The Uncooling of America* by Kallie Lasn. Copyright © 1997 by Kallie Lasn. Reprinted by permission of HarperCollins Publishers Inc. William Morrow.

Tin Le, "Enter Dragon" essay by Tin Le. Reprinted by permission of the author.

Li-Young Lee, "To a New Citizen of These United States," from *The City in Which I Love You*. Copyright © 1990 by Li-Young Lee. Reprinted with the permission of BOA Editions, Ltd.

Gabriel García Marquéz, all pages from "The Handsomest Drowned Man in the World" from *Leaf Storm and Other Stories*. Copyright © 1971 by Gabriel García Marquéz. Reprinted by permission of HarperCollins Publishers, Inc.

Student Essay by Elizabeth Matchett. Reprinted by permission of the author.

W. S. Merwin, "The Drunk in the Furnace" (New York: Atheneum, 1960). Copyright © 1956, 1957, 1958, 1959, 1960 by W. S. Merwin. Reprinted by permission of Georges Borchardt, Inc. on behalf of the author.

Scott Momaday, "The Way to Rainy Mountain" pages 105-169 by N. Scott Momaday. Reprinted with permission by the University of New Mexico Press.

Thomas Moore, "Neither Here Nor There," excerpt from *Parabola Magazine,* by Thomas Moore.

Farley Mowat, from *Never Cry Wolf* by Farley Mowat. Used by permission of McClelland & Stewart Ltd., the Canadian Publishers.

Lindsey Munro, "Dian Fossey and Me." Reprinted by permission of *The Stanford Daily Newspaper.*

Gloria Naylor, "The Two" from *The Women of Brewster Place*. Copyright © 1980, 1982 by Gloria Naylor. Used by permission of Viking Penguin, a division of Penguin Putnam, Inc.

Helena Norberg-Hodge, excerpted from *The Case Against the Global Economy*, edited by Jerry Mander and Edward Goldsmith. Copyright © 1996 by Jerry Mander and Edward Goldsmith. Reprinted by permission of Sierra Club Books.

"The Other" by Judith Ortiz Cofer, from *Reaching for the Mainland & Selected New Poems* (1995) Bilingual Press/Editorial Bilingue. Arizona State University, Tempe, AZ.

Judith Ortiz Cofer, "Silent Dancing" by Judith Ortiz Cofer is reprinted with permission from the publisher of *Silent Dancing: A Partial Remembrance of a Puerto Rican Childhood* (Houston: Arte Publico Press—University of Houston, 1990).

Fran Peavey, "Us and Them" from *Heart Politics*. Copyright © 1984 by Fran Peavey. Reprinted by permission of New Society Publishers, Philadelphia, PA.

Pratkanis and Aronson, Chapter 6, "Pictures in Our Heads" from *The Age of Propaganda.* Copyright © 1992 by Pratkanis and Aronson. Reprinted by permission of W H Freeman and Company. All rights reserved.

Rachel Naomi Remen, M.D. "Remembering" from *Kitchen Table Wisdom.* Copyright © 1996 by Rachel Naomi Remen, M.D. Used by permission of Putnam Berkley, a division of Penguin Putnam, Inc.

Liz Scheps, "Cinderella: Politically Incorrect?" Reprinted by permission of the author.

Eric Schlosser, "McTeachers and Coke Dudes," from *Fast Food Nation* by Eric Schlosser. Copyright © 2001 by Eric Schlosser. Reprinted by permission of Houghton Mifflin Company. All rights reserved.

David Sedaris, from *Naked* by David Sedaris. Copyright © 1997 by David Sedaris. By permission of Little, Brown and Company, Inc.

Idries Shah, "The Algonquin Cinderella" from *World Tales: The Extraordinary Coincidence of Stories Told in All Times, In All Places* by Idries Shah. Copyright © 1979 by Technographica, S. A. and Harcourt, Inc., reprinted by permission of the publisher.

"The Beginning of the World." *Tales from the Kojiki* from Genji Shibukawa. Reprinted without permission.

Sharon Slayton, "The Good Girl," reprinted by permission of the author.

Andrew Solomon, from *The Noonday Demon* by Andrew Solomon. Reprinted with the permission of Scribner, an imprint of Simon & Schuster Adult Publishing Group. Copyright © by Andrew Solomon.

"Knowing Spirituality" by Josh Spires. Reprinted by permission of the author.

Shelby Steele, Chapter 3 "Being Black and Feeling Blue" from *The Content of Our Character.* Copyright © 1990 by Shelby Steele. Reprinted by permission of St. Martin's Press L.L.C.

Wallace Stevens, from *The Collected Poems of Wallace Stevens.* Copyright 1954 by Wallace Stevens and renewed 1982 by Holly Stevens. Used by permission of Alfred A. Knopf, a division of Random House, Inc.

Peter Steinhart, "Dreaming Elands" *Audubon* 1982. Reprinted by permission of the author.

Amy Tan, Copyright © 1990 by Amy Tan. First appeared in *The Threepenny Review.* Reprinted by permission of the author and the Sandra Dijkstra Literary Agency.

"Tam and Cam: A Vietnamese Cinderella Story" (fairy tale.) Reprinted without permission.

Molly Thomas, "Response to Linton Weeks." Reprinted by permission of the author.

Cooper Thompson, "A Vision of Masculinity." *Changing Men,* Chapter 2 © by Sage Publications, Inc. Reprinted by Permission of Sage Publications, Inc.

John Updike, "Updike and I." First appeared in *Who's Writing This?* Edited by Daniel Halpern. Copyright © John Updike. Reprinted by permission of author.

Susan Voyticky, "Mixed-Up." Reprinted by permission of the author.

Frank Waters, "Spider Woman Creates the Humans" from *Book of Hopi* by Frank Waters. Copyright © 1963 by Frank Waters. Used by permission of Viking Penguin, a division of Penguin Putnam Inc.

Donovan Webster, "Inside the Volcano" by Donovan Webster. Published by National Geographic Image Collection Picture ID 746226.

Linton Weeks, "The No-Book Report: Skim it and Weep" from *Literacy: Read All About It,* essay by Linton Weeks published © 2001, *The Washington Post,* reprinted with permission.

Terry Tempest Williams, from *Leap.* Copyright © 2000 by Terry Tempest Williams. Used by permission of Pantheon Books, a division of Random House, Inc.

Virginia Woolf, "Professions for Women" from *The Death of the Moth and Other Essays* by Virginia Woolf. Copyright © 1942 by Harcourt, Inc. and renewed 1970 by Marjorie T. Parsons, Executrix, reprinted by permission of the publisher.

Index

568